THE PREPARATION
OF THE NOVEL

European Perspectives: A Series in Social Thought and Cultural Criticism

European Perspectives
A Series in Social Thought and Cultural Criticism

Lawrence D. Kritzman, Editor

European Perspectives presents outstanding books by leading European thinkers. With both classic and contemporary works, the series aims to shape the major intellectual controversies of our day and to facilitate the tasks of historical understanding.

For a complete list of books in the series, see pages 477–478.

THE PREPARATION OF THE NOVEL

Lecture Courses and Seminars at the Collège de France (1978–1979 and 1979–1980)

Translated by Kate Briggs

Text established, annotated, and introduced by Nathalie Léger

COLUMBIA UNIVERSITY PRESS   NEW YORK

Columbia University Press wishes to express its appreciation for assistance given by the government of France through the Ministère de la Culture in the preparation of this translation.

Columbia University Press
Publishers Since 1893
New York   Chichester, West Sussex
Copyright © Editions du Seuil 2003
Translation copyright © 2011 Columbia University Press
All rights reserved

Photos are reprinted courtesy of Fonds Roland Barthes, from the Institut Mémoires de l'Edition Contemporaine (IMEC)

"Vita Nova" in *Oeuvres Complètes V, Livres, Textes, Entretiens, 1977–1980* is reprinted by permission of Éditions du Seuil. © Éditions du Seuil, 1995 and 2002.

Library of Congress Cataloging-in-Publication Data
Barthes, Roland.
   [La préparation du roman. I et II, Cours et séminaires au Collège de France, 1978–1979 et 1979–1980. English]
   The preparation of the novel : lecture courses and seminars at the Collège de France, 1978–1979 and 1979–1980 / Roland Barthes ; translated by Kate Briggs ; text established, annotated, and introduced by Nathalie Léger.
         p. cm. — (European perspectives: a series in social thought and cultural criticism)
   Includes bibliographical references and index.
   ISBN 978-0-231-13614-3 (cloth : alk. paper) — ISBN 978-0-231-13615-0 (pbk. : alk. paper)
   1. Fiction—Authorship. I. Briggs, Kate. II. Léger, Nathalie. III. Title. IV. Series.

PN3365.B3213 2010
808.3—dc22   2010020314

Columbia University Press books are printed on permanent and durable acid-free paper.
This book is printed on paper with recycled content.
Printed in the United States of America

c 10 9 8 7 6 5 4 3 2 1
p 10 9 8 7 6 5 4 3 2 1

References to Internet Web sites (URLs) were accurate at the time of writing. Neither the author nor Columbia University Press is responsible for URLs that may have expired or changed since the manuscript was prepared.

CONTENTS

xv	Notice
xvii	Editor's Preface
xxv	Translator's Preface

THE PREPARATION OF THE NOVEL
1. From Life to the Work   1
Notes for a Lecture Course at the Collège de France (1978–1979)

SESSION OF DECEMBER 2, 1978
3   **Introduction**
      The "Middle" of Life   3
      To Change   5
      Writing Fantasy   8

SESSION OF DECEMBER 9, 1978
      The Novel   11

SESSION OF DECEMBER 16, 1978
      Two Clarifications   20
         1. As If   20
         2. Ethics / Technique   21

SESSION OF JANUARY 6, 1979
23   **The Haiku**
      "My" Haiku   23
      The Haiku in its Materiality   24
         Translation   24
         Typography. Aeration   26
         The Fascicule   27

SESSION OF JANUARY 13, 1979
      The Desire for Haiku   29
         Enchantment of Haiku   29
         The Desire for Haiku   30

    Nonclassification 32
    Nonappropriation 33
The Weather 34
    Season 34

SESSION OF JANUARY 20, 1979

The Weather 37
Individuation of the Times of Day 39
Individuation, the Nuance 42
    1. The Individual Against the System 42
    2. From the Individual to Individuation 43

SESSION OF JANUARY 27, 1979

    3. The Nuance 45
    4. The Void, Life 46
The Instant 48
    1. The Instant and Memory 48
    2. Movement and Immobility 49
    3. Contingency and Circumstance 50

SESSION OF FEBRUARY 3, 1979

Pathos 55
    1. Perception 55
        1. The Sound Is Off 58
        2. "One Art in the Form of Another" 59
        3. Synesthesia 59
    2. Affect, Emotion 60
        Emotion 61

SESSION OF FEBRUARY 10, 1979

    Animals. Digression 62
    Kireji 63
    3. Egotism of Haiku 64
    4. Discretion 66

SESSION OF FEBRUARY 17, 1979

Effect of the Real or Rather of *Reality* (Lacan) 70
    Photography 70
The Division of the Real 75
Co-presence 76

SESSION OF FEBRUARY 24, 1979
Setting a Bell Ringing 78
The Clarity of Haiku 82
The Limits of Haiku 83
1. The Concetto 84
2. Narration 85

SESSION OF MARCH 3, 1979

90 | **Conclusion**
Passages 90
1. Daily Practice of Notation 90
2. The Levels of Notation 92
Division 93
Noteworthy 93

SESSION OF MARCH 10, 1979
3. Life in the Form of a Sentence 97
4. Quiddity, Truth 100
1. Joyce: Quiddity 100
2. Proust: Truth 103

THE METAPHOR OF THE LABYRINTH
Interdisciplinary Investigations 111
Seminar (1978–1979)

INTRODUCTORY SESSION OF DECEMBER 2, 1978
113 | **Origin**
114 | **The Word, the Thing (Collating a Basic Knowledge)**
Etymology 115
The Thing 116
117 | **Fields of Presence of the Metaphor**
119 | **Symbolism**
120 | **Metaphor**

CONCLUDING SESSION OF MARCH 10, 1979
122 | **The Labyrinth: A Few Closing Remarks**

THE PREPARATION OF THE NOVEL

2. The Work as Will   125

Notes for a Lecture Course at the Collège de France (1979–1980)

SESSION OF DECEMBER 1, 1979

Preamble   127
Outline   127
Epigraph   127
Plan   128
Parabase   129
   Bibliography of the Most Frequently Quoted Authors (Authors and Critical Works)   129

130 | **1. The Desire to Write**

Origin and Departure   130
Jubilation   131
The Hope of Writing   132
   Hope   132
   Volupia / Pothos   132
   Imitation   133
   Inspiration   134
      1. A Narcissistic Distortion   134
      2. A Semiotics   135
      3. A Copy of a Copy   135
      4. An Unconscious Filiation   136
      5. A Simulation   137
The Desire to Write   138
   Mania   138
   Those Who Don't Write   139
   Anxious Desire   140
Writing as a Tendency   141
   Tendency   141

SESSION OF DECEMBER 8, 1979

Indistinction / *Poikilos*   143
Intransitive   144
To Have Finished   148
Digression—To Not Write?   150
   1. Scuppering   151
   2. "Idleness"   153
      Knowledge   154
      DIY {*Bricolage*}   154

  Nothing 155
  Wou-wei 156

SESSION OF DECEMBER 15, 1979
 "I'm Worth More Than What I Write" 160
 Ego-Ideal ≠ Ideal Ego 160
 Writing / Ideal Ego Differential 161
  1. Writing 161
  2. The (Writer's) Ideal Ego 162
 An Infinite Mechanism 165

167 **Parabase, Method, Narrative**
 Method 168
  Simulation 168
   1. Example and Metaphor 168
   2. *Mise en abyme* and Maquette 169
   3. Situation / Position 171
 Narrative 171
  The Three Trials 173

SESSION OF JANUARY 5, 1980
174 **2. First Trial: Choice, Doubt**
 Content? 174
  Philosophy of the Work 174
  The Themes of the Work 175
 The Work as Fantasized Form 176
  Fantasy / The "Volume" 176
 A Typology of the Book 178
  The Ordinary Book 179
  The Anti-Book 182
 Two Fantasized Forms: The Book / The Album 182
  1. The Book 182
   a. Mallarmé: The Total Book 182
   b. The Sum-Total Book 184
   c. The Pure Book 185
  2. The Album 186
   Circumstance 186
   Rhapsodic 186
   Diary / Structure / Method 187
   Speech / Writing 188

SESSION OF JANUARY 12, 1980
    The Stakes   189
    Dialectic of the Book and the Album   190
  Indecision and Necessity   191
    Indecisions   192
    No Necessity?   193
    After-the-Fact   193
    Finishability   194
    Need   195
    Chance   195
    "Proof"   195
  Self-evaluation: Talent   196
    Talent   196
    Misrecognition   196
    Truth-Novel   197
    Difficult / Impossible   198
  Conclusion   198
    The Blocking Fantasy   198
    "Blank in the Course"   199

199   **3. Second Trial: Patience**
  A. *A Methodical Life*   200
    The Work ≠ The World   200
      Office   200
      Society, Worldly   201
      Concupiscences   202
      Love   202
      Real Life   203
      Egoism   204
      Solution?   204

SESSION OF JANUARY 19, 1980
    Life as Work   207
      Return of the Author   207
      Return to Biography   208
      Gide   209
      Proust   209
      Life Writing   210
    Vita Nova   212
      Complete Breaks   212
      Bustle / Peace   215
        Bustle   215
        Smooth Time   216

Administration　217
　　　　　Writings　217
　　　　　Correspondence　217
　　　　　Accounts　218
　　　　　Luxury　218
　　　Defenses　219
　　　　　To Refuse　219
　　　　　Immobility　220
　　　　　A Novel to Write　221
　　　　　Originality　221
　　　　　"Workshop"　222
　　　　　Illness　222
　Casuistry of Egoism　224
　　　To Sacralize Yourself　224

SESSION OF JANUARY 26, 1980
　Casuistry of Egoism　227
　　　Regimes　228
　　　Home　230
　　　Night-Time　237

SESSION OF FEBRUARY 2, 1980
　　　Solitude　240
　　　Schedules　245
　　　The Grand Rhythm　249
　　　To Conclude　250
　B. The Praxis of Writing　250
　　　Preliminary Question: Reading / Writing　250
　　　Starting Up　252
　　　　1. Crises　253
　　　　2. "It Takes"　255

SESSION OF FEBRUARY 9, 1980
　From Starting Up to Labor　260
　　　Planning　260
　　　Brakings　263
　　　　1. The Slow Hand　263
　　　　　History of Speed　263
　　　　　Types of "Hand"　265
　　　　2. The Overall Time of the Work　265
　　　　　Parametrics　265
　　　　　Interrupting the Work　266

             3. The Breakdown   268
                    Marinade   268
                    Difficulty   268
                    Solutions   268
                 Conclusion: Boredom   271
                    Acedy   271
                    Schopenhauer   272
                    Art   272
                    Fall Outside of the Essence   273

           SESSION OF FEBRUARY 16, 1980
275   **4. Third Trial: Separation**
          Archaism and Desire   275
             Attachment to the Past   275
             Untimeliness   276
             Living Desire   276
             What Is Going to Die   277
          Signs of Desuetude   277
             1. Teaching   277
             2. Leadership   278
             3. "Work"   279
             4. Rhetoric   279
             5. Heroism   281
          The Exiled Writer   282
             1. Which History?   283
             2. Which Society?   285
             3. Which Language?   288

          SESSION OF FEBRUARY 23, 1980
             To Overcome   296
                Tragic   296
298   **To End the Course**
          1. Simplicity   299
          2. Filiation   301
          3. Desire   302
303   **A Last (but Not Final) Word**

       PROUST AND PHOTOGRAPHY
       Examination of a Little-Known Photographic Archive   305
       Seminar
305   **Editor's Foreword**

308	**1. Seminar?**
308	**2. Photographic Archive?**
309	**3. Little Known? = Unknown**
309	**4. Proust and Photography**
310	**5. "Examination"**
	1. The "World" of Proust (= of Marcel) 311
	2. The "Keys" 313

377	Summaries
379	Haiku
389	Reproduction of *Vita Nova*
397	Transcription of *Vita Nova*
407	Notes
457	Bibliography
465	Index Nominum
471	Index Rerum

NOTICE

This "Notice" is a shortened version of the general foreword that introduces the publication of Barthes's lecture courses. For more details, one should consult Comment vivre ensemble.

The organizing principle of the three volumes of Barthes's lecture courses at the Collège de France is the course session, since that was the true rhythm of the reading,[1] a rhythm that Barthes would retrospectively inscribe on his manuscript by marking the date and time where he had left off that day and where he would take up again the following week.

Unlike in the earlier courses, where the course sessions were organized by fragments, "traits," or figures, this course is composed of an infinitely long speech that unfolds continuously. Nevertheless, the lecture course is punctuated by the subtitles, pauses, and breaks that aerate and clarify that speech.

As for the "text" of the lecture course itself, the principle adopted here was to intervene as little as possible. The symbols that Barthes uses—for instance, to condense a logical construction [→, ≠]—have been retained, although we have completed abbreviations where they are a matter of a habitual shorthand (for example, *Mémoires d'outre tombe* for M.O.T.) and corrected the punctuation where it is too muddled.

Where Barthes's written argument is too obscure, we also took the liberty of paraphrasing the overall sense of the passage in a footnote, to spare the reader an unnecessary enigma. We took advantage of the wide margins in the "Traces écrites" collection: the bibliographical references that Barthes uses for the quotations appear there, at the same place on the page as in the manuscript itself. It should be added that the rare passages that Barthes crossed out have been retained but are identified as such in footnotes indicating where the deleted passage begins and ends. When a session is prefaced by remarks relating to letters received or the argument of the previous week, these remarks appear in italics. Finally, the editors' interventions in the text of the course are indicated by square brackets ([ ]). Occasionally, Barthes breaks off a quotation to make a point; these interventions are indicated by angle brackets (< >).

The footnotes are in the traditional philological style, essential in a text that is occasionally allusive. As far as possible, quotations, proper names, expressions in foreign languages (particularly ancient Greek, which we chose to transliterate into Latin characters), place names, and historical events are identified and explained in the notes, which the inclusion of a complete biographical index saves from becoming too repetitive. References to other texts or books by Barthes are to the new edition of the *Oeuvres complètes*, published in five volumes in 2002, and appear in the following form: OC 1, OC 2, OC 3, OC 4, and OC 5, followed by a colon and a page number or range.[2] In addition to the index of names and places, we have included an index of concepts, which appear in alphabetical order. When Barthes refers to an old or unlocatable edition of a text, our footnotes refer the reader to a more accessible one.[3]

A short preface places Barthes's lecture course in context and highlights its most salient features.

Éric Marty

EDITOR'S PREFACE
Nathalie Léger

> I have transmitted these things as they were then, in my passion—new, lively, blazing (and delightful to me), under love's first spell.
>
> —Jules Michelet

Here one enters the last circle of research.[1]

It is, of course, the irruption of death that retroactively renders the manuscript of this lecture course the last writing project and structures a destiny. Roland Barthes, for his part, was nurturing new projects, imagining topics for a number of future courses, putting the finishing touches to a paper for a conference on Stendhal; in short, he was working, he was constructing, he was envisaging the future. Although, when it occurs, death always confers the solemn resonance of an epigraph or an enigma upon the last words to be pronounced, in this case it can be said with certainty that it is the course that harbors the secret of a final achievement and not the other way around. It is in the perfection of its trajectory that *The Preparation of the Novel* marks the culmination of a reflection that began with *Writing Degree Zero* and, from 1953 on, constantly explored and expanded upon (in the form of the countless ruses and detours to which Barthes's oeuvre bears witness) one question and one question only: that of literary utopia. More than a response, *The Preparation of the Novel* is fully a lesson in that it stages the peregrination of a quest {*une recherche*} and dramatically sets out the law governing all quests before its audience: to know nothing of the object sought, simply to know something of oneself. Upon learning of his dismissal from the Collège de France in 1851, Michelet took comfort in the words of some of those who had attended his lectures: "We learnt nothing from your lectures. It is simply that our soul, absent, came back to us."[2] Reading between the lines, that declaration could contain Barthes's teaching program for the Collège de France, the one announced in the inaugural lecture of January 7, 1977, and exemplified in each of his lecture courses: to learn nothing—Barthes even says to *unlearn*—and to undertake that long labor of rediscovery, that return, within each individual, of a soul that has been absent for too long: "It is the *intimate* which seeks utterance in me, seeks to make its cry heard, confronting generality, confronting science."[3]

The last two lecture courses that Barthes taught at the Collège de France under the general title *The Preparation of the Novel* form a diptych—the two parts can be accessed independently of each other, yet each one is indispensable to the other. First, "The Preparation of the Novel 1: From Life to the Work," a lecture course comprising thirteen hour-long sessions that ran from December 2, 1978, to March 10, 1979. This was completed the following year by "The Preparation of the Novel 2: The Work as Will": eleven two-hour sessions that ran from December 1, 1979, to February 23, 1980. The lectures were delivered on Saturday mornings in the big amphitheater on the place Marcelin-Berthelot. Both lecture courses were linked to a seminar: for the year 1978–1979, Barthes decided to invite several outside speakers in to discuss "The Metaphor of the Labyrinth." That seminar took place on Saturday mornings from 11:30 to 12:30, immediately after Barthes's lecture. For the year 1979–1980, the seminar was supposed to begin in February (once the lecture course had finished) and to run on Saturday mornings between 10:30 and 12:30. It was to involve the discussion of a number of photographs of members of Proust's circle taken by the photographer Paul Nadar. That seminar, as we know, never took place: on Monday, February 25, 1980, Barthes was knocked down on the rue des Écoles, in front of the Collège de France; he was hospitalized for one month at the Salpêtrière and died on March 26, 1980.

The lecture course on *The Neutral* ended on June 3, 1978. At the time, Barthes envisaged devoting several years of teaching to a new project that promised to be "if not tenacious (who can say?) then at least broad in scope (ambitious)," as he explains in the first session of *The Preparation of the Novel* (December 2, 1978). Given the explicitly broad scope of that project, it is worth briefly describing the panorama of writings that form a backdrop to the two-part lecture course: texts that either anticipated it or can be read as variations on it. Since it is unquestionably the totality of Barthes's oeuvre that can be heard echoing throughout *The Preparation of the Novel*, it seems sensible to refer the reader to the five volumes of Barthes's *Oeuvres complètes*, published by the Éditions du Seuil, thanks to Éric Marty's editorial work. Here, then, we shall limit ourselves to those texts that directly preceded or were contemporaneous with the last two lecture courses. That chronology begins with the so-called general-interest lecture entitled "Longtemps, je me suis couché de bonne heure," delivered at the Collège de France on October 19, 1978—an indispensable text that condenses the issues that Barthes will discuss in his course into a few striking figures. Barthes delivered a variation on this lecture at New York University at the end of November. The week following the introductory session of December 2, 1978, Barthes's first column, or *Chronique*, appeared in *Le Nouvel Observateur*. These short texts, published between December 18, 1978, and March 26, 1979, accompanied the whole of the first lecture course. The weekly magazine would appear on Saturdays; some members of the audience can still recall how people would turn up at the Collège with the latest *Chronique* under their arms. The *Chroniques* amounted to more than the new-style little mythologies that their readers so eagerly awaited. As he states in the column dated March 26, 1979 (which marked the end of his journalistic experiment), for Barthes they were in the first instance a "writing experiment" that involved the "search for a form," "fragmented attempts at a novel." In January 1979, Barthes wrote "Ça prend" for the *Magazine Littéraire*, a text devoted to Proust's writing that repeats and anticipates some key passages of the lecture course. In the spring, between April 15 and June 3, 1979, he wrote *Camera Lucida*, a book based on analyses presented in the lecture course (notably in the session of February 17, 1979, of *The Preparation of the Novel 1*) that develops Barthes's meditation on time, on the disappearance of forms and the brief glimmers of a few ghosts. It now forms an indispensable bridge between the two parts of the lecture course. Having submitted the typed copy of *Camera Lucida* to his editor on August 21, 1979, and having in all likelihood begun work on the second lecture course, Barthes then wrote the first outline of his project for a novel, *Vita Nova*, an outline that he would spend the whole summer modifying, as he would continue to do so up until December 1979—the date that appears on the last rough sketch of that new work. The only trace that Barthes left of that new work is the architecture that also underpins the writing of the lecture course. In that same time period—between August 24 and September 17, 1979—Barthes kept the diary that posthumously would become "Paris Evenings" (published in *Incidents*, 1987) and "deliberated" whether or not it is possible for a diary to become a work. ("Deliberation," which reproduces fragments of the diary from 1977 and the spring of 1979, was published in *Tel Quel* in the winter of 1978). Late January 1980: publication of *Camera Lucida*. Late February: the last session of *The Preparation of the Novel*. At his death, a page of a work in progress devoted to Stendhal was found in Barthes's typewriter, entitled: "One Always Fails in Speaking of What One Loves."[4]

As with his two previous lecture courses at the Collège de France and all of his seminars, talks, and lectures, Barthes took great care in drafting the manuscript of *The Preparation of the Novel*. Although the text of the first course is not dated, we can presume that Barthes devoted the summer of 1978 to it, a summer spent in the seclusion of Urt, on the banks of the Ardour. As a note at the bottom of the last page indicates, Barthes completed the draft of the second lecture course on November 2, 1979, one month before the first session took place. There are very few lines crossed out and seldom any corrections in the dense and uniform writing of this ensemble of 198 pages drafted in blue or black ink (seventy-one pages for the first part, 127 for the second).[5] Occasionally, a few notes (marked with an asterisk in felt-tip pen and affixed to the margin) complete the point being made; sometimes what was clearly a deleted half-page is reintegrated into the text with a paperclip or a bit of tape. Barthes would change his mind, hesitate, and make corrections, but what is striking about the manuscript as a whole is the homogeneity and consistency of the writing. As is often the case in Barthes's manuscripts, the very frequent bibliographical references are noted in pencil in the margin. Barthes probably read over his manuscript for the last time just before the lecture course began, taking the opportunity to make a few minor annotations to the draft in ballpoint pen. It was with the very same ballpoint pen (he did not like using them but, considering them useful for making the odd note, always carried one with him) that Barthes would systematically make a note of the date of the session that had just come to an end and mark where he had left off.

Those who attended his lecture course recall the remarkable fluidity of his delivery, the deep and enveloping timbre of his voice, the warm phrasing that endowed his authority with infinite goodwill—oratorical skills that are confirmed by the sound recording of the lecture course.[6] When describing the course, many of those who attended the lectures emphasize the crowds, the fight to get a seat from the moment the doors opened, and how calmly Barthes could invent on the spot, his ability to improvise in a very consistent, sustained fashion. Very few recall him reading from a manuscript. Yet a comparison between the written version with the spoken version recorded by some members of the audience reveals scarcely any discrepancies between the two: only infrequent digressions in the spoken version and the rare last-minute changes and cuts made to the written draft (in order to adapt it, where necessary, to the technical constraints of the lecture format) suggest that Barthes was reading, taking great care not to depart from the manuscript transcribed here. That manuscript therefore contains, *without remainder*, everything that was presented in the lecture course. Several commentators have noted Barthes's unease before the packed amphitheater at the Collège de France, his awkwardness before that dense and anonymous crowd as someone who, over the preceding years, had succeeded in creating a "circulatory space of subtle, flexible desires," a closed and perhaps even isolated circle of an "amorous phalanstery" grounded in "a subtle topography of bodily relations" simply by gathering some of his disciples around a table at the École Pratique des Hautes Études.[7] However, it was indeed in the context of the Collège de France, in the context of the constraints it imposed and the ambition it embodied that—already in the inaugural lecture of January 1977—Barthes articulated his desire for this "Vita Nova." That desire, set out as the very principle of *The Preparation of the Novel*, was formulated for the first time upon Barthes's integration into the Collège and is as it were anchored to it.[8] Thus it was in the first instance the assignation of his desire to a *specific* place, a place haunted by the illustrious thinkers to whom he frequently refers (Michelet has been mentioned; one could also cite Valéry or Jean Baruzi) that enabled Barthes to sketch out the contours of a new life. However, if the inaugural lecture was placed under the sign of Michelet's teaching, the two-part lecture course that makes up *The Preparation of the Novel* was undertaken with Dante as a guide. It is well known that with *Vita Nova*, his first great work, Dante inaugurated a new form—the product of the mutual engenderment of the poem, the narrative, and the commentary. For Dante, that new form was the only one capable of expressing the power of love and the depth of mourning he experienced upon Beatrice's death. Chapter 18 of *Vita Nova* announces why it was necessary to invent that form, a form so new that it is unnerving, almost inhibiting: "And then I resolved that thenceforward I would choose for the theme of my writings only the praise of this most gracious being. But when I had thought exceedingly, it seemed to me that I had taken to myself a theme which was much too lofty, so that I dared not begin; and I remained during several days in the desire of speaking, and the fear of beginning."[9] In October 1977, a few months after delivering his inaugural lecture at the Collège de France, the death of Barthes's mother abruptly interrupted the steady progression of his work and served as a painful confirmation of his desire for a new writing life. The novel, that "uncertain form," the material of remembered as much as of desired speech, was for Barthes the only one capable of expressing what he calls the "truth of affect" whereby meaning is revealed and undone: "Moment of Truth = Moment of the *Intractable*: we can neither interpret nor transcend nor regress; Love and Death *are here*, that's all that can be said"[10]—an echo of that other figure of the *Intractable* proposed at the beginning of the lecture course, when Barthes describes that moment of illumination in which he grasped, in a sudden flash, the direction that his quest would take. For the origin of the decision to undertake the course is to be found in that abduction of consciousness that Barthes calls a *satori*, in the rapturous event of April 15, 1978, described in the introductory session. April 15, 1978, is properly novelistic not only in terms of the role that this one date plays in the architecture of Barthes's planned work, *Vita Nova*, but also because it inevitably recalls moments when the mind is completely overwhelmed, great moments of fundamental caesura, when the subject falters, whose narratives punctuate our intellectual and spiritual history. In its abruptness and its fugacity, that Barthesian *eureka*, that brief instant of incandescence and joy that, in the middle of a foreign city, oppressed by heat and boredom, suddenly lit up a banal afternoon, contains all the aspirations of the lecture course that, session after session, investigates literature's capacity to capture the passionate epiphany of the instant, to give it an absolute value, and then to reconcile the rending of the self with the creation of the self. Was it really so important whether or not the quest culminated in the writing of the novel, of *a* novel? Elsewhere, a few years earlier, in *A Lover's Discourse*, every figure of which could be read as an "Address to the Novel," Barthes wrote: "I'm not actually bothered about my chances of being fulfilled *in real terms* (I don't mind that they're nonexistent). It's just the will to fulfillment that blazes, that's indestructible."[11]

Together with the manuscripts of the two lecture courses, we are also publishing the texts of the two seminars that accompanied them.[12] As Barthes points out, the seminar at the Collège de France was in the first instance a space of exchange and dialogue, and the professor could call upon outside speakers should he wish. Barthes provided a list of those invited to discuss "The Metaphor of the Labyrinth" in his text for the Collège de France yearbook, which presents the work undertaken that year. Barthes took charge of the opening and closing sessions, and it is the nine pages of his drafted intervention (seven of which comprise the opening session) that are transcribed here. Although it never took place, the seminar on photography was drafted in the first weeks of 1980. The intention was to devote the few sessions of this seminar to a projection of Paul Nadar's photographs, with Barthes improvising a commentary based on biographical notations taken from some standard reference works on the world of Proust. The handwritten record of this undertaking amounts to a six-page "Presentation." Barthes wrote a further fifty-three pages that form a sheaf of brief notations arranged in alphabetical order. The very allusive nature of those notes means the document is full of holes and gaps. Any attempt to fill in those gaps would have been to replace it with something else. We are therefore publishing it with—in the form of an exergue—the same "warning" as the one Barthes issues in his opening session: "no non-Marcelians, please." The tenuous nature of the information provided in the document is to be supplemented by the remarkable biographical works and iconographic dossiers on Proust that have been in the public domain for over twenty years. As regards the images selected by Barthes (and conserved in his archive together with the manuscript of the seminar), they have been published many times since. Yet neither the few pages of an underdeveloped text nor the series of familiar photographs are enough to make us lose sight of the extent to which those few images, discreetly captioned by Barthes, present a vertiginous complement to the lecture course: the center of a labyrinth is always the site of an illusory goal, and the quest for the novel can only culminate in a melancholy and luminous world of apparitions.

For their libraries' resources and their friendship, I would like to thank Marianne Alphant, Bernard Brun, Anne-Sophie Chazeaux, Michel Contat, Olivier Corpet, Claude Coste, Albert Dichy, Pierre Franz, Anne Herchberg-Pierrot, Marc de Launay, Thierry Leguay, Virginie Linhard, Carlo Ossola, Claire Paulhan, Jean Pavans, Jean-Loup Rivière, and Chantal Thomas.

For the indispensable use of the sound recording of *The Preparation of the Novel*, I would like to thank Bernard Comment, Isabelle Grellet, and Christine Lemaire.

Finally, I would like to thank Jean-Claude Baillieul, Éditions du Seuil, for his invaluable assistance.

TRANSLATOR'S PREFACE
Kate Briggs

> You'll have grasped—or, rather, as you already know because I've said and written it (Cerisy): that here Wanting-to-Write relates to the Novel, the Form fantasized is that of the Novel → I've even heard it said (the path rumors usually take) that I'm writing one, which isn't true; if it were, I clearly wouldn't be in a position to propose a lecture course on its preparation: writing requires secrecy. No, I'm at the Fantasy-of-the-novel stage, but I've decided to push that fantasy as far as it will go . . .
>
> (p. 11)

By the end of the 1970s, apparently "everyone knew" that Roland Barthes was writing a novel. It was not until 1995, however, that the facsimiles of Barthes's eight-page plan entered the public domain. When they did, as Laurent Nunez documents, the general feeling was one of disappointment: What? Only eight pages? Only eight pages, amounting to eight variations on the same sketched outline of a prospective novel? Were these the pages that Barthes was proposing to "prepare" in the lecture course entitled *La Préparation du roman*, translated here as *The Preparation of the Novel*?[1] Barthes provides an oblique response to this question in the final session of the course. But for a reader as yet unfamiliar with the content of his lectures, the degree of anticipation—and disappointment—depends, at least in part, on how one chooses to read the course title. For as Nunez points out, the determination of the article is ambiguous: *The Preparation of the Novel* could of course refer to a specific novel, to the novel Barthes was planning, that is, to the project entitled *Vita Nova*. It could equally refer to any novel. Or to the novel in general. Or indeed to the Novel, to the particular conception of the novel that emerges from the course: the meaning of "Novel" expanded to include "Absolute Novel, Romantic Novel, *poikilos* Novel, Novel of the Writing-Tendency; in other words, all works of literature" (p. 144).

The question as to whether or not Barthes really intended to write *Vita Nova*—as to whether that novel would have been written had his death in 1980 not cut short what he terms a "new writing life"—has preoccupied readers of the lecture course. For Antoine Compagnon, the last session of the lecture course is "melancholic": "two years of teaching" had come to an end but, precisely, "the novel hadn't followed."[2] Other commentators have explored the implications of the peculiar "method" Barthes adopts in his lecture course: not to write a novel but to proceed *as if* he were going to write one (**p. 20**). Diana Knight argues that the novel was destined to be unrealized—that failure was built into the project from the start—and invites us to consider the creative possibilities of the plans for *Vita Nova* precisely *as* plans.[3] Thomas Clerc proposes a reading of *The Preparation of the Novel* as a work of conceptual art: the final outcome of the project is subordinate to the documentation of a mental process, especially since the sole outcome of the lecture course *was* the "preparation," that is, the lecture course itself.[4]

The decision to publish a transcription of those eight pages in the form of an appendix to this translation of *La Préparation du roman* could be seen as intervening in that debate: to append the plans for *Vita Nova* to the lengthy "preparation" of "the novel" is arguably to present the lectures in terms of Barthes's failure to pull a novel "out of his hat" (as he puts it in the final session), to link the two projects together in ways that sit uneasily with Barthes's sense of the specific ambition of the course (see, for instance, the passage quoted above). The reasoning behind publishing them here was more straightforward, however. Those pages have not yet been translated into English, and a reader of the lecture course will inevitably be intrigued as to the skeletal form of what, ultimately, did not get written. As Nathalie Léger discusses in her editor's preface, *The Preparation of the Novel* was drafted in what was an intensely productive period for Barthes: the eight elliptical plans form part of what Léger calls the "panorama" of texts, teachings, and talks that formed the backdrop to the writing of the lecture course, the majority of which are available in English translation.

The Preparation of the Novel charts the elaboration of an intensely personal writing project: the bid to kickstart a new writing practice that would both enable and amount to a radical change in Barthes's way of life, inaugurating a new life, a Vita Nova. After a long exposition of the particular features of the short form (which for Barthes is exemplified by the haiku), that elaboration takes the form of a more general inquiry into what Barthes calls "the conditions" under which a handful of writing practitioners have engaged in the "preparation" of "a literary work, for convenience called a Novel" (**p. 127**). Nunez's point with respect to the ambiguous determination of "the novel" in the course title could therefore also be made of "the preparation." Is this a concept? A specific course of action? One undertaken by writers in general, novelists in particular, or Barthes specifically, between December 1978 and February 1980, in the setting of the Collège de France, before a packed auditorium?

The "preparation" of a novel is evidently something distinct from "*the fact of writing*" one (**p. 127**): rumor may have had it that Barthes was writing a novel but, as he indicates above—and as those eight *plans* attest—this was not the case. Even so, what the "preparation" of or for writing (of *and* for writing) involves is no more immediately obvious in French than it is in English. This, perhaps, is the point: as Barthes stresses repeatedly, working out how to go about writing a novel is in reality far from obvious; it is hard going, difficult, all consuming, and often a source of pain and distress. So "preparation" is in the first instance to be understood in the sense of an arrangement, a setting out or up, an organization both of a way of life, with the series of decisions that such an organization entails, and of a certain kind of material: the various pieces of cloth that the dressmaker tacks together, the fragmented notations of the present that the would-be novelist hopes to work into one long, continuous form. Referring to the subject of the action, "preparation" can also designate the series of operations required to obtain something, and it soon emerges that here the "preparation" of and for writing amounts to a quest, an initiation, fraught with setbacks, doubts, difficulties, and trials to overcome. The "hero" embarking on that journey is a particular kind of writer: a composite figure made up of that handful of "Romantic" writers (in Barthes's sense of the term),[5] among them Rousseau, Chateaubriand, Flaubert, Kafka, Proust, and Barthes himself. Which is to say that on one level this is indeed Roland Barthes's story: he asks, "So why does this man insist on Wanting to Write (at least at this stage in my Narrative, which, as you'll have guessed, is the story of my own life)?" (**p. 160**). But the fact that this personal writing project took the form of a teaching project, that the Work and the Course came to be "invested in the same (literary) enterprise" (**p. 8**) leaves open—and even sets out to generate—the possibility that the story of *The Preparation of the Novel* is also *yours*: those amateur writers among you who have experienced or are currently under the sway of the desire to write and who are similarly compelled to embark on a journey of initiation into the writing of literary works.

The lecture course can therefore also be read as the written trace of a singular pedagogical experiment.[6] It was in order to preserve these levels of indeterminacy (which or whose preparation? of which or whose novel?), this slippage between the general and the personal (which Jonathan Culler characterizes as "a paradoxical operation: teaching a course about preparing to write a novel"),[7] that I took the decision to translate the title of the lecture course literally.

In the very first session of the course, Barthes announces: "to my mind, a lecture is a specific production: not entirely writing nor entirely oration, it's marked by an implicit interlocution (a silent complicity). It's something which, *ab ovo*, must, wants to die—to leave no more substantial a memory than of speech" (**p. 7**). This remark informed the translation strategy adopted here. For *The Preparation of the Novel* is not a book in any straightforward sense: it is the transcription of detailed, scrupulously drafted notes for a two-part lecture course and two accompanying seminars. Nor, can it be supposed, did Barthes intend it to become a book. Barthes decided not to publish the lecture course on *The Neutral* delivered the previous year for the reasons he gives here: not only does writing a course take up precious time, but: "I think that part of a life's activity should always be set aside for the Ephemeral: what happens only once and vanishes, it's the necessary share of the Rejected Monument; and therein lies the vocation of the Course" (**p. 7**). The resources of English are of course different than those of French, and the systematic use of contractions, together with translating Barthes's impersonal *on* with a general "we" or an inclusive "you" aim to give a sense of that complicity, reflecting the fact that the lectures were drafted with a view to addressing and engaging with an audience, having no ambition to outlast the moment of their enunciation.

The Preparation of the Novel shares a common vocabulary with the "panorama" of writings that Léger describes, and, as a general rule, I have sought to achieve a degree of continuity with the available translations of Barthes's writings from the same period, with one exception that needs to be noted here. In *A Lover's Discourse: Fragments*, Richard Howard translates the expression "*Vouloir-Écrire*," a formulation that chimes with "*Vouloir-Saisir*" and "*Vouloir-Vivre*" (translated in *The Neutral* as "Will-to-Possess" and "Will-to-Live," respectively)[8] as "Will-to-Write." Here, the same expression has been rendered as "Wanting-to-Write." While a "will" can of course designate a desire or wish, it can also imply a resolute intention. Now, *The Preparation of the Novel* is the dramatization of a journey: at the outset, "to write" is explicitly a desire, an urge or impulse in search of its object—specifically, an appropriate "form." It is only as the course/quest progresses—as the trials that characterize that quest are, if not overcome, then at least enumerated and examined—that the desire to write begins to look more like a resolution, and a transition is made from a generalized *vouloir* ("wanting to") to a formalized *volonté*: part 2 of the lecture course is subtitled "*L'Oeuvre comme volonté*," or "The Work as Will."

Throughout the lecture course, Barthes frequently quotes—often at length—from a small selection of what for him are key texts. Following the strategy adopted by Rosalind Krauss and Denis Hollier in their translation of *The Neutral*, I have sought, wherever possible and practicable, to reconstruct that corpus in English translation, modifying the available translations whenever the logic of Barthes's argument demanded it; I have also sought to respect Barthes's system of abbreviations (for instance, *Á la Recherche du temps perdu*, abbreviated to "*Á la Recherche*" in the lecture course, is given here in shorthand as "*In Search*").[9] However, the approach to translating the haiku quoted in part 1 of the lecture course and the biographical notes accompanying the photographs in the drafted seminar on "Proust and Photography" requires some further explanation. Since a number of the translations of the haiku quoted in part 1 of the lecture course are Barthes's own, translated directly from English versions published in R. H. Blyth's four-volume collection of haiku, *A History of Haiku* (1963), it made sense to reproduce Blyth's "original" translations here (indicated with a *). It also made sense to reproduce the translations of some of Barthes's favorite haiku found in *Empire of Signs*, translated by Richard Howard (indicated with a †). Wherever the Blyth or Howard translations differ greatly from the French versions, or wherever Barthes quotes a haiku that does not appear in *A History of Haiku* or *Empire of Signs*, the translations into English are my own. As Léger points out in her presentation of the Proust seminar, the handwritten notes intended to accompany the projection of the photographs are full of holes and gaps (see **p. 305**). The primary source for those notes was George Painter's two-volume biography of Marcel Proust, which appeared in French translation in 1966. As it turns out, Barthes is often silently paraphrasing short passages from that biography, lifting anecdotes and expressions directly from Painter in translation. In my translation of the notes I therefore chose to go back to Painter's "original" English (that is, his "original" version of events that originally took place in France and in French)

xxix **TRANSLATOR'S PREFACE**

rather than to retranslate passages from Georges Cattaui's and Roger-Paul Vial's translation: the small number of deviations from Barthes's French reflect and repeat the minor discrepancies between the English and French versions of Painter's biography.

I would like to thank Hélène Boisson, Marianne Groulez, Anna-Louise Milne, and Céline Surprenant, all of whom read sections or early drafts of this translation and provided invaluable support and advice. I am especially grateful to Diana Knight for her careful and insightful reading of the first completed draft: without her many corrections and suggestions, this would have been a much poorer translation; all the remaining errors and infelicities are my own.

THE PREPARATION OF THE NOVEL

1. From Life to the Work
*Notes for a Lecture Course at
the Collège de France (1978–1979)*

SESSION OF DECEMBER 2, 1978

Introduction

The "Middle" of Life

Subject not to be repressed

Each year, when beginning a new course, I think it apt to recall the pedagogical principle stated programmatically in the "Inaugural Lecture": "I sincerely believe that at the origin of teaching such as this we must always locate a fantasy, which can vary from year to year."[1] I'll come back in a moment to the "fantasy" for this year (and I hope for years to come, for this one promises to be, if not tenacious (who can say?), then at least broad in scope (ambitious)). The principle is a general one: the subject is not to be repressed—whatever the risks of subjectivity. I belong to a generation that has suffered too much from the censorship of the subject, whether following the positivist route (the objectivity required by literary history, the triumph of philology) or the Marxist (very important—even if it no longer seems so—in my life) → Better the illusions of subjectivity than the impostures of objectivity. Better the Imaginary of the Subject than its censorship.

Dante, age

Dante: "*Nel mezzo del cammin di nostra vita*."[2] Dante was thirty-five. I'm much older and have gone far beyond the mathematical "middle" of my life's journey[3] (and I'm not Dante! Take note: the great writer isn't someone you can compare yourself to but someone whom you can, whom you want to, identify with, to a greater or lesser extent).—But the line, so magnificently *direct*, inaugurates one of the greatest works in the world with a *declaration of subjecthood* (Writer = "I do not repress the subject that I am"). → That declaration says: (a) Age is a constituent part of the subject who writes; (b) that midway point clearly isn't mathematical: for who could calculate it in advance? It relates to an event, a moment, a change experienced as meaningful, solemn: a sort of "total" realization of precisely the kind that can determine and consecrate a journey, a peregrination in a new continent (*la selva oscura*),[4] an initiation (there's an initiator: Virgil—we'll have ours). Now, for my part, although I've gone far beyond the arithmetical middle of my life, it's today that I'm experiencing the sensation-certainty of living out the *middle-of-the-journey*, of finding myself at the kind of juncture

3

(Proust: "the apogee of the particular")[5] beyond which the waters divide, taking two divergent ways {*côtés*}. This occurred under the effect of two "consciousnesses" (self-evident truths) and an event:

Numbered days

1. First, consciousness of this: that, having reached a certain age, our "days are numbered"; counting against the tide, but its irreversible character is still more apparent than in youth. Mortality is not a "natural" feeling (which is why so many people drive headlong into trees, convinced of their immortality). The self-evident truth "I am mortal" comes with age. This reference to age is often taken the wrong way, misunderstood—it's seen as coquetry: "But you're not old!" or the sign of an obsession. The imperious need to fit the work still to be done into the confines of a ready-made box: the last box. Or rather: because the box is outlined, because there's no longer any outside-box → the work you plan to put in it = a sort of solemnity = to look *the use of Time before Death* in the face. Cf. Proust, threatened by illness (*Against Sainte-Beuve*). "Work while you have the light"[6] (probably John 12:35: "The light is among you still, but not for long. Go on your way while you have the light, so that darkness may not overtake you."), which we'll interpret in a secular sense.

Humdrum

2. Then, consciousness of this: there comes a time when what you've done, written (past labors and practices) looks like repeated material, doomed to repetition, to the lassitude of repetition. "What? From now on until I die I'll be writing articles, preparing my teaching, giving lectures—or, at best, writing books—*on* subjects, which are all that'll vary (and so little!)?" Foreclosure of anything New (= the definition of "Doing Time")? Foreclosure of Adventure (ad-venture: that which *ad-venes*, *befalls me* → Adventure = the exaltation of the subject)? Condemned to repetition? To seeing the future, until death, as *humdrum*? What? When this text, this lecture course is over, there'll be nothing else for it but to start over again, to begin another one?—No, Sisyphus is not happy: he's alienated, not by the futility of his work, but by its *repetition*.

Bereavement

3. Last, an event, sent by Destiny, can occur to painfully or dramatically mark, cut into, incise, break up that slow running aground, triggering the transformation of that all-too-familiar landscape— what I called the "middle of the journey of life": it is, alas, pain's *asset*. For example: Rancé, a dandy on horseback, rebellious, worldly, returns from his travels to find that his mistress has been decapitated in an accident!: he withdraws from society and founds the Trappist order.[7]—For Proust: the death of his mother (1905), even

if the traumatic action, insofar as it produces an active mutation, occurred later (1909, cf. *infra*).[8]—More recently: Brel, terminally ill, changed his life, his "middle of life," just a few years before he died[9] → This "apogee of the particular" can be constituted by a cruel and seemingly unique bereavement; to mark the decisive fold: bereavement will be the best of my life, that which divides it irreparably into two halves, *before / after*. Because, whatever the nature of the incident, the middle of my life is nothing other than the moment when one realizes that death is real (to go back to Dante: *The Divine Comedy* is the very *panorama* of that reality).

Acedy

All of a sudden, then, this self-evident truth presents itself: on the one hand, I have no time left to try out several different lives: I have to choose my last life, my new life, *Vita Nova* (Dante)[10] or *Vita Nuova* (Michelet).[11] And, on the other, I have to get out of this gloomy state of mind that the wearing effects of repetitive work and mourning have disposed me to → This running aground, this slow entrenchment in the quicksand (= which isn't quick!), this drawn-out death of staying in the same place, this fate that makes it impossible to "enter death alive" can be diagnosed in the following way: a generalized and overwhelming accumulation of "disinvestments," the inability to invest anew → In the Middle Ages, a word: *acedy*.[12] It can immediately be clarified that, if said and conceived of in a certain way, and despite the overuse of the word, *acedy* (a theme we'll encounter again) is irreplaceable: the inability to love (someone, other people, the world) → Unhappiness often translates as the impossibility of giving to others.

To Change

Intelligence

So, to change, that is, to give a content to the "jolt" of the middle of life—that is, in a sense, a life "plan" (a *vita nova*). Now, for someone who writes, who has chosen to write, that is to say, for someone who has *experienced the jouissance, the joy of writing* (not unlike the "first pleasure"), there can be no other *Vita Nova* (or so it seems to me) than the discovery of a new writing practice. Of course, one can imagine changing topic, doctrine, theory, philosophy, method, belief (and some people do: major doctrinal mutations occur as the result of an event, a trauma). But to change ideas is banal; it's as natural as breathing. To invest / disinvest / reinvest, there you have the very drive of intelligence in that it *desires*; Intelligence (a Proustian notion, what's more) has no other means of displaying its desire than by bestowing / withdrawing love, because its object isn't a form and therefore isn't fetishizable; even inveterate militants are hard to come by (more and more so): they always get cited as examples ≠ "faith" is different: there are those who turn to it, those who withdraw from it, but, as a general rule, it's tough, because it's linked to death. Therefore, for someone who has written, the domain of the *Vita Nova* can only be that of writing: the discovery of a new writing practice. The New expectation is only this: that the writing practice should *break* with previous intellectual practices; that writing should be detached from the *management* of the earlier movement: the writing subject is under a social pressure to become (to be reduced to) *his own manager*, to manage his work by repeating it: it's this *daily grind* that must be interrupted.

Blanchot

Blanchot (him, once again) describes this change of direction in writing in his own way, one that's both resigned and desperate: "There is a moment in the life of a man—consequently, in the life of men—when everything is completed, the books written, the universe silent, the beings at rest. There is left only the task of announcing it: this is easy. But as this supplementary word threatens to upset the equilibrium—and where to find the force to say it? where to find another place for it?—it is not pronounced, and the task remains unfinished."[13] I have experienced, still recurrently experience, and am sure to experience again, the temptation, or the *image of decision*, that Blanchot describes: last year's course bears the trace of this temptation: the dilection of the Neutral, of the Retreat.[14] Because, faced with the "daily grind" of management, two paths open up before us: (1) either to retreat into silence, rest, retreat ("Sitting quietly, doing nothing, spring comes and the grass grows of its own accord.");[15] (2) or to start walking in another direction, that is, to battle, to invest, *to plant*, with the well-known paradox: "Building a house makes sense, but to start planting at that age is downright odd!"[16] Why? On this level, any explanation of the decision will be vague because we don't know what part is played by the unconscious—or: the true nature of the desire involved. I'll say, in all consciousness: because of a sense of danger →

Petite bourgeoisie

contemporary French society: ideologically, the powerful rise of the petite bourgeoisie: it has taken over, it reigns over the media: what would be required here is an *aesthetic* analysis of the radio, TV, the popular press, to show which implicit values it promotes and which ones it rejects (aristocratic values, as a general rule). Danger that I think has become more apparent in recent times: the corroborating signs of a rise in *anti-intellectualism* (always closely related to racism, fascism), of attacks on the mass-mediatization of "jargon" (language), on art-house cinema, etc. → Sense that we have to defend ourselves, that it's a question of survival. Sollers: if he wants to survive, the writer, the intellectual, will have to be ready to administer himself with a dose of paranoia: "No favors!" → The necessity of defending the Artist. (Nietzsche)

So this is the path I've chosen. Before stating what form it will take, how it appears to me, and to you (because this Course, which is just beginning—and that will in theory go on for several years—will be my seasonal traveling companion along this writing path), I should say that the first act of this "adventure" was (and this concerns those of you who attended last year): the decision not (or at least not for the moment) to publish the course on the **Neutral**. Of course, I hesitated—but in the end I gave up the idea for two reasons:

1. On the one hand, I think that part of a life's activity should always be set aside for the Ephemeral: what happens only once and vanishes, it's the necessary share of the Rejected Monument, and therein lies the vocation of the Course (clearly there are some exceptions: Saussure, and even then! the loss didn't matter to him!): to my mind, a lecture is a specific production: not entirely writing nor entirely oration, it's marked by an implicit interlocution (a silent complicity). It's something that, *ab ovo*, must, wants to die—to leave no more substantial a memory than of speech → What is present but *will* nevertheless die: this is the nuance of the Japanese *Ma*, *Utsuroi*,[17] the flower (if I dare flatter myself in this way!) that will wilt.

2. On the other hand, to have published the Course would have been to manage the past. Now, one must move forward, time is pressing (*to write* a course takes up a lot of time); one must *walk* while there's still light, and this Proustian saying is very much like another one from the Gospels (invoked here in a very secular fashion): one has to let the dead bury the dead (Matthew 8:21–22). Let the course bury itself—the Neutral *suspend* its expression.

And now, briefly, a little personal anecdote: When was this decision "to change" taken?—April 15, 1978.[18] Casablanca.[19] The sluggishness of the afternoon. The sky clouds over, a slight chill in the air. A group of us go in two cars to the Waterfall (a pretty little valley on the way to Rabat). *The same, uninterrupted* sadness, a kind of listlessness that (since a recent bereavement)[20] bears upon everything I do, everything I think (lack of investment). Return, an empty apartment; a difficult time: the afternoon (I'll speak it of again). Alone, sad → Marinade;[21] I reflect with enough intensity. The beginnings of an idea: something like a "literary" conversion—it's those two very old words that occur to me: to enter into literature, into writing; *to write*, as if I'd never written before: to do only that → First, all of a sudden, the idea of resigning from the Collège in order to settle into a life of writing (for the lecture course often comes into conflict with writing). Then, the idea of investing the Course and Work in the same (literary) enterprise, of putting a stop to the division of the subject, in favor of a single Project, the Grand Project: joyous image: what if I were to assign myself a single task, such that I'd no longer have to keep up with all the work to be done (lectures, demands, commissions, constraints), and that each moment of my life would henceforth be integrated into the Grand Project? → That April 15: basically a kind of *Satori*, a kind of bedazzlement, analogous to (no matter if the analogy is naive) the sudden realization that Proust's narrator experiences at the end of *Time Regained* (although *his* book is *already written*!).

Writing Fantasy

All the same, I don't want to make too much of that April 15!—and so will repeat certain elements of that "decision" in a more detached, theoretical, critical manner.

Scripturire

"*To Want-to-Write*" {*Vouloir-Écrire*} = attitude, drive, desire, I don't know what: insufficiently studied, defined, situated. This is clearly indicated by the fact that there's no word for this "wanting to"—or, rather, one exists, a delightful exception, but in decadent, late Latin: *scripturire*, used just once (in the fifth century) by Sidoine Apollinaire,[22] the bishop of Clermont-Ferrand who defended Clermont against the Visigoths (major poetic work). What I mean to say is: since a word exists in one language, albeit only once, it is wanting in all the others (. . . "Fascism" . . .).[23]

To Want-to-Write
{*Vouloir-Écrire*}

Why? Probably because underrepresented, or perhaps, in a more complex manner, because here the relationship between the drive and the activity is autonymical:[24] wanting-to-write is only a matter of the discourse of someone who has written—or is only received as discourse from someone who has managed to write. To say that you want to write—there, in fact, you have the very material of writing; thus only literary works attest to Wanting-to-Write—not scientific discourses. This could even serve as an apposite definition of writing (of literature) as opposed to Science: an order of knowl-

8   FROM LIFE TO THE WORK

Proust, gesture

edge where the product is indistinguishable from the production, the practice from the drive (and, in that case, belongs to an erotics)—Or, put differently again: *writing* is not fully writing unless there's a renunciation of metalanguage; Wanting-to-Write can only be articulated in the language of Writing: this is the autonymy I referred to.

It would be good, one day, to make an inventory of the works in which this Desire-to-Write is explicit (of the *scripturire*): I'm thinking, among others, of Rilke's *Letters to a Young Poet*. I'm thinking—but is that the right word?—of Proust, for the *Scripturire* has its Comprehensive Treatise, its Monument: *In Search of Lost Time*. Proust wrote the epic—as well as the epic of the Desire-to-Write. I'll probably come back to the structure of this epic, for it's a question of a veritable Narrative—the single grand Narrative that *In Search of Lost Time* follows from start to finish—or even of a Myth: a quest, with a series of setbacks, trials (the world, love), which culminates in a final victory. Let's not forget: the *proof* that *In Search of Lost Time* is the narrative of Wanting-to-Write resides in this paradox: the book is supposed to begin at the point when it's already written—brilliant demonstration of the *autonymy* that defines Wanting-to-Write and the Act of Writing. We can go further: all mythical narratives *rehearse* (set to narrative) the idea that death serves some purpose. For Proust: writing serves as a salvation, as a means to vanquish Death: not his own, but the death of loved ones; a way of bearing witness for them, of perpetuating them by drawing them out of non-Memory. Which is why, although there are a great many "characters" in *In Search of Lost Time* (Narrative order), there's only one Figure (who isn't a character): the Mother-Grand-Mother, the one who justifies the writing because the writing justifies her. Proust is a special case in the literary world: a kind of unheroic Hero, in whom *would-be writers* recognize themselves.

SESSION OF DECEMBER 2, 1978

SESSION OF DECEMBER 9, 1978

A lecture isn't a performance, and, as far as possible, you shouldn't come here expecting a show that will either enchant or disappoint—or even—because such perversity exists!—that will enchant because it disappoints.

There's a "design" {dessein} to this course that I'm trying to keep to and an "outline" {dessin} that I'm trying to fill in, week after week—and perhaps year after year. In the first two sessions (last Saturday and today), I want to acknowledge the personal—and even fantasmatic—origins of this Course.

Last time I explained that, at a certain point in a life—which I gave the mythical name "the middle of the journey"—as a result of certain circumstances, certain devastations, the Desire-to-Write (scripturire) can present itself as the obvious Recourse, the Practice whose fantasmatic force would enable a new beginning, a Vita Nuova.

To continue:

Writing Fantasy

For a long time I thought that there was a *Wanting-to-Write* in itself: *To Write*, intransitive verb[1] —now I'm less sure. Perhaps to want to write = to want to write something → To Want-to-Write + Object. There would be *Writing Fantasies*: note the desirous force of the expression, that is to say, think of it on the same footing as so-called sexual fantasies. A sexual fantasy = a scenario with a subject (me) and a typical object (a part of the body, a practice, a situation), where pleasure is produced by that conjunction → Writing Fantasy = me producing a "literary object," that is to say, writing it (here, as always, the fantasy erases the difficulties, the failures), or, rather, being on the point of finishing it. What kind of "object"? Clearly that depends on the subject, on countless individual factors: following a crude typology, it could be a poem, a play, a novel (note that I'm saying: *fantasy* of a poem, *fantasy* of a novel); by the way, just as the sexual fantasy is coded, the fantasy may itself remain *crude*, subject to a very crude typology (literary "genres"); actually a major problem: it depends on the society;

Chubby

USA, gay small ads: an implacable code ("*Handsome, Muscular, Affectionate, Versatile, Chubby, etc.* ≠ *No Fads, Drugs, S/M, Fems.*")[2]

Code and Fantasy

→ On the subject of this "scripted" writing fantasy (Poem, Novel), I note:

Code and Fantasy: important problem. A society can be defined by the rigidity of its fantasmatic code; for example, the USA and its sexual world: catalogue of images (Images = consumer objects); code that's all the more apparent in that it bears upon so-called unconventional desires → A key feature of Homosexuality: constant recuperation through an inner code. In a sense, the Code is superior, an extension of the Law: the constraints of the "type" prevail over the Forbidden (we read a second-order, distorted form of the recreated Forbidden). "Subtle," "original" fantasies: can exist, but only in the form of an almost unspeakable marginality; they cannot make themselves heard, other than by entering the literary order = Sade: extremely, persistently aware of this problem; the meticulous elaboration of catalogues of uncoded fantasies (*One Hundred and Twenty Days*) or rather: of variations on fantasies within a strictly coded category (necrophilia, scatophilia, sadism, etc.) → Probably the same dialectic of Code / Message for the Writing Fantasy: in order to function, the fantasy (of a Poem, a Novel) must remain at the level of a crude, coded Image: *the* Poem, *the* Novel → It's only by coming into conflict with reality (with the reality of poetic, novelistic *practice*) that the fantasy ceases to be a fantasy and attains to the Subtle, the Unprecedented → Proust fantasized the Essay, the Novel (we'll come back to this), but wrote a *Third Form*; in order to begin writing his work, he was obliged to leave the rigidity of the Fantasy behind. The Fantasy as an energy, a motor that gets things going, but what it *then* goes on to produce *in real terms* no longer has to do with the Code.

Guide, model

In this way, the writing fantasy serves as a guide to Writing: the fantasy as initiatory guide (cf. Virgil and Dante).

The Novel

To Write a Novel

You'll have grasped—or, rather, as you already know because I've said and written it (Cerisy):[3] that here Wanting-to-Write relates to the Novel, the Form fantasized is that of the Novel → I've even heard it said (the path rumors usually take) that I'm writing one, which isn't true; if it were, I clearly wouldn't be in a position to propose a lecture course on its preparation: writing requires secrecy. No, I'm at the Fantasy-of-the-novel stage, but I've decided to push that fantasy as far as it will go, to the point where: either the desire will fade away, or it will encounter the reality of writing and what gets written won't be the Fantasized Novel. For the moment, then, we're still at the level of Fantasy—and obviously this completely alters the way in which (the "method" according to which) we can use the word "Novel."

What I call a Novel is therefore—for the moment—a fantasmatic object that *doesn't want* to be absorbed by a metalanguage (scientific, historical, sociological) → hence a wild, blind suspension, an *epoché*, of any commentary *on* the Novel in general → no Metanovel, which means:

Epoché

a. I'll not be discussing, I'll not be taking account of the historical sociology of the Novel, of the "Novel as the destiny of a civilization" (Lukács, Goldmann, Girard)[4] → That the Novel is "the transposition of everyday life in an individualistic society created by market forces to the literary plane" shan't intimidate me. That the mission of the Novel is (has been) to "set a universe of values (love, justice, freedom) and a social system determined by economic laws in opposition to one another," that the novelistic hero should be "a lucid and blind victim of the antagonism between a *real* story and a true ethics"—I'll not dispute any of this, but the Fantasy shan't be paralyzed by it. The Fantasy = irreducible "remainder" of any metanovelistic reductivism.

Goldmann

E.U. [*Encyclopaedia Universalis*]

b. Nor shall I let myself be daunted—at least not for the moment (= "Preparation")—by the question as to whether it's possible to write a novel *today* (that is, in historical and literary terms): novels do get written, of course, but on the one hand they don't sell well (supplanted by "testimonies," by "studies"), and on the other, truth be told, not one of them (broadly speaking since Proust)[5] seems to have "penetrated," attained the category of the Great Novel, the novelistic Monument. In the same way, it can be said that: there have been a great many tragedies since Racine and, equally: there haven't been any tragedies since Racine. *Historically*, then, the question: Is the Novel possible today? is legitimate. But, *naively* (the naivety of the Fantasy), I'm not going to ask it of myself. *For the moment*, I shan't think of the Novel—of "my" Novel—*tactically*.

Modern

In sum, I'll be proposing (on a provisional, initiatory basis) a distinction between: (1) wanting to know how something is made, *in itself*, on the basis of an essence of knowledge (= Science); (2) wanting to know how something is made with a view to making it again, to producing something of the same order (= Technology);

Science / *Techné*

12   FROM LIFE TO THE WORK

here, bizarrely, we'll be setting ourselves a "technical" problem, we'll be regressing from Science to *Techné*.

Replacing "How something is made, with a view to finding out what it is" with "How something is made, with a view to making it again"—the Essence with the Preparation—is linked to an option that's completely antiscientific: in reality, the starting point of the Fantasy isn't the Novel (in general, as a genre) but one or two novels out of thousands. For me, for example: *In Search of Lost Time*, *War and Peace*; but as soon as I start trying to read their other novels (*Jean Santeuil*, *Anna Karenina*) I want to put them down. In sum:

Giant, waste Novel

a. The fantasy seizes upon the "Novel unlike any other": the giant Novel, but also the "waste" Novel. As if the unscientific "essence" of the novel (I'll admit: the idea of an unscientific essence is bizarre! Perhaps it's a kind of existential essence? Whatever prompts the exclamation: "That's it!" Cf. *infra*)[6] were to be found in the *denial* of the genre "Novel." This is certainly the case for *In Search of Lost Time* and even for *War and Peace*, that "historical poem"—this enquiry isn't "scientific" because it isn't looking at an *average* of novels (but perhaps: *Scienza Nuova*[7]: not a science of genres, averages, majorities, but of differences?)

b. On the level of the Fantasy, it is as it were physically impossible to conceive of (to desire) a mediocre work, that is, one that belongs to an "average" → the novels sent to me for review: OK, but why *this particular* story rather than any other? In my view, the most important factor when it comes to *recognizing* a work (which is to say, quite simply and materially, to *reading* it): that it should emit a sense of *necessity*, that it should release us from skepticism: "Why? Why not?" ("Necessity"?—Perhaps what makes meaning proliferate: so that *after* reading is different from before). A curious thing: "blurbs,"[8] by telling the story so emphatically, efface any possibility of it being necessary; never make me want to read the book; they're even a bit off-putting → Rule: never tell the story; story: only to be *written*.)

First Pleasure

The Novel Fantasy: starts out from *a few* novels and to that extent rests on (takes as its starting point) something like the First Pleasure (of reading) → and, from our knowledge of erotic pleasure, we recognize the force of that First Pleasure, which traverses a lifetime.

However: the Fantasy (and the fervor of its desire) is called upon to outgrow, to overstep, to sublimate itself → The Dialectic

13   **SESSION OF DECEMBER 9, 1978**

Eros / Agapé

Novel-Recourse

Sovereign Good

Act of Love

Whom you love

To embrace the world

Gardet

Mysticism, 9

of Desire and Love, of *Eros* and *Agapé* (very familiar to the Mystics; Dionysius the Areopagite). The wounds of Desire can be healed, transcended by the idea of "writing a Novel," of moving beyond the contingencies of failure in the undertaking of a great task, a General Desire, whose object is the whole world. Novel: sort of grand Recourse → the feeling of not belonging anywhere. Would writing be my only *homeland* then? Novel (as something "to get done, to be written," *agendum*): emerges as the Sovereign Good (Saint Augustine, Dante: *Il Sommo Bene*, Saint Thomas, then psychoanalysis).

Thus, in a sense, the Novel is fantasized as an "act of love" (the expression is unfortunate, it leaves me open to accusations of sentimentality and triteness, but it's the only one we have; after all, we have to accept language's limitations). It's not (not any longer) a question of an amorous love, but an *Agapé*-love (even if there's a constant remainder of Eros). An amorous love=to speak of yourself in love=lyrical; while *Agapé*-Love: to speak of the people you love (Novel). Indeed:

a. "*To say whom you love*."[9] To love+to write=to do justice to those whom you've known and loved: to testify for them (in the religious sense), that is, to immortalize them. "To depict whom you love." Sade, in the preface to *Crimes of Love* (*Oeuvres complètes*, vol. IX–X, p. 6. "Ideas on Novels"): "Man is subject to two failings inseparable from his very existence which is defined by them. Everywhere he must *pray* and he must also *love*—and there you have the basic stuff of all novels. Men wrote novels in order to show beings whom they *petitioned*; and they wrote novels to celebrate those whom they *loved*."[10] Proust and the Mother / Grandmother (the only love objects in *In Search of Lost Time*); Tolstoy, his mother (Marie), his grandfather (that is not to say they occupy center stage: they are zones of love that *magnetize*. Novel: mediating structure).

b. The Novel loves the world because it stirs up {*il le brasse*} and embraces it {*l'embrasse*}. There's a generosity to the Novel (which Goldmannian sociology, in its language, clearly doesn't dispute), an *effusiveness*, unsentimental because mediated (think of *War and Peace*). I'm thinking of a distinction present in mystical love (Gardet):[11] (1) Either a love for someone Other than yourself, which aspires to a union with that Other (Monotheistic mystics, Lyrical poetry, the Lover's discourse). (2) Or a fundamental, obscure, ineluctable love, "ontological love" (Indian Mysticism, Novel): Novel: A means of combating the hardness of the heart, acedy.

That might seem abstract: what form can it take on the level of discourse (of the novelistic text)?

Coloration

a. Already said: the Novel is a structure—or an operation of *mediatization*. Sentimentality (unrepressed in that unbearable expression "act of love") is mediatized: induced, not declared, not proffered → cf. Freud (I can't remember where)[12] saying that the death drive is only ever perceived when colored (tinged) by libido; in the same way, the love drive *colors* the Novel: that's all.

b. The novel (always —what I'm calling "Novel": "my" Novel) needs to be situated in relation to the great logical categories of enunciation. I'm thinking of another Zen anecdote: Chou-chan (tenth century) brandished his staff before a group of disciples and said : "Call it not a *shippé* (*chu-pi*); if you do, you assert. Nor do you deny its being a *shippé* (*chu-pi*); if you do, you negate. Apart from affirmation and negation, speak, speak!"[13] Or this, from Alcidamas (the *Sophists*):[14] there are four forms of discourse: affirmation (*phrasis*), negation (*apophasis*), interrogation (*erotesis*), and *prosagoreusis* (declaration, *appellatio*, salutation). Indeed, the novel would be neither affirmation, nor negation, nor interrogation, and yet: (a) it speaks, it speaks; (b) it addresses, it interpolates (this is what *In Search of Lost Time* and *War and Peace* do to me). As to my idea of the Neutral, I'd say: the Novel is a discourse without arrogance, it doesn't intimidate me; a discourse that puts no pressure on me—hence my desire to arrive at a discursive practice that puts no pressure on anyone else: preoccupation of the course on the Neutral → Novel: the writing of the Neutral?

Non-arrogance

My weakness: Memory

However, in order to go a little further into the Fantasy (that is, in order to be able to envisage coming out the other side, into Reality), I need to try to look candidly at my aptitude for writing a Novel (my "faculties"); my only strength (at the moment) is my desire, the obstinacy of my desire (even if I've often "flirted" with the Novelistic; but the Novelistic is not the Novel, and this is precisely the threshold that I want to cross). At any rate, I can immediately see that there's a certain constitutive weakness within me, a certain incapacity to write a novel (cf. a subject whose constitution prevents them from playing sport, who can't play the piano because their hands are too small, etc.) = weakness of an organ → I'll tell you which one: Memory, the ability to remember.

Anamnestic Novels

Rightly or wrongly (I mean: subject to examination and the possibility that my opinion might change): the novels I love = novels of Memory = made out of material (of "memories") *recalled* from

15   **SESSION OF DECEMBER 9, 1978**

childhood, from the life of the writing subject. Proust made this the theory of his work (to be examined in detail, and we shall: we have the time). *In Search of Lost Time* = an *Anamnestic* Novel (culminating in Combray). Tolstoy: not so well known, not so intense, but *War and Peace*: interweaving of memories (he also wrote an anamnestic biography: *Souvenirs* (Pléiade), lots in *Childhood and Boyhood*).[15]

My lack of Memory

Whatever the facts of the matter: the conviction that I have no Memory and as a result that the anamnestic Novel is denied me → Note that Memory "disturbance" can take different forms: there's no such thing as pure, simple, literal Memory, all memory is already *meaning*. In reality, it's not memory that creates (the Novel) but its *deformation* (cf. Bachelard: imagination is that which *deforms* images).[16] Now, different types of mnestic deformation can be more or less productive → Proustian memory: recollection by way of sharp, discontinuous shocks, *unconnected by Time* (subversion of the chronological order) (cf. *infra*):[17] what's subverted is not the *sharpness* of the memory, it's the *order*; but when it comes, the memory intensely felt, torrential, that's what hypermnesia is. My weakness of memory is of a different order: it's a true weakness = an *incapacity*: "Mist-upon-Memory";[18] for example, I have great difficulty recalling the dates of my life; I'd be incapable of writing my own biography, a dated *curriculum vitae*. I probably do experience a few memory-flashes, flashes of memory, but they don't proliferate, they're not associative ("torrential") ≠ Proust. They're instantly exhausted by the short form (cf. the *Anamneses* in *Roland Barthes*),[19] whence the "novelistic" impression they can create, but also, precisely, what separates them from the Novel.

SESSION OF DECEMBER 16, 1978

Past / Present

In the *current* state of my reflection, then, my feeling is that, as far as I'm concerned, the fantasized Novel cannot be of the anamnestic kind. The novelistic "drive" (the love of the material) is not directed toward my past. It's not that I don't like my past; it's rather that I don't like *the* past (perhaps because it rends the heart), and my resistance takes the form of the mist I spoke of → a kind of general resistance to rehearsing, to narrating *what will never happen again* (the dreaming, the cruising, the life of the past). The affective link is with the *present*, my present, in its affective, relational, intellectual dimensions = the material I'm hoping for (cf. "to depict whom I love").[1]

Writing and the Present

Here we immediately encounter a problem that will orient this year's course. Is it possible to make a Narrative (a Novel) out of the Present? How to reconcile—dialecticize—the *distance* implied by the *enunciation of writing* and the *proximity*, the transportation of the present experienced as it happens? (The present is what *adheres*, as if your eyes were glued to a mirror). Present: to have your eyes glued to the page; how to write *at length*, *fluently* (in a fluent, flowing, fluid manner) with one eye on the page and the other on "what's happening to me"?

Life

This is actually to go back to that simple and ultimately uncompromising idea that "literature" (because, when it comes down to it, my project is "literary") is always made out of "life." My problem is that I don't think I can access my past life; it's in the *mist*, meaning that its intensity (without which there is no writing) is weak. What is intense is the life of the present, structurally mixed (there's *my* basic idea) with the desire to write it. The "Preparation" of the Novel therefore refers to the capturing of this parallel text, the text of "contemporary," concomitant life.

To Note

Now, although at first glance making a novel out of present life looks difficult to me, it would be wrong to say that you can't make writing out of the Present. You can write the Present *by noting it*—as it "happens" upon you or under you (under your eyes, your ears) → In this way, we at last come in sight of (I'm nearing the end of my introduction) the double problem, the key to which organizes

Notation

the Preparation of the Novel (of my Novel)—and so constitutes the first object of the course, the one for this year:

—On the one hand, *Notation*, the practice of "noting": *notatio*. On what level is it situated? The level of "reality" (what to choose), the level of the "saying" (what's the form, what's the product of *Notatio*)? What does this practice involve in terms of meaning, time, the instant, the act of saying? *Notatio* instantly appears at the *problematic* intersection between a river of language, of uninterrupted language—*life*, both a continuous, ongoing, sequenced text and a layered text, a histology of cut-up texts, a palimpsest—and a sacred gesture: *to mark* life (to isolate: sacrifice, scapegoat, etc.). Notation: problematic intersection? Yes: what notation presents is the problem of realism. To consider a practice of notation *possible* (rather than laughable) is already to concede the *possibility* of a return (in a spiral) of literary realism. Take note: this term is not to be taken in its French or political connotations (Zola, social realism) but more generally: as a writing practice that willingly submits to the authority of the Reality-Illusion. From this starting point, how to organize, to sustain *Notatio*?

Passage to the novel

—On the other hand, how to pass from Notation, and so from the *Note*, to the Novel, from the discontinuous to the flowing (to the *continuous*, the *smooth* {*au nappé*})? For me, the problem is psychostructural because it involves making the transition from the fragment to the nonfragment, which involves changing my relationship to writing, which involves my relationship to enunciation, which is to say the subject that I am: fragmented subject (= a certain relationship to castration) or effusive subject (a different relationship)? Or again, the conflict between the short form and the long form.

The Novel-Fragment?

Even so (I "daydream" over problems): whenever the mind formulates an alternative—loathing the trap it presents and savoring the simplification: for, when it comes down to it, *choosing* is easier than *inventing*—a *third form* should always be considered. Figure: something that seems impossible at first may turn out to be possible after all. In this case: possible to conceive of a *Novel through Fragments*, a *Novel-Fragment*. Such novels probably exist—or some that come close to it: everything hinges on the *dash*, on the site, on the flux, on the page upon which the caesura of the discontinuous is *marked*: here it would be necessary, it will be necessary to examine the visual *devices* of novels: paragraphs, blank alineas = *perigraphy* (cf. book by A. Compagnon, forthcoming with Seuil).[2] I'm thinking of the *cryptofragmentary* aspect of Flaubert (*blanks*)[3] and of *Aziyadé*.[4] There have to be many other examples—and, on a deeper, less formal level: there's of course Proust's discontinuous, the *Rhapsodic* (a problem for the second part of the course).

I'll naturally be dealing with these problems *indirectly* → I'll be "hooking" them onto two external experiences, onto two tutor texts:

Haiku

a. *Notation*: I might have chosen a novelist's notebooks or a biographical diary (Notation of the Present). I chose, out of personal preference and also to remain as close as possible to the problem of the short form, to speak of the short form that I love more than any other and that is as it were the very essence of Notation: the haiku. There'll therefore be a series of sessions on haiku (which is to say: on an exemplary type of Notation of the Present). Be that as it may:

Proust

b. *The Passage from the Fragment to the Novel* (to the long text): here I will (or at least I intend to) draw on Proust; more precisely, I'll be investigating that biographical episode over the course of which it seems (after agitations, hesitations, indecisions) Proust was *at last* able to launch the great river of *In Search of Lost Time*. A further point, in passing: I'm finding Proust's *life* more and more "interesting"—that is to say, worthy of investigation—*from the point of view of writing*: it's becoming increasingly necessary to conceive of a kind of "science" (so to speak) of Proust's life (the business of the film with A. T.)[5]

That, broadly speaking (I think, for I'm not yet able to calibrate the different parts), is how this year's course will be organized = two—seemingly disparate—pivots → excentric articulation—of a certain circumvolution of the Novel to be written, of the fantasized Novel: the *Haiku / Proust* (and I mean *Proust*—not *In Search of Lost Time*). I'm convinced of the validity of this opposition but was nevertheless afraid that you'd find it a little abrupt, a little elliptical, a little casual—or farfetched {*tirée par les cheveux*}[6] (an enigmatic expression: it's more a question of splitting hairs). Happily, just in time, a friend furnished me with a quotation—and it's from Proust (*Chronicles*): "Narrating events is like introducing people to opera via the libretto only. Should I write a novel, I'd endeavor to distinguish between the differing music of each successive day."[7] The differing music of each successive day → that's haiku exactly. Hence, when it comes down to it: perhaps what's fantasized is the *Novel as Opera*.

Two Clarifications

Before beginning (the session on haiku), I feel I should make two things clear—or make two confessions:

1. As If

Will I *really* write a Novel? I'll answer this and only this. I'll proceed *as if* I were going to write one → I'll install myself within this *as if*: this lecture course could have been called "*As If*."
Comments:

Risk

a. People will say to me—it's been said to me: by announcing it, you're taking a huge risk, a "magic" risk. To say something out loud, in advance, is to destroy it; to designate too early is to attract bad luck (Don't count your chickens).[8] Ordinarily, I take this kind of risk very seriously; I never allow myself to talk about the book I'm going to write. Why am I risking it this time and *provoking the Gods*, so to speak? Because the risk is bound up with the mutation I spoke of (Middle of Life's Journey): that mutation effectively involves the consideration of a kind of *Nothing left to lose*. That's in no way the motto of a "desperado" but rather of the search for a considered counterpoint to an expression that's so French (which haunts the conduct of the French): "to lose face"—French culture being more a culture of shame than of sin. Whether or not I write a novel, whether or not I fail in my attempt to write one, this isn't a "performance" but a "path." To be in love is to lose face and to accept it, hence there's no face to be lost.—Moreover:

Nothing left to lose

To be in love: is to lose face and to accept it

Method

b. *As if*: the motto of *Method* (a particular way of working used by Mathematicians). Method = the methodical exploitation of a hypothesis; here, as you'll have grasped: a hypothesis not of *explanation* (of interpretation) (meta-Novel), but of *production*.

Path, without end

c. Method = path. (Grenier, Tao = Path.[9] Tao is at once the path to be traveled and the end of the journey, the method and the accomplishment. No sooner have you set out on the path than you have already traveled its length). Tao: what matters is the path, following the path, not what you find at the end → The Quest of the Fantasy is already a Narrative → "Begin, even without hope; proceed, even without success."[10] (It's *also* a Sartrean saying).

Grand nostalgic theme

d. It's therefore possible that the Novel will remain at the level of—or be exhausted and accomplished by—its Preparation. Another title for this course (which will probably go on for several years, circumstances permitting) could be "The Impossible Novel."

In which case, the labor that's beginning = the exploration of a grand nostalgic theme. Something lurks in our History: the Death of literature; it's what roams around us; we have to look that ghost in the face, taking *practice* as our starting point → it's therefore a question of *tense* labor: at once *anxious* and *active* (the Worst is never certain).[11]

2. Ethics / Technique

Technique

Since this Course will involve investigating a practice, there'll be some *paratechnical* issues to consider (and one technique in particular: literary) → Risk that you'll be disappointed, that some of you won't find it interesting: disappointment that I'm attempting to ward off by naming and anticipating it → At first, the register will seem completely different to last year's: *Neutral = ethical* category: there's no "technique" of the Neutral, other than in Tao.

Yet: it seems to me that each thing—every action, operation, intervention, gesture, work—has three aspects to it: technical, ideological, ethical → The ideological aspect of this enterprise isn't for me to decide, it's for others to identify: The Ideological is always Other People.

Aesthetics / Ethics

But it's my hope that this labor will be undertaken at the undecidable point where the Technical and the Ethical meet. And if we consider the fact that, when it comes to writing, a Technique presupposes an Aesthetics, then this labor (this Course): situated at the point where the Aesthetic and the Ethical intersect, overlap.

Kierkegaard

This is a Kierkegaardian problem. (*Either / Or*). Let's articulate it (and correct it) with Kafka (in conversation with Janouch): "Kierkegaard faces the problem, whether to enjoy life aesthetically or to experience it ethically. But this seems to me a false statement of the problem. The Either-Or exists only in the head of Sören Kierkegaard. In reality one can only achieve an aesthetic enjoyment of life as a result of humble ethical experience."[12]

The "Technical" is basically the moral and humble experience of Writing → not, in the end, very far removed from the Neutral. Will it interest you—even those among you who don't write, or those among you who do but who aren't plagued by the same problems as I am? My hope rests on personal experience: I never tire of hearing people talk about their craft[13] the problems they come up against in their work, *whatever it is they do*. Most of the time, unfortunately, people think they're under an obligation to engage in *general conversation*. How many times have I been irritated and frustrated

Craft and general conversation

The domestic

by a conversation—that others make "general"—because a specialist whom I'd dearly love to hear discuss his specialism starts making banal cultural or philosophical remarks, when he could be telling me about his craft!—Intellectuals in particular never discuss their craft, as if they didn't have one: they have "ideas," "positions," but no craft! The amused and indulgent irony with which Rambures's survey was received (by him, by the way).[14] What? These writers who pay attention to which pen they use, to the kind of paper or the desk they write on! They're crazy, etc.

For me, there's an alliance between the Aesthetic (the Technical) and the Ethical; its privileged field: the minutiae of daily life, the "domestic." Perhaps wanting to write a novel (*the* Novel? *my* Novel?) is to enter into, to settle into a practice of *domestic* writing. Cf. Proust comparing the novel that's being written to a dress being cut, assembled, tacked together, in a word: *prepared* by a dressmaker (this is the sense in which "the Preparation of the Novel" should be understood). In Proust's time—and the time of my childhood: dressmakers working from home would go from house to house (Mademoiselle Sudour)[15] gleaning and relaying bits of news → dream of the Novelist's domestic labor: to be a Dressmaker working from home.

SESSION OF JANUARY 6, 1979

The Haiku

"My" Haiku[1]

My problem: how to pass from the Notation (of the Present) to the Novel, from a short, fragmented form ("notes") to a long, continuous form → the decision to concern myself with haiku for a short while *so as* to then be concerned with the novel is therefore less paradoxical than it might seem. Haiku = exemplary form of the Notation of the Present = minimal act of enunciation, ultrashort form, an atom of a sentence that *notes* (marks, delimits, glorifies: endows with a *fama*)[2] a tiny element of "real," present, concomitant life.

Nothing historical → "My" haiku—"*My*" doesn't refer, or doesn't *ultimately* refer, to an egotism, a narcissism (objections that, so I'm told, have been made of this course) but to a Method: method of exposition, method of speech: not *speaking* the subject but not censuring the subject either (which is completely different), changing the *rhetorical* conditions of the Intellectual—means: crystallizing theme, theme with variations, geometrical site of reflections, problems and preferences = "simulacrum," "alibi"; act of naming: "to everything that I'm about to say, I give the name haiku, *with a certain degree of plausibility*," cf. "I baptize you Carp."[3] = I baptize you haiku → something of the same vague, insistent, and probably distortive relationship as that between the classical authors and Antiquity: do we consider Racine's relationship to the Greeks to be the same as Jean-Pierre Vernant's or Marcel Detienne's? The real difference (clearly I'm not speaking of differences in values here) is that they had a good grasp of Greek and Latin, whereas I don't read Japanese at all—Even if I did! As a general rule, the translations of the classics need to be revised: a translation needs to be redone every twenty-five years. Which says a lot about the *certitudes* of philology. Here, then, it's a matter of a Discourse, not of Explanation, nor indeed of Interpretation, but of *Resonance*.

The Haiku in Its Materiality

I'm not saying: in its history, nor even its structure (technique), but such as it presents itself to a Frenchman. It's a *tercet* → French has no, or only very few, (autonomous and/or continuous) tercets; it begins with the quatrain ≠ Dante.[4] Paul Valéry: "Dante gave nothing to the French (other than *Paradiso*: a kind of abstract versification)"; cf. *Le Cimetière marin*.[5]

Japanese: a strongly syllabic language; clear, well-placed syllables (the act of syllabification has been linked to manducation: movement of the lower jawbone; we chew our words: bites); a syllabic alphabet (*Kana*) repeats the *Kanji* (especially proper names and linking words)[6] → the words are relatively easy to pronounce, which means it's relatively easy to make oneself understood: easier to take a taxi in Tokyo than it is in New York.

This tercet: 5 + 7 + 5 syllables Etiemble (5–7–5)

Furu ike ya	*Une vielle mare*
Kawazu tobikomu	*Une raine en vol plongeant*
Mizu no oto	*Et le bruit de l'eau*[7]

Very poor translation! Cf. *infra*.[8]

That 5–7–5 formula: exceptions, adaptations, liberties taken, a certain tendency toward free verse. This matters to us: if that tendency is followed, then what we're left with is pure, unversified, unmetered notation (the only constraint: the presence of the seasonal word; cf. *infra*:[9] although that too is contested) with, as always, a swing back the other way: there are those who call for a return to a strict 575 (let's agree to call haiku by what's almost the name of a cannon!);[10] now, what *we* consume is a line of free verse, and *we find it pleasing*, despite the absence of meter. Here, a problem of translation arises, which takes two forms:

Translation

1. To emphasize the enigma: what comes to me from a very foreign (very strange) language whose basic principles elude me—and furthermore from a "poetic" discourse—still manages to touch me, interest me, enchant me (yet I'm in no position to check the translation, even from a distance). I'm entirely in the hands of the translator, but he *doesn't present an obstacle* → a situation of *familiarity* that's altogether paradoxical → Think of the *exclusion* that an utterly opaque foreign language represents: Valéry in Prague. "Lost abroad

in an unknown language. Everyone understands one another, and together are human. But not you, or you . . ."[11] To me, the haiku is human, absolutely human. How is that possible (for me, who never experiences that sensation of familiarity with other kinds of translated poetry)?

This is how I explain it to myself: the haiku is the conjunction of a "truth" (not a conceptual truth, but of the *Instant*) and a form. I'm thinking of another remark of Valéry's: "to show that pure thought and the discovery of truth as such can only ever aspire to the discovery or the construction of some form or other":[12] yes, I believe that: that form (some form or other) proves, manifests truth (and not only "reasoning"). But for us, the French, the haiku isn't a form.—Or rather it *is* a form, and this can only be explained by the fact that the brevity of the enunciation—how it is *framed*—is already a form in itself; the short Form is an inductor of truth: and it is this that we sense when we read a haiku, despite all the remoteness of the language and the poetic structure. *Poetry and Truth*:[13] the appropriate syntagm. Poetry: its sole justification: truth. In Poetry, form and only form is what enables us to *touch* the truth; the tactile power of form: to touch the word, the line, the tercet.

2. Second problem: "poetic" translations of haiku. Some translators have sought to translate the 5–7–5 syllables into (unrhymed) French verse (cf. Etiemble). But to do so makes no sense. Our ability to detect a meter, a beat, a syllabic rhythm is dependent on having already had the metrical formula whispered to us by our poetic culture, on the code functioning like a route, a path, imprinted onto, incised into our brains that's then retraced, *recognized* in the performance of the poem; there is no rhythm as such: all rhythm is *cultural*; otherwise, the formula falls *flat* (it isn't a formula): it doesn't work, it exerts no fascination, it fails to *send us to sleep*. What I mean is: the function of all rhythm is either to excite or to *calm* the body, which, on a certain level, at some, distant, profound, primitive point in the body, amounts to the same thing: to excite or to calm the body by means of the formula is to assimilate the body to a nature, to reconcile it, to put an end to its separation, to *unsever* it. It's been claimed (Morier)[14] that meter (with its monotony) promotes euphoria and romance, that it's calming (≠ anarchic, stirring rhythm, exclamations, surprises, emotions, etc.).—Now French, I think (I haven't checked this): has few heptasyllables and no pentasyllables (as ever: to be checked because *everything exists*,[15] though not all of it is *memorable*).

---

46 / 1923
apropos of Eupalinos

Coyaud # 53

SESSION OF JANUARY 6, 1979

Typography. Aeration

And yet, the haikist Tercet exerts a fascination over us—not because of its meter, which is impossible in French, but because of its size, its tenuity, that is to say, metonymically, the aeration it grants the space of discourse → Haiku: the short form *par excellence*; this is a fact of reading: short forms draw the eye to the page (cf. a phenomenology of verse, even and especially of free verse: we don't read the lines as we would if they were set out end to end; the blank space attracts, reposes, distracts the eye). We're drawn to the short form as toward something that will hold our interest. Example: *Epigrams* (Martial): we go directly to the shortest ones; as soon as we spot one only two lines long, that's the one we'll pick first → aeration of the page, essential for the *picking* of haiku (in the Munier edition, for instance, there are only three per page, that's all).[16] So, to appreciate a haiku—even and especially in French, where its constitutive meter disappears—it has to be seen written down, with the line breaks: a little aerated tome, a little block of writing, like an ideogrammatical square; ultimately, on another, deeper mental level, unfettered by the superficial divisions of everyday discourse, it could be said that haiku—that *a* haiku, it alone, in its entirety, its finitude, its solitude on the page, forms a single ideogram, that is to say a "word" (and not a discourse broken down into sentences). (1) Valéry quotes these lines from Mallarmé: "I have managed to get rid of punctuation [Sollers!]; the line is an entity, a new word—never heard before, someone who punctuates needs crutches, *his sentence doesn't walk / work on its own {sa phrase ne va pas tout seule}*."[17] → The haiku walks / works on its own: it is a word. Indeed, in the corpus, it will be necessary get rid of the punctuation, to make corrections. (2) Despite, or by way of its sophistication, the haiku has a certain affinity with, is in fundamental "sympathy" with the "holophrase" (Kristeva, Lacan): a verbal gesture that can't be broken down, a nonthetic expression of desire.[18]

So: typography determines reading; it *constitutes* the haiku, even once its metrical constitution has been destroyed. Proof (so to speak): the problem Coyaud presents:[19] Are there some French poems that come close to the haiku?—No, probably not, for reasons that will resurface every now and then; but, what is certain: if here, in France, there were some form or other that might sometimes recall the haiku, it wouldn't be a poem, however short; sometimes a single line can do it—a line that resonates like a haiku: though, again, and despite it seeming childish, that line would have to be divided into three parts—it

P. V. 1741

would have to *mimic* the haiku visually, even if those divisions have no metrical reality: once again, the *aeration* of the written form is part of the haiku's mode of being. Cf. (1) Mallarmé and free verse: "it's difficult to write free verse without breaks."[20] Here, breaks: plugs of air, of white space. (2) The relationship between the written form and painting in the Orient, insofar as that relationship participates in the creation of so-called empty spaces.

For example, this line by Milosz (Schehadé)[21] is almost a haiku—later on, we'll see what makes it not quite a haiku: the *excess* that is its deficiency (the familiar *You*, the lover's interjection):

You, sad, sad sound of rain on the rain

It would gain more in haiku (in "haikuity") if we were to write it thus:

You, sad
Sad sound of rain
On the rain

I repeat: don't underestimate what the *layout* of speech on the page can do. All oriental (Chinese) art: a respect for *space*, which is to say (let's be more precise) for *spacing*. As we know: the Japanese are far from familiar with the Kantian categories of Space and Time, but with the category—which runs through them both—of Spacing, of the Interval: *Ma*.

(Larousse)

1. When we speak of the (oriental) "Void," it shouldn't be in a Buddhist sense but more sensually: as a respiration, an aeration and, so to speak, as a *"matter"*; a physicist's saying: "If there were no space between matter then the entire human race would fit into a thimble" → Haiku: the "antithimble," condensation that's antitotalizing, and it's this that the haikist tercet says. (I leave it to you to interpret this *"protestation of the Void"* (as we say: protestation of virility) thematically: respiratory drive, to be free from suffocation-anxiety, the fantasy of Oxygen, of Euphoric, Jubilatory Respiration).

2. The Japanese *Ma*: space and time (spacing and interval): haiku also involves a practice of spaced Time (cf. *infra* on the Instant).[22]

The Fascicule

There are those who'll say: you're expounding a philosophy of the *written* haiku (when of course, originally, they were *spoken*), but I'm not interested in the origins, in the historical "truth" of haiku;

my concern is the haiku *for me*; me, a French subject who reads collections of translations (it's the practice of this lecture course to always start out from the *subject*: enunciating, reading). I'm not sure that I'd know how to read a haiku (I mean: to read in a way that would *produce* an effect of truth); for that matter, in what context, in what *layer* of other discourses, according to what *Ma*? (*where* to read haiku?)—The *voice* seems impossible to me. → So, in order to articulate what I want to say about the haiku, I've prepared a small collection of haiku; I shall refer to the haiku that figure on the fascicule as and when our topic requires it; this isn't an *anthology*, then, but a *corpus*.[23]

The translations are taken from:

Blyth, Reginald Horace. *A History of Haiku*. 4 vols. Tokyo: Hokuseido Press, 1963.[24]
Coyaud, Maurice. *Fourmis sans ombre. Le livre du haiku. Anthologie promenade*. Paris: Phébus, 1978.
———. *Fêtes au Japon. Haiku*. PAF (Pour l'analyse du folklore) 38, rue de Wagram, Paris, 75013.
Munier, Roger. *Haiku*. Preface by Yves Bonnefoy. Paris: Fayard, 1978.
Yamata, Kikou. "Sur des lèvres japonaises," with a letter-preface by Paul Valéry, in *Le Divan*. 1924.

For the lines from French poems in relation to haiku:

Schehadé, Georges. *Anthologie du vers unique*. Paris: Ramsay, 1977.

SESSION OF JANUARY 13, 1979

The Desire for Haiku

Enchantment of Haiku

There is, for me—probably ever since I first started reading them, periodically, more than twenty years ago—an enchantment of haiku: tenacious desire, guaranteed enchantment → With haiku, I'm in the *Sovereign Good* of writing—and of the world, for the enigma of writing, its tenacious life, its desirability, is that it can never be separated from the world, "a little bit of writing cuts you off from the world, a lot draws you back in." We shall see, however, that the Sovereign Good of haiku is provisional; it's insufficient (and so not the Sovereign Good), which is why, and this is the argument of the Course, there's call for the novel.

Here are two haiku—among many others—that enchant me:

(1)[1]   *With a bull on board*
A small boat crosses the river
Through the evening rain

(Shiki, Blyth*)

(2)   *A day of haze*
The great room
Is deserted and still

(Issa, Blyth*)

Why these ones? No guarantee they'll enchant anyone else: the science of haikist (that is to say, "Aesthetic") beauty is an uncertain one → The proof that something is "Pleasing" = being incapable of saying why → Enchantment = a space where commentary should be, commentary left blank, its degree zero (≠ "no comment," "literality"): it's the *unsayable*, "being incapable of saying anything" as opposed to "having nothing to say." There's only a *Region* of the Pleasing: erotic region where one thing *Brushes Up Against* another: (1) a form, a sentence, with its ascetic, elliptical workings, its lack of fat (Valéry: the essential thinness of things) brushes up against (2) a referent (the room, the boat); let's be clear: as "evocation," "vision," which means already immediately worked into a sign → Brushing

Up Against, voluptuous Rubbing: a kind of sensual peace. A *perversity* of haiku? (Perversity: that which *checks* Neurosis, Obsessionality. Here, the perversion would come from what's readable: presence / absence of the Referent).

Thus, on the enchantment of haiku: no analysis but two or three approaches, or, to be more precise: kinds of *attestation*.

The Desire for Haiku

The haiku is *desired*, which is to say there is the desire to write one oneself = conclusive proof (of love): when you want to do something yourself; a desire to produce is inferred from the pleasure of the product.—This could be one criterion of a *Typology* of cultural products: especially since the historical emergence of mass media, of a so-called mass culture: a culture of pure "products" where the desire to produce has died out, has been foreclosed (left to the pure professionals); a small ideological (as well as, in a sense, an ecological) crisis in France today: the desire to produce seems to have been completely marginalized (amateurs: songs, poems); I mean (for the willingness of individuals is not at issue): in France, there are no (poetic) forms popular enough to accommodate the desire for production) ≠ the Japanese are more fortunate than us:

a. The ardent desire for haiku—the irresistible "drive" for haiku (we can probably find a few young French people possessed by this mad desire to *make* poetry).

Shiki (1866–1902) narrates:

THE DESIRE FOR HAIKU

Toward the end of 1891, I rented a house in Komagome, where I lived alone . . . spending my time reading haiku and novels rather than my textbooks. Two days before the exam, I cleared my desk and replaced the haiku and novels with my school books. Sitting at that table—which had been chaotic, and now was tidy—I experienced such violent pleasure . . . that the haiku began to emerge within me, like bubbles on the surface of my consciousness. I opened a textbook; impossible to read a line; a haiku had already formed within me. Since I'd cleared even the tiniest scrap of blank paper from my desk in order to devote myself entirely to preparing for my exam, I noted the haiku on the lampshade. But already another one was forming. Then another. Before long the lampshade was completely covered in haiku.[2]

Coyaud 33

Producing haiku (as a popular pastime): a kind of classless "national sport" (Sieffert).[3] Still, today, it plays a big part in the daily life of Japan: sixty magazines, many of them with a very large readership + columns in the papers + every Sunday, the *Asahi* (*The Dawn*): the achievements of amateur haikists are introduced by three eminent poets.

This intense pleasure taken in producing haiku, this ardent desire for haiku: perhaps linked, in Japan (which is why it would be literally unthinkable here), to the genre's (metrical) *constraint*: the seventeen syllables selected from the fifty possible consonant + vowel groups in Japanese phonetics → combinations of the fifty elements, mathematically calculable; however, if it's meaningful combinations we're after: the number of possibilities is reduced, whence the collections of thousands of haiku, enabling the poet to check that his composition hasn't already been composed by someone else → Essentially a board game, but what's at stake is not a dull performance (crosswords, Scrabble) but a *vibration* of the world (that we can call: *the poetic*): ancestral code + modern materials. Example:

(3) *The city-folk*
In the homeward train
Red maple leaves in their hands

(Meisetsu, Coyaud)

It's the right formula: in Japan, it's possible to produce modern, vital haiku. So why can't we?

1. First, due to the absence of metrical form: the great French meters have been weakened, devalorized by bourgeois, unimaginative use; the Alexandrine comes in for "ridicule" (albeit unmerited): its structure is ponderous, narrative; in order to shed some of that weight, to maintain its vitality, French poetry has been obliged to abandon meter, the code.

2. Even if we had a meter that were still alive, it would be difficult to come up with an equivalent to the haiku: here, in France, our referent-words are very weak; they've become "literary," old, and unpoetical; in Japan, there's still a vital connection with the ears of corn, the sparrows, the flowers, the leaves, etc. Let's imagine the slippage:

$$\text{Into the} \left\{ \begin{array}{c} \text{Saké} \\ \text{Pernod} \end{array} \right\} \text{hidden}$$

SESSION OF JANUARY 13, 1979

> He had secretly dipped
> A rose!
>
> (cf. Sade, rose and mud)[4]

History has outmoded the objects that we have an investment in (by the way, something to work on: what *mythical objects* do the French have an investment in nowadays? Wine? It's no longer felt to be "poetical," bucolic, hedonistic, but energy giving and "Gallic").

Yet for some of us, for those of us who love haiku, a desire for haiku persists, a haiku linguistic fantasy. Even without metrics, simply by dividing up a notation, we're playing at "haiku." But naturally it doesn't take, it doesn't come together {*ça ne prend pas*}: what's missing is the Meter, the Code (even if it's to abandon it through taking a "liberty"). What would be required is for a Poet to invent a new verse for us, one that's not yet been worn out by School: "The French demand a Poet."

Nonclassification

Second attestation of the Good Fortune of haiku: although subject to an internal constraint (metrics), it's absolutely free in its scope, its multiplicity (the only constraint, which I'll come to later: the reference to the season). As a genre, it's not defined topically by a particular type of subject (≠ the whole of Greco-Latin poetry): the tenuity, the "inconsequentiality" of the haiku ensures that it eludes all classification. There's only one traditional form of classification: by season (example: Blyth).[5]

Coyaud rejects it; he's wrong to do so, because there's no other to replace it: the haiku is the Unclassifiable, radically so → which means that the book can be opened at any page, any which way, without a scrap of meaning being lost. World in which the Syntagm is denied: not one liaison is possible → emergence of the absolutely immediate: the haiku = immediate desire (without mediation), which disrupts the legal function of Classification (= always a law) → Scarcely necessary to point out how modern that disruption is, a response to a contemporary anxiety:

Fragments, of course, but also all arts of the aleatory (risk: that the aleatory not become a sign of itself). John Cage: it's said that his interest in mushrooms stems from their place in the dictionary: *music* and *mushroom* come close to one another;[6] they're *present* to one another yet they're not connected; a mode of co-presence

Cage 38

that's very difficult to conceptualize: to conceive of a co-presence without it being metonymical, antithetical, causal, etc.; a consecution without logic yet without it *signifying* the destruction of logic: a *neutral* consecution—such would be the surface of a collection of haiku.

Nonappropriation

Third attestation, which has to do with to the freedom of the Desire for haiku. For example: "A very thoughtful friend makes me a present of a book of haiku, which he'd collected together and transcribed by hand. I recognize some of them; I'd already read them in published collections. But the other ones? Are they by authors I'm not familiar with (for there are any number of haikists)? Or had he written them himself?" → The point is, in haiku, ownership trembles: the haiku *is* the subject, a quintessence of subjectivity, but that's not the same thing as the "author." Haiku belong to everyone in the sense that it can seem as if everyone's writing them—in that it's plausible that everyone could be writing them. This is what convinces me that the haiku is of the order of Desire, in that it circulates: in that ownership—the *auctoritas*—is passed on, circulates, takes turns, as in Pass-the-Parcel.

Announcement of what I'm going to do

⁷ So there you have the haiku *for-me*, such as I'm able to make sense of it, in its materiality and my Desire. With this haiku set out before us, my role here will be twofold:

1. Not to try to directly *explain* why I love haiku—because the explanation of Desire is illusory: as you explain, you only ever manage get at what, in the subject, always recedes; there's no *end* to the explanation of Desire (of Pleasure): the subject is infinitely *layered*—but rather to *make explicit* {*expliciter*}—take note: *to make explicit* (1870) will involve giving *to explain* (ossified as "to provide a cause, to find a cause") back its etymological value: to unfold (to *make explicit*: scholastic, end of the fifteenth century)—the system of values (ideological, aesthetic, ethical, etc.) that a fondness for haiku allows us to *presuppose*, *to reconstruct* (perhaps that's what Art is, what Form is: what gives us the courage to come to terms with our Desire: making thought: *the animation of an adventure*).

2. To indicate, in keeping with the project of this Course, the path that leads—that *will lead*, since what's at stake is a program—from "Life" (and the haiku is made directly from life, *without*

remainder) to a *form* that retroactively makes it into a memory, emotion, intelligibility, "charity" (theme of the Sovereign Good).

As we journey through the territories of very indistinct themes, we'll naturally be combining these two tasks (there'll be no demonstrative performance).[8]

The Weather

Season

Cahiers Renault-Barrault (November 31, 1960): 171

In the oldest haiku, always an allusion to the season: the *Kigo*, or *Seasonal-Word*; it is either denoted: *summer* heat, *autumn* wind, or there's a clear and coded metonymy: plum blossom=spring. The *Kigo*, the base note, something like the *keynote* of the haiku. There's always something in the haiku to tell you *where you are in the year*, something about the sky, the cold, the light: seventeen syllables, but you're never separated from the cosmos in its immediate form: the *Oikos*, the atmosphere, the coordinates of the Earth's orbit around the Sun. You always have a *sense* of the season: both as a fragrance and as a sign.

As an example, two haiku (4 and 5):

(4)   Lying down
       I watch the clouds go by
       Summer bedroom

                                                        (Yaha)

The vividness of the season is made to unfold, it seems to me, in the following way:

a. Denoting it (at the end: *summer*)[9] is very powerful in itself: to say *summer* is already to see the *summer*, to be in summer (perhaps—a subtle linguistic problem—there's a differential in referential resonance depending on the words used, for example, food in novels; *champagne* when you're thirsty; *Goldfinger*,[10] the crabs and the pink champagne).

b. The summer *captured* in the bedroom is more intense: it's captured as an absence, captured outside. It's indoors, precisely where it has been driven out that summer is most powerful: it triumphs outside and intensifies→ its intensity: Intensity of the Indirect, which shows that the Indirect is the very path of communication, of manifestation of the Essence.

c. New kind of Indirect: that of an idle action, watching the clouds go by; to let the sensation of the season *burst forth*, we focus "hypocritically" on the action. In the same way, the clouds reinforce the summer because they're invoked by the gentle form of "what goes by."—There's no *description* of the summer in all of this: it's a pure *surrectum*: that which rises up, bursts forth (*surgere*), and actively: *surrector*, someone who rises up → we mustn't be misled by the haiku's tenuity: in the form of a strict *enclosure*;[11] it's the beginning of an infinite speech that can unfold the summer *by taking the path of an Indirect that*, unlike the Sentence, *has no structural reason to come to an end*; one could imagine a whole Novel (or a whole film, for film has taken up where the Novel left off) that would be the Indirect of the summer continuously. Already: in seventeen syllables, our haiku says more or less what Proust, from the starting point of the hotel room at Balbec, says about the summer in those one or two densely written pages.—Let's keep this in mind: the haiku may be *short*, but it's not *finite, closed*.

(5) The winter wind blows
     The cat's eyes
     Blink

(Basho†)

It's incredible, wonderful, the extent to which that makes me feel the winter.—It could be said: it's trying to do with *that little bit of language* what language can't do: evoke the thing itself → Haiku: language at the extreme limit of its power, of its efficacy; truly *discourse* in that it makes up for language's deficiencies, remunerates it.[12]

Therefore (even if Coyaud gave up classifying haiku according to season) the Season is fundamental: it will present itself to us in a form that's at once more vague and more precise (I mean: broader and more focused): *what the Weather is like* (was like). For my part, I'm extremely sensitive to it: cf. Proust and Meteorology (there's even a scholarly article—by Dufour—on the subject).[13] (The father's interest. Resembles his father. *In Search of Lost Time*: eighty passages displaying a fondness for Meteorology). It's like the essence of Life, of Memory. This *individual* (for example, aesthetic) investment in the Season (in the Weather) is a continuation of the interest that rural cultures take in the seasons and the weather (*Weather*);[14] men understood the seasons first, not time-duration (*Time*)[15] (their survival depended on it); they experienced *their difference and their return*, cf. the Japanese *Ma*: interval. Note that: nowadays, there's a mythical erosion of the Seasons (the theme of "*There are no seasons anymore*" is in itself a contemporary myth). The abolition of the seasons (replaced by the paradigm vacation period / nonvacation period) is one form of "Pollution" → The literature of the past becomes the Witness, the Monument to the Seasons we're no longer familiar with. Example: Amiel's *Diary*.[16] Now, *that speaks to us*, but in the form of nostalgia. I experienced the seasons in Bayonne (and even in Paris: an icy wind on the place Saint-Sulpice as I made my way to the Lycée Montaigne, whereas I don't get cold on the place Saint-Sulpice anymore), and when I'm in Bayonne, I no longer have any, or very little, sense of the season → Mythical theme: in the past, the Seasons were clear-cut, Difference reigned ≠ today, the world is *equivocal* (cf. Verlaine: "an equivocal evening")[17] → the haiku creates *clear-cut* seasons (our recent—farcical—astonishment at it being cold in winter).

SESSION OF JANUARY 20, 1979

The Weather

Point already made: our French language—which, in this respect as in others, is barbaric (because "civilized")—flattens the species onto the genus and censures the force of individuation, of difference, of nuance, of shimmering existentiality in the relationship between man and the atmosphere. I've said it, a single word: the Weather {*le Temps*}. Already, in English: *time / weather*; and Latin: *tempus / coelum*. Superiority of the Greek: *chronos / aer*, how the sky looks; *eudia*, fine weather; *ombrios*, rainy; *cheimon*, stormy; *galene*, calm at sea, etc.—In French, what-the-weather-is-like {*le-temps-qu'il-fait*}:[1] we introduce a causative, making it very clear that what's at stake in this notion is an active relation between the subject and the present.

For my part, I've always considered the Weather to be an underestimated topic (*quaestio*). But, formerly (fascinated by semiological problems in the strictly structuralist sense): the weather = exemplary phatic[2] (= pure phatic: for it doesn't bring *language positions* into play, cf. Flahault).[3] So I'd emphasize the communication that occurs by means of an empty (a trivial) enunciation → *The Weather*: false referent that enables people to communicate, to come into contact with one another, when ordinarily the subjects in question: (1) don't know each other; (2) don't feel that they belong to the same class, the same culture; (3) can't bear silence; (4) want to talk to each other but don't want to offend, to risk upsetting anyone, conflict; (5) or, at the other extreme, who love each other so much that they use the very tactfulness of the trivial expression as a means to express their love; for example, the words exchanged between the members of a family who love each other and meet (in the morning): cf. Proust, *Within a Budding Grove*, Charlus relaying a quotation apropos of Mme de Sévigné and her daughter,[4] La Bruyère, "Of the Heart": "To be close to those we love, to talk to them, to say nothing to them, it's all the same."[5] → To discuss the weather *together* = this *it's all the same* of talking / not talking about love. In this way, some absolute affections, whose defection through death causes the most terrible pain, can, have been able to move, live, breathe in the gentle triviality of this kind of talk: so *the Weather* expresses a *deficiency* of language (of discourse) that is precisely what's at stake in love: the pain at no longer being able to talk about the Weather with the loved one. Seeing the first snow and not being able to tell them, having to keep it to yourself.

[6]Brief digression. Even from the point of view of a semantics of communication, the Weather is not an innocent theme: it's frequently used by the government as an excuse to justify what's gone wrong (a rise in prices), making a mockery of the modern, technocratic State: every—or virtually every—year, something's not right with the weather: drought or rain, the food economy at the mercy of rain or fine weather; despite the fact that they keep happening, these "catastrophes" are never planned for: the *weather* only exists after the event, as a discourse of irresponsibility.

To get us moving back toward haiku: the weather (or so I now think) not only has a phatic function but also an *existential* charge; it brings the subject's *feeling-being* into play, the pure and mysterious sensation of life. This can be said within the framework of a semiological description: *the Weather is a Language* (and a language is not simply a means of communication but also a means of instituting the subject—of creation): (1) a code (a law): the Season + (2) a performance (speech, discourse) that enacts the code: *the Weather* = the code *spoken* by the moment, the day, the hour, the individuation of existence, which is to say, by what enacts, or *what baffles* {*déjoue*} (still the remunerating, compensating, rectifying function of discourse with respect to language): in France, which is a country of subtle, complex, *variation*, you sometimes (often?) see a season being disputed by the weather (winter in summer, etc.) while still being enacted, confirmed by its products (flowers, fruit etc.): here the dialectic of code and performance is very clear—the disparity between the code and the subject: the disparity and the link: I'm cold in June (performance: my epidermis, the light that my eyes see), yet there are peonies (code) → a haiku, in the form of a very brief notation, will often endeavor to situate itself on the quietly surprising border between the code (of the season) and the weather (as it's received, spoken, by the subject): a season's precocious awakenings, the languidness of a season drawing to an end: produce *false impressions* {*de fausses impressions*}: Isn't discourse the *false impression* of language, as it were? And, at the same time, doesn't language *distort* {*fausse*} discourse (all laws *distort* {*fausse*} the subject)? Dramatic contradiction that we're condemned to wrestle with.

There's an art (historically: for it's no longer practiced) that consists in the *eidetic* expression of the Weather: Romantic painting. I'm thinking of Corot and, in particular, of his *Road to Sèvres* (not exactly high culture! You can find it under "Realism" in the Petit Larousse dictionary): the individuation of the sky, the shadows, the figures, as if the painting were saying: "It was intense and yet it's gone forever"; it's unrepeatable yet intelligible (again, the dialectic of language—of the code—and discourse) → At the end of the day, the *communicable* essence of the Weather is, paradoxically, *what the Weather was like* → the Weather: of the order of Memory. Example:

(6)   *What happiness*
      Crossing this river
      Sandals in hand!

                                                          (Buson, Blyth*)

Strange: the certainty that I've lived out this scene—childhood or Morocco: a summer's day or a picnic, etc. The haiku is produced by the bedazzlement of a personal, involuntary Memory (not: applied, systematic rememoration): it describes an unexpected, total, dazzling, happy recollection—and, of course, produces in the reader the very memory that produced it. Evidently: not unrelated to Proust's involuntary memory (theme allegorized by the Madeleine), but there's a difference: haiku, close to a little *satori*; the satori produces an *intention* (whence the extreme brevity of the form) ≠ Proust; the satori (the Madeleine) produces an *extension*—the whole of *In Search of Lost Time* unfurls from the Madeleine like a Japanese paper flower in water: development, drawers opening, infinite *unfolding*. In haiku, the flower is still compact, a Japanese flower without the water: it remains a *bud*. The word (the hologram of the haiku) is like a stone in water that amounts to nothing: we don't linger to watch the ripples; we register the sound (the *plop*), that's all.

Individuation of the Times of Day

We've therefore grasped that the haiku moves toward an intense individuation, with no concessions to generality—*despite and while making use of* the code of the seasons, that is, by getting around it with the law of the lived, remembered Instant → the Instant, caught in a code (the Season, the Weather)—for what could escape the Code?—is relayed by the speaking subject → the divisions of *Time* {*Temps-Time*} become the divisions of the *Weather* {*Temps-Weather*} → natural units become subject-effects, effects of language:

1. The season as an effect of the season. I'll give an indirect example of a season-effect, not from a haiku (there are countless examples: I haven't the patience to choose) but from our own Western literature:

a. Effect of winter—not an "impressionist" effect (snow, diamonds, Gautier,[7] Symbolists) but effect for the profound, visceral, intimist, "cenesthesic" subject: De Quincey: "Candles at four o'clock, warm hearth-rugs, tea, a fair tea-maker, shutters closed, curtains flowing in ample draperies on the floor, whilst the wind and rain are raging audibly without"[8] (all that, evidently, is with a view to partaking of opium: setting the scene for pleasure): any element of that euphoria could be a haiku.

b. In the form of a digression—because it's by no means a theme typical of haiku (although the haiku is also defined by what's close to it (the Season) but that it never actually deals in)—I want to draw your attention to a dramatic effect, a heartrending season-effect: Quincey-Baudelaire (Baudelaire) → Quincey, the death of Elizabeth, his younger sister, the favorite (Baudelaire tells Quincey's story in his own way): death in the summer. Baudelaire, *Paradis*, pages 139 and 140.[9]

I've nothing to add other than this: anyone who has lost someone dear to them retains a painful memory of the season; the light; the flowers, the smells, the harmony or discrepancy between mourning and the season: how it's possible to suffer in the sun! Bear that in mind as you leaf through travel brochures!

2. Certain days (of the week) also have their own *color* (the *day's color*: haikist material): While in the country, I once noted down (Sunday, July 17, 1977): "[It's] as if Sunday morning intensifies the good weather."[10] What I meant was: one intensity reinforces another; there's a Shimmering, a differential of Intensities (of the weather); Proust described these differential Intensities very well, in his own fashion. Even if it doesn't speak of Sundays (and for good reason), the haiku is very sensitive to these subtle intensities.

3. Whence its sensitivity to the *Times* (of day): the Times of day aren't mathematical units; they're semantic *boxes*, "locks," "thresh-

olds" of "sensitivity" (cf. one's age: the actual figure only ever refers to an age bracket, we grow older in stages). Some examples:

Dawn: (7)   *The dawn of day*
On the tip of the barley leaf
The frost of spring

(Issa, Blyth*)

Noon: (8)   *Bindweed blazing at midday*
Flames
Among the stones

(Issa, Coyaud)

Evening: (9)   *The grasses are misty*
The waters now silent
It is evening

(Buson, Blyth*)

(Note that we're reading the *effect*, not the landscape, which is barely there at all: a gram of referent, a powerful diffusion of effect).

These moments are clearly very coded: the haiku is *in* the code ≠ Western "subjectivity"—on the poetic level—is less so, it goes into the details of the different times of the day; we each feel, create, appropriate a mood depending on the time of day: we all have our "good hours" {*bonne heure*} and our "bad hours" (I'm not playing on words, since "happiness" {*bonheur*} > *augurum* and not *hora*):

a. Claudel: this is more or less a haiku:

Rain
Falls
On the six o'clock forests

(Schehadé, 29)[11]

b. And, especially—because for me it's the bad time of day, the one I don't like, when I don't know what to do with myself, when I feel lazy without feeling relaxed, idle and unsociable; a *flat* hour {*heure plate*} ("washed out" {"*à plat*"}), undynamic: half-past three in the afternoon (the time of my mother's death;—as if I'd always known it would happen then—the time of Christ's death).[12] Michelet (always him): Nuns in the Convent (*The Sorceress*): "What killed them was not the mortifications they were called upon to endure, so much as sheer ennui and despair. After the first burst of enthusiasm, that dreaded disease of the cloister (described as early as the fifteenth century by Cassien), leaden ennui, the gloomy ennui of afternoons, the tenderly melancholy ennui which loses itself in vague languors and dreamy reverie, quickly undermined their health."[13] Michelet knew about a great many things; he knew about things that mattered, he knew that knowing about the leaden hours of the convent matters as much as knowing about the wool wars of Florence, etc.

The Times (of day): there's no word for *these effects of the Times of day*: it's a *pathos* that falls somewhere between *hemera* (day as limited) and *bios* (vital feeling), and it's precisely (to make the same point once again) because there's no word for it that the "discourse" (the poem) is justified, *necessary* (it compensates for language).

Individuation, the Nuance

I've spoken of *individuation* a number of times—of the Season, of the Weather, of the Times of Day as individuation. I shall dwell on this idea for a moment. Philosophically, it is, I think, an idea to which Deleuze attached a great deal of importance (in his late work). Alas, as always, I'll be taking it fairly crudely, as a *direction*: a word that acquires emphasis in relation to what it excludes:

1. The Individual Against the System

It's necessary to take this old war horse as our starting point: discredited individualism (cf. Sartrean critique of bourgeois democracy: individuals like peas in a can[14] + Marxist criticism + left-wing criticism: a real conspiracy against individualism!). As always, however, a tactic of displacement: the link between the world of "systems," that is, of reductive discourses (political, ideological, scientific, etc.) and the stifling of the "individual" → to take up the problem (the paradigm) at a different point on the spiral—here, just a few references:

Hutin 49

a. Alchemy (a parallel, marginal philosophy): Paracelsus (sixteenth century): each being has its own specific organizing principle: the *archeus* (hence the ultimate core of the subject: *irreducible*).

b. Romanticism: Michelet (preface to his *History of France*): "Among vulgar things, each soul has a special, individual suchness that never reappears in the same form and that should be noted when that soul passes and disappears into the unknown world."[15] This—bizarrely—could actually be the all-encompassing motto of the haiku: (1) *suchness* (a very Zen notion); (2) nonreturn; (3) notation; (4) the fading into the unknown of the moment, of the soul that has passed.

   c. For the record, for a reminder of the existential voice, Kierkegaard, against Hegel, against the system.

   d. Proust, of course: theoretician of individual intensities in action. Among many other sentences, I quote this one: "My realities are specific; I want to enjoy, not a woman, but such or such woman, not a Gothic cathedral, but the cathedral of Amiens . . ."[16] And this very beautiful expression (in a letter to Daniel Halévy, 1919, Kolb, 246): "It is the apogee of the particular that begets the general."[17] *The apogee of the particular*: that, too, is the haiku's emblem. Especially since everything will hinge on the passage from (the substitution of) the Individual (the traditional unit of the human being) to (by) the particular.

Note only that these references, which oppose or disrupt the system in the name of Suchness, the Particular, the Special, belong to marginal philosophies.

2. From the Individual to Individuation

Let's say, Individuation: notion that consists in relating the irreducibility, the founding nuance, the Suchness, the Specialness of the *individual* (civic and psychological subject) to a given moment of that individual: so, straight away, to the Weather, to colors, to phenomena—to the "soul" (Michelet) in that it passes, not to return.

   In a sense, it's enough to pass from metaphor to the literal meaning. Baudelaire: "People who know how to observe themselves . . . from time to time have had occasion to note, in the observatory of their minds, lovely seasons, happy days, delicious minutes. . . ."[18] It's still a question of metaphor here. But one step further and you *are* the season, the day, the minute; your subjecthood: fulfilled and exhausted by it → you become a *barometer*. Proust (Dufour):[19] "And if it were not enough that I should bear an exaggerated resemblance to my father, to the extent of not being satisfied like him with consulting the barometer, but becoming an animated barometer myself."[20] → mutation foreseen by Rousseau (this is precisely the modernism of the *Reveries*) and affirmed as a way of resisting the (psychological) system. Walk 1. "I will perform on myself, to a certain extent, the measurements natural scientists perform on the air in order to know its daily condition.... But... I will be content to keep a record of the measurements without seeking to reduce them to a system."[21]

Here, naturally, we rejoin Nietzsche (a Deleuzean author).[22] Once again I quote (MC, 53, Posthumous): "The ego is a plurality of forces of person-like forces, of which now this one, now that one stands in the foreground and assumes the aspect of the ego; from this vantage-point, it contemplates the other forces, as a subject contemplates an object exterior to himself, an influential and determining outside world. The point of the subject is mobile."[23] That's the decisive word: subjectivity mustn't be denied or foreclosed, repressed; it has to be accepted in its mobility; not "undulating," but an interweaving, a network of mobile *points*—what's important in the Nietzsche quotation is the notion of the *point* (of subjectivity): subjectivity not as a river, even an ever-changing one, but as a discontinuous (and yet unabrupt) mutation of sites (cf. Kaleidoscope).

We now have a better understanding of the ambivalence (or the dialectic) of individuation: it's both that which strengthens the subject in his or her individuality, in his or her "*reserve*" {"*quant à soi*"}—or, at least, it contains this risk, and in particular [the risk] of looking like a claim for individualism—and, at the opposite extreme, it's that which undoes, multiplies, pulverizes, and in a sense absents the subject → oscillation between extreme impressionism and a kind of mystical leaning toward the dilution, the annihilation of consciousness as unitarian: very classical and ultramodern.

SESSION OF JANUARY 27, 1979

3. The Nuance

The practice (general: mental, written, experienced) of individuation is the *Nuance* (etymology: matters to us because it implies a link with *Weather*, *coelum* in Latin → *nuer* in old French = to compare shades of color to the play of light in the clouds). The Nuance: to be taken in the strong, general, theoretical sense, as an autonomous *language*; the proof being that it is neurotically censured, repressed by today's gregarious culture. Media culture can be said to be defined by its (aggressive) rejection of the nuance. I've spoken of the nuance as a fundamental practice of communication a number of times; I even risked giving it a name: *diaphoralogy*.[1] I add these words of Walter Benjamin's: "things are, as we know, technicalized, rationalized, and nowadays the particular is only to be found in the nuance."[2]

You'll be aware of the style crisis: practice and theory (there is no theory of style, which is of concern to some people). Now, style could be defined as the written practice of the nuance (which is why style is not held in high regard today).

An example straight away, and in the haiku itself:

(10) *A summer shower*
      How hard it falls
      On the pinks

                                                    (Sampu, Munier)

Hard: this is the decisive nuance; without this *hard*, no summer, no sound: in short, only platitude, *indifference*: *adiaphoria* (*diaphoria* = nuance).

The Nuance = an apprenticeship in subtlety. Example:

(11) *The first sunrise*
      There is a cloud
      Like a cloud in a picture

                                                    (Shusai, Blyth*)

Reality and picture have been inverted: agility and subtlety → Perhaps we're now in a position to understand this: *Poetry* = practice of subtlety in a barbaric world. Whence the need to fight for poetry *today*: Poetry should be one of our "Human Rights"; it isn't "decadent," it's subversive: subversive and vital.

Nuance = difference (*diaphora*). Let's explore the notion a little further through a paradox formulated by Blanchot (and to which Blanchot provides the key): "Every artist <this is the practice we're investigating> is linked to a mistake with which he has a particular intimate relation.... Every art draws its origin from an exceptional fault, every work is the implementation of this original fault, from which comes to us a new light and a risky conception of plenitude."[3] Indeed: from an *endoxal* point of view, the nuance *is what's flawed* {raté} (from the point of view of general right-wing opinion, so-called common sense, orthodoxy). Metaphor that supports this view: the most beautiful ceramics where a flaw, where firing the glaze for too long has produced incomparable nuances; unexpected, sensual streaks. In a way, the Nuance: that which irradiates, diffuses, *streaks* (as a beautiful cloud streaks the sky). Now, there's a link between irradiation and the void: in the Nuance there's something like a torment of the void (which is why those of a "positive" disposition dislike it so much).

4. The Void, Life

The Poetics of the Void would need to be explored. For example: these beautiful lines from Joubert, quoted by Blanchot: "'This globe is a drop of water; the world is a drop of air. Marble is thickened air.' 'Yes, the world is gas, and even clear gas. Newton calculated that the diamond had . . . times more vacuums than plenums, and the diamond is the most compact of substances.' 'With its gravitations, its impenetrabilities, its attractions, its impulsions, and all those blind forces about which scholars make so much noise . . . what is all matter but a grain of emptied metal, a grain of glass made hollow, a bubble of water in which light and shadow play; a shadow, finally, where nothing weighs except on itself, is impenetrable except (for) itself.'"[4]

[5] Like Difference, the Nuance is constantly battling with, offset by what surrounds it, oppresses it, by what it seeks to distinguish itself from through a vital, sudden bursting forth, but it has a kind of *interior*, of *intimity*, of *inhabitability* that is precisely that of the void evoked by Joubert: an operator of distinction, it is within itself an operator of simultaneity. Blanchot discussing Joubert and Mallarmé: "Desire to replace ordinary reading (in which you have to go

from section to section) with the spectacle of a simultaneous speech where everything would be said all at once, without confusion, in 'a total, peaceful, intimate and ultimately uniform flash' " → and: "creation of this space of *vacancy* where, with nothing in particular coming to break the infinite, everything is as it were present in the nothingness, a *place where nothing will take place except the place* . . ."[6] (In providing these quotations, it goes without saying that I have the haiku in mind, *to which they are applicable.*)

The Nuance, the Void: a pointed theme when it comes to writing (to "creating"). Never forget Mallarmé's text (declaration made to Lefébure in 1867): "My work was only created by *elimination*, and every truth established born only of the loss of an impression which, having sparkled, burnt itself out and allowed me, thanks to the timbres it emitted, to go deeper into the sensation of the Absolute Shadows. Destruction was my Beatrice" (Blanchot)[7] → How all of this *fits* the haiku! To create (poetically) is to empty, to exhaust, to deaden the shock (the sound) in favor of the Timbre.[8]

This can be put differently (and this too fits the haiku): with Blanchot, apropos of Artaud, Holderlin, Mallarmé: "Inspiration is first that pure point where it is lacking."[9] Yes, in a sense (in *this sense*, sedimented by everything that's just been said), the haiku and any short form that's fascinated by it, all Notation, *lacks inspiration*. And here, once again, we acquire a better understanding of the Poetics of the Weather: as a kind of *absence of inspiration*, of writing, of creation: the *first* impression turned back on itself, wasted.

This path of the *Nuance* (which started out from the Weather and follows it): so what's at the end? Well, *life*, the sensation of life, the feeling of being alive; and, as we know, if that feeling is to be pure, intense, glorious, perfect, a certain *void* has to form within the subject; even when the jubilation (of love), for example, is at its most intense it's because there's a language void within the subject: it's when language is silent, when there's no longer any commentary, interpretation, or meaning that existence is pure: a "full" ("overflowing") heart=knowledge of a certain void (eminently mystical theme); the *failure*, the breakdown of discourse relates to two extreme states: the absolute wretchedness of someone who feels "distanced" from the world, the ardent jubilation of someone who feels "alive" to it → the Nuance—if not kept in check—is Life—and the destroyers of nuances (today's culture, our popular press)=dead men who, from the depths of their death, take their revenge.

In sum, *thoroughly exposed*, the Weather prompts in us only this (minimal) discourse: that life is worth living. One July morning,

1977 (the 16th), I noted: "Again, after overcast days, a fine morning: the luster and subtlety of the atmosphere: a cool, luminous silk. This blank moment (no signified) produces the plenitude of a self-evident truth: that life is worth living. The morning's errands (to the grocer's, the baker's), while the village is still almost empty—I wouldn't miss them for the world."[10] Were I a haikist I'd have said it in a *more essential and more indirect* (less wordy) way.

(12)   *As if nothing had happened*
       The crow
       And the willow

                                              (Issa, Blyth*)

The Instant

Here, I'll group together a number of remarks around "an acute dialectic of time." Why "acute dialectic"? Because, in each case, in three lines (5–7–5), a contradiction between two categories: brief, searing contradiction, like a kind of logical flash, too quick to cause any pain.

1. The Instant and Memory

   a. On the one hand, the haiku is evidently not an act of writing in the Proustian style, that is to say, one destined, through the sovereign action of involuntary memory, to "recover" (lost) Time *later on, after the event* (shut up in the cork-lined bedroom) but, on the contrary: to discover (and not to re-cover)[11] Time *at once, as-it-happens*; Time is salvaged *at once*=concomitance of the note (of the writing) and what incites it: immediate *fruition* of the sensible and of writing, the one taking pleasure in the other {*l'un jouissant par l'autre*} thanks to the haiku form (this could be transposed as: thanks to the sentence) → Therefore, a writing (a philosophy) of the instant. For example: absolute writing of the instant:

(13)   *A dog barks*
       At a peddler
       Peach trees are blooming

                                              (Buson, Blyth*)

I quote this haiku because it clearly implies that the privileged art of the instant is music; sound=the *eidos* of the Instant (Cage's theories). (Cage stakes everything on the Instant.)[12] Whence an apt metaphor (which we'll come back to): the haiku *sets a bell ringing*, a sort of short, unique, and crystal-clear *tintinnabulation* that says: something has just moved me.

b. On the other hand (the other side of the contradiction): this *pure*, that is to say, *uncompromised* Instant, which doesn't appear to be compromised by any duration, any return, any retention, any saving for later, any freezing (an absolutely *fresh* Instant: as if we were eating the thing noted down straight from the tree, like an animal grazing on the living grass of sensation), this Instant also seems to be saying: *for the record*, for when I come to read it again. Instant that aspires to be Treasured: "Tomorrow, memory" → This contradiction would be expressed in the following way: haiku: a new and paradoxical category: "immediate memory," as if *Notatio* (the fact of noting down) enabled *instant* remembrance (≠ Proust's involuntary memory: unmediated memory doesn't proliferate; it's not metonymical). This, I believe, is the function of Poetry, of which haiku is a radical form (everything Japanese: I mean, from *that* Japan, not from the Japan you find on the avenue de l'Opéra = subtlety and radicality, the *radical nuance*). This is how—transformation of the event into memory, but also the immediate consumption of that memory—I read these lines by Edgar Poe (Bachelard): "Yet now as Fate approaches, and the Hours are breathing low, the sands of Time are changed to golden grains"[13] → The haiku is truly a grain of gold made out of what would *otherwise* (if there were no writing) have been the sands of Time. (*Gold*: as I said, the haiku aspires to be treasured).

2. Movement and Immobility

Haiku: surprise of a *gesture*. I'll say: *gesture* = the most fleeting, the most improbable and the *truest* moment in any action, that is, something that the notation reconstructs by producing an effect of "*That's it!*" (= a Bell Ringing), but that we wouldn't have thought of, that we wouldn't have thought to *look at* in its tenuity. Here, for example, is a *gesture* made by a haiku:

(14) *The kitten*
Holds down the leaf
For a moment

(Issa, Blyth*)

"Politian" Poetry, trad. Mourey, p. 109

It could be said: this is a scrap, a sliver of vision (you can see how it's *simultaneously, already* a memory). (≠ Proust: here it clearly doesn't proliferate: unlike Proust's Madeleine, it's not prolific, metonymical: it's not a Japanese paper flower that, when dropped in water, etc.)—This gives us a good indication of what—in the Japanese tradition at least—constitutes a *gesture*, as illustrated by Zeami's treatise (Zeami, an actor and theoretician of the theater[14] in the Middle Ages): the paradoxical conjunction of movement and immobility (which, basically, is just what the term *immobilization* says: through writing). The gesture is suspension, it must supply the self-evident truth that it will immediately repeat (cf. the myth of Sleeping Beauty). The gesture: a kind of miniature sleeping garden, as the "marginals" of the theater world were fully aware. But no one in theater thinks about gesture nowadays. In film? I'm thinking of the (admirable) phantom-woman episode in Mizoguchi's *Tales of a Pale and Silvery Moon After the Rain* (but that again is by a Japanese).—Marginals: for example, Jacques Lecoq's mime school: "In a gesture, an attitude, a movement, one must seek immobility."[15] (This, this reference to mime gives rise to the thought that, paradoxically, haiku can be spoken in silence, without speech.) And Jacques-Dalcroze: "A gesture is not only a movement of the body but also the suspension of that movement." → the haikist gesture: kinship with the *Cartesian diver*, a little figurine suspended in water, which moves about while giving the impression of a *finality* to immobility.

> Cited by J.-L. Rivière, "Gesture" article

3. Contingency and Circumstance

The haiku's "referent" (what it describes) is always of the order of the *particular*. No haiku deals in generalities and, as a result, the haiku genre is absolutely pure of all processes of reduction.

> The General

a. Over here, that is to say, in France, in the West, in a macro-historical sense: probably a resistance to the Particular, a tendency to prefer the General: preference for laws, generalities, for the Reducible, exquisite pleasure taken in *equalizing* all phenomena rather than registering their extreme difference → cf. Michelet: abstraction, generalization = the Guelph mind ≠ the Ghibelline mind that valorizes (affective) contingency[16] → as a value, the particular has been pushed to the margins—though every now and then a thinker stands up and makes a claim for the particular, the *kairos*, the incomparable (Kierkegaard, Nietzsche), contingency. There you have two different *ways* {*côtés*}: for example, I'll always prefer the way Proust speaks of grief over the way Freud speaks of mourning. Paradoxically, it's an empiricist, Bacon (*Organum*), who provides the best formulation of this opposition: "The human understanding is, by its own nature, prone to abstraction and supposes that which is fluctuating to be fixed. *But it is better to dissect than abstract nature*; such was the method employed by the school of Democritus."[17] This is a good definition of the haiku: it doesn't stabilize movement; it divides Nature up rather than abstracts it.

Contingency

b. So, haiku: art of the contingent (*contingere*, to come about, to happen by chance) → art of the *Encounter*. In order to fully grasp that contingency is the foundation of the haiku—its peculiar feature—we need only perform a substitution test: some fragments of French poems come close to haiku, but what's missing is the contingency; the contingent has been corrupted by a desire for generality.

For example, Verlaine:

> *The long sobs of*
> *The violins*
> *of Autumn*[18]

Coyaud 25

For a haiku, it's too metaphorical; it's a metaphor, hence a generality: it's not something that once befell the subject (of the enunciation).

Likewise, Apollinaire:

> *Admiring the snow*
> *Which was like naked women*[19]

Very beautiful, of course, but the comparison is bogged down in the rhetorical production.

Schehadé 2

Different form of corruption by generality: "morality," moralized notation. Vigny: "The very infidelity was full of you."[20] This is almost a haiku, because it's a short, nongnomic form. *But* it's not sensual; it's a moral idea, and morality is always general; here there are [two] reductive propositions: (1) to be unfaithful is to abandon the other, to empty yourself of the other; (2) fidelity is a noble value, which serves as the basis for the paradox, the denial: I might appear to be unfaithful, but I'm still a "good" (faithful) guy. I'll put two haikus alongside one another, where we can clearly see the trigger of contingency at work:

> (15) *The child*
> *Walks the dog*
> *Under the summer moon*
>
> (Shoha, Munier)

The "conceit" of the contingency, here: we can be absolutely certain that the child existed → the haiku isn't fictional, it doesn't make things up; rather, through a chemistry specific to the short form, it instills the certainty that *this took place* (cf. Photography, *infra*):[21] indeed, contingency reinforces the certainty of reality; to anyone planning to tell a lie: you need to invent contingencies: the more contingent it is, the more it's authenticated → Haiku: a kind of Testimonial → the paradox: it's the "subjectivity" (of the enunciation) that grounds the authenticity of the testimony.

> (16) *"I wish to live forever!"*
> *The woman's voice*
> *The cicada's cry*
>
> (Kusatao, Coyaud)

Coyaud 17

This haiku is clever because it starts out with a generality, but the generality immediately reintroduces contingency: what, in a unique instant, once *befell* the subject: a voice, a sound (contingency defines the perishable, the mortal).

Thus far, I've spoken of *contingency*: this fits in with Basho's definition: a haiku "is simply what happens in a given place, at a given moment" (Coyaud).[22]—But in truth this isn't quite sufficient: I'd like to introduce a nuance: a haiku is what happens (contingency, microadventure), but only in that what happens *surrounds* the subject—who, moreover, only exists, and can only claim to be a subject, through this fleeting and mobile surrounding (individuation ≠ individual) → So, rather than *contingency*, think *circumstance* (think of the etymology).[23]—Thus, after "instant / memory" and "immobility / movement," this is the third dialectic (contradiction) that I want to draw your attention to: although the haiku establishes the certainty of a referent, cf. (15) it also invites us to speak of *circumstants* (a clumsy word) rather than *referents*. In a (extreme) sense, there are no referents in haiku—so, strictly speaking, no thetic:[24] it only sets out the *surrounds* (circumstants), but the object evaporates, is absorbed by the circumstance: what surrounds it, for a lightning-quick moment.

Circumstances

I think you'll grasp this nuance if we compare a haiku (that I'll provide) with the notation of the cries from the streets of Paris in *In Search of Lost Time*.

It's been said (Coyaud)—rightly—that these are almost haiku:

*"Prawns, lovely prawns,
Alive, alive-o"*

*"Lettuce, cos lettuce, not to hawk
Lovely cos lettuce out for a walk"*[25]

Compare with:

(17) *Waking from a siesta
I hear the knife-grinder
Go by*

(Bakunan, Coyaud)

The nuance is clear: in Proust, the *notation* remains realistic, it refers to a sort of reality in itself; it's an inventory, a catalogue ≠ in the haiku, the *notation*: absolutely subjective; the "referent" is a circumstant: the enunciator's torpid body, which is *stated* by what surrounds it → Of course, if we were to put the cries from the streets of Paris back into the surroundings of the Proustian enunciator, his half-sleep, the shut-up bedroom, etc., then we'd rediscover the absolute subjectivity of the body listening to those cries; we'd rediscover a *circumstance*—but, in Proust, that would require a whole narrative. → It's a question of the choice of form—and, on that level, of macroculture: we're not attuned to the short form; for us, subjectivity can only ever be *prolix* = it is an *exploration* ≠ the haiku: a kind of *implosion*.

The *circumstantial*—and not, in the strict sense, referential—nature of haiku can be discerned in its origins, or at least in its classical treatment (seventeenth century): the tercet—especially in Basho—is usually introduced and set off by a *haibun*, a piece of poetic prose, frequently an account of a journey; every once in a while, over the course of the journey, something "jumps out at language": a little satori of language: a haiku. Basho (1643–1694): *Travel Sketches*, the *Kiko*, strewn with haiku → Famously: *The Narrow Road to the Deep North* (Northern and Central mountains) = today, a route lined with upright stones that the locals have engraved with Basho's haiku. Coyaud understood this: he alternates the haiku he translates with extracts from a private diary → the haiku as an erratic debris, a relief made from the fabric of

Journey

Celebrations

individual, day-to-day existence (is in this way marked as *a double text*). Hence a personal anecdote: coming back from Gröningen, leaving the house in a hurry at eleven o'clock at night, by car. We shut everything up, we leave everything as it should be, but what about the rubbish? Holland is so clean that, even driving all night, we can't find anywhere to get rid of it: even the canals are clean. Now, I encountered this again in a modern haiku:

(18)   *The bright moon*
       No dark place
       To empty the ashtray

(Fugyoku, Blyth*)

SESSION OF FEBRUARY 3, 1979

Yami
Utsuroi

All this should show how the haiku walks—discreetly, elegantly, rapidly—along the "tightrope of Time." Of course, that trick is possible because it's prepared and determined by a specifically Japanese concept—one that, precisely, here, in France, we haven't conceptualized because we don't have a word for it: *Ma*, the Interval of Space-Time (cf. the recent exhibition).[1] Among the figures (the variations) of *Ma*, two in particular constantly nurture haiku:

1. *Yami*: that which twinkles, emerges from the darkness only to return to it; applies, for example, to *Noh*: actors emerging from the world of the Dead by way of a bridge, acting on the stage of the Living, then returning to the shadows by that same bridge (this is perhaps the best definition of Beauty: a scintillation between two Deaths).

2. *Utsuroi*: that fragile moment that separates and links two states of a thing: when the soul has left a thing and remains suspended in the void (*to cut a long story short*: that's an understatement!) before being integrated into another thing → For the Japanese, apparently it's not, strictly speaking, the cherry blossom that's considered beautiful: it's the moment when, in perfect bloom, the blossom *will* wilt → All this shows the extent to which the haiku is an *action* (of writing) between life and death.

Pathos

I'm using this word without any particular connotations, certainly none that are disparaging: in the Greek sense (which Nietzsche often goes back to) = of the order of *affect*; the haiku and affect (Emotion, Agitation, the *Emotional*).

1. Perception

Gatha

Haiku: writing of *perception*; unfortunately, in France, this word has a whiff of the Philosophy classroom, of the experimental psychology class about it.—It would be better to give the perceptual phenomenon its "Zen style" (its Zen ancestry): in Zen Buddhism,

Suzuki, I 316

there are stanzas called "*ge*" or "*gatha*" that show what the mental eye perceived or experienced the moment it opened (satori): for example, pine trees, bamboo, a refreshing breeze → "Something falls! It is itself" (exemplary definition of the haikist *Incident*:[2] what falls, what forms a crease, and yet is itself).

Tangibilia

In narrative or intellectual texts, I've long been alert to the presence of words with concrete things, objects as referents—let's say, broadly: things you could touch, *tangibilia*,[3] cf. Plates in an Encyclopaedia. Succession of sensual objects—it's rare to find *tangibilia* in classical texts (*Dangerous Liaisons*, for example); they play an important a role in the *Life of Rancé* (orange trees, gloves). (Personally, I always put them in: for instance, the lists in the text on Arcimboldo.)[4] In haiku: in every haiku, I believe, there's always at least one *tangible*. For example:

(19)   *White verbena blossom*
       And in the middle of the night
       The milky way

                                            (Gonsui, Coyaud)

In its resonance, I find the white verbena blossom enchanting, because it's not a stereotypical *Tangibile* → Even modern haiku are bound by the constraint of the *Tangibile*.

(20)   *Bank workers in the morning*
       Phosphorescent
       Like cuttlefish

                                            (Kaneko Tota, Coyaud)

To grasp the specificity of *Tangibilia* in haiku, let's once again perform the substitution test.

Schehadé

Lamartine: "Memory that returns during fretful nights";[5] there's a kind of haikist sentiment here, *sabi*, a reflection on what's happening, but what's missing is a *Tangibile*: as it result, it remains psychological.

Id.

Malherbe: "Only thorns, Love, accompany your roses!"[6] Here we have two *Tangibilia*, but (1) it's gnomic, the concrete is only there as an emblem (in haiku: there's the symbolic but never the emblematic) (2) moreover, such *Tangibilia* are stereotypical, overused: what was concrete about them has evaporated ≠ in haiku, the *Tangibilia* are *fresh*, and therefore powerful: the white verbena.

Passage of the *Tangibile*: like a flash of referent, a kind of subliminary vision: for a brief moment, the word *shows us* something (just as it's fading away: the *Ma* again, the contraction of Time, the *Utsori*, the twinkling). Rhetoric:

Hypotyposis: is what shows us, enables us to picture something ("Think, Céphise, think")[7] → Haiku's *Tangibilia*: sorts of micro hypotyposes → Thus, in the haiku, there's something like a germ, a virtuality of fantasy = short, delimited scenario, where I work myself into a state of desire, of *projected* pleasure → Type of hypotyposis in the Western (that is to say, expanded) style: the fantasy of being "in the warm in Winter." Quincey, "Pleasures of Opium": "Candles at four o'clock, warm hearth rugs, tea, a fair tea-maker, shutters closed, curtains flowing in ample draperies on the floor, whilst the wind and rain are raging audibly without."[8] (Note the abundance of *Tangibilia*.)

Now, for me, whether explicitly or secretly, haiku often contain these prospective fantasies. Thus:

(21) *Autumn moon*
Thus, on the lectern, I shall open
Ancient texts

(Buson, Kikou Yamata)

A fantasy I'm very familiar with: to work on classical texts (without the aggression of modernity), in the warm, in winter → Another fantasy, that of the rural retreat:

(22) *Little door in the trellis*
Flowers in a pot
Hut of peace

The differences in quality among haiku often stem from the force, or the deficiency, of the hypotyposis (of the *Tangibilia*). For example:

(23) *New Year's day*
The desk and bits of paper
Just as last year

(Matsuo, Blyth*)

At first, that seems utterly banal. Then I think: on New Year's Day morning, thinking hard about it being New Year's Day, activating that "little symbolism" within me that makes me thoughtful, wistful, and a little unnerved around anniversaries, I could easily have noted that down myself: *I picture myself* (hypotyposis) going to my desk fairly early in the morning (the morning after New Year's Eve, while everyone else is asleep), seeing my papers and remarking: "..." This, on the other hand, remains banal:

(24) *The dawn of New Year's Day*
Yesterday
How far off!

(Ichiku, Blyth*)

It doesn't take, it doesn't come together, it doesn't cut into me: no *Tangibile*, no hypotyposis.

Now we need to enter a little further into the dialectic—or the *redans* of perception. Among others, I shall point up three fairly complex treatments of haikist perception (which can of course also be found in other types of poetry):

1. The Sound Is Off

I said: the haiku: force of vision (of picturing): hypotyposis. Haiku frequently bring short filmed sequences to mind, but with the surprising charm, so to speak, that: *the sound is off*: in the vision, something is oddly erased, interrupted, incomplete:

(25) *The road over the autumn moor*
Someone is coming along
Behind me!

(Buson, Blyth*)

Kind of muteness to the image, which is made *dull*.

(26) *Pushing their cart*
The man and the woman
Say something to each other

(Ilto, Coyaud)

It's probably this *sound cut* which produces the "conceit" (the satori) → Given that, just imagine what was lost when they stopped making silent films (that "progress" can never be deplored enough): something that isn't silence, that doesn't *signify silence* (which is itself always significant), but—a subtle difference—the sound having been cut, speech at a distance, present and effaced, there under erasure, inaudible other than as confusion, interference, brouhaha; the source of pure inaudibility isn't a *noise*; *mute*: deaf and dumb: all painting; the Image is in this way *forcefully mute*.

2. "One Art in the Form of Another"

Classical schema: perception via one of the senses conveys a generic sensation: a sound conveys music, etc. Now, haiku can reroute these circuits, make "faulty" connections: a sound will convey a tactile sensation (heat, cold); a kind of heterogeneous, "heretic" metonymy.

(27) *The sound of a rat*
Scratching a plate
How cold it is

(Buson, Munier)

Or an odor through sight:

(28) *Summer evening*
Dust from the roads
Golden fire of dry grasses

Peculiar thing: the only haiku I've managed to find in French is of this order (that's not peculiar: it's a widespread poetic procedure), albeit written by an author who isn't (isn't reputed to be) especially "poetical," Valéry:

Schehadé, 40

The clean insect
Scratches
The dryness[9]

If it's by Valéry, this is probably because the procedure is consonant with symbolist theory. In Proust, too, theory of one kind of art being accomplished in another: Balzac and painting, *Against Sainte-Beuve*. Cf. *infra*.[10]

3. Synaesthesia

Indeed: we're dealing with a type of metonymy that's widespread in Western poetry, whose privileged field of expansion was French symbolism and that Baudelaire theorized under the metaname of *synaesthesia* in his sonnet on "Correspondences" ("There are odors succulent as young flesh," etc.).[11] But, paradoxically, despite being an art of the *tenuous*, the haiku doesn't specify, doesn't isolate the homologies of sensation; its significance lies in the production of an overall sensation in which the sensual body is undifferentiated: the aim is more *euphoric* than analytical. For example:

(29)   *Paths on the mountain*
Dusk on the pink cedars
Bells in the distance

(Basho)

Here, reconstituted in 5–7–5, is a kind of diffuse happiness, a generalized sensuousness, close, perhaps, to what Fourier called the sixth sense: the sensual, "erotic" (without it being genital) sense; so perhaps the French writer who made the best use of synaesthesia (though he's nothing of a haikist) would be Proust (this isn't, this won't be the first time that, by way of a paradox that structures this course, Proust and the haiku intersect: the shortest and the longest form). If I may be permitted to refer to personal experience: for me, this euphoria, this synaesthesic happiness is linked to two themes:

1. The "overdetermination of pleasures" (Urt diary, July 18, 1977): "this morning, a kind of happiness: the weather (very fine, very mild), music (Haendel), amphetamine, coffee, cigar, a good pen, domestic sounds."[12]

2. The augmenting, the deepening of the sensual *nuance*. For example: (Urt diary, July 20, 1977): "Around six in the evening, dozing on my bed with the window open wide onto the brighter end of a grey day (I did the shopping in Bayonne after lunch), I experience a kind of floating euphoria: everything is liquid, aerated, *drinkable* (I drink in the air, the weather, the garden); a kind of peace in the lungs. And, since I'm reading Suzuki at the moment, this seems to me to be quite close to the *Sabi . . .*"[13]

[14] Question: Why is it that I can't articulate that euphoria, that synaesthesia—make a haiku (or an equivalent short form) out of that sensation? Because my culture hasn't disposed me to that particular form—it hasn't provided me with the means to write it, which is to say: because, here in France, that form *has no readers*: I'd be accused of "affectation," for example, because the West = virility complex.

2. Affect, Emotion

J. Renard

As we know: Jules Renard: brief notations, always metaphorical, taken directly from Nature (which actually means the countryside); for example, *Natural Histories* → Whence this remark made by a journalist (Marc Legrand, 1896): "Jules Renard is a Japanese, but better than that, he's an *emotional* Japanese." (Jules Renard's re-

Coyaud, 81

sponse: "Thank you. I agree. That's quite correct, and will upset the Chinese.")[15]—The remark is wrongheaded on two counts: (1) There's nothing Japanese about Renard whatsoever; the mainspring of his short form is the *impression* (altogether contrary to the haiku). (2) In a sense, the Japanese are always emotional, but what moves them is a specific emotion: more on the side of *agitation* (which isn't a "psychological," romantic emotion).

Emotion

Japanese agitation

Watch, for example, the Japanese meet one another, greet one another, talk to one another (not here, but over there:[16] in order to understand the quality you need quantity): always, a kind of mounting agitation, a sustained "infra-panic" that's almost of the order of good manners; manners and emotion mixed up together: (1) Voices: slightly raised, making the delivery a bit childlike, frequent markers of approbation: a very "phatic" language, repeated contact, agreement. (2) Faces: the features are blank, but the eyes are extremely expressive; they dominate the whole face, which becomes a kind of fragile *shimmering*. This is very obvious in film (women's faces).[17] A kind of fear of doing wrong: not as regards the Good (God) but society (culture of Shame, not of Sin).

Tenuousness and concentration: fleeting concentration of emotion. Valéry (Yamata, 7): "The poets of the Far-East <he's thinking of haiku in particular> seem to be the past masters of the art of reducing the infinite pleasure of emotion to its essence."→ Essence, purity of affect → now, here a kind of paradox emerges: the most human (humanity at its most heartrending) rejoins the least human: plants, animals.

SESSION OF FEBRUARY 10, 1979

Supplement to Tangibilia: discovery of Proust's note (Cahiers, 53–5):[1] *"Albertine's tastes in women's fashion, theme of the presents to give her."*
  Additional note:
  "Nota Bene. Capitalissme. Every time I say 'entertainment, wealth, pleasure,' I'll put something concrete: shiny shoes, as for Mme de Guermantes; a scarf, as for M. de Guermantes; plan for a car, for a yacht."

Animals. Digression

Some modern theories: supposedly, plants are nothing more than affect. As regards animals: conspicuous = fascinating spectacle of pure affect—this is I why find dogs, in particular, interesting, fascinating; because they're pure affect: they have no reason, no redans, no unconscious, no mask; in dogs, affect can be seen in its absolute immediacy and mobility; watch a dog's tail: how quickly its movements respond to the solicitations of affect—no face, however mobile, could come close to matching the subtlety of its nuances; dogs are fascinating because, being saturated with man, they're like men without the reason (and without the madness). Imagine (true science fiction) a man endowed with a dog's expressive powers, for whom affect would be literally *im-mediate*, each and every second: what craziness! I can watch dogs for hours (and regret not being able to own one) → Error (I think) of those who, despising sentimentality, are repulsed by and reject a dogs' love. Perhaps the problem is badly formulated. We each think that *our* animal is affect for ourselves. No doubt it's pleasant—necessary?—for us all to believe that we're loved; yet a moment's reflection has to persuade you that you're not loved *in yourself, for yourself*: it's the place you occupy, not your *psyche* that's the animal's object of affect; yet, narcissism is so entrenched it still surprises us to see dogs going wild with adoration, fidelity, affection for vulgar, brutal masters who "don't deserve them" (so we think, bitterly).—No, it's not really that which interests me; what I'm interested in is affect as such; diffuse, wild, frenzied affect; to have a dog: continuous spectacle of affect → distinguish between the *affective* and the *affectionate*. In this spectacle, no doubt dogs=play the starring role. I don't want to get into the great, mythical Dogs / Cats debate. It might be that in a cat the *affective* is less obvious; perhaps a cat is more like a whole man than a dog (delayed affect)—or a whole woman (the habitual comparison): which is perhaps where this comes from: cats seem to make more *choices* (cf. Colette's *La Chatte*).

This digression: in order to separate the *animal* from the "beast." The animal is affect → often gives the impression of having a *soul*, more so than men. And also in order to give a sense of what the diffuse affective can be like: *shimmering*, rapidly changing affective (always think of a dog's tail, its super-face, as it were), an affective mode that is very specific and very rare (in the West); in Proust, for example; I don't think there are any animals in his work.[2] But in haiku: many animals, regarded with tenderness.

> Blyth, I, 377

Kireji

Thus, haiku: saturated with a tenuous agitation. This agitation has its own morphological marker: the frequent and coded use of an exclamative syllable (with an added advantage: it can also serve as an articulation), the *Kireji*=a type of poetic punctuation, as in music: *forte, crescendo*, etc., which the composer of the haiku uses to allude to his state of mind. In the classical period of haiku, there were eighteen *Kireji*, for example: (1) *Ya*: Ah! Oh! admiration, doubt, questioning; (2) *Keri*: time has gone by, something has come to an end, some of the emotion or the admiration has fallen away; can make the line heavier, can make us hear the weight of the snow, etc. (3) *Kana*: very common; has no precise meaning; emphasizes the emotion of the preceding word → However coded they may be, they still retain a necessary emotional impact → Coyaud doesn't think these *Oh! Ah!* should be translated. Personally, I like these very literary interjections: to me, they seem to *loosen up* the syntax; they create a sudden weakening of the syntax, a *forgetting* of the thetic, a suspension of the subject/predicate rule; a brief sob or sigh (as in music) → Famous haiku by Basho:

(30)   *The old pond*
       A frog jumps in
       Oh! the sound of the water

                                    (Basho†)

SESSION OF FEBRUARY 10, 1979

Suzuki, II, 775

It's been said: perhaps an account of a *satori*? Here, the *Kireji* (*Oh!*): the moment of the Satori, of language passing into the void → In France?—What comes closest to the haiku: some of Verlaine's inflections: ("*Oh* the sound of the rain . . .") And this, in Proust (a letter, Kolb?): "You think it's a question of subtleties. *Oh! No*, I assure you, quite the contrary: of realities."[3] = This *Oh! No*: a very good Kireji, because it introduces an emotional protestation into Proust's argument: the whole body is protesting that what is subtle is painful, therefore real.

3. Egotism of Haiku

Sieffert, 120
Coyaud, 34

A bit of history: originally (among men of letters), a poem composed of thirty-one syllables in two stanzas: 5–7–5 + 7–7 → became a popular parlor game called *renga*: the initiator of the game proposes a theme and the two groups compete against each other: puns, verbal conceits designed to embarrass your adversaries; the Improviser provides the first three lines → his interlocutor then has to come up with the next two → a game without end, anyone can join in: a poem production line. For example, fourteenth century: *renga* played assiduously in monasteries—then, around 1650, a double modification: (a) alongside the more dignified *renga*, a *free*—that is to say, still poetical but less solemn, without the verbal conceits—*renga* developed: the *haikai-renga*: (b) poets took the beginnings of the poems (the 5–7–5 stanza) and published collections of them; those beginnings = *hokku* → as a result, we now have either *haikai-hokku* (free, "poetic" hokkus) or haiku.

What fell away: the game played by two people, the dialogue; what was retained: the individual, solipsistic notation, the very short soliloquy; the other, the polemical other who responds and tries to outdo his interlocutor has disappeared: loss of the antagonistic function. It could be said, and it wouldn't be too implausible, that haiku sprang from a movement of egotism: the players dismissed their partners—who were only hampering Narcissus—and played by themselves. The production line (*renga*) was suspended: as soon as *I* enters the enunciation, a knot is tied, before *you* can get involved; the subject was isolated, the conflict done away with and, as a result, the ego pacified: solitary and sensual in the act of creation.

I is an effect that's always present in the haiku: pure poem of the act of enunciation. Present? Much more than that: it articulates, it reinforces the whole sensation.

It's an *I-body*. Consider these three examples:

(31) *Coolness*
I press my forehead
Against the green mat

(Sonojô, Coyaud)

(32) *A midday nap*
Putting my feet against the wall
It feels cool

(Basho, Blyth*)

(33) *I saw the first snow*
That morning I forgot
To wash my face

(Basho†)

Precise examples of what I called *individuation*: the *I* becomes the body, the body becomes the sensation, the sensation becomes the moment.

It's always a subject who enunciates overtly and who *places himself in the picture*.

(34) *Cleaning a pot*
Ripples on the water
A solitary gull

(Buson, Coyaud)

(35) *Rainy season. We watch the rain*
Me and, standing behind me
My wife

(Rinka, Coyaud)

→ A subtle type of enunciation: here we have a scene that's very easy to picture, with an actor in the midst of it, like in a realist painting, and, at the same time, that actor is me (*I*); this is very clear in (35); as *I number 1*, I can't see my wife (who's behind me), but as *I number 2* I have a clear view of the whole scene, the staggering of perspectives: rain, me, my wife → Thus, the haiku isn't a scene; rather it's a *scenario* in the fantasmatic sense → the body is present but the enunciation doesn't need to say *I*, because it can never be a question of any other body than *my own*.

> (36) *A nap in the daytime*
> *The hand stops moving*
> *The fan*
>
> (Taigi, Blyth*)

Tenuousness, delineation, micro-scopia.

Haiku: nonerotic. But, on the rare occasions when a desire is referred to, the subtlety of the enunciation is extremely complex: operating within the constraints of the *I*, the short form, discretion, the specific, the desirable.

> (37) *The young girl's scarf*
> *Too low under her eyes*
> *A wild charm*
>
> (Buson, Coyaud)

The *Being* of desire (the relationship between *I* and an object): so particular that it often takes the form of a paradox → Form's task: to discover and state this paradox. Here, it's the *too low* that makes me wild with desire[4] (it's easy to see why, since there is, or there used to be, a fashion for scarves worn too low) → Thus, the marker of the *I* (of the enunciation) = "*Too*" → This haiku successfully points up the specificity of desire, the incredibly rare, *individual* harmony between *I* and an object → At the other extreme: classical descriptions, Sade's for example, tell us absolutely nothing about the *peculiarity* of desire.

Last—still performing our substitution test: poems in which there's no enunciation fail the haiku test. The material in this one by Apollinaire is almost that of a haiku:

Anemone and columbine
Have sprung up in the garden
Where melancholy sleeps[5]

Perhaps there is enunciation here? But it's not "clear cut."

[6] In short, the haiku teaches the art of saying *I*, but it's an *I* of writing: I write *I*, therefore I am.

4. Discretion

With haiku, we're getting somewhat closer, once again, to broaching the theme, the coloration of the Neutral that here I'll call *Discretion*, since we're dealing with writing: that is to say, the suspen-

Love

sion (*epoché*) of Effect, of Pomposity, of Arrogance. Let's grasp this point on three counts:

1. Haiku: every haiku=an act of discretion. Operation that's made very obvious by the absence, in haiku, of the theme of love: it's a kind of lyricism (since it says *I*) but a lyricism that silences love—Coyaud quotes a few haikus dealing with relationships, but from such a distance (discretion) that they amount to nothing more than little tableaux *viewed from very far away*, generally with a touch of humor:

(38)   *Spring rain*
       An umbrella and a straw-coat
       Go chatting together

                                    (Buson, Blyth*)

A late haiku (1900–41):

(39)   *The greying bonze*
       Strokes a friend's head
       Veranda under the moon

                                    (Basho, Coyaud)

→ The enunciator isn't in love. Incompatibility between Love and the haiku. Love requires us to speak overwhelmingly of ourselves: crude mobilization (panic) of the imaginary. Now, the structural rule of haiku is to *divide up* the secret to the point where it is without personality; constitutive paradox, already flagged up: opposition between *individuation* and the *individual*; love, on the other hand, compacts the individual and forecloses individuation (the basic premise of the Moment)—except in its mystical extremities and excesses (for at the same time it's there that it's painful, it offers a glimpse of that suffering) → There's no imperative in haiku; this, which is very beautiful, would be impossible in a haiku: "Stammer as you kiss me with parted lips" (Ronsard);[7] neither eroticism nor an appeal to the other → Even the mention of a *You* would, in haiku, be going too far. This (by Milosz)[8] is *almost* a haiku:

Schehadé

You, sad,
Sad sound of the rain
On the rain

But the *You* reintroduces an imaginary world of relations that is incompatible with haiku's *discretion*.

Stereotype

2. Haiku: strict world of the Indirect, that we can also call (since old words are required): *pudeur*. Now, this *pudeur* bears upon things of a sexual nature (or, even more generally, upon affect) but also upon the "compromises" of discourse → although the haiku is extremely coded, it avoids stereotypes: what *should be* discussed because it's mythically important, well regarded, classical, customary, etc. For example: Mount Fuji for someone Japanese—in the whole of his oeuvre, Basho speaks of it only once—and even then!

(40) *Misty rain*
Today is a happy day
Though Mount Fuji is unseen

(Basho, Blyth*)

Admirable that the only time Basho speaks of Fuji it is to say that it's *hidden*, *concealed*: that's what writing is; it can be a tremendous, imperious, courageous force of *dis-appointment* {*dé-ception*}.

Ideology

3. There is, if not an abolition (for that's perhaps impossible) then at least a *suspension*, an *extenuation* of the Ideological: much of this is probably due to the Short form—but not just that: Maxims are heavily ideological. I see, I feel, I hear in

(41) *Dazzling moon*
Two or three clouds from time to time
To repose the eye

(Basho)

a sort of rarefaction of the Ideological that's so exhilarating and so calming it's almost intoxicating; here the account is so pure that there's no echo of arrogance, of value, nor even of the *religious* (the religious is not ideological in itself, but it *turns* very quickly—like milk turning sour).

The haiku is an *assent* to what *is*. Here it would be necessary to make a distinction (perhaps! "Subtility"? No, "reality": see the Proust quotation)[9] between *assent* and *approbation, adherence, approval* (a play by Vinaver, *Today or the Koreans*),[10] that is to say, between the path of *reality* (haiku) ≠ the path of *truth* (discourse, ideology) → Haiku = the art (an art) that "skims" reality of its ideological resonance, that is, of its *commentary*, even when that commentary is virtual. Perhaps the most beautiful haiku = those that retain a trace, a scent of this resistance to meaning. This one, for example:

(42) *The petals fall*
He shuts the great gate of the temple
And leaves

(Basho)

→ We sense that here we're being held *on the brink* of *effect*; this is precisely what Blanchot (*Conversation*) calls the Neutral: "Let us remember that neutral would be given in a position of quasi-absence, of effect of non-effect";[11] here, we're in the *quasi*, the almost: something *happens* but it's not an *effect*.

Clearly, this *Untenable* of haiku has some connections with Zen. I consider the haiku to be a sort of *Incident*, a tiny fold, an insignificant crease on a great empty surface (=satori=nonresonant account of the real). I'm thinking of this apologue: Bodhidharma (the more-or-less mythical figure who introduced Zen into China around 520), is said to have withdrawn to a monastery and spent nine years in his cell "*looking at the wall*" (*Pikuan*, in Chinese): banishing all will-to-possess from his mind; the haiku: a faint scratch on the wall of non-will-to-possess; in the haiku, I don't want to possess anything, yet there's something like a sensual fold, a joyful assent to fragments of the real, to affective inflections: this is *Discretion* → the haikist, the Man of haiku: an imperfect, lax, perhaps even a crafty Buddhist: crossed with Tao.

SESSION OF FEBRUARY 17, 1979

Effect of the Real or Rather of *Reality* (Lacan)[1]

Here, I'll be collating a few thoughts around: How does what the haiku *says* produce an effect of the real?[2] What's the particular feature of that effect? (By "effect of the real" I mean: language fading into the background, to be supplanted by a certainty of reality: language turning in on itself, burying itself and disappearing, leaving bare what it says. In a sense, effect of the real = readability → What's the *readability* of the haiku?)

Photography

To enter one art through another. Proust, *Against Sainte-Beuve*: Balzac "painting" society, not in the sense of a copy but because he had "ideas for good paintings," "an idea for a good pictorial effect," "a grand pictorial idea" "*for he often conceived of one art in the form of another*"[3] → the art form that enables us to conceive of the haiku = Photography.
Photography → Paradoxes around Photography:[4]

1. World: is full of, saturated by photographs, at every level of knowledge, of social life (public and private); multiple, heteroclite object (cf. language overwhelming Saussure)[5] ≠ And yet: no Theory of Photography, no Accession to the heights of high culture (Film, Painting).

2. Isn't considered an "Art" (≠ seventh art) and yet there are "Artistic Photographs" (which, by the way, are a negation of both Art and Photography).

3. When it comes to photography, it seems that we've not yet managed to define the *specificity* of the photographic image, the *effect* that only the photographic image (as distinct from the other arts) produces, likewise for film. We're not able to formulate the "noeme": the specific type of appearing, of being fulfilled by the noetic aim, of intentionality; this phenomenological vocabulary can be justified by the fact that for Phenomenology perception is the decisive authority of knowledge. For example (to run briefly through a few working hypotheses):

a. It can't be the (perceptive) "structure" of the Image. Photography was invented by painters (not technically, of course, but phenomenologically): the *camera obscura* reproduces Renaissance perspectival geometry.

b. It can't be its "reproducibility" (which is what distinguishes it from painting): a text is reproducible: (1) materially, ever since the printing press; (2) phenomenologically, each time it's read.

c. It can't be the "point of view": no doubt the camera offers a great many possibilities in this regard; although there are some perfect tracking shots in Flaubert—cf. Subjective camera, Pascal Bonitzer.[6]

My hypothesis (long held but never explored in depth: something I propose to do—soon—in a future work) = the noeme of photography has to be sought on the side of "that has been."[7] If that noeme fits, then it's the noeme of photography and not of film—which remains without a noeme (some will say: it gets on pretty well without one! Who knows?). Photography and film from the point of view of the Noeme: "*That has been*":

1. It's very rare for a photograph to be fictional; special case: Bernard Faucon: productions, tableaux vivants.[8] It always remains on the side of "*That has been*" ≠ film: "That *appears* to have been."

2. The share of "That has been" in film passes through the medium of photography: film artificially distorts the noeme of photography. In actual fact, "*That has been*": false, entirely fabricated, doctored, a sort of chemical "synthesis"; experience of a film set:[9] (a) the sequence of recording and reconstruction is reversed = editing; (b) image and sound are dissociated from one another: postsynchronization.

This is what makes me attach more importance to photography than to film, I mean with regard to the anthropological endeavor. A *Theory* of photography might be possible; of cinema, perhaps only a *culture*. From the point of view of a historical anthropology, the New Absolute, the mutation, the threshold, is Photography. Pierre Legendre in *Les Cahiers du Cinéma*[10] → the world divided into before / after film. I say: no: before / after Photography. Film may well dissolve into cultural history, into other forms (become Television) ≠ Photography: its noeme is always be a *shock* of consciousness: the shock (the anxiety) of "I'm certain that has been" (cf. the phenomenologists' *urdoxa*).[11]

My proposition is that haiku comes closest to the noeme of photography: "That has been" → film, too, but it's a deceitful approach, very different from the approach mediated by a heterogeneous signifier, by words, so one that's not false but whose credibility is of a different order. Film kidnaps the photograph's reliability and distorts it in the service of an illusion; haiku works with a heterogeneous material (words) with a view to making it reliable and producing the effect of "That has been." My working hypothesis, then, is that the haiku gives the *impression* (not the certainty: *urdoxa*, noeme of the photograph) that what it says took place, *absolutely*.

(43)   *Spring breeze*
The boatman
Chews his pipe

(Basho, Yamata)

It's absolutely contingent: individuation of the moment (cf. *supra*) + action in the present → Very powerful present that effectively *guarantees* the "That has taken place." But at the same time, through language, out of that pure contingency, a transcendence emerges = all Spring, all the nostalgia of the Instant *as if in relief*, never to return → The haiku presents the life of the Event and its abolition simultaneously (cf. old photographs: I'd be willing to claim that photography's mode of being is not a shiny photograph from *Paris-Match* or *Photo* but one that has *aged*).[12]

(44)   *The kitten*
Is sniffing
At the snail

(Saimaro, Blyth*)

We've seen this a thousand times: a kitten's surprise when confronted with an unfamiliar object → Same double movement: recognition, repetition = sign + keen, irrefutable sensation that this refers to *that* time (the Semelfactive).[13] Haiku: sign (since it's recognizable)[14] yet still "surprising"; perhaps a definition of writing: something of the divine (this "Sign"), epiphany.

(45)   *No sound*
Other than the summer rain
In the evening

(Issa, Munier)

Same effect: we recognize this as something that has occurred, but at the same time we see in it the "Glory" of the "That happened only once," of *suchness* (Remember: "Glory" = manifestation of the mode of being). We perceive the *particular mode of being* of *that* rain, the absence of meaning, of *interpretability* → Haiku: a sign that has no meaning. Same effect in (not transcribed in the fascicule):

A stray cat
Asleep on the roof
In the spring rain

(Taigi, Blyth*)

This, without me really being aware of it, can be plugged, not into my unconscious (that's not for me to say), but into a sort of subconscious; a region not of the Repressed but of the Forgotten: a Proustian region.

All these effects of reality can also be produced by photography. The (perhaps noematic) difference between Photography and Haiku = a photograph is *bound to say everything*: were it to speak of the boatman, it would have to tell us what he was wearing, how old he was, how dirty; of the kitten, its color. It produces excesses of meaning ≠ haiku: abstract, and yet lifelike effect (perhaps here we're leaving the Noeme of Photography behind and rejoining the Noeme of the Text).

Nevertheless, the proximity between photography and haiku remains very great. Of course, the photograph is full of, saturated by *inevitable* details—and the haiku isn't; but, in both, *everything is given straight away* → the haiku can't be developed any further (be enlarged), nor can the photograph (I'm not playing on words, since photos are *developed*); you can't add anything to a photograph, you can't *prolong* it: the gaze can linger, it can be repeated, renewed, but it can't *change over time* (except in special cases: for example, when a photograph serves as a starting point for telling a story, for dreaming, for introspection) ≠ painting, where the gaze works *directly from the image*—unlike in the dream) → The haiku and the photograph are *pure authorities* that aren't required to ground their authority in anything other than this: *that has been* → Perhaps this power comes from the short form; hypothesis: think of the photograph as a *short form* (≠ film: a rich, rhetorical form; gives rise to a desire for ellipses, for litotes).

Coyaud, 12

SESSION OF FEBRUARY 17, 1979

The "*That has been*" of Photography and Haiku can be examined under another heading: that of the temporal category they fall into → I say "temporal category" and not "tense" because it's not a matter of morphological markers: a form in the present tense can refer to an actual past (historical present).

Let's remind ourselves, with Benveniste (*Problems of General Linguistics I*, 239–240),[15] that the temporal expression of the past in general = (1) *aorist* (simple or definite past); (2) *perfect* (definite past: I read, I was); (3) *imperfect*; (4) pluperfect → Difference between the *aorist* and the perfect = the difference between historical narrative and discourse. *Aorist*: the tense of the event that occurred outside the person of the narrator = form typically used in history (disappeared from spoken discourse) ≠ *Perfect*: establishes a vital connection between the event that occurred in the past and the present in which it is evoked = tense of the person relating the facts as a witness, as a participant; tense chosen by someone who wants to make the narrated event resonate today, to link it to our present → Perfect in the first person = autobiographical tense *par excellence* → Perfect: the point of reference is the moment of enunciation ≠ *Aorist*: the point of reference is the moment of the event.

What category does haiku's "*That has been*" fall into? Although frequently written in the present tense ("the boatman chews his pipe"), they're written (in the translations) without verbs: "dazzling moon, two or three clouds"; this clearly refers to the past: not the *aorist* past (*it happened*) but to the *perfect*, the tense of evocation, of the affective link between what has taken place and who I am as I remember it (naturally, in the translations, this doesn't exclude those stylistic effects produced by the use of the simple past); see (33) → Haiku's tense = the perfect (remember: I invited him = *habet invitatum*).

What about the photograph? I don't know; something to analyze later on. Of course: on the whole, in the perfect—but there might be some aorist photographs (Larousse's vignettes, for instance).

The Division of the Real

Here are two haiku; both offer a very precise division of the real.

(46) *Peeling a pear*
Sweet drops trickle down
A knife

(Shiki, Blyth*)

To me, this is very beautiful: the pear is not "reduced" but abstracted to those droplets on the knife → Extreme metonymy.

(47) *Flies play*
On the inkstand. Spring
Sun beams

(Meistetsu, Coyaud)

Of course, the world (the Noteworthy, *Notandum*) can be divided up indefinitely (it's what physicists do)—or, at least, with no other endpoint than that of words, and even then: by combining words (syntagmatic production), I can go down even further than the fly → It follows that there's something arbitrary about stopping at notation → Language imposes its law on Nature → Haiku, in its extreme precision = at a certain point, I *put down*, I *set down* language.

At what point in the *descent* (into the infinitely subtle) did I decide to set down language? (Or: why note down this and not that?) Perhaps the *decision* (in reading, the little satori) comes from what happens when meter encounters a particular fragment of reality, makes a knot, suspends it; moment when the "real" is *raised aloft* by the 5–7–5? enabling it to be *said* with certainty?[16]

That could be the definition of Poetry: it would, in short, be the language of the Real in that it can't be divided up any further or has no interest in dividing itself up any further → Paradox? Remember Vico's (and subsequently the Romantic) myth of the anteriority of the Poetic, of the *naturality* of the Poetic.[17]

Claudel said this, I think: the "metrical raising aloft," the satori of a discovered form that *creates* the real by suspending the process of division, or if you prefer: the *formula*: Claudel says: "the mother's-touch," "the bright home . . . that organizes the concert of values, of lines, of volumes around oneself," "that seminal spark that sets the whole conception of the living being in motion" → "Only the poet holds the secret to that sacred instant when the *essential sting*

<admirable definition of the haiku> suddenly introduces, through a world of memories, intentions and thoughts suspended within us, the solicitation of a form."[18]

Co-presence

The syntactic basis of haiku is the *co-presence* of two elements (*co-presence*: a word that doesn't imply any causal or even any logical link, cf. John Cage: *mushroom* and *music*)[19] → Haiku: *paratactile* writing.—Note that here we cross paths with a language myth from the eighteenth century: cf. Vico and the anteriority of the Poetic; Condillac: originary language, speaks only in perceptible images, hence *no conjunctions* (abstract elements) = regime of the asyndeton (or the parataxis).[20]

As a test, a haiku:

(48)   *In the shadows of the foliage*
       The black cat's eyes
       Golden, ferocious

(Kawabata Bosha, Coyaud)

in which the co-presence doesn't work at all: the first term (the *foliage*) is lifeless, banal (not only that, it's a circumstantial complement) → no mental trigger, no satori, no "essential sting," no rapture → This can be put another way: the weak element is a *descriptive ornament*; now, the haiku isn't descriptive: it's beyond that, in the realm of mental experience (*photography*, not painting). That could be a description from a traditional novel: "X goes deeper into the forest and spies, glittering in the foliage, the golden and ferocious eyes of a cat." Here's another haiku (not included in the fascicule) which shows clearly that if a haiku remains on the level of description, if it avoids the co-presence jolt, then (even if it works as a description) it won't fulfill its mode of being as a haiku:

The nightingale's voice
Smooth
Rounded, long

(Toko, Coyaud)

I'll say, making a very subtle distinction, but this helps me to understand it: here there's a "That's it!" that comes from the language (the description of the nightingale's voice works very well—by the way, don't we seem to be hearing a lot more of them nowadays?) but there's no mental "That's it!"(satori).

Here, on the other hand, are two good haikus in which the co-presence dazzles:

(49) *Beings without memory*
Fresh snow
Squirrels bounding

(Kusatao, Coyaud)

Instantaneous link (though still *separated*: no logic) between being-without-memory and the snow—with a speck, a trace of humor (like a very subtle cocktail: not an Alexandra! More like Monsieur Boeuf's champagne with marshmallows!). A digression: today, marshmallow is nothing more than its negative connotation: killed by language = hollyhock.[21] In reality, there's no marshmallow in marshmallows.

(50) *A bird sang*
A red berry
Fell to the ground

(Shiki, Munier)

Here the parataxis (the co-presence) plays on two actions: singing / falling → pure co-presence, because there's no link between the two actions. (Note that, in French, the simple—false aorist-past reinforces the punctual aspect of the berry falling and the bird bursting into song: an aspectual, not a temporal, value: sensation of surprise).

Last, a co-presence that's less rigorous, since it juxtaposes a state and a process:

(51) *Convalescence*
My eyes tire
Of contemplating the roses

Clearly here we've reached one of the limits of haiku: we're moving toward something more "psychological," closer to a state of the soul than a satori: it's more *Persian* than Japanese, more Indo-European than Asiatic—more Western, more novelistic.

SESSION OF FEBRUARY 24, 1979

Setting a Bell Ringing[1]

Comparison between the haiku and the "mental jolt" (satori) → It could therefore be said: a (good) haiku *sets a bell ringing* → triggering, as the only possible remark: "*That's it!*" → I'd like to say a few words about this "*That's it*" of haiku (this setting a bell ringing), for it's contrary to Western attitudes—and thus prompts us to reflect on what, for us, is *other*.

Any "well-executed" haiku *sets a bell ringing* inside us. Occasionally, though, the *bell*, the *that's it*, is represented within the haiku itself: the sudden apparition of the referent in the walk (the walk of life) and of the word in the sentence.

(52)   *I come by the mountain path*
       Ah! this is exquisite!
       A violet!

                                                    (Basho†)

[2]And this one, with a ringing that's even purer because the *kireji* (*ah*) bears upon the apparition of the object and not the effect that it produces:

(53)   *Such a shame to pick it*
       Such a shame to leave it
       Ah, this violet

Clearly, the *bell* is anti-interpretative: it blocks interpretation. Saying "Ah, the violet" signifies that there's nothing to say about the violet: its mode of being rejects all adjectives → phenomenon that's absolutely hostile to our Western mentality, which always wants to interpret—with varying degrees of success.

As a result, (52) inevitably receives the following commentary: "Delicious and fragrant surprise: Does the haiku conceal a metaphorical meaning? Some claim that it does: one day, while walking along a mountain path, Basho is said to have encountered a Buddhist hermit, a flower of virtue" → Inveterate error: the short form, the "detail" can only ever be metaphorical: forms always have to have a signified! → Sort of Western compulsion to *hypertrophesize*

78

<small>Zola, *Oeuvres complètes* 1928, 636–37, correspondence</small>

the detail (Zola: 'I enlarge, that is for certain. . . . I have enlarged about the facts taken a leap towards the stars on the trampoline of precise observation. Truth soars upon the wing of the symbolic"),[3] a declaration that's characteristically antihaikist. In haiku, no authority of truth; the haiku can't be enlarged, its size is precise (one could speak of a *homometrics*); it makes no leap into the symbolic, it's not a trampoline—and the stars are too far away!

On this point, I wanted to cite a haiku that would appear to completely contradict what I'm saying:

(54)   *And what is my life*
Nothing more than the futile reed
Growing in the thatch of a hut

(Basho, Yamata)

It explicitly sets out a metaphor: reed = life.—Actually, this haiku is enigmatic, because it contradicts (perhaps a result of the translation? the gentle Kikou Yamata may not have been especially rigorous) not only the antisymbolic "spirit" of haiku but also, peculiarly, another haiku by the same poet:

(55)   *How admirable*
He who does not think "Life is ephemeral"
When he sees a flash of lightning!

(Basho†)

This one, in contrast, expresses the haikist doctrine perfectly. Setting a bell ringing: the (writing or reading) subject instantaneously struck by *the thing itself*. For me, immediate criterion of a haiku's success: there's no possibility of any inference of meaning, of symbolism; it doesn't "come together" as a system (metaphysical, or even "endoxal," of common sense).

Here are three explicit examples of "*That's it!*"

(56)   *In my glass of saké*
A flea swims
Absolutely

(Issa, Coyaud)

Absolutely: an audacious yet remarkable translation, for it refers indiscriminately: (a) to the referent: the flea swims with undeniable energy; (b) to the haiku itself: there's no interpretative relativity whatsoever: there's nothing to be said about it.—*Absolutely* would be the haiku's motto.

(57) In a jar of water floats
An ant
Without a shadow

(Seishi, Coyaud)

Same thing. *Without a shadow* = *absolutely* (*interpretation* would be like a *shadow* falling on the picture, the drawing: the shadow that follows the event (but let's not forget that there's been a whole tradition of painting without shadows)).

(58) "That, that"
Was all I could say
Before the blossoms of Mount Yoshino

(Teishitsu, Coyaud)

Saying that you can't say: the whole haiku tends toward this—toward "*that*." There's nothing to say, in short, other than the vertiginous limit of language, the *deictic Neutral* ("that") ≠ language as repression, dogmatism of meaning: a meaning is sought at all costs: "The frogs who asked for a meaning to make it their King."[4] Dare I extend this hypothesis around *Absolutely* to the whole of literature? For, in its perfect moments, literature (the eidetic of literature) tends to make us say: "That's it, that's absolutely it!" (cf. *infra* on the "moment of truth"[5] ≠ Interpretation makes us say: "It's not quite that"; what you're reading is not what it is: what it is has a shadow that I'll make the object of my discourse.

Clearly, the "That's it" (the bell) of haiku has a relationship with Zen: already through the satori (= setting a bell ringing) but also through a Zen notion: the *Wu-shi*: "Nothing special";[6] things are translated in their naturality, without being analyzed = the *sono-mana* vision = "Such as it is" (indeed, we've already seen, through a quotation from Michelet,[7] that *Suchness* is indeed the word that designates the spirit of haiku), or "Just as it is" → evidently this is the opposite of realism, which, disguised as exactitude, is the boundless provision of meaning.

The *Wu-shi*: a way of outwitting {*déjouer*} the desire to interpret, that is, to "talk seriously about the meaning of things." Example: one day a monk asked Feng-hsüeh: "When speech and silence are both forbidden, how can one avoid falling into error?" The master replied with two lines:

Watts, 204–5

I always remember Kiangsu in March
The cry of the partridge, the mass of fragrant flowers![8]

This: refers to *Wu-shi*, to naturality → It explains that the Zen masters would often quote poetry (classical Chinese poetry), selecting those quatrains or verses with a designative meaning (*That's it!*), then fall silent: the very definition of haiku: it designates (fundamentally: its discursive linguistic category=diectic), then falls silent.

The haiku's (or the *Wu-shi*'s) lack of interpretation—"of interpretability" (or its challenge to interpretation)—is not its naivety but rather *the third turn of the screw* it gives to language (language on the spot). I'll explain: a Zen parable says, initially: the mountains are mountains; second stage (let's call it the initiation): the mountains aren't mountains anymore; third stage: the mountains are mountains again → It spirals back → It could be said: first moment: that of Stupidity (we all have our share of it), moment of arrogant, anti-intellectualist tautology, *a spade's a spade*, etc.; second moment: that of interpretation; third moment: that of naturality, of *Wu-shi*, of haiku.—This process: in a way, the *return of literality*: haiku (a well-written sentence, poetry) would be the end of a journey, the accession to the *literal* → like the art of *speaking plainly*, the literal is difficult. (Allow me a personal, a very personal notation: it was some months after the death of a loved one before I could say, simply, nakedly, "absolutely": "I'm suffering because that person died" → In order to reach the third state, the literal II, or the return of the literal, you first have to *pass through* interpretation—to grieve a death=you have to pass through a whole "culture" of *mourning*, and *culture*=what comes first, the absolutely spontaneous.) → The first literality: an arrogance (an unthinking certainty)≠the second: a "wisdom." It can also be said that *Wu-shi*—the move beyond (or the foreclosure) of metaphor, the capturing of the *naturality* of the thing—is the accession to Difference: the capturing of all things in their *difference* from everything else. And here we encounter Basho, the haikist, again—but I'm not sure if this is a haiku or a remark: "However much you look at everything, there's nothing like the crescent of the moon"; the "truth" is in difference, not in reduction. There can be no *general truth*: this is what haiku says, one haiku after another.

Kikou Yamata, 100

The Clarity of Haiku

In general, the short (brief) form = a *shortcut* (ellipsis) that's more or less obfuscating. Now, haiku = short and extremely clear: completely readable → A kind of instantaneous, fleeting, and dazzling harmony between the *saying* and the *said*, cf. Virginia Woolf (Blanchot): "little daily miracles," "matches unexpectedly struck in the dark."[9]

1. The ephemerality of haiku: that of the saying, not that of the world; not an Epicurean philosophy: live in the moment, etc. → More an "eternity" (a stability, a return) that's perceived all at once. Cf. distich by Angelus Silesius: "The world is vanishing! It does not pass away / It's just obscurity which God does there erase."[10]

2. Fleeting clarity, fleeting emphasis: a *quality* of emotion. Emotion (or rather: *agitation*): more in the mobility of facial expressions than in the immobile weight of sentimentality (cf. *supra* on animals). Cage: "I discovered that those who seldom dwell on their emotions know better than anyone else what an emotion is." (Cage and Zen; of all the emotions: tranquility—the most important).[11]

Dialectic: we arrive at exactitude, aptness, the *That's it*—but, in the process, we reach the limit of language: the haiku *will* tip over (tries to keep itself from tipping over) or is *in the process of tipping over* (remember the *Utsuroi*) into the nothingness of the saying: the *nothing to say* → The destiny of "*That's it*" is: "*That's all it is, it's no more than that.*"

See:

(59)   *In the winter river*
Pulled up and thrown away
A red turnip

(Buson, Blyth*)

Is that really worth saying? (Well, yes . . .)

(60)   *It's evening, autumn*
I think only
Of my parents

(Buson, Blyth*)

Even harder to analyze. Yet . . . an *event* occurs: like a ball of emotion (sadness, nostalgia, love), here, in my throat → The ultimate transformation of "*That's it!*" into "*There it is!*"

The haiku, being very conscious of the limit of language, can state it:

(61) *Nothing else today*
Than to go into Spring
Nothing more

(Buson, Munier)

This tenuousness of haiku's language is in all likelihood related to this conspicuous phenomenon: most of the time, impossible to say why I like a haiku, why it "suits" me, why "it works," why it "sets a bell ringing" + intuition that other people won't necessarily feel the same way. At any rate, in order to sketch out an explanation of "good" haiku, I constantly find myself having to refer, not to the Beautiful as such, but to an absolutely personal disposition: the most subtle of individual specifications; for example:

(62) *Everyone is asleep*
Nothing else
But the moon and me

(Seijugo, Coyaud)

For me, the enchantment, the "truth" of this haiku has to do with a *hyperconsciousness* (cf. Neutral):[12] acute, pure consciousness, with no interposition.

"Difficult to say why I find it beautiful"; what this actually represents is not an incapacity on my part but, on the contrary, the *founding premise* of haiku; its nature (its aim) is to *silence*, at last, all metalanguage; therein lies haiku's *authority*: perfect harmony between *this* speech and my (rather than anyone else's) "incomparable" self → I = someone who can't speak of himself / who can't be spoken {*celui qui ne peut se dire*}, not because he's unlike anyone else but because he's unlike "anything" else: no generality, no Law. *I* is always a *remainder*—and it's there that it encounters haiku.

The Limits of Haiku

À propos of a line of French verse, I've often said: "It's *almost* a haiku, but . . ." → We've been carrying out a kind of commutation test[13] → There are *limits*, then: it's not enough for a form to be short for it to be a haiku, far from it → certain textual *forces* (certain temptations) can pull the haiku off course, distance it from itself → I'll indicate two areas adjacent to the haiku that remain, to my mind, exterior to it.

1. The Concetto

Here's a haiku that I "almost" like:

(63)   *In the house of the solitary nun,*
Indifferent to her indifference, blooms
A white azalea

(Basho, Yamata)

Very beautiful: the white azalea is metonymically linked to hermetism. But one element seems suspect to me (though it might be an addition of the translation): "indifferent to her indifference" is a *verbal conceit*, a *concetto*.

In my view: haiku shouldn't contain any "conceits" → There are (at least) two short forms contrary to haiku:

a. The epigram functions on an aggressiveness: spitefulness, an absence of generosity *put into form*: this is the "*conceit*"[13] (instrument of aggression); Martial (I, XXXIII):

Non amo te, Sabidi, nec possum dicere quare;
Hoc tantum possum dicere: non amo te[15]

The conceit: the beginning and the ending literally echo one another → The epigram = an antihaiku → A haiku would be more likely to say: "I love you haiku, and I can't say why / all I can say is: I love you, haiku" → Haiku has two enemies: generality and spite.

b. The *concetto*, the (sophisticated) verbal conceit, the *agudezza*: so *subtle* (that's its law) that it is sometimes concealed; hidden finesse, *acutezza recondita*, that's the watchword of Manierism → *concetto* (etymologically: an *idea*, an essence; ideal representation of a hidden connection) → essence of all literary Manierisms (early seventeenth century): Gongorism (Spain), Marinism (Italy, the poet Giambattista Marino), euphuism (England, *Euphues*, a novel by Lyly, 1580), affectation (France) → cf. pictorial Manierism (Parmigianino, sixteenth century): the verticals are lengthened, the horizontals foreshortened, accelerated perspective, *serpentinata* (sinuous style) → cf. Michelet's *vertical style*.[16] This: the opposite of the haiku's *naturality*, its *horizontal* language (therein lies the paradox: the source of the *satori*, the vertiginous sensation is not an abyss, a depth, but a quick spreading out, given all in one go). Every now and then you come across a concettist haiku—but there aren't many I like. Thus:

Hocke, 17

84 FROM LIFE TO THE WORK

(64)   *Bat, you live*
Hidden under
Your broken umbrella

(Buson, Coyaud)

These exceptions are what legitimized the rapprochement between haiku and Jules Renard.[17] A member of the audience is quite right to make the link, citing: "*The cockroach. Black and sticky, like a keyhole.*" "*The spider. A little hand, black and hairy, clutching strands of hair. All night long, on behalf of the moon, it affixes seals.*" *Natural Histories* (I don't like Ravel very much either):[18] "*The raven. Grave accent on the furrow.*" "*The lark*: It lands, dead drunk from having flown into the eye of the sun / poked the sun in the eye again."{*ivre morte de s'être encore fourrée dans l'oeil du soleil*} (pursue this form of wit and you get to *Le Canard enchaînée*)—But Jules Renard's metaphors don't reconstruct anything; they don't individualize a moment: kind of algebra of the signifier; for haiku, a kind of danger, for example:

Evening moon
The snail
Bares his chest

(Issa)

The sole haikist resonance: *evening moon*, happening upon a snail: that's all → perhaps it's that the haiku is basically *realistic*: it believes in the referent.

2. Narration

Second limit: narration. Some haiku contain the germ of a story, a "narreme." For instance:

(65)   *The moon-viewing boat*
I dropped my pipe
Into the river shallows

(Buson, Blyth*)

→ a "story," that is to say, already a nebulous tangle of causalities-consequences: someone is distracted, he drops his pipe, but because the water's shallow it can be recovered, etc.

Here's a haiku that's explicitly linked to a story:

> (66) *I remember*
> *The old woman left to cry*
> *With the moon for company*
>
> (Basho, Coyaud)

And Coyaud, *Fourmis sans ombre*:

THE MOUNTAIN WHERE OLD PEOPLE WERE ABANDONED

There once lived a very pious son. In those times, old people were considered a burden. They were taken by piggy-back to the mountain, and there left to their fate.

The father of this son was sixty years old: it was therefore time to be rid of him. The son took him on his back and walked, walked, zunzun, *with great strides toward the foot of the mountain. But the father began to worry about his son: what if he gets lost on his way home? So it occurred him to break off the tips of some the branches of the trees,* pakipaki, *and to scatter them along the path. At the foot of the mountain, the son built a roof of leaves to protect his father from the rain. Then he said:*

"Papa, here I must leave you."

The father replied:

"So you wouldn't get lost, I marked the way with broken branches."

The son burst into tears, suddenly full of pity for his father. He lifted him onto his back again and took him home. Anxious to conceal what had happened from the authorities, he hid the old man in a hole behind their hut, and would bring him food.

Now, one fine day, the Prince of the realm presented his people with a riddle:

"Bring me a rope woven from ashes," said he.

Not even the cleverest villagers were able to find the solution to the riddle. From his hole, the father said to his pious son:

"Weave a solid rope, put it on a tray, and burn it."

The son followed his instructions to the letter. He made a rope out of ashes and presented it to the Prince, who showered him with praise.

Some time later, the Prince summoned the son and presented him with the trunk of a felled tree: the tree-trunk was black, and perfectly round. It was impossible to tell which end had been planted in the ground, but that was precisely what the Prince asked the son to find out. Once again the son went and asked his father in the hole.

"Plunge the trunk into water: the end which bobs up isn't the right one; the other end, the one still under water, is the end with the roots."

Once again the son did as he was told, and once again he was praised by the Prince.

Next, the Prince asked him to make a drum that makes a sound without being struck. The son went to his father yet again, who said:

"Ha! That's easy! Go into the forest and find a bee's nest."

While the son was seeking the nest, his wife went to the tanner's to buy a skin. The son simply stretched the skin and put the bees inside the drum—and the drum sounded by itself: boron boron. He took it to the Prince, who was delighted:

"You've solved the three riddles. You're truly cunning."

The son said:

"Listen: it wasn't me who solved the riddles, it was my father, who lives hidden in a hole. Old people are full of wisdom."

"Ah, truly," said the Prince, "old people do know such wonderful things! Well, from now on we'll no longer abandon them on the mountain! Ja mi Shakkiri, *that's the end of that*."[19]

SESSION OF MARCH 3, 1979

Between haiku and narrative, a possible intermediary form: the scene, the little scene. Cf. Brecht, street scenes and the *gestus*[1] → Kind of anecdotal pulsation of the haiku:

a. Diastole: calls for de-contraction:

In tears, seated
He recounts
His mother listens[2]

(Hasuo, Coyaud)

b. Systole: lends itself to contraction; for example, the whole of the beginning of *In Search of Lost Time* can become:

Nevertheless, his mother came
To wish him goodnight
Happiness

Ellipsis
╲╱
╳
╱╲
Catalysis[3]

Here we come back to where we started: the relationship between Notation and the Novel, between the Long Form and the Short Form.

In putting Narration as a (the last) limit of haiku, I wanted to point up the extreme proximity between the two, via the category of the *Incident* (I'll come back this), but also what seems to be the inherent impossibility of *extending* the haiku in the form of a story: it's as if there were an invisible, insurmountable wall between the two—or, put differently, as if their waters didn't mix:

a. Example (from personal experience) → I want to narrate a party: as a rule, anecdotal material: people I'd not met before, particular characters, conversations, rituals, etc. But when I set about telling the story, I find myself weighed down by the "necessary" details (necessary for the logic of the narrative) that I personally find it tiresome to recount. I only really need "retain" two notations from the party: the yellow dress worn by the hostess (a kaftan) and the sleepiness of the host's eyes, the droopiness of his eyelids, sorts of realistic haiku that exhaust the *saying* and don't belong to narrative discourse (at least not my practice of it) because they're: *not functional*.

b. Conversely, I can find something in a story that jumps out at me, like a film jumping, a sliver flying off, something that has all the spirit of haiku but in fact is in no way related to the story: something that *sets a bell ringing*, that brings with it all the particular features of haiku I've tried to articulate:

FLAUBERT, *A SIMPLE HEART*

There was a gentle breeze, the stars were shining, the huge wagon-load of hay swayed from side to side in front of them and dust rose from the feet of the four horses as they plodded along. Then, without any word of command, the horses turned off to the right. He kissed her once more and she vanished into the darkness.[4]

The Short Form is its own necessity and suffices in itself: *it can't be stretched*.

Conclusion

Passages

Let's now go back, little by little, to our initial task: how to pass from a fragmented Notation of the present (of which we've taken the haiku as the exemplary form) to a plan for a novel? That is: what, of haiku, can pass in(to)[5] our Western thinking, our writing practice? I'll indicate some of these *passages*.

1. Daily Practice of Notation

Honor to whom honor is due: the problems of daily practice:

a. "*Instrumentation*." Why is this a problem? Because Notation = *Notatio* (act), and *Notatio*, because there's the necessity of capturing a *sliver* of the present as it *jumps* out at observation, at consciousness: (1) *Sliver*? Yes: my personal and internal *scoops*[6] (*scoop*: to shovel, bale, action of lifting with a spade, to swipe, to scoop into a net, the first news in) → the (very insignificant) bits of news that I consider sensational and I want to "swipe" directly from life. (2) Suddenness: cf. the *satori*, the *kairos*, the right opportunity, a kind of "reportage," not of what's happening in general terms but of my own personal little current affairs: the drive of *Notatio* is unpredictable. (3) *Notatio* is therefore an *outdoor* activity: not at my desk, but out in the street, in the café, with friends, etc.

The "Notebook" → My practice, already long established: *notula* and *nota*. I simply take a note of the word (*notula*) that will remind me of my "idea" (let's say no more on that for the moment), which I then copy out onto a piece of paper (*nota*) at home the next day → Noteworthy phenomenon: if I don't make a note (*notula*) of it, even one that's absolutely elliptical, I forget the idea; on the other hand, once the *nota* is taken, I can easily recall the whole idea and even its form (its sentence) → Quite a vertiginous sensation: that an "idea" should be of no more importance, no more *necessary*, than the very short time it takes to remember it? It can return to nothingness, having had no effect whatsoever? That's a good definition of the *luxury* of writing (or at least of my writing!).

I don't want to play down the *inconsequentiality* of this microtechnique of *Notatio*: the notebook, not very thick (→ pockets? Modern clothing, no one wears jackets anymore ≠ Flaubert's notebooks, oblong, in beautiful black moleskin; Proust's. Summer: fewer notes!) → Pen: a Biro at the ready (speed: no need to take the lid off): this isn't real (weighty, muscular) writing, but that doesn't matter, because *Notula* is not yet writing (≠the *Nota*, copied out) → All that means: the image of a single, fluid gesture whereby a notebook would be instantaneously produced, open at the right page, with the scriptor ready to write: *like a gangster pulling a gun* (cf. the *pen-camera*; though it's not a matter of showing but of hatching the germ of the *Sentence*; cf. *Infra*).[7]

b. *Readiness / Availability {Disponibilité}*. Whatever the objective, whether it's taking notes directly from life (rather than directly from a book)—or directly from the book of life: Novel, essay, or just the pleasure of noting down—this needs to be understood: in order to practice *Notatio* in its most *consummate* form, in order for it to give a feeling of plenitude, of enjoyment, of being worthwhile, there's a condition: you need time, lots of time.

Paradoxical: you'd think that a Note wouldn't take up much time, that it could be taken whenever, wherever; that it would only accompany, supplement, another, primary activity: walking, waiting, attending a meeting, etc. Yet experience tells us that in order to have "ideas" you have to be mentally ready. Difficult: for you mustn't go for walks solely with the purpose of having your notebook at the ready (→ sterilizing), but you do need a *measure* of readiness, like a humus. Even, a type of *free-floating attention*: not *focusing in on* that attentiveness and yet not getting too invested in what's going on elsewhere → Almost: an empty existence (voluntarily empty), wiled away on café terraces → In a sense: the activity of someone with a private income, who doesn't have to work (Flaubert, Goncourt, Gide): preparing a lecture, for example=contrary to *Notatio*.

Logic of this paradox: someone who devoted himself entirely to *Notatio* would end up refusing to invest in any other sort of writing activity (even if he thought of *Notatio* as the preparation for a work): *don't let yourself get distracted*→ *Nihil nisi propositum*.[8]

c. I sometimes notice this: if it's been a while since I've taken any notes, since I've taken out my notebook, I feel frustrated, as if I'm drying up → To go back to *Notatio*: like a drug, a refuge, something reassuring. *Notatio*: like a *maternity*→ I go back to *Notatio* as I would return to a mother; psychical structure that's perhaps attributable to a certain kind of culture (of education): *interiority* as a reassuring, safe place; cf. a "Protestant" tradition of interiority

> H.-J. Martin *Pour une histoire de la lecture*

and of the practice of *Notatio*: autobiographical diaries (Gide, Amiel). Historical divide: Northern Europe (end of the Middle Ages), adepts of *Devotio moderna*: the Brothers of Common Life and the canons of Windesheim→ cultured layman (the business classes): replacing the liturgical prayer with solitary meditation, direct contact with God → birth of solitary reading → *Notatio*: absence of a mediator (priest or work): the direct articulation of the thinking subject and the sentence-making subject.

d. So far, I've spoken of *Notatio* as a capturing directly *from life*, as if there were an instant harmony between what's seen, observed, and what's written → In reality, there's very often an *after the fact* to *Notatio*: *Nota*, that which, after a sort of probationary latency, returns despite ourselves, insists → What Memory must preserve is not the thing but its return, for this return already has something of a form—of a Sentence (cf. *infra*) → *Nota*: somewhat similar to the phenomenon of being incapable of thinking of a good rejoinder until the moment has passed {"*l'esprit de l'escalier*"}: untimely quick wittedness, quick-wittedness-come-late.

e. For *Notatio*, there's a first test of viability: the moment of transition from the notebook to the piece of paper, from the *Notula* to the *Nota* → Copying out devalorizes whatever isn't good enough: we don't have the muscular motivation to copy out, because our muscles start us wondering whether it's worth the effort → The birth of *writing* (as a complex and complete act) probably coincided with the *copy* (*Nota*): enigmatic links between writing and copying; the copy as endowment of value: you can write "for yourself" (*devotio moderna*) but you're already copying for someone else, with a view to external communication, social integration (hence the paradoxical impact of *Bouvard and Pécuchet*: they end up copying *for themselves*; closed loop: the ultimate mockery of writing).

2. The Levels of Notation

Cf. "Division" of the real.

We're aware of how important the "Level of Perception" is for the identification, the recognition, the naming of an object = dossier on "Size." Architecture: the art of scale—*Encyclopaedia* plate: a flea enlarged under a microscope → terrifying animal—Nicolas de Staël = 5cm² of Cézanne, etc.[9]

Variétiés, 1924

Division

Order of literature = the levels of Notation: how far down can note-taking go? We've seen this with respect to haiku, which descends as far as the extremely tenuous—But take note: the capturing of the tenuous is not necessarily linked to the short form → Sometimes lots of language is required to take account of a force of division (of divisibility).

Proust. Valéry: "What other writers are accustomed to pass over, Proust divides—and gives the impression of being able to go on dividing indefinitely."[10] Proust's hyperperception: comes from his hypersensitivity (smells) and his hypermnesia → Paradoxically, in order to divide up, he has to *enlarge*, to multiply: the experience of the tenuous is an experience of the large. Overvaluation, not trivialization: the smallness of Illiers, the expanse of Combray. Illiers, the garden: it wouldn't be possible to take a walk there in the rain: in order to "descend" as far as the notation "The grandmother's walk in the rain" he had to make the garden bigger.

When never-ending notations come quickly one after the other, there's a transformation of temporality. Baudelaire, the subject under the influence of hashish: "One's sense of temporal and existential proportions is disturbed by the innumerable swarms of intense feelings and ideas. One lives several lifetimes in the space of an hour. In that state, are you not like a fantastical novel that would be living rather than written?"[11]

Noteworthy

Baudelaire's metaphor clearly states that, on the horizon of division, that is, of the dense proliferation of Notations, lies the Novel.—But, for us, for this year at least, we'll remain on the level of the isolated Notation, the short form whose exemplary form is the haiku → Of what order is the *unit* of Notation? In other words: what possible justifications are there for the *Noteworthy* (*Notandum*)?

SESSION OF MARCH 10, 1979

1. *Functional*. In the classical novel, as a general rule, the Noteworthy has a semantic value: it's a sign, it refers to a signified, its purpose is to make us understand something that's necessary for the system of the Story.

Maupassant, *Pierre and Jean*: "Pierre's arms were hairy, a little on the thin side but sinewy; Jean's were plump and white with a touch of pink, a knot of muscles rippling beneath the skin."[1] → Functional features as regards the psychological system that structures the plot: Jean, strong, embittered, rejected by his mother ≠ Pierre, the slightly effeminate favorite → and the story, which, by the way, I've forgotten, follows on from this. (Inversion of the signs: endoxally impossible.) Balzac (*The Girl with the Golden Eyes*, p. 286): Henry de Marsay, who "was at that moment having his beard brushed with a soft brush rubbed with English soap."[2] → sign of Dandyism.

2. *Structural*. The thing to take note of = *notandum*; can be determined not by its content (functionality) but by the rhythm of its appearance → We take note (a) either of something that's repeated a great many times (repetition as an indicator of something being interesting: a law underlying it); in which case, notation is of the order of interpretation, of decoding (b) or of something that isn't repeated, that happens only once: the singular; probably of the order of supernatural Narration—the watchword would be: *Semel vel multum*[3] → You might ask: So what falls between the *Semel* and the *Multum*: zone of the *Unnoteworthy*?—Dazedness, depression of "What's the point in noting?": the always dangerous zone of the insignificant, when notation doesn't have the energy to pick it out, for *What's the point?* = "Why live?" (which is why it's depressing) → There are two kinds of "futile": (a) the futile that falls outside of writing, into nothingness = the vain, the *Vanitas*; (b) the futile picked out by writing; Cioran (*La Tentation d'exister*): "Why not admit it? The futile is the most difficult thing in the world, by which I mean conscious, accepted, voluntary futility."[4] This (structural) noteworthiness is evidently *relative* to the subject's position: his identity, his alterity. Medina of Marrakech: in a hut blackened with soot, a kind of filthy Buddha slumped on a heap → I take note of

this, but in doing so, I connote my status as a foreigner → Category of the *picturesque*: only happened to me once (*Semel*), but in the context of an ordinariness (for others) that I'm very much aware of = two discourses rubbing up against each other.

3. *Aesthetic*. Here's an incident (a *nota*): July 1, 1978. Waiting for the number 89 bus in front of the Sénat: two women, with a little boy trailing along behind; one of them is wearing a kind of off-white blouse. She walks exaggeratedly, swinging herself along. Now, for this incident to be noteworthy in my eyes, it must in some sense take a detour; I first need to note that, to express her exaggerated walk, I'd have to say: were a man to walk like that, we'd all think: he walks like a woman! An authentic noteworthy because it involves the following principle: in order to tell the *truth* (of a gesture) you have to try to express its effect: it's in its excess that a gesture reveals its essence. Cf. Baudelaire: "The grandiloquent truth of gestures on life's great occasions."[5]

4. *Symbolic*. Determination opposed to the Functional-Semantic (which refers to a signified). Noteworthy: what can be perceived as a *sign* (the signified remaining in the shadows). Here, I'll simply cite this anecdote relative to Kafka:

NOTEWORTHY (JANOUCH, *KAFKA*, 115–6)

> *Kafka suddenly stood still and stretched out his hand:*
> *"Look! There, there, can you see it?"*
> *Out of a house in the Jakobsgasse, where we had arrived in the course of our discussion, ran a small dog looking like a ball of wool, which crossed our path and disappeared round the corner of the Tempelgasse.*
> *"A pretty little dog," I said.*
> *"A dog?" asked Kafka suspiciously, and slowly began to move again.*
> *"A small, young dog. Didn't you see it?"*
> *"I saw. But was it a dog?"*
> *"It was a little poodle."*
> *"A poodle? It could be a dog, but it could also be a sign. We Jews often make tragic mistakes."*
> *"It was only a dog," I said.*
> *"It would be a good thing if it was." Kafka nodded. "But the only is true only for him who uses it. What one person takes to be a bundle of rags, or a dog, is for another a sign."*[6]

All this: determinations of intentionality, the Noteworthy determined by a certain aim. But, as far as extending the haiku is concerned, it is once again necessary to go back to the problem of *quantity*: relationship between the Noteworthy and the Short Form → Indeed, everything hinges on the syntagmatic *size* of the Notation: the *quantity of syntagm* imprisoned in the Notation.

Valéry *formulated* the determination of form very well: apropos of haiku—or similar short poems—he wrote, in a letter to the translator Kikou Yamata: "The little pieces you offer us are of the *order of the grandeur* of a system of thinking." Paul Valéry doesn't say a *thought* (= Maxim ≠ haiku), but the stance he takes is original: he conceives of thought in terms of syntagmatic quantity; extremely paradoxical for the time (Paul Valéry's originality lay in his *picturing* of textual forms: the reasoning behind in his chair in Poetics).[7]

In a more "technical" manner, the Notation (as a short form) could be defined as *what can't be summarized* → It goes without saying that this criterion is purely "endoxal," for to think of a text (whether long or short) as summarizable, that is, as an essential kernel of content padded out with pleasing but inessential forms, is already to adopt an ideological stance; "ideology" seems justified here because the *summary*, under the euphemism *contraction de texte*,[8] is deployed as a pedagogical weapon in technological universities ("techniques of expression"). Be that as it may: a haiku (a Notation) can't be compressed. Note that this resistance to summary is also a characteristic of the modern text (*Paradis*)[9] → the Summary: a very good test of (social) *integration*.

Of course, extending far beyond *Notation*: a whole dossier on the Short Form (I've often thought of it as a possible topic for a course)—As a form of preparation, the dossier would have to be compiled along two axes:

1. An inventory of short forms. In literature: maxims, epigrams, short poems, fragments, diary notes—and perhaps especially in music: Variations, Bagatelles (Beethoven at the end of his life, turned down by his publishers), Intermezzi, Novelettes, Fantasiestücke (Schumann, especially 1849, opus 73, clarinet / piano then cello / piano), all this as it relates to the capturing of individuation (as in the haiku). → But the musician of the Short Form = Webern of course: his ultrashort pieces + the dedication to Berg: "*Non multa, sed multum*," his radical art of silence, of the *plug of silence* (= the Ma, the interval). Schönberg on the *Short Pieces for Piano and Violin*: "A whole novel in just a sigh," and a critic, Metzger, who spoke

Cage, 31

of the "irrepressible cough which seizes the public each time it hears a silence in Webern."[10]

2. Examination of the *values* invested in the Short Form, and therefore of the *resistances* to it: very few Short Forms in Modernity, which, textually, tends to be more wordy (haunted by the idea that it's being prevented from speaking) → Valorization of verbal *abundance*, ancient in the West: Cicero (a good representative of the doxa). Thrasymacus and Gorgias cut speech up into rhythmical elements that were too disjointed; Thucydides went even further: not smooth enough → Isocrates: the first to craft smoother expressions and sentences with more fluid rhythms.[11]

→ I'll say it again: as to the prospect of a Theory of literature (still to be written) and of Modernity, all the *quantitative* phenomena of discursivity (in all the arts) would have to be examined: *length* (elongation), *brevity, shortcuts, copious, unending, tenuous, scanty,* "*trifles*" {"*rien*"} (with their corresponding mythologies: the doxa's distain for someone who writes "trifles" {"*de petits riens*"}) → Norms as regards length (of books, films) → And also the phenomena of *density*: the *Rarus* (scattered), cf. the *Ma*: notion that would authorize us to speak of painting: Twombly, the Orientals.[12]

3. Life in the Form of a Sentence[13]

Here, again, as for Short Forms, an ongoing dossier that I can always make the topic of a lecture course: the Sentence.[14] Restricting myself here to the Theory of Notation, the argument I want to advance is the following: the sudden bursting forth of the Notation is the sudden bursting forth of a Sentence → drive, physical pleasure taken in Noting Down = drive, physical pleasure taken in producing a sentence.

The aim of a lecture course on the sentence would be: to define the *sentence-object*.—Here, as the crow flies — and at top speed —I'll give the coordinates of that object:

a. An entity that's *both* linguistic and aesthetic (stylistic), mobilizing *both* a science of the message and a "science" of the enunciation.

b. Until it receives renewed critical examination: the Sentence fulfills the *Thetic* (subject + predicate). Thetic: what's necessary and sufficient for there to be a Sentence.

So the sentence: logical, psychological object (since it involves the accession from infancy to an adult matrix) and an ideological object (Society practices a *normativity* of the sentence-form: censuring

Sophistes, 134

nonsentences; the "competence" that distinguishes man is the ability to produce sentences—Chomsky).[15]

c. As an object, the Sentence can be the site of investments that can be described in metapsychological terms; you can have a fetishism of the sentence.

d. Such investment can be so radical that you end up with a kind of metaphysics of the sentence: the absolute sentence (Sovereign Good): Flaubert is the key author here.

e. All this notwithstanding, it's possible to think of the sentence as an *artifact* (cf. *infra*, last question).

Let's go back to notation → Latin authors: three successive operations: (1) *Notare* (to take notes). (2) *Formare* (to write up, even if it's just a first draft or a detailed plan). (3) *Dictare* (texts were always intended to be read in public) → In *Notation* (in my conception of it), there's a condensation of *Notare* and *Formare*: the positive side of *Notatio* is to conceive (to imagine, to feign, to make up) a sentence (a well-written sentence). (*Dictare*: has since become the correction phase: to objectivize in the form of the shift to typewriting.)

Notion of the *Notebook* (for example, the Notebooks of the virtual Novelist): means only: what matters is not so much the eye (I referred to the pen-camera, but the metaphor is misleading) as the pen: the pen-paper (the hand) → Notebook = observation-sentence: what's produced in a single movement as *Seen and already a Sentence*.

Here, a whole "philosophical" problem: the human subject only defines himself as "speaking" (modern epistemology), *capable of speech*: which means he can't help but speak, he speaks all the time; to live is to speak (externally, internally). On the level of the unconscious, ridiculous to oppose language and life: I speak therefore I am (someone speaks, therefore I am) → But among the many different kinds of human being, through education, sensibility (as well as social class), there are those who've received the *imprint* of literature, *order of Sentences* → On that level, to live in the most active, the most spontaneous, the most sincere and, I'd say, the most primitive sense is to receive the *forms* of the life of the sentences that preexist us—of the absolute Sentence that's within us and that shapes us → Distinguish between: talking like a book ≠ living as a book, as a Text.

There would therefore be cause to examine (and it would be a vast undertaking, because by no means limited to "good" literature) what we might call the *literary or textual Imaginary*: at issue

H.-J. Martin, *Revue française d'histoire du livre*, no. 16, 1977 is not the "imagination" (making up adventures in the way that children do—or the theme of the Family Romance) but the formation of Images of the Self through the mediation of *Sentences*: for example, the whole problem of the erotic (or the pornographic) text, the *Sentences* of the erotic fantasy (of the fantasized practice): Sade and sentences, subordinate clauses.

→ The prototype of the Character for whom life in the most urgent, devastating sense is *formed, fashioned* (remote controlled) by the (literary) Sentence: Madame Bovary; her loves, her dislikes come from Sentences (see the passage on the books she reads in the convent and what follows), and she dies by the Sentence (this whole field could be called *Sentence-ology*, not in the oratory sense of the term: more the little corpus of well-written sentences listed at the end of an dictionary entry).

Many—if not all—of us are *Bovarys*: the Sentence directs us as a fantasy (and often as an illusion).—For example, on the basis of a Sentence, I can *decide* what kind of holiday I want to take: "Two weeks of peace on a Moroccan beach, feasting on fish, tomatoes, and fruit." Apart from the menu, which is *precisely* literary (Epicureanism), that's Club Med through and through; as an illusion, the Sentence does away with, scotomizes all the other bits: the weather, the boredom, the wretchedness of the cabins, the empty evenings, the vulgarity of the other holiday makers, etc. But I'll buy my ticket nevertheless → It could be said that, as a producer of sentences, the writer is a master of illusion; but he's immune; he's aware of the illusion; he's *inspired* but not *deluded*: he doesn't confuse the real with the image, the reader does it for him: Ruskin's sentences about Venice, the cathedrals, may have made Proust "hallucinate," but Proust *stated* that hallucination: Ruskin only inspired him → Yet, at the same time, *at the level of illusion*, the literary Sentence initiates something: it leads, it teaches, first Desire (Desire is learned: without books, no Desire), then *Nuance*.

This dossier I'm planning on the Sentence—the absolute Sentence, storehouse of literature—wouldn't be, won't be complete without considering its future. For the Sentence might not last forever. Already, there are signs of wear: (1) in spoken language: constructions have been lost, the stacking up, overlapping, decentering of subordinate clauses → To describe spoken French, perhaps a new technique will be required; (b) in textuality: "poetic" texts, texts of the avant-garde, etc: destruction of the thetic (of centered consciousness), of the "laws" of language → Flaubert, artist and metaphysician of the absolute Sentence, knew that his was a mortal art: "I write . . . not for the reader of today, but for all the readers who may present themselves, as long as language lives."[16] I like this letter because it's modest ("the readers who may present themselves") and because it's realistic, pessimistic even: language won't live forever and, for Flaubert, language is not style (contrary to what people think: Flaubert is not a theoretician of fine style), it's the Sentence → Flaubert's "future" is under threat not because of the historical, outmoded nature of the content he describes but because he's thrown his (and literature's) lot in with the Sentence.[17]

The future of the Sentence: there you have a *real* social problem—which, as it happens, no one is making any forecasts about.[18]

4. Quiddity, Truth

We're approaching the Novel (Utopia, Fantasy, Sovereign Good)—and the end of this Course: the last "passage" (from the haiku to, if not the Novel, then at least the modern *Nota*) is the most important: it concerns something which has to do with *Truth* → To "pass," you need *ferrymen* {*passeurs*}. We'll have two ferrymen here: Joyce and Proust.

1. Joyce: Quiddity

(Notes thanks to Patrick Mauriès), cf. Ellmann's biography.[19]

a. *Biography*: between 1900 and 1903 (Joyce was around twenty years old (he was born in 1882)—he published *Ulysses* in 1922—the year Proust died), Joyce wrote what would come to be called "prose poems," though he didn't want to call them that, he wanted to call them *Epiphanies*; I'll say in a moment what became of those *Epiphanies*.

b. *Definition*. Epiphany = manifestation of a god (*phainô*, "to appear"); but in Joyce it's not that—even though (through his Jesuit education) Joyce's experience was always semantically linked to the theology and the religious philosophy of the Middle Ages, St. Thomas in particular, "the greatest philosopher because his reasoning was 'like a sharp sword,'" and Duns Scott.[20] Joycean Epiphany: "the sudden revelation of the quiddity (*Whatness*) of a thing" → No need to spell out what this shares with haiku: what I called the "*That's it*," the *setting a bell ringing* of "*That's it*" (quiddity: "the ensemble of conditions that determine one being in particular"). Or: "the moment in which 'the soul of the commonest object seems to us radiant.'" Or indeed: "a 'sudden spiritual manifestation'"[21] (cf. satori).

c. *Mode of appearing*: (1) To whom do Epiphanies appear? To the artist: his role is to *happen to be there*, among men, at certain *moments*. (A strange and beautiful definition of the writer: "*to happen to be there*," as if he were chosen by chance; a kind of magical mediator of certain "revelations," a sort of "spiritual" reporter).— (2) What are these epiphanic *moments*?—They're not defined by beauty, success (in the Apollonian, Goethian sense), surfeit of meaning → fortuitous, discrete moments that can be moments of plenitude, of passion, or vulgar and unpleasant (let's bear that in mind for *infra* on the "moment of truth"): vulgarity of a gesture, of a remark, an unpleasant experience, things that it's important to reject, examples of stupidity or insensitivity that can be "easily captured in an exchange of two or three sentences" (3) Their function vis-à-vis Joyce himself?—a work function: to check his lyrical tendencies, to render his style even more meticulous. (4) An example of a Joycean epiphany:

> *High up in the old, dark-windowed house: firelight in the narrow room; dusk outside. An old woman bustles about, preparing the tea. . . . I hear her words in the distance . . .*
> *— Is that Mary Ellen?*
> *— No, Eliza, it's Jim.*
> *— O . . . O, goodnight Jim.*
> *— D'ye want anything, Eliza?*
> *— I thought it was Mary Ellen . . . I thought you were Mary Ellen, Jim—*[22]

d. *What has become of these Epiphanies?* There's a collection of them: edited by A. O. Silverman, Buffalo University; but we don't know whether it was collated by Joyce himself—because Joyce's explicit thoughts on these *Epiphanies*: in 1904, Joyce stopped using the fragments as they were and decided to include them in a novel, *Stephen Hero*; a question of "forming these isolated spasms <*spasm*: the word *sets a bell ringing*: Haiku, Satori, Incident> into a linked chain of moments in which . . . 'the soul is born'" and "instead of being the author of short works, he must pour them into long ones, without waste."[23] Here: a precise formulation of the problem set out throughout this—and next year's—lecture course.

Joyce's experience of these Epiphanies is very important to me; it fits in exactly with my personal quest for an analogous form that I call the *Incident*: form I experimented with in a piecemeal fashion in *Pleasure of the Text, Roland Barthes by Roland Barthes, A Lover's Discourse: Fragments*, an unpublished text (*Au Maroc*), and my columns in the *Nouvel Observateur*; which is to say I've been circling around it, intermittently but insistently—and I'm therefore familiar with its difficulties and its attractions.

Affinity with the haiku—even if the "philosophy," or rather the "religion," is evidently not the same (here pagan, there theological) → If I've dealt with the haiku at such length, it's clearly only insofar as it relates to the *Incident* (to appear, to happen *upon*).

Same problematic of meaning in the haiku, the Epiphany and the Incident as I'm conceiving of it: instantly meaningful event (cf. Nietzsche, *Will to Power*: "There are no 'facts-in-themselves,' for a sense must always be projected into them before there can be 'facts'")[24] and at the same time no pretention to a general, systematic, doctrinal meaning → which is probably why there's a refusal of *discourse*, a retreat into the "fold" (*incident*), the discontinuous fragment—cf. what Ellmann, Joyce's biographer, says about *Epiphanies* and their homogeneity with the modern Novel: a technique that's "arrogant yet humble, it claims importance by claiming nothing."[25] The strict consequence of this, which is also what gives the *particularity* (the quiddity!) and the difficulty of the haiku, of the Epiphany, of the Incident, is the constraint of *no-commentary*; apropos of Joyce: the (epiphanic) technique "seeks a presentation so penetrating that any comment from the author would be an intrusion" → Extreme difficulty (or bravery): not to provide the meaning, a meaning; deprived of all commentary, the inconsequentiality of the Incident is laid bare, and to stand by inconsequentiality is almost heroic. (Thus, in my *Chroniques*[26]—given the context: a major weekly publication, five hundred thousand readers—, I couldn't see how I could avoid giving each "incident" a *moral*; so from that point of view the project was a failure → But it also taught me to cope with failure, to understand it: "there are triumphant defeats rivaling victories."[27] → Once again: in the West, we are overwhelmingly conditioned to furnish every reported fact with the alibi of an interpretation: culture of Priests; we interpret, we're incapable of tolerating *short* forms of language (in the sense of *ending abruptly*, of "it's a bit on the short side, young man"). Here in France, short forms are required to be overmeaningful: maxims, lyrical poems → for us, the haiku (or its substitutes) is impossible.

Hence, perhaps, Joyce's failure and the transformation of this failure: *to pour* the Epiphanies into the Novel, to drown what we find intolerable about what's brief, short in narrative: calming, reassuring mediation, elaboration of a grand meaning (Destiny). Cf. what Lévi-Strauss says about the dialectical function of Myth, which allows for contradictions.

2. Proust: Truth

As a "ferryman," Proust presents us with two problems; present in Joyce, but in another style of experience:

1. Proust never showed any interest in the Short Form; his "spontaneous" writing was just the reverse: "at a gallop"; on the side of the *inexhaustible*: additions, paperoles, etc.; on the side of Catalysis, not Ellipsis (catalysis writers, that is, writers for whom corrections are additions: relatively uncommon, Rousseau, Balzac).—But for a very long period of time he only wrote texts that were, if not short, then *limited* at any rate: short stories, articles, chronicles, fragments → Proustian problem (or Marcelian problem, for it concerns his biography) which I intended to discuss in the second half of this lecture—now postponed—and that I merely flagged up in the lecture and the short *Magazine Littéraire* article:[28] at a given moment, those bits of text *took*, *came together*, setting in motion a *long* writing: from that point on, the writing of *In Search of Lost Time* continued without interruption → this is the theme of "*It takes*." I thought the decisive moment of "*It takes*" could be dated: very brief interlude between the rejection of the *Against Sainte-Beuve* essay, rejected by *Le Figaro* in August 1909, and the seemingly lightning-quick speed with which *In Search of Lost Time* got going in October 1909 → The enigmatic month of "*It takes*" would therefore have been September 1909 → a simplistic and overly dramatic way of looking at things, justified because it formulates the (personal) problem set out by this lecture course: how to, when to get a handful of Notations *to take*, to come together to form a great, uninterrupted flow?—In actual fact: as the research group working on Proust's manuscripts has shown (Centre d'histoire et d'analyse des manuscrits modernes, rue d'Ulm):[29] more distant determinations make dating the start of *In Search of Lost Time* in a precise, punctual manner difficult. This is to be expected, for in all likelihood the kickoff didn't depend on a biographical circumstance: the biographical foundation of *In Search of Lost Time* is, I think, the death of the mother (1905) → Transmutation of values—but with long-term effects; no doubt nothing spectacular happened in September 1909, but a number of, not biographical, but "poïetic"

determinations had reached maturity, had ripened → I advanced the following hypotheses: (a) the discovery of an *appropriate* way of saying *I*; (b) establishing a system of proper names; (c) the decision to alter the size of the planned work, to make the transition to a long, a very long work (the whole of *Time Regained*: full of the obsession with dying before the long work is complete); (d) "structural" discovery inferred from a Balzacian procedure: recurring characters, *marcottage*.[30]

All of the above would have to be checked (scholarship would come in useful here).—I note, I stress: Proust, nonheroic hero of the adventure of writing; in the same way as the main character of *Ulysses* is actually language (even the color version of the *Petit Larousse* says so), the story Proust narrates is that of *Writing*.

2. The second problem that Proust "passes" on to us is very different—in some ways related, not to Joyce's decision to pass from Epiphanies to the Novel (*Stephen Hero*), but to the very nature of Epiphany: the revelation, the reconstruction of "quiddity" (*Whatness*). Only with Proust it's not, or at any rate not in the first instance, a matter of the quiddity of things but of the *truth of affect* → the two are related, however; for, as in the haiku, what's at stake or staged is the "*That's it*," the *Setting a Bell Ringing* → haiku: for me, a sort of propredeutics to what I call (and what I'll say something about): the *Moment of Truth*.[31]

First approach → "Moment of Truth" = a phenomenon of reading, not of writing. It therefore doesn't depend on a *realistic* technique. Moment of a story, of a description, of an enunciation, a sudden knot in the path of reading that assumes an exceptional character: conjunction of an overwhelming emotion (to the point of tears, to the point of distress) and a self-evident truth giving rise, within us, to the certainty that what we're reading is the truth (has been the truth).

Moment of Truth: that which, in my reading, happens *to me*, a subject in the literal sense: which means I can only make sense of it by referring to my own experience—which is what I'll do.—But the encounter between a character and a moment of truth drawn from a book is sometimes related within a book, the former appearing *en abyme* in the latter; two examples:

a. Dante, *Hell*, V: in the second circle (Lust), Francesca de Rimini and Paolo Malatesta: together they read about Lancelot's and Guinevere's love for each other (Chrétien de Troyes: Lancelot of the

Lake, one of the Knights of the Round Table, brought up by Viviane, the fairy at the bottom of the lake, fell in love with Guinevere, King Arthur's wife; Galehaut had favored Lancelot's love).

Dante, *Hell*, V.[32]

Moment of Truth: the proof of it is that it prompts a conversion, an undertaking.

b. Larmartine, *Graziella*: the projective, or rather the *homological* character of the Moment of Truth is obvious here.

Graziella, 96 and 99.[33]

$$\frac{\text{Paul}}{\text{Virginie}} = \frac{\text{N}}{\text{Graziella}}$$

(To dwell on *Homology* ≠ Analogy for a moment. At issue is a structural relationship between forms, situations, configurations—not between characters, contents).

As I've already said, for me, two moments of reading imposed themselves as moments of truth: (1) the death of old Prince Bolkonski in *War and Peace*, in the old house, with the French threatening to arrive at any moment—his last tender words to Marie, his daughter (with whom he'd always had what seemed a cantankerous relationship): "My dear, my friend"; Marie taking great care not to disturb him the night before, when in fact he'd been calling for her all night long, etc. (This, like the next example: "moment of truth" that doesn't *reproduce* the cruel death of a loved one; this isn't a realistic copy of what happened to me: reading can precede the actual bereavement). (2) Indeed, second moment of truth, exemplary (for me): the Death of the grandmother (Proust, *Guermantes*, II, 1, Pléiade, II, 314, *sq.*). There's nothing dramatic about this death: it's not a Greuze;[34] nor is it "realistic" (literal copy of a referent); biographically, probably a number of sources: death of Madame Nathé Weil, January 2, 1890, death of the Father (1903), death of the Mother (1905). I simply want to pick out two *determinations* that intensify the Moment of Truth—to the point of it being unbearable:

1. What can be written about Death is the *Dying*—and Dying can be drawn out. Proust describes the episodes, the degrees, the passages of dying admirably. I mean he always adds in something concrete, as if he were going to the root of the concrete: the little attack on the Champs-Elysées: the flushes, her hand in front of her

mouth; during her illness: it hurting when Françoise combs her hair, etc. Why is this *true* (and not just *real* or *realistic*)? Because the radicality of the concrete designates *what will die*: the more concrete it is, the more it is alive, and the more alive it is, the more it will die; this is the Japanese *utsuroi* → a kind of enigmatic *surplus-value* bestowed by writing.

2. It's the grandmother who dies. Her death, central in discursive terms, actually structures what gets written before: all that contributes to the portrait of the grandmother from the garden at Combray onward participates in this sort of eminent concreteness, this kind of violent emotion, pity, "compassion" that sets up the moment of truth → *In Search of Lost Time,* Vol. I, 10, *sq.*; we can paint a psychological portrait from this: she loves nature, she has ideas about education, she's the odd one out in her family, she's "humble of heart," etc. But all of that is (or would be) tedious, it doesn't take account of the unique connection I feel with her; this connection = very tenuous, but for me it's heartrending; again, the absolutely concrete: when her husband is given cognac to drink, "pushing back her disordered grey locks"; "my poor grandmother would come in and beg and implore"; "she would go out again sad and discouraged, but still smiling"; "her handsome face . . . its brown and wrinkled cheeks, which with age had acquired almost the purple hue of tilled fields in autumn."[35] In a sense, all that that says, from the beginning (p. 12), is that *she's going to die* and the Concrete Fact of the Body in the Garden is the same body as the Body that falls ill and dies: likewise, her cheeks and her hair.

Those two moments of truth: moments of Death and of Love; probably what the creation of a moment of truth requires → I'm thinking of other moments of truth (for me, in my own reading): Gide, *Et nunc manet in te*: Madeleine's hands, the clock to be put back on the wall, always that memorable concreteness. I've said this elsewhere: the automaton in Fellini's *Casanova*: its make-up, how thin it is, the feather, the white gloves that don't quite fit, the way the arm moves, too high.[36]

So, *Moment of Truth*: (a) On the level of the subject: emotional rending, visceral cry (without hysteria): the body rejoins the metaphysical (all those systems that try to transcend human suffering); in the moment of truth, the (reading) subject is exposed to the human "scandal": the fact that death and love co-exist ("God should not have created death and love; if only he had created one or the other, but not both.").[37] (b) On the level of writing: Moment of Truth = solidarity, compactness, concision of affect and writing, intractable unit. The Moment of Truth is not an unveiling; on the contrary, it's the sudden *bursting forth* of the uninterpretable, of the last degree of meaning, of the *after which there's nothing more to say*: hence its affinity with the haiku and the Epiphany → the two levels (that of the subject who's suffering and that of the subject who's reading) only come together around an idea: *Pity*. I know, a very bad word: who'd dare to speak of *pity* nowadays (in a newspaper, for example)! It would be just about acceptable if we were talking about pity for an animal. But *pity* is an old word: it's *written affect* in that it justifies *catharsis*, that is to say: *Tragedy*.

Moment of Truth = when the Thing itself is affected by the Affect; not imitation (realism) but affective coalescence; historically, we're in the realm of pre-Socraticism, of a thinking that's *other*: pain and truth are active—not reactive (ressentiment, sin, contestation) → Moment of Truth = Moment of the *Intractable*: we can neither interpret nor transcend nor regress; Love and Death *are here*, that's all that can be said. And it's precisely the motto of haiku.

Here, a more methodological note to conclude our discussion of the *Moment of Truth*, which will indicate how the Moment of Truth is not only a "subjective, arbitrary impression" but can also relate to a general concept—this is to compensate somewhat for my extreme imprudence in speaking of truth outside of a system that tells us how to ground it → Probably connected on an analytical, intellectual level, to two anterior notions: (a) Diderot, Lessing: the *pregnant instant*, the condensation of meaning that transports the spectator's emotions and beliefs.[38] (b) Brecht: the social *gestus*: the social schema present in all represented action[39] → There would be: moral *gestus* (Diderot), social *gestus* (Brecht), affective *gestus* (moment of truth)—the moment of truth would be related to what are called "*pregnant forms*"; René Thom, the mathematician of catastrophe theory, speaking of language (*Ornicar*, no. 16, p. 75): "A form is pregnant if the observing subject is to some extent able to identify with it in what I would call a symbolic sense" or "A form is pregnant if it provokes reactions which, from a quantitative point of view, are of an entirely disproportionate intensity when compared to the intensity of the stimulus."

Let's go back, in conclusion, to writing, to this projective—and prospective—complex that I've been trying to knot together and to attach to two different poles, one that has been explicit throughout the course, the other that has always been present too, but indirectly:

Notation (the Haiku, the Epiphany, the Incident, and also the Moment of Truth) and the Novel.

First, this: it wouldn't be impossible to theorize a reading—and therefore an analysis, a method, a mode of criticism—that would be concerned with or that would start out from the *moments* of a work: *powerful* moments, moments of truth or, if the word doesn't frighten us, moments of *pathos* (bearing in mind the link with the Tragic) → Pathetic criticism: rather than logical units (structural analysis), would start out from affective elements → one could go so far as to judge the values (the value) of a work on the basis of the *power* of its moments—or of a moment: the whole of Fellini's *Casanova* (which I don't particularly like) redeems itself because the automaton sets a bell ringing—in me, of course, so taking no account of the cultural consensus: For me, I know that there are pathetic elements in *Monte-Cristo* from which I could reconstruct the whole work (I've thought of doing a course on that novel) → presuming we'd be willing to devalue the work, to not respect the Whole, to do away with parts of that work, to *ruin* it → in order to make it live.

Indeed, the Novel (since it's a question of the novel), in its grand and extended continuity, can't sustain the "truth" (of the moment): that's not its function. I see it as an interweaving (=Text), a vast, extended canvas painted with illusions, fallacies, made-up things, the "false" if we want to call it that: a brilliant, colorful canvas, a veil of Maya punctuated by, scattered with Moments of Truth that are its absolute justification; those moments: *Rari* (*Rarus*: scattered): apparent rari (*nantes*) → When I produce *Notations* all of them are "true": I never lie (I never make anything up), but the point is: I don't produce a Novel; it's not that the Novel would start out from *falsehood* but rather from the point at which truth and falsehood mingle without warning: the true (striking, absolute) and the false (colorful, brilliant, of the order of Desire and the Imaginary) → the novel would be *poikilos*, many colored, variegated, daubed, speckled, covered with paintings, pictures, an embroidered, complicated, complex garment; etymology of *pingo* [to paint], to embroider with different threads, to tattoo; cf. *pigmentum* > Indo-European *peik*, to decorate, either with writing or by applying color → the *poikilos* of the novel = a heterogeneity, a heterology of Truth and Falsehood.

Perhaps, then: managing to write a novel (such is the *prospect*—the vanishing point—of our lecture course) comes down to conceding to lie, to being capable of lying (it can be very difficult, lying)—to telling that second-order and perverse lie that consists in mingling truth and falsehood → Ultimately, then, the resistance to the novel, the inability to produce a novel (to engage in the practice of writing one), would be a *moral* resistance.

THE METAPHOR OF
THE LABYRINTH

Interdisciplinary Investigations
Seminar (1978–1979)

INTRODUCTORY SESSION OF DECEMBER 2, 1978

Origin

A few years ago, not long after '68, a theory was trying to get itself established, a theory of plural Power, of networks of power, and also a challenging of centered Structures: the idea of decentered networks. Now, just as the "impressive advertising"[1] for this thinking (Deleuze, Foucault, possibly Derrida) was coming together it was, away from any trend, very quietly "overtaken" (as it were) by an interdisciplinary colloquium—the initiative of a mathematician, Pierre Rosenstiehl[2] (who, by the way, will be joining us at the end of the seminar)—around the notion of the "*Ant-Hill*," a notion that exists in mathematics, in ethnology, but has also emerged as a good metaphor for any discipline in which networks, decenterings of power are at issue → A process of mutual exchange that I found extremely interesting:

(1) The human sciences make use of a notion that originates in the formal, physical, or exact sciences. (2) They metaphorize what's already a metaphor (as we know, mathematicians, physics, have the genius—and the courage—for a good metaphor: Tastes / Colors / Trees / Trellis / Asymptotic Freedom / Catastrophe, etc.). This theme of the relationship between Metaphor (in the banal sense of an image that makes a comparison) and scientific discourse: I've always been alert to it—insofar as, for the human sciences, the *normative* distinction between science and writing (the essay) turns on the rejection / admission of Images; now, as it happens, the exact Sciences do resort to Metaphor and what's more tend to come up with very good ones → Whence the—already long-held—desire to explore a Metaphor (a metaphorical process), chosen precisely because it *already* seems to have a presence in very varied disciplines → The stakes are threefold: exploration (1) of the word in each of the disciplines; (2) of the notion of Metaphor; (3) of the notion of "discipline" → Naturally, the stakes {*l'enjeu*} reveal themselves through a "game" {*un jeu*}: the word will be dealt with directly, Metaphor and Discipline indirectly (which isn't to say they're any less interesting) → Whence the principle of this seminar: a word and invited speakers from very varied disciplines who are going to

come and as it were *testify* to the word → Take note: I have no *theory* and scarcely any *"idea"* of the labyrinth of my own; I'm even forcing myself not to have one, to listen to others, to let something like a new landscape gradually form around the word; my role here is therefore merely to start things off (today), to conclude (the last session), and to make some brief concluding remarks after each of the eleven presentations.

The Word, the Thing (Collating a Basic Knowledge)

A word has a whole range of "resonances": it "chimes" culturally → there's a sort of immediate phenomenology of the word, a phenomenology that could be called cultural (so to speak) since it depends on the subject's culture (vague, diffuse, embodied). On the basis of this phenomenology, for me, *labyrinth* chimes at two extremes:

1. The commonly used, almost popular Metaphor; for example, the subject heading of a reader's letter (*Libération*, November 15, 1978): *Labyrinth*: the subject vexaciously to-ing and fro-ing between her alienating day job (as a switchboard operator), her neurosis, and psychiatric hospitals → Obvious semes: twists, detours, an enclosed space that, once inside, you struggle to find a way out of.

Legend, *Phaedrus* **II, 5**

2. At the other extreme: the Greek word, the legend relayed in these lines by Racine: "And going down into the labyrinth / Phaedra would have returned with you, or else / Been lost with you." "My sister, Ariadne / Stricken with love, upon a desolate coast / Despairing died."[3]

S 16

Although Marcel Detienne will be inviting us to reflect on the Greek myth this coming Saturday, I think it would be useful to remind ourselves of the mythic anecdote now, because, for us, culturally speaking, this is what the labyrinth is: Greece (and not Egypt), Minos, Daedalus, Ariadne, Pasiphae. So: in the form of a white bull, Zeus abducts Europa takes her to Crete, where he fathers Minos, who extends his rule to the Cyclades islands and part of Peloponnesus (civilization, thalassocracy). Minos weds Pasiphae, daughter of Helios, the sun god. Minos suffers from a serious illness, brought on by Pasiphae's jealousy: whenever he makes love to another woman, hideous animals spring from his body: snakes, scorpions, centipedes. Minos's children: Phaedra the Resplendent, An-

dregeus the Luminous, and Ariadne (Ariagne) the Pure, the Saint →
Minos asks Poseidon to consecrate his power with a sign. Poseidon
accepts, on the condition that Minos sacrifice the being he sends:
the sign is a white Bull that emerges from the sea opposite Knossos.
But Minos keeps the bull for himself: perjury. Poseidon's anger
and revenge: he makes Pasiphae fall in love with the Bull. But how
are they to make love? Daedalus (*daidalléin*: to build well), an Athenian of royal stock, was Minos's court architect (he invented the
awl, the set-square, the drill, the spirit level, the sail, automata); [he]
comes to Pasiphae's aid; out of wood and wicker, he builds a simulacrum of a cow, and Pasiphae gets inside. The Bull is deceived and
impregnates her; she gives birth to a monster, a Minotaur. Minos
imprisons the monster within a labyrinth that Daedalus built for
the purpose. A war breaks out between Minos and the Athenians,
who are defeated. Conditions of Peace: the annual sacrifice of seven
young men and seven young women to the Minotaur. In order to
free the Athenians from their obligation, Theseus will fight the Minotaur; arrives at the court of Minos, Ariadne falls in love with
him, and presents him with the infamous thread; he kills the Monster
and returns, abducts Ariadne, then abandons her (at Naxos).—
According to a different version: the danger of the labyrinth has
less to do with its twists and turns than its darkness; Ariadne accompanies Theseus, the golden glow from her head-dress lighting
the way.

For us, Labyrinth = Greece. But there are labyrinthine drawings
on Egyptian seals. Egyptian labyrinth: always associated with the
Pharaoh's tomb, a labyrinth (with the King's remains at the center,
thereby protected) → There's probably a connection between the
two labyrinths, the Cretan and the Egyptian: 2000 BC, the first
Minoan architects, more or less contemporary with the Hawara
labyrinth[4] and the temple of the Sphinx.—We should also bear in
mind that: "intentional" labyrinths exist in all cultures: Cretan,
Egyptian, Babylonian, Rupestrian, Scandinavian, Amerindian, Zulu,
Asian—contemporary (Facteur Cheval, the Surrealists); initiatory
labyrinth. Maeght exhibition, 1947.[5]

Etymology

Unclear:

1. *Labrus*: double-headed axe; recurring motif of the Palace of
Knossos, sacred, menacing, or cruel sign; weapon and symbol of

power; iron that kills the beast; justice dispensed to the right and to the left: the two horns of a bull? Human face?

S 66

2. *Labra*, *laura*: cave, mine with different chambers (the words are probably of Anatolian origin) + *inda* (Aryan root) = children's games, "Basilinda" = to play at being the King → the Cave Game, the Mine Game.

→ The second etymology is generally preferred.

The Thing

A fundamental issue is whether or not a labyrinth can be *structured*: that sounds like a contradiction in terms, yet can be retained as a defining condition: presence of a factor of intentional and *systematic* construction. Let's set this problem, which might be dealt with in the presentations, to one side. I'll simply note this:

1. The first stage in the intellectual appropriation of a thing = the classification of all its possible forms—this has been done for labyrinths (Santarcangeli):[6] for instance, *natural* labyrinths (Postumia, Yugoslavia, near Trieste: hollow chambers in the chalky rock) / *fortuitous* labyrinths (chambers of a mine) / *artificial* labyrinths →

S 48 *sq.*

Other classifications, which couldn't be any less interesting: geometrical / irregular, with rectangular / rounded corners, a-centric / mono-poly-centric, with simple or complex bifurcations, etc. → All this, at least on this simplistic level: of no use at all, fails to make the phenomenon intelligible.

S 119

2. There's actually a simple principle to the *production* of a labyrinth: a German scholar has shown that you can make a Minoan labyrinth (without systematic irregularities) by cutting one or two paths through a series of concentric circles.[7] Yet we can be more specific in our approach (rather than rush into the question of Symbolism) by drawing out the *structural* function of the labyrinth:

S 188

to what basic function does it respond?—Function that's clearly *hermeneutic* (broadly speaking). Brion: "What characterizes the labyrinth . . . is the combination of dead-ends which offer no way out and bifurcations which require the traveler to be constantly choosing his route from among the many options he is presented

116 INTERDISCIPLINARY INVESTIGATIONS

with,"⁸ that is to say, on the one hand, paths that leave us with no choice (there's a wall at the end) and, on the other, bifurcations that sustain our freedom: the obstacle will be created by our choices, not by destiny.

To bring our discussion of the word to a close, let's remind ourselves of the term's lexicography. *Littré*:⁹ (1) Term from Antiquity: edifice composed of a great many rooms and passages arranged in such a way that, once inside, it's impossible to find a way out. (2) Little wood in a Park that's cut with so many intersecting paths it's very easy to get lost (Jardin des Plantes). (3) Anatomy: inner ear. (4) Quarry labyrinth: when a quarry has been in use for a long time the tunnels can create a labyrinth. (5) Archaeology: designs made out of mosaic tiles, etc. (vases, coins, ornamental tiling). (6) *Figurative* (note that, for *Littré*, the Figurative comes very far down the list): great confusion, complications of muddled affairs, difficulties, obscure questions, contradictory thoughts. Note that the syntactical figure (cf. Freud's syntactical figure, for example the "*yes, but*" of Fetishism: "I know very well, but even so . . .")¹⁰ of the labyrinth would appear to be "*so much so that*": so well designed that we no longer know where we are; in other words: so well made, so perfect, that the outcome can only be failure = figure of this kind of intensity and the fall that comes after it.

Fields of Presence of the Metaphor

Randomly, what comes to mind (without consulting my memory or any books), direct from my culture: *edifices* (of course), *cities* (Paris, the labyrinths of the central areas of the city and of the faubourgs opened up by Haussman; labyrinths and guerrilla warfare: fortifications), *gardens* (art of *topiary*: *topia*, *orum*, elaborately designed gardens; *topiarus*: garden designer).—*Dances*: the *Geranos* (crane) dance, a Delian dance derived from the legend of Ariadne, comprises *parallaxeis* and *anelixeis*: circular movements, sometimes moving forward, sometimes backward, mimicking the detours of the Labyrinth at Knossos, the crane dance (boys and girls holding hands or holding onto a rope, like a sedge of cranes in flight).—*Games*: for example, glass labyrinths, nightmare; trying to get to someone but you can't reach them; labyrinths made out of mirrors (fairgrounds). Pachinko, slot machines: pinball, jukeboxes. And above all, *Snakes and Ladders*: emerged around 1650; progression *per*

S 325

S 37

S 352

accidentia (the dice); square number 42, very dangerous = the house of the labyrinth.—And, of course, all the "arts" of language: (a) the world of *Psi* (Nietzsche: "If we willed and dared an architecture corresponding to the nature of *our* soul ... —our model would have to be the labyrinth!");[11] (b) the work, to the extent that involves a peregrination, an initiation; for example, *Divine Comedy*: circles → purgative process that gets progressively more intense → union with the *Summum bonum*; (c) style, the sentence; Proust (Preface to *Tendres Stocks*)[12] saying that style is his *Ariadne's thread*; (d) Narrative: narratology; indeed, the forks in the path are what drive a Narrative forward (*proairesis*);[13] of course, the author guides, chooses the bifurcations, but he sometimes goes back on himself, chooses a different path; confusion, complexity, the feeling of being lost in a story; it can be useful to study Narrative as a labyrinth (the acceptable degree of complexity).—To go back to the Greek legend: in terms of language, the myth of the labyrinth seems linked to two *betrayals*, two broken promises: (1) Minos's promise to Poseidon, that he will sacrifice the Bull-Sign; promise that he doesn't keep. (2) Theseus and Ariadne.

So, straight away, at first glance: the field of expansion and of application of the "Metaphor" (let's put it between scare quotes, since one of the aims of the seminar could be to point up the problematic nature of the word): extremely vast. By inviting a series of speakers, I've attempted to cover part of this field (for, in reality: it's infinite). At the end of each seminar I'll announce who will speak the following week. For the moment, here are the "disciplines" (the "discourses," types of discourse) that will be represented here:

1. Greek Mythology
2. Nietzsche (as we know, there's an important figure in the late Nietzsche: Ariadne).
3. The history of the theory of plastic forms.
4–5. The history of literary corpuses: Russian and Spanish (there could be many others).
6. Film
7–8. Urban topography, architecture / urbanism
9. Gardens
10. Math
11. Psychoanalysis

→ Eleven invited speakers[14] (so long as no one withdraws); I'll take charge of the last seminar (March 10) → A not uncommon para-

S 279
Pierre-Quint, 132

dox: as it turns out, the discipline I took the idea of the labyrinth from won't be represented: ethnology. Practically: I wasn't able to find anyone, not among my friends at any rate—and, as you know, for me, it's important that I counterbalance the risk of pure knowledge, of the Pure discipline, with a kind of preliminary (if vague) consensus among the interventions. (An interesting figure, by the way: when the *origin* of a thing is rejected in the development of that thing; this comes up all the time: image of the booster rocket that's then "dumped" → "The Rejection of the Origin.")

Symbolism

I don't know what will be said. My role in this introduction is to state the endoxal basics of the labyrinth (perhaps to get it over with); now, there is a basic and endoxal symbolism of the labyrinth.

Metaphorical material: (a) the Cave, the *penetralia*: Freud (*Introduction to Psychoanalysis*): "the legend of the Labyrinth can be recognized as a representation of anal birth: the twisting paths are the bowels."[15] Cave: death (with a view to a rebirth: the "exit"), someone's inner journeying toward the light (real life). However, although rare, open-air labyrinths: Fellini's *Satyricon*, deliberately designed so that the subject (the camera) can see the other person struggling: theurgic position. (b) The thread: Theseus fastens one end of the thread to the entrance of the labyrinth, where he leaves his companions; first, he *unwinds*; then, having killed the beast, he *winds* the woolen thread → Thus, the movement of unwinding, unraveling (= getting lost) ≠ winding (= finding one's bearings) → All myths of orientation (Daedalus) are linked to the thread; especially those involving animals. (c) The Center: Monster or Treasure; it's the *something*, the divine *Quid*; the hidden, the sacred, what's encountered at the end of a peregrination strewn with obstacles → Middle Ages: difficulty in getting to Jerusalem; invention of alternative pilgrimages: Rome, Compostela—and then, failing that, on cathedral floors, a symbolic itinerary, long and complicated: the "Road to Jerusalem." A familiar symbolism, then: *labyrinth* covers a whole network of themes: interior, center, secret, monster—initiation, *iter pefectionis*—hampered peregrination, anxiety dream, *irremeabilis error* (the point of no return)—orientation, disorientation, where what's at stake is life / death.

Metaphor

In a certain sense, "labyrinth" Indirectly sets out a problem that's perhaps more important (to me) since it involves a theory, something like an Ethics, of language: Metaphor → Vast "scientific" dossier (especially over the last twenty years). I won't provide a synthesis of it—but will only propose, to round off this introduction (whose primary aim is *not to inhibit* what will be said, what will emerge, and what is as yet unknown to me), some points of reflection on Metaphor, prompted by *this particular Metaphor* that is the Labyrinth.

1. "Infinite" metaphor: the list of signifiers is endless. An object for which the labyrinth becomes the metaphorical signifier can always be found → A friend (Éric M.) tells me that he's just read a book in which genealogy is conceived of as a labyrinth[16] → No doubt there are some very simple forms whose metaphorical power seems eternal *but* constraints of quality, which are in fact constraints of complexity, still apply; for example, anything protuberant can serve as a Metaphor for the Phallus, from the Eiffel Tower to a penholder, but it's not very interesting → "infinite Metaphor": means, on the one hand, there's a certain specificity to the signifier (it's not just anything), and, on the other, *over time*, labyrinth-objects can always emerge. In other words, a "good" metaphor: one where language labors, struggles, isn't inert → That remark would lead to a "genealogy of metaphors" (Nietzsche: differences between forces of meaning); a "hive," banalized metaphor, one that lends itself to banalization ≠ "ant-hill," better → Basically, one would have to analyze the *force* that, within an image, makes it more or less resistant to stereotyping.

2. *Labyrinth*: the original object is mythical. Cf. "Nectar." → Affinity with the problem of the class of Metaphors with no denotative word (≠ "Night traveler" = old age) → Perhaps it's the case with patronyms. Middle Ages: Philosopher = Aristotle; imagine if he didn't have a patronym: "Philosopher" would become his "Denoter," so to speak, while still being a metaphor (so he would become Mr. Philosopher – cf. Lebrun, Charpentier, Lefebvre[17]—or "Barthez"). The emblematic figure of all of this would be a particular variety of metaphor: *catachresis* (the arms of a chair, the sails of a windmill)[18] → kind of rhetorical paradox: indeed, it can be said that, once a metaphor is established (for *labyrinth* has been received as a metaphor from the outset), invention over the centuries has paradoxically

amounted to coming up with varieties of denotations for that metaphor: gardens, constructions, games → This would lead us back to Vico: metaphor as the original form of language; in the beginning there was metaphor.[19]

3. Another aspect of this "genealogy" of Metaphor (to be undertaken) would be to ask ourselves whether (in the world, among the innumerable objects of the world) there aren't "metaphorogenic" "features" (the prodigality of metaphorical development: that, basically, is the problem common to all these remarks). In North Africa, I remember often seeing those small white wading birds. For a long time (to myself) I mistakenly called them *ibises* but they were in fact "cattle-egrets": birds that follow the cows, that perch on their backs and eat their vermin (moving at the same pace as their guardians, *amicably*); a precise example of a *metaphorogenic* feature: parasitism, indelicacy, amiability, the contrast between the pure white bird and its function. What's more, it can serve as a metaphor for metaphor → And, once again, the problem of what makes a good metaphor: the signifying form has to be sufficiently *complex* but again its complexity should arise from *episodes*, *times*, *phases*; in other words, the form should (for it's a hypothesis) be *anecdotal* in structure (link between Metaphor and Myth, specifically that of the Labyrinth).

4. Last, final avatar (for me), not of metaphor (which is infinite) but of the Labyrinth-Metaphor theory: let's imagine a Labyrinth without a central *quid* (neither Monster nor Treasure), so one that's a-centric, which basically means a labyrinth without a final signified to discover → Now, that might be the Metaphor for Meaning, in that it disappoints → Interpretation (detours, investigations, orientation) like a kind of mortal game, possibly with nothing at the center; here, again, the path would be equivalent to the goal—*but only if you manage to get out* (Rosenstiehl: the only mathematical problem presented by the labyrinth is how to find a way out). Imagine Theseus *not finding* the Minotaur at the center and yet still turning back in the direction of . . . Ariadne, Love, Infidelity, "Life to no avail."

I'll say no more on this: so as to not in any way prejudice what will be said in the eleven seminars.

Next week, December 9: Marcel Detienne, Director of Studies, 5th Section, EPHES, honor to whom honor is due: "Greek mythology: the Minotaur."

CONCLUDING SESSION OF MARCH 10, 1979

The Labyrinth: A Few Closing Remarks

I

There won't be a "conclusion." *To conclude* would mean manipulating the series of interventions with a view to making a "synthesis" out of them after the fact; it would mean transforming those "co-presences" into elements of an organic, rational whole. In short, it would mean submitting the labyrinth to a Metalinguistic discourse → For a few years now, constant opposition on my part to metalinguistic treatment—for "philosophical" reasons that I'll not go back on and that stem from the necessity of not repressing the subject → plus, here, the labyrinth's particular resistance to becoming the object of a metalinguistic synthesis:

Encounter with Merleau-Ponty:[1] clothing is a "pseudo good topic." The expression often comes back to me: I find it both helpful (delicate operation of deciding what you want to work on) and that it makes me very hung up (how to know whether it's an *authentically* good topic and, above all, *when* do you know?) → Pseudo good topic? = exhausts itself or is exhausted as soon as it's begun; restricts the "exposition" to a repetition of the topic-word (the labyrinth is a Labyrinth) or a disavowal (the labyrinth, there's no such thing) → I believe that on the metalinguistic level (that of a synthesis) the labyrinth indeed = a pseudo good topic (which doesn't preclude the truth, the yield of the successive labyrinths that have been presented here—on the condition that the seminar, that is to say the consecution of papers, is allowed to retain the status of simple co-presences). The labyrinth would be a "pseudo good topic" for two reasons:

a. Labyrinth: a form so well put together that whatever you find to say about it easily *falls short* of the form itself; the specific is richer than the general, the denoted richer than the connoted, the letter richer than the symbol. Cf. what Mannoni was saying about *literality* (poetry).[2] This power of the labyrinth is that of Narrative: powerful, incandescent narrativity → A vague narrative: good symbolic terrain (semiogene), while a powerful narrative, one that's very well put together, blocks the symbolic → A subfield of Narratology would be required to deal with the *differential of narrative intensities* → Labyrinth (cf. Detienne) = *muthos* = *single story* (with no ramifications): absolutely memorable → excess of memory: fixes, fascinates, blocks metalinguistic *transformation*—what Mannoni calls "comprehension" → Labyrinth = nothing to understand (can't be *summarized*).

b. And as a metaphor (we might also want to know something about the metaphor)? It doesn't really work here either; the labyrinth is everywhere: in monuments, gardens, games, cities, tricks, in the mind; as a result, it loses all metaphorical specificity. Of course, a simple metaphor can proliferate, generate new metaphors through a complex play of transformations (the paternal Metaphor, for example); here, the metaphorical power is both applicable to everything and weak (due to the power of narrative, of myth).

A study of Metaphor (a rhetorical, not a psychoanalytical study) might well begin by dividing semiogenesis into two contrary movements: (1) Objects, beings that attract a great many metaphors: sex, in French, around 450 words (metaphors that are all more or less slang expressions) = *attracts* metaphors. (2) Forms that serve as metaphors for everything: the labyrinth = *supplies* metaphors (but, as we've seen, this supply is as it were blocked by Narrative).

Ultimately, the truth of the labyrinth would be on the side of Play, that is to say the Derisory. It's only a game, nothing more! Zulus: Game of the labyrinth. At the end of the game: *Wapuka Segexe*, we fooled you with the labyrinth!

II

The Metalinguistic (blocked or obstructed route) has to be set against the Nietzschean question: what's meaning *for me*? What's the labyrinth *for me*? I'll offer two responses, one of them affective, the other more intellectual (although there's bound to be a region where they meet: region unknown to me and that it isn't for me to name).

1. Labyrinth. Sole resonance in me: wanting to reach the loved one (who's at the center) and not being able to. Typical form of this nightmare, childish form: not being able to get to your mother; theme of the lost, abandoned child → It's a labyrinth of the way in → But ambivalence: the anxiety of the labyrinth can be reversed, it can be made into a supremely safe enclosure. Traditionally, we identify

with Theseus ≠ it's also possible to identify with Minos: to remain shut up, *protected* (to sleep); no one ever talks about the labyrinth as a form of protection.

2. I'd like to go back to Mannoni's presentation → Striking that the only presentation not to deal explicitly with the labyrinth should be given by the Psychoanalyst (it matters little whether this was an oversight or a liberty taken on his part). I'll say: (a) Probably (or presumably) psychoanalysis has very little to say about the labyrinth—absent, by the way, from Freud's texts, despite dealing in so many objects; (b) Psychoanalysis never speaks of what it's asked to speak of: that's its golden rule. And Mannoni behaved like a good psychoanalyst.

However, Mannoni's presentation directed me not toward the labyrinth, but toward a *new question* concerning the labyrinth, on which I'll finish—leaving it open:

Mannoni: literality (what doesn't admit of any possible transformation → "Obscurity," Poetry) ≠ comprehension (what's transformable, Prose). Which is to say, Mannoni spoke of the dialectic of Readability and Unreadability—or even of the *vanishing points* of readability (in the perspectivist sense of the term). Now, this urgent question relates to the exclusions, alienations of language: How do you decide whether or not an enunciation is readable? And then you have the question: Where does readability begin? Which, for me, reveals the labyrinthine question: not: What is it? How many are there? Nor even: How do you get out? But: *Where does a Labyrinth begin*? We come back to the epistemology of degrees of consistency, of thresholds, of intensities: the *viscosity* of forms.

THE PREPARATION OF THE NOVEL

2. The Work as Will
Notes for a Lecture Course at the Collège de France (1979–1980)

SESSION OF DECEMBER 1, 1979

Preamble

If you're agreeable, we're going to think of the Course that's beginning as a film or a book, basically as a story, the narration of which will, I think, occupy us for the ten two-hour sessions and of which, as a rule, I'll be the only narrator. Therefore, as for the majority of films and books, there'll be:

Outline

The kind of *abstract*, outline, intellective summary that gets sent out to the papers, on a roneotyped sheet (film) or put on the back of the book (="blurb"): it's what we look at first; often it's not very convincing or enticing but, for better or worse, it allows us to *classify* the product; being unable to classify is the worst kind of social unease; a society—and, acting on behalf of society, the being as a social being (*socius*)—unable to classify is *panic stricken*: classification is a powerful means of integration, normalization. The outline or the blurb of this film, of this book, could therefore be stated in the following way: for the last year, in front of you, with you, I've been investigating the preparatory conditions of a literary Work, for convenience called a *Novel*. First I examined the relationship between the Work and that minimal act of writing that is Notation, chiefly through an exemplary Form of Notation, the Haiku. This year, I want to track the Work from its Projection to its accomplishment: in other words, from *Wanting-to-Write* to *Being-Able-to-Write*, or from the *Desire-to-Write* to the *Fact-of-Writing*.

Epigraph

Epigraph or Credits; more an *epigraph*, because I'm not sure how the thing could be filmed—which goes to show that film can't do everything: it can't, among other things, *evoke an odor*, which the text can do perfectly well (contrary to what I might have said: Sade).[1] This epigraph is indeed a *scent*: I'm putting a *scent* as an epigraph.

Chateaubriand, *Memoirs from Beyond the Grave*: in 1791, Chateaubriand wants to go to America to see the North-West passage and is encouraged by Malesherbes, a friend of the family. He sets sail from Saint-Malo (and will dock at Baltimore); his ship stops off at Saint-Pierre Island.

CHATEAUBRIAND, *MEMOIRS FROM BEYOND THE GRAVE*

I dined two or three times at the Governor's house, an officer full of kindness and good manners. He grew a few European vegetables on the hillside. After dinner, he showed me what he called his garden. A sweet and subtle scent of heliotrope was exhaled by a little patch of beans that were in flower; it was brought to us not by a breeze from our own country but by a wild Newfoundland wind, unrelated to that exiled plant, without sympathy of shared memory or pleasure. In this perfume, not breathed by beauty, not cleansed in her bosom, not scattered where she had walked, in this perfume of a changed sky and tillage and world there was all the diverse melancholy of regret and absence and youth.[2]

Plan

As regards the Film, the Book, the Course itself, its structure will be somewhat like that of a play—or a Rite (affinity, link), or even a little (domestic) Tragedy, which means there'll be:

a. a Prologue: the *Desire-to-Write*, as the point of departure of the Work to be written;
b. three chapters (book), three acts (Tragedy or Comedy?) or three trials (Rite, Initiation) = the obstacles that will have to be overcome, the knots that will have to be untied in order to write the Work;
c. a Conclusion? An Epilogue? No, not in the strict sense: more a *Suspension*, a final Suspense—I myself don't know how it's going to turn out (alas, suspense for me alone, for I can well imagine that, narratively speaking, you couldn't care less whether or not the Work gets written).

Parabase

Between the Prologue and the Narration proper (Book, Film, Rite, Tragedy), I intend to insert a brief intervention or digression (in the literal sense) on the Method of exposition. This will be more or less in keeping with the comparison Course=Theater (or Film); in Greek Comedy (and the Course might turn out to be a Tragi-Comedy), you would have an interval during which the actor representing the author would come to the front of the stage and address the audience as the author himself: the Parabase. There will therefore be a short *parabase*, a moment when I'll speak as the author of the Course rather than as the hypothetical author of a Work to be written.

The bibliography? = all literature—at any rate, all Metaliterature: those writings in which an author confides his plans, his projects, his concerns as regards the work to be written: correspondence, diaries → Here, I'll only provide the references to the few most frequently quoted books → I'll read them out:

Bibliography of the Most Frequently Quoted Authors (Authors and Critical Works)[3]

CHATEAUBRIAND
——. *Mémoires d'outre tombe*. Gallimard, Bibliothèque de la Pléiade, 2 vols.

FLAUBERT
——. *Extraits de la correspondance, ou Préface à la vie d'écrivain*. Introduced and selected by G. Bollème, Seuil, 1963.

KAFKA
——. *Journal*. Translated by Marthe Robert, Grasset, 1954.
Wagenbach (Klaus). *Kafka*. Seuil (Écrivains de toujours), 1968.

MALLARMÉ
Scherer, Jacques. *Le Livre de Mallarmé*. Gallimard, 1957.
Mauron, Charles. *Mallarmé*. Seuil (Écrivains de toujours), 1964.

NIETZSCHE
——. *Ecce Homo ou Comment on devient ce qu'on est*. In *Œuvres philosophiques complètes*. Gallimard, 1974.

RIMBAUD
——. *Lettres de la vie littéraire d'Arthur Rimbaud (1870–1875)*. NRF, 1931.

ROUSSEAU
——. *Confessions*. Charpentier, 1886.

TOLSTOY
———. *Journaux et carnets.* Gallimard, Pléiade I, 1847–1889.

Polytechnique Presentation

[4] Ten years ago, I could have given an up-to-date and timely presentation of the field of literary criticism → That rich and diverse field: Marxist (Lukács, Goldmann), thematic (Bachelard, Sartre, Richard), structuralist, or rather semiological (because, *strico sensu*, only Dumézil, Benveniste, and Lévi-Strauss are structuralists) with its two branches: Narratology and the analysis of Figures (often strongly influenced by psychoanalysis) → Some of those critics are now dead; happily, others are still very productive—but, in most cases, on their own individual accounts: they're all still working, but—as is the case in many of the other spheres of French cultural life today—there's no longer any collective, systematic force that would allow me to present a meaningful synthesis of the discussion of literary works. I therefore gave up the idea of dealing with Criticism—since it would only have been a dull and outmoded account (and I don't know how much you already know about these things): there's nothing more difficult than trying to muster interest in *Recently* (≠ *Long ago, Now*): people are interested in Retro trends, but not that of 1970 = Retro is never about the *Recent* past.

In actual fact, *Criticism*—if we don't count criticism of the latest thing, which is a matter for the Media and not the Book = a *Theory of Literature* (exists in Germany and the USA ≠ France obsessed with the *History of Literature*) → Better than an ideology (= criticism of the latest thing), all the (serious) critical approaches I spoke of involve: a philosophy, an epistemology, a systematic conception of the human subject, of society, of History → I therefore propose that for the duration of this short paper we occupy a very small canton of literary theory; even then, I'll be dealing with this point subjectively; I'll be speaking for myself and not in the place of science, I'll be asking questions of myself, as someone who loves literature → The corner of that canton is in effect the *Desire to Write*.

1. The Desire to Write

Origin and Departure

Why do I write?—It could, among other reasons, be out of obligation: for example, in the service of a Cause, a social, moral end, to instruct, enlighten, militate, or entertain. These are not negligible reasons, but to me they look a bit like justifications, excuses, in that they make *Writing* contingent upon a social or moral (external) demand. Now, to the extent that I'm capable of lucidity on this point, I know that I write to satisfy a *desire* (in the strong sense): the *Desire to Write* → I can't say that *Desire* is the *origin* of Writing, because I've not been granted extensive knowledge of my Desire or of its every determination: one Desire can always stand in for another, and it's not for me, a blind subject, buried in the imaginary, to trace my Desire back to its original impulse: I can only say that there was a certain point of departure to the Desire to Write, which I'm able to identify.

Jubilation

That point of departure is the pleasure, the feeling of joy, of jubilation, of fulfillment that reading certain texts written by others produces in me → *I write because I have read* (and at the beginning of the Chain? The first person to have written? There you have a *general* question that I can't and don't want to answer: cf. Who was the first person *to speak*? Origins of language? The question I'm asking is existential, not anthropological). In order to pass from the *Pleasure of Reading* to the *Desire to Write*, it's necessary to pass through a differential of *intensities* (Science of Shimmers, of Intensities); it's not a matter of the "*Joy of Reading*," a banal expression that could easily be the name of a bookshop (there must be bookshops called this)[5] → that kind of joy produces readers who remain readers, who don't become scriptors ≠ the productive joy of writing is a different kind of joy: a jubilation, an ex-stasy, a mutation, an illumination, what I've often called a *satori*, a shock, a "conversion." For instance, that short text by Chateaubriand (*Memoirs from Beyond the Grave*),[6] I have no desire whatsoever to explain it, to analyze it (clearly it would be possible to do so); it produces a bedazzlement of language, a fit of pleasure in me; *it caresses me* and that caress produces its effects every time I read it (renewal of the First Pleasure): like a sort of eternal, mysterious incandescence (explaining it wouldn't get to the bottom of it); true happiness of a *loving desire*, because I'm very conscious that the object of my desire, this text, just one among a thousand other possible texts, has come to adapt itself to my particular desire; there's nothing to suggest that someone else could desire it as I desire it: moreover, this loving desire takes different forms in different subjects, giving everyone a chance—for if we were all in love with the same person, what torture that would be!—for us and for them! Likewise for books and fragments of books: there's Dissemination of Desire, and it's insofar as this is the case that there's impetus to and a chance of procreating other books; my Desire to write doesn't stem from reading as such but from certain readings in particular, local readings: the Locality of my Desire → [7] Like meeting someone and falling in love: what defines that Encounter? *Hope*. From meeting and falling in love with a handful of texts the *Hope to write* is born.

The Hope of Writing

[8] Hope

Especially that Time of reading and of jubilatory reading that occurs in Adolescence—but also throughout a Writer's Life, where nothing is given, and Desire is constantly being reborn. *Writing* presents itself as a Hope, the color of a Hope—let's remind ourselves of Balzac's very beautiful formulation: "Hope is a memory that desires." Every beautiful work, or even every impressive work, functions as a desired work, albeit one that's incomplete and as it were lost *because I didn't write it myself*; in order to recover that work, I have to rewrite it; to write is to want to rewrite: I want to *actively* add myself to something that's beautiful but that I lack, that I *require*.

Volupia / Pothos

This dialectic of Memory-Hope, of Pleasure-Desire: illustrated by two ancient words, one Latin, the other Greek: *Volupia*, goddess of fully satisfied Desire, of Fulfillment ≠ *Pothos*, poignant desire for the absent thing.[9]
→ Three modes of Pleasure:

    a. Pleasure satisfied by reading, in that it isn't tormented by the desire to do likewise: *Volupia*.
    b. Pleasure of reading that's tormented by a lack: desire to write: *Pothos*.
    c. Pleasure of writing: is clearly not without its anxieties (difficulty, frequent pitfalls), but it's an anxiety of Producing, not an Anxiety of Being → *an* anxiety, not anxiety. Not *Volupia*, but on the side of *Volupia*.

Picon, 61

Reading and writing: they each start the other off; perhaps that's what the Force of all Creation and even of all Procreation amounts to: in the procreated child, I add myself to the person I love → Relationship between *Reading* and *Writing*: would be nuptial → Rapprochement between Creation and Procreation: it's been done countless times, but it's inevitable; it's therefore necessary to give it its anthropological meaning: to Procreate and to Create = not, strictly speaking, a Triumph over Death but a dialectic, the Dialectic of the Individual and the Species: I write, I "finish" (the work), and I die; in so doing, something lives on: the Species, literature → Which is why the threat of decline or extinction that can weigh on literature tolls like an extermination of a species, a sort of spiritual genocide.[10]

Imitation

Clearly, the passage from reading to writing, following in the wake of desire, can only be achieved through the mediation of a practice of *Imitation*. But no sooner has the word been said out loud than it has to be abandoned: because, in the passage from reading to writing, what takes place is an Imitation so particular, so rebellious, so distortive that a different word is needed to identify the relation between the book read (the book that seduced) and the book to be written.

In the strict sense, *Imitating a book* can only cover two practices, which are like caricatures of writing: both are represented in *Bouvard and Pécuchet*:

1. To Imitate the book = To Apply the book: to take a book and "realize" it literally, point by point, in life; it's what Bouvard and Pécuchet do for a series of books. We know what disasters this kind of Imitation leads to, and what feelings of madness, or at least of "Craziness," arise from it (cf. Don Quixote) → A radical version of this Imitation = Application = "Imitation according to . . ." Jesus Christ (but also according to Sade).

2. To Imitate the book = to Copy the book: to remain within Writing and to literally copy it out; Bouvard and Pécuchet do this too. I'm convinced—but what sociology is interested in this?—that there are book copiers who do it out of love, or there were at any rate: in the past, those who loved poetry would copy out poems (→ whence notebooks full of poems copied by hand). A metaphorical use of "Copying the book" = Pastiche → I refer you to Genette's

work[11] → To be honest, I find this theme quite tiresome: the only pastiches I like are Proust's, because in themselves they're actually acts of love—and for this reason they come under imitation done out of desire; I'm not interested in pastiches done out of irony, out of mockery (I've been subjected to a few).[12]

Inspiration

It's necessary to leave those literal and as it were immobile imitations behind, which means abandoning the word itself and proposing that the *dialectical* passage from a loving reading to a writing productive of a work needs another name; I'll call this passage: *Inspiration*. I'm not taking this word in a mythical, Romantic sense (Musset's Muse), nor in the Greek sense of *enthusiasm*, a complex notion that Antoine Compagnon has been working on,[13] but in the sense = to be inspired by. Of this notion, I'll give the following sketch: *Inspiration* =

1. A Narcissistic Distortion

For the other's work to pass in me I have to define it within myself as written *for me* and, at the same time, I have to distort it, to make it *Other* by dint of love (challenge to philological truth). A comparison: I happened to hear (on France-Musique, July 11, 1979) a Bach movement that I like very much being played by a harpsichordist (always this contemporary obsession with playing Bach on the harpsichord, because it's closer to historical "truth"); when I play the movement, I play it slowly (and for good reason). For all that I play badly, to my ears the movement is profound, soft, melodious, sensual, lyrical, tender; now, the harpsichordist (Blandine Vernet) was playing it three or four times faster, to the point where it was a while before I recognized it (I always struggle with the *Tempo* of works; whether or not I agree with an interpretation always hangs on this) → all the characteristics I usually associate with the piece had disappeared; they were *lost*, had vanished, as if down a trapdoor; such and such melodious "little phrase" no longer sang; it wasn't even identifiable; a song had been silenced, and with it Desire: bitterness that this should happen at the hands of a professional (although it does: What a shame! What a disappointment! This isn't conceitedness, but an Amateur's truth, for his Desire is indubitable). The movement was being played *in itself* (no doubt correctly, historically speaking) but not *for me*: it had no meaning *for me* (Nietzsche)—and so *nothing happened, nothing was created* (nothing was transformed). Now, what I'm looking for, what I want from the work I desire, is for something to happen: *a love affair*, precisely the dialectic of a conjunction of lovers whereby their love for one another will distort them both and create a third term: either the relation itself, or a new work, *inspired* by the old.

2. A Semiotics

Paradoxically, although in theory I'm a "semiologist," my sense of the term "semiotics" is very irregular, strictly Nietzschean. I'm referring to Nietzsche's remark (*Ecce Homo*): he's discussing his relationship to Schopenhauer and to Wagner, whom he's identified as signs of himself: "It was in [precisely] this way that Plato used Socrates, as a semiotic for Plato."[14] God knows Nietzsche "imitated" Wagner and Schopenhauer! And yet the relationship is there: the author who counts (or even: who's loved) is present, to me, as a person who wants to write, as a *sign* of myself—and, as we know, a sign isn't an analogy but merely an element of a *homological* system in which, according to Lévi-Strauss's formulation, it's the systems, the relations of differences that resemble one another.

3. A Copy of a Copy

This is clearly not the same thing as a pure imitative copy (Bouvard and Pécuchet, Pastiche). I refer you to Proust's very intelligent idea about Balzac (in *Sainte-Beuve*): I'll read out the passage; not all of it directly relates to our problem, but it's very beautiful (and, in my opinion, so true):

> PROUST, *AGAINST SAINTE-BEUVE*
>
> *Now, Balzac set out not simply to paint, or at least not in the simple sense of painting faithful likenesses. His books resulted from beautiful ideas, ideas for beautiful paintings if you like (for he often conceived of one art in the form of another), from a beautiful pictorial effect came a grand pictorial idea. Just as he could see a beautiful idea in a pictorial effect, he could see a beautiful effect in an idea for a book. He envisaged a picture which would have something strikingly original about it, which would amaze. Imagine a writer today coming up with the idea of treating the same subject twenty times, in*

> *different lights, and feeling like he was doing something profound, subtle, powerful, crushing, original and arresting, like Monet's fifty cathedrals or forty water-lilies. An amateur passionate about painting, he sometimes took pleasure in thinking that he too had a beautiful idea for a picture, a picture that everyone would go wild about. But it was always an idea, a dominant idea, and not a preconceived painting as Sainte-Beuve supposes.*[15]

This gives a good sense of what occurs in the Passage between an anterior Book and an ulterior Writing: (a) There's a very diffuse kind of imitation, which mingles several different authors as the need arises, not a unique and maniacal form of imitation; what *inspires* the reader-writer (someone who *hopes* to write) is already, beyond a given lovingly admired author, a sort of general object: Literature (as Proust says: Painting). (b) *Inspiration* works *via relays*; there's a relaying of aesthetic concepts (I'll say of *fantasies*): "the idea of beautiful painting," "a beautiful pictorial effect," etc. (c) It is this copied "idea" (and not what it represents) that's *preconceived*: you have to conceive of it before writing begins, to conceive of it *between reading and writing* → this *third* relation (which has different levels) is what distinguishes inspiration from straightforward imitation and is illustrated in the nine or ten words of this haiku by Issa:

> More marvelous
> Than the real cormorant
> Is the child who imitates it[16]

There's the cormorant, the child, and the poet: the poet doesn't *imitate* the child imitating; he *says* it, he enunciates it: literature isn't born of direct imitation but of the proliferation, the enunciation of the world as a movement of Mirrors.

4. An Unconscious Filiation

I was recently sent a short "poetic" text—I say "poetic" because it was neither narrative nor intellectual=vertigo of images or of a single image with no referential basis or aim: I *recognized* this text as coming from Rimbaud or, more accurately, as coming from a language, a mode of discourse that was impossible before Rimbaud, and only possible after him; but I think I'm right in thinking that the author of the short text hadn't read Rimbaud, or at any rate

Munier, 79

didn't know his work very well → Therefore: diffuse filiation, via relays that the person writing is unaware of; this concept of nonpaternal filiation, one that doesn't acknowledge the Father, would need to be refined → Some Authors function as writing Matrixes: Rimbaud certainly does: the "modern" text (of contemporary Modernity), the text that's still called "poetic" today is a descendant of this Line → Diffracted filiation, on the outer edges of the Name: feature of the Inter-Text.

Two things, it seems to me, are clear: (a) There's no text without filiation. (b) All filiation (of writing) is unidentifiable (for example, contemporary texts, "contemptexts" {*textes actuels*, "*textuels*"}: they can't be "wild," there's no such thing as spontaneous generation; and yet, where do they come from? I can't say: the most appropriate formula (because it's the most modest, the least arrogant) would be: they're *authorized* by the writing mutations that preceded them.

5. A Simulation

This word might surprise you, since I'd ruled out *Imitation* as a notion that's too strict, too literal, and simulation is one step up from imitation. I understand it as follows, based on what happens to be the precise meaning of "Simulation": to inject the "true" with the "false," the "same" with the "other." In his forthcoming book, Severo Sarduy reflects on (classical) Painting[17] and replaces the commonly used notion of the "copy" with the concept of the "simulation drive": a drive that isn't an impulse to be *an* other but to *be other*, it doesn't matter who: the impulse to liberate an Other within myself = force of alterity that comes from, that's contained within Identity → To pass from a loving reading to the Act of Writing is to draw out from the imaginary Identification with the text, with the beloved author (who has seduced us), not what is different to him (= the dead-end of the *effort* of originality) but what, within me, differs from myself: the beloved stranger urges me, actively compels me to affirm the stranger who is within me, the stranger I am to myself.

Such are some of the modes of "creative influence" or, if you prefer, some of the paths that the transformation of Pleasurable Reading {*Lecture de joie*} (as people used to say: *Fille de joie*)[18] into Writing can take.

The Desire to Write

There, then, you have the subject who's first touched by, fascinated by the Hope of writing, accepting the Desire to write and inhabiting it.

Mania

Desire to write as the *sole desire*: Kafka thinking of his nocturnal "scribbling" as his *sole desire*; Flaubert speaking of the "indomitable fantasy of mine to write"[19] (1847, he's twenty-six years old). Here, we'd need to pick out from post-Romantic literature (the argument advanced in *The Literary Absolute*)[20] the excessive features of the desire to write—or those that ensure that this desire is only ever excessive = that is to say, that could turn the writer into one of La Bruyère's caricatures.—Chateaubriand, in conversation with Monsieur de Marcellus, his embassy secretary (London), having spontaneously come out with what he finds is a "good" sentence: "Monsieur Chateaubriand had only just pronounced this sentence during one of our literary tête-à-têtes in London when he interrupted himself to go and write it down.":[21] like an attack of polyuria! I'm possessed by that madness when, in the company of a friend, I find myself getting out my notebook to scribble down a sensation-sentence or an observation-sentence, completely disregarding the protocols of good manners (though in reality I only ever do this when the friendship releases me from those little niceties, from society's little super-ego) → there's therefore an maniacal aspect to the Desire to Write.

The Writer (whom for the moment I'm defining as someone who has the desire to write), a comical character to *observe*: "he itches with desire" {"*il a le désir aux fesses*"}; there's something ridiculous about this maniacal desire (but, if you look below the surface, which is what those who mock fail to do, there's something grand about the ridiculous, in that it's an exclusion, a solitude): Friedrich Schlegel (*Fragments*): "If, in thrall to a sacred vocation and with a smile on one's lips, one should have overcome ridicule to become a writer, it remains only to be mocked for minor things, and I'm not concerned by that in the least."

Where, locally, do I sense the desire to write?—Not in books—but rather in the unknown manuscript that gets sent to me anonymously, in the ardent letter that accompanies it, in the fear that the manuscript might have gotten lost (reminder letter), etc. → Now, inversion: the proof that the Desire to write is present in manuscript, that it's offered, held out, *imposed* in its pure state, having not yet been mediated by publication—the proof is that whatever the manuscript's worth, *it's boring, it bores me*; because it's very difficult (euphemism for "impossible") to communicate with someone else's desire, to be interested in someone else's desire → *all manuscripts*—whether by Dante or Alexandre Dumas—*are boring*: each one is a block of pure Desire, and I've no need of that block, for the bundle of desire that gets set down before me ≠ the work written *and* published = what mediates the Writer's Desire, takes some of his Desire away, so that I, the reader, can bear it.

Those Who Don't Write

A moment ago I "identified" with Chateaubriand rushing to note down a sentence (identified with: not compared myself to). Allow me to prolong this "infatuation" by offering an account of my own feelings as a "writer" (as a subject putting himself in the position of a "writer"): my life is in a sense devoted to *Writing*; I'm constantly anxious about finding the time, the energy for it; anxious = desirous and guilty if I don't manage to. Now I often have this monstrous (schizoid) feeling: when I see people around me, often friends (who should, given their professions, have time to write), going about their business, their leisure activities, basically passing their time, and often extremely well, *without writing*, without thinking about it or, put differently, without having made *writing* a key feature of their lives. More than surprised, I'm: *uncomprehending*; I can't understand what they can be doing with their time, *toward what time* they can be turning, an opacity that's the sign of an obsession; for me, the *opposite* of writing could never be a mere contingency: I only know it as a Philosophy (cf. *infra* on "idleness")[22] → A different form of this incomprehension (or this naivety), a question that I sidestepped by discussing the dialectic of *reading* and *Writing*: if *Writing* comes from *reading*, if there's a binding relationship between the two, then how is it possible to read without being bound to write? In other words, monstrous question: How is it that there are so many more readers than writers? How can anyone be content to just read, even to set themselves up as a great Amateur of reading, and never go on to Write? Is it repression? I don't have an answer to this question; I only know that I keep coming back to it; deep down, I'm always surprised to *have readers*—that is to say, readers who don't write. Always the same question, which is the essence of noncommunication (not that the "message" isn't getting through, but): How to *understand* the desire of the other (How to identify with that desire—with that pleasure)? Kind of question that *liberalism* (pretending to understand a desire that you don't understand) masks.

Anxious Desire

The Desire to write = anxious Desire. Of this anxiety, two great witnesses and a *metteur en scène*. Witnesses:

1. Flaubert: I refer here to the whole correspondence, where writing is passionately presented both as a *Jouissance* or, better, as a *sweetness*—Flaubert (1873, fifty-two years old): "I have not written for a long time (soon it will be a year), and to make sentences seems sweet to me"[23] (which explains the persistence of the activity),—and as a terrible Ordeal (both lurk in sentence-making)—Flaubert (1853, thirty-two years old): "Damned profession! Confounded obsession! Yet, bless this treasured torment. Without it, I should die. Life is tolerable on the condition of having nothing to do with it."[24]

2. Kafka: to write, life's only goal, in conflict with life (the world, marriage, we'll speak of this again): the Sovereign Good from which he is constantly being separated; but, at the same time, the terrible fear of writing—correspondence, 1907: "but it isn't laziness alone, it's also fear, generalized fear of writing, of this horrible pursuit; yet all my unhappiness is now due to being deprived of it."[25]

3. The *metteur en scène* of the Desire to Write, Proust: I've said it a number of times (because it's always struck me): *In Search of Lost Time*: the work only has one narrative (in the classical sense: with trials, suspense, and final victory): that of a *subject who wants to write*: *In Search of Lost Time*: the novel of *scripturire*[26] → What's more, perhaps that *great drama* of Wanting-to-Write could only have been written at a time when literature was in a period of decline, was withering away: perhaps the "essence" of things only emerges when they're about to die.

Polytechnique Presentation

[27]To interrupt (but not to conclude) these reflections on the desire to write, this: the theme can be pursued in two directions:

1. Passing from the desire to write to the work: a whole series of *operations*: organization (= protection) of the hours in the day, plan-

ning, overcoming the difficulties, doubts, stallings (cf. my lecture course for this year).

2. The sometimes painful, sometimes vertiginous confrontation between the desire to write (I've been trying to articulate how powerful it is) and the sociocultural mechanism that it usually has to be integrated into, that is, *literature* as an Institution or Commerce → Now, currently, it seems to me: drop in literature's value (this would be another topic) → Desire to write: functions as a social Separation, a separation that's all the more difficult to accept because literature looks like an object of the past (one that's in the process of going out of fashion: end of transference) → Desire to write: retrograde, archaic.—But perhaps all desire is like this?—Moreover, in a world that has made a myth out of Innovation (since the eighteenth century: Neomania), the past is always what's hardest to stand by.

Writing as a Tendency

Tendency

I refer here to a distinction that Freud makes, that I don't have the reference for (I don't want to spend a morning going through the whole of Freud to find it, a real needle in a haystack: it's in this sense that I'm *a bit cavalier {léger}*, experiencing my culture as an incomplete recollection): sexuality defined by its object (for example, Man ≠ Woman) ≠ sexuality defined by its tendency (indifferentiation of the object; for example, for Freud, the homosexuality of the ancient Greeks).[28] With respect to the tendency, the object takes second place: it doesn't establish a Category, an Ethics; for example, desire is detached from the object, hence from procreation, from the species ≠ consideration of the object introduces a greater number of norms, classifications, exclusions → Now, it seems—this is the point I now want to make—that *Writing* was initially incorporated into a Desire for the Object (to write *such and such* a thing), but at a certain point, there was a break, a disengaging; the Object was now of secondary importance, having been supplanted by the Tendency: *to write something* → to write, period, with the intermediary *to write this and that*. I'll come back in a moment to this short form of the verb *To Write*, but let's first note that, as a *Tendency*, *Writing* easily fits the image of a natural, physiological Need, as it were independent of any intention or deliberation on the part of the subject → Flaubert, the most explicit witness to this visceral condition of Writing (the importance of Food, see Jean

Préface, 45

43

Pierre Richard);[29] at twenty-six years old, in 1847, he writes (*Correspondence*): "I write solely for myself, as I sleep or smoke" <Not quite the same thing: today he'd have his knuckles rapped by the Anti-Tobacco League, as I did when I protested against No Smoking signs: *Nouvel Observateur*.>[30] "It is so personal and private, almost an animal function."[31] And this (from the same period): "And not having the ability needed to attain success, nor the genius to conquer fame, I am condemned to writing solely for myself, for my own private diversion, as one smokes <he insists on this> or rides on horseback. It is almost certain I shall never have a line printed . . ."[32] (another theme we'll be taking up again later on). Aristotle: reading and writing, peculiar to man; but here, *writing* is detached from *reading*, detached from the manual function and, by way of a sort of historical "perversion," becomes an autonomous function: an organic function for some people (of Flaubert's ilk).

SESSION OF DECEMBER 8, 1979

Indistinction / *Poikilos*

When the object retreats or fades into the background in favor of the Tendency (*Writing*), distinguishing between objects of Writing, that is to say the "genres" of literature, clearly becomes less of a concern; the division of the genres: here the question is sexual, there rhetorical; over the course of the nineteenth century, rhetoric fades away; there's a push toward the indifferentiation of writings, stalled by publisher's categories.

The privileged field of that Indecision is the one marked out by the fragmentation of the Novel, or at any rate by its deformation (like that of a topological space) → A dossier to be compiled; think (here's simply what comes to mind) of: (a) Proust hesitating *in extremis* (the notorious summer of 1909)[1] between the Essay (*Sainte-Beuve*) and the Novel, admiring this hesitation in his favorite authors, who want several genres at once (Nerval, Baudelaire),[2] and laboriously producing an atypical work, as if *Writing* (Tendency) had long been stalled by the law of the Object (To write what? A novel? An essay? Cf. Bouvard and Pécuchet's comical hesitations: What to write? A tragedy, a biography, etc.)[3] (b) From its canonical form, the beginnings of a transcendence of the Novel: the category of the *Novelistic*, which, as the relevance of the canonical novel declines, becomes ever more compelling: *Monsieur Teste, Artificial Paradise, Nadja, Madame Edwarda* → All of this works in favor of a new word, in itself not at all generic, but that serves to designate a work of unidentifiable genre: the Text.

Historically speaking, what comes closest to the Text or at least in a certain sense prefigures it theoretically, making a case for the mixing, the "motleying"[4] of genres: the (German) Romantic theory of the Novel → Novel (Novalis, Schlegel) = mixture of genres, with no hierarchy or distinction made between them = Romantic Novel or Absolute Novel. Novalis (*Encyclopaedia*, Book 2, Section 6, fragments 1441 and 1447): "*Art of the Novel*: Shouldn't the novel include all kinds of styles, variously linked to and animated by the common spirit?"[5] "The art of the novel excludes all continuity. The novel should be an edifice that is built anew in each of its eras. Each

Servière, 51, 95

little fragment should be something cut out—something circumscribed—a whole worth something in itself." "Properly Romantic prose—changeable at its highest peak—marvelously strange turns of phrase—sudden leaps—altogether dramatic. Likewise for brief presentations." Beautiful definition of the Fragment as Novel: we see here how the object is already divided, supplanted by a shimmering of writing energies: *Writing* as a tendency means that the objects of writing appear, glitter, disappear; what remains is basically a force field.

Thus it's to be expected that we should come up against the problem of fragmented and motleyed writing in Nietzsche.— Nietzsche diagnoses Plato's stylistic plurality (*Birth of Tragedy*): "downright necessity . . . compelled him to create a form of art which was intimately related to the existing forms of art he had rejected. . . . If tragedy had absorbed all previous artistic genres, the same can be said, in a paradoxical sense, of the Platonic dialogue, *which was created by mixing all available styles and forms together*, oscillating between narrative, lyric, and drama, and *constituting a third term between poetry and prose*, thus breaking the strict older law of the unity of style."[6] → Plato's dialogues: to take the word in Bakhtin's modern sense, dialogism, the mixing of voices.[7] With regard to the motley, Nietzsche's position is conditional; he defends the motley (the mixings, the indecision of genres) in terms of strength and weakness; pre-Socratic mixings: strong ≠ Platonic mixings: weak → *motley*: key notion—I forgot to give the Greek word: *poikilos*, daubed, spotted, mottled—the root of *pikilia* in modern Greek: various *hors-d'oeuvres*—we could also cite the Rhapsodic,[8] the tacked together (Proust: the Work as made by a Dressmaker) → the Rhapsodic distances the Object, magnifies the Tendency, the *Writing*.

I had something of this extension of—or defection from—the Novel in mind when I titled the Course "The Preparation of the Novel": *Novel* should slowly expand to include Absolute Novel, Romantic Novel, *poikilos* Novel, Novel of the Writing-Tendency; in other words, all works of literature.

Intransitive

Thus, at some point (to be identified; *historical* research: probably began with Romanticism but also, perhaps, here and there, earlier works: Montaigne and the book as offspring, see Antoine Compagnon)[9] *writing* was no longer, or no longer simply, a "normal" activity: aim + object, aim adapted to the object, incorporating it in a

Servière, 64, 94

single movement, but also, there and here, a tendency, whose object mattered less than the possibilities offered by *Tending-toward*, of a Force that sensuously and dramatically seeks its point of application.

A possible trace of this sudden emergence (of this little revolution in the intentionality of the verb), a grammatical trace: passage from *to write* + direct object → without a direct object "in the absolute sense" as we say → "And what are you writing for us today?—I'm writing" or "What do you do?—I write," etc. → It could be said: *to write* is an intransitive verb[10] since what's now the regular construction of the verb lacks a complement (this was already somewhat the case in seventeenth-century usage, especially in and ever since Chateaubriand). Although in reality there always is a complement: one always ends up writing something ("I'm writing *Paludes*");[11] curious grammar: the complement remains *suspended*, either in the future or in uncertainty, in the impossibility of discerning, of naming what it is you're writing. Nevertheless, it's on the side of grammar—of linguistics—that we find a good image of absolute *Writing*: not from French but from Indo-European (Benveniste):[12] *Voices*, or diatheses. Diatheses = the basic position of the subject in the verb, *through* (*dia-*) the process. We know and think it natural that there should be two basic voices in our languages: *Active / Passive*. Now, in Greek, there's a third voice, that the (late) Greek grammarians called: the *Middle* voice (*mesotes*: between *energeia* and *pathos*). As comparatists are aware, the passive is actually only one modality of the Middle. In Indo-European, there are two basic diatheses: *Active / Middle*. In order to grasp the distinction, you need to know that what's particular about the Indo-European verb is it *refers to the subject, not to the object* (≠ American Indian or Caucasian languages, where other indicators signal the end of the process); in Indo-European, everything is presented and arranged with respect to the subject → If we're "subjective," if our philosophies start out from or debate the subject, if we return to it as often as we do, this could be because the subject is inscribed in the very foundations of language (of our language) → Thus, *Active / Middle* refer to two different attitudes of the subject in relation to the process: the difference (Pānini)[13] is between doing something for someone else, on someone else's behalf ≠ doing that thing for yourself, on your own behalf.

Sanskrit *Yajati*: as a priest, he is sacrificing for another →	*Yajate*, as the one making the offering, he is sacrificing for himself

= Active	→	= Middle
= the subject is the starting point of the process, which is accomplished outside of the subject.	→	= the process is accomplished within the subject, the subject is the seat of the process.
		(We were taught, though it would be years before I'd understand why: *louimai*, "I untie for myself." I untie the laces of my shoes for myself? Obviously! It was absurd—risky to translate this as "for myself.")
The subject effects		The subject effects while being affected
nomous tithénai "to establish laws"		*nomous tithésthai* "to establish laws and include oneself therein" = "to give oneself laws"
polémon poiéi, "he produces war" (for example by giving the signal for it)		*polémon poiétai*, "he wages or takes part in war"

Note: explained in this way, we see clearly that (1) the Middle can have a direct object; (2) in the Active, the subject's participation is not required: thus, however paradoxical it may seem, in Indo-European the subject isn't required to participate in *being*, to be self-affecting in being: *to be* is active (like *to go*, or *to flow*), in the Middle, on the other hand, the subject is the center and agent of the Process.

Benveniste proposes, rather than *active / middle*: external and internal diathesis.[14]

You'll have already grasped how this analysis relates to *Writing*, which, in the absolute sense, is clearly a middle: *I write, and in doing so I'm affected*; I make myself the center and the agent of the action; I establish myself in the action, not by adopting an external position (like the priest) but an internal one, where the subject and the action form one and the same bubble:

Préface, 64
1852, thirty-one years old

1. "To Write something": such was the case for centuries; generally on behalf of someone, someone generic, or someone fictional, for whom the writer was simply the procurator; I'd take up the sacrificial knife, the sword, the pen for a Cause: to instruct, convince, convert, make people laugh; to write a realist novel is to become a procurator, a priest *for* the people ≠ "To Write" is to take the knife from the priest's hands and perform the sacrifice for yourself. Of course, the direct object (the *what*) is possible, even inevitable, but it's always bound up with, has always embraced the writing subject, not as a subjective character but as someone affected by the act of writing: in this way, a "subjectivity" of writing, rather than of character, emerges. The practical level corresponding to this subjectivity of affected action is what we now call *enunciation* → (Let's say, to simplify things): the classical writer would lend his pen to a cause, to an external end (religion, for instance): he was in an *active* diathesis ≠ Flaubert, as the classic writer of *writing* (not the first: Chateaubriand was there before him and, a singular case, possibly Montaigne), is no longer distinct from his pen: "I am a man-pen, I feel through the pen; because of it, in relation to it and so much more with it."[15] *Absolute Writing* becomes an essence, the essence with which the writer burns and identifies, in a sort of mysticism of the Purity of Writing, uncorrupted by any end. Flaubert (1860, thirty-nine years old): "The works of art which please over and above all others are those where the *art is in excess*. In painting, I like Painting; in verses, Verse."[16]

2. *Writing* as Middle (internal diathesis) corresponds to a historical period: broadly speaking, Romanticism (my understanding of the word isn't in the textbook, restricted sense), that is to say, from Chateaubriand (or even from the late Rousseau) up to and including Proust. It's possible to go beyond *Writing*, just as it's possible to go beyond the Middle, and one endeavors to go beyond it, to radicalize it; this might even be a good description of the efforts as well as the failures of contemporary literature (but all that still hangs in the balance). I'd use it—if this were my intention, but I'm simply a man narrating his decision to write in a "Romantic" manner—to describe the texts (note that I'm not saying the "books") that I sometimes get sent, that some people are kind enough to send me, along the lines of the following typology:

a. To Write is a very strong Middle: the affectation of the subject through the act of Writing is the only thing that really counts; diathesis that's more than internal = *intestinal*; thus, for better or worse, the object becomes unclassifiable, unidentifiable, and as it were unnamable; it's a *text*, a trace of an activity, a "graffiti" that, as a general rule, falls outside the norms of readability: neither narrative, nor argumentative, not even "poetic"; it's a kind of "Anything" (in the eyes of the reader), whence the tension when it comes to its "publishability."

b. A different path: pushed logically, to the point where the subject is negated, dialectically dissolved in the universality of writing, *to write* (in the Romantic manner) is no longer the ultimate aim: like the subject, it has been done away with → no longer a question of stopping at the book, at the Work as offspring, the substitute for a line of descendants, since the written is "socialized" to excess → Present-day temptation of anonymous and/or collective writings: (1) in the generalized practice of Writing,[17] where *to write* is no longer a middle verb but more like a passive: writing gets written, using certain techniques; (2) in anonymous or collective writing efforts; the Name of the author having been sacrificed in a very Hegelian manner to timid figures of the Universal (notably the Idea: for the Idea is impersonal, the bourgeois law of literary copyright says so).[18]

These forms have not yet proven themselves (with the exception of Writing[19] of course), because reading resists. The man whose story I'm telling has set himself the problem of a writing that's both readable and absolute—of a romantic writing. Thus we take up our narrative again, which is that of *To Write, middle verb: I write, and in doing so I'm affected* in the very process of writing.

To Have Finished

Writing as absolute brings with it a particular existential movement: *to finish (the work) in order to start again* = the Fantasy of "Having finished." You labor on the work like a maniac, *in order to finish it*—but as soon as it's finished, you start another one, under the same illusory conditions (George Sand would finish a book at two in the morning, and by three have started another one); the "tendency" is indeed inexhaustible.

The wish "To Have Finished" presents itself at every stage: Gathering material, Drafting, Correcting, Typing up, Publication; at every stage: ardor, impatience to get it over with, then, when it's done, a kind of disappointment, the object ends up looking dull, banal: *what, is that all it is?* (the first rereading is agonizing), *quick, on to the next thing!*—It can be said (I can say): once I've begun writing something, I write only in order to have finished it.—It wouldn't be too much of an exaggeration to say that the joy I get from a book is the finishing of it—to have properly finished it; the rest (its reception): satisfying in terms of image but not in terms of the doing—and therefore unreliable, because an image can't be accurate (the only true satisfaction I'm able to get from a published piece of writing is when, thanks to a few letters from unknown readers, I can convince myself that *it responded to an unconscious demand* = definition of a *living* book).

It's in keeping with the logic of the *Pro-ject* {*Pro-jet*} (of throwing something out ahead of you, from springboard to springboard) to fantasize a final endpoint, a definitive end: a time when you'll stop writing, when you'll finally take a break, less from writing than from the perpetual reactivation of the desire; Rousseau, fantasizing a *complete idleness* (Saint-Pierre Island)[20] → Whence the fantasmatic privilege accorded to the Last Work, a last Testament: another work! This will be the last, the one in which I'll say everything and then be silent, etc. Fantasy of the Testament, Reality of the Testament that's constantly being reworked.

Jean Pavans

This concept or, more modestly, this Fantasy of *Having Finished* might provide the basis for a new typology of *Writing*—what's more, a timely one; the case of Jean P.: his manuscript didn't fall into the categories of the first typology: neither "textual" (unreadable) nor anonymous; an elegantly written narrative novel, a first novel.[21] I asked him (though, as always, I was secretly thinking of myself): Did he envisage his future life as the life of a writer? Did he imagine building up a body of work on the same scale as his life (that is, an infinite sum of works)?—His response to me was: *no*. What he wanted to do was capture a moment (of his life) in a work, that's all; in other words, he had no hangups about going back to "*writing something*"—*albeit at a different point on the spiral*. I consider, perhaps mistakenly, everything young (as in the case of this young novelist) to be modern. I therefore felt "outmoded" in that the feeling I have for *Writing* is absolute (it doesn't end with the work but begins it again) or *lifelong* (on the scale of my life) → *Writing*, or my writing at any rate, is *protensive*: it's constituted on the basis of the future, and the future has no content, it's never full, its by nature hemorrhagic, since it's constantly getting time (and the object it mediates) going again; I'm illustrating what Montaigne (quoted by Chateaubriand) says: "humanity [is] always gaping toward the future."[22]

To bring *To Have Finished* to a close, I'd like to remind you of an extreme case: that of Proust. *In Search of Lost Time* = a struggle against Death, to finish before dying; therefore, it inevitably has the character of a testamentary work; it's a *To Have Finished* limited by Death, an intense Protensivity (a whole regime, a life's asceticism), but one that's nevertheless granted with a final loop. Which then raises the question of *reprieve*: if Proust hadn't died, having only just finished the work, *what would he have written*? What *could he* have written? A reprieve is never put to good use: it's an *excess* of time, a time of boredom (Michelet and the nineteenth century, the Reprieve of the Revolution as it were, cf. After the Thousandth year).[23] In a sense, Proust could do nothing but die; if he hadn't, he probably wouldn't have written anything new but only have kept *adding to* the work, through a process of "*marcottage*"[24]: paperoles, and yet more paperoles; endlessly adding more oil to the mayonnaise. His last word, written on a sheet of paper stained with Veronal: *Forcheville*.[25]

Digression—To Not Write?

Since *Writing* is taken here to be a Desire, a Passion (this is how I began speaking of it), it's necessary to posit the theoretical possibility of a break or cessation of that Desire, of that Passion—we must, in other words, evoke the possibility of a *Counter-Writing* and of a *Not-Writing*, of a *Para-graphy* (to redirect the desire into something other than writing) or of an *A-graphy* (to dominate or exhaust the Passion, to enter a state of Wisdom, because *Writing isn't wise*). This isn't a logical clausula: it happens—it rarely happens to me, but still, every time it does I feel a great fear, the fear of something that it's nevertheless possible to get acclimatized to—thus it happens that I sometimes feel the wing of Not-Writing pass over me: a black wing of Misfortune but also a gentle wing of Wisdom. So, this—in truth, singular—question, that hardly ever gets asked (we've considered that other singular question: How can anyone not write?): How do you stop writing? How to interrupt the practice and the craft of the writer? I'll evoke two cases: (1) the diversion of the Desire; (2) the calling into question of the Desire itself, as a Desire.

1. Scuppering

Dates

In French literature, a spectacular scuppering of Writing: Rimbaud (1854–1891; Verlaine's gunshot: 1873). Total break: on the one hand, readings, letters, verse, theories (that of the Visionary), and then, all of a sudden, absolutely nothing: literature consigned to the Void, radical, sudden, and definitive Assassination → Why? There hasn't been, as far as I'm aware, any explanation for this, and to tell the truth I'm very conscious that the very idea of a *motive* would be useless, insufficient here: *that's how it is, period, that's it*. Rimbaud, a very difficult thing to achieve, impressed upon all his commentators (seeing there's been a Rimbaud myth): the absolute impenetrability of his decision: an opacity similar to that of faith as Kierkegaard sees it (cf. Abraham)[26]—the Scuppering, the squandering is total. Upon his return to Roche in 1879, Ernest Delahaye asks Rimbaud if he still thinks of literature; in response, this absolutely dull sentence, devoid of all affect, a neutral state of desire: "*I no longer concern myself with that.*"[27] The scuppering leads to breaking off all contact with the Charville friends who represented the past, literature—and of course the total shipwrecking of the books; to his friend Pierquin: "To buy books, especially those kind of books <published by Lemerre> is completely idiotic. You have a head on your shoulders, which ought to stand in for all books. Once they're on your shelves, the only purpose those books will serve is to hide the peeling walls!"[28]

Carré, 166

Lettres, 160

The only thing to have been debated: the date when this scuppering occurred:

  a. The long accepted version (Carré):[29] 1870: *Poésies*. 1871: *Poésies*. 1872: *Les Illuminations*. May 1873: *Une Saison en enfer* → November 1873: cessation of literary activity.
  b. New version, following the work of Bouillane de Lacoste[30]: *Les Illuminations* written after *Saison*. 1873: *Saison* → 1874: *Illuminations* → 1875: cessation of literary activity.

If the aim is to uncover a creative "logic" to this break, then it matters whether or not *Saison* was written after *Les Illuminations*, but for us, who are happy to simply note and to contemplate with stupefaction the total Shipwrecking of a Desire, we need only situate it roughly between 1873 and 1875, that is, very precisely, when Rimbaud was about twenty years old → he still had almost twenty years left to live: a different Rimbaud.

What's striking: Rimbaud casts aside one Desire (that of Writing), but replaces it with another, one that's just as violent, radical, and, I would say, maniacal: *travel*.

a. It's literally mad; already, in his adolescence, incredible journeys on foot: walking, walking, without a penny (Today, wouldn't he just have hitchhiked? Although: Perhaps he wanted to walk by himself?). Then, a maniacal desire to learn languages: English, German, Arabic, Spanish, Dutch, Hindustani. And especially after 1873: England (after Verlaine, with Germain Nouveau), Germany (Stuttgart), Italy (Milan) via Switzerland, trips back to Charleville, cutting across Europe, Java (alone in the forest), Austria, Cyprus (supervising workers in a quarry), Red Sea: all that, between 1875 and 1881.—All the characteristics of a *mania*.

b. This desire for Travel was eventually replaced by a second libido: exploration, colonization (in Abyssinia); at the time, 1887–1889, which is precisely the era of grandfather Binger (though he was nothing of a poet, not even a wrecked one!),[31] exploration and colonization were intimately linked; I mean: were *still* linked. Rimbaud was conscious of the impact of his efforts at exploration; he established the main route into Abyssinia: it would be the route of the first Ethiopian railway; he also grasped, immediately, the geographic and economic significance of Djibouti → The poet and the Traveler (still a romantic figure) were replaced by another role: colonizer and geographer (the true antithesis of the Poet). He didn't write a single line: "absurd and distasteful childishness"[32]; we only have two writings from this period: a two-page summary of this trip to Harrar in 1887 (for the Geographical Society), very dry, altogether prosaic, and a letter in a minor French paper published in Cairo, *Le Bosphore Égyptien* (1887).

Lettres, **186**, *sq.*

As I said: for me, this scuppering still has something stupefying about it, something that defies analysis; it can in no way constitute a cultural model because clearly everything was played out on the level of Desire: there was a carousel, a circus, circles of Desires; but Desire itself or, better, *Will* (in the Nietzschean sense) was never scuppered—and the Desire for the Other is probably the very essence of the *Unanalyzable*—the *Scandal*. Just two remarks:

a. We are very ready to be surprised—given that for us Rimbaud is a literary being—at Rimbaud the colonizer and businessman (dealing in coffee and guns) *emerging out of* the successful writer. But we would be equally justified in turning the question around:

Given what he became, how, at a certain point, was he able to *write*, and to write so well?—The evolutionary model ("Destiny") has to be unlearned: how to not privilege one or other moment in a man's life; it's a Christian tradition to privilege the ending, to judge a man by his death (the idea of the "good end"). Pascal against Montaigne: "Now throughout the whole of this book he thinks only of dying in a cowardly and weak manner."[33]

b. Rimbaud is modern (a founder of Modernity) not thanks to his writings—or less thanks to his writings than to the dazzling nature, the *madness* of his break. It's not even the radicality, the purity, the freedom of the break that's so modern; it's the fact that it enables us to see, it shows us how the subject—the linguistic subject—is split, divided, like a track with each rail running straight ahead, in parallel to the other; as if there were two "conditionings" within Rimbaud, sealed off from one another: one to poetry (through his lycée), the other to travel (through the Mother's rejection? Banal? Who knows?); he spoke two, discontinuous languages: there's no *connection* between the poet, the traveler, the colonizer, and the believer he would turn out to be (Paterne Berrichon, Claudel),[34] and it's this schism that behaves like a modern incitement: Machiavelli, speaking of Laurent de Medicis (serious and sensuous), says that there were two different beings inside him, "*joined by an inconceivable jointure.*"[35]

| *H.F.*, VIII, 36

2. "Idleness"

Opposed to this *Paragraphy*—the desire to write redirected into a different desire—there remains the possibility of a pure *Agraphy*: a cessation of writing linked to a voluntary cessation of Desire. The opposite of *Trade* (*Negotium*), that is to say, Labor, Activity, Bustle, is *Otium*, Leisure, or, if you like, *Idleness*, but on the condition that the term is taken to mean a fully developed Force, not a lesser and more relaxed image of Labor but a fully fledged (and, moreover, a difficult) Philosophy.

| **Will-to-Possess**

| **Manipulation**

The idea of (total) Idleness as a system for living can occur to the writer whenever the written work—regardless of what it is he's writing—is felt to be a *Will-to-Live* that inclines toward the (hidden) violence of a *Will-to-Possess*, a *manipulation* of other people's Desire (however pure his intentions). Then comes the temptation to suspend all written work on the grounds of it being, statutorily, whatever the content, an "enterprise," an "offensive," a "domination"; next, the desire to say no more, to annul all ambition, all social

Rousseau, *Confessions,* 600

(Not publishing)

libido → With its worries, its struggles, its scruples, *writing books* can seem like a "fatal profession" (Rousseau)[36] that the writer dreams of renouncing—whence the fantasmatic solution: *to write* (since it's a pleasure) but *to not publish* (because publishing is a worry; a theme we'll come across again in Flaubert); naturally, it's not existentially viable.—Of course, the problem of "subsistence" still remains, but today it's relatively uncommon for a writer, and especially a "serious" writer, to be capable of making a living from his books: he can give up writing and still live.

The path of *Idleness* = an initiatory path, which goes from straightforward "leisure" as the freedom to do whatever you want (being no longer subject to the harsh law of the Labor of writing) to a Profound Philosophy of Good and Evil, of Power and Powerlessness. Let's indicate some of its stages:

Knowledge

Knowledge

Picon, 128

The most acceptable form of Idleness (we're running through a hierarchy that will lead us down to its most scandalous form, that of complete *For nothing*): study, reading, "for itself," with no transformable gain. Expressed in this beautiful sentence from *The Wild Ass's Skin*: "*Will* burns us and *power* destroys us: but *knowledge* leaves our weak organization in a perpetual state of calm."[37] It is indeed a matter of "philosophical" *Idleness* (since this is our topic), since *Knowledge* is only a Commodity to the extent that it's in conflict with *Will* and *Power*. Let's remind ourselves of St. Augustine's three *libidos: sentiendi, sciendi, dominandi*. The libido of knowledge is in conflict with that of the senses (desires) and that of domination, thereby introducing, as it were dialectically, the possibility of *calm*, that is to say of *non-libido*.

DIY {*Bricolage*}

Busy Idleness
Rousseau

Busy (full, occupied) *Idleness*: the kind that replaces *tasks* with *occupations*, like those of a Retiree keen on DIY. Tempting description in Rousseau: (1) Idleness = fantasized as a *Grand Project*, a *New Life—Vita Nova*[38] (we'll encounter these notions again in the actual writing process itself, for the truth is: the *Labor of Writing* and the *Idleness of Writing* are two sides of the same fantasy). 1765, Rousseau, at fifty-two (†1778), plans to settle on Saint-Pierre Island (Lake Bienne): "the age of romantic schemes was past and with it the fumes of vainglory, which had bemused rather than flat-

154   THE WORK AS WILL

Confessions, 634
630 sq.

tered me, my last remaining hope was that I might live a life of unconstrained and eternal leisure."³⁹ He visits the island, it enchants him, and he stays there: "I was thus in some sense taking leave of my century and my contemporaries and was bidding farewell to the world <hence the solemn theme of conversion> in confining myself to this island for the rest of my days; for this was what I was resolved to do; and I was counting, moreover, on at last being able to realize there that *grand scheme* for living a life of idleness to which I had hitherto devoted, in vain, all the little energy that the heavens had apportioned me."⁴⁰ (2) This idleness is full of plans for activity (I spoke of the do-it-yourself-er; Rousseau expresses this very well:

Confessions, 634

"The idleness I like is not that of a lounger, who sits there, arms crossed, wholly inert <though, as we shall see in a moment, such *total inaction* can be fantasized in a much better way, in the Oriental style> and who thinks no more than he acts. It is at once that of the child, who is always in motion and always doing nothing, and that of the driveller, who rambles on endlessly while never stirring from his seat. I like to be busy doing nothing, to begin a hundred things and to finish none, to come and go as the whim takes me, to change my plans at every moment, to follow each twist and turn of a fly, to dig up a rock to see what is underneath it, to embark with ardor upon a task of ten years and to abandon it without regret at the end of ten minutes, in short, to while away the whole day without plan or purpose and to follow in everything the caprice of the moment."⁴¹ → Thus it's not "labor" that's rejected (labor is a sacrosanct value), it's constraint → Rousseau wants idleness because it is "free" (this is how we usually conceive of idleness: *social*, not metaphysical disalienation).

Nothing

Komboloï

A degree further in the dissolution of tasks and occupations → activity as a pure form that produces absolutely nothing: no return whatsoever, not even an internal one.—You'll have probably seen, in Greece, or in North African countries, men sitting doing nothing, endlessly manipulating what looks like a rosary composed of big beads: this is the *komboloï*;⁴² your fingers fiddle with it without you realizing, it has no religious function; it's not an instrument nor is it merely a trinket. It is as it were the active emblem of *Doing Nothing*. For, without it, *Doing Nothing* might not be discernable; subtle dialectic of Being and Nothingness; for *nothing* to be seen, known, felt, it requires a prop; otherwise, no paradigm, no meaning; *Nothingness isn't anything!!* Something thought finds unbearable.

Wou-wei

It is, however, something that has to be *borne* in the total (and final) experience of Idleness: to fantasize a certain experience, if not of nothingness (too emphatic, too metaphysical), then at least of *Nullity* {*Nul*}. We could give it the epigraph of these two Zen lines, lines I've always been so struck by and so fond of that, unusually for me, I know them by heart:

> *Sitting quietly, doing nothing,*
> *Spring comes, and the grass grows of its own accord.*[43]

(The anacoluthon enchants me: there's no longer a subject, only a "Sitting"). I experienced this state absolutely, not for myself unfortunately—indeed, therein lies the problem—but by proxy, upon seeing, on a day when I was in the car by myself, driving slowly toward Ben Slimane along a very minor road in Morocco, a child sitting on an old wall—and it was spring. Three forms:

1. This one, of course: the Oriental *Wou-wei* (Non-Action),[44] desire for a life that, seen from the outside, is unchanging, where there's no struggle, no ambition that anything should change. To describe this, this basic premise requires discredited, not especially flattering images. That of the *Heap*: to be like a *Heap*—why not like a *Cowpat*? A Philosophy of the Heap? A *Sorology*,[45] *Soritophilia* (*sôros*: *sorites*, syllogisms through accumulation), or a *Bolitology*[46] (*boliton*: cowpat?)—Or indeed a *larva*—but—with everything there, so to speak—a *sentient* larva, which is to say, in a sense—things are reversed: interiority is restored to its absolute, its barest affirmation. And what we encounter is, precisely, *Wou-wei*: a "sort of humble passivity," removed from any desire for violence or rivalry (writing, then, is clearly quite impossible) but that's grounded in a kind of "spontaneous and inexhaustible activity." Sentient larva, thinking Heap: the only contact between the Heap and the outside: *pressure* from the atmosphere, barometric sensitivity.

2. It can also be said, in a more Western manner, that fantasized in this way (as against *Writing*: fantasy set against fantasy), radical, ontological *Idleness* is *Natural*. Here's a quotation from Heidegger (*Essays*, XXVII, "Overcoming Metaphysics"): "The unnoticeable law of the earth preserves the earth in the sufficiency of the emerg-

ing and perishing of all things in the allotted sphere of the possible which everything follows, and yet nothing knows. The birch <the tree, that is!>[47] never oversteps its possibility. The colony of bees dwells in its possibility. It is first the will which arranges itself everywhere in technology that devours the earth in the exhaustion and consumption and change of what is artificial. Technology drives the earth beyond the developed sphere of its possibility into such things which are no longer a possibility and are thus the impossible"[48] → that, I think, is a good description of the Conflict between *Writing* (will, exhaustion, wear, variations, whims, artifices, in short, the *Impossible*) and *Idleness* (Nature, development—"sensitivity"—within the sphere of the Possible).

Russian fatalism

3. Third example of *Wou-wei*. Nietzsche, talking about himself (*Ecce Homo*): he likens *Ressentiment* (reactive Force, on the side of the Priest) to a restlessness, a hindrance, an illness: "Freedom from *ressentiment*. . . . Being sick is itself a kind of *ressentiment*—Against this the invalid only has one means of cure—I call it *Russian fatalism*, that fatalism without rebellion with the Russian solider for whom the campaign has become too much at last lies down in the snow. *No longer to take anything at all*, to receive anything, to take anything *into* oneself—no longer to react at all . . . a kind of will to hibernation . . . nothing burns one up quicker than the affects of *ressentiment* . . . this was grasped by that profound psychologist Buddha."[49] Superior, transcendent passivity, which remains in harmony with Nature: more Tao-like than Buddhist → clearly involves a difficult Ethics of Non-Response to Evil, which can be found in Tolstoy (today's world seems unprepared for this to say the least; we're living in the Era of generalized *Ressentiment*: Priests, Popes, Ayatollahs, Political Moralists).

SESSION OF DECEMBER 15, 1979

Personal Temptations

In order to explain how a man who wants to write can feel, within the most irrepressible and tenacious Desire to write, that other desire pass through him, that of Doing Nothing (of *Wou-wei*)—though perhaps they're cut of the *same cloth*, perhaps they're made of the same stuff—that is, so that I might understand it myself, it's necessary for me to go through some of the things I've felt within myself (the rule = offer the *intimate*, not the *private*).

1. The observation, petty but often repeated, that in life the tiniest little things are always a struggle (the big conflicts, that's all anyone ever talks about); the number of little exertions that life forces upon you over the course of the most ordinary day is quite incredible: parking the car is a struggle; finding a table in a restaurant is a struggle; getting your wallet out when its corners have wedged it inside an inside pocket {*poche revolver*}; buttoning a button. On the flipside (or the right side) of these struggles would be an idyllic civilization—no longer heroic; either absolutely aristocratic or absolutely "ascetic": no cars, no buttons (robes, only robes), no wallets, no pockets, no guns {*revolvers*}! → A Civilization of *gliding*? Where everything would "glide along"? Of the same order, a summer morning in Paris, glancing over the pages in my diary for the next few days = ease, freedom, jubilation, sense of a *truth* to life, because they were completely empty: not one Appointment, no other commitments → this is the unhoped-for *Wou-wei* (that said: for what purpose?—That's precisely it: none).

2. This *Wou-wei* = absolutely antisocial; that is to say, you can't explain it or, more prosaically: it can't serve as a *reason*, as an *excuse*; a broken leg is a valid excuse to refuse an invitation, the desire for *Wou-wei* isn't. In my village, this summer, a dinner invitation: I'm trapped, because when I'm there I have no excuses at my disposal: they know I'm not "busy," that I don't have anything else arranged. I splutter because I don't know how to explain without hurting anyone's feelings that here my desire is to be *like an immobile heap*: to lie back, to stretch out and as it were to take root in the house or the countryside; *to be an essence of inactivity*, shielded from that terrifying thing (according to this Philosophy): *initiative* (my fear of people with "get up and go").

One evening, this feeling took a "romantic" form (because it had to do with "Nature"): on the evening of July 14, after dinner, a drive in the countryside: on an incline, on a road that leads only to a farm (between Urt and Bardos), we stopped the car and got out; we were surrounded by rolling countryside, with the Adour in one direction and the Pyrenees in the other; the air was completely still, inert even: not a sound, a few brown and white farms in the Basque style (without the terrorism!) dotted in the distance, the smell of cut hay. I folded my arms, and I surveyed the scene. But not so as to say, like Rastignac looking over Paris: "It's between you and me now!"[1] On the contrary, what I was experiencing was a sort of degree zero of Desire; everything within me was as still as the landscape: force, splendor, truth as sovereign as the Desire-to-Write.

3. Less "romantic," more "conceptual" because it's urban: what I'd call "the fantasy of an August 15 spent in Paris": Empty Day, Public Holiday of Emptiness, of Disaffiliation; (nonclimatic) pinnacle of the summer social calendar; tomorrow, the descent will begin (back down toward gregariousness); the streets were deserted, as in wartime, the silence—and, that year, the grey, the rain, the pavements empty of cars (more significant than when there's less traffic); I felt the 15th of August to be the true bridge between one year and the next; neutral day, buffer, blank, parting of the waters, deserted summit: singular Day of Disaffiliation, Public Holiday of *Wou-wei*.

Préface, 258

4. A final remark on the Desire for Idleness as a Counter-Desire to Write: the enemy of this Fantasy, or of this Philosophy, or of this Practice if it were attempted is: Boredom (the risk of boredom). Flaubert, completely taken over by the Desire to Write, expresses this very well (1873, fifty-two years old); he wrote to George Sand: "I do not share the kinds of distain you profess. And, as you say, I am absolutely unacquainted with 'the pleasure of doing nothing.' The moment I'm not holding a book in my hands or not thinking about writing one, I'm so bored I could scream. Life seems bearable only when it's being conjured away. Otherwise one would have to give oneself over to dissipation—and even if I did that!"[2] We'll speak of Boredom elsewhere, for it's ambivalent; it is, or can be: (1) what compels you to write, so as to escape it (Flaubert); (2) it can suddenly appear, in the midst of the very act of *Writing*, and eat away at it: there's a boredom in not writing and a boredom in writing.

As regards the act of *Writing*, *Wou-wei* is ambivalent: when the Will-to-Possess of Writing encounters *Wou-wei*, it dies, but within Writing itself *Wou-wei* can also be a strength of attachment to the labor of writing that, when seen from the outside, will appear inert and in conflict with the bustle of the World → Flaubert doesn't use the metaphor of the Heap but one very close to it: "I live absolutely like an oyster. My novel is the rock that I attach myself to, and I know nothing of what is going on in the world." (cited by Kafka, *Journal*, 249)[3]

I'm Worth More Than What I Write

The man I'm speaking of therefore occasionally catches a glimpse not only of the seduction but also of the validity of *Wou-wei* (of absolute Idleness). So why does this man insist on Wanting to Write (at least at this stage in my Narrative, which, as you'll have guessed, is the story of my own life)? To understand it, we'll have to enter into the dialectic of Writing and the Imaginary.

Ego-Ideal ≠ Ideal Ego

For that, I shall revert—something I haven't done for a long time—to Psychoanalysis—or at least to two concepts. We have a double concept, proposed by Freud and developed by Lacan: *Ichideal* = Ego-Ideal ≠ *Idealich* = Ideal Ego.[4]

Safouan, 143
Lacan, 97, 116

a. Ego-Ideal: site of exigencies; the status of this authority is therefore inconceivable without language. With respect to the *Ego-Ideal*, the *Super-ego* is nothing more than a secondary introjection: the super-ego is constraining ≠ the *Ego-Ideal* = thrilling. *On the side of the Symbolic.*

Safouan, 143

b. Ideal Ego: form in which the subject appears, or wants to appear, as determined by the Ego-Ideal. *On the side of the Imaginary* → The Ideal Ego's dependence upon the Ego-Ideal, like that of the Imaginary upon the Symbolic.

Freud, *Essais*, 161, 137

Balance between the *Ego-Ideal* and the *Ideal Ego*: subtle and stable; if it's upset, the subject is destabilized; for example, (a) cyclical affective states (Freud) = ego-ideal, after having exerted a very strict control over the ego, finds itself absorbed by, dissolved in it; (b) state of being in love: the whole situation can be summed up in this formula: the object has taken the place of what was the ego-ideal (perhaps this is why writing can't coincide with Love = it comes *after*).

160   THE WORK AS WILL

Writing: evidently on the side of the Symbolic, on the side of the Ego-Ideal. But the other authority is present: the Ideal Ego, more or less successfully dominated. A differential is set up between the postulation of the Ego-Ideal (Writing) and the postulation of the Ideal Ego (Imaginary outside of writing) and it's this that gets the subject *going*, *moving* in the direction of writing, obliging him write *infinitely*.

In a word—I'm summing up what I'm going to develop a little further—it could be said that the writer reasons (or "works," functions) in the following way: "*I want to be a good guy* (Ideal Ego) *and I want to be seen to be a good guy, I want everyone to know I'm a good guy* (Ego-Ideal).

Writing / Ideal Ego Differential

I'll take the differential from the opposite direction and begin by saying a word about writing and its *failure to completely satisfy the Ideal Ego* (the Imaginary of the subject who writes / wants to write).

1. Writing

For the writer, writing is first (first and continually) an absolute position of value: introjection of the Other in the form of an essential language. Whatever becomes of this sentiment (and it's not straightforward), the writer possesses, is constituted by an initial narcissistic belief → I write, therefore I'm worth something, absolutely, whatever happens. This belief would traditionally be called: Pride; there's a writer's pride, and that pride is a *primitive*. Consider the example of Chateaubriand: he led a political and a literary life; his political life was very important to him, his *Memoirs* are full of it → countless manifestations of political self-satisfaction (the soundness of his liberal positions, the loyalty and rigor of his actions, etc.); and yet, in him, the primitive is the absolute pride of the writer; in 1822 he returns to London as ambassador to Louis XVIII: "However, there was another cloud over my head in London. My political standing overshadowed my literary reputation; there is not a fool in the three kingdoms <that is, Great Britain> who would not prefer the ambassador to Louis XVIII to the author of *The Genius of Christianity*"—This "pride" (an old word, though not necessarily an old thing) can be expressed in gentler, less arrogant terms. Kafka: "This evening I was once again filled with anxiously restrained abilities."[5] Paradoxically, this pride can actually be *modest*, because it doesn't necessarily bear upon a contingent work (both Chateaubriand and Kafka were always doubting the quality of their works) but always, inevitably, upon the *act of Writing* itself: it's the *act of Writing*, as Ego-Ideal, that's sovereign, thrilling; to write is an act which Bestows Value → Of course, that Value is constantly being undermined by the doubt that bears upon the contingent work, but it's never destroyed; there's an ongoing strategy that turns doubt itself into something that Bestows Value: I could, for example, write a work (a Diary) in which I announce the loss, the degradation of my talent, and in doing so movingly come to terms with it;[6] but if I *write* that I'm worth less, then what I'm actually doing is declaring that I'm worth more. Yet, contradictorily—and this marks the start of the dialectic that gets the writer going, that engages him an infinite writing, more powerful than any dream of *Wou-wei*, the dialectic that I'm attempting to describe—the Value bestowed by Writing is shot through with a sense of disappointment, of a loss of value: I write, therefore I reassure myself of who I am (ego-ideal), but at the same time I'm aware that: no, what I've written is not *all me*; there's a remainder, extensive to writing, that I haven't yet said, that makes up my total value, and that I must say, communicate, "monumentalize," write, at all costs: "I'm worth more than what I write." This remainder or this surplus, this leftover of writing that writing must make good, this *reprieve* that I must exploit by writing again, endlessly, is the *Ideal Ego*, the *pro-tension* that it imposes upon the Ego-Ideal, upon Writing.

2. The (Writer's) Ideal Ego

"Entirely"

In this way, a process of *upping the stakes* is set in motion: set against writing, which is felt to be almost parsimonious, is the ardent wish for a writing to come (in my future) that would be a *total* writing, a writing that would say who I am *entirely*, that would project the *whole* of my Imaginary onto the stage of language.

Let's listen to Kafka formulating the demand of *Entirely*: "I have now, and have had since this afternoon, a great yearning to write all my anxiety *entirely* <my emphasis> out of me, write it into the depths of the paper just as it comes from out of the depths of me, or write it down in such a way that I could draw what I had written into me *completely*. This is no artistic yearning."[7] Artistic yearning would be on the side of the Ego-Ideal, and here we're beyond that,

Journal, 161 (1911)

or below it, in the vast realm of the Imaginary, of the Ideal Ego. It's therefore a matter of an *extensive* proposition—which is why the formula I'm proposing is not "I'm *better* than what I write" but "I'm worth *more* than what I write." → The aim of the work is therefore never uniquely and purely artistic—except as a theoretical pretext, in Flaubert for example; its aim is existential, or even topological: it's a matter of exhausting a space—which is in reality inexhaustible (we'll come back to this in a moment, for it's in this *exhaustible / inexhaustible* that the *workings* of the writer reside).

Meanwhile, what can this *entirely* that would have to be said consist in? I'll tell you how I understand it, and if I'm reinserting myself here (and not Kafka or Flaubert), there's a logic to it: in order to remain true to the sentiment—to the proposition—at the origin of the Course and that I announced at the beginning of last year, in my explanation of what I understand by "Preparation of the Novel": as a *Work of Love*, work through which the writer expresses a particular love of the World.[8]

The Loving Soul

1. As a general rule, the *Ideal-Ego* I'm referring to, which is as it were the unexpressed surplus of writing confronted with the "hardness" of writing, tends toward what isn't "hard," toward emotion, sensitivity, generosity, "heart" as we once might have said. Mallarmé himself says of writing: "An ancient and very vague but jealous practice, whose meaning lies in *the mystery of the heart*." It's the—in theory, infinite—space of the *loving soul*. Writing = I want to express myself, but I want to express my loving self. The movement of the Ideal Ego, reined in by the Ego-Ideal of Writing, is to go beyond egotism, less in the service of a generality (a deceptive ideology) than of a general love, for instance *to transform Eros* into *Agapé*. It seems to me that it's because underlying the Ego-Ideal that constrains Writing there's always an Ideal Ego in perpetual expansion that literature has always had something to do with Love → Pascal: "We have to please those who have humane and tender feelings." (*Pensées* II, p. 167)[9]—and ultimately, it seems to me, the writer doesn't write in order to be admired, approved of (or criticized). For my part, I don't like people saying good or bad things about me; I write to be loved: by a few, but *from a distance*.

Herbart, 58

Man / Work

2. The Ideal Ego is always the ego of a man, a subject, not of a writer; as far as he's concerned, writing should be subordinate to the manifestation of the individual being, of whom Writing is merely an appendage. Once again: "I'm worth more than what I write" → A writer such as Gide played with precisely this dialectic—this turnstile

between the Man and the Work—in a very sophisticated way: he worked tirelessly to ensure that we'd cherish him (or that we'd be interested in him) in the face of the work, in connection with the work: *Diary*, role of friends, testimonies, etc. The problem is that as soon as the *ideal ego* is written, as soon as it becomes writing, it's reified, it dries up, it loses its "value" (this is obvious in Gide's case), and the whole process has to be begun again, endlessly.

To Testify

3. The Ideal Ego, considering himself to be "greater" than the writing ("I'm worth more"), would like to be able to *testify to himself*: to his intentions, his qualities, to the fact that he's a *good guy*. He wants someone to *bear witness* for him, to do him justice, to be his guarantor, *auctor*, author; he wants to be his own *author*, he wants his writing to testify to everything that, in him, exceeds the writing. In this way, in my own case—I make a point of not using rhetorical formulae: "forgive me for speaking about myself," "I wouldn't like to appear self-obsessed," etc., reminding myself of one of Pascal's remarks (*Pensées*, II): "I am always ill at ease with such civilities as: 'I have given you a lot of trouble'; 'I am afraid I am bothering you'; 'I am afraid this is too long'—We are either persuasive or irritating."[10]—as a result, in my own case, I note with sadness that my writing is reproached for intellectualism, I'm told that it lacks instinct, warmth, reproaches directed at someone who's too muted {*feutrée*} (I'm well aware that *Feutre* {Felt} is one of the only possible rhymes with *Neutre* {Neutral}, along with *Pleutre* {Cowardly}), and I dream of a counter-Writing that would say the opposite about me, a Writing that I can feel bubbling up inside me: emotivity, sympathy, indignation, etc; my Ideal Ego doesn't fit my writing; this pains me (sometimes) and I want to reduce that discrepancy, to be rid of it by at last producing a new, *accurate* writing, one that really expresses the *whole* of me.

The Novel

4. And so the movement starts up again: the testimony I give of myself can't satisfy me unless I extend it to include others, for what can I be worth if I don't do justice to other people? Now, to create the Other, knowing how to, this is the role of the Novel. Whence the wish (and the decision, announced at the beginning of the 1978–1979 Course) to turn the Novel into a project, with the stipulation that what I'm calling Novel is not a particular historically determined genre but any work in which egotism is transcended, not in the direction of the arrogance of generality but that of *sym-pathy* with the other, sympathy that's in some sense mimetic. "Compassion": Rousseau's Philosopheme → the "Novel" as the expansion of the Ideal-Ego.

To Testify to the Other, in what sense? Where?—Broadly, it seems to me, to testify:

a. to his *"wretchedness"* (I'm using very classical words because they're very general; 'wretchedness' encapsulates both alienation and distress). For example, in Kafka's *Diaries*, a little experience that's altogether "novelistic" because, without stating it explicitly, it establishes the author's generosity: it's a fair description, there's nothing mean about it (Kafka, *Journal*, p. 16);[11]

b. to his *strength*. Kafka again: letter to Max Brod, used again in *Description of a Struggle*. A kind of epiphany (cf. last year's course):[12]

KAFKA

When I opened my eyes after an afternoon sleep . . . I heard my mother calling down from the balcony in a natural tone: "What are you up to?" A woman answered from the garden: "I'm having my tea-time in the garden." I was amazed at the stalwart technique for living that some people have.[13]

Thus the "Novel" looks—this, at least is how it looked to me at the beginning of this Course—less like a fixed literary form than a form of writing capable of transcending writing itself, of enlarging the work to the point where it serves as the total—albeit dominated—expression of the *Ideal Ego*, of the imaginary Ego; it was indeed a *Project*, a work projected out ahead, whence the title of the Course: *The Preparation of the Novel*.

An Infinite Mechanism

From the moment you start writing (I must stress this), a mechanism of starting over, "catching up" or "upping the stakes" establishes itself between Writing and the Ideal Ego (the Imaginary Ego), that compels you to keep on writing, to keep going further, to keep projecting forward, and makes it difficult—bar some serious psychological mutation—to stop, whether by scuppering everything or converting to *Wou-Wei*. This "upping of the stakes" can be described in the following way: (1) Love me because I'm worth more than what I appear to be worth: just look at my writing. (2) Love me because I'm worth more than what I write: just look at my new work, my future work → The Ego-Ideal and the Ideal Ego regulate each other: when the Ideal Ego, wanting to say Everything, to express Everything in a burst of love, finds itself hampered by some obstacle (this is a major cause of writing aphasia), the Ego-Ideal intervenes and imposes a viable Form: writing ≠ when the Ego-Ideal goes too far, leaving the writing subject with the feeling that he could say more, that he could speak better of himself, the Ideal Ego starts up again, it reanimates the writing process. This is how Writing works.

> Sartre
> Morin, p. 319

1. I've outlined this mechanism using psychoanalytic notions. But I can also describe it, I think in a more striking fashion (I'm talking about the mechanism, not the terms used) in Sartrean terms. For Sartre, once you're dead, you only exist through the other (if that: *exist* is already the wrong word). The Other, for Sartre, is whatever looks at you objectively, being forever ignorant of your Subjectivity, that is to say your freedom → *Writing* isn't *wise* (as I said at the beginning), because it involves subjecting yourself entirely, completely to the Other's gaze (= reading) (To Write = Ego-Ideal, Symbolic, Language); when I write, once my writing is finished, my subjectivity is objectively determined by the Other; he denies my freedom: he puts me in the position of someone who's Dead. Now, someone who writes evidently finds the position that writing inevitably puts him in difficult to accept, or at least to accept once and for all: he stands by the monument momentarily, because the monument is flattering, but since it also embalms, the writer works to dismantle it; with the work written, and its writer dead, the writer still wants to affirm a supplement of subjectivity, of freedom; *he wants to live again*: this is the book he wants to write. But the work he then goes on to write solidifies in turn and so it goes on until actual, bodily death. It's for this reason that, contrary to all wisdom, someone decides to write and to keep on writing; it's for this reason that there are so few, really so very few, writers who've scuppered themselves.

2. On the basis of this analysis—of this proposition for an analysis—we can intimate a—very tentative—typology of writers (from the past):

a. Writers whose *Will for a Work* includes, incorporates the protensive workings of the Ideal Ego and who therefore keep on writing because they want to do this ego justice, following the schema I've described: exemplarily, Rousseau, Chateaubriand (clearly, there's a tendency toward Diaries, Confessions, Correspondence). This covers a whole range of intensities: Flaubert and Proust can be said to be writers who haven't broken with the Ideal Ego, who haven't mutilated it, but who instead have dialectized it through a great novelistic writing.

Mondor, I, 20

Livre à venir

Lautréamont, Seuil, 5

b. Writers who've come to terms with the death of the Ideal Ego, of the individual, of the "Mr.," in the writer they want to be, who've come to terms with the fact that the work is Dead, a Monument. The prototype would be Mallarmé (though, rather than death, he says Nothingness; see the role that Hegel plays in his thinking). Mallarmé to Camille Mauclair, who'd inquired about his origins (in other words, about his individual Ego): "I'll say nothing, for there's nothing worth saying. I only exist (and, even then, so little) on the page. Preferably one that's still blank."[14] Today, the pure figure of this kind of writer would be Blanchot: "Each time the artist is preferred to the work, this preference, this exaltation of genius signifies a degradation of art, a decline in its power, the search for compensatory dreams."[15] → I admire this but think it sticks too rigidly to the opposition personal / impersonal → There's a dialectic inherent to literature (with, I think, future potential) that makes it possible for the subject himself to be presented as a work of art; art can be involved in the very making of the individual; there's less of a conflict between the man and the work if he makes himself into a work.

c. We could also imagine outlining a historical typology of different types of writing corresponding to different types of *I*, pronoun of the Imaginary (close, as we saw, to the Ideal Ego):

1. The *I* is detestable → Classics
2. The *I* is adorable → Romantics
3. The *I* is outmoded → "Moderns"
4. I'm imagining a "Modern Classic" → the *I* is unspecified, dodged

In this Book-Course, or Play-[Course], there's the end of my Prologue: I've tried to *ground* the preparation of the Work—which I want to discuss—in the Desire to Write. I now need to say a word, here, about the *method of exposition* I shall adopt. So, like the lead actor in the Comedies of antiquity, I'll stop now, I'll step in front of the curtain, which is about to be raised, and perform what was once called the *Parabase*.

Parabase, Method, Narrative

[16] This year, I want to think about the very strange "mental thing" (*cosa mentale*) that makes one man in a million, if not a billion, start desperately wanting to write that real thing that we call—or used to call—a work.

This Course comes out of a general interest—which I've already written about apropos of music, and of painting—in the *Amateur*, in the practices and values of the Amateur.

Amateur = someone who *simulates* the Artist (on occasion, the artist would do well to simulate the Amateur).

Method

Simulation

Method? The one I set out at the beginning of last year's course: *Simulation*; I'm simulating someone who wants to write a work.[17] I'm not methodological; if I were to present my methodology I suppose there'd have to be a whole chapter on Simulation since, as a method, it exists in the experimental sciences as a way of conducting research: you build a device, you provoke causes in order to produce effects, in order to study the relationship between the two (example: little artificial basins, storm simulators) → the object produced by and for the Simulation: a *maquette* (*machietta*), a little stain, sketch; there would be some philosophizing to do around the notion of the work, of certain works as *marks* (*macula*) to be made out, cf. the mark on Leonardo da Vinci's wall[18] (≠ *tâche* {task}: *taxare* "piece work to be completed within a given time frame," whereas *tache* {stain, mark} > *tèche* (Middle Ages) "distinctive mark," very complicated etymology: gothic—but I only like Latin, southern Indo-European etymologies (no idea why). Note that:

1. Example and Metaphor

In the order of epistemology, there are demonstrative forms that have an affinity with the Maquette, that is to say, with the Simulation of an artificial object for the purposes of reflection, analytical manipulation:

a. The example. For example, the grammar example (or the linguistic example, since transformational linguistics makes use of examples) is a Maquette of a Sentence, from which we infer or illustrate a "rule."

b. The illuminating metaphor. For example, when Diderot describes the stocking-making machine (in the *Encyclopaedia*), he turns it into a metaphor, that is to say, into the maquette of reasoning (the tangible face of the device).

DIDEROT

The stocking-making loom is one of the most complicated and rational machines there is. It can be regarded as a single and unique reasoning of which the fabrication of the piece of work is the conclusion; so great a dependence reigns among its parts that to remove a single one, or to alter the form of those considered the least important, would damage the entire mechanism. . . . Those who are endowed with enough genius, not to invent such things, but to understand them, are astonished to see the almost infinite number of springs from which the machine is composed and their great many different and extraordinary movements. When we see a stocking being knitted, we admire the flexibility and dexterity of the laborer's hands—despite only being able to make one stocking at a time. What it is then to see a machine that can do hundreds of stitches at once; that is, that can perform in a single instant all the different movements that it would take the hands many hours to accomplish. All those little springs pulling the silk thread then letting it go only to pick it up again in order to thread it through another one in an inexplicable fashion—and all that happening without the laborer who works the machine understanding anything about it, knowing anything about it, and not even thinking about it. In this respect it can be compared to the most excellent machine that God ever made, etc.[19]

(What an admirable metaphor—maquette—for *expressing* the psyche: a great many elements; varied and extraordinary movements. Pulling → letting go. Threading the thread in an inexplicable fashion. Unconsciousness of the subject.)

2. *Mise en abyme* and Maquette

In the order of literature, of the text, the work itself, the product that gets sacralized and consecrated as the *work* can sometimes be explicitly presented as a *simulation of itself*: works that stage their own fabrication → Distinguish between *the "mise-en-abyme" structure ≠ the maquette work*.

a. "Mise-en-abyme" structure: a work within a work, like a painting within a painting (Watteau's *Picture Gallery*). Examples: *Paludes* (the title of 1 reappears in 2),[20] the novel Roquentin is working on in *Nausea*,[21] the reference to painting (heraldic, "*abyme*")[22] clearly suggests that what's at issue is a flat, static relationship, the privileged form of a failed return (*Paludes* doesn't get written: in the end, only the *Paludes* of *Paludes* gets written).

b. The work-as-maquette presents itself as its own experimentation; it stages a production, or at any rate a strategy to facilitate actual production (rather than just the vague compulsion to produce); for example, Dante's *Vita Nova*: the narrative drives the poem (although it is actually supposed to have been written after the fact), and the poem is retroactively crowned with the rhetorical exposition of its composition (production). Or Gide again: *The Counterfeiters*+*The Journal of the Counterfeiters*; or Poe, "The Raven" and its productive commentary (written after the fact, which means it was rigged). A very sophisticated case: *In Search of Lost Time*: virtually, both a work "*en abyme*" (the novel that the narrator wants to write, whose failure he's documenting (the failure of wanting-to-write))+work-as-maquette, because the novel in question turns out to be *In Search of Lost Time* itself. As if the maquette were dissolving, fading into the background to make space for all that it draws in and attracts: a world (or a triple world: of love, of worldliness, and of art). There's an instability, an unstable slippage between the *mise-en-abyme* and the *maquette*—the issue being production (action). Example, a porn film: on the screen, a scene: the movie theater in which a porn film is being screened = "*mise-en-abyme*"; no movement other than what's happening on the screen in the film → the spectators in the movie theater in the film begin to reproduce the gestures of the scene they're watching → "maquette" (third degree, if the real spectators were to become erotic partners).

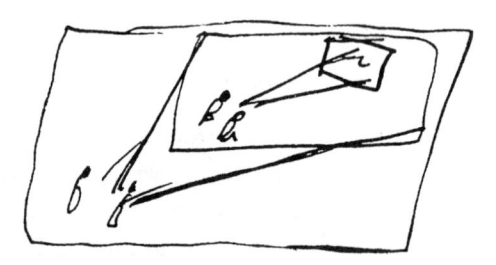

I'll leave you to complete this little dossier of "*mise-en-abyme*"-works and maquette-works.

3. Situation / Position

In the order of criticism, of literary theory, of teaching, I'm not aware of anyone resorting to simulation as a method. However, I see an advantage in it: a new combination of intellectual analysis and subjectivity as a force of Desire; to say that in my attempt to simulate the preparation of a work I'm putting myself *in the situation* of producing one is an understatement; it would be better to say: I'm putting myself *in the position*; "situation": empirical condition of producing (which isn't quite the case: I'm not going to produce a work—other than the Course itself, but my topic isn't the Preparation of the Course; one year, perhaps? ≠ "position": I'm playing a role, I'm exercising and revealing an imaginary; the waiter who brings me a drink in a café is *in the situation* of bringing me a drink, but if he thinks about his role, plays it up a bit, slips, goes flying, and still manages to hold onto his tray (see Sartre's description at the beginning of *Being and Nothingness*), he is *in position*: he's positing an imaginary (of his function) and making the most out of it (life is less dull, you have to make what you can out of the alienation of work) → I understand the simulation of the Novel in the same way: something which I, as a "professor," that is to say, associated with a *paid* profession, am undertaking *as a positioning* (and not a *situating*, which in any case could only take place in the seclusion of my study): I'm giving free rein to my imagination, I'm "responding to my nature," *the Course concerns me*—my only hope is that it also concerns you. In more general terms, simulation (the method) becomes a means *of telling stories*: it places itself at the door of the Novelistic. Montaigne: "*I am not teaching; I am narrating.*"[23] Here, the theme of Narrative makes its appearance.

V. Woolf, Seuil, 65

Narrative

This ten-week course (since the last three weeks will be given over to a seminar on an entirely different topic) will indeed be occupied with a story, a *narrative*: an intellectual narrative, with weak narrative links, one that, unfortunately, will have nothing of the *thriller* about it, since it will be the internal story of a man who wants to write (to write a work or to write, period? We shall see), a man who's deliberating the best way to realize that desire, or that will, or indeed that *vocation*: *his calling* → It's therefore a matter of a *Deliberation*, a genre once recognized by rhetoric (epidictic, juridical, deliberative: in actual fact, politics)[24] → A deliberative journey, the episodes of which will be, broadly speaking: (1) *Writing*; where, within me, does the Force, the Will to write come from? (2) The trials I must undergo in order to write the work = an initiation.

This man—my not especially heroic hero—will obviously be a composite man, a pseudonymic man, for he'll have several proper names; he'll be called, in turn, Flaubert, Kafka, Rousseau, Mallarmé, Tolstoy, Proust—and so that things aren't made too easy for him, given the *final achievement* that these names represent, he'll also be called: *me* → How can I, could I dare to include myself among those names, to draw on their authority? What, you really consider yourself a writer?—Well, yes, in a way, I do take myself to be a writer, in the same way as *I take myself in hand* in order to work, to live (advantage of "*putting oneself in position*"): anything goes (apart from evil, violence, arrogance) when it comes to *daring to live* → What's pretentious: *comparing yourself to*; but I'm not comparing myself. *I'm identifying with*: my imaginary isn't psychological, it's desirous, loving; it is, precisely, an imaginary, and not a paranoia, and what's more, it's an imaginary of labor, not of being; I'm identifying with a practice, not a Social Image, which, for that matter, isn't really all that prestigious anymore: go and ask Khomeiny, Carter, Marchais, Giscard, or the woman I buy my chickens from (I know what she thinks because she's very chatty) what they think of Kafka!

This man, whose narrative is beginning, will be all these names: them, me. But will he be *you*, or even one of you?—This isn't a rhetorical question, an invitation for you to protest, a *captatio benevolentiae* through *excusatio propter infirmitatem*[25] (in this case, the individual specificity of my project). The question, which has historical breadth, is this: whether a reflection on *wanting-to-write* can interest and be of concern to *those who don't write*. It's therefore all the uncertainty of literary transference—by means of literature—that will be set down as a foundational anxiety, one that serves the very basis of this Course: perhaps this amphitheater will gradually empty out as your curiosity or your loyalty begins to flag.

From the moment the would-be writer—for whom I'll be mapping out a specific route—leaves the space of Hope and Desire, or indeed the time of *Indecision* (some never leave it: Amiel for example),[26] as soon as the would-be writer makes the transition from *writing* to *writing something*, he finds himself confronted with painful problems: deliberations; half-made, difficult decisions; tribulations of will and of desire; doubts, despondency, trials, obstacles, obscurities → A whole *peregrination* begins; like an initiatory path: *things to overcome*. I'll attempt to define and to describe *three trials* (I said: lecture course = like a play: cf. *Turandot*[27]—trials that the would-be writer encounters on his journey:

The Three Trials

1. An abstract (mental) trial: deciding *What to write*; that is to say, *choosing*; this is the trial of the object; the *Tendency* (*Writing*, cf. *supra*)[28] must fix upon an Object, that is to say, it must discount other objects: it must *choose well*, because the object it chooses will be the would-be writer's traveling companion for some time, and to abandon it for another along the way will be a failing, a possible cause for depression.

2. A concrete, practical trial: the step-by-step management of *Writing* (the writing of the chosen object); whence the need for the writer to organize his life in accordance with the labor of writing and to overcome countless obstacles, both external and mental, on the way to achieving this; this is the trial of Time: Patience.

3. A moral trial: evaluating how the work will be judged by society, that is, the problem of how the work *fits in* with the social (the historical social), or, if the would-be writer is obliged to come to terms with what's deemed a lack of harmony (singularity, a solitude), the trial of a Schism with society.

→ Three trials, then: Doubt, Patience, Separation (Secession).

SESSION OF JANUARY 5, 1980

2. First Trial: Choice, Doubt

What does someone who wants to write fantasize about in the work to be written? What kind of work is envisaged? What is it about the work that makes him want to write it, to the extent that becomes *possible* (for everything hinges on this) for this desire to be pragmatically transformed into a concrete (and patient) labor? Put differently, what *guiding-image* will he choose to "set down" in his plan for the Work to be written?

The Content?

The first thing to be planned out would usually be the *Content* (the subject = *quaestio*, in English: topic). Content: I won't take sides on this word, which is no longer in fashion, I won't define it; I need it because it immediately points us toward a certain combination of things as *opposed* (paradigm) to something else that I'll have even greater need of: *Form* → Now, it's not clear that it's *Content* that's fantasized, that is to say planned out in accordance with Desire.

Philosophy of the Work

Many writers of the past (the "romantic" period of *writing*, the one I'm most interested in) covered themselves, so to speak, with a *philosophy*. Yet, reading the work they produced (the sum of works), one often gets the impression that their philosophies were uncreative, that they weren't the driving force behind getting the work going (it's this "getting going" that interests us). Philosophy: sincere belief, but on the ideological level an alibi; a sort of after the fact of the work; a seal of solemnity that's affixed to the work in order to blot out its statutory gratuity (the work is largely *outside-society*):

- Zola and heredity: we don't read and enjoy Zola for his philosophy of heredity.
  - Chateaubriand and religion: likewise.
  - Flaubert and Art: likewise.

Kolb, 198

• Proust? More complex. Proust seems to have anticipated my reservations, my lack of interest in self-confessed philosophies, their feeble credibility; he says that he quite deliberately refrained from setting out his philosophy of truth (the Telescoping of Time). To Jacques Rivière, 1914: "I thought it more honorable and tactful as an artist not to let it be seen, not to proclaim that I was setting out precisely in search of the Truth, nor to say what it consisted in for me. I so hate those ideological oeuvres in which the narrative is a constant betrayal of the author's intentions that I preferred to say nothing. It's only at the end of the book, when the lessons of life have been grasped, that my design will become clear."[1] → Proust, of course, conscious of his philosophy, but whether the writing of the book was contingent upon Proust setting this philosophy out before him and attempting to plan out its gradual conversion into a novel, into narrative, is another issue. → The philosophy of the work can be *concomitant* but not necessarily a *driving force* (besides, is it really this that we enjoy in Proust?)

The Themes of the Work

Besides—and this is a problem for method, or for literary theory—the criteria for designating what we consider to be the *theme* (*quaestio*) or content of the work are variable, arbitrary → There are a number of possible "themes" (contents) in any given work; for example (to run through them quickly):

1. Tolstoy, short story *Master and Man*.[2] It could be said: everything leads to the story's ethical crowning: the charity shown by Vassili, the servant: when lost in a snowstorm, he sleeps on top of his master so that he might stay warm and be saved from dying of cold (he dies anyway), but I'd be equally justified in claiming that the theme of the work is Snow, the Black Snow.

2. Proust, *In Search of Lost Time*. A great many themes can be attributed to it: (a) a noble theme: the philosophy of time (cf. *supra*);[3] (b) a dramatic theme: I want to write but can't; (c) a "naïve" theme: why not think of the whole of *In Search of Lost Time* as the shimmering, the subtle and insistent development of a simple proverb: "It's a small world!" (we're constantly "rediscovering" characters); (d) a "mythological" theme: sleep, being half-asleep or half-awake, posited as the *starting point* of the immense work, sets up a general perceptive condition—and, metonymically, a moral and metaphysical condition of the world: *decompartmentalization* →

Proustian sleep

There you have a possible *explanation* of the whole work: (a) very peculiar kind of sleep: giving rise not to a hallucinosis but a *false consciousness* (which is actually inductive of truth): unsettled, unsteady consciousness independent of the logic of the narrative syntagm and of chronology (decompartmentalization of the different stages of the Narrator's life); this is by no means the "deep" topology of Freudianism but a psychology of the expansion and the permutation of specific places (the theme of the bedrooms); moreover (very quickly), there's the key fact that sleep is connected to the mother's first kiss, that is to say to the whole affective continuum; the kiss: what enables him to get to sleep, to "rediscover" Nature (to sleep at night); and not forgetting the powerful role that soporifics played in Proust's life.

3. As a general rule, the work doesn't let us uncover its point of departure, the figure of its *impetus* = the image that the author set out before him, the image he desired, a desire that enabled him to pass from *writing* to *writing something*.

4. The question we're asking in this Course is the question of a *practitioner*: the man who wants to write, who, in concrete terms, wants to get to the *practical* stage of writing a future work. Now, the "content" (the subject matter, the *quaestio*) is probably not, or at least not initially, a *poetic category* (*poïetic*: from "Making"), it's a "Meta" category: category for the critics, the professors, the theoreticians → We could widen the scope of the question by going back to the grand Nietzschean typology: *Priest / Artist*; there's no way round it: the problems of "content," of "subject matter," are on the side of the Priest, while we who are on the side of producing ("producing the work" and not illustrating an idea, a faith) are on the side of the artist: Apollo or Dionysus, but not Socrates;[4] a *different* truth, by *different* means → To employ a Mallarméan terminology: it's a matter of passing from the *Metaphysics* to the *Physics of the book*.

The Work as Fantasized Form

Fantasy / The "Volume"

Since I keep talking about the Fantasized Work, I want to remind you of the psychoanalytic definition of *fantasy* (even if I'm using it in a somewhat metaphorical manner): "imaginary scenario where the subject is present that features the fulfillment of a desire" (Conscious = Fantasy / Unconscious: Phantasy) → When someone who wants to write (whose story I'm telling) "fantasizes" a work to be written, *where* does he take pleasure in situating himself? What's the *scenario* of his imagined action? It seems to me—for here I don't have much more than my own experience to go on—that what I fantasize is the *fabrication of an object*; in my fantasy, I'm making that object, planning the stages of its fabrication in the manner of an artisan: think of the *masterpiece*, the piece that *compagnons*[5] make for nothing, in view of a final object, envisaged in its material totality; in the manner of an artist, or a romantic artist at any rate: that object, is it the book? Yes, in a sense, but since I'll be needing to oppose that word to another written form, I'll say more generally: the *Volume*: pure surface of writing, formally structured, though not as yet by the content → At first, then, it's not a content or a theme that's fantasized and "visualized" (which isn't to say that contents and themes aren't already buzzing around in my head): it's a surface, an organized *unfolding* (*volumen*)[6]—and it's the organization of this space of writing that constitutes my scenario, my pleasure. Thus, in my opinion (or for me), what's fantasized is a form (and not a content). On this question, here are two explicit testimonies, and what's more from two of the masters, albeit relative to a time that's perhaps, or now appears to be, in the past (this question will shape our third and final trial).

Mallarmé, Scherer, 126

a. Mallarmé: dossier on the "book"[7] compiled by Jacques Scherer (we'll come back to this). "Book" planned by Mallarmé: dossier of notes, of sketches. *But*, according to that dossier, before he knew what he was going to discuss in the book he was planning, Mallarmé reflected upon the structure of his work and the abstract conditions of all literature; very few pages of the manuscript deal with what the book should say—Mallarmé, very struck by Poe's "The Raven" and "The Philosophy of Composition" (Baudelaire: *La Genèse d'un poème*), actually written after the fact but that recounts the invention of the poem from the starting point of a form and not a content.[8]

Flaubert

Préface, 62

b. *Flaubert*: somewhat different, because what he fantasized (at least at the start, at around thirty-one or thirty-two years old) wasn't a structure, a series of permutations, but a *writing*, pure stylistic action—but for him too, in the absence of any content. 1852 (thirty-one years old): "What seems beautiful to me, what I should like to write, is a book about nothing, a book dependent on nothing external, which would be held together by the internal strength of its style . . . a book which would have almost no subject, or at least in which the subject would be almost invisible, if such a thing is possible."⁹ And 1853 (thirty-two years old): "I should like to write books where there would be nothing to it but *writing* sentences (so to speak) just as, to live, one only has to breathe air. What I don't like are the stratagems of the plan, the combinations of effects, all the underhanded calculations."¹⁰

As these two examples show, "form" (depending on the particular nature of the fantasy) is an array of possible *presentations* of the volume = from the "structure" (Mallarmé) to the "grain" of writing (Flaubert)—If I dare insert myself between these two giants (but, as I said, there's nothing pretentious about *identifying with*, for identifying with is not comparing yourself to, and I am, after all—like them—defining myself, here, by my pleasure, my desire to write), in my fantasy form is neither structure nor style: rather, it's the *rhythm* according to which the volume is *divided up*, that is, form insofar as it comes down on the side of the *continuous* or the *discontinuous* → the forms that I'd have to choose between (were I to write this volume) would therefore be something like the Narrative, the Dissertation (the Treatise), Fragments (Aphorisms, Diary, Paragraphs in the Nietzschean style), etc.; those are the *types* of forms that my writing fantasy tends toward and therefore that I have to choose between; for desire doesn't necessarily recognize itself straight away; my fantasy can *hesitate*, want many forms at once, and choosing between them is the first trial—the trial I'm discussing at the moment! Insofar as the vision, the taste for, the *appetite* for a Form is what triggers the fabrication of the work—here, form is very close to *Formula*: the formula of a medicament, a construction, a magical operation; it offers a way out, it releases, frees up the would-be writer.

A Typology of the Book

Many typologies of the book—of the volume—are possible. The one that interests me is that of the forms that someone who wants to write fantasizes about. But, before outlining that fantasmatic typology (with Mallarmé's help), I want to remind you of the existence of a vast, mythical, transhistorical landscape of the book → the great mythological functions of the Work as volume.

The Ordinary Book

Those grand mythical functions—which I'll describe—stand out against an indistinct background: *books*, gregarious plural, accumulation of mercenary objects; artificial space in which books are collected together: shelves of a library, of a bookshop, books piled up, spread out (in *La Hune*, in PUF)[11] → the ordinary book: *liber communis*, *vulgaris*, the Altogether-Common-Place {*le Tout-Courant*}.

In today's society: by dint of repeating itself, multiplying itself, piling itself up, the book scarcely exists any more, even as an object (for example, the decline in bibliophilia: people who cover their books with coated paper are borderline eccentric nowadays; bookbinders have disappeared—a profession that enabled my mother to support us as best as she could during my adolescent years). General feature of the society that we prudishly call *consumer* but that's more crudely the society of *advertising* (in the broad sense: not only commercials, billboards, but also criticism, what makes things sell, or not) → Striking: in *Le Monde*, some advertisements are written in the newspaper's own style: the distinction between the article and the Advertisement is dissolving. Now, the effect of advertising is to vaporize the object in favor of its discursive counterpart: *the object is reduced to the two or three things that get said about it* → Everything becomes a language-commodity: what's sold is language; before the thing, a washing machine is first handled by the buttons on the TV that make it exist (there's a pollution through language) → The book, sacred site of language, is desacralized, flattened: books get bought, admittedly, a bit like frozen *pizzas*, but the book is no longer *solemn*. Authors themselves, carried away by this *secular Reification*, no longer seem to believe in the book: they no longer think of it as a Grand Sacred Object (I feel this about the manuscripts I get sent: most of them are a bit "slapdash"). For example, the notion of *Introit*. Who, today, would be brave or mad enough to offer the grandiose *Introit* that Rousseau gave to his *Confessions*: "I am resolved on an undertaking that has no precedent and will have no imitator. I want to show my fellow-men a man in all the truth of nature; and this man will be myself"?[12] The Mythical Functions, which I'll now say a word about, can of course survive (they're by definition transhistorical), but they're no longer revived—or authors are increasingly resistant to renewing them, to letting themselves be fertilized by them. → Here are three of these mythical functions, of these great figures of the book:

Bible

1. *The Ur-book*: the Arché-Book, the Origin-Book, for a religion, and therefore for a civilization—(a) *Ahel el Kittabi*, "the people of the Book": Bible, Gospel, Avesta, Koran → What would be interesting would be to study the fascination—or the creative irrigation—of the Bible—with respect to this question: *Ta Biblia*,[13] since it's a collection of works called "books" from different genres, written in two or three different languages, drawn from oral traditions over nine centuries → Bible: in some great literary works, the Bible (*the Book*) plays the complex role of a maquette of forms and contents as well as, more structurally, that of original abutment: the reference, the *Arché*; clearly I have Dante's work in mind (a work without an title: *Divine Comedy* was added after the fact), the one that was inspired by the Bible, in the sense that Dante endeavored to achieve the "depth of meaning of biblical writing, the polysemy of the letter,"[14] but I'm also thinking of what Marthe Robert wrote about the relationship between Kafka, the Kafkian book, and the Bible-book. Authors who've been fascinated by the Bible (outside of any religious connection): undoubtedly a great many; dossier that you can complete.—(b) In our culture, a writer who manages to conceive of, to plan an essential, prophetic work, the essence of the book, cannot but assimilate it to the Bible: Nietzsche, *Ecce Homo*, that is to say, just before he went mad, a time of Christ-like histrionics judging from his *Zarathustra*: "Within my writings my *Zarathustra* stands by itself. I have with this book given mankind the greatest gift that it has ever been given. With a voice that speaks across millennia, it is not only the most exalted book that exists, the actual book of the air of the heights . . . it is also the *profoundest*, born out of the innermost abundance of truth, an inexhaustible well into which no bucket descends without coming up filled with gold and goodness";[15] and in a letter of 1888, on *Ecce Homo*: "In it I will shed light for the first time on my *Zarathustra*, the first book of all millennia, the Bible of the future, the strongest eruption of human genius, in which the fate of mankind is grasped . . . my *Zarathustra* will be read like the Bible."[16] With respect to the Bible, Mallarmé, who spent the whole of second half of his life thinking about the Total Book, effected a shift: his Total Book was intended to be read aloud in public, with permuting the lines (and letters); the reference was therefore not the (immobile) book, but the book transformed through ritual, through theater ("The Theater is, by essence, superior");[17] for Mallarmé, then, the Ur-book is not the Bible but, so to speak: Mass.

Scherer, 43

2. *The Book-as-Guide*: unique, possibly secret book that directs the life of a subject; the classic example of this is clearly the religious book, the holy book, and so very often the *Ur-Book*, the origin-book, but not necessarily: *Imitation According to Jesus Christ* (fifteenth century, in Latin) → This would require (but all this is no more than a brief digression) an inventory of the "secular" candidates for the book-as-guide. For example:

a. Dante: Paolo and Francesca discovering their mutual love and desire for each other while reading the love-story of Guinevere and Lancelot. *Hell*, V, 155, *sq.* (second circle: lust).[18]

b. Some friend of ours heading off to Mexico because of *Under the Volcano*.[19]

c. Think of the ridicule that following a book comes in for when it's blind, mechanical: it's what *Bouvard and Pécuchet* is all about. Bouvard's and Pécuchet's idea of the book is absolute: they read a great many, and their gentle form of madness stems from immediately and literally applying whatever book they happen to be reading at the time. (The Book-as-Guide is not the only promotion of the book. Let's read Kafka: "we would be just as happy if we had no books, and as for the books that make us happy, if necessary we could write them ourselves. On the other hand, we do need the books that affect us like some affliction that grieves us deeply, like the death of someone we loved more than ourselves, like being banished into forests far from everyone, like a suicide. A book must be an axe for the frozen sea inside us.")[20]

d. Last, a mention of *The Book-as-Key*: the book that appears to unlock the understanding of a country, an era, an author. Mallarmé: "the work, *par excellence*." For him, in Shakespeare: *Hamlet*. For the whole of Italian literature: *The Divine Comedy* (book of the origin). We don't have a book like this in French literature. For the ancient Greeks: *Iliad* and *Odyssey*. For Spain: *Don Quixote* (Severo Sarduy has pointed out that this is a bit of a shame: it would've been more amusing had it been *La Celestina*: a country can "choose the wrong book").

All this—which is why I've said something about it—marks out, for the would-be writer, *the space of the book my gaze is directed toward*. I'm convinced that there always is such a book (cf. *Supra* on Imitation), in most cases it's kept very secret; critics don't uncover it because, as a general rule, they're preoccupied with *influence*, whereas what we're dealing with is the fantasmatic imposition of a matrix, a formula → Perhaps I have one of my own, or at least—and here I go back to my original point—I have several of them in mind and I have to, I shall have to chose between them.

The Anti-Book

(And not forgetting, of course, the Contradictory: this subjection to the Master-Book, to the book as Master, can be countered by Rebelling against the book: Lautréamont, Artaud; the impossible task, the acrobatic feat that this requires is to say No to the book by means of the book; a form of bad faith that makes me a little uneasy, that only Rimbaud knew how to avoid by scuppering all the books inside him once and for all *without even explaining why*—for to do so would have been to revive the book under the pretence of negating it).

Two Fantasized Forms: The Book / The Album

What you have there are fantasies of civilization, so to speak, the book being a collective myth: origin, guide, or reflection (meaning) → Now we need to go back to the more modest, the more pragmatic forms: which form do I desire for the work that I want to set about writing? I said that as far as I was concerned this form situated itself in relation to the continuousness / discontinuousness of discourse. Here I encounter an opposition between two types of work advanced by Mallarmé (this is a theory and not simply an empirical classification): (1) *The Book*: "architectural and premeditated," "a book that really would be a book," or "*the Book*, persuaded when all's said and done there is only one, attempted unwittingly by whoever has written." (2) *The Album*: "an anthology of chance inspirations, however marvelous."[21] I'll go back over those two types, one after the other:

1. The Book

So, "architectural and premeditated."

a. Mallarmé: The Total Book

Mallarmé (1842–1898): apart from *Le Coup de dés*, Mallarmé only produced "Albums" → Idea of *Book*, then, for him: like a fantasy of contrast. *Total book*: idea around 1866; in roughly 1867,

[margin: Scherer, XV, 18]

[margin: Total Book]

[margin: Scherer, XII, 150]

182   THE WORK AS WILL

Scherer 22, 23

thinks of a work of synthesis (*Herodiade*, opening + four prose poems on Nothingness):[22] cf., he'd say, the great work of the alchemists. But it isn't the total book: Mallarmé would have begun working on it in around 1873; reflects on it between 1873 and 1885; then the pace of work slows down; picks up again in 1892–1893. In 1894: retirement: devotes his mornings to it → What remains is a manuscript of two hundred pages: not *the Book* but thoughts on the Book; as I said, we don't know very much about the content, only the ritual: public readings, an admission fee (a whole financial plan of theater and publishing), permutable verses or lines, the combinations varying with each performance, multiplying the dissemination of the book → Features of this total book: objective (impersonal), not circumstantial (= the totality of living things, the sum of essences), organized in accordance with a structure (≠ album) → Hence this paradoxical, specifically Mallarméan position: the *book* is metaphysical (it's the "hyperbole" of all excellent books), it amounts to an explosion of the mind ("There is no explosion but a book"), it's a *pure* work (almost bordering on madness) and at the same time it's a disseminating device (through the performances and the system of differing permutations, "I sow, so to speak, this entire double volume here and there ten times")—but, paradox, that metaphysics is formed entirely of a *Physics of the Book* → which, for that matter, is what we ought to be calling this reflection on the fantasized form: a physics of the book → This Mallarméan physics is revolutionary; to be sure, it establishes the book as a pure Object, but an object that's limitless; it's an infinite mechanism, a renewable Ritual: "A book neither begins nor ends: at most, it pretends to."[23]

Seuil, 26

Scherer, 73

→ Mallarmé's *Total Book*: limit-experience, for the Book is "empty" (in the state we know it, but there was surely an infinite movement of *disappointment*: twenty-five years spent on just the Form, pure fantasy) and yet at the same time very concrete: the price of seats, calculating the sale price of the book, etc. Cf. "madmen" who "rave" and have very powerful *egos*, are competent travelers, know how to manage their accounts, etc. Cf. *infra*[24] on the fantasy as blockage.

24

→ On this side of that limit-experience, it seems to me that two forms of the *Total Book* can be desired (let's stop saying "fantasized," we want to give them a chance of coming to something):

183   **SESSION OF JANUARY 5, 1980**

The Sum-Total Life	b. The Sum-Total Book

Desire, at a given stage of your life (I'm not specifying which: not necessarily old age), for a book that you'll put *Everything* in: the *Whole* of your life, your sufferings, your joys, and therefore, of course, the *whole* of your world and perhaps the *whole* of the world → Sum of Knowledge: encyclopedia transcended by a *meaning* given to the world and to your own work, that is to say, in my view, by a writing; this *meaning* is like the *color* of the book—for all knowledge is colored (all discourse is connoted); it can be, for example:

Drive
Préface, 263

1. The drive for knowledge (there's a satisfaction—a *jouissance*—of knowledge) → Flaubert: for each novel "I have to learn many things of which I'm ignorant";[25] for example, for *Salammbo*, a vast archaeological, historical knowledge; frantic, manic, crazed (never mind the aesthetic pretext) → I'm dwelling on this, I mean: I'm isolating this urge because at times I experience it very powerfully. The desire to immerse myself in a new or only imperfectly mastered science (for example, the desire to study semantics or etymology in depth); that desire is initially in conflict with writing; hence the next phase: the desire to resolve the contradiction and to amalgamate knowledge and writing, that is to say, to write a "novel" (bearing in mind the *atypical* meaning that this word has for me),[26] which would require learning many things about the world and, in some sense, setting about "learning" the world (Audrey: viral hepatitis and jaundice)[27]—The eponymous hero of this drive: Flaubert, toward the end of his life, adopts quite a subtle strategy with respect to this desire: he accepts it on a practical level (reads hundreds of books) but distances himself from it by way of an elaborate mechanism of derision = *Bouvard and Pécuchet*.

Chateaubriand

2. A different color: a total *Ego* takes possession of all the history he's lived through: *Memoirs from Beyond the Grave*; project validated by the fact that Chateaubriand had known two worlds, the ancient and the modern, one on either side of the Revolution, and had played his two roles to the full: politician (actor and witness) and writer (a Malraux with a bit more of the genius, a Malraux if he'd had style) → *Memoirs from Beyond the Grave*: a sum-total but, thanks to Chateaubriand's talent, a sum-total of concrete objects: historical figures, places, clothes, symbolic objects (a soldier's musket, a traveler's stick, a pilgrim's staff), etc.—I refer you to the admirable testamentary preface, which I don't have time to read out.

Testamentary Preface

Protensive and Apocalyptic

Gardair, 46

3. *A different color:* the total book presents the sum of knowledge as opening onto a new world; example: Rabelais; what could be called a *protensive* encyclopedia, tending toward the future (as Diderot's collective *Encyclopaedia* would at a later date): progressive book. Symmetrically: the sum-total can be apocalyptic. End of history and the theological prophesy of a palingenesis of humanity: Dante = rhetorical, poetic, moral, political, scientific, theological knowledge.—Apocalypse of the bourgeoisie, with no protensivity: Balzac.

4. *And today?* And today? It would appear that the sum-total of all knowledge—a masterable, scriptable sum-total—is impossible: (a) because of the expansion and multiplication of knowledge; (b) because epistemology has changed: we now have *sciences—Science* in the singular no longer exists; (c) knowledge is immediately divided, ideologically tainted (an end to universality) → Which is perhaps why the last encyclopedic project was a *Farce* (*Bouvard and Pécuchet*).—Proust? In one sense: sum-total of psychological knowledge (with its amorous, worldly, and aesthetic aspects); in one sense, it's a sum-total book, but in a superior sense it's essentially an *initiatory book*, the story of an initiation—which is different, for it's a matter of a knowledge of the soul.

c. The Pure Book

Scherer, XVI

These sum-totals are massive (thick books, numerous volumes): it's their status to be *accumulations*. At the opposite extreme from the total book, there's the possibility of the short, dense, pure, essential book: the little book, the Pure book or, as Mallarmé says (1869): alongside the grand project, an idea for a "strange little book, very mysterious, rather in the manner of the early Fathers <the religious book still serves as the matrix>, very distilled and concise."[28] I'll give, as an example of the Pure Book, one that's to my liking: Valéry's *Monsieur Teste*, a dense book, in a sense "total" in that it elliptically summons up the very experience of total consciousness.

So there you have a few reflections on—or "glimpses" of—the first fantasized form of the "volume": *the Book*, "architectural and premeditated"; a *Book* that's either infinite (in its permutations: Mallarmé's Total Book), summative (Sum-Total-Book: Dante), or compact and essentializing (*Monsieur Teste*).

2. The Album

The antagonistic, or paradigmatic form—giving rise to the necessity of choice—is the *Album* → opposed to the *Book* as a "structure founded on the nature of things."[29] Album: used by Mallarmé and strongly condemned by him: "That condemnatory word"[30] → Two elements, two criteria make the Album:

Circumstance

Scherer, 18

1. The circumstantial. Album = inventory of circumstances. (2) The discontinuous. Either a thread running *from day to day* (all forms of Diary), or an anthological dispersion of pieces (poetry collection) → Absence of structure: artificial grouping of elements whereby the sequence, the presence or absence of a given element, is arbitrary → A *page of an album* can be moved or added at random; procedure absolutely contrary to the Book: articles, occasionally sonnets = "to send a visiting card to the living"[31] (unfortunately that's just how it is: to write a preface for someone = to slip your visiting card into someone else's book) → Type of Album: Mallarmé's *Divagations*: "A book just the way I don't like them, scattered and with no architecture"; same defect as journalism: "Decidedly, no one escapes journalism"[32] → Indeed, today everything draws us into it, forces us into it.

Rhapsodic

For Mallarmé, Album: very pejorative (hence his fantasmatic conception of the Book; or rather: the ambition of the Book compelled him to retroactively discredit the Album; or again: the stakes aren't the same, it's not the same philosophical option, cf. *infra*)[33] → Of course, it's possible to feel the other way and to exalt the Album as the equal of the Book: then you would have the ardent—and often revolutionary—defense of the *Rhapsodic* (Idea of the *Stitched, Tacked together, Patch-work*); Poe, translated by Baudelaire "a magnificent and multicolored procession of disorganized and rapsodic thoughts," and Baudelaire: "the word *Rapsodic* <*Rhapsodic*>, which is such a good definition of a train of thought suggested and ordered by the external world and the chance of circumstance."[34] → There are great creators on the side of the album: Schumann, for example → The Album doesn't imply a lesser thinking. Album: perhaps the representation of the world as *inessential*.

Baudelaire, 57

Diary / Structure / Method

This is why "Fragments" aren't necessarily on the side of the Album; the notion of the "fragment" can easily be specious → Last year, a member of the audience pointed out to me, quite rightly, that *In Search of Lost Time* is actually an interweaving of fragments. There is an *architecture* (in the musical sense) however, one that isn't of the order of a plan but rather of a return, a *marcottage*: a return *foreseen* by Proust ("the book, architectural and *premeditated*"). Nietzsche: writing in fragments (his paragraphs), and yet (see Deleuze),[35] complex superimposition of constructions → In actual fact (let's examine the fantasy, since that's what we're dealing with), the emotional response it provokes (refusal, attraction, intolerance) is directed at the *ongoing* mode: a circumstantial, chronological, unstructured *continuation*, realized eidetically in the *Diary*, can present problems as a *creation* (it can have other functions); Proust disapproves of the *Diary* for this reason (have we marveled enough at the fact he didn't keep one?); to his friend Guiche (whom we'll see a beautiful photograph of in the seminar):[36] "Above all, don't bother replying to me. Another letter, and it would mark the beginning of an *ongoing* correspondence, an awful thing, worse only than 'writing in one's diary day after day.'"[37] (Proust: vast, but not *sustained* correspondence: "scattered" interlocution, Madame Straus to her concierges). Here, on this subtle problem of the Fragment and the Album, we could draw on Cage's distinction between *structure* and *method* apropos of Schönberg: (a) *Method*: Schönberg would worry about the movement from one sound to another. "That's not a question of structure, but what I call method. Method consists in taking one step after the other, the right then the left. You can walk like that with twelve tones, can't you? Or even with counterpoint. Schönberg's course was essentially methodological."[38] In this sense, the Diary is a matter of method: it moves from one day to another, as from one sound to another. (b) *Structure*, in Schönberg = the division of the work into parts. "When one makes use of tonality, the structure depends on the cadence, because it's only the cadence that enables us to delimit the parts of a musical work."[39] Right: the structure isn't the plan, it's the tonality (a single system, whose unity forces itself upon us *at the end*) → Album: atonal, *without cadence* ≠ Book: there is a *cadence* (think of the books referred to: *The Divine Comedy*, *In Search of Lost Time*, *Monsieur Teste*).

Clermont-Tonnerre, 21

Cage, 28, 66

Speech / Writing

Journal, 30–31

Whenever the Album—and especially the Diary—is met with suspicion, this suspicion (I'll say, for me: this *unease*) actually has to do with *Speech* (≠ *Writing*).—The major issue with Speech: its *value* is precarious; it loses its value in the very process of actualization; the regime of Speech = deflation ≠ Writing = probably what checks the exhausting hemorrhage of the imaginary (there are downsides to this "cure" as I keep pointing out: writing is *hard*, difficult) → Now, if the basis of the Album is the *notation* (as in the case of the *Diary*), then as an *intermediary* between Speech and the Writing it can easily disappoint: the notation is *already* writing yet still *speech* → Kafka speaks of the notation whose "worthlessness [is] recognized too late"[40] (disappointment typical of speech), and Mallarmé describes this disappointing process, this deflation admirably: 'or some other blather that becomes so whenever you elaborate it <in the writing of the Album, of the *Diary*>, but is persuasive, dreamy, and true when you mutter it to yourself."[41] (Speech: that very short-lived inner moment when it still has a *value*) → Of course, all is not lost: a dialectic is possible; Kafka again: "When I say something, this thing immediately and definitively loses its importance <the curse of speech>. When I write it down, it also loses it, but sometimes gains another importance."[42] The chance, the vagaries, the miracle of writing: but it's by no means guaranteed ("sometimes").

Scherer, 124

Journal, 278

SESSION OF JANUARY 12, 1980

The Stakes

Everything, up until this point, has hinged on the *Forms* of book. It's from among these Forms that I'll have to choose the work I want to write. However, above "content" (which hasn't been dealt with), something other than Form is involved or, if you will, something of the order of ideology comes spiraling back, in the place occupied by content but at another level: the *responsibility* of the form; *Book* or *Album*, each form has its stakes and ultimately it's the stakes that you're having to chose between; all the high drama of the choice of Form really does constitute a *trial* (the first), and a solemn one, for it has to do with *what I believe*.

    1. In its most elevated conception (Dante, Mallarmé, Proust), *The Book* is a representation of the universe; the book is homologous to the world. To want the "architectural and premeditated" Book is to conceive of and to want *One* universe, one that's structured, hierarchically ordered → Dante = to represent the totality of reality and history from the perspective of Transcendence. Mallarmé: "My work <in the masculine = the Total Book {*le Livre Total*}> is so well prepared and ordered, representing the universe as best it can, that I couldn't have removed anything from it without damaging some of my layers of impressions.'[1]

    2. In its way, *The Album* represents the opposite: a universe that is not-one, not-ordered, scattered, a pure interweaving of contingences, with no transcendence → You can:

    a. either reject that dispersion, and for that very reason be averse to the Album, to the Diary. For the Album is of the order of "Just as it is," "As it comes" and comes down to believing in the absolute contingency of the world. Tolstoy, 1851: "For a long time I was tormented by the fact that I had no heartfelt thought or feeling to determine the whole direction of my life—I took everything *just as it is*, as it comes."[2] And Mallarmé: occult traditions, powerful influence on him; they've always taught that any fragmentation of totality is a betrayal and a sin;

Gardair, 46

Scherer, 23

Préface, XV

Scherer, 148

Deleuze, 26

Cage, 45

b. or go along with the glory of this scattering, this shimmering, and reject the myth of depth as opposed to surface—Nietzsche (of course): "It is necessary to disperse the universe, to lose respect for the whole"[3]—and say, with Cage: "In any case, the whole will make a disorganization."[4] You can experience the appeal of the *rhapsodic* as the appeal of a truth about the world.

In short, you can't chose the form of the work (and so can't write) without deciding upon your own personal philosophy → The idea of the Book implies a Monist philosophy (structure, hierarchy, ratio, science, faith, history); the Idea of the Album implies a pluralist, relativist, skeptical, Taoist philosophy, etc., → "What do I believe in?" Wanting to write is to be suddenly and violently confronted with that question from the outset, and that sudden violence is a trial you have to overcome!

Dialectic of the Book and the Album

You're probably thinking that this opposition, this Book / Album alternative, is a little rigid, a little forced; I've expressed it as I've been experiencing it, in keeping with the methodological convention of the Course. But that opposition can be relaxed, generalized, that is to say, it can be thought out not at the level of someone who writes but at the level the history, the genesis of works. And there it will emerge that if there's a conflict between the Book and the Album, ultimately it's the Album that's the stronger of the two, for the Album is *what remains*:

Pensées, I, 10

a. A mass of notes, of unconnected thoughts, form an Album; but that mass can be collected together with the Book in view; the future of the Album, then, is the Book; but the author can die in the process: what remains is the Album, and, through its virtual design, that Album is already the Book; you'll have recognized Pascal's *Pensées* → It is indeed a matter of a *Book*: *Apology* (for the Christian religion), guided representation of Man, transcendence, hierarchy, "architecture" (unknown to us: disputes over Pascal's plan)[5] and "premeditation," yet at the same time it is indeed a matter of an Album. Florin Périer, Pascal's brother-in-law: "What was found among his papers ... amounts to scarcely more than a mass of unconnected thoughts about a large-scale work he was musing over, thoughts he would produce in the snatches of free time between other occupations or over conversations with friends."[6] → The Album vanquished the Book: Death vanquished it.

b. At the other end of the time-scale, the completed Book becomes an Album again: the future of the Book is the Album, just as the ruin is the future of the monument → Valéry: "It is strange how the passage of time turns every work—and so every man—into fragments. Nothing whole survives—just as a recollection is never anything more than debris, and only becomes sharper through false memories."[7] Indeed, the *Book* is destined to become debris, an erratic ruin; it's like a sugar cube dissolving in water: some bits sink, others remain upright, erect, crystalline, pure, and brilliant. This is what's called a *karst* relief (in geography).[8]

[sidenote: Valéry, Pléiade, 34]

What remains of the Book is the *quotation* (in the very broad sense): the fragment, the remainder that is *transported* elsewhere. For *The Divine Comedy*, it's: "Abandon all hope ye who enter here," etc.—The ruin isn't actually on the side of Death: as a Ruin, it's living, it's consumed as such, aesthetically constituted, germinative → We are constantly creating ruins (through the activity of remembrance, see Valéry) and feeding off them; in order to feed our imagination, our thinking. What lives in us of the book is the Album: the Album is the *germen*; the Book, however grandiose, is merely the *soma*.[9]

A sort of drive compels us to take the Book apart, to make it into a piece of lace. Absurd traces of this drive can be seen every day: (a) July 8, 1979, on the number 21 bus, crowded, Sunday evening, around 9 pm, next to me, an imperturbable man of around forty, armed with a ruler and a black Biro, underlining *almost every single sentence* in a book (I didn't get to see which one). (b) Chateaubriand's portrait of Joubert: "As he read, he would tear out the pages of the books he disliked, thereby creating a personal library composed of works with the cores removed, contained within oversized covers."

Thus exit (*exeunt*) the Book and the Album, the one constantly referring us back to the other—yet suspended before me, like the two options of a difficult decision.

Indecision and Necessity

The practice of writing is constitutively shot through with *hesitations* (so let's broaden and move beyond the hesitation between

Necessity

Kolb, 163

Book / Album). We call the miraculous absence of indecision by a loaded name: Inspiration—and I'd like to say a word about this, because it falls within the first trial (in truth, co-extensive to the whole labor of writing). For the record, let's recall the sites of indecision:

Indecisions

1. *Between general "forms"*: Book / Album, or, as in Proust's case, Novel / Essay. 1908, to the Countess of Noailles: "I should like, although I'm very ill, to write a study on Sainte-Beuve. The idea has taken shape in my mind in two different ways between which I must choose <either an essay → Fragments of *Against Sainte-Beuve* or a novel → *In Search of Lost Time*>; but I have neither the will-power nor the clear-sightedness to do so."[10]

2. For the record: *between "words"* → the "pangs of style."[11] I say *for the record* because this isn't our topic for this year; perhaps, probably—next year.

3. Between notations: What *has to be noted down* (this takes us back to last year's course)?[12] Why note down this and not that? What is the *noteworthy*, the *notandum*?—We usually make a note of something because we see a meaning (that, at the same time, we don't want to give away), or indeed because it comes to us in the form of a *sentence* (but what motivates a sentence?). But also, sometimes, and this is hesitation in the strict sense, something is just purely, gratuitously, inexplicably, enigmatically noteworthy: for example, waiting for the number 48 bus, Place Saint-Germain, I see a couple go by, the young woman is wearing incredibly high high heels; she manages, nevertheless, despite wobbling quite a bit; I wonder: how can women walk like that? In one sense, not interesting at all, but at the same time calls for notation, for this is "life" in all its tenuousness.

4. Last but not least, on the question of a novel (or a film): *why this story and not another?* I feel this very keenly when I look at the majority of contemporary novels and films, even the good ones; a depressing feeling: it's "good," but I don't see why it was *necessary* to tell that story, to have chosen that as the object of a tremendous labor of fabrication → In logical terms: the world presents me with "terms" linked together by the relation of indifference or irrelevance: *Vel . . . vel*; but, as a creation, for me the work has to assert the relation *Aut . . . aut*, exclusive disjunction, that of *Reality*. For the story to be necessary in my eyes, it has to have an

allegorical density: presence of a palimpsest, of *another meaning*, even if we're not sure which one.

No Necessity?

Every writing practice, therefore, is grounded in a generalized indecision around values → *Indecision* doesn't mean that you're not happy with what you write or with what you're planning to write; it means, literally, *you're not sure*: there are no reliable criteria that would enable you to determine whether it's good or bad; for example, Kafka rereading his Diaries: "I have found neither that what I have written so far is especially valuable nor that it must be thrown away."[13] Once again, it's Kafka who sees it and says it: "'It's the fire I warm myself by this weary winter.' Metaphors are one among many things that make me despair of literature. The literary creation lacks independence, its dependence on the maid who tends the fire, on the cat warming itself by the stove, even on the poor old man warming himself up. All these are independent activities ruled by their own laws; only literature is helpless, cannot live in itself, is a joke and a despair."[14] This lack of independence, this lack of any possibility of *self-assurance*, comes from the fact that literature is language, and is pure language, participating fully in the status of language, *order without proof*; out at sea with no points of reference; Pascal: "Language is the same in all cases. We need a fixed point in order to judge it. The harbor decides for those who are on a ship. But where will we find a harbor in morals?"[15] For me, language = generalized morality. This absence of *points of reference* = constitutive lack of *Necessity*; where's the Necessity in telling this story rather than that one, in retaining this word over that one, in planning an Album and not a Book? On the one hand, there's no *Necessity* but, on the other, in the writer, in someone who reads or who wants to write, there's an invincible demand that what gets written should be grounded in necessity, should be *guaranteed (auctor)*.

After-the-Fact

Nevertheless, as readers of certain works, we experience the certainty of their necessity; there's no way, so we think, that the author could have hesitated, it must have forced itself upon him; it was *necessary* that that particular story and not some other should have been told, that *that* word should have been chosen, etc. → This *self-evidence of*

Necessity: even clearer in music than in literature; certain airs, certain melodies (for instance *Carmen* or the *Ode to Joy*) are so pleasing to the ear, so "welcome" it's as if they were created not by the Author but by Nature; *it could not have been otherwise*: it was Necessary → Obviously, in the case of the consumer—of the reader—Necessity comes *after-the-fact*; Pascal provides a good description of this illusion, of this *after-the-fact*, apropos of the Saints:

PASCAL, *PENSÉES*, II

What spoils us in comparing what once happened in the Church with what we see there now is that we usually regard Saint Athanasius, Saint Theresa, and the others as crowned with glory and their judges as black like demons. Now that time has cleared things up, it does so appear. But at the time when he was being persecuted, this great saint was a man called Athanasius and Saint Theresa a mad woman. Elias was a man like us, subject to the same passions as we are, said Saint Peter, to disabuse Christians of the false idea that makes us reject the example of the saints as disproportionate to our state. They were saints, we say; they are not like us. What actually happened then? Saint Athanasius was a man called Athanasius, accused of several crimes, condemned by such and such a council for such and such a crime. All the bishops agreed, and finally the Pope. What did they say to those dissenting? That they were disturbing the peace, causing a schism, etc.[16]

Someone who writes: a Saint before he's been consecrated a Saint; *he doesn't know* where the Necessity is.

A few criteria

Whence the search for "criteria" for your own personal use—criteria that are often vague: hesitant, ultimately challengeable adjuncts to that impossible sense of Necessity → For example:

Finishability

At a certain point, the work imposes the sense that it's finished: impossibility of adding anything to it, of carrying on (not the same thing as lassitude); that goes without saying for the architectural Book: to structure a work is to foresee that it will be finished at a certain point: it's to substitute an ending imposed by lassitude or death for one by logic (cf. the paradox of the sentence, which is both structured and virtually interminable; cf. *In Search of Lost Time*). But what about the unstructured Album? It's possible to have the (vague and powerful) "feeling" that it's done, that *that no more is required* (that feeling probably comes from an aesthetic *culture*; obvious in the case of the Painting that has been declared finished ≠ anxiety and failure of painters who don't manage to finish, thinking it isn't finished → What destroys the creator, sterilizes him = "But it's not finished").

Need

Someone who writes can project his feeling onto that of the potential reader and write as if at least *one* reader *needed* this text. The *Necessity* of a work would be that it *responds* (in the mathematical sense of "correspondence") to a reader's need, somewhere in the world → Proof *a contrario*: "to reject" a text, a book, a manuscript (out of boredom, irritation), is to declare that it's not needed, that it doesn't respond to any need in me → "You send me your manuscript. But, at this point in time, I have no need of it. At this point in time, I need Pascal, etc." → *Necessity*: what someone requires at a given point in time (= idea that runs counter to any possibility of "Marketing" the book because it's an idea that's grounded in subtlety, fugacity, and individuality—but one that would be enough to justify writing).

Chance

Scherer, 19

In my attempt to breach the difficult notion of the *Necessity* of the world, I'm basically only really managing to describe the *demand* for Necessity, not establish the basis for the response. For example, the feeling (Mallarmé) that true literature abolishes chance:[17] the work is an anti-chance (that's really the meaning of *Necessity*) → Feeling of unease that comes over me whenever I get the impression that, yes, certain authors, or certain people, say intelligent things—but only by chance.

"Proof"

Scherer, 91, *sq.*

Apropos of the Book, Mallarmé had a strong sense of necessity . . . of the work's Necessity → In other words, strong version of necessity: *Proof*; the work must be endowed with *Proof*. That Proof can't be about the meaning: a text has no *true meaning* (Mallarmé, Valéry); meaning can't be *proven*, nor can it have to do with how far it resembles reality, because the Book is unrealistic (a-figurative); at the very most it's *homologous*, not analogous.—For Mallarmé, Proof is probably dependent on the process of confrontation and comparison; in the Book, two "aspects" have to come together: what's subjective is unique ≠ what's objective is what can be arrived at by at least two different means: objectivity is a *junction* (for example, for Proust, the *proof* of *In Search of Lost Time*—which, what's more, is probably what got it going in the first place—is that elements from the beginning are rediscovered at the end: this is the hiving off, the *marcottage*). So Proof can't be in the detail (Verism); it has to be total. In 1867, Mallarméan vision of the Work: "I contemplated it, without ecstasy or terror and, closing my eyes, *I realized that it existed*."[18] Ultimately, the work's Necessity = affirmation of existence: the certainty that *it exists*, certainty that comes from the superimposition of (or the encounter between) two distinct aspects; Proust again: the work can be said to *have existed* when the two ways meet[19] (then it could *finish*) → Since Necessity = Existence, there are no degrees, no such thing as *more* or *less* (this is really what Necessity is): *yes or no*; either it exists totally or it doesn't exist at all: "We'll see if it's something or nothing" → In short, there's a logical progression: from *causality* (there's a reason for this to exist, this work has to exist, this work is necessary) to the *stating of the fact*: it *exists* (mystical movement).

Self-evaluation: Talent

Talent

To reach the point where you feel that the work to be written or that's in the process of being written is *Necessary* = an uncertain, intuitive labor that's more or less fed by expedients: there's no *recipe*. But what is conceivable is a certain *propedeutics* to that feeling: rule, disposition that has to be observed in itself for the Necessity to suddenly burst forth (and with it the work). Generally speaking, self-evaluation of your own *talent*. Talent = a limit that can't be breached without prompting failure, that can't be overstepped: a *limit* to your resources.

Misrecognition

There is, constantly looming, the threat of the writer (this is the name I'm giving to someone who wants to write) *failing to recognize* his talent. Flaubert (1852, thirty-one years old): "There is how-

Préface, 65

ever, at bottom, something which troubles me: not knowing my capabilities. This man who appears so calm is full of self-doubt. He would like to know how high he can go, the exact power of his muscles."[20] (very well put; unfortunately, in literature, there are no dynamometers) → We can try to name this limit (this ceiling): Flaubert again (1853, thirty-two years old), *Madame Bovary*: "If I tried to insert action, I would be following a rule, and would spoil everything. One has to sing in one's own voice; and mine will never be dramatic or attractive."[21] → In all likelihood, what we call a writer's maturity, the success of his works once the beginnings are out of the way, has nothing to do with an increase in his powers (physiological image) but rather with the precise, subtle discovery, which comes from experience, of how best to apply them; Kafka says that you can "admire the energy with which a man misuses his talent";[22] this is often the impression given by first manuscripts: a double energy, of language and of misrecognition → "Mastery" would be more like a managed depletion, an *Epicurean* economy of the pleasures the writer is capable of giving (and of giving himself) through writing.

Truth-Novel

Talent (= knowing what you're good at) has a moral function; for me, it consists in remaining within the bounds of "my truth," that is: refusing, in my writing, to give in to superficial, secondary incitements (the pull of the latest thing, of fashion, or a whim, a fad, or an illusion of myself); in short, in refusing *pretences*, *pretence* (pressure of the images I'm surrounded by). For example (as I suggested at the end of last year's course), I can have the tenacious desire to write a novel (hence the generic title: *Preparation of the Novel*), only to realize that I'm incapable of doing so, for this reason: *I don't know how to lie* (not *I don't want to* but *I don't know how to*); that's not to say that I know how to tell the Truth; what's beyond me is the *invention* of Falsehoods, luxurious Falsehoods, Falsehoods that create a stir {*fait de la mousse*}: Storytelling, Mythomania → Is this a cultural trait? Religious? Calvinist? It would be interesting to see whether there've been any great Calvinist novelists → This isn't a guarantee of morality; for the Imagination that can make up stories is a generous force (*to create the other*), and the refusal "to lie" can belie a Narcissism: my imagination, it seems to me, is merely fantasmatic (it doesn't tell tales), that is to say: narcissistic.

Difficult / Impossible

A different Voice of the Necessity (of the work)—all this is a problem of *Precision*—can be heard on the side of how far Talent is *Stretched*: to stretch talent to its extreme limit, without it snapping and tipping over into pretence, a "Puppet Show" → The work to be written shouldn't be easy (the Diary, for example, is an easy genre, except when it comes to turning it into a sophisticated work after the fact), but nor should it be impossible: between difficult and impossible, then → You remember the citation from Heidegger: in Nature, each thing remains within the allotted sphere of the Possible; only "will" takes us outside of the Possible.[23] I said that Writing, as Will, was an Impossible (which I was opposing to *Idleness*, as Nature).—We can now say: even within the will to write, that is, within its Impossible, the task of Talent is to remain within its Possible: to precisely delineate the Nature within this Non-Nature that is Writing.

Conclusion

The Blocking Fantasy

We've now reached the end of the first Trial, not its resolution (it remains a trial) but the end of its exposition. It essentially has to do with the *optional* texture, at every level, of the operations of writing: at every moment—and from the outset: *written large* (for example, *Book / Album*)—you have choose, and there's no God (of Writing) to impose or even to guide you in your choice → Writing: vertiginous freedom. This practical freedom comes into conflict with the fantasy of the work, which is the affirmation of desire: the fantasy "initiates" the work by making it "visible," making it "shimmer" in the distance like a mirage, but, of course, since it's still only a fantasy, what is made visible is not a real work: it's a generic image in the distance, a tone, or perhaps some bits of the work, some aspects, some inflections (I refer here to Balzac's short story, which deals with this problem with considerable precision: *The Unknown Masterpiece*) → The fantasy gets the work going, but it also blocks it: for it keeps *repeating* a pleasure to-come without getting to the stage of planning out its realization in real terms; it can't get past the Reality of execution in its essential form, the obligation to chose, to exploit a freedom → the *Preparation of the Work* can also be a pure, immobile fantasy, of which the writer has only a few fragments (a few notes); this is what Joubert is describing when he

Chateaubriand, *M.O.T.* I, 450

says, "I am like . . . an Aeolian harp which makes some beautiful sounds, but does not play any tune."[24]

"Blank in the Course"

So how to get out of this situation?—I've no idea, because it's the state I was in on the day I drafted this Course: I desire a Work, but I don't know how to choose it, to plan it (besides, even if I had chosen the work to be written, I wouldn't say so; cf. *infra: secrecy*)[25] → Thus there is, here, at this point in the Course, a *blank* → I've not resolved the first trial (which is often paradigmatic of the ones to come), yet I have to proceed as if the Work to be written was chosen, I have to speak of the other trials that await me as if the first, the main one, had been overcome.

3. Second Trial: Patience

Let's imagine, then, that the man whose story we're telling ("someone who wanted to write") had chosen, fixed upon the Form of the work he's going to get started on. In theory, he's now capable of answering: "What are you preparing for us at the moment?" But then he encounters the obligation of *secrecy* (cf. *infra*) → Formidable trial: he'll be making the transition—necessary, at some point—from the fantasy to its realization, which is to say to a *practice* (*praxis*); he'll no longer have to struggle with *indecision* (a quasi-obsessional position) but with *Time*, with a *duration*: the time it takes to fabricate the Work. It's long: (a) on the one hand, it's bound to last as long as the existential duration of life itself—and a life, even the life of a writer, isn't all about writing: there's an underlying conflict between the duration of existence and the duration of writing; (b) on the other, the praxis itself, even supposing that ideally it would somehow be purified of all other time, comprises internal difficulties, obstacles, misunderstandings → The second trial is therefore that of *patience* (of writing). That patience comprises two "fields": external patience (with respect to the world, to the "worldly") and internal patience (with respect to the task itself). There will therefore be two parts to this second trial:

> A. The material organization of the life of writing, what could be called a *methodical life*. Chateaubriand, in Rome, his

ambassadorship: "The Romans are so accustomed to my methodical life that I serve as their timepiece."[26]

B. The *praxis* of writing: its obstacles, its resistances, its internal threats, *its stallings* (since it's a matter of patience).

A. *A Methodical Life*

The Work ≠ The World

In order to have the time to write it's necessary to do mortal battle with the enemies that threaten that time; it's necessary to wrench that time from the world, both through a decisive choice and constant vigilance → There's a *rivalry* between the world and the work; Kafka is the key figure of this conflict, this tension: he always experienced the world as something hostile to literature, that made him suffer, sometimes to the point of panic; the world, that is to say, for him, the figures of the Father, the Office, and the Woman. What is the world, what can it be?

Office

For Kafka it is (partly) the Office: "That I, so long as I'm not freed of my office <legal advisor to an insurance company>, am simply lost, that is clearer to me than anything else, it is just a matter, as long as possible, of holding my head so high that I do not drown."[27] (whence the diary). And this:

> KAFKA, *DIARIES*
>
> (Kafka, writing or dictating a sentence for the Office, with great repugnance:) . . . *Finally I say it, but retain the great fear that everything within me is ready for a poetic work and such a work would be a heavy enlightenment and a real coming-alive for me, while here, in the office, because of so wretched an official document, I must rob a body capable of such happiness of a piece of flesh.*[28]

The Office stands in for all forms of daily alienation ("going to the office everyday"): all that's obligatory, the *price* that has to be paid to society in order to live; writing = my own blood → the price is that of blood. Note: as always, no psychological principle is completely reliable, universal. I recall that Queneau wrote better because he was obliged to wrench the book from the Office.

Kafka

Seuil, 151

Journal, 20

Picon, 94

Society, Worldly

"Society," or the world in the sense of "worldly": parties, the visits you get paid, meetings with friends, private views, screenings, etc. → Figure: Proust, *before / after 1909*,[29] or the ideal figure of Daniel d'Arthez: "The whole existence of Daniel d'Arthez is entirely consecrated to labor; he sees society only in snatches; to him it's like a dream..."[30]—Note that here too it's ambiguous (or "dialectical"): the dilemma "World / Work" doesn't have the fine rigor of the Jansenist choice (Bedroom ≠ Entertainment, that is to say Good ≠ Evil, each of them pure).

1. The World's subtle offensive: the observation, hence the frequentation of the world in its different forms is necessary for the elaboration of the work = storehouse of material and stimuli: worldly social settings (Proust), reading the papers (Sollers?), even the willingness to take a stand, through writing, against "what's wrong with the world": the work as anti-Stupidity, anti-Evil. There can be an exhausting oscillation that goes round in the following circle: necessity of withdrawing from the world in order to write the work: onslaught of ambient, intraworldly stupidity → the need and as it were the obligation to react → participation in the World (for example, the *Nouvel Observateur* columns)[31] → reinvestment through Melancholy, withdrawing into yourself, the desire to retreat from the world → renewed onslaught (André T.'s film)[32] → renewed desire to react (To Start up a Journal), etc.

2. The "World" is not only the General-Social; it's also the Personal-Relational: meetings with friends, private views, friends' films → Now, the peculiarity of the "Personal," of the Affective Personal, is that it can't be generalized, synthesized; it's a collection of different cases, each of them *irreducible*; this plunges you into an irresolvable contradiction: the "relationship" is in conflict with the Work because it's repetitive; the meetings with friends are what keep you from writing; but if you itemize the collection, each relationship is worth maintaining and wants to be maintained—so you're back where you started, for: (a) friendship is of the order of the Incomparable, (b) but, adding all those Incomparables together, you produce a general constraint. Whence the temptation—and what's more one that's crazy because the price paid would be too high—of an *All or Nothing*.

Concupiscences

Pensées, II, 121

Another form of the "world": the "attachment" to "transitory creatures" (Pascal),[33] or, to use the eighteenth century term, *concupiscences* → in modern language, all forms of *cruising*; cruising = irresistible combing for pleasures, quests, wanderings, giving in to one desire then flitting to the next; the very image of *wasting time*: it's here that abandoning the work gives rise to the most immediate and the most banal kind of guilt; probably because the breaching of the *Sacred* of the work (postulated as an absolute end) is compounded by a cultural breach, inherited from religion: sin, weakness of the flesh. The conflict *Concupiscence (Cruising) / Writing*: something subtle—and even ambiguous—about it, because it has to do with the nature of *"the small differences"* (Freudian notion): (a) Pushed to a radical extreme, Cruising is like a life writing: it "crosses out," inscribes, marks out, inhabits the terrain of Time through an energy of inscription that's wholly perverse (more so than Writing) because it isn't productive (it doesn't "engender" anything). (b) "Cruising" can be experienced—can have the same allegorical shape—as a quest, an Initiation: which is what Writing is → Conflict between two isomorphic forces.

Love

Love, or rather (to make clear that we're on a different level from that of concupiscences), the *loved one* → Romantic myth: the loved one, as the presumed dedicatee, is someone who *inspires*, that is to say, who enables the work; there's a fusion between the work and the loved one ≠ Reality: can be more complicated; an almost inexpiable rivalry between the loved one and the Work; for the loved one, the work is an object of jealousy; for the writing subject, it's the much-loved favorite (and so the source of "egoism"'s guilt) → Kafka, torn between his fiancée (of the time) and literature; it's not a specific work that's at issue: it's a rivalry, a permanent tension.

Seuil, 108–9

Kafka, of course, lucid on this point, and suffering because of it, recites a Jan-Tsen-Tsaï poem that he was familiar with to Felice:

IN THE DEAD OF NIGHT

*In the cold night, while poring over,
my book, I forgot the hour of bedtime.*

*The scent of my gold-embroidered bed-covering,
has already evaporated, the fireplace burns no more.
My beautiful mistress, who hitherto has controlled
her wrath with difficulty, snatches away the lamp
And asks: Do you know how late it is?*[34]

Jealous, jealous of a book? It must happen more often than we think (I've been quoted examples of it).—This opposition: for Kafka, pure, painful—because he's tempted by marriage but dares not agree to it, whence his fine scruples with respect to broken engagements, for he can never go as far as marriage → Add to that the contradictions of the imaginary; example, Balzac: professes on the one hand that to write his work the writer must avoid and live in absolute separation from love and on the other sincerely believes that his true goal is not literature but the happiness that love can bring (≠ the young Hugo: "to be Chateaubriand or nothing"); he places love above the work; installing Madame Hanska in the rue Fortunée matters more to him than having written masterpieces: "If I am not great from the *Comédie Humaine*, I shall be through this success, if she comes"[35] (1849) → It would be a terrible test, a solemn and dramatic trial for a love affair: "Are you willing to sacrifice your work for me?" Seemingly, a moment of truth; but the fact of the matter is, if anyone were to blackmail the writer in this way, they'd instantly and in so doing lose all *value*, they'd become unworthy of love—they'd simply lay bare the other's alienated desire (after all, doesn't the writer always somehow manage to *mess up* his love affairs from the moment they present a real threat to the future of his work?)

Real Life

The devotion to the work, the sacrifice it presumes, can be experienced romantically, if not as a curse, then at least as an exaggeratedly marginal, fanciful, abnormal, mad life. For example, Van Gogh would have preferred "real life": but here real life is not a life lived in true solitude (that would be more like the status of the work) but paradoxically a life that some would judge artificial; "real life" = the life that everyone lives, a normal life with a home, wife, children, a profession, ordinary dignity; so it's this happiness that has to be sacrificed to the work.

Picon, 140

Mallarmé, Seuil, 7

Egoism

Journal, 281

Such is, broadly speaking, the "world" that rivals the work (to be written) → For someone who writes, this "rivalry" is distressing not only for practical reasons (obstacles, the time sacrificed) but also for psychological ones:

1. I can experience the work to be written as a kind of disturbance, a madness, an obsession that cuts me off from everything else, a "schism." Kafka [July] 1913: "I hate everything that does not relate to literature, conversations bore me (even if they relate to literature), to visit people bores me, the sorrows and joys of my relatives bore me to my soul. Conversations take away the importance, the seriousness, the truth of everything, I think."[36]

Picon, 20

2. The devotion to the work (as opposed to the World): experienced as a painful hardness of the heart, a restriction, a constriction. Here's Balzac describing the cruel life of the slave to literature: "The egoism of a man who has to depend on his ideas for his livelihood is something appalling. To be a man apart from the rest, one has to begin by really cutting oneself off from them. Is it not martyrdom for a man who loves to unburden his heart, for whom affection is the breath of life, who longs for someone who will shield him from the world, is it not, I say, martyrdom for such a man to be always meditating, comparing, inventing, seeking, voyaging through strange seas of thought, when all he really longs for is to love and be loved?"[37]

3. Indeed, what's most distressing is the accusation, or at any rate the self-accusation, of *egoism* (I don't know if this word is still used); for, to set his mind at ease as regards this "egoism" in the eyes of the world, the writer must: (a) brave incomprehension, no one really understanding why he seems to be living solely for "work," thinking it unreasonable, unwise etc.; "accepting" egoism = accepting that people will think you egoistic; (b) overcome this devalorization by making the work—and the worst of it is: *your own* work—into something Supremely Valuable, an overvalorization that the social consensus is increasingly reluctant to accept.

Solution?

So what do you do?—I am not fully a writer and am not worldly—yet I'm not someone who manages to reconcile labor and the world, or only unsatisfactorily; I'm constantly complaining about what the world takes away from my labor—I can't tell you what the solution is—since I'm seeking it, without success, but also without giving up. I can only say this, which is both very beautiful and, unfortunately, very general—it's from Kafka: "*In the struggle between you and the world, back the world.*"[38] What does that mean?—To my mind, this: the writer—at least the one I'm referring to: the "romantic" writer who writes *in his own Name* (that is to say: neither anonymously nor collectively)—, the writer is obliged to affirm his "singularity": conflict with the world is therefore inevitable (and perhaps this is the case for every man, insofar as he's *singular*) → The certainty of the singular is set against that other certainty: "Truth resides not in the individual but in the chorus";[39] in a sense, whatever it is, the world is on the side of truth, because truth is in the indissoluble unity of the human world → which means singularity has got it wrong → So? *Backing the world* means:

1. Recognizing the truth of the Chorus and, for the writer, somehow setting the world to music: *lovingly* incorporating the world into his work (this can also be done in a vengeful manner); lessening or "transforming" the pressure of his *egotism* (the world ≠ *ego*); for example, making use of what, of the world, seems to be precisely contrary to the devotion to the work in the writing of the work; if the loved one is impeding the Work, reverse the equation: make the loved one the guiding, initiating spirit of the Work; this is what Dante did with Beatrice, who opened up the three worlds of that age for him: the worlds of sin, of penitence, and of recompense (In parenthesis—and I'm not in any way being ironic here; rather, I find the idea distressing: had she lived, it's not clear that Beatrice would have liked *The Divine Comedy*; she might have been *shocked*, *offended* at being turned into an *image*, however beautiful, an image deprived of her voice, for everyone always claims to be themselves, not an image of themselves; better my real *ego*, however modest, than its image, however grandiose → In this way, and you'll recognize the allusion:[40] someone writes a book about Love in order to get closer to the loved one, in order to include him in the work but, and this is *precisely the point*, the loved one doesn't love the book because it doesn't let him speak; if he reads it all, it's in bad humor, with ressentiment; the Work of love separates the two partners even further; the Work has triumphed: it *separated*, although it's possible that it brought other readers out in the world closer together).

Backing the world means guiding the work toward the presence of the world, making the world co-present to the Work: the world, that is, basically everything I've described as temporal obstacles to writing: society, the worldly, concupiscences, love, the norm.

2. But, at the same time, and despite doing everything you can to welcome the world into the Work (affectively, intellectually), you have to be *tough* with the world; you mustn't let the practices of the world (its "dailiness") stifle and kill the practice of writing like a cancer, and to do this you probably have to come to terms with a certain toughness on your part, which means adopting, among others, the image of someone who's unavailable, distant, lacking in generosity → The paradox of "backing the world" and "devoting yourself to the Work" can be expressed in this nuance: not being *egotistic* but accepting that you have to be *egoistic*.

SESSION OF JANUARY 19, 1980

Life as Work[1]

Rivalry, conflict between the World (Life) and the Work: a *derivation*, a dialectical solution is possible, which I'll indicate in the form of a digression: it involves the writer *making his life into a work, his Work*; obviously, the immediate form (without mediation) of this solution is the *diary* (I'll say at the end of this [development] why that solution is unsatisfactory).

Return of the Author

In the history of French literature, there have been several "*returns of the author*" of varying types and of varying value:

1. "Isolated" returns, sorts of erratic monuments, over the course of a literature that's "officially" (that is to say: in schools: see the manuals) suspicious of the *ego* (or rather of the *I*): Montaigne's *Essays*, Chateaubriand's *Memoirs from Beyond the Grave*, and, in way that's more diffuse, already more subtle, Stendhal, who is said to have written with his life and to have lived through writing (*Memoirs of an Egotist*) ≠ Balzac, who writes by suppressing his life in order to live otherwise (in accordance with an imaginary of superhuman strength).—I'll set these *returns* to one side since they belong to an ongoing history.

2. When, in accordance with a positivist spirit, literary history was established (end of the nineteenth century, University), scholars were primarily interested in the author, who can therefore be said to have "returned"; but, cruel and erroneous distortion, the author who returned in these studies was the *external author*: his external biography, his influences, the sources he may have consulted, etc., that return was in no way considered in the light or in terms of the prospect of the act of creation: it was neither the *Ego* nor the *I* who returned, just the *He*: the "Mr." who wrote masterpieces: a particular branch of descriptive History.

3. The *return to the author* I want to discuss is something to look out for even today; I say *to look out for* because I'm not sure: it might be something that I'm making up and projecting

Picon, Balzac, 20

onto reality. This would be the movement: ever since a certain type of modernity (of the sixties) became interested in Mallarmé again, in his relationship to literature, there's been a tendency to erase the author in favor of the *Text*, conceived either as a pure process of enunciation referring to the body of the person writing (and no longer to the metaphysical or psychological subject (texts such as Artaud's)) or, on a theoretical level, as a *structure* that transcends the author—a very active period of literary structuralism, of semiology; at the time, as a sign of what I'm describing, I myself wrote an article, the title of which summarizes this trend: "The Death of the Author"[2] → Neocriticism repressed the author, or at least deprived him of consciousness; the opening paragraph of a little book by Bellemin-Noël testifies to this: "Everything <in his book> comes out of a lack of curiosity with regard to authors. For me, this is of the order of fact, I am not touched, drawn to, even less am I mobilized by the lives or the personalities of writers . . ."[3]; a good quote (even if today I take the completely opposite view) because it uses the right expression: *lack of curiosity* with regard to the author → Death, Lack of Curiosity → Return of curiosity, return of the author.

Return to Biography

For me (once again, I'm not sure if I have the right to generalize), the sudden about-face occurred at the time of *The Pleasure of the Text*:[4] weakening of the theoretical superego, return of much-loved texts, "release" or "de-repression" of the author → I also thought I could detect, here and there, a fondness among some of my peers for what could be called—to avoid the problem of definitions—*biographical nebulae* (Diaries, Biographies, personalized Interviews, Memoirs, etc.), a way, no doubt, of reacting against the coolness of generalizations, of collectivizations, of socializations and putting a little bit of "psychological" affectivity back into intellectual production: to give the "Ego" a bit of an opportunity to speak, rather than always the Super-Ego or the *Id* → That biographical "curiosity" then developed freely in me:

a. Paradox: I'd sometimes come to prefer reading about the lives of certain writers to reading their works; for example, I'm more familiar with Kafka's *Diaries* than with his oeuvre, with Tolstoy's *Notebooks* than with the rest of Tolstoy (apparently this is a very "camp" attitude).[5]

b. Different form of the paradox: I'd sometimes imagine a perverse Author who'd written works simply so that he might, one day be authorized to write his autobiography.

c. Last, I had a very strong desire to write a biography, but because the biography I wanted to write was that of a musician, namely Schumann, and since I don't speak German, I gave up on the idea.

Naturally, you have to go beyond my own particular case and take a brief look at how a certain transformation of the Biographical is currently being effected, following in the wake of a few of the important works of the last fifty years—notably, to go very quickly, for this is no more than a digression: Gide and Proust.

Gide

Gide, his *Diary*: a great work that many people prefer to the rest of his oeuvre (personally I was already very fond of it in 1942: one of my first texts was on this diary).[6] Why? Hard to say, because it's a very subtle text, but the point is that the *modern* reason for this preference is the complexity of its network of enunciation, that is, the uses, the roles of the *I*: complexity on different levels: (1) The *I* is sincere; (2) The *I*'s sincerity is artificial; (3) Sincerity is irrelevant, it becomes a quality of the text to be placed between scare quotes.—We can put this differently and say that what emerges from Gide's *Diary* is the author is not a *witness* (as the Goncourt brothers were) but an *actor of writing* (what's misleading is that Gide's writing is classical, retrograde and "precious") → It's probably the *Diary* that gives meaning to the entirety of Gide: indeed, it makes a *creative whole* out of Life+Work: his oeuvre is not among the greatest, and there was nothing heroic about his life (that of someone of independent means who loved literature and had a few "well-connected" friends), but the life asks to be read as entirely oriented toward the formation of the oeuvre: and the achievement lies in that tension, that insistence, that permanence.

Proust

Proust: this is gradually becoming clearer—for the Proustian landscape changes over time—, Proust marks the intensive, audacious entrance of the author, of the writing subject as *biographologist* into literature; the work, which doesn't fall into the category of

v. Herbart, 79

Painter I, 25

Chevrier, Cerisy, 383

biography (Diary, Memoirs), is entirely woven out of him, out of his places, his friends, his family; that's literally all there is in his novel—despite all the theoretical pretexts: condensations, absence of real-life sources, etc. Rightly so, since Proust's problem was to regain the Time lost to him (and not Time in general) → His work: not a philosophy, but a *Salvation*, a personal "every man for himself": "*How can I survive the death of someone I love?*" (Answer: by writing the contraction of Time, before and after the Mother's death). *In Search of Lost Time* has been called "a symbolic story of his life,"[7] a symbolic biography; no chronological narrative: it isn't a bio-chronography → The distinction (or the confusion) between Marcel and the Narrator is unhelpful → The innovation of the *Life / Work* relationship, the positioning of the life as work is now slowly emerging as a veritable historical shift in values, in literary prejudices; it's today, in Proust, that the biographical intensity, the biographical force seduces and transports (biographies, albums, iconographies; the Pléiade edition is out of print, unfindable) → The Proustian myth has shifted toward the apotheosis of the biographical subject → what I termed *Marcelism* (different from Proustianism).

Life Writing

Testamentary preface

Seen in its new light, the experiment—Proust's work—ushers in *life writing*, the life written (in the strong sense, which transforms the word "writing"), which is not the same thing as biography: the "*biographematic*"[8] (which is also, inextricably, as in Proust, a thanatography). The new principle enabling this new kind of writing = the division, the fragmentation, indeed the pulverization of the subject. Proust saw this already: "<The method of *Sainte-Beuve* fails to recognize> that a book is a product of a *self* other than that which we display in our habits, in company, in our vices."[9] → That division is a necessary detour, a necessary deviation on the path to finding an adequation between, not writing and life (straightforward biography), but writings and fragments, bits of life. Chateaubriand knew this, and his *Memoirs from Beyond the Grave* (the model of life writing) inverts the roles of life and writing: "Of the French writers of my date <well put: less hollow than "generation">, I am the only one whose life resembles his works <well put: the work doesn't resemble life; writing *leads*: poetically, transcendentally, it's Charlus who's the model for Montesquiou>: traveler, soldier, poet, publicist, it is in the woods that I praised the woods, on ships that I painted the sea, in camps that I spoke of weapons, in exile that I learned about exile, in the courts, in business, in assemblies that I studied Princes, politics, law and history."[10] Life Writing = as writing and life become more fragmented (stop misguidedly trying to form a unified whole), the more homogenous each fragment becomes; thus, on the horizon: the *poikilos* of the Romantic Novel.

We could—but I say this only in passing—outline a typology of the *roles* that life writing brushes aside, that is in fact to say, of the *I*s that write, successively:

a. *Persona*: the everyday, empirical, private individual who "lives," without writing.
b. *Scriptor*: the writer as social image, the one who gets talked about, who gets discussed, who gets classified according to school, or genre, in manuals, etc.
c. *Auctor*: the *I* who considers himself the *guarantor* of what he writes; father of the book, accepting his responsibilities; the *I* who, socially or mystically, considers himself to be a writer.
d. *Scribens*: the *I* who's engaged in the practice of writing, who's in the process of writing, who lives writing everyday.

All of these *I*s are woven into, shimmer in the writing that we read, though some are more dominant than others → But *life writing* clearly involves attributing a particular creative value to the *persona*: writing springs from the part of life that's unwritten, it constantly brushes up against what's not writing and the relationship it establishes with that unwritten part is of the order of a distorted analogy, or *allegory*; this is absolutely the case for Proust, who fulfils Keats's saying to the letter: "A man's life of any worth is a continual allegory."[11]

Persona and *Scribens* can be instantly bracketed together; "life" becomes work "immediately" (without mediation): the Diary, the Album → The major risk is *egotism*: only half-heartedly "backing" the world → In which case, the Diary becomes a kind of *labor*:[12] so we come back to the law of labor, of transformation through writing, the law of the Book (≠Album) (Montaigne's *Essays*, *Memoirs from Beyond the Grave*, Proust) → and in this way, following this digression, we come back to the problem of *writing* as a radical practice, an obsessive labor, a *way of life*: the problem of the Methodical Life.[13]

Painter, I, 26

Vita Nova

Complete Breaks

In the thread of my narrative (the story of the man who wants to write, who wants to set about writing a Work), the idea of the Work (of this particular Work, solemnified) is linked to the idea of a Complete Break, a Reinvented Way of Life, the Organization of a New Life: *Vita Nova* (or *Vita Nuova*) (I'm aware of two *Vita Nova*: Dante, Michelet)[14] → I'll explain what I mean by this idea of *Vita Nova* in a little more depth.

All of us, I believe, have experienced or periodically experience the Fantasy of a Complete Break: a break from a way of life, a break from habits, liaisons (often it remains a fantasy) (you only have to read the "Change your life" column in *Libération*) → There are two elements to this fantasy: *to shake off* . . . the past, the present that adheres (= freedom, a liberating breaking of ties: mythical image of shedding one's skin, of desquamation, of rebirth, path to immortality) + *to create something new*: total, grandiose, triumphant. Keeping within the order of literature:

Picon, 91

1. Balzac: at the end of *Lost Illusions,* Lucien, who's on the point of committing suicide, meets Carlos Herrera; he discovers that his life can begin again on a different basis: with Carlos, he'll "write" a triumphant novel.

2. A *Break* means: I shall produce, radically, without concessions, at the cost of total extrication, a different *I* (I'll say a word about the *religious* nature of this movement at the end of this [passage]); of course, by giving up literature completely and turning to travel, then to trade, the break (and the *Vita Nova*) that Rimbaud lived through was exemplarily—even staggeringly—rigorous. But it's not the complete break I want to draw your attention to; rather it's the break he describes in the *Visionary Letter* (to Georges Izambard, May 31, 1871), the one that occurs within the very will for a work (and so, for literature): "Now I am degrading myself as much as possible. Why? I want to be a poet, and am working to make myself a *Visionary*: you will not understand this <God knows whether we understand it now! How many 'visionaries' did Rimbaud make of himself!>, and I don't know how to explain it to you. It is a question of reaching the unknown by the derangement of *all the senses*. The sufferings are enormous, but one has to be strong, one has to be born a poet, and I know I am a poet. This is not at all my fault. It is wrong to

Rimbaud, *Lettres*, p. 55

say: I think: One ought to say: people think me . . . I is someone else."[15]

The fantasy of a complete break can be converted into "sub-fantasies"; let's not forget the fantasy is a scenario; there are therefore "scenes" that get played, replayed, caressed (always the same, seemingly immobile scenes; the fantasy is a film made up of stills), for example, to go and shut yourself away in total "solitude" (in the geographical sense, as in landscape painting); Senancour's *Oberman*:[16] after an unhappy life, the hero describes the ideal site that is *Imenstrôm*, the pastoral sanctuary where he'll take refuge. What can make a Refuge even better is when it's absolute, but there's also somewhere busy, "worldly" nearby: Rousseau: ("Seventh Promenade") finds a total refuge in the mountains—and he describes it delightedly—only to realize that the place in question is very close to a mill (just one of the surprises that mountains can hold in store);[17] Rousseau isn't happy; for my part I have this fantasy of an absolutely secluded, sheltered place in the middle of a big city; I don't like the countryside, or the provinces: ideally, it would be a hidden, almost secret place in a very big city; this is why Paris suits me: a city of quick, bold modulations between the city's center and its more provincial areas; between Saint-Germain-des-Prés and my (provincial) street, the place Saint-Sulpice (a few meters away) is a modulation that's as difficult and as effective as going from D major to F sharp minor.—Or again, very similar to the preceding fantasy, that of the "dive": nothing is more sensuous than "diving" into a big city and suddenly finding yourself in an area you know very well (Tokyo is conducive to these sensuous delights). Of the same type, the fantasy of spending a fortnight tucked away in a hotel in a completely different neighborhood of Paris: to disappear but to still be *close by*; because all it takes for a man from Saint-Sulpice (in other words, from Saint-Germain) to feel he's somewhere else entirely is to go and have a coffee at the bar of a café in another neighborhood to pass the time before the cinema opens (for example), a cinema such as the "Templiers" near the place de la République (for example); on that particular evening, a Sunday, around eight o'clock, in the café, young working-class men, one with his neck laden with charms, the other with enormous sideburns; an accordion, the old-fashioned kind; at the end of the bar, two old women, the concierge-type, and an old man in a cap, all three of them tipsy, merry (from repeated Pernods); to one side, a father lets his kid

Castex Surer, **19th c., p. 14**

Painter, II, 192

have a go on the jukebox → The theme of *Flight*, which is the first step toward a *Vita Nova*.

Different subfantasy of the Complete Break: saying your goodbyes; Proust actually did this before withdrawing from society to devote himself to his Novel: November 27, 1909, he hires three boxes at the Théâtre des Variétés for the performance of *Circuit*, a comedy by Feydeau and Croisset and invites his friends to come along,[18] a very peculiar form of adieu: a *Party* to mark starting work on a book—and not its publication.

This fantasy of a Complete Break, of a *Vita Nova*, can probably occur at any age, but it's most interesting when it happens on the threshold of old age; every "retirement" (in the social and now unionized sense of the word) contains the germ of the fantasy of a *Vita Nova*; my point is banal, but the thing is, if you don't tone it down, socially speaking, by resorting to the slippers-and-pipe model, there's something violent, subversive about this fantasy; I always find it sinister when I hear people speaking admiringly of an "oldie," saying *he keeps himself in good shape*, that he's *still* doing all the things he used to do (for example, playing tennis, going for his walk, or, like Hugo, making love); but *carrying on* isn't an act of vitality; what old age needs (whenever possible) is, precisely, a Complete Break, a Beginning, a *Vita Nova*: *a rebirth*. Michelet had his *Vita Nova* (the expression comes from him) at fifty-one years old, upon meeting a frail young woman of twenty, Athénais (who, at his death, unfortunately turned into an overpossessive widow, falsifying his manuscripts); he then *changed* his Works completely and wrote his books about Nature (and stopped writing about History): *The Bird, The Sea, The Mountain*,[19] frequently strange, beautiful books.

I want to come back briefly to that opposition between "Carrying on" (living as before, sempiternally) ≠ Breaking with, changing, being reborn, becoming someone else, a different *I* (*Vita Nova*) → There are two types of immortality; the desire for immortality that's within all of us takes two contradictory forms: (1) To be immortal (or: in order to be immortal): *staying still* (carrying on); this is the philosophy of the heap (*Sorophilia*),[20] but I related that philosophy to absolute idleness, the *Doing Nothing* of the Zen Poem and the Moroccan child;[21] so it's not that kind of immortality that the devotion to the new work (which is force, labor, struggle) is aiming for. (2) To be immortal is to be completely reborn; the work to be written is the mediator of this second kind of immortality →

What follows from this is a peculiar thing, something I experience at any rate: I don't like it when people shut me up, so to speak, in the first kind of immortality—the immortality of *always being in the same place*—, however immortal that immortality may be! Now, this happens all the time: people, especially doctoral students, suddenly resurface having not been in touch for years and, without asking how you are (what you might have become), ask you something to do with who you were when they last saw you—something that, as it happens, you're no longer remotely involved in ("iconic structuralism," or a mythology of Toys, or of Fashion); from their point of view, it goes without saying that people don't move, that they stay in the same place, that you should still be here, immobile, like a statue, awaiting them, available. I change places, I want to be reborn; I'm not where you expect me to be → So there's an unpleasant kind of immortality, which the *Vita Nova* protests against.

Bustle / Peace

Several different *ethoses* of *Vita Nova* are possible (there's a good doctoral thesis to be written on the different types of complete break!): *Vita Nova* through adventure, a change of scenery, action, etc. ≠ *Vita Nova* sought, fantasized through the Work to be Written = *Vita Nova* of enclosure, of peace and quiet (paramonastic model); this turns, I think, around the notion of *Bustle*.

BUSTLE The "Peace" of daily life = absence of "assaults" (in all senses of the word: intervention of the "Wicked," Rousseau's language, cf. *infra*[22] + the whole range of "disturbances") → I see three motives in this:

1. In order to write the work, the would-be writer must not be disturbed. Chateaubriand: "A year or two in some corner of the earth was enough for the completion of my *Memoirs*; but the only time I have ever known peace was those nine months I spent sleeping life <admirable expression> inside my mother: I will probably only experience that pre-natal rest again after-death, in the womb of our common mother."[23] (The work, with its capital W, is like the womb of the blessed life, of life before birth.)

2. Nonactivity is necessary for thought. Kafka: "I have too little time and quiet to draw out of me all the possibilities of my talent."[24] I'd put it more radically: difficult (for me) to cope with life without philosophizing about it (to *deaden* myself to it would

make things worse). And, in order to philosophize, you need time; whence the anxiety of an overfull life, when you don't have time to "reflect" on life, on meaning, in other words to elaborate a *consolation*: working on the Work and having peace and quiet *for* reflection go hand in hand.

3. However, everything is ambiguous, dialectical: distressingly, I'm aware that I'm basically *incapable* of busying myself (because to busy yourself is also to invest in, a positive value); I can experience calm as a privation of Desire, an Acedy → So I decide to accept this inaptitude vis-à-vis busying myself, to reinstate my own capacity (or incapacity): bustle frightens me, as something over which I have no control.

Préface, 125

SMOOTH TIME   What's desired in the *Vita Nova* associated with the Work is a particular kind of time, a particular kind of daily temporality; the writer must, almost despite himself, bind himself to a time with no rough patches, no "disturbances." Flaubert (1853, thirty-two years old): "In order to write, I require the *impossibility* of being disturbed (even when I might want to be)."[25] The writer must be bound to Time by a law over which he has no control, a *Nature*—and for that reason, however *practical* he wants it to be, the temporality that the writer's *Vita Nova* desires is a philosophical category; indeed, what he wants—an almost mystical, paradisiacal desire—is a *smooth time*: a time with no endpoint, with no expiration date, which contains, for instance, no appointments, no "things to do" to interrupt *the thing* to be done → The image that might approach this Smooth Time would be that of Drifting. Rousseau on Saint-Pierre Island (Lake Bienne): he often jumps into a little boat "which the attendant had taught me to manage with a single oar; I would make straight for the open water. The moment I left the shore, I felt joy so intense as to leave me trembling, and whose cause I cannot begin to tell or even to comprehend, unless perhaps it came from some secret feeling at finding myself, in this place, beyond the reach of human wickedness."[26] (Rousseau is already old; he's lived through a lot; he's at the age when what you want more than anything else is for "people to just leave you alone": age of *innocence*, of No Harm, which corresponds to Childhood; the child is the one who mustn't be harmed) → This Smooth Time mustn't be interrupted, but it does have to be scanned, to be subjected to a *Rhythm*, to the Strophes of Labor; regular tempo: that of *Rule* (cf. infra[27] → Whence, *a contrario*, Bustle = *Rhythm-less*).

Confessions, 637

Administration

From the point of view of Temporality, what's unrelated to the Work, to its Fabrication, to the Smooth Time of the Work to be Written = *administrative tasks* (≠ creative tasks): all kinds of life, and especially a social life, require effort, tasks if they are to carry on, to be sustained.

WRITINGS Managing writings: translations, new editions, *writings*,[28] proof corrections. This kind of management is irritating because, for the writer, once the work is written, it falls into the inessential, to be supplanted by the as yet unwritten work → The finished Work becomes *artificial*. Flaubert (1862, forty-one years old): "Once a work is finished, you have to think of writing another. As for the one which has just been completed, I lose all interest in it; if I show it to the public, it is out of stupidity and in compliance with a received idea that *one must publish*, something which I personally don't feel the need to do." (this overstates it, I think; cf. *infra* on "Not publishing")[29] → All administrative tasks come down to *copying out* (= recopying); I spend weeks at a time *recopying*: *writings*, reports, repeating what I've said, reworking what's already been done ≠ creation: nonrepetition; creation of an *Original-Writing*: before Duplication.

Préface, 222

CORRESPONDENCE Managing your social circle: not necessarily a "worldly" circle (that's easily avoided, you only have to not like that kind of thing) but a network of relations: network in which your relationships within a certain milieu (for example, intellectual) and your affective relationships are interlinked. Often impossible to tell apart. For example, the difficulty of getting someone else to deal with your letters → *correspondence* is indeed a laborious administrative task, a real *crux*: for me? Yes, to be sure, but also—keeping things in proportion—for Flaubert; 1878 (fifty-seven years old), to Caroline, his niece: "And on the subject of letters, people *pester me* to write them! I have a mind to announce in the papers that I won't answer anymore: four today! Six yesterday! Just as many the day before! My time is eaten away by this idiotic scribbling." (what he doesn't say: those were *real* letters, ultimately an important part of his oeuvre; but this is an *a posteriori* point of view; he only knew the distress at being kept from the work to be written).—And Rousseau (Saint Pierre Island, 1765): "After breakfast, I would write, hurriedly and grudgingly, a few wretched letters, thinking longingly all the

Préface, 283

Confessions, 636

while of the happy moment when I would never have to write another."³⁰ → Why is letter writing such a "cross" to bear? Precisely because it represents an affective constraint, that is to say, a constraint on the good side, on the side of affection; I'm torn between the necessity of meeting the demands of the affection that I can't do without, the affection that is my precious, vital possession and the "madness" that makes me desire the lifting of all constraints: the work is *intolerant* (and, in that, "mad"); just as in some extreme cases even a mouthful of Vichy water can disagree with a dyspeptic (Aunt Léonie)³¹ in a movement of excess even the obligation to write a postcard to a friend disagrees with me—let alone a whole day spent writing letters.

ACCOUNTS   To grasp how heavily this Management weighs, we need only make a few calculations; to a "writer's" day (ideally, a writer who doesn't have another job) day, four parts: (1) The part for Basic Needs: eating, sleeping, washing (already cultural!). (2) Part for creative Labor: the book (the Course? Yes, but it's already less creative than the real writing, that of the book). (3) Part for Administration: letter-writing, manuscripts, *writings*,³² the inevitable interviews, proof corrections, shopping (hairdresser's!), private views and friends' films. (4) Sociality, Conviviality, Friendship. All that, as reduced, as restricted as one could make it. Over twenty-four hours: ten hours given over to Basic Needs, four to conviviality (for example, the evenings), five to creative work, five to administration. It's absurd: administration, pure maintenance, takes up as much time as creation → Is it base to make such calculations (especially to calculate the Time for Friendship)? Yes, but as I said: an egoism of the Work imposes itself very quickly, because, in a sense, the world doesn't want anything to do with it; to the world, the labor of the Work is both *respectable* (a liberal belief) and *un-desirable* (ab-normal). The other's resistances to being disturbed are put down to *ill-temper*: as if it were *natural* (= the Unmarked) to disturb / to be disturbed—and interfering with that natural order were abnormal; it requires an explanation.

LUXURY   You therefore have to be constantly *wrenching* the Work from an antagonistic force that's of the order of Nature—or Social Nature, in the sense that the Work is a pure *Individual*: for it's *normal*, or at least, in the life of Humanity, it has been up until now—and the point of Socialism would be precisely to *alter* that Nature, that Normality—that the administration of life should absorb the time of life itself; we live just to carry on living; what has to be *wrenched from life* is the remainder, the surplus, the *luxury* (not in the ostentatious sense) → even for a social individual as sophisticated as the writer, administrative tasks only manage to maintain a life, they aren't capable of producing this surplus, which for the writer is the essential thing → Everything about social life forces the writer to engage in Administration; if he enters old age, for example, we expect (*we* = Opinion, Myth) old age to be the time for *managing* past achievements: the time for repeating, reviewing his work, for chairing committees, etc. (I said, on the contrary, the *natural* movement of old age, in the *individual* sense, was the *Vita Nova*).[33] Actually, at the other extreme, someone who works solely for the surplus is in the ambiguous position (morally, mythically ambiguous) of a Queen Bee: monstrously idle and yet a participant in the organization of social movement (so far, at any rate): she's well looked after and productive, but [*illegible*]. Those who refuse administration = discredited marginals. Figures of what could be called *Anti-Administration* (less prestigious than *Self-Administration*): the Tramp, the Parasite, the Scrounger and, in a more philosophical mode, the man of Tao (of the *Heap*).

Defenses

TO REFUSE How can the writer (the one I'm discussing: who wants to write a Work) protect himself against the encroachments, the onslaughts of Administration (in the very broad sense of the term, broader than just professional administration), against *life's demands*? → The advice is: *Refuse, Refuse* (the demands, the invitations, the desires) → Clearly, whether we wanted to or not, the solution, the *Defense*, is on this side → Michelet talks somewhere about a community in Antiquity that perishes because they can't say *no* → Let's imagine, in the mode of a fantastic Novel, a man (a hero or a saint) who fell ill every time he said no and as a result was prevented from refusing anything. Imagine the at once grotesque and dramatic way in which his life would unfold (this could be a good outline for a plot, along the lines of Voltaire's *Contes*) → To refuse: question of life or death → So why is it difficult? Grammatical question, if I may say so: *to refuse* is classed as a transitive verb (with a direct object): you refuse *something*; but what really matters is the complement: you always refuse *someone* something; it's not possible to refuse no one; the real transitivity is not that which links the subject to an object (what's refused) but that which links the subject to another subject (who is refused); Latin expresses this well: "to refuse someone your door" = *prohibere aliquem janua* (or *domo*), "to refuse, to deprive someone *of* door." And so, of course, it all begins: intersubjectivity, the play of images, fear, desire, friendship, etc. → Such a slippery slope, so dangerous for the work, that the writer (who I'm discussing, the *scripturus*, someone who wants to and is going to write) is constantly trying to come up with *defenses* (ways of protecting himself) against the exigencies of Management → Defenses = sorts of relays that cut the demand short but without having to accept direct responsibility for the ultimate aggressive act of saying *No* → I'm not talking about the contingent *lies* that everyone weaves into their lives with a view to refusing something tiresome: illnesses, trips abroad, and all the made-up details ≠ I'm talking about the basic defenses that can serve beyond such and such contingency—for it's easy to lie just once, but repeated lying, now that signifies something, which is precisely: I lie (the whole mechanism of lying in Proust). I list, among others:

Préface, 36

IMMOBILITY   Stubborn immobility (with respect to and against everything): what I said about Idleness, the Heap, but now in the service of the Work; not replying to letters (other than bills, if only to avoid an even bigger interruption at a later stage), not turning up to appointments, cutting off the telephone, etc. Flaubert (1846, twenty-five years old): "I regularly read or write for eight hours a day; and if I'm disturbed, I'm ill. Many days go by without going to the edge of the terrace; the boat is simply not floating."[34] (Me in Urt)[35] → Probably an untenable position, but one that's worth considering in that it forces us to consider "disturbances," "movements" from the point of view of *consequentiality* or *inconsequentiality*, which is to say it makes clear what is of no consequence, what has to do with habit, and what has to do with the vague pressure of the Image; we often allow ourselves be disturbed through rashness, habit, or for fear of doing damage to our Image (even though it's rare for refusing to be interrupted to have any repercussions). We could—one day, another time—reflect upon a kind of *Typology of Retreats* or, if you prefer, of *Immobile Times* → There'd be:

1. Monastic time: profound interiority;[36]
2. Epicurean time: Planting ("the Retiree");[37]
3. Sterile time, no longer autarchic, but autistic: narcissistic to the point of sterility: the time of frozen exile, illustrated by Mallarmé's (and Valéry's) bird: *the Swan*; cf. sonnet: "The lively, lovely, and virginal today." Last lines:

> *Phantom whose pure white dooms it to this place,
> swathed in futile exile with a chill
> dream of contumely, the Swan is still.*[38]

A NOVEL TO WRITE   The Work to be written can itself be a declared motive for refusal; paradoxical return to the truth: "I'm sorry, I've got a novel to write" (since we're dealing with the Preparation of the Novel) → "I'm writing *Paludes*." Unfortunately, no one is ever convinced by the truth, or at any rate the truth is often less convincing than a lie (this is the basic principle of rhetoric); moreover, for such an excuse to serve as grounds for Refusal (that is, for it to neither arouse suspicion nor be contested) it is necessary for a society or a milieu to recognize the work as something important, vital—vital, if we can expect this, which is now infrequently the case → Paradox, a journalistic one at any rate: the Work exists (has a "value") only in order to be frittered away in interviews, prefaces, etc.—as if the work had written itself, as if no one had spent any time on it; people expect you to play the role of the writer (still necessary for a certain kind of journalism), without thinking about the fact that it takes time.

ORIGINALITY   Perhaps the most powerful defense (but you have to have the talent for it) is that of *originality*: make it clear to the world that you're an "original," and, by virtue of this, of it being a recognized and categorized role, they stop making demands → It's possible that Proust's originality (not to say his eccentricity) served unintentionally to protect and assist him in the fabrication of the work by enveloping the subject in a sort of cloak that was *looked at* but never attacked or breached. Simply dressing in an original way can be enough to make you *different*, to distance and in a sense *exempt* you from being solicited (Proust, on the boulevard Haussman: uneven moustache, dark-brown dressing gown; a pad of cotton-wool over his shirt-collar, floss silk gloves, knitted slippers.[39]—Rue Hamelin: in bed with a scarf around his neck; when receiving visitors, he'd get out from under the covers fully dressed, wearing white or black cotton gloves, several pairs of stockings, and a ruffled shirtfront.);[40] to say nothing, of course (but we'll come back to this), of the inversion of day and night → What's more, there's a kind of individualistic freedom in all that which would be difficult to achieve today, in the context of an increasingly overbearing State: complete self-sequestration isn't easy; even though his eyesight was failing, Proust didn't want to see an

L. P.-Quint, 90

115

Rivane

L. P.-Quint, 113

oculist (because he could only go out at night). Today, he'd be taken by force in an ambulance (social security, etc.); likewise, upon the declaration of war in 1914, he was embarrassed because he wanted a doctor to call on him *at night* (since he couldn't go out in the day): can you imagine such naivety today! On occasions, Proust would use excessive and calculated courtesy as a form of protection (still within the context of his originality); Rue Hamelin, Proust, extremely sensitive to noise, which prevented him from working (it was a busy house), was at the point of despair: the children who used to stomp about in the rooms above him; he made them a present of felt slippers.

"WORKSHOP" Why does administration present such a weighty issue? Because these are the bitty, repetitive tasks that come round and round again, that—like Sisyphus—you can never get to the bottom of, that interrupt the flow, the continuity of creative work → Now, this continuity is experienced as necessary, vital; the work is socially gratuitous: you can only believe in it, devote yourself to it by shutting yourself away in it, by creating a sort of schizophrenia, an autism within yourself → Administrative tasks (letter writing, appointments, small commissions): so many little demons that come along to upset, break up the unity of the work in the process of being written → Solution that's often toyed with, favored: to set aside, for example, one day a week for administration so you then don't have to think about it=to block off, to sacrifice a day so that you can have your mind free for the rest of the week → At one time, together with a friend who was experiencing the same problems, I envisaged (probably only as a joke, since we still haven't made it happen) spending one day a week blitzing our administrative tasks side by side, tasks that are probably less tiresome when you do them in the company of someone else; we would thus have created an embryo of a weekly *workshop* {*ouvroir*} (> *operare*, "to work"), a place where everyone works collectively ("charitable" connotation), a kind of prefiguration of how time ought to be organized in a good society: one day for work, six days either for daydreaming or for your obsession—as long as it's inoffensive.

ILLNESS To bring the "Defenses" against the world to a close, there's one supreme and paradoxical defense against administrative tasks, and especially against the guilt that gnaws away at you when you don't manage to finish them—for we are all responsible for our presence in the world—, a defense that releases you from all sin and leaves you alone and free before an endless daily writing: *illness.*

Seuil, 137–138

1. Kafka, back from Hungary, August 1917: coughing, spitting up blood; September: it's clear that it's tuberculosis. Kafka is almost happy about this: "It's almost a relief"; released from all obligations (what I'm calling administration): office, family, fiancée (Felice). "Freedom, freedom above all else." Sets off for Zürau, a little village in Bohemia. To Max Brod: "In any case, my attitude to the tuberculosis today resembles that of a child clinging to the pleats of his mother's skirt.... I am constantly seeking an explanation for this disease, for I did not seek it. Sometimes it seems to me that my brains and lungs came to an agreement without my knowledge."[41] → I know that feeling: ill twice (with tuberculosis): (a) The first time I was seventeen years old, it was in May of the year of my philosophy class; difficult personal circumstances, which my illness released me from → but free cure at Bedous:[42] the solitude, sadness, frustration of adolescence. (b) Relapse during the Occupation (1941): a way of releasing myself from anxiety? → Sanatorium: happy; friendships, a long time spent reading the classics (but no writing). I've often wondered—cheap psychoanalysis—whether I fell ill with tuberculosis *in order to* protect myself from a distressing familial, then national, situation. Yet, I didn't write anything when I was ill—only made notes on what I was reading → It was only when I returned to the active world that I started writing (1946, *Combat, Degree Zero,*[43] etc.) → It goes without saying that the protection provided by illness is incredibly ambiguous; you're aware of how dangerous it is; in Kafka's time and that of my youth you died of tuberculosis; that's what lay at the end of it—or if not that then the life of a patient whose condition is stable but who isn't "cured," who's destined to spend the whole of his life in the mountains: sanatorium librarian, or doctor (I considered it).

2. Proust's illness must *also* (that is to say, must not only) be interpreted as a Defense: the discourse of Complaint abounds in Proust = discourse of the Retreat from the World → his illness (clinically quite complex, not to say enigmatic; there's a book on this):[44] both what prevented him from working and what enabled him to write.—And, with Proust, this terrible sign: he died as soon as the Work was complete → Never has the Work / Illness (and Death) coupling been more dialectical—or more nuptial.

3. Charles-Louis Philippe: "Illness is the poor man's travel" (Madame Bocquet, not at all concerned about the prospect of going to

the hospital: *preparations* for the journey)⁴⁵ → for the writer, illness can be not *a vacation* but a fantasized *vacancy*, the worldly void in which the Work fantasmatically comes to reside.

Religious

Before going into the practical details of the *Vita Nova*, I want to point out (or don't want to suppress the fact) that there's clearly a connection between the very idea of a *Vita Nova* (in which to write the work) and the religious: the writer "sacralizes" the Work (I'll come back to this) and by putting himself in its service, by becoming a "convert" to the work, endeavors to effect a spectacular change in his way of life.

As regards the worldly / the world, the subject accepts, comes to terms with a form of *Resignation* (something that's never well regarded) → I'm thinking of Eliot's wonderful expression: "*The awful daring of a moment's surrender*"⁴⁶ → However committed it might be *after the fact*, writing a work gives the appearance of a *surrender* to the forces of desire or guilt, which in the world's eyes look like healthy, sound, natural forces. This surrender: to substitute one moral authority for another, in other words, to undergo a *conversion*. Affinity with the *mystical* movement, for the mystic always chooses the "de-valued," the *Darkness*. But, once again, why a Work? Why this relentless effort, these sacrifices, this absolute? To go back once again to Mallarmé's response: "Do we know what it is to write? An ancient and very vague but jealous practice, whose meaning lies in *the mystery of the heart*. He who achieves it, wholly, is strengthened."⁴⁷

Seuil, 7

Casuistry of Egoism

I want to go back to the *Egoism* that the Work forces us into:

To Sacralize Yourself

A moment ago I said that the writer has to be willing to *sacralize* the work (to consecrate it)—The problem we're setting ourselves isn't that of the *finished work*—the work for others (at which point it doesn't matter whether it's sacred or not; even: the finished work is no longer *sacred* in the eyes of its author); our problem is the *work to be written*, *opus agendum*, hence the work that *I* must write; therefore, by means of a voluntary and provisional stratagem, it's the would-be writer that has to be sacralized; you have to make yourself into a sacred being *in terms of what you do* (and not who you are), so that when the world attacks the *worker* (the *operator*)[48] that I am those attacks are *serious* (this isn't all that strange or over the top; there are many traces, scraps of sacralization in secular life; look at political language: attacks on the *worker* in the current communist—I mean nonrationalist— context, for example, are implicitly considered to be acts of "blasphemy").

Préface, 282

For example, you have to "figure yourself," to see yourself as a *figure*: I project an image of myself playing a role, and the strength of that role will help me to do I want to do. Flaubert makes this point (1878, fifty-seven years old: so it's just not a feature of adolescence): "You have to act the part of a strong man in your own eyes; that's the way to become one."[49] → I act the part of a writer, in the fully sacred sense of the role, *as a way* of enabling myself to become one.

Préface, 14

A different means—or a different trace—of that sacralization: to *solemnify* the act of writing—of starting, of finishing the work; cf. the first stone laid or the flag unfurled on top of a finished roof → Flaubert again, on completing The Temptation of Saint Anthony: "Wednesday, September 12, 1849, at 3:20 in the afternoon, a sunny and windy day. Begun May 12, 1848, at 3 and a quarter hours." (The extent to which this solemnification is of the order of the *symbolic*; humiliatingly disputed by the reality of the situation; the work Flaubert is announcing and triumphantly signing off had more avatars than any other: censured by his friends Maxime du Camp and Bouilhet (who recommend a more down-to-earth topic→ *Madame Bovary*), revised in 1856, published in 1874, that is to say, twenty-five years after the solemnification of its completion). Once again, I want to make clear that the one to be sacralized is the *Operator*, the one who produces, not the *Scriptor*, the one who produced. Whence an amusing misunderstanding: when people rudely (more or less aggressively) set about desacralizing a writer who in their view is sacralizing himself, dressing himself up as a writer → Episode with Henri ** on the train to Cabourg:[50] he quite clearly thought I considered myself a consecrated writer, and took pleasure in desacralizing me. But after a while I realized that what he was actually doing was sacralizing me and challenging me on the basis of a false position: I don't consider myself a writer, but I have to consider myself someone who wants to write. I watched him get more and more embroiled in an operation that I knew in myself wasn't about me: he was off target but would only have taken any protestation to be a suspect disavowal on my part → The correct response was to explain that there was indeed "sacralization" at work, but elsewhere: of the work to be done, of schedules, appointments, etc.

Reminder of the fantasized Form:

"... *the idea and the first form of a book has to be a space, a simple site where the material of the book will be placed, and not material to be placed and arranged.*" (Joubert)[51]

SESSION OF JANUARY 26, 1980

Casuistry of Egoism

Why "sacralize" yourself? Because it provides you with the strength of a certain egoism, without which the Work can't be written → kind of self-manipulation = replacing charity (or, if you don't like that word, *generosity*) (having time for everyone) with another authority that also partakes of the "religious," that is to say, that also has a fundamental link with nature, with the world—and which is Writing → if I'm using the word "egoism" it's because it allows us to enter into a series of practical issues (to do with the practice of writing) that are knotted around the *ego* → Indeed, someone who wants to write must *organize* his writer's ego (*scribens*) on the basis of a systematic set of calculations or, more generally, of *life traits*: what Nietzsche curiously terms "*the casuistry of egoism*" → In *Ecce Homo*, his last work, Nietzsche, with bombast, passion and verve, holding nothing back, provides a detailed breakdown of his preferences, habits, and opinions: "I shall be asked why I have really narrated all these little things which according to the traditional judgment are matters of indifference.... Answer: these minor things—nutriment, place, climate, recreation, *the whole casuistry of egoism*—are beyond all conception of greater importance than anything that has been considered of importance hitherto. It is precisely here that a *re-education* has to begin."[1] (*Casuistry* = justificatory construction).

The *Vita Nova*, that is to say, the point of entry into the Making of the Work, entails an *education*, a *self-education*, and therefore a *re-education*, for it's a question of passing from one way of life into another → It's a matter of conceiving of the *finer details* of your life (of your way of life), without fear of a super-ego that would condemn such details as trivial; whence the notion of *casuistry*: a force that dares to make such subtle *distingos* in the order of a way of life.

Let's take a look, then, at some elements of this "*casuistry of egoism*" (clearly I'm only talking about this *simulacrum*, this *eidolon* of the writer, a composite made up of several writers and, on occasion—this is the rule I set down at the outset—of myself).

Ecce Homo, 273

Regimes

I'm taking this word in the general sense: the day-to-day organization of your everyday needs (Nietzsche = the horror of a life where everything would have to be improvised): *eating, dressing* (*sleeping:* all too important to the writer, *all too related to the head!* We'll deal with sleep separately).

1. *Diet.* A peculiar thing: very little is known about the relationship between writers and food (other than when food appears in the work: see J.-P. Richard's very fine studies of Flaubert, Huysmans, Proust, etc.):[2] What did they eat? How did they eat? As a general rule, we don't know, or we only know bits and pieces (for example, we know what Proust ate, thanks to his servants)—it's as if this were the ultimate inconsequential detail, so very insignificant that it would never be worth the effort of discussing it—Nietzsche, however, explains his food.

NIETZSCHE, ECCE HOMO[3]

I am interested in quite a different way in a question upon which the "salvation of mankind" depends far more than it does upon any kind of quaint curiosity of the theologians: the question of nutriment. One can for convenience's sake formulate it thus: "how to nourish yourself so as to attain your maximum of strength, of virtù in the Renaissance style, of moraline-free virtue?"—My experiences here are as bad as they possibly could be; I am astonished that I heard this question so late. Only the perfect worthlessness of our German education—its "idealism"—can to some extent explain to me why on precisely this point I was backward to the point of holiness.

Exemplary passage, for, at first glance, purely egotistical confidence, but in fact every detail = a *sign* that refers back to a philosophy, to precisely what gives Nietzschean thematics their distinctive character → this is the "casuistry." Following on from this, a dossier would have to be opened on "styles of food," on how it's possible to fantasize a style of food in accordance with the style of the work (= the *Vita Nova*); what we lack is not a *sociology* of Food (some do exist) but its Philosophy, or its Philosophies—not on the scale of a religion (fastings, vegetarianisms, etc.) but that of the individual: the more or less analogical connection between a food system and a fantasmatic or, more precisely, a symbolic system; for example, Joubert: his fondness for the fragment, for the *uncon-*

structedness of thought, of the work. Now, we know that he observed (albeit in an anarchic, capricious fashion) what countless weight-loss regimes (though in fact there's only one: hunger) now call: the *dissociated diet*. Chateaubriand: "M. Joubert was constantly modifying his diet and regime, living off milk one day and minced meat <already!> the next . . ."[4] → I must stress this: symbolic meaning, not necessarily of a specific food (the issue of "taboos" is somewhat different), but of systems, of dietary styles, the *gestalt* of menus (the ways in which food is consumed). Thus, powerful affect in this: the fact that, at the end of his life, thinking of the way his mother nursed herself, Proust went on a diet: nothing more than a little milky coffee.[5]

2. An individual, especially nowadays, can be defined by his *Pharmacopoeia*; everyone has one; a little medicine cabinet, independent of actual treatments for actual illnesses; what you can buy at the pharmacy without a prescription, or with repeat prescriptions; what accompanies life (*something for the journey*), relieves the little aches and pains, makes the body more comfortable—or more tolerable. Whence the current debate (Social Security): I'm convinced that the need for a personal pharmacopoeia belongs to an Imaginary; can Social Security reimburse the Imaginary's expenses? This actually has to do with the historical evolution of the body; Progress gives rise to both Social Security and a new demand from the Imaginary, and that demand rapidly comes to coincide with a Need; if I couldn't rely on Optalidon, Eno, Aturgyl, and Optanox,[6] my body wouldn't be as comfortable → Pharmacopoeia: veritable prosthesis for the body, can fit in a suitcase.

As regards the writer, this is the whole dossier on his *drugs* (I discussed this, I think, in another lecture):[7] either stimulants, or soporifics, or paradoxically—but quite commonly—both at the same time: Proust, terrible insomnia (sixty hours without switching off the electric light) → Veronal: massive consumption: three grams per day, plus caffeine (not actually used as a stimulant, but to combat his fear of suffocation; but who knows? an excuse?), his preferred medication, seventeen cups of coffee to relieve a suffocation attack: "my steps, trembling from the caffeine" → I won't go into this dossier in detail; I'll simply make a note of the fact that when faced with the exigency of the Work the writer's body feels powerless, inadequate, incapable of finding a *balance*, an appropriate equilibrium between the Sentence and the Body (cf. *infra* on the Slow Hand);[8] the body feels simultaneously and contradictorily sleepy, opaque, "out of it," sluggish, lazy, uninventive—it has to be roused, stimulated—and yet at the same time the stimulation has to be controlled, for it has the tendency to go on interminably: insomnia—I've never been able to work in the evenings, because afterward I can't sleep; I need a sort of social (or, in the countryside, televisual) *buffer* between work and sleep; I need (this isn't very kind of me!) something to "make me yawn" (to relax me); now, however thankless, labor never makes you (makes me) yawn.

3. *Dress*: of note since it's one aspect of the writer's (albeit fantasmatic) *ease*. Rather than dress, *outfit*. Some outfits are legendary: Proust (I've discussed this already), Balzac (his dressing gown) → Dressing Gown? Could imply, if not taken literally, a long *robe*: an item of clothing that envelops, protects, while also (Flügel)[9] suggesting importance, authority (*robe*: not in any way feminine, Middle Ages, the Orient) → Rousseau at Motiers-Travers: "I adopted the Armenian dress. This was not a new idea. It had presented itself to at various times during the course of my life, especially at Montmorency, where the frequent use I made of probes, confining me often to my room, had made me more aware of the advantages of long clothes. . . . I thus had a little Armenian wardrobe."[10] (Which is why people would throw stones at him: eccentricity isn't always a protection.)

Confessions, 594

Here we could in all seriousness (though still with a smile on our lips) raise the question of the "Novelist's outfit," or that of the realist novelist at any rate, someone who observes and takes note of what he sees outdoors (Zola, three days in Rome, notes down everything for his book) → Necessity of a *notebook* that can be speedily taken out of a pocket, like a camera (coded in commerce, such things as *reporter's bags* do actually exist) → A jacket with pockets, not just a pullover: frustration at trying to get a notebook and a pen out of a trouser pocket → Now, an idea not noted down immediately = idea forgotten, that is to say, annulled, that is to say, void: literature can't do without notation (→ dossier to be continued, to be completed) (think of Flaubert's long moleskin notebooks, written in pencil: necessity of *shirt-tails*).

Home

Here's a key theme for the *Vita Nova*, and for the Preparation of the Work (though that doesn't mean I'll be discussing it in depth): *setting up home*; if it were me, this would be most powerful scenario of the *Vita Nova*: to go and set up home somewhere; the fantasy bears upon the preparations for this setting up: choosing the place, getting the things you need to take together, etc.; novelistic fantasy of those erstwhile long voyages by boat: the houseboat, theme of the *Nautilus*.

What's required (fantasmatically speaking) is a new location: *Vita Nova, Locus Novus* → Model of Setting Up Home in order to start a new life: *Bouvard and Pécuchet* → infallible: despite all its comic, absurd aspects I can never read the scene where they set up home at Chavignolles[11] without experiencing the most intense envy and delight. Note that Bouvard and Pécuchet move house not in order to compose a work of writing—although their project is closely related: they want to embark on an *education*; at the intersection between the book and its application; it is indeed a matter of a *Vita Nova*, one that follows in the Shadow of the book.

Another fantasized feature of the new location: *autarky*; [the location] must be isolated and, as far as possible, I need to be able to be self-sufficient; which means "living off the set-up" in the same way as one might "live off the land"; now, the countryside (a house) is more self-sufficient than an apartment, thanks to its "reserves" (the store cupboard, the wine cellar): garden + store cupboard + tools = autarky → not going out for days on end → creation of a stable microsystem, like that of a boat → Material autarky amounts to a moral value of the epicurean sort: *moderation*, *modesty*, a sober life → to be self-sufficient = to make do with not very much → *Vita Nova*: a kind of rounded life, one that runs on its own, off the same elements and, because it looks after itself, one that leaves enough energy left over for the work → Total autarky, described in Plantin's sonnet:

THE HAPPINESS OF THIS WORLD

To have a home of comfort, neat and clean,
A garden carpeted with fragrant vine,
Few children, many fruits, the best of wine,
To own a faithful wife and live unseen;

To have no debts, or loves, or quarrels mean,
And not to share with kindred what is thine,
Be pleased with little, vanity confine,
Not on the great but on true justice lean;

To live ambitionless and openly,
To give oneself to piety unquestioningly,
To tame thy passions with thy every breath;

To keep thy judgment strong and spirit free,
Tell thy Rosary, tend thy flowers with care:
This is to wait full tranquilly on death.[12]

That sonnet has enchanted me ever since reading it as a child (it hung in a frame on the dining-room wall at Bayonne): I've never felt cut off, fantasmatically, from the circle of life—from the rounded life—that it represents, despite the necessary "adaptations," for those "adaptations" are easily made: *piety* (I almost prefer piety to "Faith") can relate to small-scale symbolism, to regulated spiritual occupations; *rosary*: formal, regulated occupations, the form of which can be adapted to something else → I adore the fragrant vines, the house neat and clean, the fruits, the hard graft—and the last verse, which has always made me envious (the only problem: the wife; but you could say "we all have our problems" or "that's your problem") → The whole sonnet, not an ascetic vision—retreat into homemaking: flowers in beautiful vases, for instance, fruit in elegant ceramics, etc.—but an Epicurean vision (one that doesn't exclude pleasure but that moderates it, makes it *reasonable*, regular) of an immobile time, where the *New* (that is, Adventure) is no longer made into a value; and for precisely that reason the New is completely interiorized: it is the Work.

To go back to the productive, creative *Vita Nova*: the *Vita Nova* (fantasmatically) associated with a House or, failing that, what I'll call: "the cavernous apartment" = out-of-the-way, enclosed. I know of one: peaceful neighborhood + courtyard + back garden + very big room with a window: grandeur and seclusion, shelter (Mallarmé) → I have wondered: where does this fondness for Home, for doing intellectual work at Home come from (lost, uprooted and inefficient in the Library, incapable of working in an Office, for instance here in the Collège)? Perhaps from this: as a schoolboy (at the Lycée Montaigne and then the Lycée Louis-le-Grand), I delighted in being ill, that is to say, in being obliged to stay at home on those days when everyone else was at school; that is to say, in having access to a privileged domain, in discovering home-time outside of mealtimes and holidays, the mornings especially (I still like mornings: I don't like staying in bed) → Perhaps it was this that made me want to become a schoolteacher: not having spent *as much time* at school as my classmates; having had, compared to other workers, a *supplement* of home.

This exploration of the work-space follows the order of an ever-increasing *proxemy* (*proxemics*: space where all objects are within

Home

Bedroom

reach: armchair, bed, table). I discussed this in the first course)[13] →
More proxemical than the House or the Apartment: the Bedroom.

The "*Vita Nova*" Bedroom (that could be a style, like Lévitan style)[14] is an extension of the Home through its *archaism* → For the act of withdrawing into yourself implies a certain regression (others would say: to the womb), and that regression is precisely what characterizes the style → *Vita Nova*: has much to gain, I think, from a certain attachment to the past → Because of this mixture of childhood and "the old days," I now want to quote Proust's beautiful page on the bedroom (remember that the whole of *In Search of Lost Time* is presented as a shock, coming in ever bigger waves, of remembering bedrooms once occupied in various different places); the page is from *Against Sainte-Beuve*, the chapter is called "Bedrooms":

PROUST, *AGAINST SAINTE-BEUVE*

My body, still too torpid to move hand or foot, lay guessing at its surroundings. All those which it had known from childhood onward offered themselves in turn to its groping memory, reassembling round it every place I had ever slept it, even those which for years I had not called to mind and might never have called to mind til my dying day, although they were places I ought not to have forgotten. It remembered the room, the doorway, the passage, the last waking thought which reappears as the first thought on waking.[15]

Préface, 32

The bedroom-study comprises two mythically decisive elements: the fire and the lamp (replacing the erstwhile candles) → Flaubert (1845, twenty-four years old): "I have said an irrevocable farewell to practical life.... From now until a day that is far distant I ask for no more five or six quiet hours in my room, a good fire in winter and a pair of candles to light me at night"[16] → the good fire, this is a *style*: results in a very definite work, a plan to be executed (this is our theme); a sort of Benedictism of labor; imagination taking the place of erudition—or rather, in Flaubert's case, of the labor, the crafting of style: Can you imagine Céline, Artaud, needing a good fire in order to write?

As for the lamp: three civilizations (not so long ago, if you took a train across France, you could watch them file past): that of the light bulb (farmhouse kitchens), that of the ceiling light (petite-bourgeois dining rooms), that of the lamp → Paradoxical but significant fact: Proust's bedroom—during the manic fabrication of

Rivane, 46

the Work, that is to say, while living on boulevard Haussmann and rue Hamelin: window always closed against hermetically sealed shutters, curtains drawn, because any unfamiliar smell (the chestnut trees on the boulevard Haussmann) → attack of suffocation—a single light bulb, the room poorly lit; but (a) here the space in question isn't the bedroom but the bed (cf. *infra*, I'll come to it in a moment); it therefore wasn't a matter of creating a *cavernous*, shadowy space, the *tenebroso* of a private realm; (b) and therefore, perhaps: the Work was so absorbing that "aesthetic" or mythical considerations of space were of little importance (and then there's the aesthetic refinement of culture ≠ the living space) → At the opposite extreme of everything I've been saying: once it starts coming together, the Work transports the writer beyond his immediate surroundings; it's possible to write a Work on a café table; and so, *a contrario*: perhaps overthinking the Bedroom, the House, the *Vita Nova* amounts to artificially filling in a certain emptiness in the Work, a certain sterility = in some ways the strategy is unproductive (fantasmatical nature of the exploration I'm undertaking here).

To go back to the mythical force of the Bedroom: it has two functions of *harmony*, of pacification: (a) It's where the subject is released from all pretence; its aesthetic is therefore not immediately apparent; it's not a decorative aesthetic; an absolutely solipsistic aesthetic, *for the subject's eyes only*: whence a mixture of practical, symbolic, biographical, maniacal elements, outside of any aesthetic *code*; for example, Schopenhauer's bedroom in his house in Frankfurt: sixteen engravings of dogs and, alongside a portrait of his mother, his poodle's death-mask, deceased in 1843 (his will: the main beneficiary: his poodle, Atma). Likewise, Proust's bedroom: disorder and unaestheticism.—(b) The miracle of the bedroom is to simultaneously figure (to unite) two logically contradictory values: the enclosure (is to say, the shelter, safety) and the absolute freedom of being in your own company → Proust again (*Against Sainte-Beuve*): "a bedroom I had in Brussels whose proportions were so pleasing, so spacious and yet so cozy, that it seemed a nest to hide in and a world to explore."[17]

Seuil, 103

Desk

Continuation and coming almost to the end of the movement toward proxemy: the *table* (the work desk).

Seuil, 100

1. It's truly the umbilical cord of writing. Kafka refused to go on holiday with Max Brod: "my fear of the journey is partly compounded by the thought that I will be kept away from the desk for

several days. And this ridiculous thought <though Kafka is actually in the process of finishing *The Castle*> is really the only legitimate one, since the existence of the writer is truly dependent on his desk and if he wants to keep madness at bay he must never go far from his desk, he must hold onto it with his teeth."[18] The paradox is well put: a madness (a mania) in order to escape madness → The Desk becomes a vital center.

2. What is this Desk? Or, more importantly, what *must* it be (for what might look like an object invested with a function is in reality invested with a *value*)? I think it's essentially a *structure*, which is to say a localization of functions and connections between microfunctions, for example, the writing surface, lighting, writing instruments, paper clips, blank index cards, written index cards, papers stapled together, a clock, etc.:

a. The complexity of this structure varies with the subject: ascetic subjects and luxurious subjects, maniacal subjects and indifferent subjects, do-it-yourself-ers (structuralists!) and conformist subjects (whose offices look like a CEO's); a typology is possible, a reading of the Desk as a body of signs referring us back to the subject's relationship to his work (an erotic, sublimated, dilatory, etc. relationship.) → I personally experience a very strong sense of alterity whenever I see empty desks or rooms without the usual objects lying around.

Journal, 22

b. The relationship between structure and order or disorder: structure takes precedence over tidiness; a desk can look disorganized, but if the structure is respected, then its untidiness isn't contingent (correctable, "tidy-able"): there are structured messes, which as a result function very well, indefinitely → Disorder must be in keeping with the structure, and I like to think this is what Kafka meant when he complained of his desk being *in a certain kind of disorder:* "I have now examined my desk more closely and have seen that nothing can be done on it. There is so much lying about, it forms a disorder without proportion and without that compatibility of disordered things which otherwise makes every disorder bearable . . ."[19]

Bed

There's a variation on the desk: the *bed*; in a way it's the *éidos* of proxemics (of the retreat) since you can work, eat, and sleep in it.

Préface, 69

1. For Flaubert, it corresponds to the phase of *reflection* (when there's no point in writing). 1852 (thirty-one years old): "I have to

be completely immobile in order to write. I think better lying on my back and with my eyes closed . . ."[20]

2. The legendary bed, the one in which Proust wrote *In Search of Lost Time*. Before describing what look to us like appalling, or at least absurd, working conditions, remember—ambivalence—that for Proust the bed was a source of energy. 1907 (that is, before the grand departure of *In Search of Lost Time*), after an exhausting stay at Cabourg, he rediscovers his creative powers in his bed; to Montesquiou: "You were . . . perspicacious in your letter in what you said about the physical reserves which I rightly build up in my bed."[21] → Writes in extremely impracticable conditions: outside, people falling ill from the heat, but he writes under seven woolen blankets, wearing a fur coat, with three hot-water bottles and a lighted fire, to say nothing of the thick layers of Rasurel and Pyrenees cloth → So he writes in bed, with a leaky schoolboy's penholder, an inkpot that's almost always empty (and, as I said, his sight was failing). Would write page after page in an awkward and strained position: sheets of paper scattered, spread out over the bed like enormous pieces of confetti; making it very difficult to retrieve a page in order to reread it or correct it (some have said: whence the complicated sentences, but I don't believe a word of it). Once again, I infer from this acrobatic organization: a passion for writing that takes precedence over everything else, a "maniacal" investment, tetanization → cf. bodily insensitivity of certain mystics.

3. I myself know what it's like to work in bed—in the sanatorium: bed-table, a makeshift pulpit to rest the book on; I probably derived all the physical pleasure of a close "proxemics" from doing so (I hadn't written anything before going into the sana), from organizing what *surrounds* the bed (cf. Matisse at the end of his life, very comfortable): bed = perfect for reading and taking notes, but not for writing. Perhaps *bed / desk* → gives rise to in different *types* of writing, or they can be inferred from this distinction: hurried, flowing, spontaneous (= bed, in whatever position) ≠ careful, well-thought through, difficult (desk) → "the bed and syntax."

Is all this trivial? A bit farfetched?—I always look at things from the perspective of Nietzsche's *Ecce Homo*: postulation of a profound *Philosophy* linked to seemingly insignificant choices: the choices of the body.[22]

Bonnet, 49

Rivane, 47

L. P.-Quint, 89

Night-Time

Night-time writers

We'll be looking at the problem of the *schedule* a little later on (since it has to do with the theme of *Rule*) → Schedules: cinesthesia or existentiality of the *division* ≠ *Day / Night*: mythical theme, concerns the imaginary, not Law, Obsessionality.

Everyone who knows a bit about "Writers' legends" (the memorable features of their life stories) knows that there are Day-time writers (morning writers especially) / Night-time writers. Morning writers: the purest is Valéry; five o'clock in the morning, coffee, lamp, every morning for a whole lifetime → *Cahiers*. Night writers: better known.—Flaubert (in part: though he was day and night).—at one time, Rimbaud; in Paris, 1872, a letter to Ernest Delahaye offers a very good description of the "poetics" of nocturnal work: "Now, it is night-time that I work {*travaince*}. From midnight to five in the morning. Last month, my room on rue Monsieur-le-Prince looked out on a garden of the Lycée Saint-Louis. There were huge trees under my narrow window. At three in the morning, the candle went pale <the *right* time, not yet the perverse time of summer, which is two hours behind the sun>: all the birds in the trees start singing at once: it is over. No more work. I had to look at the trees, the sky, seized by that unspeakable hour, the first of the morning. I saw the lycée dormitories, absolutely muted. And already the jerky, sonorous, delightful noise of the carts on the boulevards <boulevard Saint-Michel, access road for the market farmers coming from Arpajon to the market at Les Halles; I remember the train on rails>. I smoked my hammer-pipe, spitting on the tiles, for my room was a garret. At five o'clock I would go downstairs to buy bread; it was the time. There were workmen everywhere. For me, it was the time to get drunk at wine-merchants'. Then I would go back to my room to eat, and go to bed at seven in the morning, when the sun prompts the woodlice to come out from under the tiles. What has always delighted me here is the early morning in summer and the December evenings."[23]—Kafka's joy at having written "The Judgment" in one sitting, from ten o'clock in the evening to six o'clock in the morning: "as if I were advancing over water";[24] and always the marvel of dawn.—Proust: so well-known I won't dwell on it; complete inversion of day and night: "People would bid me good evening after the post came" (perhaps this is the real inversion Proust effected); his friends would visit this "Midnight Sun" at night; he would to go the Ritz at two o'clock in the morning and ask Olivier for a "a really strong black coffee, one that is as good as

Lettres, 89
"Parshit Junish 72"

Journal, 262

L. P.-Quint, 76, 81

Journal, 63

Mythical satisfactions

Chateaubriand, *M.O.T.*, Book III

Seuil, 95

Picon, 17

two"[25] → Every mythical dimension (cf. *infra*, I'll come to this in a moment) has its empirical, rational side: Proust believed his asthma attacks occurred less frequently at night.

The morning looms menacingly over the night. Kafka: "I . . . feel, especially toward evening and even more in the morning, the approaching, the imminent possibility of great moments which would tear me open, which could make me capable of anything, and *in the general uproar that is within me and which I have no time to command*, [I] find no rest."[26] → And a member of the audience (J.-F. Faguet), who tells me that he finds writing hard-going, that he only manages to write the moment he wakes up, before getting out of bed, before eating anything, as if there were an advantage in somehow "administratively" prolonging the night (stopping the clocks so that it's still daytime).

To work at night? Of course there are sound, practical reasons for doing so (silence, calm, lack of interruption). But I'm interested in the mythical images it conjures up (for, as I explained, I've never been able to do so myself, not even in the evenings)—and that, ultimately, is the subject of the course: the whole mythical space of Wanting-to-Write → A few of those images:

1. Perhaps the very old idea that, compared to Day, Night is a primordial substance: Mother-Substance, an Anterior Substance; according to Tacitus, the Germans believed that the night was older than day:[27] *Nox ducere diem videtur.*[28]

2. The unifying virtue of the Night → Opposition between Daytime, which separates, and Night-time, which unites. Tristan and Octavian (*Knight of the Rose*) bemoan the Day that separates, divides the lovers as opposed to the Night which brings them together. Octavian: "I don't want this day, why this day?"[29]

More concrete theme: the wish for an unbroken, continuous stretch of work. Kafka could only work with a continuous run ahead of him, so only at night, in the most complete isolation (hence the uneven arc of his output, for there were times when he was prevented from writing at Night); cf. Balzac unable to work unless he had at least three clear hours ahead of him. (I'm very susceptible to this constraint, which comes at a price: it means you can't make use of any "empty" time—an hour between going to the shops and a meeting—, such time is lost).

3. Night-time: sort of space homologous to profound interiority; interiority is experienced as real life, the subject's veritable experience, Night-time is lived as real life; for the Night writer, real life

begins when, like the stranger in Balzac's *Exiles*: "returning to his abode, the old man shuts himself up in his room, lights his lamp of inspiration <see how important the lamp is: you have to choose the right one: like the power of Aladdin's mysterious lamp, it will release the work>, while asking words of silence, ideas of the night."[30]

4. It might be that a perverse pleasure is taken in nocturnal work: that of inversion: to invert Day and Night and vice versa, inversion that's anti-nature (no domestic animals do this, with the possible exception of cats, a specifically literary animal) and antisocial → There's *metanoia*, reversal, conversion → Indeed, there's a religious aspect to it, Ramadan for example, inversion of day and night (you eat at night, doze in the day) → Inversion of the sun and the moon: the moon becomes the planet of the Day, it "rises" and gives the signal for supernatural life to begin → Eponymous hero of this inversion: Proust.

(That said, I'm not speaking from experience, but from my imagination: I'm a "writer"—or *scribens*—of the morning, never of the night, which is why I'm so good at imagining it: I *want* to work at night, but my body disagrees).

SESSION OF FEBRUARY 2, 1980

Solitude[1]

Last part of this "casuistry of egoism": the nature and degree of the writer's solitude; not metaphysical or artistic solitude (that's not what we're dealing with at the moment) but empirical solitude: practical relationship with others insofar as they allow you to or prevent you from "living alone."[2]

Friends

It seems to me that there's a study to be written (or at any rate a dossier to be compiled) on *writers' friends*; in the *aura* that surrounds a writer, the same names, or a single name, often crops up: correspondents, confidants, judges; for Flaubert, Bouilhet, Maxime du Camp; for Kafka, Max Brod, etc. (Proust: lots of friends, correspondents, but there doesn't seem to be anyone who was exclusively linked to the work) → What would be required is an analysis of the *existential* situation of those partners: devotion, loyalty, lack of jealousy (?), literary incomprehension too, perhaps. All that subtly influencing how the writer behaves with respect to his work: a word from a friend, spoken in passing, can illuminate, alter, or even destroy a work (Bouilhet and *The Temptation of Saint Anthony*). And therefore, also, the writer's more or less mute resistance to his friends: the experience—or the apprenticeship—of solitude isn't undertaken in relation to the world, to those bearing you ill will, but those closest to you, your friends → terror, abyss that sometimes opens up when a word from a friend suddenly betrays an incomprehension, a distance, an appalling state of *noncomplicity*.

But since we're considering the prospect of *actually engaging* in the labor of writing, there is the more straightforward problem of *Time for Friends*: the time given to or required by friendship → Perhaps, broadly speaking, two temporal microsystems: (1) Gathering your friends together in little groups, parties; extended conviviality, similar to "worldliness": "days" (Mallarmé's Tuesdays), "evenings" (at Médan), the idea being that you set aside a regular slot to deal with all your relationships at once, as a way of soaking them up, of "paying your dues" and then having the rest of the week to yourself, reinstating a strict *privacy*. (2) Spacing them out; bilateral, noncollective relationships; seeing one friend at a time.

Bibesco, 20

19

M.O.T, I, 450

Solitude

L. P.-Quint, 118

Journal, 281

Proust: "I disperse [my friendships] too I admit, but not all at once; I do it successively, giving much more, but for a shorter time." The tension, then, arises from the accumulation, and therefore from the congestion, of those spaced-out friendships. Proust: "Emerson [tells us] that we should always be changing friends."[3] → We immediately see the beginnings of a conflict between the Work (the Time of the Work) and Friendship (with its endoxal-type value: Fidelity).

Of course, the relationship between the Work and Friendship can't be reduced to a question of time; there is that "time of the soul" that has to be devoted to the people you love: to think about them, to be affected, at times overwhelmed, by their anxieties; forces of affective participation that come into conflict with the—egoistic—anxiety of the Work → Friendship: a sort of gaping hole, an open hemorrhage in the barrier erected around the work → Chateaubriand puts this very well in his description of Joubert ("selfish" and "original"): "He was careful to keep those emotions of the soul he considered dangerous for his health in check, and still his friends would come and disturb the precautions he had taken, for he could not help but be moved by their sadness or their joy: he was an egoist who thought only of others"[4] → Even as regards the cynical, monstrous prospect of a total sacrifice to the work, this gaping is necessary, it's necessary for the work, which probably requires that underlying, loving pulsation which, through the mediation of the other, opens the Work up to the World.

Whence a subtle use of Solitude; the optimal balance would be achieved through this formula: to be alone and yet *surrounded* (with the affective nuance) by others (personally, I need solitude, but I'm not fanatical about it: I like it when other people are there, *around* me). The image, a bit forced, but very powerful, would be this one taken from Proust's life: at the end of his life, Proust, in the porter's lodge at the Ritz, a well-heated glass box, bent over his papers, correcting the proofs of *In Search of Lost Time*; all around him, the comings and goings of the guests in the hotel.[5]—Kafka, who'd been cruelly confronted with the problem (constantly deliberating the pros and cons of marriage), describes it well: "Inability to live alone, which does not imply inability to live, quite the contrary, it is even improbable that I know how to live with anyone, but I am incapable, alone, of bearing the assault of my own life, the demands of my own person, the attacks of time and old age, the vague pressure of the desire to write, sleeplessness, the nearness of insanity—I cannot bear this alone."[6] (From this perspective, Friendship is a better solution to the problem than Marriage or coupledom—

indeed, the evolution of social mores makes us feel the absence of a word: Marriage? That doesn't cover all unions. Coupledom? Concubinage? Not a very pretty word. And what about homosexual "conjunctions"?)

The solitude of someone who writes: I don't know what functions it has, but it would appear to be experienced according to different, concomitant, or alternate images (images are peculiarly capable of contradicting one other):

Journal, 281

a. as a *Necessity*: condition that's both statutory of and transcends the Making of the Work. Kafka: "I must be alone a great deal. What I accomplished was only the result of being alone."[7]

24

b. as an *opening up*, an unfurling, a loosening of the "constrictions" imposed by the world. Kafka (1910): "Two and a half days I was, though not completely, alone, and already I am, if not transformed, at any rate on the way. Being alone has a power over me that never fails. My interior dissolves (for the time being only superficially) and is ready to release what lies deeper. A slight ordering of my interior begins to take place and I need nothing more, for disorder is the worst thing in small talents."[8]

Seuil, 115, 270

c. as a *madness*, for better or worse; as the risk and the temptation of madness. Kafka (1913): "I'll shut myself off from everyone to the point of insensibility. Make an enemy of everyone, speak to no one."[9] → And once again this theme of a loss of consciousness: in 1918 Kafka gets engaged for the third time, to Julie Wohryzeck; ill with tuberculosis, he lodges at the Stüdl boarding house in a village; thus, once again, he contemplates renouncing his "desire for a solitude to the point of insensibility" → *Solitude*: it basically functions like a drug → The Work is a Madness, an expiration of (worldly) consciousness; it's a *conversion*, a *metanoia*, an inversion of reality that comes out of solitude (cf. Eremitism).

Secrecy

To bring this dossier on the writer's solitude to a close, I must indicate one last theme in connection with it: the secret or half-secret, the secrecy or half-secrecy in which, often, it seems, the writer shrouds the Work he's in the process of writing.[10]

Seuil, 44

To be sure, there are some writers (or there *were*? for the literature I'm discussing is probably of the past, has disappeared) who read their works-in-progress aloud to their friends as they go along: Flaubert, Gide; Kafka did this too, but, it seems, with a certain reluctance; his friends sometimes managed to persuade him to read from his manuscripts, but they were never invited to make a single comment.—But, a point worth noting: it appears, at least in the cases of Flaubert, Gide, and Kafka, at issue were important works, but not the Work in the monumental sense of the term: the writer keeps quiet about the fabrication of that Work; however long it takes to produce it, he seems to keep it shrouded in secrecy; when it comes down to it, we know very little about *In Search of Lost Time*. Proust—despite the vast correspondence—actually revealed very little about his grand project and its trajectory, its adventure; and the funny thing is, Proust makes exactly the same point and expresses the same degree of surprise about Balzac (*Against Sainte-Beuve*): "The one slightly alarming thing in this interpretation of his work <Balzac according the 'countless things in life that had hitherto seemed to us too contingent' a literary value> is that these are the very things <the transformation of Balzac's reality, of his day-to-day into Balzacian reality> of which he never spoke in his correspondence. . . . But all this may depend on the accident of which letters we have, or even of which ones he wrote."[11] I don't think so. I think there's a hiatus, a break, rupture of homogeneity between affective life and the Great Work (Great in that it's the one being written at the moment): whence the writer's silence on the subject of his "preparations," as if he quite simply didn't like speaking of the Work he's in the process of writing; that might even be a kind of criterion: the writer can discuss a Plan for a work with friends if it hasn't yet come together, if it's still fantasmatic, still all talk, but as soon as it takes, as soon as it gets serious, the writer becomes secretive and as it were jealous. *What are you writing at the moment?* If I'm telling you it's because there's a very good chance I won't write it; if the labor has already properly begun, if I'm already investing the whole of myself in that labor, then my response will be evasive. Reasons for this tendency toward secrecy (on the subject of the Preparation)?

1. Either modesty or an inability to really grasp what's happening, the fact that the work is actually in the process of getting written; reluctance or resistance on the part of the *Scribens* to allowing anyone a glimpse of the "cooking" of the Work—many cooks chase you out of the kitchen in this way—basically because the preparation is often not very appetizing and is in no way related to the excellence of the dish that gets pompously set down on the table; a "preparation" is actually composed of repetitions, back-trackings, uncertainties, mistakes; it's pointless to want to isolate a specific moment by providing a progress report, for, as we well know, that moment will no doubt have already passed by the time you come to

Préface, 262

describe it; the work in the process of being written: of the order of the *Unnamable*—and the worst of it is: wanting to name it, you feel that doing so so reifies and damages it, blocks it → at her request, Flaubert (1874), sends the first sentence of *Bouvard and Pécuchet* to his niece Caroline, but adds: "So much for that, and you won't know a word more for a long time to come. I'm floundering, scratching out, feeling generally desperate."[12]

2. As I said, prior to *In Search of Lost Time*, Proust would read his work-in-progress aloud to his friends, but when in the process of writing *In Search* he only very rarely discussed his book → Perhaps it was only then that the Work, experienced as monumental (the Work of a Lifetime), passed into the category of the *Sacred* →

L. P.-Quint, 89

The movement of the writer: the Work is alive to him when he's writing it; once it's finished, it dies (at the precise point when it comes alive for other people): it's living and sacred, jealously hidden, like a love or like a God: *Deus absconditus*[13] → The work making itself *abscondita*, or *Opus absconditum*.

3. Perhaps also, return to some psychological motive (in any case we're still in the Imaginary of Writing). The writer can have a desire for Anonymity: doesn't want to conform to any social image and so doesn't want to give anything away → That desire for anonymity can be seen as a form of hysteria: "Don't take any notice of what I'm doing = pay attention to me" → But, from our point of view, that's of no consequence; what does matter is the distress that any breach of anonymity can cause. In that event, to preserve the secrecy of the Work (in the process of being written), the writer can pretend to be working on something else: can agree to play a particular kind of social game, to accept a particular kind of image imposed by society.

Seuil, 98

Kafka anticipated the advantages of this game: he considered any solution other than "a life dedicated to literature" <with its corollary: solitude> an *artificial construction* intended "to satisfy the outside world" and "to avoid attracting attention to himself."[14]

4. Last, the will for secrecy can amount to the philosophical acceptance of a tragic fact: that, in the end (I'll say: in the bitter end), the writer is *responsible* for his writing; he alone inhabits that responsibility: as long as the Work is unfinished, it's impossible for him to hand it over to someone else. Who's responsible for the Text?—Me, first of all: when it comes to the Text, the most indelible wounds, the failures, the panics, etc. come from me—Of course, a friend can read over the finished work carefully and point up any errors, oversights—can, *on occasion*, before the text is published,

offered up to the public, intervene over sentences, paragraphs if need be; but such tasks are a matter of polishing, not the actual elaboration of the work → "Advice" (we'll come back to this) has its place, but only much further *down* the line, or much further *up*.

Schedules

To work

All this, all that the elaboration a *Methodical Life* entails (the fantasized figure of which is the *Vita Nova*), is with a view to a formidable activity, rich in the ambivalences of pleasure and of unpleasure, of law and of enjoyment: *to work*, intransitive, like *to write* ("I can't see you, I have to work") or possibly partitive: "What are you working on at the moment?" In other words, what part of the absolute universe of work as such are you cutting out for yourself?

First I'd like to point out that all the "great writers"—those who produced a monumental work (a whole work or fragments of a work)—were animated by or endowed with an *unfailing will* (in the most flatly psychological sense of the term): will for labor, for corrections, for copying out that functions in all possible conditions: in health, in discomfort, in affective misery, a veritable bodily energy: Chateaubriand's and Michelet's travels, staying awake, bouts of insomnia, etc. → The writer's labor: somehow *unsinkable* → The simple and powerful image this stubborn determination of labor conjures up = that of the "good workman" → Flaubert (1845, twenty-four years old): "Ill, agitated, prey a thousand times a day to moments of an terrible anxiety, without women, without wine, without any of the tinsel the world offers, I continue my slow work like a good workman who rolls up his sleeves and sweats away at his anvil, indifferent to rain or wind, hail or thunder."[15] Sort of division of psychological labor; two distinct waves that neither intersect nor impact on one another: the laborious wave, the passionate wave (or two parallel furrows) (cf. my own personal astonishment: intense crisis in my love life; looking at the dates: while all that was going on, month after month, I was writing *Mythologies*).[16]

Préface, 34

Law and Rule

Two other images are possible; they can be found in Flaubert, and I'll say a word about their relationship, their contradiction, and their dialectical resolution:

a. The convict or the ascetic: the writer's labor = a sentence to hard graft or to a mad asceticism. Flaubert (1852, thirty-one years old): "I love my work with a love that is frantic and perverted, as an ascetic loves the hair shirt that scratches his belly."[17]

Préface, 69, 43

b. The Benedictine monk; 1846 (twenty-five years old), to Louise Colet: "Try working patiently every day for the same number of hours. Get into the habit of a studious and calm life, initially you'll find it charming, and it will give you energy."[18] → The image of the Ascetic (or the Convict) suggests being dominated by the Law. In some ways, that's an appropriate starting point: the Work is desire, a protension of *Jouissance*, but there's no Desire without Law somewhere or other (the growing number of people with no Law and with no Desire); the Work is therefore also like the necessary Shadow of the Law → Terrifying ("Work constantly: every minute lost to the work is a sin"), the law is then dialectized, it takes on the form of a law that's bearable, a law that the subject wants, and who submits to it precisely because it's not suffocating: it becomes *Rule* (the Benedictine monk) → And the incarnation of the Rule is the *Schedule*.

Schedules

Types of writer's (of the Writer-Laborer's) schedules: we all know of a few (or at least I know of a few); for me, they have a kind of charm; insofar as they're "Rules" and Rules I believe were followed, I like the idea of them; each one has its own shape. I'll discuss several of them, even if that sounds monotonous—but if just two or three of you are interested in schedules then I'll be justified in giving an account of those I'm familiar with:

1. The most famous is Proust's: spectacular because strictly inverted (cf. "Night"); I'll say no more about it.

Picon, 20

2. Balzac (1833): "I go to bed at six or seven in the evening, like the hens; I am called at one a.m. and work until eight. At eight, I go to sleep again for an hour and a half; then I have something very light, a cup of pure coffee and harness myself to my cab until four. At four, I receive guests, have a bath <no washing before starting work>, or go out. After dinner, I go to bed."[19]

Préface, 204

3. Flaubert (1858, thirty-seven years old): "You ask what I'm up to. Here's your answer. I get up at noon and go to bed between three and four in the morning. I take a nap at about five in the afternoon." (→ "My existence is extremely unsociable; I love its uneventfulness, its quiet. It is complete and objective nothingness.")[20]

Seuil, 105

4. Kafka (especially after 1912, a productive period, "his laborer's existence"): Office: 8 am–2 pm. Siesta: 3 pm–7 pm.—Walk: one hour.—Dinner with the family: late.—11 pm–3 am or later: writing.

Seuil, 103

5. Schopenhauer (habits, end of his life, Frankfurt, Glory (1788–1860): In both winter and summer, gets up at eight o'clock.—Washes

in cold water (his eyes, especially: beneficial to the optic nerve)—Prepares a copious breakfast (won't have a servant in the mornings). Works until eleven o'clock.—At eleven, friends visit (articles and discussions of his philosophy).—Before lunch: a quarter of an hour of flute (Mozart and Rossini).—At twelve on the dot: shaves.—Lunch.—Short walk in his dinner jacket and white tie.—Short siesta or a coffee.—Afternoon: long walks around the outskirts of Frankfurt (with his poodle) or a swim in the Main.—Cigar (but only half, because of the nicotine).—6 pm: to the Casino to read the papers.—Dinner at the Hotel d'Angleterrre (cold meats and red wine; no beer because of the Cholera).—Evening: occasionally a concert or the theater.[21]

Kafka, *Journal*, 631

Let's get away from literature for a moment: Liszt, in Weimar, would work between five and eight o'clock in the morning, go to church, then go back to bed; from eleven o'clock on, he'd receive visitors.[22]

One possible direction an analysis could take: examine how far these individual schedules fit in with the general Schedule of the Time, of the Country, that is, ultimately, to what extent they were *individualistic*, indicative of: (a) a professional constraint (Kafka) or not (Flaubert, Balzac: but he had his Debts!); (b) an *eccentricity* (which, as I suggested, can serve as a form of protection); (c) and possibly even a differential constraint to do with the type of writing in question (Philosophy ≠ vast Novels ≠ Short stories, etc.). But, in keeping with the *existentiality* of the Schedule (for that's basically my angle here: existential, not sociological), I see a double justification in the Schedule, in the Regulation of the hours in the Day:

Picon, 20

a. To ensure, at all costs, a continuous stretch of time for labor, to protect it from all interruptions (I'll say: precisely because it's artificial); Balzac is quite clear: "I find it impossible to work when (here I was interrupted by a friend paying a visit) I have to go out and I never work for just an hour or two."

b. And, at the same time, to the extent that Schedule involves regulated, authorized interruption = Rhythm → Bachelard: "What has most duration is what is best at starting itself up all over again." Bachelard again: "To have duration, we must entrust ourselves to rhythms, that is to say systems of instants."[23]

This is not to say that a schedule is the answer to everything; as a Rule, it's a bearable, not a mad Law, a corner of Law, but a bit of Law all the same (= a source, an energy of Transgression):

35

32

28

Préface, XIV

Journal, 20

a. It could be said: absolute Law = sort of Psychosis (we saw this in the case of Flaubert) ≠ Rule, trapped in a Neurosis: obsessionality → Schedule: experienced as a manic apportioning, classification of the hours in the day; Tolstoy is a classic example: "Have a purpose for your life as a whole, a purpose for a certain period of your life, a purpose for a certain time, a purpose for a year, a month, a week, a day, an hour and a minute, sacrificing the lower purposes to the higher ones . . ."[24] → The obsession clearly involves a form of calculation (cf. Loyola using signs to count and gauge how often he weeps).[25] "Always keep a table in which to define all the most trivial circumstances of your life, even how many pipes to smoke a day."[26] → When it's obsessive, the schedule essentially becomes a *Plan*: it's lived in the future, it's perfected in the future. Tolstoy, 1847 ("Rules for Developing the Will"): "(1) To get up at five, go to bed at nine or ten, and perhaps sleep for two hours during the day; (2) To eat in moderation, nothing sweet <he couldn't stop eating raisins>; (3) To walk for an hour; (4) To fulfill all my written injunctions; (5) To [have] one woman only, and then only once or twice a month; (6) To do as much as possible for myself." → This obsession with the Schedule is related to the execution of (to the obsession with?) Plans, Papers set out in front of you, "Rules of Conduct" (Tolstoy, from the age of fifteen), "Rules for Developing the Will," "Rules of Inner Development," "Rules of Life."[27]

b. The problem of the Schedule is actually how to *keep to it*, for its very regularity—without which it would be nothing—is destroyed, threatened by interruptions (that is, by other people: "*Ci-gît moi, tué par les autres*"),[28] by "exceptional" circumstances (individual cases), by dislikes, by bouts of laziness—and, the ultimate Ruse: the occasional disheartening glimpse of the futility of the strategy, the undertaking, the aim → To be unconcerned by any interruption to the Schedule—there you have the ultimate difficulty created by the demon. Kafka: "The fact that today I did not adhere to my new time schedule, to be at my desk from 8 to 11 pm, that at present I even consider this as not so very great a disaster, that I have only hastily written down these few lines in order to get into bed, shows just how difficult that task <combining life with the Office: keeping your head just above water so you don't drown> will be, what strength it will drain me of."[29] → Hence, the solution, or rather a modest sort of recipe: be concerned, but don't turn a single lapse into an excuse to give it all up; in other words, don't get disheartened. You let things go for a day? A week has been thrown off schedule? As soon it's practicable, take up the Schedule again; the secret of Labor (the labor of writing): *to bureaucratize writing*. Kafka found the Office draining? Switch things around: make the Desk into an Office, somewhere to go and work at regular times → Struggle against the paradox that would mean giving into the alienation of the professional Office, that is to say, of regularity, for what we wouldn't want to defend the writer can't do without → Writing should always be thought of in terms of music. Tolstoy, *War and Peace* (1865): "I must work like a pianist."[30] Could anyone learn how to play the piano or how to sing without working *every day*? The *fits and starts* approach brings no return whatsoever; for example, it's important to know that, for singing, half an hour a day is enough (for an amateur), but it really does have to be *every day* ≠ the piano (at least an hour) → You can "think" by dint of inspiration; you can only write by dint of *labor*.

The Grand Rhythm

I spoke of the Schedule as a rhythm within a day. What gives a day its rhythm.—A different question remains, just as vital, that of Regularity over an extended sequence of days: the Grand Rhythm.

The two rhythms

I imagine two conceptions: (a) "Epicurean" rhythm: a *little bit* of work everyday (or a moderate, aerated labor, a sensible, realistic, accommodating schedule that makes allowances for things *in advance*). But, implacably rigorous, that *little bit* is never put off. (b) Rhythm that I'll call—inappropriately, for want of a better word, or while awaiting a better one—*Orphic*: where periods of rigorous asceticism are followed by periods of excess, of Dionysian abandon, absolute Festivity → Greek opposition (and succession) of *ascesis* and *telete*.[31]

Préface, 36

At the risk of ruining the suspense of a choice, the right answer would appear to be a moderate combination of the two: Epicurean rhythm comprising *breaks*: a regular schedule with, at certain times, stops, suspensions, changes → Why these *breaks*? Because every now and then you have to regenerate the *desire to work* within yourself. Flaubert (1846, twenty-five years old): "I'm going to get down to work, at last, at last! I want to."[32]—I experience that desire myself, for instance in the evenings, at about eleven o'clock, after a dinner with friends (in other words: after having had a *break*): I want to go home and work (but I don't, I convince myself that I'm too tired, and riskily put it off until the next morning); in reality, Labor: figure of desirable Interiority, which calms, orders, strengthens—symbolized by the Lamp and Silence.

To Conclude

To conclude these remarks on the "Methodical Life" I'd like to correct an impression I may have given: that all these measures are put in place in view of an immediate *return* in terms of the Work (I even used the term): how to produce a Work and to succeed in the eyes of the Public → It's more subtle than that; of course, there's *calculation* or a tendency toward calculation, even the temptation to keep accounts, but that calculation isn't an *exchange*, asceticism for success; the Work is a *value*, an ethical object; the labor of the Work is therefore a course of action that takes the form of an initiation, the aim of which is not success but what I'll call (bearing in mind how the expression is used in Nietzsche) a *Noble Life*.[30] Proust, who warns against the image of *Exchange*, puts this in a striking way: "That a writer should have moments of genius <let me add: should exercise an asceticism of Labor> *so as* to be able to lead an agreeable life of literary dilettantism the rest of the time is as false and naive a conception as that of a saint living the most elevated moral existence so as to be able to lead a life of vulgar pleasure in paradise."[31]

That's it for the first part of the Second Trial: *the Methodical Life*.

B. The Praxis of Writing

I should remind you that we're working our way through the Trials of Writing: we started with the first one, that of Choice; then the second, that of Patience (or Duration); we divided the second trial in two parts: the first part, the methodical organization of a writing Life; we're now going to deal with the second part: the practice of writing in real terms, day after day. In some sense, the trial becomes more precise, more *localized* (for the problems of a *methodical life* are not confined to the field of literature); we're passing from the temporal, spatial *context* and "everyday habits" to the body in the process of writing, the hand poised over the blank page.

Preliminary Question: Reading / Writing

The question is the following: when you devote yourself to a Labor of writing, can you (or, even, must you) read? When you *enter into Writing* (such is the *Retreat* I'm describing), can you keep reading, maintain a reading practice? Must (should) the writer's egoism go so far as to deny all other books—and, metonymically: culture?

Remember, or remind yourselves, that at the concrete origin of writing there's a love of the book, of the book-Object, an *aesthetic* (in the strong sense of the term) fondness for a type of Object: so I believe (this is my doctrine at any rate); I always think it a pity that, for the most part, the writers of the texts I sometimes get sent or of the proposals to publish doctoral theses don't think: "book." To write—according to my desire and in my experience, at least—is to *see* the book, to visualize the book: *On the horizon, the book*. Kafka had a sort of physical relationship with the book; he explains that there's one reliable thing about him: his "greed for books"; it's not really a question of wanting to own them or to read them: he wants to see them (even in a bookshop window), to be persuaded of their existence; a sort of perverse appetite[32] (here, digressing, the problem of the book as *Decor* would present itself: bookcases, built-in shelving, doctor's books; books fill the walls, if not the mind).

As a general rule (moving beyond the case of the Work that's in the process of being written) → *scriptor / reader?*—it's not a question of value, but of "*realization*": I realize the best of myself (=I realize the Other that's within me), either as reader or as scriptor: I had a friend, a marvelous reader who taught me many things, whom I'm greatly indebted to, who had a very difficult time writing the one book he did publish (which, by the way, wasn't a success), and it must always be remembered that Socrates was the ultimate Agraphic (though, it must be said, according to a different opposition: writing / speaking, not writing / reading).

And on the level of the Work in the process of being written, of this phase where "I enter into writing"?—I think there's a rejection of reading, of sustained reading, of reading as labor: writing pushes reading aside; a question of time, of investment, but probably also the more prickly question of a kind of *rivalry*: "not enough room for two"; therefore, in this phase, you can only read books that are unrelated, heterogeneous to what you're writing → Insofar as writing wants to be *active* (Nietzsche's vocabulary), it has to protect itself against the *Reactive*,[33] avoid having to *react* (other than in the phase of materials, which is entirely different and not the *praxis* aimed at here) → Nietzsche: "Another form of sagacity <he's listing the forms of self-defense: climate, diet, types of recreation> and self-defense consists in *reacting as seldom as possible* and withdrawing from situations and relationships in which one would be condemned as it were to suspend one's 'freedom,' one's initiative, and become a mere reagent." Example: the scholar who does nothing but read books: "If he does not trundle he does not think." In his case, the self-defense instinct has been eroded → On the horizon: reading, for Nietzsche, a decadent occupation that mustn't absorb Active time, the time of Freshness: "Early in the morning at the break of day, in all the freshness and dawn of one's strength, to read a *book*—I call that vicious!"[34] I interpret the conflict between writing / reading in the following way (thinking of J.-L.,[35] who never stopped reading): *reading* is a metonymical, all-consuming activity; you're gradually pulling the entire continuum {*nappe*} of culture toward you; as into the sea at high tide, you plunge into the Imaginary of Culture, into the chorus, the polyphony of a thousand other voices, to which I add my own: a book (in truth, not all books, unfortunately: let's say a book that *takes*), is like a loose thread → Now I believe that writing=that enigmatic thing which, *not being speech, is nevertheless language*, checks the hemorrhage of the Imaginary → When I was a child, I'd see women all around me obsessed by the risk of getting a nick in their knitted stockings (no nylon), causing a loose thread to suddenly start unraveling down the length of the stocking, and I can still picture that slightly vulgar but necessary gesture whereby they would moisten a finger in their mouths before applying it to the loose thread—checking the ladder by cementing it with saliva (what's more, at the time, there were still those flimsy little "mender's" stalls) → This is what Writing is like: a finger pressed onto the culture's Imaginary, and [which] checks it; in a way, writing is the immobilization of culture (perhaps so that it can append itself to it) → Whence, I believe, a sort of necessity, from the moment you undertake the Work, of putting a stop to reading, of effecting a reading Blank.

Starting Up

In the long Patience of Fabrication, of Writing, not from day to day but *day after day*, there are two "regimes" (two types of difficulty): (1) The Start, Starting Up the work (which is different from its Projection), Inaugurations. (2) The cruising speed, and the "accidents" that affect that speed: (a) Obstacles. (b) Depressions and imaginings.

Let's begin by thinking about those moments when the work *gets going*, moments that have often held the attention of historians: "how a work is born," "how a work takes off" → Therefore, for just that reason, a *mythical* moment (even if, for someone who writes, the moment in question is very real, painfully real); because a work=something that's not easy to begin, to *inaugurate*: a good word, since it hints at a quasi-anthropological, *ritualistic* dimension).

Crises

1. Crises

I don't know what literary histories are used in secondary schools nowadays, nor indeed whether French literature still gets taught in them. But, if I consult a famous literary manual, the *Castex et Surer*[39] (at once thoroughly mythological and well conceived): one thing that's both surprising and amusing in its regularity, a veritable *tic*: almost all the writers' lives are organized around a central *crisis* (regardless of whether it occurred in the middle of their lives), crisis that's the source of the renaissance of their oeuvres, that is to say, that serves as the point of departure of the triumphant, regenerated Work.—That crisis is presented visually:

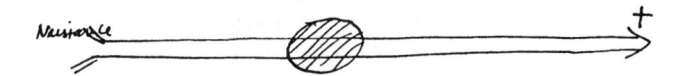

Fateful circle! And one that adds value, for the rare lives in which it doesn't appear look altogether mediocre: disadvantaged, marginal authors who didn't even know how to generate a creative crisis in their lives: such writers aren't the heroes of literature because they're not martyrs to the Act of Creation, to Drama.

Types of "crises" that reveal the degree to which—in order to meet the requirements of the myth—the notion is unstable, artificial, formal:

1. *Anecdotal crises* (biographical accidents): Baudelaire: his mother remarries, 1828, he was seven years old!—Nodier, 1830: "a cruel year" (money worries + plus his beloved daughter's marriage).—Hugo, 1843: Léopoldine's death (Hugo = rich: he'll have two crises).—Flaubert, 1843, nervous illness.—Stendhal and Gide: decisive journeys, discovery of Italy (1800) and Biskra (1893).

2. *Crises of the heart, sentimental crises*: Lamartine, 1816 (sentimental).—Musset, 1833 (likewise)—Apollinaire, 1901: Rhinean love affair.
3. *Political or historical crises*: Exiles (Madame de Staël, 1803; Hugo, 1851.—Dreyfus Affair (1893–1899): Barrès, France.
4. *Spiritual crises* (the best kind): Chateaubriand (rediscovers his faith upon his mother's death, 1798–1800).—Renan, 1846.—Taine, 1870 ("moral" crisis).

→ The myth of the productive crisis is so necessary for the smooth functioning of literature that it's sometimes presented as a *joker* that can be invested with any kind of value, any kind of content: we simply speak of *inner crises* (Sainte-Beuve) or of the *crisis years* (Verlaine).

Seen in this light, the crisis a *value* (a Romantic value): therefore, over the twentieth century—which, from the point of view of secondary-school teaching, isn't or at least never used to be considered a good century (at once difficult and dangerous, "modern")—the number of "crises" has declined.

I'm not disputing the fact that, in a writer's life, there can sometimes be a profound connection between certain "critical" events and the inauguration of a new work, a new body of work. What is more doubtful is the systematic nature of this recourse and above all the idea that it could serve as a straightforward explanation: there can be no question that death of Proust's Mother coincided with a profound "crisis," but, on the one hand, the writing of *In Search of Lost Time* started up only well after her death; Proust went on living, went on writing in the meantime; and, on the other, it's impossible to say that it was his sorrow that produced a new work: some extremely complex relays → As a result, we see the same "crisis" being decorated with heterogeneous explanations: Mallarmé; there's supposed to have been a big "Crisis" in 1866—but also in 1862 and 1869; despite the contours of the actual episode being ill-defined it's invested with a number of different explanations: (a) A psychiatric explanation: at the time, Mallarmé was bordering on psychosis: nervous complaints, hypochondria, melancholy; consults Dr. Béchet in Avignon. (b) A metaphysical explanation (Michaud[40] and, generally, literary critics): "discovery of Nothingness," "loss of Christian faith"; the Man and the Universe: mere substances. Mallarmé is supposed to have been cured by reading Hegel → New faith, conscious and atheistic; renounces petty individuality. Energy to conceive of an immense work, with its "architecture eternally ordered, in keeping with that of the Universe" (this will be "the Book").

2. "It Takes"[41]

Second "starting up," or second form of the problem of how to get started, of Inauguration: hesitation, attempts, failures, like an engine trying to get going, when "all of a sudden" (an "all of a sudden" that may have something mythical about it), the engine starts up → the Work takes.

State anterior to *it taking* = state of *unconnectedness*; the possible materials, the fragments, the bits of work are all there (this is what we're modestly calling the "Preparation"), but you can't seem to connect them together, to give them *a continuity* → Tolstoy experienced this problem: with *War and Peace*, he had all the fictional and imaginary characters in his head but wasn't able to connect them: "*It's no good, it's not coming.*"—It was thought that *Les Misérables* triggered the connection—*trigger* is inappropriate, because, to achieve that connectedness, he labored for the whole of 1865. At last, October 20, "It's working."

Probably, on occasion, the different *topics* start competing with one another, and that competition produces a block; you have the obscure sense that *it all connects up* somewhere: you await the manifestation of that connection. And all the time you spend waiting for it you have the sense that it's "*Not quite that*"; as a general rule, that sense is very reliable.

The *It takes*: experienced as somewhat miraculous. Mythically, and often retroactively, in quite a deceptive manner, it takes the form of a sudden, immediate bursting forth: a flash of inspiration, or a spurt. Flaubert (1861, forty years old): "A good subject for a novel is one that comes all at once, in a single spurt."[42] (I'm not sure if that's true) → It's like an *intoxication*; you've been stuck for so long and yet you're so close to the work that you sometimes wonder whether, with just a little wine, a drug, it might *take off*; for once a long, rich Preparation is established, the missing element is something like a *gracefulness*. The *It takes* clearly initiates a good *flow* of writing: before, the pen would keep stopping; now it goes faster, or at least pursues a more even course; I've discovered that in paleography the formation of the written letter (and the pleasure it affords) used to be called the *Ductus*.

This type of "starting up" (of the Grand Work), though still enigmatic (I mean in the context of literary historical research), is to be

Préface, 221

found exemplarily in Proust (I've spoken and written about this): when did Proust first have the idea for *In Search of Lost Time*? When did he get started on it? When did the writing of *In Search* take? The elements of the dossier—of the suspense—are: (a) The biographical facts in as much detail as possible: especially how they're described in Henri Bonnet's *Marcel Proust de 1907 à 1914* (Nizet, 1971, 2 Volumes); this is almost Proust day by day over the period of "it taking." (b) More recently: research carried out at the *Centre d'histoire et d'analyse des manuscrits modernes* (CAM, 45, rue d'Ulm), or the detailed study of Proust's notebooks.[43]

1. Biographically, an apparent hiatus in 1909 between completing *Against Sainte-Beuve*, sending it to the publisher, it getting rejected, and getting started on *In Search of Lost Time*: intensive writing labor from October 1909 onward → I had inferred, dramatically, a sort of mysterious blank in September 1909: sort of *intermediate space* in which Proust passed from the *Essay* (which already contained some novelistic fragments) to the *Novel* (*In Search of Lost Time*) → The connections between *Against Sainte-Beuve* and *In Search of Lost Time* are extremely complex: not only did the two overlap but what Proust initially conceived of as *Sainte-Beuve* is already *In Search*—and what, in 1911, he was still calling *Sainte-Beuve* belongs uniquely and fully to *In Search*. This solemnification, this suspense of September 1909 has been politely contested (an academic call to order!) since bits and pieces of *In Search* were already underway well before that date:[44] of course! But I remain convinced that at a certain point in time the Project, the Starting Up came together, that there was a kind of *active crystallization*: an almost violent start to the writing, pages (of *Swann*) were written in a matter of weeks, and Proust's handwriting even changed, became dense, complicated, crowded.

2. Despite, or alongside this biographical mutation, clearly the starting up (the *It takes*, the Inauguration) could only have taken place under the pressure of certain creative, aesthetic *discoveries* ("finds") that are more difficult to pinpoint, to localize in time. I have indicated four of them:[45]

Names

a. The discovery of Names—of *Good* Names, of the right Names, of fitting proper names, such that the network of proper names now looks to us like the very Nature of *In Search of Lost Time*. It's been brought to my attention that Proust came up with some of the important names only after he'd gotten going on *In Search*: Montargis → Saint-Loup in the summer of 1913; Guercy → Charlus,

Mme B., 273

1914. Nevertheless, I believe that at a certain point a demand for a *System of Proper Names* presented itself, one that, for the writer, is the definition of Novelistic euphoria. Coming up with Names is evidently decisive: while traveling in the Orient, Flaubert was obsessed by the task that lay ahead of him (the novel that will be called *Madame Bovary*); now, with Maxime du Camp, on the border of lower Nubia, on the banks of the Nile, he exclaims: "I've got it! Eureka! Eureka! I'll call her Emma Bovary."

SESSION OF FEBRUARY 9, 1980

Proportions

b. Accepting, that is, being certain of having come up with, a *change in the proportions* of the book to be written. *Against Sainte-Beuve* → *In Search of Lost Time*: the proportions are inverted. Indeed, it's enough to suddenly *think big* what had been conceived small for the Work to be written to reveal itself as Necessary—or the other way round; for *Proportion* is not a quantity, it's a quality (cf. Architecture).

Faillois, *S.B.*, 25

"I"

c. Invention of a specific "I": a new, sophisticated, subtle, subject of the narrative enunciation, the biographical enunciation and the symbolic enunciation→ This Proustian *I*: imitable → To come up with the right *I*: that's the key thing → There's therefore no point in wondering whether it's better to write *he* or *I*; it's a specific *I* that has to be invented (or a specific *He*); the miracle of the Proustian *I* is that it isn't egotistic; ultimately, then, it's something *moral* that had been invented: a *generosity*?

Hiving off

d. Probably more decisive: the "find" of having characters reappear, sometimes after long intervals, despite the work not being subject to a strict narrative logic (canonically analyzed by Narratology):

S.B., 259

1. This trigger, this "find" may have come from Balzac; "Balzac's admirable invention of having kept the same characters in all the novels": condemned by Sainte-Beuve; Proust defends Balzac: "What Sainte-Beuve here failed to recognize was an idea of genius of Balzac's. It may be said, no doubt, that he did not have it right away. Some parts of his great cycles were only attached to them after the event. What does that matter? The "Good Friday Spell" is a piece Wagner wrote before he had the idea of doing *Parisfal*, into which he inserted it later. But are they not among his finest intuitions, these addings-ons, these beautiful inlays, the new connections his genius has suddenly perceived between the separate parts of the oeuvre that now join up, are alive and could never again be separated? Balzac's sister has told us of the joy he felt on the day he had his idea, just as great this way I find as if he had had it before he set out on his work. It is a shaft of light that has appeared

Castex, p. 147

Special Vol., Kolb

and has come to settle on various hitherto drab parts of his creation simultaneously, has unified, enlivened, illuminated them"[1] (the idea occurred to Balzac in 1833 and he exploits it systematically in *Père Goriot*, 1834; clearly it relates to the concept of the *Comédie Humaine*, title chosen in 1842): perfect description of the illuminating, punctual nature of the "Find."

2. Proust calls these recurring characters "prepared" characters. Proust prepares them in such a way that some surprises are held in store for us. Letter to René Blum (1913): "There are a great many characters; they are 'prepared' in this first volume, in such a way that in the second they will do exactly the opposite of what one had expected from the first"[2] (example: Vinteuil). (Here, a second theme emerges: that of inversion, of the inverted recurrence; cf. my article:[3] Charlus, initially seen as Odette's lover, turns out to be the classic figure of homosexuality; a brothel madam spotted on the little train → the princess Sherbatoff, etc.) This preparation (the reappearance of certain characters): what Proust calls *construction*, the constructed nature of his novel. The critics have done their utmost to uncover the "plan" of *In Search of Lost Time*, and Proust always insisted that his work was constructed; his kind of construction, however, wasn't rhetorical (a plan for a work that's then carried out: this is probably how Flaubert would proceed), but dialectical: movement back in time, spatial nonorganization, what I termed *marcottage*.[4]

Last remark on Starting Up by means of "Crystallization" (*It takes*): it's unlikely that a title would trigger this kind of crystallization. It took Proust a great deal of effort to come up with *Swann's Way* {*Du côté du chez Swann*}; in the end, he stuck with his banal title "because it is the name of a path in Combray"; "earthy reality and local veracity" → "I considered that title modest, drab, like a ploughed field."[5] → So Proust had his own part to play in the mediocrity of the title, which sheds no light on the work whatsoever. As a general rule, either you come up with a very good title but don't write the book, or you write the book with no title in mind and then, for want of anything better, make do with a neutral title → The title is actually a *retroactive* value; when it comes to creation, the best title is a working title, under which you file your index cards, your pages.

From Starting Up to Labor

Once the trigger is assured (or perceived to be at least—concretely enough for the subject to avoid being plunged back into that state of uncertainty described as the "First Trial"), it's then a matter of passing from the excitement of a discovery, of a vision, to the patience of a daily labor; the work glimmers in the distance, but it's still very much *in limbo*: somewhat like the beginning of Ravel's *Valse*.⁶ This passage, this delivery from limbo is distressing, dramatic even, for *nothing can ever be taken for granted* → Flaubert (1853, thirty-two years old): "To not write anything and to dream of beautiful works (as I'm doing now) is a charming thing. But how dearly one pays for such sensuous ambitions! What *come-downs!*"⁷

Préface, 144

Planning

To go from the Projected Work to its Fabrication: where's the difficulty?—in the *Planning*, which means, specifically, this is the Project I've selected; I'm going to set to work → *What shall I work on tomorrow?* Which operation? Sit at my desk, remain there, with my arms folded, thinking? It's a truth test: sometimes a project is exciting, appealing but when your back's against the wall you have no idea how to divide it up into the *multiple* operations that will gradually advance its realization: it's a question of coming up with a daily procedure, an *agenda* of things to do, which *cashes in*, *converts* the Project.

I don't have the recipe because the possibility of conversion is the seal of a project's validity, which means that the actual planning of it is of the nature of *kairos*, of the Good Project → I shall pick out, perhaps, two types of project, which give rise to two types of planning, of working practices:

Biography, 69

Alternative that Valéry puts very clearly (Lecture at the Collège, May 5, 1944); two possibilities for the creator of a work: "in the first, the work is answerable to a predetermined plan, in the second, the artist fills in an *imaginary rectangle*."⁸ → So there are two different kinds of plan: (1) the plan that proceeds by logic, *unraveling*, deduction; (2) the plan that proceeds by filling in a grand fantasized ("imaginary") form: an activity that has more to do with aesthetics than with logic (cf. the Oriental painter or writer) → On the horizon of this dichotomy, two domains: (a) narrative logic, the regular novel and the essay; (b) poetry, the heterodox novel (Proust).

1. In the readings I did for this Course (limited: they couldn't have been exhaustive), this curious thing: very few accounts of the labor of Planning the Work to be written (which can differ from the Plan of the finished work → always Pascal's saying: "The last thing we discover when writing a book is what to put first"),[9] that is to say, the Plan of the Plan: obvious example, Flaubert (I think I've said this already), *Madame Bovary*: thanks to scholars, we know a great deal about the formation of the Great Project; from Flaubert himself, we learn about the almost daily pangs of style, of the Sentence, but he tells us nothing about working on the Plan: remarkable hiatus; Flaubert discusses the episodes he's working on putting into sentences (dialogue with the Priest, the Ball, Agricultural Show, etc.), but tells us nothing about when he first had the idea for those episodes (= typical operations of *conversion*) → Notations are rare and elliptical: 1853 (thirty-two years old): "I'm very tired this evening. (I've been making *a plan* for two days now...)"[10] → Yet there's everything to suggest that Flaubert's mode of Planning was of the logical kind; there's an idea (for a Novel) and the episodes derive logically from it. 1861 (forty years old): "A good subject for a novel is one that comes all at once, in a single spurt. It is a matrix idea, from which all the others derive."[11] → Flaubert opposes— quite rightly, I think—two *inspirations* (and, as a result, two "plans"): that of the autobiographical note, of the lyrical or aphoristic fragment (→ Album) and that of a logic of the Imagination (canonical novel ≠ Proust) (→ Book); 1853 (thirty-two years old): "When one writes something of *oneself* <something that comes from you, from your own experience>, the sentence can be good in *spurts* (and lyrical minds achieve this effect easily, following their natural inclination), but the *whole is lacking* <this is the Album>, repetitions, needless repetitions, commonplaces, banal locutions abound. When, on the other hand, one writes something *imagined*, since everything has to derive from the idea, and even the commas are answerable to the overall plan, your concentration bifurcates"[12] (that "bifurcation" = conversion, multiplication).

2. At the other extreme, this technique: the *Rectangle*, that is to say, a fantasized form of the book that is gradually *filled in* with spots of color, fragments, bits and pieces, like certain painters before a rectangle of canvas.

a. Technique demonstrated exemplarily in Mallarmé: according to Valéry, Mallarmé (Poems, that is to say, *Album*) would begin some of his poems by putting words down on paper at random, discontinuous spots of color; then they would work on inventing the links that turn them into sentences.

    b. On a larger scale, a Proustian operational procedure: Proust would take notes and draft little bits of text; he would compose "passages" at a time; for example, the "*Within a Budding Grove* passage," composed in winter 1908–1909 and completed in the summer of 1909 → Technique of "concretions," "flocculations" → whence the problem, the difficulty of assemblages that can seem "artificial," that don't work. "It's not taking": *Against Sainte-Beuve* can be considered an attempt at assemblage that *didn't take*.

> Bonnet, 59, 94

    Proust composed by nonsequential fragments that he'd begin work on simultaneously in several different Notebooks, in several different versions → This "promotion" of the Passage of Text over the composition as a whole occurs again in reading → Rhapsody at the point of departure, rhapsody at the destination → Type of recollection of our reading: sorts of "flecks" remain in our memory: the grandfather's cognac, something about a Chinese vase, but we can't recall the consecution: this is why it's possible to reread Proust → There's something *epic* about the Proustian monument: the "evenings" (or afternoons, or receptions), like the battles in an epic work: an *in-itself* that works independently of the whole; and there's also something *disintegrated* about it, which means that, in Proust, the index of episodes remains something that's very much alive; the index (Pléiade) is not just a means of orientating yourself around the work: it represents a "truth" of the work; something like an X-ray of the Ur-text.

> Tadié

    What remains enigmatic, of course, is problem of soldering and montage → What would be required is an analysis of the *transitions* (or the nontransitions); I don't think such an analysis exists, for the critics have been obsessed by the conformist desire to uncover a classical "construction" to *In Search* (in the shape of a star, for example), but on the contrary it's the awkwardnesses, the naiveties, and the not-quites of the transitions that we should be paying *attention* to. The "Rectangle" = space of flocculation; as the importance, the freedom of the *additions* confirms; Proust, as we know— this is an essential component of the *operational status* of his writing— *was constantly making additions*; this is the *mayonnaise* technique: once it starts coming together, you can keep adding on more and more oil; constantly, alongside a passage, this note: "add somewhere" → Proust, very conscious of this technique, of its constitutive value;

> S.B., 27

Kolb, 244

to Gaston Gallimard (1919) who, like any editor anxious to avoid coughing up for so-called author's corrections, had probably made some objection: "Since you're good enough to see a certain richness that you like in my books, remind yourself that it is precisely due to the extra nourishment with which I re-infuse them through living, and of which these additions are the material form."[13] It's likely that, once the work was finished, had Proust lived, he wouldn't have written anything else; he'd have spent the rest of his life *making additions* → The status, the *eidos* of *In Search of Lost Time* is to be an *infinite* work.

Brakings

At the outset: the Work to be written, in the radiance of the Fantasy; this is how it starts off → Yet the fantasy (this is its "teleological" definition) comes up against reality. Ultimately, that reality is *Time* (Duration) as a force of delay, of braking, and so of modification, infidelity (to the Project), of versatility → Two figures of modificatory Time: (1) the Time of writing (of the act of writing): microtime, the rhythm of the Pen = "the slow Hand"; (2) the overall Time of the Work: macro-time; seconds, tenths of seconds ≠ months, years.

1. The Slow Hand

My text on writing

HISTORY OF SPEED[14]   Speed of the graphic act = a real cultural issue. Why? Because to be able to write faster (at a time when professional writing was still done by hand) was to gain time and therefore money → Many new types of writing derived from the need to write faster:

a. The Egyptian demotic = hieroglyphics simplified and speeded up by the use of ligatures (for, and I'll repeat the point again in a moment, taking the pen off the page takes up more time than following one continuous line).

b. In order to write faster, the Sumerians drastically modified their first writing system: they passed from the pictogram to the cuneiform, from using an awl to a beveled reed, avoided curves and changed the orientation of their tablets. + to save space (because the surface you write on costs money): Tironian notes (Tiron, Cicero's freed slave); a great many, from the ninth to the fifteenth century: *ff = filii* → It's sometimes better to save space over time: in the

Middle Ages, words were shortened, and accents (which don't take up any room) embellished. In order to save time, you first need to know what absorbs the time of writing = *taking the pen off the page*; nibs are expensive → The ligature is therefore an economical rather than an aesthetic operation. We tend to think that the normal state of the letter is the lower case (which occasionally gets enlarged and schematized in capitals); historically, it's the other way around (Greeks and Latins): first, capitals; then, in order to write faster, they linked the letters together, they accepted there would be irregularities and furnished their letters with hastes and tails, indicators of the hand moving faster, more freely → Lower cases were a product of the essential act of functional writing, of *cursivity*: that writing should race ahead! Race after what? Time, speech, money, thought, bedazzlement, affect, etc. If only my hand were as quick as my tongue, my eyes, my living memory: demiurgic dream; all of literature, all of culture, all of "psychology" would be different had the hand not moved at a slower pace than the inside of our heads.

Pensées, I

Thus, relative to literature, there's a whole dossier to be compiled on the speed of the graphic composition of Works; a *historical* dossier for it seems there were variations: (a) First, the testimonies are difficult to reconstruct: in the seventeenth century, for example, no one kept their drafts, their preparatory notes, their plans: the manuscript wasn't sacred → whence the exceptional character of Pascal's *Pensées*, where the writing (the written form) can be traced (with difficulty) in its abandon, its speed, its "free wheeling." (b) For lots of writers, the form would present itself straight away, and as a result the work (after what could be a long preparation) would often be written at a speed that seems almost inconceivable today, for that impression of speed is compounded by how quickly things would be published. Michelet would have what he was writing printed as he went along (mad audacity); for example, the *History of the Middle Ages* (final volume on Louis XI): November 6, 1843: begins the last chapter—December 4: finishes the book—December 6: the book is printed—January 4: it's on sale[15] → Perhaps writers' bodies were different in those days? Musset would often write a play (for example *Les Caprices*) in a night, assisted by alcohol (absinthe) and the presence of a naked prostitute in the room. Stendhal dictated the five hundred pages of *The Charterhouse of Parma* over fifty-two days: we have a version in his secretary's shorthand.

Monod, *Michelet*, ǂ165

My text on writing

Certain "intellectuals" (Quintilian, the Surrealists; Germany, end of the nineteenth century) have taken an explicit interest in this problem of writing speed—which competes with mental speed: some try to start a movement in favor of shorthand—Husserl had his own shorthand.

TYPES OF "HAND" The essential point of this "dossier" = to establish whether there two different types of "handwriting" exist and, on that basis, perhaps, two different types of "style": (1) the whole of Proust's oeuvre, its wordiness, the almost infinite character of his sentences, the abundant correspondence, the appearance of his handwriting suggests that Proust wrote very quickly by hand, and the whole of his oeuvre owes much to that muscular facility. Proust was aware (letter to Robert Dreyfus, 1888) that he wrote *at a gallop* → The "gallop" presupposes a kind of asymptotic rapprochement of the manual (the muscles) and the mental (the affective): the hand seems plugged directly into the mental; it's no longer a means to *reduce speed*. (2) ≠ Slow writing: (a) writing that is constantly lifting the pen from the page, either due to the super-ego of mulling things over, or to aphasia, the inability to come up with the right word straight away; (b) writing that, due to its homology with a particular mental attitude, needs to *press down*, to put pressure on the paper (this is what takes time): *to inscribe / to paint* → Therefore, the desire to pass (even fantasmatically) from a work that presses to a work that races ahead (from the Essay to the Novel, for example) involves having to learn how to *write fast*.

Kolb, 30

We could risk defining the work in general terms as a *kinetic relationship between the head and the hand* → Perhaps *writing* consists in not thinking any faster than your hand can write, in mastering that relationship, in making it optimal → On that basis, the obsessive care (or so it appears to others) taken over which pen, what kind of paper, etc. to use is comprehensible, an "obsessive behavior" that's foolishly derided by those who see in it only an absurd extravagance, particular to writers, who, as we know, are a breed apart.

2. The Overall Time of the Work

Préface, 257

PARAMETRICS One of Flaubert's most singular remarks is his calm announcement that the book he must write will take him six years. Now, how can anyone know where they'll be in themselves, in their relationship to the world, in six years? The book, a fixed object, since it's finished, structured, premeditated, is produced by a subject who can never guarantee his own immutability. Once the Planning Stage has come to an end, and the slow work of Writing begins, there's therefore a concern. Proust: Will I have time to finish it before I die? = Will I have time to realize it in the form I envisaged before I change myself? Sort of Einsteinian problem: the non-identity of the self has to produce an object that's defined by its identity → Non-identity formulated by Pascal in the following way: "I feel in myself a malice that prevents me from agreeing with what Montaigne says, that vivacity and firmness weaken in us with age. I would not wish that to be so. I am envious of myself. This self at twenty years old is no longer me."[16] Whence the impatience to finish the work as soon as it has begun: precaution against yourself. Frequent feelings of revulsion, of disarray, because I no longer fit the work and yet I have to see it through, in the way it was planned → Unless, of course, the variability of the subject and the parametrical variation of the Work is factored into the Plan of the Work; but, in classical literature, that's very uncommon, the only form that makes allowances for the "parametrics" of the subject is the Diary, the Album; but, precisely, that's not the Book.

INTERRUPTING THE WORK   The change: the modification of the *self* can be so pronounced that the writer *changes the Work* that's in the process of fabrication → Interrupting the Work; I can think of a conspicuous case: Michelet finishing his *History of the Middle Ages*; he's got to Louis XI; according to his plan, he should follow Louis XI with the monarchic centuries; now, he has a sort of flash of inspiration, or of radical impatience: he feels, decides (1842) that he must start writing the *History of the Revolution* straight away; as a result, he stops and drastically alters the course of History (he wrote the history of the sixteenth, seventeenth, and eighteenth centuries at a later date, in a completely different style, one that's violent, biased, a bit mad). His self had changed and that change forced a change in the work: What provoked that change, that mutation of the subject? There are some scholarly, biographical explanations: (a) influence of Quinent (left-wing militant); (b) influence of the revolutionary students who attended his classes at the Collège (very lively classes); (c) attacks from the ultramontanes who urged Michelet to radicalize his attitude—or rather his position (as we say nowadays): to give up on the Middle Ages and the Church.[17] There's Michelet's own explanation, an explanation that's more mythical than biographical, or

Monod, II, 43

rather of a mythical psychology that stages the weakening of the Imaginary:

MICHELET, *HISTORY OF FRANCE*

I entered through Louis XI into the centuries of Monarchy. I was about to undertake this study when an accident made me reflect deeply. One day, passing through Reims, I examined in great detail the magnificent cathedral, the splendid church of the Coronation.

The interior cornice from which you can walk around the church at a height of eighty feet makes it appear enchanting, of flowering richness, a permanent hallelujah. In the hollow vastness, you always think you hear the great official hubbub, spoken by the voice of the populace. You think you see at the windows the birds which were released when the clergy, anointing the king, made a pact between the Throne and the Church. Going back outside over the arches in the immense panorama which embraces all Champagne, I came to the last little steeple, exactly above the chancel. There a strange scene amazed me. The round tower was wreathed with tortured criminals. One has a rope around his neck. Another has lost an ear. The mutilated are more wretched there than the dead. How right they are! What a frightful contrast! What! The Church of festivals, this bride, has taken this lugubrious ornament as a wedding necklace! This pillory of the people is set above the altar. But could not their tears, through the arches, have fallen upon the heads of kings! Fearful anointing of the Revolution, of the anger of God! "I will not understand the centuries of monarchy if first, above all, I do not establish within myself the soul and the faith of the people." I spoke these words to myself and, after Louis XI, I wrote the Revolution.[18]

I want to point out in passing that "changing" is an act that presents the Doxa with a great deal of problems; fickleness is never well regarded—I'll say: even when it can be called a "conversion"; what the Doxa admires is immutability, the persistence of an opinion (Why? Perhaps left over from feudal morality) → Possibility of a typology of intellectual "changes": (1) Never change = Militant. (2) Change but dogmatize each change = Clovis's complex: worship what you have hitherto burned, and vice versa. (3) Change, vary, but in a nondogmatic way, like the shimmering of mottled silk (that is to say, without fanfare) on the curtain of life (the Maya):[19] cf. the "versatility" that Nietzsche speaks of in *Ecce Homo*.

3. The Breakdown

Préface, 69

MARINADE   These brakings → often and in a more contingent manner: writing *stalls*, breaks down → for Flaubert, this would translate bodily into "marinades": abandoning his desk (whose "sacred," fetishistic nature I've discussed), he would throw himself onto his couch and lie there limply (this is why you should always—or never—have a couch in your study). So, Flaubert, (1852, thirty-one years old): "Sometimes, when I am empty, when words don't come, when I find I haven't written a single sentence after scribbling whole pages, I collapse on my couch and lie there dazed, bogged in an inner swamp of ennui . . ."[20] (I provide this quotation with a certain degree of indulgence because, alas, I too am a marinader (but take note: I'm identifying with, not comparing myself to)

Scherer, XXII

→ And Mallarmé (1893): relieved of his teaching, had hoped "to really make a start in literature" but is aware of "a laziness in the pen itself" taking hold.

DIFFICULTY   What causes the Breakdown? For Flaubert: when the words don't come; breakdown of style, his sole obsession → Other sorts of incapacity are possible: to do with ideas, with the plan; doubts or sterilities rise up within you and overwhelm you, like a blush: despondency, "sinkings" (Flaubert) → however, I'd like to give the Breakdown a more precise definition: the sudden realization that writing is difficult to the point of impossibility (Flaubert, 1857, thirty-six years old): "Writing seems more and more impossible to me")[21] or else suddenly encountering a difficulty in writing

Préface, 193

of indeterminate origin and nature (cf. Unconscious); whence the disheartening impossibility of fighting it.

SOLUTIONS   Solutions to the Breakdown? (or at least ways of shortening it; for the Breakdown is really like a broken heart: in the end it goes away by itself). For example (this depends on the subject as well as on the book):

Drugs

a. Drugs, of whatever kind: for Musset, absinthe, nowadays, amphetamines → the role of Tenuate[22] → facility, intrepidity even, euphoria at vanquishing sterility; but, once the effect has worn off, you reread what you've written and feel disheartened at how uninteresting it is, or at least at how much less interesting it is; drugs don't bestow genius but they do offer a fleeting impression of genius; a useful blast of mythomania to get things going again: sort of artificial choke.

Autonym

b. Sometimes (it depends on the book), autonymic (= "when the word refers to itself and not to its referent") trick: "I'm drying up; very well then, I'll write: 'I'm drying up' " → In some sense, all contemporary literature is autonymic; it consists in designating itself as literature, in writing the impossibility of *writing*: Blanchot → Let's imagine an immense Breakdown from which you would emerge (without actually emerging from it) glossing the Breakdown (as I'm doing now, but in passing).

Neurosis

c. It's possible to imagine, as a solution, a sort of neurotic stratagem or plasticity: depending on the nature of the problem or of the breakdown, you exploit the different neuroses within yourself; for example, breakdowns at the outset: defeating the page, coming up with ideas, provoking the *spurt*, etc. = hysterical activity ≠ the phase of Style, of Making Corrections, of Protection = obsessional activity.

Not publishing

d. When it's a matter of a breakdown caused by the Other's (the Great Other's) Imaginary Gaze being fixed upon what you're writing, the sense that your writing is being monitored (anxiety of being watched while doing something difficult), the Imaginary provides a solution: you artificially divide writing up into Pleasure and Fear (of the Other); you write (pleasure) but tell yourself (pure imaginary) that you're not going to publish it: this frees writing up (so you tell yourself). Flaubert (1871, fifty years old): "I'm still taking notes for my *Saint Anthony* <this will be the third version>, which I have resolved not to publish when it's finished, *which means I'm working with complete freedom of mind*";[23] the problem is well formulated, because the desired outcome of this line of reasoning isn't not publishing (*Saint Anthony*, finished in June 1872, published in April 1874) but *freeing the mind* (the pen). "*Not publishing*," a kind of half rhetorical, half-magical figure, used by lots of writers:

Préface, 249

Préface, 126

222

38

Flaubert, of course; countless declarations: "Publishing is basically a very stupid thing to do" (1853, thirty-two years old); "If I show it <the finished work> to the public, it is out of stupidity and in compliance with a received idea that *one must publish*, something which I personally don't feel the need to do" (1862, forty-one years old); and 1846 (twenty-five years old): "But I don't want to publish anything. This is a stand, an oath I took at a solemn time in my life. I work with a total disinterest, with no agenda or ulterior motive."[24]

Rousseau: "Let them spy out what I am doing, let them worry about these pages, let them seize them, suppress them, falsify them <= description of the Other's Gaze perceived as Manipulative>;

henceforth none of that bothers me. I neither hide nor show them. If they take them away from me while I am living, they will not take away from me the pleasure of having written them, nor the memory of their content, nor the solitary meditations of which they are the fruit."[25]

Baudelaire: "Is it even very necessary, for the author's satisfaction, that a given book be understood by anyone except the person for whom it was written? <Illusion of the Dedication, which Baudelaire punctures in the next sentence> Is it, in the end, absolutely vital that it should have been written for *someone*?"[26]

Pensées, I, p. 11

There are variations on *Not publishing*: (a) Notes to yourself, with no intention of them being read by another: Pascal's papers found at his death; private reflections not meant for publication, notes for the Apology = just the necessary amount of information for Pascal to be able to understand them himself. (b) Publishing as a minimal act, a *dull* act unburdened of any imaginary vibration. Vigny (*Journal*, 164): "There is only one thing for a man who has any respect for himself to do: publish, see no one, and forget about his book."[27] Gide (1947): "The truth is, at bottom I don't really believe in the posthumous."[28]

I'll set this against an attitude that's the extreme opposite: the *innocent* frenzy of publication; anecdotally, because it's quite extraordinary: Swedenborg[29] (a contemporary of Voltaire's), a bishop's son, upper middle class, member of the Elite, Money, Favors, Connections, always abroad. Now, it appears he travels because he has a system in place whereby he writes his books *in the town where they'll be printed* (in Latin): he lives where he writes, writes where he publishes (that's—that *was*—Europe for you!).

These solutions: artificial ≠ the real, modest, not especially triumphant, humbly moral solution (Morality of Labor): to identify, that is to say, to *work out*, to *isolate* what doesn't work and to remedy it (or to delete it) → Very important: you reread a page—very bad impression → breakdown, marinade: "none of this is any good, I don't know how to write, I'll never do it," etc. → Here: to get up, go back to your desk and identify *where* it's not working; generally, only a few passages don't work at all, but they contaminate the rest; it's a matter of not getting discouraged and constantly reminding yourself that it is the *nature* of the text to be an interweaving of *details*. Solution to the Breakdown: the *identification* of "what doesn't work."

Conclusion: Boredom

The difficulties, the delays, the temptation to give it all up, the recurrence of which constitute the Second Trial of Writing, the Time of Patience, have a hidden relationship with an ambiguous power, both an incentive and a force of destruction: *Boredom*.

Acedy

Boredom {*Ennui*}: the word itself manages to be the mockery of its own etymology: *ennuyer* {to bore} > *inodiare* > *in odio esse*: to be an object of hate. Now, if the word had a much stronger meaning in the seventeenth century (unbearable pain, intolerable torment, violent despair), today it means the complete opposite: a state without hate and without love, a loss of drive. (Note, for this kind of semantic problem is very important to me: the productiveness of misreadings: "*Dans l'Orient désert, quel devint mon ennui*"[30] = (1) "Correct" philological version: what becomes of my violent despair. (2) Version that's philologically wrong but aesthetically correct, considering the word's modern connotations: harmony between the Orient and boredom {*ennui*} in the sense of the vague unease of an unoccupied mind → It's actually a very subtle word: it refers to the strength, as it were, of a weakness, to the intensity of a lack of intensity. With that in view, from the perspective of an Ethics of Energy (and they all are, with the exception of Buddhist ethics) Boredom = a serious Sin: *acedy* (cf. First course),[31] privation of desire and of hope; and the nullity of Desire is a more serious Sin than the nullity of Hope; indeed, those who lived in Desire but with no Hope Dante places in limbo (the first circle), but the *Accidiosi*, those who lived with no desire and with no hope, are placed in the fifth circle, much lower down. Their *contrapasso* is to suffocate in the mud of the Styx: they are literally stuck {*vaseux*},[32] which brings us back to the writer at a standstill, that is, in the grip of Boredom + different root: *accedia* → in theological Latin: *pigritia*, capital sin; to translate this as *laziness* is to understate it: it's not clear why laziness should be as serious a sin as killing someone, but it should be taken in the sense of a black laziness, the unnatural state of Man without desire, without protension, without moral seed, and this is also what the stalled writer experiences: a hopeless *laziness* → The whole of Christianity considers Boredom to be a kind of appalling Evil. Pascal: "Nothing is so intolerable for man as to be in complete tranquility, without dealings, without diversion,

Inferno, VII

Pensées, II, 122

without effort. He then feels his nothingness, isolation, insufficiency, dependence, weakness, emptiness. Immediately there arises from the depth of his soul boredom, gloom, sadness, chagrin, resentment, despair."[33] (Note that Christ momentarily bore the burden of this sin, saying: *Tristis [est] anima mea usque ad mortem.*)[34]

Schopenhauer

Schopenhauer made Boredom the metaphysical condition of Man; desire's profound truth, the secret truth within each of us: "Life swings like a pendulum to and fro from pain to boredom."[35] → Two symptoms of Boredom (among others): games and Sundays. Pascal's notion that entertainment is itself boring; boredom = nest of tables, one inside the other, a construction in the form of a *Mirage*; the young Chateaubriand, on his way to see a play in Paris, puts this very well: "boring myself so as to relieve my boredom."[36] Starting with Schopenhauer and with what came before and after, a whole dossier on Boredom: in the works of the Romantics, then the Symbolists → Novel by Moravia: *Boredom* → More generally, I had thought of doing a Lecture Course on the *Mal du siècle*, or variations of the "*Mal du siècle*," because nowadays, too, lots of people profess to being bored. But all I'm doing here is merely *offering a sketch*: relationship between Boredom and Writing.

Art

Now, it appears that in the case of many writers—the ones who've furnished us with the majority of our quotations (# 1850 1920)—the will for a Work emerges out of a context of Boredom—from Chateaubriand to Flaubert and beyond (Mallarmé). Flaubert, 1846 (twenty-five years old): "I was born bored; it is the leprosy that eats away at me. I tire of life, of myself, of other people, of everything."[37] → Note that the Doxa is very resistant to this way of looking at life; it discredits it as "pessimism" and thinks it healthy to respond with a kind of boy-scoutism of energy, of *joie de vivre*, of bravery, etc. (but pessimism is as stupid as optimism). Out of this context, then, writing emerges as *Art*: Art is indeed this surprising power that *relieves boredom*: it *cuts off* (short-circuits) Boredom, a different kind of Metaphysics acting upon the first → once again, in his own fashion, Chateaubriand puts this very well—in a sentence that's strange and beautiful in its own right: "If I had shaped my own clay, perhaps I would have made myself a woman, for love of

M.O.T., I, 121

them; or if I had made myself a man, I would first have endowed myself with beauty; then, *as a precaution against boredom, my bitter enemy*, it would have suited me to be a great, but unknown artist, using my talent only for the benefit of my solitude"[38] (still the *Not publishing*) → This cutting off, this breach that Art makes into Boredom can be found, converted, in the humble practice of writing: to write, every day, relieves boredom. Flaubert (the same quotation, where he began by saying he was born bored; he goes on): "By dint of will-power, I eventually got into the habit of working; but, whenever I stopped, all my troubles would break the surface again, like a bloated carcass displaying its green belly and poisoning the air that one breathes."

Fall Outside of the Essence

It's probably necessary to put things in radical terms: Art is the essence of Anti-Boredom, of Relief from Boredom; or rather, to avoid falling into the "anti" trap, this can be put the other way: Boredom = a reactive force to which Art (Writing), as an active force, is opposed. It follows that the "breakdowns" of writing (the brakings, the difficulties): repeated falls outside of the essence, which means, even if they get lost in the dailiness of everyday life, they are experienced as repetitions of a serious sin → Therein lies the fragile ambivalence of Boredom; as you write you emerge, so to speak, out of the context of Boredom, but once engaged in the labor of writing all of a sudden a second Boredom rises up (perhaps a hypostasis of the first) that prevents you from writing. Mallarmé (1864): "I haven't written for a long time, because I was in a state of utter dejection" and "Yet I do indeed feel dead: tedium has become in my case a mental illness, and my lifeless impotence makes the lightest work painful to me."[39]

Last remark; lucid, I think: it's not "autonymic" recuperation that's at stake here. I said: possibility of saying "I'm drying up, very well, then, I'll write that I'm drying up"; many—perhaps a whole century—of writers have said: "I know about boredom, very well then, I'll write about boredom": it's what lots of the Romantics did (for me the "Romantic" period dates from Rousseau to Proust): Chateaubriand, Byron, Baudelaire, Mallarmé; with the ultimate ironical treatise, the Writing of Boredom: Gide writing *Paludes*. But the point is, even if it's the same Boredom (there's probably only one kind), it isn't the same *intentionality* of boredom; it's one thing to intentionalize human existence as Boredom (as a condition) (but don't animals get bored?) and another to want to write that intentionality and, within that labor, that activity, to sometimes intentionalize the labor itself as Boredom, as a little bit of Boredom that then treacherously, perversely, comes to figure in the Portrait of Boredom, but *en abyme* → As I've said, to counter that "lesser" Boredom there's only one solution: one that's *pragmatic* (to struggle on, detail after detail, moment after moment) and *active* (to trust in Writing, in Art).

SESSION OF FEBRUARY 16, 1980

4. Third Trial: Separation

We've now reached the Third Trial. The first was more or less punctual, or in any case inaugural: Choice. The second is in some sense permanent, or in any case enduring: Patience (of Writing). The third is, so to speak, recurrent; it comes up again and again, throughout the labor, like an uneasy feeling that can never be definitively shaken off: someone who gives themselves up to writing feels *separated* from the world not only by an act of physical retreat but by a feeling, almost a guilty feeling, of rupture, divorce, separation in terms of *values*; the writer retreats from the recognized values of the world, cuts himself off, renounces a complicity; if he remains *co-present* with the world it's by way of a detour that he sometimes has difficulty coming to terms with: he feels himself to be in a state of (secular) *apostasis* → It's therefore a matter, so to speak—or so we once might have said—of a *moral* trial.

Archaism and Desire

What's now breaking the surface of the collective consciousness—or semiconsciousness—is a certain *archaism* of literature and therefore a certain marginalization (marginalities are always discussed as if they were statutorily "young," more or less avant-gardist, but there are fringes of Time, of History that would be just as interesting to identify, to understand). Now, therein lies our problem: this "archaization" of literature is co-present with (concomitant with) a powerful Desire for precisely that literature (cf. the beginning of the Course).

Attachment to the Past

The kind I've been discussing: conspicuous and—since I'm announcing it—conscious archaization = fondness for the material quoted, and therefore for the concepts and gestures, for the proposed working practices → hardly anything I've quoted is more recent than Proust, that is to say, a writer—perhaps the last—totally integrated into the canonical concept of literature (in actual fact: Romantic literature, cf. *infra*)[1] → 95 percent of the books written today probably elude the problems I've been dealing with.

Untimeliness

Another symptom of archaization: sudden awareness of there being a discrepancy between what for me is the burning timeliness of what I'm doing (Writing) and what's going on in the world around me; neither sphere is really contemporaneous with the other → cruelly gives rise to a sense of embarrassment, of being laughed at → For example, on the day (October 10, 1979) when I was working on the section of the Course that deals with this serious problem: "Can you keep reading books once you've decided to start writing?" I glanced at the "world" (*Libération*) and that world jumped out at me, making a mockery of my personal little investments: police blunders, bikers getting beaten up, nuclear waste, clashes in Cherbourg, Guattari's noble letter to the President of the Republic in which he refuses the invitation to attend Children's Day and recalls all the leftist themes (immigrant workers done over in police stations, Piperno's extradition, Goldman's assassination, etc.)[2]—all this while I was expounding at length on how you might go about shutting yourself away with a view to producing a literary Work! → What's going on in the world exercises a kind of permanent blackmail over someone who forgets about it.

Living Desire

However (a strong "However," of the *Eppur si muove* sort),[3] at the root of this guilty retreat into anachronism, into the Untimeliness of *Writing*, is an inflexible desire, one might be compatible with literary Archaism insofar as the desire in question is itself archaic: (a) in the first instance because all desires are archaic, they originate in the occulted—and uncultured—zones of the self; (b) and then, more specifically, because the desire to write is, if not puerile, then at any rate *adolescent*; it's been noted that the awakening of the literary "vocation" more or less coincides with puberty; there's a kind of—not infantile, but adolescent—fixation upon a semiarchaism, more amorous than strictly Oedipal.

This no doubt explains why the Desire to Write resists all pressure from the Timely as the Figure of Good Integration, and why it always emerges alive: extraordinarily alive, immediate and vitalized by its own timeliness, its own ardent uncompromising timeliness.

Mallarmé, Seuil, 21

Reading Pascal on the plane (August 29, 1979, on the way to Biarritz), and being transported by his text, by its *truth* (the truth of a text is not the truth of what that text says; it is—paradoxical notion—*the truth of its form*), I thought to myself: to love literature is, from the moment you start reading, to chase away all possible doubt as to its presentness, its timeliness, its immediacy, it's to believe, it's to see that there's a living man speaking to me, as if his body were here, next to mine, more real to me than Khomeini or Bokassa; it's Pascal fearing Death, or being overwhelmed by it to the point of vertigo, it's discovering that those old formulations (for example, "Wretchedness of Man," "Concupiscence," etc.) perfectly express the present-day things that are within me, it's *not feeling the need for another language* → In fact, the *present* = notion distinct from the *topical*; the *present* is alive (I'm in the process of creating it myself) ≠ the topical can only be a *noise*.

What Is Going to Die

In addition to the above: this desire for literature is all the more keen, all the more alive, all the more present within me precisely when I can sense that literature is on the decline, in the process of dying out: it's then that I love it with a penetrating, even an overwhelming love, in the way one loves and embraces something that's going to die.

Signs of Desuetude

This feeling that *literature*, as Active Force, living Myth is, not in crisis (too facile a formula), but perhaps in the process of *dying* = a few signs, among others, of desuetude (or breathlessness); perhaps very subjective; single dossier to be completed; a few points to follow up.

1. Teaching

The very first thing to do would be to take a serious look at how literature is currently taught, School (more than University) being the place where both a love of literature and its mythology, that is to say, both a respect and a disdain for it used to be instilled: Proust and Gisèle's dissertation[4] → Now, I'm not qualified to do this: I can't testify to the attitudes of the teachers nor to those of their pupils; on this last point, I can't imagine that the assessment would be glowing → The dossier is very complex:

a. because literature's image is directly dependent upon political (economical and social) factors: the Powers that be wanting to make cuts in "literary studies" in favor of the "technical" professions (=technocracy), Malthusianism of teaching posts, etc. → here it would be necessary to study the evolution, the decline of the Figure of the Literature Teacher: think what Proust's literature teachers meant to him;

b. because any writing practice associated with "School" now has a Bad Image, it's associated with a rigid, formal style; ideologically speaking, literary writing is dealt a bad hand, it's tarnished simultaneously: (a) by the fact of being the property of the ruling classes; (b) by the contemptuous devalorization of anything to do with the Past; (c) by the myth, prevalent in some quarters, that the exercise of form is a sophisticated, "decadent" activity; (d) by the fact that literature's survival is now in the hands of the academics → This explains how the attacks can come from within the intelligentsia itself; Foucault calling for the "sovereignty of the signifier" to be abolished at last and for "outdated academic methods of textual analysis and all the concepts which are the appanage of the dreary and scholastic prestige of writing"[5] to be shunned → "Modernist" rejection of "style" because of its association with school. Céline: irony with respect to what he calls "*school-boy*" style, the French sentence as illustrated by Voltaire, Renan, France (but what if I personally had a *perverse* fondness for that style?).

2. Leadership[6]

Another obvious change—but I'm only outlining the shape of the dossier: the disappearance of literary leaders; for at least two hundred years, literature: a grand, hierarchical structure of major, minor figures; every ("committed") intellectual was consubstantially a Writer → the Writer = mythical figure in society, crystallization of "values." Between the two wars, you still had great leaders: Mauriac, Malraux, Claudel, Gide, Valéry → They've disappeared but not been replaced: Malraux, the last; or Aragon → This mutation would have to be tracked and analyzed in relation to Sartre as the figure of the myth's self-destruction → This disaffiliation can be summed up in a fairly crude, derisory manner: in France, there are no longer any "Nobelizables."

Order of Discourse
Psy à Université vol. 4
I, Pierre Rivière

3. "Work"

This course is so fundamentally "archaic" that in a sense its object—that is, the notion of the *Work*—no longer has any currency in the field of letters. It would appear that those who write produce, want to produce *books* but what's disappeared, or what's more or less disappeared, is the intentionality that characterizes the Work as a personal monument, a mad object that the writer is totally invested in, a personal cosmos: *stone* that the writer constructs over the course of History (whence the exceptional and ultimately *anachronistic* nature of Sollers's *Paradis*). Why? (Actually, with these sorts of phenomena, it's never clear whether it's a matter of traces, of signs, or of causes). Probably because: writing is no longer the dramatization of a Value, of an active Force; it's no longer or is now only loosely attached to a system, to a doctrine, to a faith, an ethics, a philosophy, a culture → writing is produced in an ideological outpouring (of the world) with no *stop mechanism*: now, the Work (and the Writing that mediates it) = precisely: a *stop mechanism* that checks that *free wheeling*; the free wheeling of stereotypes or the free wheeling of Madness; the Work: not nihilistic (Nietzsche: nihilism = when the loftier values depreciate).

4. Rhetoric

Writing is no longer the object of a *Pedagogy* (in the very broad sense of the term):

a. As we know, *Rhetoric*, that is to say the *teachable art* (from *Techné*) *of speaking with the aim of producing certain effects* no longer exists: it's no longer possible to conceive of language as a mechanism for producing effects. I'm not going to dwell on the institutional Death of Rhetoric, since this was the topic of my EHESS seminar in 1965–1966.[7] Rhetoric has been degraded, technocratized → "techniques of expression" (what ideology!), summaries, *writings*,[8] etc. Now, there used to be a direct link between rhetorical teaching and the writing by the writers I've been discussing. Rhetoric = the art of writing (≠ art of reading → arts of language no longer exist).

b. A superior form of this *Pedagogy* (Psychagogy) of Writing, not on the level of institutions, of teachings: writers discussing the problems of the Practice of Writing among themselves → Rhetoric *inter pares*: correspondence (Flaubert, Kafka, Proust) and, from an elder to a younger writer: "advice"; remember Rilke's beautiful text, *Letters to a Young Poet*. Now those "words of advice" have disappeared: there's no longer any "transmission" → The surprising and anachronistic character (which, by the way, I find touching) of Cortazar's declaration (surprising to read this today) (in the Leguay manuscript, *Le Club des amis du texte*, p. 22):[9] "I would advise a young writer who is having difficulty writing—if it is amicable to offer advice—that he should stop writing for himself for a while and do translations, that he should translate good literature, and one day he will discover that he is writing with an ease he didn't have before" (*Conversationes con Cortazar*, Edhasa, 1978).

c. The "essential" form of the Advice offered to a Writer ultimately concerns not the practice of writing but the very Will to Write: Writing as the *Telos* of a life = in answer to the question "Should I write? Continue to Write?" they all say (Flaubert, Kafka, Rilke): it's not a matter of a gift, of talent, but of *survival*: write, but only if you're absolutely convinced that, if you don't, you'll perish (what we call a *vocation* probably refers to this kind of survival): Flaubert (1858, thirty-seven years old), to Monsieur X: "I should like to write you a very long letter. . . . If you feel an irresistible need to write, and you have the temperament of Hercules, then you're doing well. But otherwise, don't! I know the profession. It isn't easy!" etc.[10] → The "Advice" therefore consists in directing the other back to his desire or, better, to the *knowledge of his Desire*; but it's not easy to know your desire; lots of people wrestle with the intention to write and don't manage it (= Indecisiveness); perhaps it's just that, when it comes down to it, they don't really have the desire: the false desire to write masks another, unknown to the subject himself; it's merely a *transferable* symptom → But that's something only the subject himself can know: the person offering Advice stops short of delivering the narcissistic blow he knows he'd inflict on the other were he to say him: *Don't write* or *It's not worth it* → for *Agraphism* isn't well regarded—But what about Socrates?—Yes, but Socrates had his *Telos* directed away from writing in the form of Plato.

To bring this to a close: today, in my experience, there's no longer any demand for *practical* advice, but there's still a powerful demand for recognition through writing → What has changed, the desuetude = not the desire to write (so perhaps it transcends a definite sociality) but the loss of the sense that writing is linked to a *labor*, a pedagogy, an initiation. The urge (to write) manifests itself

Préface, 200

as a sort of unrealistic innocence: refusal to think out the *Mediation*; *labor* isn't fashionable any more!

5. Heroism

I said: disappearance of literary *leaders*; this is still a social idea; the leader = figure in the organization of Culture → But within the community of writers (the calling into question, not to say the decline of which I'm outlining now), another word imposes itself, less social, more mythical: *hero*. Baudelaire on Poe = "one of the greatest literary heroes" → It's this Figure—or this Power—of the literary Hero that's dying out today.

> *Mondor, Mallarmé, I, 9*

a. If we think of Mallarmé, of Kafka, of Flaubert, even of Proust (the Proust of *In Search of Lost Time*), what is "heroism"?—(1) Literature is accorded a kind of absolute exclusivity: monomania or, in psychological terms, obsession: but also, put differently, a transcendence that proffers literature as the full expression of an alternative to the world: literature is Everything, it's the Whole of the world; radical declarations—consciously, philosophically radical—from Mallarmé: "Yes, literature exists and, if you will, alone, to the exclusion of everything"—and in the interview with Jules Huret (*Revue Blanche*, 1891): "Everything in the world exists to end up in a book"[11]—and, in a less doctrinal, more existential, more heartrending manner, Kafka (letter to Felice Bauer, 1912): "should I ever have been happy outside of writing and whatever is connected with it (I don't rightly know if I ever was)—at such times I was incapable of writing, with the result that everything had barely begun when the whole applecart tipped over, *for the longing to write was uppermost.*"[12] (2) Heroism = uncompromising attachment to a Practice = the declaration of an autonomy, a solitude with respect to the world; that is to say, paradox: starting out from an *Imitation* (Imitation according to literature, according to the beloved Author), what's then required is what Husserl calls a *refusal to inherit* (= a "dogmatism"):[13] cf. Nietzsche (*Ecce Homo*, 299): "At that time <the first Festival of Bayreuth, around 1876> my instinct decided inexorably against any further giving way, going along with everyone else, confounding of myself with what I was not."[14] (3) Third attribute of the Heroism of solitude: an apprenticeship in literature is an apprenticeship in how to be alone, to the point of it becoming a curse, which is to say, to the point of it inviting the world's ironic disapproval. Kafka began writing around

> *Lautréamont*, Seuil, 5
>
> Scherer, XV
> Seuil, 100
>
> Seuil, 40

1897–1898: one Sunday afternoon, he writes something about two brothers (one in America, the other in prison, etc.); one of his uncles reads the text out to the family, then comments: "The usual stuff" → "To be sure, I remained seated and bent as before over the now useless page of mine, but with one thrust I had in fact been banished from society, the judgment of my uncle repeated itself in me with what amounted almost to real significance and even within the feeling of belonging to a family I got an insight into the cold space of our world which I had to warm with a fire that first I had to seek out."[15]

b. Does this kind of "Heroism" exist today? Perhaps, probably even, but we can say with certainty that literature itself (let's prudently say what gets written) no longer bears the trace of it, no longer testifies to it. Unique and final testimony of this "Heroism": Blanchot → But perhaps the point is that nowadays Heroism is compelled to be *secret*, to be unsaid; for clearly such Heroism has none of the arrogance of social (military, militant) Heroism; it's *not a particularly attractive* Heroism, for it's shot through with distress, with difficulties, to such an extent—and therein lies *the desuetude*—that society no longer recognizes it, that is to say, society no longer identifies it and no longer recognizes its *value*, its right to be acknowledged. The literature of today: brings to mind the last movement of Haydn's *Farewell*: one after the other, the instruments stop playing; only two violins remain (they carry on playing the third); they remain on stage but snuff out their candles: heroic and melodic.[16]

The Exiled Writer

On the basis of those few signs of Desuetude—this is how I experience them at any rate—, I (this *self* who wants to write a Work) am continuously weaving into my work, my writing practice, a sense of separation from—broadly—the world, the present, as Theater of History: my third trial is therefore the phantom of a certain kind of Exile → I conceive, I plan, I labor, but I'm obliged to do so while immersed, so to speak, in an intellectual "biosphere" that I don't feel is or don't believe to be in keeping with my labor, with my desire. Of course, this "Exile" isn't clear-cut: it results from a sort of *coalition* of questions: as someone who wants to write a Work, who has decided to sacrifice everything to it, I'm wondering *where* to situate it: (1) In which History? (2) In which Society? (3) In which Language? → A sketch of those questions:

1. Which History?

There are two problems here:

To Represent History

a. The first: how does the writer "represent," how does he "express History" (=his present insofar as he wants it to be intelligible)? This is an *aesthetic* problem: it would be a completely different topic for a course, requiring a historical theory of literature—which isn't my concern; my concern has been existential, not aesthetic. I can only make the following suggestion: be wary of the sublime idea that Great Works are the expression of Great History as seen from its great vantage points. It can happen. It is, for instance, the aim of *War and Peace*, which is a vast historical poem, an epic of Russian society in Napoleonic times. But great works very often have a marginal, indirect, fragmented relationship to History: is there a more *historical* writer, a writer more engaged with his time than Dante? Yet, read *Inferno*: you have a few quarrels between some small-scale gangs, between families from a few towns or even villages surrounding Florence: and it's all set in the absolute Transcendence of Evil → Those are the *modes* of representation that would have to be studied, which would not only involve establishing whether a determining relationship exists but identifying how that relationship *operates*: homology, parcelization, miniaturization, mediation through intermediary concepts, etc.—But, once again: this isn't our topic.

Exclusion and Jointure

b. The second problem, closer to an *existentiality* of the writer (rather than of an aesthetic technique)=what, in History, in *my* History, spurs me to action? How does my existence *structure* my History, articulate it, in such a way that that articulation inflects my Work or, even better, my relationship to the Work? For example (for I am only outlining the shape of a "dossier"): if we take a writer who had a very strong existential relationship to his History, Chateaubriand (so not at all the ethereal author of *René* or *Atala* but a vehemently "committed" writer, more so than Sartre and Malraux put together), we'll see that there's a sort of oscillation between two propositions:

Testamentary preface

1. I'm viscerally excluded from my present, I'm rejected, by the very fibers of my being, by the History that's happening now, I'm passionately, desperately sent back to obliterated History, to the Past. I neither love nor understand anything contemporary, I love and understand what is noncontemporary; I experience the passage of Time as a degradation of Values = "Attachment to the Past" or Nostalgia. Chateaubriand: "France has barely nothing left of its

Préface, 260

past, once so rich <written in 1833, that is to say, as the bourgeois Powers took hold>; it is beginning a new era: I remain behind to bury my century, like the old priest who, in the sacking of Béziers <Albigeois, 1209> had to ring the bell to mark the death of the last citizen, before dying himself."[17] → This "attachment to the past" has all the ambivalence of a passion: pleasure and guilt. This absolute attachment to the past could also jokingly be called "polycarpism." Why? Because Flaubert, who couldn't stand the age he lived in (and yet what could be more "historical" than *Madame Bovary* or *Sentimental Education*?), wanted to adopt Saint Polycarp, who was always indignant and would always say: "Oh God! Oh God! In what age hast thou made me live!"[18] as his patron saint.

2. This grandiose, impassioned obstinacy in claiming *not to be present* can go hand in hand with—and indeed does go hand in hand with: second proposition—the keen sense that you're both *in the present* and *not in the present*; that is to say, that you're at the very jointure between the new world, between the absent world of the past and world of the present that's in the process of being created—and that jointure is ultimately conceived as the *thing to write*. What remains is to know, to decide upon, to designate (to be conscious of) the fracture of the world, of History, that you experienced, that you experience profoundly, in a way that's totally alive → For Chateaubriand it was straightforward; he was strictly contemporary with the major event of modern history: the French Revolution—my sense of "strictly contemporary" is when there's a concomitance between the *Acme* of the Event and the subject's passage from adolescence to adulthood; now, Chateaubriand (1768–1848), born the same year as Bonaparte,[19] was twenty-five years old in 1783 (the acme wasn't 1789: the Bastille was actually a trivial event) → This chronological positioning is what enabled Chateaubriand to present his Life as a confluence of the Old and the New in the Testamentary Preface to *Memoirs from Beyond the Grave*: "I would represent . . . the principles, the ideas, the events, the epic of my time, all the more so in that I saw a world end and begin and in that the contradictory characteristics of that end and that beginning can be found mixed up in my own opinions <indeed, since he was both a legitimist and a reformist>. Like at the confluence of two rivers, I found myself between the two centuries; I plunged into their troubled waters, regretfully distancing myself from the old shore of my birth, and swimming, full of hope, towards the unknown bank upon which new generations will land."[20]

The Historical Fracture

→ Does every writer's life have its historical fracture? Probably not;

but we should be wary of evaluating the Event of a Complete Break solely in terms of change in politics; what counts=there being a *mutation in sensibility*, even if it's not followed up by a political transformation (as was the case with the Revolution); for example, the Dreyfus Affair (Proust, Zola); for me, it has to be *May 68* (and not the war); creatively, what matters, what's of consequence is if History gives rise to the necessity, the anxiety, and therefore the active labor of *self-adaptation* → Whether the continuity is interrupted or not, History=a *constant adaptation*: the Young Man adapts biologically, but the Old Man has to adapt existentially, and if we combine that task with the task of writing then you'll find, I think, a particular chemical formula for the Work as a thing to be done: difficult, vertiginous formula, for it's a subject who is himself changing who has to adapt to change; Einsteinian problem: me and the world are both changing at the same time but with no fixed point to gauge, by rights or by nature, the *legitimacy* of that change → "I don't like this": but is it me or the world that's changed? What should I complain about? The world or myself?

2. Which Society?

Answering this question would be satisfying only if we were to apply ourselves, with conviction and patience, to an in-depth sociological analysis, and to do so would inevitably involve making a political decision—a choice—at the outset, for the "thinking" of society is inevitably "optional," "doctrinal." Now, I'm not sure of my own views on that thinking → So I can only risk a few remarks, which have both the crudeness and the vagueness (the nonverifiability) of a conversational remark:

Lukács, Goldmann

E. U.

1. The most "social" theory of literature, for modernity: within Marxist discourse, that of Lukács-Goldmann[21] (other possibilities: Sartre, Structuralism, which was primarily concerned not with the nonsocial but rather the *transsocial*: the code); apropos of the Novel, thesis (*Encyclopaedia Universalis*): for the great Western novelist, conflict and incompatibility between two ideas: *being* and *becoming*: without him being conscious of it, the character in the novel (Julien Sorel, for instance) remembers that mythical state of humanity when individuals lived in harmony with the world; the hero undertakes to rediscover that lost harmony in a modern world that has been warped, altered by the laws of modern capitalism (emerging: *Don Quixote*, or dominant: *Anna Karenina*), laws that isolate

And the Petite Bourgeoisie?

men from one another → The novel's mission would therefore be to oppose a universe of values (love, justice, freedom) to a social system determined by economic laws → Logically, the hero must succumb (this is often what happens: Julien Sorel); but it's also often the case that the novel = the working out of a compromise between some unrealizable values and an unacceptable social history → Hero = victim of an antagonism between a *real* history and a *true* ethics (*Encyclopaedia Universalis*).[22]

2. This schema is fairly convincing, both in its confidence and its dialectical force, something that the first cultural systematizations of Plekanovian-style Marxism lacked[23] → Yet it raises some very important questions, this one in particular, which is *our* question: the novels of today, that is to say a great many novels and not a single "great novel," no longer appear to be the storehouse of any *worthwhile* aim, any ethical project or passion; as far as I am able to judge, they are no more than fragmented expressions of specific situations, of specific issues: decline or suspension of a *true* ethics → in this sense, regressive: absence of a novelistic Transcendence (→ there are no "great" novels anymore) → Now, these novels crop up in a society that hasn't ceased to be capitalist, where the dreams of harmony are loudly refuted by the real world → I think (once again: conversational remark) the point, the nub of this complexification is this:

a. Politically, at the very heart of Marxist thinking, there's a great Repressed: the Vulgate always sets the Bourgeoisie and the Proletariat against one another: the Repressed is the *Petite Bourgeoisie*. Where is it? What does it do? How, on what does it act? Marx designated its *pivotal* role apropos of the 1848 Revolution, explaining that the Revolution, triumphant in the phase of the alliance between the Petite Bourgeoisie and the Proletariat (March), floundered when in an about turn the Petite Bourgeoisie formed an alliance with the Bourgeoisie (June). The deunification of the Proletariat and the Petite Bourgeoisie (PS) always costs the left its victory—as we say in the Vulgate: "you can see where I'm going with this . . ."[24]

b. Now, this is important for literature. Why? Because the social status of the writer is ambiguous, falling halfway between the Bourgeois and the Petit Bourgeois → Take Flaubert: he's constantly fulminating against the Bourgeoisie, but what he's really attacking is petit bourgeois aesthetics (or ethics, or discourse) → What Flaubert really finds distressing and suffocating is the historical rise of the Petite Bourgeoisie → The history of present-day France (and prob-

Préface, 254

ably of Europe) is marked by the cultural rise, the cultural flourishing of the Petite Bourgeoisie (via the media, controlled by petit-bourgeois Powers), whose cultural interests capitalism evidently takes care of; this explains Flaubert's outburst, which I'm about to quote: he could utter the same cry today, given the cultural and pedagogical politics of the Powers that be; in 1872 (fifty-one years old), to Turgenev: "I have always tried to live in an ivory tower <that is to say, as a pure bourgeois isolated from the rise of the petite-bourgeoisie>, but a tide of shit is beating at its walls, threatening to undermine it. It is not a question of politics but of the *mental state* <we'd say: the ideology> of France. Have you seen Simon's <Minister of Public Instruction> circular, with its plan for the reform of state education? The paragraph about physical exercise is longer than the one about French literature. There's a significant little symptom!"[25]

Journal, 151

c. Between Flaubert and the present day, there's been a long period of transition, over the course of which literature as a (bourgeois) value has continued to exert an influence, in the form of Literary History; cf. what Kafka says about the literature of small nations (which is probably what we are: the Bohemia of Kafka's time); literature continues to create by making an inventory of dead writers: "These writers' undeniable influence, past and present, becomes so matter-of-fact that it can take the place of their writings. One speaks of the latter and means the former, indeed, one even reads the latter and sees only the former.... Literary history offers an unchangeable, dependable whole that is hardly affected by the taste of the day."[26] → My view, obviously, is that that whole is no longer unchangeable and that the "taste of the day" causes this bastion to fall into ruin and destroys it → Whence the anxiety of *separation*, of *abandonment* (third trial) of someone who's still inside it.

d. Perhaps what needs to be retained, to conclude this brief survey of the relationship between literature and society today, is this: *literature is no longer supported by the moneyed classes*. Who supports literature? You, me, that is to say those of us without means: distanced from the "bourgeoisie" (if it still exists) by our lack of economic power although not incorporated into the petite bourgeoisie, the new class in pursuit of power, because we consider its ethics, its aesthetics to be inadequate, something to criticize → Literature: supported by a clientele of the *de-classed*: we're social exiles and we carry literature about with us in our flimsy luggage.

Commitment

3. It's because the writer is De-classed that he energetically, sometimes hysterically, sets himself the problem of Commitment:

Oblation

"The world 'exited' me, I want to get back into it at all costs" = this is commitment. And because I'm a kind of reject of Reality, I can only force it to acknowledge me at the cost of a certain *oblation* → I leave it to be seen to what extent the activity of commitment of today's writers' and intellectuals' is *moral*; there are countless signs of this *morality*: signatures, declarations, proscriptions → My point is simply that there's a constitutive link between the writer's real *separation* and his *commitment*: it's because he no longer *fits in* that he *rallies*. Chateaubriand (testamentary Preface) notes that in the Middle Ages there was an adequation between the life and the work (indeed, we only have to think of the quite brilliant interweaving of life and work in Dante: no one today comes anywhere close to this incandescence): "but since Francis I, our writers have been isolated individuals whose talents could express the spirit but not the events of their times."[27] (Chateaubriand says this because he's conscious of the singularity of his commitment). → Hence the kind of *erethism* (for those who can't be bothered with dictionaries = "violent excitation of a passion")—therefore, erethism of commitment in today's writer; every time he fails to take up an invitation to commit himself, he risks the anxiety of missing the boat of Reality, of being left behind on a beach while everyone else sails off, or on a different solitary planet (*Sirius*, obviously). (I'm not describing "what he should do"—perhaps that will be outlined in a moment—, but a fact, a situation of separation).

3. Which Language?

History (Historical Time) and Society (organization of the social masses): all this weighs literature, a living, active, exultant milieu, down and carries it off course, contemporary forces that tend toward *separating* the Writer → Here we have a third trial (within the Third Trial): in order to produce the cherished Work, in which language shall our writer write?

Native language

Everything, it seems to me, rests on a paradox, or at least on a contradiction between two natures (or two hypotheses) of what could be called the *language of writing*—literary language having been until now necessarily written: literature is by definition not spoken; "oral literatures" are, for us, folklores, distant fringes (≠ But what about *Paradis*?)[28]

a. First requisite feature of the language of writing: it's *native*; it partakes, in the form of a subcategory, of the subject's mother tongue (let's set aside the altogether exceptional case of those writers who produce a Work in a language other than their mother tongue; I say, spontaneously: Conrad, Beckett, Cioran). I believe that this *native* character, what I'll call the pathetic essence of a language; the mother tongue (we don't say "father" tongue) = the one learned in the presence of the Mother; in a sense, it's the language of Women; it's the transmitted language, the hereditary language, referring, I believe unconsciously, to a Matriarchy → I consider this *pathos* (in the good sense of the word) of the native language to be so important that I can't bear translated works, however great, however well translated; Kafka, for example, it's still sometimes, *scripturally*, a bit unrewarding; criterion: I get no pleasure from pleasure *copying it out*.

b. Second feature of the language of writing: it's learned, not through childish automatism, but through teaching, education: at School (in Antiquity, the educational system made a very clear distinction between the language of "Nannies" and the language of "Pedagogues": see Quintilian).[29] In actual fact, Classical language (I'm using this expression in a broad sense: all literary language) is *taught*, or at least, *it used to be*, I learned Classical language in the same way as I learned English (with more success, by the way).

Seuil, 6

→ Ambivalent character of the language of writing: a language of the *outside* and the *inside*, an inherited language yet one that's in each instance "*self made*,"[30] spontaneous, constructed: particular and universal, in the sense that we're convinced this *group language* contains an *essentiality*: Mallarmé had the vague notion (with respect to himself)—an idea announced with a smile, of course—of an inherited nobility (some of his ancestors wrote): filiation of *letters* →+ also a nostalgic language, since it's fixed in the subject by (1) Childhood, (2) Adolescence.

Rending of Time

Several different time periods are inscribed within the language of writing (and therefore, I should say straight away: several deaths):

a. The subject's native language ages—all the move because it's always the language of the class origins of the parents—at a rate that's difficult to measure because the changes occur daily; there are some words in my spoken language, some colloquial expressions that come to me from my childhood and as a result, all of a sudden, I see that my younger interlocutors are a bit taken aback by them; some literary works take account of these subtle discrepancies in the way they reconstruct characters' dialogue (Balzac): the slightly vertiginous effects of language, to be pointed out, to be "studied."

b. Learned language, Classical language, ages more violently or, without aging in the strict sense, is in any case dealt a severe blow by rejection, expiration: it goes *out of fashion*, drawing anyone who remains loyal to it into the solitude of the outmoded (the outmoded is distressing, other than when it's artificially rehabilitated: retro-kitsch); for example, the new generation don't appear to be affected by certain words anymore: What "young man," for example, would you overhear saying he feels "sad"? Where today would you hear the Pascalian expression: "the Wretchedness of Man"? (and yet the content hasn't changed and the expression remains simple and accurate) → There's an irremediable Rending of Time, and this Rending is inscribed in language.

Apocalypse

M.O.T., I, 250

For a subject (a writer) who has the tendency to live intensely, to *reflect on* Time (a Theme, as we've seen, which permeates our Third Trial), this Rending of Language as a Rending of Time can take on the grandiose and heart-rending allure of a linguistic Apocalypse: Chateaubriand (him, of course) put this magnificently, that is to say exaggeratedly, apropos of the disappearance of some of the American Indian languages (Iroquoian, for example). I quote: first this gloomy Introit: "A Prussian poet <we're never told where Chateaubriand gets his countless examples from>, at a banquet given by the Teutonic order, recited the heroic deeds of the ancient warriors of his country in old Prussian, dating from around 1400: nobody could understand him and as payment he was presented with a hundred empty walnut shells" → And then this, grandiose and absurd: "There are Orinoco tribes that no longer exist; all that remains of their dialect is a dozen words uttered in the treetops by a few parrots enjoying their new-found freedom, like Agrippina's thrush warbling Greek words from the balustrades of the Roman palaces. Such will be, sooner or later, the fate of our modern jargons <understand here: classic French>, the debris of Greek and Latin. Having flown out of its cage, some raven belonging to the last Franco-Gallic priest will address foreign peoples, our successors, from the heights of a ruined bell tower, saying: 'Hark the inflections of a voice once familiar to you: you shall put an end to all such speech.' Be Bossuet <prototype of classical writing> then, so that in the final outcome your masterpiece shall outlive your language and man's remembrance of you in the memory of a bird!"[31]— The bird, raven or parrot, is not so very metaphorical, or barely metaphorical at all: it's the phonographic document; the story of the old lady's parrot (three hundred years old?) who used to say:

***Préface*, 255**

"*Le Rouè, c'est Mouè!*"³² → Literature is language, a particular language → Therefore, if the writer reflects for a moment, it makes sense that he should think of his eternity, or at least of his posthumous life, not in terms of content or aesthetics (for such things can be repeated, using other methods, at another point on the spiral), but in terms of language → And the prognosis is harsh, for not only is language not eternal, its future, that is to say its decline, is irreversible; if Racine were to go out of fashion one day (as is already more or less the case), it wouldn't be because his description of passion is or will be out of date, but because his language is as dead as Latin is for the Conciliar Church → thus, Flaubert's prudence and intelligence (1872, fifty-one years old): "Because I write . . . not for the reader of today, but for all the readers who might present themselves *as long as language lives.*"³³ (I note with amusement that this idea has *already* ceased to resonate, its form no longer considered admirably direct and impressive: I devoted one of my little columns in the *Nouvel Observateur* to it, but it didn't elicit any kind of response = moment when a language, without having weakened, is no longer *heard*).

Division

Language {*la langue*} (I'm using this word in the complex but I think precise sense of "discourse originating in a linguistic system {*la langue*}, which itself originates in language {*le language*}," that is, in fact, in the Saussurian sense: the linguistic system {*la langue*} minus "speech" {"*parole*"}), so language = a *temporal space*, that is to say, the synchronic divisions, following the divisions of social space, are bound up with the divisions of historical Time (whereby some things fall into decline, others live on, regrets, etc.) → It's therefore reasonable to situate the division of the French language within "the Sufferings of Time" → There would be (to simplify things) three French languages:

Spoken language: difficult

1. *Spoken*, or rather *conversational*, language, for there is a such a thing as a rhetorically coded spoken language (which, for all that, isn't a written one): the language of politicians, of teachers and more generally of Radio-TV → This conversational language, *interlocutory* (that's its defining marker): as I've said several times, there are probably a great many unidentified, un-*described* (in the linguistic sense) subvarieties (and this is one of my regrets) → I won't be discussing them, this isn't the topic of the Course → The most I'll say is this: something that's always struck me in daily life: the theoretical, methodological possibility of an analysis of a spoken language that would take account of the following (point of view that would have

some affinity with Nietzsche's idea of the Forces = the *Drama* of language): the fact that, very often, the subject seems to struggle with language, to struggle immensely with its nullity, with aphasia; a great many subjects seem to have difficulty using language, finding it distressing, hard going; this depends, of course, on the level of culture as well as on regionalization (as compared to School French); in "my" village, I often hear subjects (the gardener, the road worker) and even in Paris, the concierge, expressing themselves in such a terribly embarrassed, rough, stilting, slow, sporadic manner, trying unsuccessfully to grasp the *form* of language; it could be said that, for them, French is like a second language they haven't quite mastered (as in my case when I speak English)—but which one is their first? which virtual patois? I noticed that the young hairdresser in my village—who did his hairdressing training in Tarbes, so who had spent time somewhere other than the village, but still—spoke two different languages depending on how a topic was broached; I asked him about the risks of going to Saint-Sébastien: on the risks themselves, uncertainty, an embarrassed, harsh, laconic language; but on Basque or anti-Basque terrorism in North Euskadi (as it's called nowadays), his language loosened up—and why was that? Because he could draw on *stereotypes*: news gleaned from the Radio, gossip from the local policemen who come to him for a haircut (Basque assassinated in Saint-Jean-de-Luz, something to do with procuring: History viewed from very minor vantage points) → In other words, to give this anecdote a methodological ending: a good linguist, a subtle linguist wouldn't make a distinction between language and discourse! To speak in a fluent, sovereign language is to have access not to the *treasure chest* of the language spoken by linguists but to that of stereotypes: the stereotype is not only an ideological fact; it's an *absolutely* linguistic fact.

SESSION OF FEBRUARY 23, 1980

Universal Reportage

Seuil, 63

Écrivance

Collective writings

[1]2. Opposed to that conversational language, there's a group of spoken (Radio, TV) or written (the press, scientific writing, literary writing) languages. This group is characterized by its strict recourse to the code → these are the languages that can be studied; the code can be divided into two main codes—two languages; to distinguish between them, I'm making use of an opposition advanced by Mallarmé: "An undeniable desire of my time is to distinguish two kinds of language according to their different attributes <important, we'll come back to this>: taking the double state of speech <here=language {*langue*}>—brute and immediate here, there essential."[2]

a. "*Brute or immediate state*" of language (spoken and written language mixed up together). Mallarmé is thinking of a very broad category of social linguistic activity, which elsewhere he calls *journalism* or, even better, "universal reportage." This powerful, even imperialist language, which is increasingly dominant today, has the following characteristics: (1) It's reputed to be "spontaneous" (Mallarmé = "immediate"), that's actually to say "instrumental"; language should merely be the instrument of a mental or dramatic content, it has no substance in itself: or you don't *see* it; it presents itself as "natural." Given that criterion, *Universal Reportage* can be linked to scientific writings, which don't present themselves as writings but merely as transparencies whose sole aim is to report, to relate an account of the thought process: effectively a kind of superior, serious *Reportage* (in the past I've called such instrumental language: *écrivance*, opposing it to *writing*).[3] (2) The language of journalism (in the very broad sense of the term): clearly doesn't comprise any archaism, any sense of Origin, any Ritual (of language), any *liturgy*, in short, any *religiosity*: language of the present ("immediate"), it doesn't have a sacred link to the Past (of language): an absolutely secular language. (3) It doesn't originate in the body of the person writing (or reading) it; it's therefore a nonindividual language, it doesn't demand that a name take responsibility for it: *nameless* language, semianonymous (as in the case of pure journalism)—and if we consider the field of the book, a writing that manages to be *collective* and even tends to be more and more so: generalized practice of *writing*,[4] collective book collections, books that are the work of several different people → the Author is rapidly going out of date, determination that the Name should no longer be inscribed in the Sentence → Conspicuous trend among certain publishers to produce *authorless books* (even if there's a name on the cover): very obvious books on "topics," on "themes." This "Universal Reportage" is the dominant force now, which means that as language-body, the Author is increasingly *separated* (our third trial).

Essential language

Scherer, 36

141

b. For, opposed to this, but threatened, reduced, ridiculed even, is what Mallarmé calls (so as to defend and to incarnate it), the *essential state* = the absolutely literary state of writing. My aim is not to describe this writing (perhaps that will be objective of a future course). I simply want to remind you that in Mallarmé's view this "essential language" invalidates the opposition between Prose and Poetry. Essential Prose is Verse: "So long as there is stylistic effort, there is versification" and "Actually, there is no such thing as prose: there is the alphabet, and then there are verses that are more or less closely knit, more or less diffuse."[5] And again: "the prose of any luxurious writer . . . counts as broken verse"[6] → This is not to say that *essential* writing is driven by hidden alexandrines. But rather, opposed to Universal Reportage, that there's a writing grounded in ellipses and *formulae* (the word refers both to the poetical and the magical enunciation); a writing that's *radically, voluntarily, and gloriously* removed from "brute, immediate" social language: a writing *apart* (excluded?).

→ This is precisely the exclusion that the Writer (whom I have in mind) has to come to terms with, and that acceptance is his third trial, for not only is the support he receives in that exclusion dwindling (no longer a social class to support him) but also, because he's keen to do something, he finds he keeps being tempted to join forces with Universal Reportage himself—in order to regain a form of social acceptance. To be *Exiled from a language* is never easy, for language is a *link {lien}*—like religion (as the word implies): it's therefore like a form of Excommunication.

The two languages

cf. p. 99

On the level of Language, the Trial of Separation comes down to this: *is it possible write in classical language today?* (I mean without risking being out of step with the times). Yes, if society were to accept a plurality of languages, a coexistence of different languages → In the Mallarmé quotation: "An undeniable desire of my time *is to distinguish two kinds of language according to their different attributes*: taking the double state of speech—brute and immediate here, there essential" → what's unsatisfactory is not the division of languages (and thus the existence of a language "apart"); on the contrary, it's the fact that the *difference of their attributes* is not respected → This problem: which Dante touches on in the *Convivio* in his defense of the legitimacy of a differential use of Latin and the vernacular[7] → The French subject should have a right to two languages, without *the one intimidating the other*: and especially to essential language, to its ellipses, in a word: to its "jargon," or instead: let there be no more accusations of jargon.

For a long time, "essential language" (that is to say, classical language, the language of writing) was the dominant one; associated with the ruling classes, it had a preeminence that sanctioned class divisions → condemnations of the badly spoken and the badly written. But today, there's a reversal: implicated in the aesthetic debacle of the bourgeoisie, the "well written" is no longer "respected," which is to say that it's no longer *observed* (you hear any number of grammatical mistakes on the French Radio), nor is it *loved* → on its way to becoming a very minor and excluded language → Our attitude, our decision: we no longer have any reason to think of *classical writing*—as an outmoded, legal, conformist, repressive form, etc.,—as a form that needs to be defended; on the contrary, it can be considered a form that the circumvolution and the *inversion* of History is in the process of making new; like a language deemed artificial, *set apart*—equivalent to poetry in verse, which is probably impossible—or very difficult—today: a way of creating a distance, a linguistic *act* by means of which you make it clear that you want to distance yourself from the bad faith of universal communication and the *libido dominandi* that lies, that lurks like a monster within Universal Reportage (I'm writing this on the morning of the suicide of Boulin, the Minister, October 31, 1979)[8] → In other words, it's *today* that we need to be thinking of Classical Writing as released from the *Durable* in which it was embalmed → Now that it's no longer caught in the Durable, it becomes *New*: what's fragile is always new; this Classical Writing needs work done to it if we are to make manifest the *becoming* that it conceals. Remember Nietzsche: "Linguistic means of expression are useless for expressing 'becoming'; it is accords with our *inevitable need to preserve ourselves* to posit a crude world or stability, of 'things' etc."[9] → "There is no will: there are fulgurations of will that are constantly increasing or losing their power." Once again, it's because literary writing is no longer durable that it's relieved of its conservative weight and can be *actively* thought as a *becoming*, as something light, active, intoxicating, fresh: where is the New, the *Original*? Is it in the sen-

Will, power

tence I wrote in my diary this morning (Universal Reportage) or in this sentence from Chateaubriand (apropos of America), written, plucked from countless others: "Everything was dazzling, radiant, golden, opulent, saturated with light"? Where's the diversity of what's Living? In the writing, I should say the *writing*[10] of Present-Day stereotypes or in this Stylistic Principle (Flaubert, 1854, thirty-three years old): "The sentences in a book must stir like leaves in a forest, all dissimilar in their similarity."[11]

M.O.T. I, 264

Préface, 173

To Overcome

Tragic

So there are three separations in this Third Trial: from History, from Society, from Language → This feeling of separation, which has to be continually overcome in order to write, isn't simply a feeling of guilt at being absent from the world in times of conflict but, on the contrary, a complex sensation of difficult presence: active and impotent, true and ineffective. Before the world, the Writer, such as I've tried to imagine him, someone who devotes himself to the *Literary Absolute* (the *Romantik*, as the Jena Romantics would say),[12] feels himself to be both a *truthful* (he sees the truth) and an *impotent* witness.

Impotence

1. Why *Impotent*? At issue isn't the hackneyed and pointless theme of the writer's (or, today, the intellectual's) influence over the public, over politics, ideas, etc. but rather the capacity to master the world through thought or art, in other words, the capacity intrinsic to the Book. It's the question of the *Masterable*, a historical question; for example *Knowledge*; in the seventeenth century, it was possible for just one man (Leibniz) to master Knowledge, the whole of Human Knowledge, but already by the eighteenth century, the mastery of Knowledge required many men = the *Encyclopaedia*; ever since, Encyclopedias have expanded, multiplied, but not one of them is satisfactory; in place of science in the singular, we now have *sciences: branches of knowledge*.—Likewise, in a slightly different context, for a long time a single author was (fictionally) capable of mastering the world; Proust was probably the last one to do so; today, this would no longer be possible: no novelist could master the planetary breadth of the world, the complexity of its problems, of its structures, such that no single philosophy is capable of mastering them—complexity, what's more, that's immediately dramatized and dis-

Truth

torted, trivialized by the media, the News day-to-day, taking us in.[13] (*Paradis*? = great Novel of the day-to-day).

2. Yet—this is what's distressing—the Writer of the Literary Absolute knows that *he's telling the truth*; or, if you prefer a less pretentious assertion: when he reads other Writers, and especially Writers from the past, he's often struck by the truth and, as it were, the durability of what literature says → Let's do a test; I'll read you a text, which reports a speech—the reported speech of Feminism.

FLAUBERT, *A SENTIMENTAL EDUCATION*[14]

According to Mademoiselle Vatnaz, the emancipation of the proletariat was possible only through the emancipation of women. She wanted the admission of women to all types of employment, investigation into the paternity of illegitimate children, a new legal code, and either the abolition of marriage or at the very least "a more intelligent regulation of the institution." In her opinion, every French woman should be obliged to marry a Frenchman or adopt an old man. Wet-nurses and midwives should become civil servants; and there should be a jury to examine books by women, special publishers for women, a polytechnic school for women, a National Guard for women, everything for women! And seeing that the Government did not recognize their rights, they would have to conquer force by force. Ten thousand citizenesses, armed with good muskets, could make the Hôtel de Ville tremble!

With the exception of the last sentence, that little speech is impossible to date: it cuts across the ages; it is "true"; since it was reported in 1848 and remains plausible in 1980, it ought to have a demystificatory force: to see that we still speak as we did in the past, doesn't that "weaken" the arrogance of Modernity, of the Timely?—Not at all: literature is constantly delivering a *Critique of Discourses that goes unheard*; probably a terrible thing, men are never aware of their discourse: *showing* them their discourse achieves nothing—even if that demonstration is that of the Truth (of languages) → Writer: sort of Cassandra of the past and of the present; truthful and yet never believed; vain witness of the Eternal return.

Will that ever prevent Newspapers from investigating the Private Lives of Ministers, or from adhering to Joseph de Maistre's superb and horrible saying (superb as a saying, horrible as an idea): "You have not countered opinions until you have attacked those who hold them"?

Cassandra

Tragic

Cassandra = impotence and truth → Tragic figure. Well, I actually think that the Tragic is the very being of the Timely / Untimely Writer, his fate and also his freedom, what gives his labor its essential difficulty but what also enables him to overcome the Third Trial, that of Separation; the Writer draws his strength from the tragic status of literature today; for Tragic = active Force → What is the Tragic? = to come to terms with your Fate in such a radical way that it gives rise to a freedom; for *to come to terms with is to transform*; nothing can be said, *accepted*, if it isn't bound up with a labor of transformation; to come to terms with a loss, a bereavement, is to transform it into *something else*; Separation shall be transformed into the very material of the Work, into the concrete labor of the Work (cf. to come to terms with one's Homosexuality = to transform it) → This might help us to understand why the Tragic is not a form of pessimism—nor of Defeatism, nor an Abstentionism—but on the contrary an intense form of Optimism: an Optimism without Progressivism.

The writer's *place*: the Margins? There are so many: there ends up being an arrogance of the Marginality—I prefer to replace it with the Image of the *Interstice*: the Writer = man of the Interstice.[15]

To End the Course

I'm saying: *to end* and not *to conclude*.

Indeed, what would the *conclusion* to this course be?—The Work itself. In a good scenario, the material end of the Course should have coincided with the actual publication of the Work, whose progression we've been tracking at the level of its projection, its will.

Alas, as far as I'm concerned, there'll be no question of that: I'm unable to pull any Work out of my hat, and quite obviously certainly not this *Novel*, whose *Preparation* I wanted to analyze →[16] Will I manage it one day? It's not even clear to me, on the day I write these lines (November 1, 1979) that I'll write anything else, anything other than those things that are already underway, already known, in the mode of repetition and not of Novelty, Mutation. (Why this doubt?—Because the bereavement I evoked two years ago, at the beginning of this Course, has profoundly and obscurely altered my desire for the world.)

However, with a last attempt at formulation—and this will be the end of the Course—I can try to give a sort of profile of the Work that I should like, either to write, or to see written today, so that I might read it with the same satisfaction as I read certain works from the past; I can try to get as close as possible to that blank Work, to that Degree Zero of the Work (empty box but extremely significant in the system of my life): I can approach it *asymptotically*.[17]

I shall say, then, that the desired work has to be *simple, filial, desirable*.

1. Simplicity

This is to be taken in the strong sense: not as a vague quality of the Work, the kind that might be remarked upon in conversation or a literary review in a Newspaper, but as a veritable aesthetic principle, a principle of a School: a new Aesthetic→ It seems to me that, *in contrast to certain modern endeavors*, simplicity would be defined by the following three writing behaviors:

> *Readability*

1. *Readability*. Today, texts are easily reputed or declared *unreadable*. (There's a nice way of saying "not very readable": *difficult*. Criterion that's spreading fast: (a) Newspapers that have a critic specializing in "difficult books". (2) Radio: "the books that fall under the radar." (3) The dispute between Lindon and the Government, Fnac).[18] I don't want to go into the dossier on *readability*, which is very complex, since every text, even the most traditional, I'm thinking of Pascal, or the most modern, Rimbaud, can be experienced as both readable and unreadable: everything depends on the *level at which the text is perceived*, the *rhythm of reading*, its *intentionality* → Not one repression should be made to weigh down on a text's readability → for me it's a question of conceiving of a work as voluntarily, constructively subjected to an aesthetics of readability, an aesthetics that today would be set *alongside* other works, other aesthetics, other instances of the language of modernity: a readability that wouldn't be the *commonly readable*, the readability of Universal Reportage, that would have the *quality* of the Superior Text → We could define it in the following terms (I'm extracting these points from "Notes on the Notions of Norm and Readability" by Philippe Harmon;[19] I say "I'm extracting" because these norms are set out for the genre of the Novel and I want to be more general, not knowing whether "my" Work will be a novel or something else, for I don't believe that uncertainty as to the genre of a work is a feature of unreadability). So: (a) An overall narrative or logico-intellectual framework, that is to say, underlying every

work, even if it isn't a novel, a *design*, a schema, that is to say, a *protensive force*, the best incarnation of which is Narrative—but intellectual Narratives exist: *Monsieur Teste, Artificial Paradise*; (b) An anaphoric system that isn't deceptive: anaphor = that which, at a given moment in the discourse, refers to another moment, in principle anterior to the first (otherwise it's called a *cataphor*), for example, "as I said" or "the man" → There's *deception* when we're led to believe that we're being referred back to something that was said when it wasn't → logical vertigo that can extend to the sentence if it's broken down, if each word is an isolat with no anaphoric links → The real criterion would be, if I dare risk such an outrageous remark, that the author should understand himself, that is to say, that he should, without dissimulation, take full responsibility for his own readability; now, this criterion isn't infallible: some authors, I'm convinced, aren't altogether capable of reading their own work; "folds" can remain in a text for reasons other than that of readability: the euphoria, the cadence, the triumph of an expression whose *excipient* is opaque.

Non-Irony

2. Second condition of "simplicity": that the work should cease to be, or be only discreetly, a *discourse of the work about the work*; common modern procedure: I can't write a work, there's no longer any work to be written, the only thing left for me to write is that there's nothing to write. Model: Pascal's saying (I'm quoting from memory): "I had a thought, I forgot it. I write that I forgot it."[20] → Blanchot, admirable theoretician (even if my project rejects his) of this form of deception, of the tragic extenuation of literature: now the work can only be what I have to say about it. (Tatiana Lipshitz, doctoral student: "Irony" in the sense of calling into question.)[21] This second clause of simplicity = to renounce the metalinguistic code.

Take note: there is Irony, the Metalinguistic in *In Search of Lost Time*; the Narrator narrates the Work *that's in the process of not being written*, and in the process of writing that, he manages to write the work, but that design is not actually made explicit to the reader, who takes *In Search* literally, that is to say, *referentially*.

Without scare-quotes

3. The third clause: to renounce what's insinuated by the autonymic code (Autonymy: the word taken as a word and not as a sign: the word put between scare quotes). Now, simplicity doesn't mean doing away with scare quotes, for to delete them, to insinuate autonymy without warning, is a sophistication that runs the risk of weakening the effect of the text → I'll explain what I mean: I recently received a manuscript that I thought was good but, after reading it,

left me with a vague impression: I found parts of it very difficult to read, yet after speaking with the author, I discovered to my great shame that the text was a deliberate, though not explicit, pastiche of certain authors (whom in truth I'd barely heard of) → I then understood that today we (me included sometimes) spend our time furnishing our texts with complex systems of scare quotes that in reality only we can see but we're convinced will protect us, will prove to the reader judge that we've not been not taken in by ourselves, by what we've written, by literature, etc. Now, this protection actually serves no purpose, for I have no doubt that if they're not inscribed on the page in black and white then no one sees the quotation marks; we have to face facts: *everything gets read at face value*; what simplicity wants, will want, then, is for us to write, as much as possible, *at face value*.

2. Filiation

Lineage

The work must be *filial*: let's be clear that it must accept (and thereby, as I said, *transform*) a certain *filiation*. Nietzsche: no beautiful things without *lineage* → *lineage* ≠ inheritance; it is not a matter of renewing, of recopying, of imitating, of conserving; it's a matter of going back to a kind of heredity of noble values, in the same way as an aristocrat with no money, with no inheritance, is still an aristocrat; a writing requires a *heredity*. There are times when it's necessary to say, along with Verdi: "Let us turn toward the past, that would be progress" (letter from 1870). → The filiation has to be effected by *slippage*; it's not a matter of pastiche: you have to transpose the writing of the past, fine like an old wine, and yet be willing to slip some new words, some new metaphors in between the lines → *Slippage* as opposed to an avant-gardist slogan that it's clearly necessary to set to one side (for the avant-garde can be mistaken): *deconstruction*.[22] *To deconstruct?* Admittedy, the slogan's tempting, because to deconstruct is to resist the political alienations of language, the prevalence of stereotypes, the tyranny of norms, but perhaps now's not the time: society isn't following suit. And, moreover, perhaps it never will, either because it will always be alienated or because a language will never let itself be deconstructed from the outside.

Slippage

Aristocracy

Filiation: to accept the *aristocracy* of writing → This brings me back to the conception of the Book in Mallarmé. (Don't say [that] I'm upholding a century-old slogan; for those hundred years it was nowhere to be seen; it's a matter of bringing it back *at another*

Scherer, 108

point: in a spiral). Now, Mallarmé's conception of the book was universalist and aristocratic; remember (for it's a point generally ignored or forgotten in the mythology of the Mallarmé-Figure; I remember Vittorini's suspicion, believing Mallarmé to be spiritualist, Catholic, "right-wing"),[23] that Mallarmé took an interest "with passion, sometimes with anxiety, in social questions": thinking about the current state of the world was by no means an unfamiliar activity; given his "essential" idea of literature—or of literature as essential—his stance was felt to be ambiguous, paradoxical: How could he on the one hand be a "republican and a strike supporter" and on the other, in literature, a refined aristocrat? Contradiction that has to do with the major Problem with literature over the last hundred years: Mallarmé didn't provide a solution to it, he accepted it, by accepting the *division* of the subject, that is to say the division of languages (which the Doxa always resists): "Let man be democratic; the artist must separate and remain an aristocrat."[24]

3. Desire

Desire

This course = leisurely analysis of all the efforts, sacrifices, perseverances that literature (or Writing) demands of you from the moment you give yourself up to it, that is to say, from the moment you devote yourself to it, under the active figure of the *Work to be written*. And, to bring things to a close, this: when all's said and done, *for what purpose*? Let's write that down: *for what purpose?*—Mallarmé (him again) said that the world was made to end up in a book → But what's the purpose of the book? What should the book end up as?—In itself, within itself, a *desirable* book: something that gives rise to desire. (I consider Desire to be, paradoxically, the very being of Joy—not of Pleasure, and even less of *Jouissance*: a paramystical view: see Ruysbroek's admirable formulations, quoted in *A Lover's Discourse*[25] → For me, Paradise = radiant blaze of Desires, light saturated with Desires = "Glory.")

Chateaubriand

I profoundly, that is to say, stubbornly, believe—that is to say, I still believe, from the moment I started writing and now more than ever: the Desire that must be deposited in the Book = desire for language—a certain desire for language—which, for me, as I said, is Desire for the French language (which explains the choice, which I've made repeatedly clear throughout the Course, of a *filial* work) → Chateaubriand shows us the way: there's a spectacular discrepancy in his oeuvre (particularly in *Memoirs from Beyond the Grave*), between the datedness of his political (or ideal) activities—

though in his eyes it was an enormous investment: he thought of himself as a politician, advisor to the Prince—and the vivid, sumptuous, desirable seal of his writing → What dates is the politics (in the very broad sense of the term: the relation between *Power* and the World): the *libido dominandi* dies along with the subject, but the *libido sentiendi* (of the senses) has a capacity for (although I'm not saying it guarantees) endurance; it seems to me that, for a writer, the issue isn't how to be "eternal" (mythological definition of the "great writer") but how to be desirable after death.

Nobility

Ultimately, the only Revolution that literature could evince is to be constantly reminding us anew, that is to say, to bring us around to the idea that there can be Nobility in Desire → much more than that: that it's possible to make Desire Noble.

Aesthetics

There's an Order, a category that society considers to be—or concedes is—the guarantor of Noble Desire: *Aesthetics* (at least, that's how I define it) → Mallarmé (him, for the last time): "there are only two ways open to mental research, where our need bifurcates, aesthetics, on the one hand, and political economy on the other."[26] We mustn't be let old words frighten us: the Work as desirable is one of the active forces of that active Force: Aesthetics, not to be discarded, for it's an irreducible, un-confusable Force, as Mallarmé says and as Nietzsche affirms in his typology by making the *Artist* (as opposed to the Priest (Politics, Ressentiment)) an absolute type that cannot be reduced.

Such, for me, is the most proximate ("asymptotically") "Profile" of the Work to be written.

A Last (but Not Final) Word

So, this work, why am I not writing it—not straightaway, not yet?—I've already outlined the Trial of Choice, a trial that I've not yet overcome → All I can add is a particular notion of mine of "waiting" (for the decision, for the "embarkation"): Perhaps a certain "moral" embarrassment; the Course states it often enough, being entirely restricted to a desirous consideration of the works of a broadly conceived Romanticism (Flaubert, Mallarmé, Kafka, Proust) → The Works of contemporary modernity were set to one side. Sort of Fixation on, of Regression into the Desire for a particular past; blindness with respect to the contemporary, the transfer of Desire back onto forms that have no knowledge of the countless labors of today: something that's difficult to come to terms with, or that

Fixation

we're always convinced we've not yet come to terms with: the solitude and poverty of Stubbornness.

Thus, what I'm waiting for (as I said) is a trigger, a chance event, a mutation: a *new ear* for things → I quote Nietzsche (still without comparing myself to, but identifying myself with on a practical level); Nietzsche conceived of *Zarathustra* in 1881 while strolling though the woods that border Lake Silvaplana; resting beside an enormous block of stone = the idea of the Eternal Return. *But* (and this is what interests us), premonitory sign: *sudden and radical modification of his taste in music*: "Rebirth of the art of hearing"[27] → The New Work (new with respect to yourself: this is the postulation of the Work to be written) will probably only be possible, probably only get going in real terms when an old liking is transformed and a new one emerges → Perhaps what I'm waiting for, then, is for my Hearing to be transformed—and perhaps that will happen to me, unmetaphorically, through music, which I'm so fond of → Then I might achieve the real dialectical becoming: "To become what I am"; Nietzsche's saying: "Become what you are," and Kafka's saying: "Destroy yourself . . . in order to make yourself into that which you are"[28] → Thus, in this way, the distinction between the Old and the New would quite naturally be abolished, the path of the spiral marked out, and these words from Schönberg, who founded contemporary music and reinvigorated the music of the past, honored: it's still possible to write music in C major. There, to bring things to a close, you have the object of my desire: *to write a work in C Major.*

(November 2, 1979)

Ecce Homo, 306, sq.

Journal, V

PROUST AND PHOTOGRAPHY

Examination of a Little-Known Photographic Archive
Seminar

Editor's Foreword

We took the decision to publish Roland Barthes's biographical notes on some of the key figures in Proust's circle, photographed by Paul Nadar (for an introduction to the seminar, see the preface to this volume), as he left them. To fill in the gaps would have required so great a number of annotations they would have inevitably overtaken the text itself. We refer the reader to the quantity of source material on Proust that is easily accessed today, in particular to the standard reference work to which Barthes refers: Anne-Marie Bernard, *The World of Proust, as Seen by Paul Nadar*, trans. Susan Wise (Cambridge, Mass.: The MIT Press, 2002). We took the decision to modify the small number of dating errors that appear in Barthes's papers, basing the changes on the revised and corrected second French edition of *Le Monde de Proust* (2003). The photographs published here are taken from the Roland Barthes archive held at the Institut Mémoires de l'Édition Contemporaine.

Contents

Alfred Agostinelli (1888–1914)
Marquis, then Duc Louis d'Albufera (1877–1953)
Lydie Aubernon de Nerville (1825–1899)
Maurice Barrès (1862–1923)
Julia Bartet (1854–1941)
Mme Benardaky (died in 1913)
Monsieur Nicolas Benardaky
Marie Benardaky (1871–?)
Sarah Bernhardt (1844–1923)
Professor Édouard Brissaud (1852–1909)
Albert Arman de Caillavet
Gaston Calmette (1854–1914)
Marquis Boni de Castellane (1867–1932)
Comtesse Adhéaume de Chevigné, née Laure de Sade (1860–1936)
Lieutenant Comte Armand-Pierre de Cholet
Nicholas Cottin (died in 1916)
Alphonse Daudet (1840–1897)
Claude Debussy (1862–1918)
Lucie Delarue-Mardrus (1880–1945)
Gabriel Fauré (1845–1924)
Anatole France (1844–1924)
Prince of Wales (1841–1910)
General Marquis Gaston de Galliffet (1875–1966)
Anna Gould, Marquise Boni de Castellane (1875–1966)
The Gramont children
Comte Henri Greffulhe (1848–1932)
Comtesse Henri Greffulhe, née Élisabeth de Caraman-Chimay (1860–1952)
Duc Armand de Guiche (1879–1962)
Gyp, Comtesse de Martel (1849–1932)
Charles Haas (1832–1902)
Reynaldo Hahn (1875–1947)
Laure Hayman (1851–1932)
Willie Heath (died in 1893)
Marie de Heredia (1875–1963)
Abel Hermant (1862–1950)
Mrs Meredith Howland
Madeleine Lemaire (1845–1898)
Stéphane Mallarmé (1842–1898) and Méry Laurent (1849–1900)

Princesse Mathilde (1820–1904)
Robert de Montesquiou (1855–1921)
Louisa de Mornand (1884–1963)
Comtesse Potocka, née Emmanuela Pignatelli
Jeanne Pouquet, the future Mme Gaston Arman de Caillavet
Dr. Samuel Pozzi (1846–1918)
Prince Boson de Sagan (1832–1910)
Gabrielle Schwartz
Mme Émile Straus, née Geneviève Halévy (1849–1926)
Comte Louis de Turenne (1843?–1907)
Nathé Weil, the grandfather (1814–1896)
Adèle Weil, née Berncastel, the grandmother (1824–1890)
Georges Weil (1847–1906)
Amélie Weil, née Oulman (1853–1920)
Adrien Proust, the Father (1834–1903)
Jeanne Proust, the Mother (1849–1905)
Robert Proust (1873–1935)
Marcel Proust (1871–1922)

I shall unpack the title, which will allow me to address some prejudices or rumors ("a seminar on Photography") and to anticipate some likely disappointments.

1. Seminar?

(a) Because a sort of *practical* on nonverbal material (the slides); (b) because restricted to a presentation of the materials, making no attempt to theorize them; source material that anyone (anyone with an interest in Proust) could make use of; not a private, more a collective activity: everyone conversing *in petto* with the photos → For the most part, I'll be keeping my interventions to a minimum; I simply prepared and organized the materials in the laboratory.

2. Photographic Archive?

In the Ministry of Culture, rue Valois, there's a Service of Photographic Archives of Historical Monuments (unsurprising: if we want our monuments to be preserved they need to be photographed—as they have been systematically since 1880). In addition to its own photographic campaigns, this Service (rightly) set about acquiring the photographic archives of well-known photographers → In 1951, the State acquired the archives of the Nadar Studio (Félix and Paul) from Paul Nadar's widow (Paul Nadar, Félix's son, who worked with his father): four hundred thousand glass plates → currently being inventoried; it's already been possible to collate the portraits (taken by Paul Nadar) of the personalities Proust would have been familiar with (roughly between 1885 and 1910, Paul having taken over his father's studio in 1886) → Photos that you're going to see: taken by Paul Nadar, who didn't have his father's genius but was still a very good photographer.

I'd like to thank Mme Bernard,[1] who informed me of the existence of the archive and whose knowledge of Proust was indispensable in helping to identify the personalities in the photographs—aristocracy, upper middle classes (to which Proust's family belonged) going along to have their photographs taken at Paul Nadar's studio (like Harcourt's[2] twenty years ago): remember that the Portrait is a sign of wealth, of social standing (nineteenth century: people would wear their finest clothes to have their portraits painted and it's the same in the photographs that follow: note the beauty of the clothes).

3. Little Known? = Unknown

a. It's not secret: you can apply to the Service to view the Photographic archives and to make prints—in return for copyright fees.

b. A number of the personalities you're going to see have been photographed elsewhere, and their photographs can be found in the iconographic albums on Proust: there are a great many of them, and they're very sought after (Pléiade: out of print); so the faces you're going to see (already a disappointment!) are faces that you (or some of you) will be familiar with.

c. A number of these photographs were the subject of a little touring exhibition in 1978—with a good catalogue (*Le Monde de Proust*)[3]—which I've drawn on.

d. Little known nevertheless: (1) The Exhibition didn't cause much of a stir (*little known* to me at any rate). (2) Some of the photographs I'll be showing didn't feature in the Exhibition due to photographic imperfections, ones that interest me precisely because they reveal the photographic *process*.

4. Proust and Photography

It will by no means be a case of drawing out and analyzing the active links between Proust and Photography: allusions to Photography in *In Search of Lost Time* (the grandmother), Proust's obsession with owning a photograph of the people he loved (Jeanne Pouquet).[4] Nor will it be a question, or at least not directly, of "Proust" as a literary name, the author of *In Search of Lost Time* → I've already indicated the emergence of a specific investment in Proust as a social being: his life, his friends, his eccentricities: his *Marcelism* → The seminar is aimed at Marcelians → Like in the small ads, I'll say: no non-Marcelians please; non-Marcelians would inevitably find it deeply boring. A seminar, then, not on Photography, nor on Proust, but on "Marcel."

On this topic, let me remind you (since the photos are dated):

Proust	1871–1922
Dreyfus Affair	1894 (conviction)
	1906 (exoneration)
In Search (publication)	1913–1927

5. "Examination"

We're going to *examine* these Photographs, one by one, in alphabetical order. What does that mean?

a. We're not going to "analyze" them: there'll be no ideas, no literary or photographic remarks, no attempt will be made to locate the passages in *In Search of Lost Time* that may correspond to the person represented (or scarcely any). Simply a few brief biographical details on each person: taken from Painter[5] (I'm not a "Proustian") → Information and images → "recreational" seminar: leafing through images → So what's the profound, serious point, what's the chance, the kairos of these sessions?

b. To my mind, it's to produce an intoxication, a fascination, an action particular to the Image:

An image is, ontologically, what we can't say [anything] about: to talk about an image requires a special, very difficult art, that of the Description of images (≠ imaginary descriptions). Cf. J.-M. Gérard's texts.

The aim of this seminar isn't intellectual: it's simply to intoxicate you with a world, as I'm intoxicated with these photographs, and as Proust was with their originals.

To be fascinated = to have nothing to say: "We fail to speak about what fascinates us."[6]

Intoxicated with what? With the accumulation of these faces, these gazes, these figures, these clothes; with a sensation of falling in love with some of them; with nostalgia (they were alive, all of them are dead).

The few words I'll be saying point to something that I'm not saying; I'm not speaking there where it is, *I'm speaking to one side of it*;[7] this is the particular feature of Fascination, of Stuttering (cf. Marceline Desbordes-Valmore).[8]

Before submitting these photographs to your "examination" and, possibly, to your "Fascination," two general remarks, of *theoretical* import (for there'll be no "theory" in the rest of the presentation):

1. The "World" of Proust (= of Marcel)

In French, unhelpful division of the lexical field: *monde* {world} = a social totality → *mondain* {worldly} = a milieu of recreational activity. Now, in Proust, the *worldly* contains a *world*.

Proust's world = a *population*, a "social ethnic group": (1) monarchical aristocracy and an imperial aristocracy, losing money; many "mixed" marriages, Jewish (Rothschild) and American money; (2) upper middle classes → mingle in the salons, often with a mediating element: artists (musical evenings) → That ethnic group is to be reconstructed (and this is precisely what Proust did) in the way an ethnographer would go about it → small, very structured communities (already in the "world" of La Bruyère and "already" in Lévi-Strauss).

We say the "faubourg Saint-Germain." That isn't very precise: it was more like the faubourg Saint-Honoré; almost all the people in that real world and all the characters in *In Search of Lost Time* lived on the Right Bank: (a) the Prousts themselves, in the Malesherbes-Courcelles / Haussmann / Capucines-Madeleine triangle; the Champs-Élysées: *their* park; Condorcet (Saint-Lazare): *his* secondary school. (b) The rest, in the same neighborhood + spread into other neighborhoods (close by): Monceau, Trocadéro ≠ Saint-Germain: the Duc de Guermantes's aged cousins, "damp" part of the city where they were afflicted with rheumatism, hence their canes = aged aristocracy of the past → Proust, a man of the Right Bank; he practically never crossed the Seine (not even for the Mazarine, where he only stayed two months).[9] All the names of the streets of the apartments of the people you're going to see: Haussmann, Malesherbes, Courcelles, Messine, rue d'Astorg, Miromesnil, Monceau, etc.: the regeneration of the area was linked to Orleanist Finance (César Birotteau and the Madeleine); that's where the real-estate money was.

Proust's experience of the compactness, the powerful existence, the *nature* of that world couldn't have been more tense, more intense; the movement of being drawn into this world (in life then in the work) = like a love affair, a frenzy: *a wild desire*.

The greatest of paradoxes, which is the very inexhaustible Paradox of literature: that the greatest work of the twentieth century should have emerged from (should have been determined by) what in other circumstances can be the lowest, the least noble of sentiments: the desire for social advancement (it's altogether possible for a *desire* to be fictionally dramatized, represented, figured from a critical or ironic point of view) → In order to appreciate the relationship between Proust and the worldly "world" of high society (social classes far superior to his own), you should keep reminding yourselves of the social differential: on one side (his mother), Jews who were very well-off, but outside "society" (the Weils: you'll see what Aunt Oulman looks like);[10] on the other (his father), provincial shopkeepers (Illiers); to grasp this, you only have see Aunt Léonie's house today:[11] dinky little house (and literature's admirable powers of transformation); the rise in social status suddenly accelerated with the Father, who not only became a Professor of Medicine but a "notable" (political connections, missions).

Even before turning it into the precious metal of an unforgettable work, Proust transformed social desire into something very serious (you'll see the trace of this in the photographs): an intense life (so-called life of a socialite) transformed by an ennobling power: madness, mad desire → Don't forget that—before he shut himself away to write *In Search*—Proust's social life was *exhausting*, like a veritable profession. More than a professional, a virtuoso of high society: *a militant*. Putting as much hard work, as much "attendance" into society's get-togethers as a political or trade-union militant at committee or branch meetings → In both cases, it's a phenomenon that would be worth analyzing (as a neurosis): the "meeting-ite" {"*réunionite*"}.

A question you could ask: can the *social* be discerned in the photographs you'll be looking at? Not directly, obviously, but perhaps there are some keys to decoding (to reading) them:

a. Morphology (of the faces). This goes back to a contentious notion, that of "distinction." I'll simply say that you'll see all sorts of faces in these portraits: pure-breed Dukes and common Dukes, distinguished cocottes and exceedingly cocotte cocottes, sophisticated members of the bourgeoisie and vulgar members of the bourgeoisie, and that very mix in Proust's own family—you'll see, on an extra slide, the unforgettable beauty and *distinction* (I'll keep using that word, despite Bourdieu!)[12] of Proust aged fifteen or sixteen. What's more, Proust himself deals with this issue apropos of the grandmother's views on *distinction*: she introduces the idea, but for her it has no social meaning.

b. A classic social *marker*: dress. Note it in the men particularly, because it's there that the social dialectic is established (≠Women: immediate "display," instantly flaunting the owner's—I mean the husband's—social standing). Monarchical society: dress, coded sign of a person's social standing, no problem ≠ Democracy: egalitarianism, men's clothing is all of the same design, Quaker in origin, in general, something that's suitable to work in. Necessity of *discreetly* reintroducing a measure of "distinction": social → aesthetic → beauty of the fabrics + "glamour" of the "details": collars, cuffs, cravats, canes, etc.—You'll see the *glamour* of Proust's watch chain[13] (I wish some of these forms, some of these details, would come back into Fashion).

c. A more subtle marker: the *pose*; generally very *coded* by the photographic code of the time: facing the camera, so there's nothing particularly distinctive to be discerned from the poses. Yet, occasionally, by chance or by genius, a subject (or the photographer) transforms the pose into a complex sign that refers to a subtle yet definite social position: this is what Brecht called the *gestus*[14] (which he sought in his staging, his costumes, etc.) → For example, Laure Hayman, her way of presenting herself to the image[15] is in my eyes a *gestus* = the distinguished kept woman, gentle and reserved, of superior feeling (this will come up again in her biography).

2. The "Keys"[16]

Problem that concerns us here since these are Photographs of the people Proust frequented:

Proust himself ambiguous and contradictory; for example: (a) letter to Lacretelle: "It is the fate of books to become *romans à clef* after the event, however spontaneously they were conceived"; and (b) acknowledges (in a dedication, also to Lacretelle)[17] that certain characters and places were drawn from real life; the "keys" we can be sure of are Montesquiou, Agostinelli, Illiers, and Cabourg.

My own attitude: itself ambiguous, in the way I'll describe; it's pointless, absurd, and almost ridiculous to "reconstitute" the keys or, at any rate, to believe in them in a positive (and positivist) way:

a. because, in literary matters, it involves an exorbitant theoretical option: a theory of the copy, of the source, of the depiction, and that option could only be taken up in a serious, wide-ranging way: a smattering of theory:

b. because, in the case of Proust, there was clearly such a mix up in his mind, such an extraordinary, proliferating power, such a muddle of exaggerated and subtle features that a cryptology of that world would be both impossible and disproportionate with respect to what is really at stake, which is reading.

But, at the same time, as we look at these photographs, we shan't refuse to (discreetly) play the game of identifying who's who (no revelations: just the ones Painter suggests—who in fact goes too far). Why?

Let's come back to this: the issue of the Keys to *In Search of Lost Time* has been a source of excitement for a minor branch of literary history: monographs identifying such and such distant key as a secondary character, etc.; thrill of erudition that I couldn't compete with (and won't attempt to); but this excitement, this cryptological energy constitutes a *symptom*: *the keys don't refer to Proust but to the reader; the keys, the desire for, the pleasure taken in identifying the keys is a symptom of reading.*

Here, by way of this problem of the keys (it's an intuition of mine and at a later date I'd like to develop it theoretically, working toward a theory of reading): the Keys are of the order of a deceptive *illusion*, but that illusion functions as a Surplus-Value of Reading, the keys strengthen and develop the *imaginary* link with the Work; they partake of a theoretical object to be posited, the *Imaginary of reading* (a different argument for that Imaginary: the projection of the reader in the work). It's on this account that we shan't repress the problem of the Keys, for illusion is the very foundation of reading.

The couple "character in *In Search* + his or her real-life source" = indeed an imaginary object, subjected to the Technique of *Condensation* (several heterogeneous features condensed into a single figure); but in fact—this is what reading, as the "end" of writing, involves—beyond Proust, we're the ones doing the condensing, we're the ones doing the dreaming → We'll see at once that Photography both assists in and hinders this condensation—this dreaming.

Condensation = multiplicity of features, different types of key. Broadly:

- physical (there are actually very few of these): Castellane, Chevigné;
- fragmentary: Turenne's monocle, Sagan's hair;
- situational: Marie Benardaky (Champs-Élysées);
- structural: the Benardaky parents.

When they happen to co-exist in a single character, the keys contradict one another: vulgarity of Monsieur Benardaky = Swann.

The Photograph—and herein lies the originality, the novelty (I believe) of this seminar—will function as a confrontation between the Dream, the Imaginary of reading and *Reality* → With respect to reading, then, there'll essentially be the phenomena of disappointment, of uneasiness, of surprise (but there'll also be compensatory phenomena, other points of interest):

• As a general rule, the photographs *work against* the character: Daudet as Bergotte (to say nothing of Agostinelli as Albertine); very few photographs fit (don't work against) the character. Haas has Swann's face exactly (note that, bizarrely, I'm not saying the opposite): it's no longer possible to picture Swann with anything other than Haas's face.

• Disappointments: what, that's all it is?! Even for the good keys: Chevigné → Duchesse de Guermantes. The excessive power of literature, a sumptuous, ample garment, too big for the small-scale reality of the photograph.

• The discrepancy not only has to do with physical nonconformity but also with moral distortions: How could Gilberte's father be as vulgar as Monsieur Benardaky? Cf. nightmare of discovering you have vulgar parents.

• But, at the same time—this is the intoxication I'd like to effect—these Photos have a *hold* over us: *we dream, therefore we start a process of transference* (Mannoni);[18] we're frustrated when a character from *In Search* doesn't have his or her photograph: the box remains empty; Montesquiou is Charlus, but the physical appearance is all wrong; for the physical appearance, see Baron Jacques Doason;[19] but there's no photo, or not here at any rate → We haven't got *all* of Charlus: we only get that in *In Search of Lost Time*.

Alfred Agostinelli [on the right]

Born in Monaco in 1888. Son of an Italian from Livorno. His mother, from Provence, a bit of Arab blood.

Stay in Cabourg, 1907. Jacques Bizet runs the Unic Taximeters of Monaco (branches in Paris and Cabourg) → Proust wants to begin visiting churches again, as he did with the Bibesco brothers in 1902 → Hires a taxi with its three chauffeurs, who included Odolon Albaret and Agostinelli (who's nineteen years old).

Importance of inventions; passion for the latest things; how they find their way into his work: telephone, car, theatrophone—signs up to a service: you can listen to a show over the telephone; February 21, 1911, from his bed, the black receiver pressed to his ear, Proust listens to *Pelléas* at the *Opéra-Comique*; loved the scene where they emerge from the vault under the castle: the roses.

"... had cloaked himself in a black rubber cape and the hooded helmet which enclosed the fullness of his young, beardless face <indeed: note that the shape of his face is almost square>, made him look like a pilgrim, or rather, a nun of speed."

(Cf. the falling-in-love scene, Werther).

→ Proust's secretary

Agostinelli leaves Proust [in] December 1913 to enroll in a flying school under the pseudonym Marcel Swann.

May 30, 1914, his monoplane crashes into the Mediterranean, off Antibes.

Two months later, Proust asks Nadar's studio for a copy of this photograph (the father, Émile, the young brother, who'll replace his brother as Proust's secretary for a short time → Rostand's chauffeur, killed at Gorizia in May 1915). August 8, 1914.

He'd be ninety-two years old.

Marquis, then Duc Louis d'Albufera
(= Albu)

Born 1877.

Accepted into the little Saint-Loup band in 1903, at the same time as Guiche and Léon Radziwill (Loche) (he was twenty-six at the time).

The only aristocrat in Proust's circle who wasn't an intellectual (indeed, he doesn't really look like one), "the loyal Albufera never reads anything," and the only one who was an anti-Dreyfusard (devoted to the Church). Passionate about cars and travel. In love with an actress (cf. Saint-Loup): Louisa de Mornard (cf. later on); at one point, Proust effects a reconciliation.

Proust didn't like Albu calling him "Proust." (Cf. Guiche → My dear friend or my dear Marcel.)

Gatherings with friends in the evenings, initially at Weber's or Larue's, then later in Proust's bedroom: conversations, iced cider, and beer from the Pouchet Tavern beloved of Proust.

Albu doesn't understand Proust, who's a Dreyfusard and defends the Churches (Canon Marquis in exile, Saint-Jacques secularized!), Illiers → Combray (Combe's Laws, 1903); he asks Proust to explain the Affair.

As regards the problem of the Keys, Montesquiou guesses that Saint-Loup is more Albu than Guiche.

War → Joffre's chauffeur.

Lydie Aubernon de Nerville (1825–1899)

Photo 1883.

= Mme Verdurin: one of the most homogenous and convincing keys.

Rivalry between two salons: Mme Arman de Caillavet; the stakes: Anatole France, pinched from Mme Aubernon in 1886 → The friendship breaks down.

Held her salon at rue de Messine, then rue d'Astorg.

Friends + squadron of old ladies, widower friends of her mother's (cf. the pianist's aunt and Princesse Sherbatoff = the leading lights).

Her day: Wednesdays (cf. Mme Verdurin); reception preceded by a dinner for twelve; topic of conversation announced in advance: "What do you think of adultery?"—(Mme Laure Baignères): "I'm so sorry! I'd come prepared for incest." D'Annuzio implored to talk about love: "Read my books, Madame, and let me get on with my dinner" → Little silver bell to secure the attention of the speaker.

Salon with no pretty women: I provide conversation, not love. Like Mme Verdurin, presides over executions, then pardons-reinstatements.

Little band of those loyal to Aubernon: Cottard (Pozzi), Brichot (Brochard). Little train to her house in the country (Louveciennes). Unfaithful.

Physical appearance? As you can see: plump little woman, lively, chubby arms, showy dresses → Montesquiou: "She looked like Queen Pomare on the lavatory seat."

She—who'd done so much talking, invested so much in conversation—died of tongue cancer.

**Maurice Barrès
(1862–1923)**

Photo 1916.

Proust meets him in 1892: likes his melodious diction—a trait he shares with Bergotte.

But the three Bergottes we're going to see: Barrès, Daudet, and France: not especially interesting keys; nothing, at any rate, can be inferred from or superimposed onto their physical appearance.

Julia Bartet
(1854–1941)

Photos # 1885 and 1887

Member of the Comédie-Française.

= "distinction": the Grand Duc Paul, a "foul-mouthed" character, starts applauding her: "Bravo old girl!" Cf. *In Search of Lost Time*: Grand-Duc Vladimir, at Princesse de Guermantes' home, claps his hands as though at the theater and roars "Bravo old girl!" when Mme d'Arpajon gets splashed by the fountain in the garden.

Incomparable diction = the Divine.

1893, evening at Madeleine Lemaire's where Proust met Montesquiou; recites *Les Chauves-Souris*.

= Roxane (but particularly renowned in Andromache).

Dressed for town: I adore it, I'm in love.

(To be in love with a photograph.) Cf. Guiche.

Of all the photos shown here, I'm in love with three faces: Bartet, Guiche, and Proust at fifteen years old.

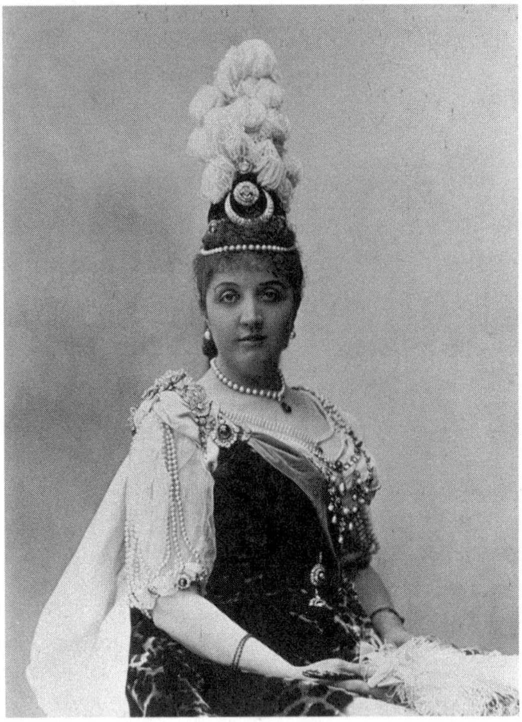

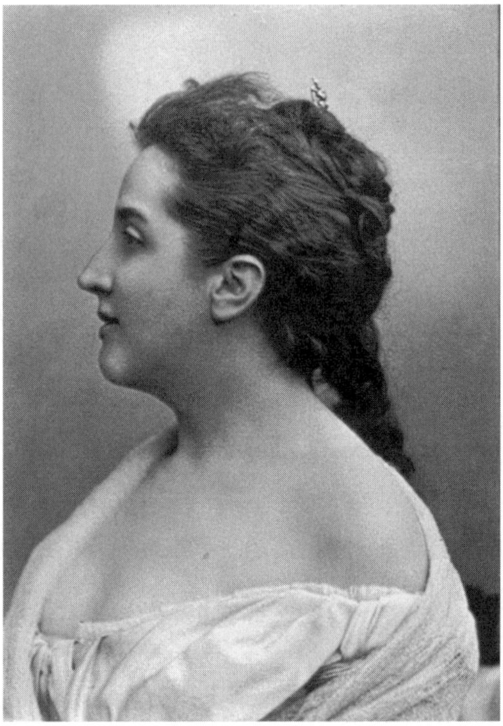

Mme Benardaky

Photos 1888, 1891

Same remark: this is Odette, but only by dint of the place she occupies in the structure (=mother of Marie-Gilberte).

Was only interested in champagne and love, cf. Odette's louche salon at the beginning.

Numerous photographic disguises in the service of the myth: the "beautiful woman," sculptural beauty (≠ Odette, Miss Sacripant).

As a Valkyrie (dress made by Worth): noted, in this guise, at a fancy-dress ball → Imagine poor Chéreau if he'd had to dress up Brunehilde like this!

[Second] photo: myth of the just-out-of-bed, of the still-undressed; sculptural beauty (profile), with no adornment: the baring of the "bosom"; the eroticism, in that period, of unadorned hair.

Monsieur Nicholas Benardaky

Aberration of the keys, if we were to take them literally: father of Marie. Now, Marie=Gilberte (Champs-Élysées), so Monsieur Benardaky=Swann! This fat, coarse, dull-witted man: impossible (the same can be said for Mme Benardaky).

Photo April 11, 1900.

Marie and Nelly: daughters of a Polish nobleman, Nicholas de Benardaky; considerable fortune as a tea merchant; formerly master of ceremonies at the Tsar's court="Excellence."

65 rue de Chaillot (Marceau—Champs-Élysées); known for his arrogance.

Richer social sphere than the Prousts'—but socially dubious. Proust's parents are not keen on Marcel's visits.

Marie Benardaky

Probably born in 1871 (=Proust).

So, fifteen years old when Proust sees her on the Champs-Élysées in 1886–1887 and falls in love.

Here, 1893: six years later, she's twenty-one or twenty-two.

Long black hair and a rosy, laughing face ≠ Gilberte, sullen, freckles.

But, again, no one *falls* in love with a physical appearance (with a "type"); you fall in love with an image in a setting (Charlotte and the slices of bread and butter): here, arrival of a small young girl on the Champs-Élysées; dedication to Jacques de Lacretelle that discusses the keys (thirty years later): "For Gilberte's arrival on the Champs-Élysées in the snow, I thought of someone who was the great love of my life . . . Mademoiselle Benardaky."

1897 (?), marries Prince Michel Radziwill, cousin of Léon (Loche); should have had a girl, Léontine, like Gilberte (but here interference with Jeanne Pouquet, Mme Gaston de Caillavet).

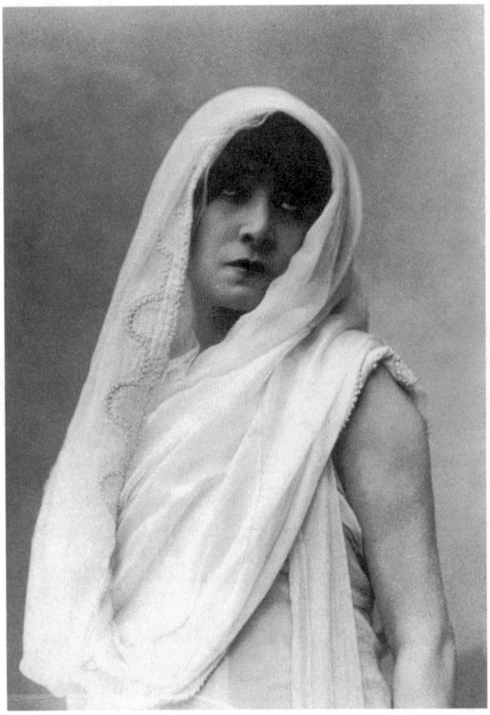

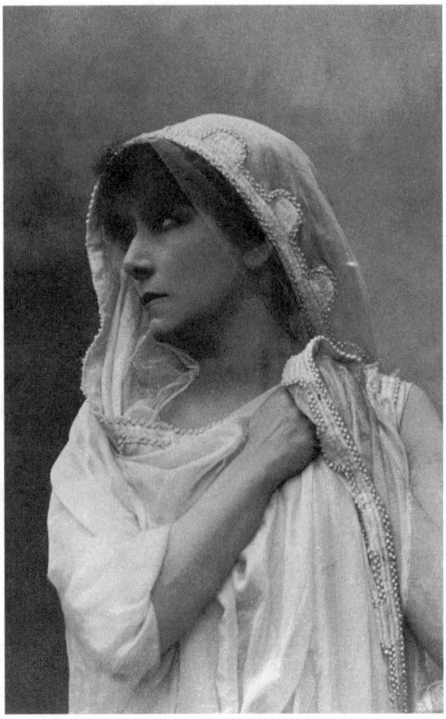

Sarah Bernhardt
(1844–1923)

Montesquiou's party (May 30, 1894) in honor of Sarah Bernhardt and her protégé, Yann Nibor, a Breton sailor who sang some poems, where for the first time Proust met the personalities from the faubourg Saint-Germain (important elements of *In Search*).

Sarah Bernardt's summer house on Belle-Ile, Yann Nibor's birthplace; advises Proust on his trips to Brittany (with Reynaldo Hahn).

In *Phèdre* (restaged in 1893, year of the photos): "How these vain adornments, how these veils weigh me down!" → Berma.

(Unsettling hiatus between the total kitsch of the dramaturgy and the acute modernism of Proust's descriptions, *as if he couldn't see the kitsch*; well, that's precisely what kitsch is: you never see it when you're inside it; kind of selective hysteria.)

Professor Édouard Brissaud
(1852–1909)

Colleague of the Father's—Neurologist, founder of the *Revue neurologique* → Book: *L'Hygiène des asthmatiques*. Proust consulted him in 1905. Loved literature.

→ "Prof. E." who habitually quotes a few lines before examining the Narrator's grandmother.

→ Something of Brissaud in de Boulbon (the Anti-Cottard): "A touch of the Brissaud type of great doctor, more eloquent and skeptical than clinical."

Photo May 14, 1899.

Personal connection:

=The father of Dr. B. who treated me—Rue Garancière, eau de Cologne: severing of adhesions.[20]

Mme Brissaud, sister of Henri Franck, Anna de Noailles's [lover] ("La Danse devant l'Arche") (died in 1912).

Jean and Henri: very much part of my life as a young man (→ our apartment [illegible]).[21] Genetic morphology.

Albert Arman de Caillavet

Monsieur Verdurin.

Proust admitted to Mme Arman's salon in 1889. Is introduced to Anatole France (Bergotte), who disappoints him.

12 avenue Hoche.

Mme de Caillavet=Léontine Lippmann. Married the rich Albert Arman in 1868 (=Mme Arman). Then the husband added the name of an estate, a Bordeaux vineyard, and gradually got rid of the *Arman*. She thinks this ridiculous and continues to call herself Arman Caillavet.—Imperious manners.

Cf. Mme Verdurin.

The Husband: would suddenly appear, in an alarming and inopportune manner; wart on his nose; the bows of his cravat=like the sails of a windmill. Yachtsman like Monsieur Verdurin. Brusque, mischievous, but controlled by his wife—anti-Dreyfusard (≠France).

Gaston, the son, will marry Jeanne Pouquet, whom Proust was in love with (cf. later on).

**Gaston Calmette
(1854–1914)**

Photo 1889.

Writer for, then editor-in-chief of *Le Figaro*.

Commissioned and published many of Proust's articles.

Rejected *Against Sainte-Beuve*.

Dedicatee of *In Search* (*Swann's Way*, Grasset, 1913). "To Monsieur. G. C., in recognition of my profound and affectionate gratitude." On the copy itself: "I have often felt that you did not like what I was writing very much. If ever you have the time to read a little of this book, especially the second part, I think you would at last make my acquaintance."

Murdered March 16, 1914, by Mme Caillaux, the wife of the Minister for Finance.

Marquis Boni de Castellane

Very like Saint-Loup: elegant silhouette, dazzling pink complexion, cold *lapis-lazuli* eyes, pale skin, hair "so golden that it was as if it had absorbed all the sun's rays," monocle flying about, darting movements.

Remarkable young socialite. A royalist and anti-Semite.

His fortune dwindling, he marries Anna Gould, an American millionairess (cf. later on) → Monumental house on the avenue du Bois (in the style of the Grand Trianon at Versailles). Receptions of a megalomanic lavishness → Ruin: "You need to be used to it, if you're going to handle all that money" (Baron Alphonse de Rothschild).—His wife ends up divorcing him just in time and marries another nobleman—this one makes his living from antiques (commerce in disguise).

Comtesse Adhéaume de Chevigné, née Laure de Sade

Photo 1885.

Duchesse de Guermantes.

Very distinguished salon.

Proust caught his first glimpse of her in 1891 at Madeleine Lemaire's and Mme Straus's: profile like that of a bird, azure eyes and golden hair.

Spring 1892, Proust watches out for her on her morning walks: "I had a heart attack every time I saw you," walk on the avenue de Marigny (lived 32 rue de Miromesnil).—Is irritated by Proust's little game.—Then everything falls into place, they remain friends for twenty-eight years; but she's hurt by her portrait as the Duchesse de Guermantes in the second volume of *In Search*; Proust is affected by this and complains to Cocteau: "When I was twenty years old, she refused to love me; now, at forty, having made from her all that is best in the Duchesse de Guermantes, must she refuse to read me?"

Lieutenant Comte Armand-Pierre de Cholet

Photo 1888.

Proust's military service at Orléans in 1889: under Cholet's command.

Cf. Robert de Saint-Loup: met Proust in the street, pretended not to recognize him.

Nicolas Cottin

Photo August 8, 1914.

Young, stocky peasant, taken into his service in 1907 along with his wife Céline (= Françoise) for seven years (followed by Céleste and Odilon Albaret).

Mocking, sly, would poke fun at Proust when he wasn't there; "I have a horrifying suspicion that Nicolas drinks."

Creative phase 1907–1914. January 1909: snow on the Boulevard Haussmann. Tea + toast brought by Céline → madeleine.

Would go to bed at four in the morning so he'd be awake while Proust was working; then Céline would take over.

Would organize loose pages in a binder, write down what was dictated to him. "His sentences are as irritating as he is but, mark my words, when he's dead he'll be a success."

Died at the front from a pleurisy in 1916.

**Alphonse Daudet
(1840–1897)**

Bergotte? (Cf. Barrès, France).

Proust taken to their house by Reynaldo Hahn.

Photo 1891.

Was slowly dying, victim of syphilis contracted in his youth.

Magical readings by the fire in the dining room at Illiers, or in the garden (the Pré Catelan).

**Claude Debussy
(1862–1918)**

Photo April 3, 1909.

Vinteuil Septet > *La Mer* and *Quatuor*.

Relations between Debussy and Proust.

Proust's love of Debussy's music, from 1890 on. Even stronger after *Pelléas* (1902).

But incompatibility between Debussy's and Reynaldo Hahn's conceptions of music (Hahn's: academic). And Debussy's gloomy, prickly character (you only have to look at the obtuse nature of his brow, his closed countenance).

Debussy: on the fringes of Daudet's circle at Café Weber. Debussy was suspicious of Proust's group: "He's long-winded and precious and a bit of an old woman." Proust invites Debussy to a dinner for writers and artists, 45 rue de Courcelles; Debussy refuses: "You see, I'm an absolute bear in company. I'd rather we just went on meeting at Weber's. Don't hold it against me, my dear sir, I was born like this!"

**Lucie Delarue-Mardrus
(1880–1945)**

Photo February 27, 1914.

Dr. Mardrus's wife.

Poetess = "Muse"; reads her verses at Montesquiou's last receptions.

Between 1914 and 1921 or thereabouts, little coterie of charming women; preferred their own company to that of men, though they continued to go out in the world; restrained version of Gomorrah; a band, not a ghetto: Mme de Noailles, Colette, Liane de Pougy, Émilienne d'Alençon, Renée Vivien and her friend Evelina Palmer; the leader: the Amazonian Miss Barney; late encounter between Miss Barney's idyllic Gomorrah and Proust's gloomy Sodom, but the meeting was not a success. When Miss Barney read the last volumes of *In Search of Lost Time* she thought that Albertine and her friends "were not so much charming as improbable" (not badly put): "Not everyone is able to infringe these Eleusinian mysteries."

Gabriel Fauré
(1854–1924)

Photo November 29, 1905.

Proust's love of Fauré's music: "My dear sir, I not only love, admire, and adore your music, I was, I still am, in love with it."

Sonata for the piano and violin heard at the Prince de Polignac's, very much a musician and composer.

Would get the Poulet Quartet to come to his house in the middle of the night to play him some Franck and some Fauré.

Keys: the Vinteuil Sonata:

- incidentally: Prelude to *Lohengrin*, Fauré's *Ballade*, "Good Friday Spell," "a piece by Schubert";
- but essential: little phrase: Saint-Saëns's Sonata in D minor and, for the sonata as a whole, Sonata by Franck.

(So Fauré: very indirect.)

**Anatole France
(1844–1924)**

Photo 1893.

Relations between Proust and France: very well known.

- 1889: Proust taken to Mme Arman de Caillavet's salon—Mme Arman de Caillavet was France's muse.
- Dedicates *Pleasures and Days* to him.
- Probably the main source for Bergotte.

**Prince of Wales
(1841–1910)**

Photo 1894.

Son of Queen Victoria → Edward VII in 1901.—Initiated the Entente Cordiale.

Very much a socialite, his mother was suspicious of him; Swann and Haas, his friends.

General Marquis Gaston de Galliffet (1830–1909)

Photo 1893.

Greffulhe's coterie. Close friend of Charles Haas's: *Cercle de la Rue Royale* (Crillon), Tissot's painting.

Known for his role in the Mexican War.

- Led the cavalry charge at Sedan.
- Savage suppression of the Commune.
- Minister of War (1899), following the Dreyfus Affair.

Vain and opportunistic; nicknamed *Silver Belly*: silver plate in his abdomen, wounded in Mexico in 1863; successful with the society ladies because of this plate, curious as to its real dimensions (twenty-franc piece?).

Froberville and his monocle.

(Really very uptight. Peculiar uniform of the time: slim, austere, tight, *maschio* in its austerity: a *baton*, a stick.)

Anna Gould, Marquise Boni de Castellane

Photo July 24, 1901.

We've seen Boni de Castellane: his fortune dwindling, he marries a skinny sallow American millionairess; a line of black hair down her spine, "like an Iroquois chieftainess"; Boni depilated, rouged her, taught her how to reply "Nice of you to say so" when paid a compliment—Boni = "the other side of the coin."

For Anna's twenty-first birthday, lavish ball in the Bois de Boulogne, rented from the City, 1896 (the year Great-Uncle Louis Weil and Grandfather Nathé died): three hundred thousand francs of Anna's fortune— eighty thousand Venetian lanterns hung in the trees of the Bois; the full corps-de-ballet from the Opéra; twenty-five swans released among the lanterns and illuminated fountains.

Anna put a stop to it all before her fortune was completely frittered away. "You can't divorce him!—I don't see why. I 'ate him, I 'ate him"{"*Je le hé, je le hé*"}.—January 26, 1906: leaves, taking her children with her. April: divorce → Marries Boni's cousin: Hélie de Talleyrand-Périgord, Prince de Sagan.

The Gramont Children

1896.

Duc de Guiche → cf. *infra*.

Louis René de Gramont.

Mlle de Gramont (a future Noailles).

Comte Henri Greffulhe
(1848–1932)

Greffulhe or Greffeuille? The swells would say "Greffeuille"—but Montesquiou wrote:

Comtesse Greffulhe
Is two dark glances wrapped in tulle

Photo May 24, 1881.

→ Duc de Guermantes.

Family of Belgian bankers, very rich, obtained French nationality, ennobled under the Restoration. His great-aunt, Cordelia, wife of the Maréchal de Castellane = Chateaubriand's mistress. His father: one of the founders of the Jockey Club.

Blond beard, majesty and suppressed violence = a king in a pack of cards (Jacques-Émile Blanche), Jove the Thunderer (cf. the Duc de Guermantes). Condescension of a lord. Member of parliament for Melun (cf. Duc de Guermantes and Méséglise).—Jealous and unfaithful husband. Has little time for his wife's coterie (Montesquiou). "They're a lot of Japs" (= the aesthetes). Insisted on his wife being home by eleven thirty.

Comtesse Henri Greffulhe, née Élisabeth de Caraman-Chimay (1860–1952)

Photo: probably from before 1900.

Supreme social beauty of her time; fully conscious of it; sculpted by Falguière, painted by many painters, lauded in verse by Montesquiou, her cousin: mutual admiration and affection. Was considered very intelligent but never read a book: picked up what she knew from dinner conversations with men of science, artists, musicians.

Duchesse de Guermantes=Mme de Chevigné.—But Mme Greffulhe: position in society, marital relations, cousinship Charlus-Montesquiou; chiming, silvery laugh, coterie exclusively made up of her men-friends (Haas was among them as an old man).

How did she age? How did she die? 1952. That's not long ago. I was writing *Degree Zero*!

Duc Armand de Guiche
(1879–1962)

Photo 1900, that is, before he knew Proust.

We know that around 1903 Proust frequented a band of young aristocrats, the "Saint-Loups," Albufera (cf. *supra*) and Léon Radziwill (Loche) and Guiche among them.

Half brother of Élisabeth de Gramont → the wife of Clermont-Tonnerre: Memories of Proust—Son of Agénor, Duc de Gramont and a Rothschild.

Black curly hair, pale complexion, empty eyes. Sporty, artistic (painting), and a scientist (optics and aerodynamics) → international scholar.

Meets Proust at Mme de Noailles's: struck by the brilliance of his conversation. Writes to him to invite him to his parents' house: "My dear Proust"—"Of course, I realize you can't call me 'My dear Marcel' but you might at least put 'My dear friend,' which commits you to nothing, not even to friendship."

(Guiche. Montauzer!)

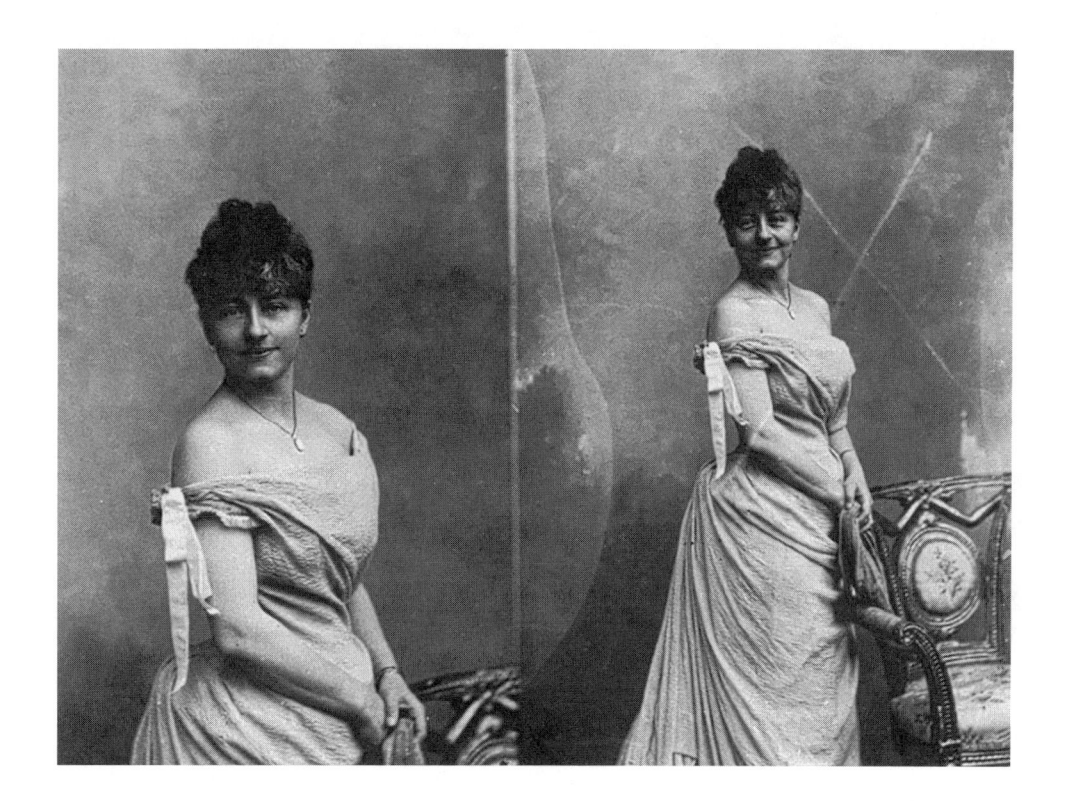

Gyp, Comtesse de Martel (1849–1932)

Probably from around 1890.

Two poses: I think one of the photos (the one on the left) has been touched up.

Mirabeau's great-grand-daughter.—Woman of wit: a number of highly subversive books criticizing the society of her time.

Had often seen Marcel playing on the Champs-Élysées: epoch of Marie Benardaky and Antoinette Faure: sees him on another day buying the complete works of Molière and Lamartine in the Calmann-Lévy bookshop, rue de Gramont (bookshop frequented by Haas and France).

Another day, in the Parc Monceau, sees a very cold Proust clutching a hot roasted potato (it was customary for Parisian women to buy a hot potato before going to the Opéra; they'd keep it in their muffs during the performance).

Anti-Dreyfusard. French-Fatherland League (in response to the League of Human Rights): Maurras, Barrès, Heredia. Those happy days when such things as right-wing intellectuals and writers existed!

Charles Haas (1832–1902)

Photo December 26, 1895.

= Swann (Haas: fits the image).

Would say of himself: "The only Jew ever to be accepted by Parisian society without being immensely rich."

Yet nowadays he'd be rich: his father, stockbroker.

Bravery, 1870 war → accepted into the Jockey Club.

Had frequented the Tuileries court.

Red, frizzled hair; as he got older, salt and pepper, arched eyebrows, nose barely curved at all, became "Jewish" again in old age (Proust's famous remark about Swann as an old man, as if old age were a return to *eidos*).

Straus's salon (1880–1890), Princesse Mathilde and the Greffulhe-Montesquiou coterie.—Friend of the Prince of Wales and the Comte de Paris, in exile in Twickenham.

Life of a socialite, painting and women.

Had a Spanish lady for a mistress, with whom he had a daughter, Luisita?

Had the courage (compared to his clan) to be a Dreyfusard.

Everyone recognized Swann-Haas.

(Taut skin, constriction.)

Reynaldo Hahn
(1875–1947)

How recent it all is.

Photo # 1898.

Hahn's personality and relations with Proust: well known.

Friendship: from 1894 until Proust's death.

Massenet's pupil, composer, pianist, and singer (tenor). A few records that we poke fun at now as ridiculously kitsch. Jew from Caracas, lived in Paris with his parents and sisters. Musical attraction of Madeleine Lemaire's afternoons (song cycle on Verlaine's poems: *Les Chansons grises*).

Very good conversationalist.

Passionate friendship for two years—then less intense but loyal (the usual pattern). Trips to Brittany, then to Venice. Proust kept him up to date on his work, and was the first person he read *Swann's Way* to, which Hahn was enthusiastic about.

Laure Hayman

Photo # 1879.

= Odette.

Born in 1851, on a ranch in the Andes; her father, an engineer, died young; her mother tried to get by by giving piano lessons, then set her up as courtesan → "cocotte," cultured prostitute, intelligent, with good taste (≠ Odette), a talented sculptress until her death, from a mysterious sorrow, in 1900. High-society lovers: Duc d'Orléans, King of Greece, the heir to the throne of Bulgaria = "the educator of young Dukes."

Like Odette, lived in a little townhouse on the rue La Pérouse, with the servants' entrance on the rue Dumont-d'Urville. Proust met her in 1888, when he was seventeen (she was thirty-seven).

Blond hair, black eyes that tended to open disproportionately wide when she was overexcited. Paul Bourget (lover) described her in a short story: *Gladys Harvey*.

Gave Proust a copy of *Gladys Harvey*, bound in a piece of embroidered silk from one of her petticoats.

Liaison with great-uncle Louis Weil (the one who owned the house at 96 rue La Fontaine, demolished to make way for the avenue Mozart).—Accepted by the Prousts, received by Dr. Proust.

1922, before Proust's death, quarrel: Laure Hayman told that she's Odette. Furious. Letter. Proust's now famous response: ". . . but since some people whom you don't name have been spiteful enough to reinvent this fairy tale, and you credulous enough to believe them (which, in you, astonishes me), I'm obliged to protest once again, with no more hope of success but as a point of honor. Not only is Odétté de Crécy not you, she is your exact opposite."[22]

(Ye-es! But she's definitely Odette all the same, but a more respectable version).

Willie Heath

Photo 1889.

Proust met him in 1892. Died a year later.

1892: collection of ardent but platonic friendships.

Closely resembled a very dear friend, Edgar Aubert, Genevan and Protestant (the Protestant set: caste like the faubourg Saint-Germain, notion of "good family"), who died in 1892.

Heath: English, religious (initially Protestant, then converted to Catholicism at twelve years old), serious and childlike.

Met in the Bois de Boulogne: "It was in the Bois that I'd often meet you in the mornings, you had spotted me and were waiting for me, erect yet reposing, like one of those cavaliers that Van Dyck painted, whose pensive elegance you shared."

Died from typhoid in 1893.

Proust dedicated *Pleasure and Days* to his memory.

Marie de Heredia
(1875–1963)

Photo 1889.

Around 1893, Proust was a regular at José Maria de Heredia's Saturdays, rue Balzac. Three daughters; the eldest, Marie, organized a party of friends, the "Académie Canaque" {"the Cannibal Academy"}: Pierre Louÿs, Léon Blum, Henri de Régnier (who she married in 1895); Proust = "perpetual secretary."

→ Novels under the name of Gérard d'Houville.

Abel Hermant
(1962–1950)

Novelist, columnist, *Le Figaro*.

Purist writer, wrote the *Grammaire de l'Académie Française*.

Ridiculed by Ferdinand Brunot.

Linked to Rachel de Brancovan's children (among them Anna de Noailles), friends of Proust. Villa at Amphion (Proust at Évian).

It's said: some elements of Bloch. Not obvious from the photo; probably to do with language.

Here with his adopted (?) son. Photo 1904.

Mme Meredith Howland

Personality of the faubourg, linked to Haas, Montesquiou—and Degas.

Well known for her dresses.

Very sought after. *Time Regained*: the Narrator reminds the Duchesse that a society hostess had spoken ill of Mme Howland; she bursts out laughing: "Why, of course, Mme Howland had all the men in her salon, and your friend was trying to lure them to her own!" (III, 1026).

Madeleine Lemaire (1845–1928)

= Mme Verdurin.

Villeparisis (because of the roses).

Bourgeois salon: all of Paris (all but the most exclusive members of the aristocracy): artists + the faubourg Saint-Germain.

Tuesdays, 35 rue de Monceau: crowd, streets blocked with carriages. Garden with lilacs in it. Receptions in the glass-roofed studio.

Tall, energetic woman, untidy hair, lots of rouge, as if she'd dressed in a hurry.

Would spend all day painting flowers, roses (five hundred francs for a painting).

= "la Patronne," "the Mistress."

Country house in Seine-et-Marne: Chateau Réveillon.

Musical recitals.

Stéphane Mallarmé and Méry Laurent

Photo 1896.

1897, Proust taken to Méry Laurent's salon by Reynaldo Hahn.

Méry Laurent: extra at the Théatre du Châtelet.

Dr. Evans's mistress, who was dentist to Napoleon II (generous and not a bit jealous).

Manet's mistress, then Mallarmé's.

Perhaps a little of Odette: Japanese decor in her living room.

Vers de circonstance, p. 115 ["White sardonic Japanese woman / as soon as I rise I tailor for myself / A dress from a turquoise blue piece / Of sky to make others dream."]

Princesse Mathilde

Photo (1865–1870) taken by Dallemagne, a photographer who interested Nadar and whose collection he bought.

Daughter of Napoleon's brother Jérôme (died in 1860). Her dates = 1820–1904.

Famous salon (often referred to in the Goncourts's *Diary*): Flaubert, Renan, Sainte-Beuve, Taine, Dumas fils, Mérimée.

20 rue de Berri: nucleus of Bonapartists + the Strauses, Haas.

Looked like Napoleon. "If it weren't for him I'd be selling oranges on the streets of Ajaccio."

Proust's first introduction to her salon was a success. The Princesse gave him a piece of silk from her dress to make into a cravat.

In *In Search of Lost Time*: appears as herself in the famous scene in the Bois du Boulogne; the words are hers.

→ Princesse de Parme; stupid lady-in-waiting: Mme de Varambon; cf. Mme de Gallois, Princesse Mathilde's maid of honor: knitted at the Princesse's side for thirty years; stupid remarks that made their way into *In Search* ("It's the most amazing thing I've ever seen—other than table-turning of course" (I, 333 [347]) (Comtesse de Monteriender on hearing the Vinteuil Sonata at the Saint-Euverte reception).

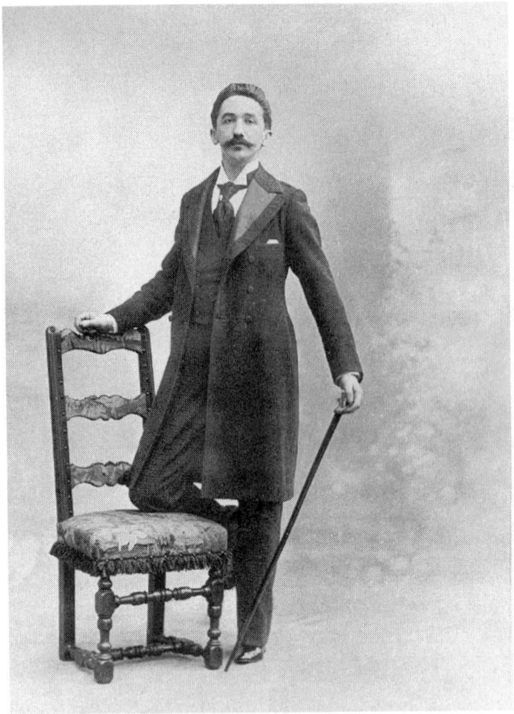

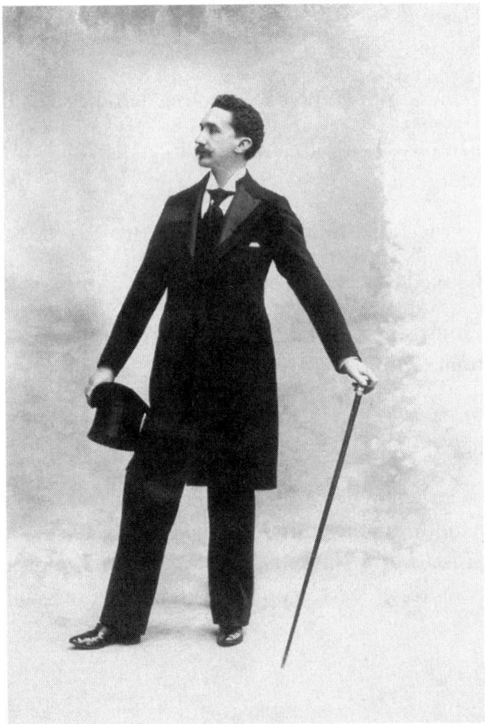

Robert de Montesquiou

Charlus = Doasan (Baron Jacques): Mme Aubernon's rich cousin who ruined himself for a Polish violinist; tall, looks like a knight-at-arms in the Hundred Years War = but a bloated, heavily powdered face: didn't dye his hair and his moustache at the same time.—Hostile remarks about homosexuality.—Brochard (Brichot) tried to improve his behavior in society: "It can't be helped, I prefer my vices to my friends."—Stared at Proust, the first evening, as Charlus stares at the Narrator.

+ Montesquiou (probably the model for Des Esseintes in Huysmans's *Against the Grain*).

Very old French nobility—Chateau d'Artagan, Hautes-Pyrénées (refuge for Montesquiou). Countless traits of aestheticism and dandyism (read *Against the Grain*); legendary eccentricities and rude behavior.

Small, red mouth. Little black teeth, that he'd hide with a quick movement of his hand whenever he laughed.

Proust and Montesquiou: mutual interest in one another and quarrels.

(Has something of Dali about him. Everything repeats itself.)

Louisa de Mornand

→ Rachel (Saint-Loup's mistress).

Albufera's mistress.

Actress (light comedies): (the Code dictated that one should take an actress as a mistress); one of her maids was called Rachel.

Friendly and affectionate relations with Proust until she died.

(Compare her with Laure Hayman.)

Comtesse Potocka, née Emmanuela Pignatelli

Artist's salon; "beautiful and cruel Comtesse"; counted Maupassant and Jacques-Émile Blanche among her lovers.

The Siren, la Patronne.

Turn of the century, moves to Auteuil to spend more time with her greyhounds, which she walks in a pack in the Bois. Hahn: "Take care, you're too malicious to live so far out." Society follows her, but grumbles: "It's charming out here. Is there anything worth seeing in the vicinity?" One by one, they desert her.

Dies during the Occupation, of old age and hunger, left alone in her house at Auteuil with her last greyhound—found eaten by rats.

(Tragic: not only is her profile is like that of a rat, she was eaten by them.)

Jeanne Pouquet

→ Mme Gaston Arman de Caillavet

→ Gilberte (though she doesn't have anything of her physical appearance).

The homology doesn't have to do with age but with Proust's feelings of love.

During his military service, introduced to the fiancée of the son, Gaston, at Arman de Caillavet's salon. Proust assails her with compliments, and she doesn't like him at first.

Fascinated by her plaits of dark hair (cf. Gilberte: "Gilberte's plaits seemed to me a matchless work").

Proust's insistence: invites her to Orléans, stoops to anything to get a photo.

Married to Gaston, 1893. Their daughter Simone: Gilberte's and Saint-Loup's daughter.

Here, as a fortune teller.

(Face I find very moving. I like the little girls from this period. Cf. Gabrielle Schwartz. Perhaps because it's more or less that of my mother's childhood.)

Dr. Samuel Pozzi

Photo 1898.

→ Cottard.

The most fashionable doctor of the upper classes + Saint-Germain faubourg. Friend and doctor to Montesquiou.

Robert Proust was very fond of him and was his assistant at Broca.—Proust met him at his parents' home (when he was fifteen), and his first invitation to dine in town was at Pozzi's house.

→ Straus's salon and Princesse Mathilde.

Daudet: he was "talkative, hollow and reeked of hair oil."

Notoriously unfaithful; Mme Aubernon: "*L'Amour Médecin.*"

Vain of his good looks, but opinions varied as to his talents as a surgeon.

His wife = Mme Cottard exactly, mute and loyal.

Mme Aubernon: "Pozzi's Mute."

"I didn't deceive you, my dear, I supplemented you."

Died in 1918, murdered by a deranged patient.

Prince Boson de Sagan

Photo July 28, 1883.

Uncle of Boni de Castellane.

Arbiter of elegance. Frequents the foyer of the Comédie-Française, where the friends would meet: Gallifet, Haas, Turenne.

→ 1908: paralytic stroke → wheelchair, mane of white hair → Charlus recovering from a stroke, arriving at the Guermantes's afternoon on Jupien's arm.

Gabrielle Schwartz

Photo February 19, 1883.

I'm showing this photo because I'm very fond of this little girl's face.

Link to Proust, tenuous: summer 1891, with Gaston de Caillavet et Jeanne Pouquet, would often go to the tennis court on Boulevard Bineau at Neuilly.—Rather than playing, would sit with the young girls; those who played would disdainfully call the group "gossip's corner" or the Court of Love. In charge of refreshments: would turn up with an enormous box of cakes, beer, and lemonade.

→ "Little band" (→ the budding grove of girls), Gabrielle Schwartz among them.

**Mme Émile Straus,
née Geneviève Halévy**

Photo April 21, 1887.

→ Duchesse and Princesse de Guermantes.

Very well known to Proustians, due to a collection of letters. As a reminder:

First marriage to Georges Bizet, whose son Jacques is a friend (and condisciple) of Proust's; then married Rothschild's lawyer, Émile Straus.

Intelligence and charm.

Comte Louis de Turenne

Photo July 17, 1884.

Accepted in many circles: Chevigné's and Straus's salons, friend of the Prince of Wales.

His monocle → Bréauté.

Nathé Weil, the grandfather (1814–1896)

Wealthy stockbroker from Metz.

Spent his whole life in Paris, leaving only once to take his wife to Étampes for safety, 1870.

Grouchy, grumpy, with a heart of gold.

→ M. Sandré, in *Jean Santeuil*.

Adèle Weil, the grandmother, née Berncastel (1824–1890)

Derision and vertigo: this ill-favored face, pitiful in its ugliness, in its absence of nobility, is the beloved grandmother, the finest, the noblest of the characters in *In Search of Lost Time*.

Either the photo itself is hideous, badly taken (it's not one of Nadar's), or what we rediscover here is that same abyss between reality and literature.

Yet, in *In Search*, heart-rending descriptions of her physical appearance (her tears), her cheeks, the purplish-brown of the tilled fields → (people always say it's a Mother's kiss; but it's the cheek that's the enduring site of the maternal body).

Her relationship to photography, her death (which is above all that of Proust's mother). Her trip to Cabourg with Marcel.

Same personality as in *In Search*: kindness, selflessness, love for her daughter, fondness for music, for classical literature, for Mme de Sévigné.

Georges Weil

The Mother's brother. Solicitor. Beloved brother of Mme Proust.

When great-uncle Louis (the one from *In Search*, the great-uncle of Laure Hayman and Miss Sacripiant) dies, he leaves his apartment to his son Georges: 102 boulevard Haussmann—building where Proust will live after his mother's death.

Had great affection for Proust, whom he would go and console after his mother's death.

Died in 1906—while Proust was staying at the Reservoirs at Versailles.

Amélie Weil, née Oulman

Wife of the solicitor uncle, Georges.

1906: upon the solicitor's death, his share of 102 boulevard Haussmann goes to his widow. Proust lives on the first floor.

Sale of the building: the aunt outbids her nephews and becomes the owner; she rents the apartment to Proust.

1919: the aunt sells the building to a banker, Varin-Bernier. Disaster for Proust (the place is connected to his mother).

(→ Apartment [in] Réjane's house, then Rue Hamelin.)

**Adrien Proust, the Father
(1834–1903)**

**Jeanne Proust, the Mother,
née Weil (1849–1905)**

Photo 1904, a year before her death.

**Robert Proust
(1873–1935)**

Robert, square face = the Father

**Marcel Proust
(1871–1922)**

Marcel, thin face = the Mother

APPENDIX

Roland Barthes's Summaries for the Collège de France Yearbook

Course: The Preparation of the Novel (I)—From Life to the Work

This year marked the beginning of what is likely to be an extended investigation into the (internal) conditions under which a writer today might conceive of undertaking the preparation of a novel. It is therefore by no means a question of analyzing the genre "Novel" from a theoretical or historical perspective, nor indeed of collating information on the techniques that have served various novelists from the past in the preparation their novels. What is more, it is not even clear whether it is a question of the "novel": this old term was chosen for the sake of convenience in order to suggest the idea of a "work" that states its connection to literature on the one hand and to life on the other. The point of view adopted here is that of a fabrication undertaken by a particular subject: in order to find out what the Novel can be, let us proceed *as if* we had to write one.

The first year of this course was devoted to the first practical stage of all writing (whether novelistic or poetic): notation. With a view to writing a work, what is noted from life? How is this activity of notation organized? What is this act of language that is called a notation? Rather than investigate "novelist's notebooks," a long detour via a form that is in no way novelistic but that emerges, in the universal history of literatures, as the exemplary achievement of all notation, was preferred: Japanese haiku. The haiku was therefore the chief concern. The position adopted was not that of a specialist of the history of haiku, and even less of its language. Rather, the haiku was dealt with as a "short form" captured in some recent French translations (principally Munier and Coyaud).

First, the *haiku* was studied in its materiality (versification, typography) and its desire (it is possible to be enchanted by *haiku*). Three domains of notation were then explored: the individuation of the seasons and the times of day; the instant, contingency; mild affect. Finally, two limits were indicated, beyond which the haiku loses its specificity: the *concetto* and narration. Passing, in conclusion, from the *haiku* to some more modern and more Western forms, the problems of a daily practice of notation and the seemingly decisive role of the "formed" sentence as the very dynamic of notation were evoked.

Seminar: The Metaphor of the Labyrinth—Interdisciplinary Investigations

The idea of the seminar was to select a seemingly very rich word and to track its metaphorical development when applied as a metaphor to very different kinds of objects. It was therefore as much an invitation to reflect on the notion of metaphor as on the Labyrinth itself.

Various speakers contributed to this investigation, outside of any rationally preconceived program and making no claim to comprehensiveness: MM. M. Detienne, director of studies at the École Pratique des Hautes Études (Greek mythology); G. Deleuze, professor at the University of Paris-VIII (Nietzsche); H. Damisch, director of studies at the École des Hautes Études en Sciences Sociales (Egyptian Labyrinths and chessboards); Mme Claire Bernard and Mme Hélène Campan, university lecturers (Russian and Spanish literature); MM. Pascal Bonitzer (film); H. Cassan, professor in the department of law at the University of Lille and Fèz (the Medina of Fèz); Mme F. Choay, professor at the University of Paris-VIII (architecture); MM. J.-L. Bouttes (assistant professor at the University of Paris-X (Labyrinths and ruses); P. Rosenstiehl, director of studies at the École des Hautes Études en Sciences Sociales (mathematics); and O. Mannoni (Labyrinths and enunciation).

After listening to such very different presentations, it was noted that the Labyrinth is perhaps a "pseudo" metaphor in the sense that its form is so particular, so pregnant, the literal meaning predominates over the symbolic: the Labyrinth engenders narratives, not images. The seminar ended not with a conclusion but with a new question: not "What is a Labyrinth?" nor indeed "How do you get out of one?" but rather "Where does a Labyrinth begin?" In this way, the seminar shares an affinity with what would appear to be a timely epistemology of degrees of consistency, of thresholds, intensities.

Mission: lecture and seminar at New York University ("Proust and the Preparation of the Novel"), November 1978.

Collège de France
1978–1979

HAIKU

The majority of the haiku cited are drawn from the following collections:[1]

Coyaud, M. *Fêtes au Japon. Haïkus* (Paris: PAF, 38 rue de Wagram, 8th arrondissement).
——. *Fourmis sans ombre. Le Livre du haïku. Anthologie. Promenade* (Paris: Phebus, 1978).
Munier, R. *Haïkus* (Fayard, 1978).
Yamata, K. *Sur des lèvres japonaises* (Paris: Le Divan, 1924).

The other haiku were collated and translated from the English by the Professor.[2]

(1) With a bull on board,
A small boat crosses the river,
Through the evening rain.

(Shiki, Blyth*)

(2) A day of haze—
The great room
Is deserted and still.

(Issa, Blyth*)

(3) The city-folk
In the homeward train
Red maple leaves in their hands.

(Meisetsu, Coyaud)

(4) Lying down
I watch the clouds go by.
Summer bedroom.

(Yaha)

(5) The winter wind blows
The cat's eyes
Blink.

(Basho†)

(6) What happiness
Crossing this river,
Sandals in hand!

(Buson, Blyth*)

(7) The dawn of day:
On the tip of the barley leaf,
The frost of spring.

(Issa, Blyth*)

(8) Bindweed blazing at midday
Flames
Among the stones.

(Issa, Coyaud)

(9) The grasses are misty
The waters now silent
It is evening.

(Buson, Blyth*)

(10) A summer shower
How hard it falls
On the pinks.

(Sampu, Munier)

(11) The first sunrise
There is a cloud
Like a cloud in a picture.

(Shusai, Blyth*)

(12) As if nothing had happened,
The crow,
And the willow.

(Issa, Blyth*)

(13) A dog barks
At a peddler
Peach trees are blooming.

(Buson, Blyth*)

(14) The kitten
Holds down the leaf
For a moment.

(Issa, Blyth*)

(15) The child
Walks the dog
Under the summer moon.

(Shoha, Munier)

(16) "I wish to live forever!"
Woman's voice
Cicada's cry.

(Kusatao, Coyaud)

(17) Waking from a siesta,
I hear the knife-grinder
Go by.

(Bakunan, Coyaud)

(18) The bright moon.
No dark place
To empty the ashtray.

(Fugyoku, Blyth*)

(19) White verbena blossom,
And in the middle of the night
The milky way.

(Gonsui, Coyaud)

(20) Bank workers in the morning
Phosphorescent
Like cuttlefish.

(Kaneko Tota, Coyaud)

(21) Autumn moon,
Then, on the lectern, I shall open
Ancient texts.

(Buson, Kikou Yamata)

(22) Little door in the trellis,
Flowers in a pot,

Hut of peace.

(23) New Year's day—
The desk and bits of paper
Just as last year.

(Matsuo, Blyth*)

(24) The dawn of New Year's Day,
Yesterday,
How far off!

(Ichiku, Blyth*)

(25) The road over the autumn moor,
Someone is coming along
Behind me!

(Buson, Blyth*)

(26) Pushing their cart,
The man and the woman
Say something to each other.

(Ilto, Coyaud)

(27) The sound of a rat
Scratching a plate—
How cold it is!

(Buson, Munier)

(28) Summer evening,
Dust from the roads,
Golden fire of dry grasses.

(29) Paths on the mountain,
Dusk on the pink cedars,
Bells in the distance.

(Basho)

(30) The old pond,
A frog jumps in—
Oh! the sound of the water.

(Basho†)

(31)   Coolness,
       I press my forehead
       Against the green mat.

                                    (Sonojô, Coyaud)

(32)   A midday nap,
       Putting my feet against the wall,
       It feels cool.

                                    (Basho, Blyth*)

(33)   I saw the first snow
       That morning I forgot,
       To wash my face.

                                    (Basho†)

(34)   Cleaning a pot,
       Ripples on the water,
       A solitary gull.

                                    (Buson, Coyaud)

(35)   Rainy season. We watch the rain,
       Me and, standing behind me,
       My wife.

                                    (Rinka, Coyaud)

(36)   A nap in the daytime,
       The hand stops moving,
       The fan.

                                    (Taigi, Blyth*)

(37)   The young girl's scarf
       Too low under the eyes
       A wild charm.

                                    (Buson, Coyaud)

(38)   Spring rain.
       An umbrella and a straw-coat?
       Go chatting together.

                                    (Buson, Blyth*)

(39) The greying bonze
      Strokes a friend's head,
      Veranda under the moon.

                                    (Basho, Coyaud)

(40) Misty rain.
      Today is a happy day,
      Though Mount Fuji is unseen.

                                    (Basho, Blyth*)

(41) Dazzling moon,
      Two or three clouds from time to time,
      To repose the eye.

                                    (Basho)

(42) The petals fall;
      He shuts the great gate of the temple
      And leaves.

                                    (Basho)

(43) Spring breeze:
      The boatman
      Chews his pipe.

                                    (Basho, Yamata)

(44) The kitten
      Is sniffing
      At the snail.

                                    (Saimaro, Blyth*)

(45) No other sound
      Than summer rain
      In the evening.

                                    (Issa, Munier)

(46) Peeling a pear—
      Sweet drops trickle down
      A knife.

                                    (Shiki, Blyth*)

(47) Flies play
      On the inkstand. Spring

Sun beams.

(Meistetsu, Coyaud)

(48) In the shadows of the foliage
The black cat's eyes,
Golden, ferocious.

(Kawabata Bosha, Coyaud)

(49) Beings without memory,
Fresh snow,
Squirrels bounding.

(Kusatao, Coyaud)

(50) A bird sang—
A red berry
Fell to the ground.

(Shiki, Munier)

(51) Convalescence—
My eyes tire
Of contemplating the roses.

(52) I come by the mountain path
Ah! this is exquisite!
A violet!

(Basho†)

(53) Such a shame to pick it!
Such a shame to leave it!
Ah, this violet!

(54) And what is my life?
Nothing more than the futile reed
Growing in the thatch of a hut.

(Basho, Yamata)

(55) How admirable,
He who does not think "Life is ephemeral"
When he sees a flash of lightning!

(Basho†)

(56)   In my glass of saké
       A flea swims,
       Absolutely.

                                            (Issa, Coyaud)

(57)   In a jar of water floats
       An ant
       Without a shadow.

                                          (Seishi, Coyaud)

(58)   "That, that"
       Was all I could say,
       Before the blossoms of Mount Yoshino.

                                       (Teishitsu, Coyaud)

(59)   In the winter river,
       Pulled up, and thrown away,
       A red turnip.

                                            (Buson, Blyth*)

(60)   It's evening, autumn;
       I think only
       Of my parents.

                                            (Buson, Blyth*)

(61)   Nothing else today,
       Than to go into spring,
       Nothing more.

                                           (Buson, Munier)

(62)   Everyone is asleep,
       Nothing between,
       The moon and me.

                                         (Seijugo, Coyaud)

(63)   In the house of the solitary nun,
       Indifferent to her indifference, blooms
       A white azalea.

                                           (Basho, Yamata)

(64)   Bat, you live
       Hidden under
       Your broken umbrella.

                                    (Buson, Coyaud)

(65)   The moon-viewing boat,
       I dropped my pipe,
       Into the river shallows.

                                    (Buson, Blyth*)

(66)   I remember,
       The old woman left to cry
       With the moon for company.

                                    (Basho, Coyaud)

REPRODUCTION OF *VITA NOVA*

21 VIII 79

Vita Nova
Méditation · Bilan
Morale sans espoir d'application

Prologue : Deuil

I. Le Monde comme objet contradictoire de Spectacle et d'indifférence [comme Discours]
  — Objets archétypiques : — [le Mal?]
         — le Militant
         — la mauvaise foi

I bis — que les "plaisirs" sont insusceptibles de ...
         — la Musique

II — la décision du 15 Avril 78
   — la littérature comme substitut d'amour
   —
   — Écrire

III. Imagination d'une V.N.
    — Régimes

IV La litt. comme déception (c'était une Initiation)
    — le déjà fait : l'Essai
    — le Fragment
    — le Journal
    — le Roman
    [le Comique ?]
    — la Nostalgie

V L'Oisiveté *compacte* [le Neutre ? le Tas/Tao]
      le Rien faire philosophique

Épilogue : la Rencontre

22.VIII.79

Vita Nova
Méditation Bilan
Morale sans espoir d'application

*Rendre dialectique
plus edifiant
Schéma trop et dirigeant
not accepté*

Prologue — Deuil
— le problème vital de l'Agir (pertinence de ce qui suit ; que faire ? Comment faire ?)

I. L'acédie amoureuse
  — Suite de RH
  — quêtes velléitaires

II Que les "plaisirs" sont insusceptibles de force ⎫ la Drogue
  — la Musique
  — Abandon de la peinture
  — Dérisions : le Tricot, le kobolo ⎭

III Le Monde comme objet contradictoire de spectacle et indifférence. Examen et Typologie des Discours.
  le "Mal" ? Le Militant. La mauvaise foi

IV La déception du 15 Avril 1978. La littérature comme substitut, répondant d'amour

V Imagination d'une V.N
  Régimes

VI Littérature : il ne s'agit que d'une initiation ? Déceptions, impuissances ?
  — le Déjà fait : l'Essai
  — le Fragment. le Journal. le Roman.
  — le Complexe
  — la Nostalgie

VII L'Oisiveté pure : le "rien faire philosophique" (le Neutre, le Tao/ le Tas.
  — les Amis (Fantasme de ne s'occuper que d'eux)
  — le Retour aux places antérieures. Continuer. Pas de VN

Épilogue : la Rencontre

22 Août 79
II
10x

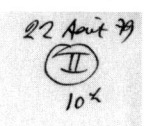

Prologue — Deuil
— Rêve.

— Vivre, agir, investi, désirer   Champs, Cercles, traversés
le "Retour   → Quête Perte du vrai guide, la Mère
à l'Enfance"   Maestri e Auctori *   Drague Soirées
(Caro Père)   Vaches Soirées
              — L'Écrivain (Jamais un philosophe ne
Marches du   fut mon guide)
Bescam   ⎧   — le Gigolo — comme Autre + Peuple
         ⎨   la Boulangère
         ⎩ ⚹— l'Ami —
              le jeune homme inconnu
— Figures   — la Femme — comme Agacement
Anti-
Discours   ? — le Militant — comme Autre - Prêtre

? — la décision du 15 Avril 78   Maestro Tolstoï se substitue à Proust ?
   la Litt
? — V N

? — l'absence de maître | L'Enfant marocain du Poème Zen écrit
                            | l'Oisiveté pure

? Epilogue   La Rencontre

Index des lieux et des personnes (rue de Flore) 139-42
                                     * Enfer II

23 VIII 79

Prologue : — Deuil
— la porte du Guide (la Mère)

— vivre, agir, investir, désirer, fantasmer
— Quête : quel force, quel forme, quel discours pour faire ?

— Anti-Discours :

    — la Femme comme Agacement

    — le "Savant"

    — le Militant (Prêtres du Pouvoir)

— Médiateurs : "Maestro et Autore"

    — le Gigolo
    — le Jeune Homme inconnu
    — L'Ami

    — L'Écrivain   → Vita Nova

    — L'Enfant (marocain) : le Sans-Guide
                                  l'Oisiveté

26 VIII 79

V N

– Prologue
↓   Mam. comme Guide
——— Vaines Soirées
        + Politique (le Monde au Flore ?)
        "Telles étaient mes soirées"

? ——— Recherches
        ~~Voyages~~ Cercles   Dialectique – Mal et Bien mêlés
        Guide   – Positif et Insuffisant
                                           – Fantasmes de nécessité de
                                             chaque voyage. Don jusqu'au bout

            – Le gigolo
            – Le jeune homme inconnu
            – L'Ami
            – L'écrivain

            – Mm. reste le Guide

↓   Décision du 15 Avril 78

    _ V N
    "Je me retire pour entreprendre une grande œuvre
    m'serait dit .... L'Amour.

{ Je le savais
  pas si
  Je me
  retirai
  pour
  cela au
  contraire } ≠

    L'enfant (marocain)   Le Sans Guide
                          L'Oisiveté

Apologie   2 Sept 79

— Idée du Rockefes, du Roman Romanesque
  du Roman absolu. v. Fiches à Cours 79-80 # I 11

Formes :

— Le Récit, la relation de quête (intellectuelle)
  cf Photo

— La Relation de soirée (Vanité de la dia-
  chronie qui s'étire)

— Les Fragments d'une "grande œuvre" (cf Pensées
  de Pascal) # observations, aphorismes
  Fragments : comme reliefs d'une Apologie de
  quelque chose

— Faux dialogues (serait bon pour le
  Politique, qui est ratiocination contesta-
  trice sans fin)

[VN]
3 sept 79

[lisant Pascal] Envie de :

– Faire comme si je devais écrire ma grande œuvre (Somme) — mais Apologie de quoi ? là est la question. En tout cas pas de "moi ") — et qu'il n'en restât que des ruines au linéaments, ou parties erratiques, (comme le pied peint par Porbus) : des fragments d'inégale longueur, (ni aphorismes, ni dissertations)

– Ces Fragments : réaliseraient la théorie du Mochlos, du Roman romantique, du Roman absolu : de rédaction dense, voire elliptique, toujours très "intelligente" (surveillance rigoureuse) → Travail lent, acharné — pas seulement de la forme, mais aussi (nouveau pour moi) de la Pensée

– Renoncer au jeu s/ la Bêtise, les guillemets, le refus de prendre position sur l'énonciation (alibi du Romanesque, de la diversité de mon moi). Sans Complaisance. Pas de Semblant

– Quelle Loi ? celle, absolue, de mam.
  [Le Neutre ? en tout cas : ferme et courageux]

– Plus de Je. En tout cas, pas plus que Pascal.
  – Ce sera difficile : lui pouvait dire : l'homme, les hommes

– Classement ? "liasses" : plan indéchiffrable et cependant pas de désordre.

– L'idée s/ les Cercles, Médiateurs, par ex. ne sera pas enflée ; elle sera ce qu'elle peut être : un fragment – Apologue de 2 pages etc

– "Pensée" dans lesquelles la Référence aux Écriture (citations) serait remplacée par la Référence à la Littérature (citations)

– Tout ceci voudrait dire qu'on abandonne l'enfantillage du Récit Vita Nova : ces efforts de grenouille qui veut se faire aussi grosse…

V. N   12 XII 79

ou
à la fin [= Deuil]

— L'Acédie

— Hypothèses de vie   [Vignette]
    — Prague. Bolge   Gig
    — Rencontre. Fête.   le Jh inconnu
    — Lutte (Politique H etc)   Militant
    — Charité   L'ami JL
    — le Tas.   L'enfant marocain
    — Musique Peinture Retraite

— [Mam. comme guide]   Journal de Deuil
  " le Cercle de mon possible " * = la litt.
— Désarroi du 15 Avril 78 : La littérature

* v. citation Heidegger de le Cours §3 s/ Oisiveté

TRANSCRIPTION OF *VITA NOVA*

Vita Nova comprises eight sheets of paper in 21 x 29.7 format. The first seven pages were written on typewriter paper, the eighth on squared paper. The pages were filed in a red cardboard folder marked VITA NOVA in capital letters. The first draft was written in ink; additions were made in black or red pencil.

Abbreviations Used

< > word crossed out
<illeg.> word rendered illegible
{ } interlinear addition
Italics indicate additions made in black pencil, **bold** indicates those made in red pencil.
The square brackets [ ] are Barthes's.

21 VIII 79

<u>Vita Nova</u>

Meditation. Taking stock
Morality with no hope of application.

<u>Prologue</u> – Bereavement[1]

I. The World as a contradictory object of spectacle and indifference [*as Discourse*]
  —Archetypal objects: —[Evil?]
    —The Militant
    —Bad Faith

I. (a) *"pleasures" are impervious to . . .*
    —Music

II.   —The decision of April 15, 78[2]
    —Literature as a substitute for love
    —
    —Writing

III. Imagining a V.N.
    —Regimes

IV. Literature as disappointment (it was an Initiation)
    —Done already: the Essay
    —The Fragment
    —The Diary
    —The Novel
    [—Humor?]
    —Nostalgia

{*compact*}

V. <The> Idleness [The Neutral? The Heap / Tao]
  {*philosophical* <u>Doing Nothing</u>}

<u>Epilogue</u>: The Encounter

22 VIII 79
(I)
9 a.m.

<u>Vita Nova</u>

Make
more dialectical
Plan too edifying   Meditation. Taking stock
   too disappointing   Morality with no hope of application

<u>Prologue</u>   —Bereavement
            —The vital problem of <u>Action</u> (with respect to what ensues: what to do? how to act?)

I.   Amorous acedy
      —What came after RH[3]
      —Half-hearted pursuits

II.   "Pleasures" are impervious to force
       —Music   Cruising
       —Giving up painting
       —Derisory things: Knitting, *Komboloï*[4]

III.   The World as a contradictory object of spectacle and indifference. Analysis and Typology of <u>Discourses</u> "Evil"? The Militant. Bad faith.

IV.   The decision of April 15, 1978. Literature as a substitute, <illeg.>[5] of love.

V.   Imagining a V.N.
Regimes.

VI.   Literature: is only an initiation? Disappointments, incapacities?
         — Done already: the Essay.
         — The Fragment. The Diary. The Novel.
         — Humor.
         — Nostalgia

VII. Pure Idleness: "philosophical doing nothing." (The Neutral. Tao / the Heap).
  —Friends (Fantasy of devoting myself entirely to them)
  —*The Return to former positions. Carrying on.* No V.N.

Epilogue: The Encounter

August 22 79
Ⓘ Ⓘ
10 a.m.

Prologue — Bereavement
— <To Live, A⁶>

—To live, to act, to invest, to desire Fields, Circles, crossings
→ Quest
The "Return————Loss of the true guide, the Mother
to Childhood" —Maestri e Autori*   ⎫ Cruising
(without Mother)   ⎬ Futile
                                          ⎭ Evenings

Masters of—The Writer (*Never was a philosopher
Discourse*   *my guide*)
         ⎛—The Gigolo – as Other—Ordinary People
         ⎜   the Baker
         ⎜—The Friend
         ⎝—*the unknown young man*

—Figures – Woman – as Irritation
  Anti-
  Discourse ⎛ <Proust?>
               ⎝ ? – the Militant – as Other-Priest

?   ⎛—The decision of April 15, 1978 Maestro Tolstoy takes the
     ⎜   place of Proust?
     ⎜   Lit.
?   ⎜
     ⎜ ? — VN
     ⎜
     ⎝ ? — *The absence of a master* │ The Moroccan Child
                                      │ from the Zenrin
                                      │ Poem⁷
                                      │ Pure Idleness

? Prologue   The Encounter

Index of people and places (e.g., *the Flore*)

*Inferno II 139–42⁸

401 TRANSCRIPTION OF *VITA NOVA*

23 VIII 79

<u>Prologue</u> – Bereavement
        —The Loss of the Guide (the Mother)
—To live, to act, to desire, to fantazise
—Quest: what force, what form, what <u>discourse</u> in order to write?

— Anti-Discourse:
    — Woman as Irritation
    — The "Scholar"
    — The Militant (Priests of Power)

— Mediators: "Maestro et Autore"

    — The Gigolo
    — The unknown Young Man
    — The Friend

    — The Writer → *Vita Nova*

    — The (Moroccan) child: the Guide-less
                                           Idleness

VN　　　　　　　　26 VIII 79

-Prologue

　↓　*Mam.[9] as guide*

___ Futile Evenings
+ Politics (Le Monde at the Flore?)[10]

"This is how I spent my evenings"

? ─── –Quests[11]

    Journeys, Circles   Dialectic: —Evil and Good Mingled
        Guides   —Positive and Insufficient
    _____   —Fantasies where every
                                            journey is a success.
                                            Talent to the very end

    —The gigolo
    —The unknown young man
    —The Friend
    —The writer

    —*Mam. still the guide*

↓ Decision of April 15, 1978

    —VN
    —"I'm withdrawing from the world to begin a great work that will be an expression of . . . Love"

I didn't know whether I was withdrawing do to this or its opposite { ≠ the (Moroccan) child   *the Guide-less*
                                                                         Idleness

<u>Apology</u>　　　　　　　　　Sept 2 79

-Idea of Poikilos,[12] of the Romantic Novel, of the absolute Novel. See notes for the 79–80 <u>Lecture</u> <u>Course</u> # p. 11

<u>Forms:</u>

—Narrative, account of an (intellectual) quest
cf *Photography*
—Account of my evenings (endless, futile diachrony)

—The Frgmts of a "great work" (cf Pascal's <u>Pensées</u>)
observations, aphorisms
Frgmts: like the remains[13] of an Apology for something
—Fake dialogues (would be good for Politics, which is interminable contestatory hair-splitting)

[VN]
Sept 3, 79

[Reading Pascal] Desire to:

— <Frag> Proceed as if I were writing my major work (Summa) <the illeg.> but an Apology for what? That is the question! Not for "me" at any rate!)—of which only ruins or contours, or erratic portions would remain (like the foot in Porbus's painting):[14] Fragments of varying lengths, <possibly illeg.> (neither aphorisms, nor essays)

—The Frgmts: would bear out the theory of *Poilikos*, of the Romantic Novel, of the Absolute Novel: densely written, elliptical even, always very "intelligent" (a tight watch to be kept on this) → Slow, unremitting labor—not only of the Form but also (new for me) of the Thinking.

—Give up playing the Foolish game, the scare quotes, the refusal to assume a position in relation to the enunciation (excuse of the Novelistic, of the diversity of my ego). Without Self-indulgence. No <u>Pretence.</u>

—Which law? the absolute law of mam.
[The Neutral? at any rate: firm and brave]

—No more *I*. At any rate, no more than Pascal.
—That will be difficult: he could say: <the> man, men

—Organization? "Sheafs": indecipherable plan that's still ordered.

—The idea about the Circles, Mediators, e.g. <Illeg.>
won't be *inflated*: it will be what it can be:
a Fragment—a two-page Apologue, etc.

—"Pensées" in which, References to the Scriptures (quotations)

[would be replaced by References to literature (quotations)

—All of this would mean giving up the childishness of the Vita Nova Narrative: those efforts of the frog who wished to make itself as big as . . . [15]

| | VN | 12 XII 79 |

or   *[-Bereavement]*
at the end

   —Acedy

   —Life hypotheses   [Virgil]
      —Cruising. Bolge[16]   Gig.
      —Encounter. Celebration   The unknown ym
      —Struggle (G[17] Politics etc.)   Militant
      —Charity   The friend JL[18]
      —the Heap   The Moroccan child
   —*Music Painting Retreat*

—[Mam. as guide]   *Journal of Mourning*[19]
—'*The Circle of my possible*'* = Lit.
—Decision of April 15, 78:[20] Literature

*See Heidegger quotation in the lecture § on Idleness[21]

NOTES

Notice

1. 1977: Roland Barthes, *Comment vivre ensemble: Simulations romanesques de quelques espaces quotidiens*, ed. Claude Coste (Paris: Seuil/IMEC, 2002); 1977–1978: *Le Neutre: Cours et séminaires au Collège de France, 1977–1978*, ed. Thomas Clerc and Éric Marty (Paris: Seuil, 2002); 1978–1980: *La Préparation du roman I et II: Cours et séminaires au Collège de France 1978–1979 et 1979–1980*, ed. Nathalie Léger (Paris: Seuil, 2003).

2. {The references to the *Oeuvre complètes* have been retained here in the same format. Whenever Barthes's works are quoted directly, reference is also given to the available English translation.}

3. {Barthes's own bibliographical references in the margins of his notes have been retained. They have been completed for the English reader by footnotes that, wherever possible, provide references to an available English translation or, if the reference is to an English text, the original.}

Editor's Preface

1. {The epigraph to this preface is cited by Roland Barthes in "To the Seminar," in *The Rustle of Language*, trans. Richard Howard (New York: Hill and Wang, 1986), 340.}

2. Jules Michelet, lecture of March 6, 1851, *Cours au Collège de France* (Paris: Gallimard, 1995), 2:694.

3. "Longtemps, je me suis couché de bonne heure," paper delivered at the Collège de France on October 19, 1978, a few weeks before the first session of *The Preparation of the Novel*, of which it is a kind of abstract. In Barthes, *The Rustle of Language*, 284.

4. {The available English translations of the texts discussed are as follows: "Longtemps, je me suis couché de bonne heure," "Deliberation," and "One Always Fails in Speaking of What One Loves," in *The Rustle of Language*, trans. Richard Howard (New York: Hill and Wang, 1986); *Camera Lucida: Reflections on Photography*, trans. Richard Howard (New York: Hill and Wang, 1981); "Soirées de Paris," in *Incidents*, trans. Richard Howard (Berkley: University of California Press, 1992).}

5. Manuscripts conserved in the collections of the IMEC (Roland Barthes archive), class-mark BRT2.A08–04, BRT2.A09–02.01.

6. Now available through the Éditions du Seuil in mp3 format.

7. Barthes, "To the Seminar," in *The Rustle of Language*, 333 {translation slightly modified}; *OC* 4:503.

8. "I too am entering a *vita nuova*, marked today by this new place, this new hospitality." The "I too" refers to Michelet, whose *vita nuova* Barthes evokes a few lines above. (Barthes uses both the Latin and the Italian forms of the expression.) "Inaugural Lecture, Collège de France," in *A Roland Barthes Reader*, ed. Susan Sontag, trans. Richard Howard (London: Jonathan Cape, 1982), 478; *OC* 5:446.

9. Dante, *La Vita Nuova*, chap. 18, trans. Dante Gabriel Rossetti (New York: Dover, 2001), 17.

10. See the last session, p. 107.

11. Roland Barthes, *A Lover's Discourse: Fragments*, trans. Richard Howard (New York: Hill and Wang, 1978), 55 {translation modified}; OC 5:86.

12. Manuscripts conserved in the collections of the IMEC (Roland Barthes archive), class-mark BRT2.A09–01, BRT2.A09–03.

Translator's Preface

1. See Laurent Nunez's account of the reception of Barthes's plans for *Vita Nova*: "Vie nouvelle, roman virtuelle," *Le Magazine Littéraire* 482 (January 2009): 74–75.

2. Antoine Compagnon, "Roland Barthes's Novel," trans. Rosalind Krauss, *October* 2005 112:23–34.

3. Diana Knight, "Idle Thoughts: Barthes's *Vita Nova*," *Nottingham French Studies* 36 (Spring 1997): 88–98.

4. Thomas Clerc's lecture, "Barthes conceptuel, *La Préparation du roman*," was delivered at the conference entitled *Colloque Roland Barthes: Littérature et philosophie des années 1960* (March 28, 2009, École normale supérieure, Paris). A sound recording can be consulted online at www.diffusion.ens.fr.

5. See p. **147**.

6. For a discussion of the generic status of the written lecture course, see Andy Stafford, "'*Préparation du romanesque*' in Roland Barthes's Reading of *Sarrasine*," in *Roland Barthes Retroactively: Reading the Collège de France Lectures*, ed. Jürgen Pieters and Kris Pint, *Paragraph* 31, no. 1 (2008): 95–108.

7. Jonathan Culler, "Preparing the Novel: Spiraling Back," in *Roland Barthes Retroactively*, 100.

8. Roland Barthes, *The Neutral*, ed. Thomas Clerc under the direction of Éric Marty, trans. Rosalind Krauss and Denis Hollier (New York: Columbia University Press, 2005).

9. Rosalind Krauss, "Translator's Preface," in *The Neutral*.

Session of December 2, 1978

1. Roland Barthes, "Inaugural Lecture, Collège de France," in *A Roland Barthes Reader*, trans. Richard Howard, ed. Susan Sontag (London: Jonathan Cape, 1982), 477; OC 5:429–446.

2. "In the middle of the journey of our life": the first verse of canto 1 of Dante's *Inferno*, *The Divine Comedy of Dante Alighieri*, ed. and trans. Robert M. Durling (New York: Oxford University Press, 1996), 27. Barthes is quoting from André Pézard's translation ("Au milieu du chemin de notre vie") (Paris: Gallimard, "Bibliothèque de la Pléiade," 1965), 883.

3. Barthes was born in 1915. He was sixty-three at the time of writing.

4. This is the "dark wood" that opens the *Inferno*: "*Nel mezzo del cammin di nostra vita / mi ritrovai per una selva oscura / ché la diritta via era smarrita*" ("In the middle of the journey of our life / I came to myself in a dark wood / for the straight way was lost.") Dante is lost and finds in Virgil an attentive guide to lead and instruct him throughout the great journey of *The Divine Comedy*.

5. Marcel Proust, letter to Daniel Halévy (July 19, 1919): "it is the apogee of the particular that begets the general" Marcel Proust, *Selected Letters*, vol. 4, *1918–1922*, ed. Philip Kolb, trans. Joanna Kilmartin (London: HarperCollins, 2000), 86. {translation modified}

6. In his analysis of "The Method of Sainte-Beuve" (1908), Proust invokes the fear of a "bankruptcy of talent," of "no longer finding the strength to say what one most wanted to say": "And one would like to counter the force of an earlier indolence by obeying Christ's beautiful commandment in St John: 'Work

while ye have the light.'" Marcel Proust, *Against Sainte-Beuve and Other Essays*, trans. John Sturrock (London: Penguin, 1988), 10.

7. In his *Life of Rancé*, Chateaubriand recounts the exemplary journey of Amand-Jean de Rancé (1625–1700), a young socialite who frequented the social circles of the Hôtel de Rambouillet and whose life was turned upside down by the tragic death of his mistress, Madame de Montbazon. Rancé renounced his fortune and withdrew to La Trappe. Barthes wrote the preface to an edition of the *Life of Rancé* (OC 4:55–65). Note that Rancé was not, as Barthes writes, the founder of the Trappist Monastery (1140) but a dedicated reformer who returned to the fundamental rules of Benedictine and Cistercian monarchism.

8. See, in particular, 154, sq.

9. Upon being diagnosed with lung cancer, Jacques Brel quit the world of music and, in July 1974, embarked on a sailing trip around the world. He died on October 9, 1978.

10. *Vita Nova* (1292), a text alternating between prose and verse, is Dante's first work, written after Beatrice's death. *Vita Nova* is also the title of the plan for a novel that Barthes wrote out on eight loose sheets of paper between August and December 1979, in between preparing the two halves of the course entitled "The Preparation of the Novel" for the Collège de France.

11. "'Vita Nuova,' Michelet said, marrying at fifty-one a young girl of twenty and preparing to write new books of natural history," writes Barthes in his paper "Longtemps, je me suis couché de bonne heure," in *The Rustle of Language*, trans. Richard Howard (New York: Hill and Wang, 1986), 286 (OC 5:459–470). Barthes uses either the Latin or the Italian form of the expression, depending on the text.

12. *Acedy*, from the Greek *akedia*, "prostration," and *kedeuo*, "to take care," is prefixed with the privative "a," which gives *akedes*, "neglecting, neglected," and *akedestos*, "abandoned." Barthes expands on this notion at length in the preceding lecture course, "Comment vivre ensemble" ("How to Live Together"), his first course at the Collège de France: "State of depression: vagueness, lassitude, sadness, boredom, discouragement." "In akedia, I am the object and subject of abandonment: hence the sensation of blockage, feeling trapped, at a dead-end." *Comment vivre ensemble*, ed. Claude Coste (Paris: Seuil, 2002), 53–54.

13. Maurice Blanchot, *The Infinite Conversation*, trans. Susan Hanson (Minneapolis: University of Minnesota Press, 1993), xv.

14. The lecture course Barthes taught at the Collège de France the previous year was entirely devoted to this question. See *The Neutral*, ed. Thomas Clerc, trans. Rosalind E. Krauss and Denis Hollier (New York: Columbia University Press, 2005).

15. A poem from *Zenrin Kushu*, translated by Alan W. Watts in *The Way of Zen* (London: Thames and Hudson, 1957), 134. *Zenrin Kushu* is an anthology of some five hundred thousand two-verse poems collated by Toyo Eicho (1429–1504). Barthes quotes this poem a number of times throughout his oeuvre. See, among others, *A Lover's Discourse: Fragments*, trans. Richard Howard (New York: Farrar, Straus and Giroux, 1978), 233; *Vita Nova*, OC 5:994–1001; infra. **pp. 397–406**.

16. Jean de la Fontaine, "The Old Man and the Three Young Men," in *La Fontaine: Selected Fables*, trans. James Michie (London: Penguin Books, 1982), 127. {translation modified}

17. In a text entitled "The Interval," Barthes defines *Ma* as "all relation, all separation between two instants, two places, two states" and *Utsuroi* as "the moment when the flower will wilt, when the soul of something is as if suspended in the void, between one state and another." OC 5:475–480. An attentive reader of Taoist writings and the masters who popularized them (notably Daisetz Teitaro Suzuki and his *Essais sur le bouddisme zen*, trans. Jean Herbert [Paris: Albin Michel, 1940–3]; and *Essays in Zen Buddhism*, ed. Christmas

Humphreys [London: Rider, 1950]), Barthes makes direct and indirect reference to Zen Buddhism in his work from *L'Empire des signes* (1970) on. See Roland Barthes, *Empire of Signs*, trans. Richard Howard (New York: Hill and Wang, 1982). See also infra., **p. 55**.

18. This date—April 15, 1978—appears several times on the eight pages that constitute the plan for a novel entitled *Vita Nova*, drafted between August and December 1979; OC 5:994–1001.

19. In the spring of the same year, after leading a research seminar on the theory of reading at the Universities of Fez and Rabat, Barthes to went Morocco for the second time, staying in Casablanca.

20. Barthes lost his mother on October 25, 1977.

21. In "Flaubert and the Sentence," Barthes comments: "When the depths of agony are plumbed, Flaubert throws himself on his sofa: this is his 'marinade,' an ambiguous situation, in fact the sign of failure is also the site of fantasy, whence the work will gradually resume, giving Flaubert a new substance which he can erase anew." In *New Critical Essays*, trans. Richard Howard (Berkeley: University of California Press, 1990), 70. The idea of the Flaubertian "marinade" probably comes from the correspondence; see, for example, the letter to Ernest Chevalier (August 12, 1846): "I throw myself down on the green leather couch that I recently had made. As I seem destined to marinade there, I decorated the pot to my taste and lie there like a dreamy oyster." Gustave Flaubert, *Correspondence*, ed. Jean Bruneau (Paris: Bibliothèque de la Pléiade, 1973), 1:293.

22. Sidoine Apollinaire (431–490) was the author of twenty-four poems and 146 letters (*espistulae*) that were organized into nine books and disseminated between 469 and 482. The word *scripturire* appears in a letter addressed to his "dear Constantius" (book VII, 18, p. 1), written in Clermont in 477. Discussing the publication of his letters with his friend, Sidoine explains that "his mind, once set off, constantly wants to write again" (*quamquam incitatus semel animus necdum scripturire desineret*). See Sidoine Apollinaire, *Lettres (Books VI to IX)*, ed. and trans. André Loyen (Paris: Les Belles Lettres, 1979), 79. In "Comment vivre ensemble" ("How to Live Together"), his first course at the Collège de France, Barthes refers to Apollinaire's biographical notice in the *Dictionnaire de la spiritualité ascétique et mystique*, vol. 15, ed. Marc Villier (Paris: Beauchêne, 1937–1995).

23. Barthes is making an implicit reference to his "Inaugural Lecture," delivered January 7, 1977: "But language—the performance of a linguistic system—is neither reactionary, nor progressivist: it is quite simply: fascist; for fascism does not prevent speech, it compels it." "Inaugural Lecture, Collège de France," in *A Roland Barthes Reader*, 461. Orally, he adds: "When a word exists in one language but not in any other, there's a power struggle."

24. Autonymic, meaning "in its own name," "referring to itself"; when a word refers to itself and not to its referent.

Session of December 9, 1978

1. Barthes developed this idea in a paper delivered at Johns Hopkins University in 1966: "It would be interesting to know at what point the verb *to write* began to be used in an apparently intransitive manner, the writer being no longer one who writes *something*, but one who writes, absolutely. . . . This passage from the verb *to write*, transitive, to the verb *to write*, apparently intransitive, is certainly the sign of an important change in mentality." "To Write: Intransitive Verb?" in *The Languages of Criticism and the Sciences of Man*, ed. Richard Macksey and Eugenio Donato (Baltimore, Md.: The Johns Hopkins University Press, 1970), 141–142.

2. {In English in the text.}

3. On June 22–29, 1977, the Centre culturel international de Cerisy-la-Salle hosted a conference organized by Antoine Compagnon entitled "Prétexte: Roland Barthes." During the discussions, Barthes spoke of his desire to write a novel a number of times. See *Prétexte: Roland Barthes. Colloque de Cerisy*, ed. Antoine Compagnon (Paris: Éditions Christian Bourgois, 2003). Barthes's paper, "The Image" is published in *The Rustle of Language* (1986); OC 5:512–519.

4. See György Lukács, *The Theory of the Novel*, trans. A. Bostock (London: Merlin Press, 1971); Lucien Goldmann, *Towards a Sociology of the Novel*, trans. Alan Sheridan (London: Tavistock Publications, 1975); René Girard, *Deceit, Desire, and the Novel: Self and Other in Literary Structure*, trans. Yvonne Freccero (Baltimore, Md.: The Johns Hopkins University Press, 1976). All the quotations below are taken from Goldmann's "Introduction to the Problems of the Sociology of the Novel" in *Towards a Sociology of the Novel* {translation modified}.

5. Oral: "I'm speaking crudely and I concede all objections."

6. See p. 76 and p. 78 *sq*. On the formulation "that's it!" as the movement whereby the object is recognized in all its heartrending particularity, see Roland Barthes, *Empire of Signs*, trans. Richard Howard (New York: Hill and Wang, 1982) ("Tel," OC 3:415). See also *The Neutral*: "The key word of satori=the exclamation: *Ah, this!*" {a translation of the slightly different formulation *c'est cela!*}, trans. Rosalind E. Krauss and Denis Hollier (New York: Columbia University Press, 2005), 174. See also *La Chambre claire*: *Note sur la photographie* (1980): "A photograph always follows on from this gesture; it says: '*that, that's it, that's what it is!*'" (OC 5:793). {This sentence is omitted from Richard Howard's translation, *Camera Lucida: Reflections on Photography* (New York: Hill and Wang, 1981). See p. 5.}

7. Barthes is referring here to Giambattista Vico's major work, *Scienza Nuova* (the first edition was published in 1725), which he read in Jules Michelet's translation.

8. The "blurb" {*le rempli*} is the outline that the editor writes when the book is to be published; it often appears on the back cover.

9. Barthes is referring here to the lecture "Longtemps, je me suis couché de bonne heure," which he delivered at the Collège de France a few weeks earlier, on October, 19, 1978. The novel must "permit me to *say* whom I love (Sade, yes, Sade used to say that the novel consists in painting those one loves), and not to say *to* them that I love them (which would be a strictly lyrical project); I expect from the Novel a kind of transcendence of egotism, insofar as to say whom one loves is to testify that they have not lived (and frequently suffered) 'for nothing.'" In *The Rustle of Language*, trans. Richard Howard (New York: Hill and Wang, 1986), 288; OC 5:469.

10. Marquis de Sade, "Essay on Novels," in *Crimes of Love: Heroic and Tragic Tales, Preceded by an Essay on Novels*, trans. David Coward (Oxford: Oxford University Press, 2005), 5.

11. Louis Gardet (1904–1986), a Christian philosopher, disciple of Louis Massignon and Jacques Maritain, and writer of a number of essays on Islam and Christian mysticism, among them *Études de philosophie et de mystique comparée* (1972).

12. The origin of Barthes's reading is probably Jean Laplanche and J. B. Pontalis, *The Language of Psychoanalysis*, trans. Donald Nicholson-Smith (London: Karnac Books and the Institute of Psychoanalysis, 1988). See especially p. 99, where Laplanche and Pontalis cite Freud—the death instinct "eludes our perception . . . unless it is tinged with eroticism"—and refer to the *Gesammelte Werke*, vol. 14 (London: Imago, 1940–1952); *The Standard Edition of the Complete Psychological Works of Sigmund Freud*, ed. James Strachey (London: The Hogarth Press and the Institute of Psychoanalysis, 1961), 21:120.

13. Daisetz Teitro Suzuki, *Essays in Zen Buddhism* (New York: Grove Press, 1961), 1:275.

14. Alcidamas, a Greek Sophist and rhetorician, Gorgias's pupil and successor. See *Les Sophistes. Fragments et témoignages* (Paris: PUF, 1969), 26.

15. Leo Tolstoy, *Childhood, Boyhood, Youth*, trans. C. J. Hogarth (London: Everyman's Library, 1991).

16. "We always think of the imagination as the faculty that *forms* images. On the contrary, it *deforms* what we perceive." Gaston Bachelard, *Air and Dreams: An Essay on the Imagination of Movement*, trans. Edith R. Farrell and C. Frederick Farrell (Dallas: Dallas Institute of Humanities and Culture, 1988), 72. Emphasis in the original.

17. See pp. 104 sq., 150, 175, and 263.

18. As Barthes explained to Alain Robbe-Grillet at the conference held at Cerisy in June 1977, Mist-upon-Memory is an allegory: "I mused that, on our way here as we passed through Normandy, we crossed a river called the river Memory and that, rather than Cerisy-la-Salle, the name of this place was Mist-upon-Memory. In actual fact, the nature of my amnesia is not entirely negative; it is an incapacity of memory, a mist." *Pretexte: Roland Barthes* (Paris: Éditions Christian Bourgois, 2003), 278.

19. Following the fifteen anamneses that form a kind of "pause" in the middle of *Roland Barthes* ("At the afternoon snack, cold milk with sugar in it. At the bottom of the old white bowl there was a defect in the glaze"), Barthes writes: "I call *anamnesis* the action—a mixture of pleasure and effort—performed by a subject in order to recover, *without magnifying it or sentimentalizing it*, a tenuity of memory." Roland Barthes, *Roland Barthes*, trans. Richard Howard (Berkley: University of California Press, 1977), 107, 109.

Session of December 16, 1978

1. See p. 14.

2. Antoine Compagnon defines *périgraphy* as "a scenography that brings the text into view, with the author at its center. . . . Notes, tables, bibliography, but also prefaces, forewords, introductions, conclusions, appendixes, annexes. These are the headings of a new *dispositio* enabling us to judge a book without having to read it or get inside it." Antoine Compagnon, *La Seconde Main ou le travail de la citation* (Paris: Seuil, 1979), 328.

3. Barthes is probably referring to Flaubert's use of temporal ellipses—*Sentimental Education* being the most striking example: the whole history of the Second Empire is contained in the blank space between chapters 5 and 6, which opens with the lines: "He traveled the world. / He tasted the melancholy of packet ships, the chill of waking under canvas, the boredom of landscapes and monuments, the bitterness of broken friendship. / He returned home." The effects of the ellipses are also frequently reinforced by alineas in the writing itself. See Gustave Flaubert, *Sentimental Education*, trans. Robert Baldick, rev. Geoffrey Wall (London: Penguin, 2004), 451.

4. There are many blank spaces in the typographical presentation of Pierre Loti's novel *Aziyadé*. Barthes wrote one of his *New Critical Essays* (1972) on Loti's novel: "Pierre Loti: *Aziyadé*," *OC* 4:107–120.

5. Barthes is referring here to a film about Marcel Proust that he intended to write in collaboration with the director André Téchiné.

6. {Literally, "pulled by the hair."}

7. "Vacances de Pâques" was first published in *Le Figaro* (March 25, 1913). "Easter Holidays," in *Marcel Proust: A Selection from his Miscellaneous Writings*, trans. Gerard Hopkins (London: Allan Wingate, 1963), 163. {translation modified}

8. {Barthes writes "*La Peau de l'ours*," from the expression "*Il ne faut pas vendre la peau de l'ours avant de l'avoir tué*" ("Don't sell a bear's skin before you've killed it"). The equivalent English expression is "Don't count your chickens before they hatch."}

9. Jean Grenier, *L'Esprit de Tao* (Paris: Flammarion, 1957), 14.

10. This saying is attributed to William the First of Orange, Count of Nassau (1533–1584), who instigated the Dutch uprising against the Spanish.

11. {Barthes writes "*Le Pire n'est pas sûr*," referring to the expression "*On peut s'attendre au pire, mais le pire n'est jamais sûr*," which translates as "We can expect the worst, but the worst is never certain."}

12. Gustav Janouch, *Conversations with Kafka*, 2nd ed., trans. Goronwy Rees (New York: New Directions, 1971), 81.

13. {In French, Barthes writes "*métier*," which can mean either "profession" or "craft," "acquired skill." Since Barthes is talking explicitly about questions of technique and practice here, *métier* has been translated as "craft" throughout.}

14. In 1973, Jean-Louis Rambures interviewed a number of contemporary writers about their writing practice and published the series under the title *Comment travaillent les écrivains* (Paris: Flammarion, 1978). The text of his conversation with Barthes was first published in *Le Monde* (September 27, 1973). "An Almost Obsessive Relation to Writing Instruments," in *The Grain of the Voice: Interviews 1962–1980*, trans. Linda Coverdale (Berkeley: University of California Press, 1991); OC 4:483–487.

15. Mademoiselle de Sudour was Barthes's grandmother's dressmaker in Bayonne.

Session of January 6, 1979

1. For Barthes's early reflections on haiku and zen, see "The Breach of Meaning" and "The Exemption from Meaning," in *Empire of Signs*, trans. Richard Howard (New York: Hill and Wang, 1982); OC 3:403, 407.

2. *Fama*: here, "renown," "reputation."

3. Barthes is evoking the scene in Alexander Dumas's *The Three Musketeers* (1844) where Aramis, disguised as a priest, renames a hearty meat dish that he is served on a Friday.

4. The rhyme scheme for *The Divine Comedy* is the *terza rima*, whereby the middle line of a tercet (a group of three lines) rhymes with the first and third lines of the following tercet.

5. Paul Valéry, letter to his brother, Jules Valéry (March 29, 1922). Paul Valéry, *Oeuvres 1*, ed. Jean Hytier, "Biographical Introduction," by Agathe Rouart-Valéry (Paris: Gallimard, "Bibliothèque de la Pléiade," 1957), 45.

6. The *kana* are used to transcribe the sounds of Japanese and serve as its alphabet. They are organized into two writing or syllabic systems, the *hiragana* and the *katakana*, and are considered to be the basis of Japanese writing. The *kanji*, also called "ideograms," are the characters of the Han dynasty that are used in Japanese and borrowed from Chinese. A Japanese sentence is made up of an association of *kanji*, to which the syllabic signs (*kana*) provide a kind of grammatical envelope and guide to how they should be pronounced.

7. {This is one of Basho's (1643–1694) most famous haikus; a literal translation of Etiemble's translation would read: "The old pond / A frog in a flying leap / And the sound of the water."}

8. Etiemble sought to conserve the haiku's metrical form (5–7–5). Orally, Barthes comments: "Personally, I think this is very poor." He explains his reservations concerning translations that respect the meter below. See also Etiemble, "Du Japon" (1976), especially the chapter entitled "*Furu ike ya*," reprinted in *Quelques essais de littérature universelle* (Paris: Gallimard, 1982), 57–130.

9. See p. 34.

10. An allusion to the "75" cannon, a famous piece of artillery used by the French army in World War I.

11. "Ephémérides" (October 1926). Valéry, *Oeuvres 1*, "Biographical Introduction" by Agathe Rouart-Valéry, 50.

12. Paul Valéry, letter to Paul Souday (May 1, 1923), on the subject of *Eupalinos*, quoted by Agathe Rouart-Valéry, in ibid., 46.

13. An allusion to *Poetry and Truth* (*Dichtung und Wahrheit*), Goethe's autobiographical narrative begun in 1811.

14. See Henri Morier, *Dictionnaire de poétique et de rhétorique* (Paris: PUF, 1961).

15. From courtly poetry to La Fontaine's fables, from Musset to Valéry or Rimbaud, there are countless examples of the use of the heptasyllable (a line with seven feet) in French poetry. The pentasyllable (a line with five feet) tends to be used in heterometrics (the use of two or more types of verse in the same poem) but can also be found in other kinds of poetry.

16. For the presentation of the haikus in one of the works that Barthes refers to here, see *Haiku*, ed. Roger Munier, preface by Yves Bonnefoy (Paris: Fayard, "Documents Spirituels," 1978).

17. Note taken by Valéry after his first visit to Stéphane Mallarmé, cited by Jean Hytier in Valéry's *Oeuvres*, 1762. Barthes's aside refers to the work of Philippe Sollers and specifically to his book *H* (1973), a text stripped of all punctuation marks.

18. The holophrase is a syntactical structure realized on a level below the syntactical demands of the sentence; it is a linguistic operation without a predicative thesis. The very first morphemes that a child utters are examples of the holophrase. The term is used in psychoanalysis to designate what, in discourse, is motivated by the drives and is organized around a concatenation of nouns, where the verb is often signified through gesture, tone of voice, and attitude rather than language. See Jacques Lacan, *Le Séminaire*, book 11, lesson 17 (June 3, 1964) (Paris: Seuil, 1973); see also Julia Kristeva, *La Révolution du langage poétique* (Paris: Seuil, 1974), 267 sq.

19. Maurice Coyaud, *Fourmis sans ombre. Le Livre du haïku* (Paris: Phébus, 1978), 25. Coyaud evokes the "frequently wordy Western poets" and discusses some exceptions, notably Verlaine.

20. Note taken by Paul Valéry in October 1891, after his first visit to Stéphane Mallarmé, cited by Jean Hytier in Valéry, *Oeuvres*.

21. Georges Schehadé, *Anthologie du vers unique* (Paris: Ramsay, 1977). For Barthes, the lines of verse that Schehadé selects from across the history of poetry are examples of lines that can "sound like a haiku." In his introduction to the *Anthologie du vers unique*, Robert Abirached writes: "In putting this anthology together, Schehadé neither crammed a lot of books nor immersed himself in the history of literature . . . quite simply, he collated all the lines of verse that he knew *by heart* . . . floating all alone and unsigned on the white page, deprived of their contexts and their props, they regain a peculiar virginity, come to life again, and taken together, compose a singular, unexpected melody that is at once the song of a single line and of them all." The line by Oscar Milosz, taken from "Les Terrains vagues" ("The Wastelands") in *Andramandoni* (1918), is cited on p. 48.

22. See p. 48.

23. [Orally]: "These haiku are neither the most beautiful nor even the ones I like best; they're the ones I require for my work." The fascicule was distributed in the following lecture. Since Barthes considered it necessary to remove the punctuation marks from the translations he selected, they have also been removed here. Where the sources of the haiku are not given, they were taken from R. H. Blyth's *A History of Haiku* (Tokyo, 1963) and translated from the

English by Barthes. Those where the name of the author or translator is not indicated were probably extracted from popular anthologies of haiku. See the appendix for a complete transcription of the fascicule that Barthes distributed, which retains the original punctuation. {For an account of the translation strategy adopted with regard to the haiku in English, see the translator's preface.}

24. {The bibliographical reference that Barthes provides here appears to be erroneous. R. H. Blyth's *A History of Haiku* was published in 1963 in two volumes rather than four; given the reference to R. H. Blyth's organization of haikus according to the seasons, it seems likely that Barthes also consulted Blyth's earlier anthology, entitled *Haiku*, which appeared in four volumes between 1949 and 1952 (Tokyo: Hokuseido Press, 1949–1952)}.

Session of January 13, 1979

1. All the haiku on the fascicule that Barthes distributed were numbered. This enabled Barthes to discuss a haiku and refer to it by its number rather than quote it. The same numbers are given in brackets here.

2. Maurice Coyaud, *Fourmis sans ombre. Le Livre du haiku* (Paris: Phébus, 1978), 16.

3. René Sieffert, *La Littérature japonaise* (Paris : Armand Colin, 1961), 35.

4. Barthes is alluding both to the rose motif present throughout Sade's oeuvre (from Rose Keller to Rose, the young woman molested by Saint-Ford, from the rose-colored tongue to the whip made from rose branches, etc.) and to Georges Bataille's text on Sade: "the disconcerting gesture of the Marquis de Sade, locked up with madmen, who had the most beautiful roses brought to him only to pluck off their petals and toss them into a ditch filled with liquid manure." Georges Bataille, "The Language of Flowers," in *Visions of Excess: Selected Writings, 1927–1939*, trans. Allan Stoekl with Carl R. Lovitt and Donald M. Leslie Jr. (Minneapolis: University of Minnesota Press, 1985), 14. Barthes does not mention that he replaced the chrysanthemum that appears in the original poem cited by Coyaud with a rose. Coyaud, *Fourmis sans ombre*, 34.

5. See R. H. Blyth, *Haiku*, 4 vols.: *Eastern Culture, Spring, Summer–Autumn, Autumn–Winter* (Tokyo: The Hokuseido Press, 1949–1952).

6. This reflection on co-presence and the randomness of the series is one of the key elements of John Cage's musical investigations. See Daniel Charles's interviews with John Cage in *For the Birds: In Conversation with Daniel Charles* (Boston: Marion Boyars, 1981); Cage's passion for mycology is also well known.

7. Beginning of a passage crossed out by Barthes.

8. End of the passage crossed out by Barthes.

9. {In the French translation of the haiku, the word "summer" comes at the very end: *Couché / Je vous passer des nuages / Chambre d'été.*}

10. Barthes is referring to Ian Fleming's novel *Goldfinger* (1959, filmed by Guy Hamilton in 1964); one of the scenes describes dining on crab and champagne: [Orally]: "The vividness of that short menu is still very sharp in my mind." For an analysis of certain episodes in James Bond novels, see, among others, "Introduction to the Structural Analysis of Narrative" (1966); OC 2:828–865.

11. {In English in the text.}

12. This is an explicit reference to Stéphane Mallarmé: "[Poetry], philosophically, makes up for language's deficiencies, as a superior supplement." "Crisis of Poetry," in *Divagations*, trans. Barbara Johnson (Cambridge, Mass.: The Belknap Press of Harvard University Press, 2007), 206.

13. See Louis Dufour, "Marcel Proust et météorologie," *Revue de l'université de Bruxelles* 3–4 (1950–1951).

14. {In English in the text: Barthes is using English to distinguish between *le Temps* (the weather) and *le Temps* (time).}

15. {In English in the text: see note 14.}

16. Henri-Frédéric Amiel (1821–1881), a Swiss writer who wrote in French; his major work remains his *Diary* (1839–1881), which runs to over seventeen thousand pages and contains a great many notations on the weather, such as: "Moody sky, day of cloud and rain" (July 3, 1851), and "Cloudy. Spring shower. Leafy wind" (March 12, 1878).

17. Paul Verlaine, "Evening fell, an equivocal autumnal evening: / The lovely girls in a dream on our arms / Murmured such empty words so low / That ever since we've trembled with delight." From "Les ingénus" ("Without Guile"), in *Fêtes galantes* (1869). In *Paul Verlaine: Selected Poems*, trans. Martin Sorrel (Oxford: Oxford University Press, 1999), 41. {translation slightly modified}

Session of January 20, 1979

1. {In the expression "*le temps qu'il fait*," French introduces a modal verb (*faire*: to do or to make), which allows a distinction to be made between *weather* and *time*.}

2. In his description of the act of communication in *Essays in General Linguistics*, Roman Jakobson identifies a "phatic function" whose aim is to establish or to maintain contact between speakers ("hello," "ha," "don't you think . . . ?"); through its very existence, speech is thereby experienced as an affect.

3. François Flahault, *La Parole intermédiaire* (Paris: Seuil, 1978); preface by Roland Barthes, OC 5:487–490.

4. "'Once she was with her daughter, she probably had nothing to say to her,' put in Mme de Villeparisis. 'Most certainly she had [Charlus replied]: if it was only what she calls "things so slight that nobody would notice them but you and I." And anyhow she was with her. And La Bruyère tells us that this is everything.'" Marcel Proust, *In Search of Lost Time*, vol. 2: *Within a Budding Grove*, trans. C. K. Moncrieff and Terence Kilmartin, rev. D. J. Enright (London: Chatto and Windus, 1992), 396.

5. "To be with the people one loves is enough: to daydream, to speak to them, not to speak to them, to think about them or about less important things, it's all the same, so long as one is with them." La Bruyère, *Les Charactères*, "Du Coeur" ("Of the Heart") (Paris: Gallimard, "Bibliothèque de la Pléiade," 1951), 135.

6. Paragraph crossed out by Barthes.

7. See Théophile Gautier, "Symphonie en blanc majeur," *Émaux et camées* (1922) (Paris: Librarie Gründ, "La Bibliothèque Précieuse," 1935).

8. Thomas De Quincey, *Confessions of an English Opium-Eater*. Vol. 3 of *The Collected Writings of Thomas De Quincey*, rev. ed., ed. David Masson (Edinburgh: Adam and Charles Black, 1890), 407.

9. In his discussion of Quincey's *Confessions of an English Opium-Eater*, Charles Baudelaire writes: "Any great irreparable misfortune that comes upon us at this beautiful time of year seems to be invested with a more deadly, sinister character." Baudelaire recalls the circumstances of Elizabeth's death and quotes De Quincey: "The summer we see, the grave we haunt with our thought!" Charles Baudelaire, "An Opium-Eater" (1860), in *Artificial Paradise*, trans. Ellen Fox (New York: Herder and Herder, 1971), 152.

10. Barthes is referring here to the "Urt Diary" (July–August 1977), fragments of which—this note included—appear in "Deliberation" (1979), in *The Rustle of Language*, trans. Richard Howard (New York: Hill and Wang, 1986), 364; OC 5:668–681.

11. Georges Schehadé, *Anthologie du vers unique* (Paris: Ramsay, 1977), 29. Barthes presents it as three distinct lines, in keeping with the method set out on p. 27.

12. Matthew 27:45–50: "Now from the sixth hour [that is, noon] there was darkness all over the land until the ninth hour [three o'clock in the afternoon]."

13. Jules Michelet, *Satanism and Witchcraft: A Study in Medieval Superstition*, trans. A. R. Allinson (New York: Citadel, 1946), 168.

14. "In society as conceived by the analytic cast of mind, the individual, a solid and indivisible particle, resides like a pea in a can of peas: he is round, closed in on himself, uncommunicative." Jean-Paul Sartre, "Introducing *Les Temps Modernes*," in *"What Is Literature?" and Other Writings*, trans. Jeffrey Mehlam (Cambridge, Mass.: Harvard University Press, 1988), 256.

15. Jules Michelet, preface to *Histoire de la France* (Paris: Librairie internationale, 1871), xv.

16. Marcel Proust, "The article in *Le Figaro*," in *By Way of Sainte-Beuve* [*Contre Sainte-Beuve*], trans. Sylvia Townsend Warner (London: Chatto and Windus, 1958), 53.

17. See p. 5.

18. The first line of "The Taste for Infinity," which opens "The Poem of Hashish," in Baudelaire, *Artificial Paradise*, 33.

19. Reference to Louis Dufour's article "Marcel Proust et la météologie," mentioned on p. 35.

20. Marcel Proust, *In Search of Lost Time*, vol. 5: *The Captive, The Fugitive*, trans. C. K. Scott Moncrieff and Terence Kilmartin, rev. D. J. Enright (London: Chatto and Windus, 1992), 82.

21. Jean-Jacques Rousseau, *The Reveries of a Solitary Walker*, trans. Charles E. Butterworth (New York: NYU Press, 1971), 7.

22. The reference is to Gilles Deleuze, *Nietzsche and Philosophy*, trans. Hugh Tomlinson (New York: Columbia University Press, 1983).

23. Barthes takes this citation from *Vie et vérité*, an anthology of texts edited by Jean Grenier (Paris: PUF, 1971), 73. (The pagination that Barthes provides refers to this anthology, which was listed in the inventory of his library). The citation is in fact from an unpublished note taken from the *Oeuvres posthumes* [*Nachgelassene Werke*], trans. H-J. Bolle (Paris: Mercure de France, 1939), 185–186.

Session of January 27, 1979

1. *Diaphoralogy*: a neologism combining the Greek *diaphora* ("that which distinguishes one thing from another") with the suffix "-ology" ("theory, discourse"), which Barthes uses to designate a science of nuances and shimmerings, notably in the "Urt Diary" (July 21, 1977), published in "Deliberation," in *The Rustle of Language*, trans. Richard Howard (New York: Hill and Wang, 1986); OC 5:668–681.

2. This citation is probably taken from "The Work of Art in the Age of Mechanical Reproduction" (1936). Barthes is probably quoting from memory since, despite consulting a number of different editions of the works of Walter Benjamin, we have not been able to identify the source.

3. Maurice Blanchot, "At Every Extreme," in *The Book to Come*, trans. Charlotte Mandell (Stanford, Calif.: Stanford University Press, 2003), 107.

4. Maurice Blanchot, "Joubert and Space," in *The Book to Come*, trans. Charlotte Mandell (Stanford, Calif.: Stanford University Press, 2003), 57. The Joubert quotations are taken from his *Carnets* (1805).

5. Paragraph crossed out by Barthes.

6. Maurice Blanchot, "Joubert and Space," 60. {translation modified}

7. Maurice Blanchot, "Where Is Literature Going?" in *The Book to Come*, trans. Charlotte Mandell (Stanford, Calif.: Stanford University Press, 2003), 226. {translation modified; see note 8 below}

8. {Barthes appears to have misquoted the extract from Mallarmé's letter to Eugène Lefébure quoted by Maurice Blanchot, in ibid., 226. While the letter has "*grâce à ses ténèbres dégagés*" (translated by Charlotte Mandell as "thanks to its liberated shadows"), Barthes writes: "*grâce à ses timbres dégagés*," translated here as "thanks to the timbres it emitted." Note that Barthes refers to the notion of "timbre" again in the following sentence.}

9. Maurice Blanchot, "Artaud," in *The Book to Come*, trans. Charlotte Mandell (Stanford, Calif.: Stanford University Press, 2003), 40.

10. "Urt Diary" (July–August 1977); note reprinted in "Deliberation," in *The Rustle of Language*, 363–364 {translation modified}; OC 5:668–681.

11. The terms Barthes uses here are *trouver* and *retrouver*, which refer explicitly to the final volume of *Á la Recherche du temps perdu*, entitled *Le Temps retrouvé*, usually translated as *Time Regained*.}

12. On "applying Zen to music" and the themes of the instant, duration, and repetition in the music of John Cage, see John Cage, *For the Birds: In Conversation with David Charles* (Boston: Marion Boyars, 1981), 47–48.

13. These lines, taken from Edgar Allan Poe's play *Scenes from Politian* (scene 6, lines 39–41), are quoted by Gaston Bachelard in *The Dialectic of Duration*, trans. Mary McAllester Jones (Manchester: Clinamen Press, 2000), 53. For Bachelard, the "knowledge of duration" is possible only by emphasizing "the contingency of an innermost experience," "isolating the centers of psychic crystallization." Barthes gives the reference to the bibliographical note provided in Bachelard's text.

14. An actor, dramatist, and theoretician of Nô theater, Zeami (1363–1443) wrote a collection of treatises on the theater, the most famous of which is *The Mirror and the Flower* (1424).

15. The article entitled "Gesto" by Jean-Loup appeared in the *Enciclopedia Einaudi* (1979), 775–797. The quotation from Jacques Lecoq (1921–1999) comes from Odette Aslan's *L'Acteur au XXe siècle* (Paris, 1974); the quotation by Jacques-Dalcroze (1865–1950) below comes from Georges Mounin's *Introduction à la sémiologie* (Paris, 1970).

16. In "To the Seminar," Barthes writes: "Michelet opposed the Guelph to the Ghibelline. The Guelph is the man of the Law, the man of the Code, the Legist, the Scribe, the Jacobin, the Frenchman (shall we add the intellectual?). The Ghibelline is the man of the feudal line, of the oath sworn in blood, the man of affective devotion," *The Rustle of Language*, 340; OC 4:509.

17. Francis Bacon, *Novum Organum*, in *The Works of Francis Bacon* (Philadelphia: Carey and Hart, 1841), 3:348.

18. The first line of Verlaine's "Chanson d'autumn" ["Autumn Song"], in *Poèmes saturiens* (1867), in *Paul Verlaine: Selected Poems*, trans. Martin Sorrell (Oxford: Oxford University Press, 1999), 25.

19. Guillaume Apollinaire, "Poem Read at the Marriage of André Salmon" (1909), in *Alcools* (1913), in *Selected Writings of Guillaume Apollinaire*, trans. Roger Shattock (New York: New Directions, 1971), 88. Cited by Georges Schehadé, *Anthologie du vers unique* (Paris: Ramsay, 1977), 16.

20. Alfred de Vigny, "Dolorida," in *Poèmes antiques et modernes* (1826). Cited in Schehadé, *Anthologie du vers unique*, 16.

21. See p. 70–72.

22. Maurice Coyaud, *Fourmis sans ombre. Le Livre du haiku* (Paris: Phébus, 1978), 17.

23. Circumstance: from the Latin *circumstantia*, "the action of surrounding" (*circumstare*, to surround).

24. *Thetic*: from the Greek *thētikos*, "what is set down, laid out, arranged"; the origin of *thesis* in philosophy.

25. Marcel Proust, *In Search of Lost Time*, vol. 5: *The Captive, The Fugitive*, trans. C. K. Moncrieff and Terence Kilmartin, rev. D. J. Enright (London: Chatto and Windus, 1992), 136–137.

Session of February 3, 1979

1. Exhibition entitled "*Ma*. Espace / temps du Japon" ("*Ma*. Space / Time of Japan"), organized by the Musée des arts décoratifs de Paris (Autumn 1978). At the organizer's request, Barthes wrote an itinerary of the exhibition for the catalogue in which he links each space to a figure of *Ma* (see OC 5:479–480). See also "L'Intervalle," *Nouvel Observateur* (October 23, 1978); OC 5:475–478.

2. On the links between the incident and the haiku, see the chapter on this topic in *Empire of Signs*, trans. Richard Howard (New York: Hill and Wang, 1982), 77–84. In a text on Pierre Loti written in 1971, Barthes also wrote: "The incident . . . is simply *what falls* gently, like a leaf, on life's carpet; it is that faint, fugitive crease given to the fabric of days; it is what can be *just barely* noted: a kind of notation degree zero, precisely what is needed to be able to write *something*." In "Pierre Loti: *Aziyadé*," in *New Critical Essays*, trans. Richard Howard (New York: Hill and Wang, 1980), 108; OC 4:107–120. The notations that Barthes wrote in Morocco during 1969–1970 were also entitled "Incidents"; OC 5:955–976.

3. *Tangibilia*: from *tangibilis*, "what can be touched, is palpable." On the object reduced, tamed, made familiar by the encyclopedic enterprise, see "Image, Reason, Unreason," preface to *L'Univers de l'Encyclopédie* (1964), reprinted in *New Critical Essays* (1972); OC 4:41–54.

4. Barthes lists a number of objects in a text entitled "Arcimboldo ou rhétoriquer et magicien," preface to *Arcimboldo*, ed. Maria Ricci (Parme-Paris: "Les Signes de l'Homme," 1978); OC 5:493–511.

5. From "La vigne et la maison" (1856), in *Poèmes du cours familier de littérature*. Cited by Georges Schehadé, *Anthologie du vers unique* (Paris: Ramsay, 1977), 5.

6. From "Alcandre plainte la captivité de sa maîtresse" (1609). Cited in Schehadé, *Anthologie du vers unique*, 6.

7. "Think, Céphise, think, of that cruel night which proved / For our whole nation an eternal night." From Jean Racine, *Andromache*, act 3, scene 8. In Jean Racine, *Five Plays*, trans. Kenneth Muir (New York: Hill and Wang, 1960).

8. Thomas De Quincey, *Confessions of an English Opium-Eater*. Vol. 3 of *The Collected Writings of Thomas De Quincey*, rev. ed., ed. David Masson (Edinburgh: Adam and Charles Black, 1890).

9. Paul Valéry, "Le Cimetière marin," in *Charmes* (1922).

10. "His books resulted from good ideas, ideas for good paintings if you like, for he often conceived of one art in the form of another, from a good pictorial effect, then, a grand pictorial idea." Marcel Proust, "Sainte-Beuve and Balzac," in *Against Sainte-Beuve*, trans. John Sturrock (London: Penguin, 1988), 68.

11. Synaesthesia: from *sunaisthēsis*, "simultaneous perception." The citation is from Baudelaire's poem "Correspondences," in *Les Fleurs du mal*, trans. Richard Howard (Boston: Godine, 1982), 15.

12. "Urt Diary." A different version was published as "Deliberation," in *The Rustle of Language*, trans. Richard Howard (New York: Hill and Wang, 1986); OC 5:668–681.

13. Ibid., 365 {translation modified}. For Daisetz Teitaro Suzuki, the Sabi is "the spirit of Eternal Loneliness which is the spirit of the Zen expresses itself under the name of sabi in the various artistic developments of life such as landscape gardening, tea ceremony, tea-room, painting, flower arrangement, dressing, furniture, in the mode of living, No-dancing, poetry. This spirit comprises of [sic] elements such as simplicity, naturalness, unconventionality, refinement freedom, familiarity singularly tinged with aloofness, and everyday commonness which is veiled exquisitely with the mist of transcendental inwardness." Daisetz Teitaro Suzuki, *Essays on Zen Buddhism* (London: Luzac, 1934), 3:320.

14. Paragraph crossed out by Barthes.

15. Marc Legrand, "La Fraternité" (April 8, 1896). The article was written to mark the publication of a new collected edition of the *Histoires naturelles* (Paris: Flammarion, 1896) that had previously appeared as a series. Maurice Coyaud probably found this anecdote in Jules Renard's *Journal* (entry dated November 20, 1895). Jules Renard, *Journal, 1887–1910* (Paris: Gallimard, "Bibliothèque de la Pléiade," 1969), 301. One example of Renard's "brief notations" would be the last passage of "Une Famille d'arbres" ("A Family of Trees"): "I already know how to watch the clouds going by / I also know how to stay still / And I almost know how to keep quiet." Jules Renard, *Histoires naturelles*, in *Oeuvres* (Paris: Gallimard, 1971), 163.

16. Barthes went to Japan for the first time in 1966 and returned on a number of occasions between 1966 and 1970. See also *Empire of Signs* (1970); OC 3:347–444.

17. Sentence crossed out by Barthes.

Session of February 10, 1979

1. Kazuyoshi Yoshikawa refers to this "discovered note" in his article "Vinteuil ou la genèse du Septuor," *Cahiers Marcel Proust* 9 (Paris: Gallimard, 1979), 259–347. The reference comes from a partial transcription of notebooks number 53 and 55, which are held in the Bibliothèque Nationale de Paris. The "additional note" is a transcription of notebook 53, p. 15v, extracted from Kazuyoshi Yoshikawa's doctoral thesis, *La Genèse de la Prisonnière* (Paris-Sorbonne, Vol. II), 208.

2. Though let us not forget Mme de Sazerat's or M. Galopin's dog, fetched from Lisieux ("A very friendly animal," Françoise observes); see *In Search of Lost Time*, vol. 1: *Swann's Way*, trans. C. K. Scott Moncrieff and Terence Kilmartin, rev. D. J. Enright (London: Chatto and Windus, 1992), 68.

3. Interview with Marcel Proust by Elie-Joseph Bois, *Le Temps* (November 13, 1913). Published as an appendix to *Choix des lettres*, ed. Philip Kolb, preface by Jacques Lacretelle (Paris: Plon, 1965), 288.

4. In his discussion of Eisenstein's photograms, Barthes introduces the notion of "obtuse sense" (that "which carries a certain emotion"). In his attempts to describe what touches him (what *pricks* him), Barthes can only come up with the haiku, which is both "elliptical and emphatic," "an anaphoric gesture without significant content." "The Third Meaning," in *The Responsibility of Forms*, trans. Richard Howard (Berkeley: University of California Press, 1985), 56; OC 3:501.

5. Apollinaire, "Clotilde," in *Alcools: Poems 1898–1913*, trans. William Meredith (New York: Doubleday, 1964), 69. {translation modified}

6. Sentence crossed out by Barthes.

7. Pierre de Ronsard, "Maîtresse; embrasse-moi . . ." in *Sonnets for Hélène* (1578). Cited in Georges Schehadé, *Anthologie du vers unique* (Paris: Ramsay, 1977), 18.

8. Oscar Vladislas de Lubicz-Milosz, "Les Terrains vagues," in *Andramandoni* (1917). Cited in Schehadé, *Anthologie du vers unique*, 48.

9. See p. 64.

10. *Aujourd'hui ou les Coréens* {*Today or the Koreans*} (1958) by Michael Vinaver narrates the story of a French solider injured while on patrol in North Korea; the solider is taken in by Korean peasants and remains with them. Barthes was very taken by Vinaver's writing and wrote a number of texts about the play when it was staged by Roger Planchon, notably in *Théâtre Populaire*: "*Aujourd'hui* presents a new ideological problem: that of an assent to the world, postulated outside of humanist alibis and mystifications" (April 1956). See "Notes sur *Aujourd'hui*" and "*Aujourd'hui ou les Coréens*," OC 1:646–649, 1:666–667.

11. Maurice Blanchot, "The Absence of the Book," in *The Infinite Conversation*, trans. Susan Hanson (Minneapolis: University of Minnesota Press), 303. {translation modified}

Session of February 17, 1979

1. Orally, Barthes makes the following distinction: "The real is what's demonstrable, reality is based on illusion." For the distinction between the "real" and "reality" according to Jacques Lacan, which Barthes only mentions here, see Lacan's Seminars V and XX, published by the Éditions du Seuil.

2. On the power of the "notation" to signify the real, Barthes writes: "just when these details [in Flaubert or Michelet] are reputed to *denote* the real directly, all that they do—without saying so—is *signify* it; Flaubert's barometer, Michelet's little door finally say nothing but this: *we are the real*; it is the category of the 'real' ... which is then signified." "The Reality Effect," in *The Rustle of Language*, trans. Richard Howard (New York: Hill and Wang, 1986), 148; OC 3:25–32.

3. Passage already cited by Barthes; see the note to page 59.

4. This passage on photography constitutes the outline of what Barthes would develop further a few months later in *La Chambre claire, note pour la photographie*, written between April 15 and June 3, 1979, after the Course was finished. *Camera Lucida: Reflections on Photography*, trans. Richard Howard (New York: Hill and Wang, 1981) See, in particular, the attempt to identify the "noeme of photography." These remarks can also be read alongside Barthes's other writings on photography from 1953 onward; for the links between photography and Zen teachings, see his text on Richard Avedon, "Tels" (1977); OC 5:299–302.

5. In a text on Ferdinand de Saussure, Barthes evokes the difficulties that Saussure encountered when founding a linguistic model. Barthes talks of a "little scientific crisis, in that the lacuna of signification caused the linguist so much suffering." He also mentions Saussure's work on anagrams: "[He] can already *hear* the modernity in the phonic and semantic buzzing of archaic verses: so, more agreement, more clarity, more analogy, more value.... We know how much hearing this panicked Saussure, who as a result seems to have spent his life oscillating between anxiety over the lost signified and the terrifying return of the pure signifier." "Saussure, le signe, la démocratie" (1973); OC 4:329–333.

6. Reference to the seminar following the lectures; that year, the theme was the "Labyrinth." See Barthes's introductory text, p. 000. Pascal Bonitzer was invited to participate in the session of January 27, 1979.

7. These reflections are developed at length in *Camera Lucida*, esp. 76–77.

8. "Bernard Faucon *arranges* the scene that he is going to photograph. With great precision, he produces a tableau vivant. Now, he entrusts this immobile scene to the very art of the Immobile ... he makes a photograph which *doubles up* as a tableau vivant: he accumulates two immobilities." Roland Barthes, "Bernard Faucon" (1978); OC 5:472.

9. Barthes is referring here to his experience of filming *Les Soeurs Brontës*, directed by André Téchiné (which came out in 1979), in which he plays William Thackeray, the English novelist and critic (1811–1864).

10. See Pierre Legendre, "Où sont nos droits poétiques?" *Cahiers du cinéma* 297 (February 1979).

11. The *urdoxa*, the foundation of phenomenology, is "the study of 'phenomena,' of *that* which appears to consciousness, of *that* which is 'given.' It is a matter of exploring this given, 'the thing itself' that we perceive." Jean-François Lyotard, *La Phénoménologie* (Paris: Presses Universitaires de France, "Que sais-je?" [1954], 1976), 5.

12. Although the argument of *Camera Lucida* (which Barthes wrote a few weeks after "The Preparation of the Novel I") is based on a selection of photographs

drawn from a number of different works and revues—notably from *Photo* (nos. 124 and 138)—Barthes's analysis is particularly linked to some photographs of his mother as a child, to which he is probably referring here.

13. *Semelfactive*: "what took place once." From *semel*, adverb "once, the first time, initially."

14. Reference to Emile Benveniste's definition of the sign: "Taken in itself, the sign is pure self-identity, pure alterity with regard to anything else, meaningful basis of language, material necessary for enunciation. It exists when it is recognized by all members of a scientific community." In "La Communication," *Problèmes de linguistique générale* 2 (1969) (Paris: Gallimard, "Bibliothèque des idées," 1966; "Tel," 1974), 64.

15. Émile Benveniste, *Problems in General Linguistics*, trans. Mary Elizabeth Meek (Coral Gables, Fla.: University of Miami Press, 1971), 208.

16. Orally, Barthes put these two questions differently, saying: "It's the moment when the real is elevated by a 5–7–5. The meter is the operator that suspends the descent into the real."

17. See Giambattista Vico's *New Science*, esp. book 2: "Poetic wisdom." According to Vico, "poetic science founded the human race." The history of ideas has its source in "man's natural disposition" to interpret the world and to make sense of it using his imagination. See also the book that Barthes consulted and that features in the inventory of his library: Jules Chaix-Ruy, *La Formation de la pensée philosophique chez Vico*: "Vico . . . makes imaginative knowledge or poetic wisdom the primary form of all knowledge; for this reason, he considers it more profound and more creative than intellectual or considered knowledge" (Paris: Presses Universitaires de France, 1943), 68.

18. Paul Claudel, "Lecture d'*Odyssée*," *Le Figaro Littéraire* (September 20, 1947). Quoted by Georges Cattaui in his preface to George D. Painter's *Marcel Proust* (Paris: Mercure de France, 1966), 21.

19. See note 6, p. 32.

20. The asyndeton is a particular kind of ellipsis characterized by the absence of linking words, conjunctions, or adverbs between propositions or syntactical groups that are nevertheless linked by a logical connection. The parataxis is a juxtaposition of propositions dependant on one another but where there is no explanation of what links them. The great originality of Etienne de Condillac's (1714–1780) thought was to assign language a function not only of expression but also of structuring thought: the relationship between a language's signs and ideas is arbitrary, a product of our faculties of abstraction and combination—this last idea played an essential role in the development of Condillac's theories, which went so far as presenting the psyche as an effect of the combination of sensations and the expression of their transformation in language. For Vico, see note 17.

21. The Alexandra is a cocktail made with crème fraîche. Monsieur Boeuf is a famous restaurant near Les Halles, in the first arrondissement in Paris, that Barthes frequented and where they serve a champagne and marshmallow cocktail. The marshmallow is a plant of the Malvaceae family; the hollyhock is a variety of marshmallow.

Session of February 24, 1979

1. {The expression Barthes is using is *tilt*, the bell-signal that goes off to indicate the end or momentary interruption of a game of pinball. *Faire tilt* means to set that signal off and, figuratively, to suddenly capture one's attention.}

2. Sentence crossed out by Barthes.

3. Extract from Émile Zola's famous letter to Henri Céard on the subject of *Germinal* (May 22, 1885). {This passage partially is quoted (and translated) by

Roger Pearson in his introduction to his translation of *Germinal* (London: Penguin 2004), xxxv. See Émile Zola, *Correspondance*, ed. B. H. Bakker (Montreal, 1978–1995), 5:249.}

4. Paraphrase of the fable "The Frogs Who Asked for a King" (Jean de la Fontaine).

5. See p. 104.

6. On the subject of *Wu-shi*, Alan Watts also says: "lack of affectation," "simplicity." See *The Way of Zen* (London: Thames and Hudson, 1957), 148.

7. See pp. 42–43.

8. Watts, *The Way of Zen*, 182–183.

9. Maurice Blanchot, "The Failure of the Demon: The Vocation," in *The Book to Come*, trans. Charlotte Mandell (Stanford, Calif.: Stanford University Press, 2003), 100.

10. Angelus Silesius, *The Cherubinic Wanderer*, trans. Maria Shrady (New York: Paulist Press, 1986), 62.

11. John Cage, *For the Birds: In Conversation with David Charles* (Boston: Marion Boyars, 1981), 56. On the Hindu theory of emotions, Cage explains: "For there to be . . . an aesthetic emotion on the part of the listener, the work must evoke one of the permanent modes of emotion"; he goes on to list "the nine permanent emotions," one of which is tranquility: "Tranquility lies between the four 'white' modes and the four 'black' modes; it is their normal propensity. That is why it is important to express it before the others, without even worrying about expressing the others. It is the most important emotion." Cage, *For the Birds*, 103.

12. See *The Neutral*, ed. Thomas Clerc under the direction of Eric Marty, trans. Rosalind E. Krauss and Denis Hollier (New York: Columbia University Press, 2005), 95–105. The session on "Consciousness" proposes two objects of study: "(1) Intellectualist hyperconsciousness, entirely absorbed by its own reflexivity. (2) This hyperconsciousness insofar as it stands out against an affective background."

13. In linguistics (Hjelmslev), commutation is an operation of substitution on the paradigmatic axis that enables the identification of phonological units that are otherwise difficult to dissociate. Barthes uses this procedure in order to identify the qualities particular to the haiku.

14. {The French term *pointe* (which translates the Italian *concetto* or, in English, "conceit") can also mean a jab or prick.}

15. Barthes translated this epigram into French during the lecture. {A translation of his translation would read: "I don't love you, Sabidius, but I can't say why / I can only say: I don't love you."}

16. Although not by name, Barthes is referring to a critic who—advisedly, in Barthes's view—spoke of Michelet's "vertical style."

17. See the passage on Jules Renard, p. 60.

18. Jules Renard's *Natural Histories* inspired Maurice Ravel to write his song cycle for the piano (1907).

19. Tale from the Nagoya region of Japan, extracted from *Choix de cents contes japonais* (Tokyo: Sanseido, 1975) and quoted in Maurice Coyaud, *Fourmis sans ombre. Le Livre du haiku* (Paris: Phébus, 1978), 39–40.{A shorter version of the story, in English, can be found in Keiko Sheigo, *Folktales of Japan* (Chicago: Chicago University Press, 1963), 183–186.}

Session of March 3, 1979

1. The *gestus* is at the center of the Brechtian theatrical dialectic; it designates a figure of the body that expresses the state of social relationships and, in a singular fashion, translates the determining relationship between the individual and the community.

2. "This could work as the outline of a chapter of a novel," comments Barthes, explaining the phenomenon of "diastole," that is, relaxation, the possibility of extending a haiku.

3. Orally: "Between haiku and narrative, there is this movement, this double movement, which is so important for our understanding of the theoretical problem of enunciation, or at least of discursivity; a double movement that could come under a double rhetorical figure: ellipsis, a figure of condensation, and catalysis, a figure of expansion."

4. Gustave Flaubert, "A Simple Heart," in *Three Tales*, trans. Roger Whitehouse (London: Penguin, 2005), 5. This extract does not appear in the manuscript; Barthes read it aloud during the lecture.

5. {*peut passer dans* can mean both "pass into" and "pass" in the sense of "be accepted"}

6. {*Scoops* in English in the text.}

7. See pp. 97–100.

8. After a short digression on the different temptations that sometimes distract him from his work, Barthes tells the audience that he had wanted the Latin saying to be inscribed on his letterhead. Although the formulation would appear to say, "Nothing, other than what I am told to do," Barthes clarifies that what it really means is "Nothing, other than what I tell myself to do."

9. Barthes often refers to this image; see, among others, *All Except You* (on Saul Steinberg): "All of Nicholas de Staël's work comes out of a few square centimeters of Cézanne, assuming they were enlarged: meaning depends on the *level of perception*." OC 4:968; for other contexts, see also OC 4:230 and 4:395.

10. Paul Valéry, *Variety*, trans. Malcolm Cowley (New York: Harcourt, Brace, 1927), 172.

11. Charles Baudelaire, *Artificial Paradise: On Hashish and Wine as Means of Expanding Individuality*, trans. Ellen Fox (New York: Herder and Herder, 1971), 21–22.

Session of March 10, 1979

1. Guy de Maupassant, *Pierre and Jean*, trans. Julie Mead (Oxford: Oxford University Press, 2001), 21.

2. Honoré de Balzac, *The Girl with the Golden Eyes*, trans. Carol Cosman (New York: Carroll and Graf Publishers, 1998), 56.

3. *Semel vel mutum*: "once or many times."

4. E. M. Cioran, *La Tentation d'exister* (Paris: Gallimard, 1956), 117.

5. "Always the agitated, anxious crowd, the clash of weapons, the pomp of the outfits, the grandiloquent truth of the gesture on life's grand occasions! . . . for no one, since Shakespeare, excels like Delacroix in dissolving drama and daydream into a mysterious unity," writes Charles Baudelaire on *Les Croisés* by Delacroix (1855); *Oeuvres complètes* (Paris: Gallimard, "Bibliothèque de la Pléiade," 1961), 970. Barthes cites this passage from Baudelaire throughout his work, from the text on the mythology of wrestling to the lecture entitled "Longtemps, je me suis couché de bonne heure," delivered in 1978.

6. Gustav Janouch, *Conversations with Kafka*, 2nd ed., trans. Goronwy Rees (New York: New Directions, 1971), 115–116.

7. Paul Valéry taught at the Collège de France between 1937 (his inaugural lecture was delivered on December 10) and 1945. Barthes often mentions attending some of Valéry's lectures. See Paul Valéry, *Introduction à la poétique* (Paris: NRF-Gallimard, 1938), which contains the programmatic text from February 1937 entitled "De l'Enseignement de la poétique au Collège de France" and the inaugural lecture "Cours de poétique." Barthes has also said with reference to himself: "I have a disease: I *see* language." Roland Barthes, *Roland*

Barthes, trans. Richard Howard (New York: Hill and Wang, 1977), 161; *OC* 4:735.

8. {A "*contraction de texte*," literally a "contraction of text," is a précis or summary.}

9. Philippe Sollers, *Paradis* (Paris: Seuil, 1978).

10. Along with his fellow disciple Alban Berg (1885–1935), Anton von Webern (1883–1945) was a student of Arnold Schönberg's from 1904 on. An emblematic figure of modernity, Webern radicalized the propositions of the Vienna School through the refinement of musical structure. Brevity (his longest work, *Cantate* [opus 31], lasts only eleven minutes), the stretching-out of intervals, and the use of silence were the key features of his aesthetic. Anton von Webern presented *Five Pieces* [opus 1] to Alban Berg in 1913, and the dedication reads: "*Non multa sed multum* [little in quantity, much in quality], how I wish that could apply to what I offer you here." Guided by that same motto, Barthes makes a link between Webern and Cy Twombly's painting. See "Cy Twombly ou *Non multa sed multum*," text for the catalogue of Cy Twombly's works on paper (1979); *OC* 5:703–720. The reference to the German music critic Heinz-Klaus Metzger is taken from John Cage, *For the Birds: In Conversation with David Charles* (Boston: Marion Boyars, 1981), 39.

11. Barthes frequently refers to the standard work *Les Sophistes: Fragments et témoignages* (Paris: Presses Universitaires de France, 1969), which contains references to these authors.

12. See Roland Barthes, "Cy Twombly ou *Non multa sed multum*," together with "Sagesse de l'art," text written for the catalogue of the Cy Twombly retrospective organized by the Whitney Museum in 1979 (*OC* 5:688–702), in which Barthes develops the notion of *Rarus* as "the key to Twombly's art. . . . Rarity engenders density and the density of the enigma." Both of the texts on Twombly conclude with an evocation of *Tao*.

13. This is the last lecture of the Lecture Course: running out of time, Barthes skipped a few pages of notes: "There's no great loss, this will perhaps be the subject of another lecture later on."

14. "We are delivered to the sentence," wrote Barthes in 1973 in *The Pleasure of the Text*, trans. Annette Lavers and Colin Smith (New York: Hill and Wang, 1973); *OC* 4:250. For Barthes's different approaches to this subject over the course of his career, see, among others: *Sade, Fourier, Loyola* (1971); "Style and Its Image" (1971); "Flaubert and the Sentence" (1972); *Roland Barthes* (1975); *A Lover's Discourse: Fragments* (1977); "Tant que la langue vivra" (1979).

15. Noam Chomsky, American linguist (born in 1928). Chomsky's works develop a theory of linguistic structure based on a universalism of linguistic forms: we all possess an innate general linguistic competence, exercised in a singular linguistic performance. See his *Syntactic Structures* (1957) and also *Aspects of the Theory of Syntax* (1965).

16. Gustave Flaubert, letter to George Sand (December 4, 1872), *Correspondance*, vol. 4 (Paris: Gallimard, "Bibliothèque de la Pléiade," 1998) {translation modified}. Barthes is probably citing from the selected correspondence edited by Geneviève Bollème, *Préface à la vie d'écrivain* (Paris: Seuil, 1963). Barthes devoted one of the columns published in the *Nouvel Observateur* to Flaubert's declaration; *OC* 5:643.

17. On this, see "Flaubert and the Sentence" (1968), written in homage to André Martinet. Republished in *New Critical Essays* [1972]; *OC* 4:78–85.

18. End of the passage cut by Barthes.

19. Patrick Mauriès, writer and art critic, was Barthes's student and one of his closest friends. Richard Ellmann, *James Joyce* (Oxford: Oxford University Press, 1959).

20. Thomas Aquinas (1228–1274) was an extremely important influence on James Joyce's works, as is already clear from *Stephen Hero* (1904). The quotation is given in Ellmann, *James Joyce*, 353. John Duns Scott (c. 1265–1308) was a philosopher and theologian, a talented dialectician and a critic of Aristotelianism and Thomism; he was Scottish, though he was often thought to be Irish.

21. All these quotations are taken from Ellmann, *James Joyce*, 87.

22. An extract from a notebook held in the Joyce collection at Cornell; cited in ibid., 88.

23. Cited in ibid., 132.

24. Friedrich Nietzsche, *The Will to Power*, trans. Walter Kaufmann and R. J. Hollingdale (New York: Vintage, 1968), 301.

25. See Ellmann, *James Joyce*, 88.

26. Between December 8, 1978, and March 26, 1979, Barthes published a weekly column in *Le Nouvel Observateur* (OC 5:625–653).

27. Michel de Montaigne, book I, chapter 31, "On the Cannibals," in *The Complete Essays*, ed. and trans. M. A. Screech (London: Penguin, 2003), 230.

28. The lecture in question, entitled "Longtemps, je me suis couché de bonne heure," was delivered at the Collège de France on October 19, 1978 in *The Rustle of Language*, trans. Richard Howard (New York: Hill and Wang, 1986); OC 5:459–470. The article, entitled "Ça prend," appeared in *Magazine Littéraire* 144 (January 1979); OC 5:654–656.

29. {Center for the history and analysis of modern manuscripts}. Now the Institut des textes et manuscrits modernes (ITEM), Paris.

30. *Marcottage* is a horticultural term; a method of propagating trees or bushes whereby one of the higher branches is planted in the ground and forms another root. Barthes gives this name to "composition by enjambments where an insignificant detail provided at the beginning of the novel reappears at the end, having as it were grown, germinated, blossomed." See "Ça prend"; OC 5:656.

31. See aspects of the paper "Longtemps, je me suis couché de bonne heure" (OC 5:459–470) that Barthes repeats and develops here.

32. "We were reading one day, for pleasure, of / Lancelot, how love beset him; we were alone and / without any suspicion. / Many times that reading drove our eyes / together and turned our faces pale; but one point / alone was the one that overpowered us. / When we read that the yearned-for smile was / kissed by so great a lover, he, who will never be / separated from me, / kissed my mouth all trembling Galeotto was the / book and he who wrote it: that day we read there no / further.' Dante, *The Divine Comedy of Dante Alighieri*, vol. 1: *Inferno* (canto 5, lines 127–138), ed. and trans. Robert M. Durling (Oxford: Oxford University Press, 1996), 93.

33. *Graziella*, by Alphonse de Lamartine, was initially conceived in 1844 as a commentary on the poem "Le Premier regret" but, in 1849, became one of the episodes in *Confidences*. As in Bernardin de Saint-Pierre's *Paul and Virginie* (1788), the narrative of *Graziella* is based around the tension between the paradisiacal island and the hell of society, between the ambiguity of the twins' love for each other and the heroine's angelic identity; in both cases, an elegiac and mournful love story binds two lovers with what is professed to be a pure, brotherly love, and in both cases the lovers' separation will have fatal consequences. It is precisely "a moment of truth taken from a book, related within a book, the former appearing *en abyme* in the latter" (evoked by Barthes above), that sets up the thoroughly "homological relationship" between the two works, since it is having *Paul and Virginie* read aloud to her every evening that awakens Graziella's passion: "When I came to that part of the book where Virginia, recalled to France by her aunt, feels as though her very soul is being rent asunder, and forces herself to console Paul under the banana trees, speaking to him of a return, and pointing out the sea that is to carry her away, I closed the vol-

ume and postponed further reading til the morrow. This was a blow at the very heart.... Graziella fell on her knees before, then before my friend, to beg of us to finish the story. But she pleaded in vain. We wished to prolong the interest for her, and the delight in watching it for ourselves. Then she snatched the book from my hands; she opened it as if she would, by the very force of her will, decipher the characters before her. She talked to it; she kissed it; she returned it with a respectful air to its place on my knees, while she joined her hands and looked up at my face pitifully. Her features, usually so serene and smiling, but a little severe in their impassibility, had suddenly taken from the passion and sympathetic tenderness of the recital something of the animation, the confusion and pathos of the story. It seemed as though a sudden revolution had metamorphosed this beautiful piece of marble into humanity and tears. The young girl felt her soul, that had slept until this time, revealing itself to her as the soul of Virginia." *Graziella: A Story of Italian Love*, trans. James B. Runnion (Chicago: Jansen, McClurg and Co., 1886), 98–99.

34. {Reference to the French painter Jean-Baptiste Greuze (1725–1805), who initiated the mid-eighteenth-century vogue for sentimental and moralizing anecdotes in paintings.}

35. Marcel Proust, *In Search of Lost Time*, vol. 1: *Swann's Way*, trans. C. K. Scott Moncrieff and Terence Kilmartin, rev. D. J. Enright (London: Chatto and Windus, 1992), 10–12.

36. Barthes evokes the automaton in Fellini's *Casanova* in *La Chambre claire*: "my eyes were touched with a kind of painful and delicious intensity ... each detail, which I was seeing so exactly, savoring it, so to speak, down to its last evidence, overwhelmed me." *Camera Lucida*, trans. Richard Howard (New York: Hill and Wang, 1981), 116; OC 5:882.

37. In the lecture "Longtemps, je me suis couché de bonne heure," Barthes asks: "What Lucifer created *at the same time* love and death?" In *The Rustle of Language*, trans. Richard Howard (New York: Hill and Wang, 1986), 287; OC 5:468.

38. This is a key notion in Diderot's theory of painting as he develops it in the "Response to Mademoiselle Delacroix," *Lettre sur les sourds et muets* (1751), and the article on "Composition" in the *Encyclopaedia* (1753): according to Diderot, in his treatment of his subject, the painter must identify the instant or moment that condenses the events of the past and contains those about to happen. In Courtin's 1866 translation of *Laocoon* into French, Lessing calls this instant or moment the *fecund* instant. Roger Lewinter, the author of the "Introductions" to Diderot's *Oeuvres complètes*, qualifies this instant of "artificial, syncretic time, a reflection on the past, exposition of the present and announcement of the future." Lewinter stresses Diderot's influence on Lessing and, rather than the *fecund* instant (Courtin), talks of the *pregnant* instant. See Denis Diderot, *Oeuvres complètes* (Paris: Club français du livre, 1970), 542.

39. In *Diderot, Brecht, Eisenstein* (1973), Barthes explains: "It is a gesture, or an ensemble of gestures (but never a gesticulation) in which an entire social situation can be discerned." OC 3:341.

Introductory Session of December 2, 1978

1. In "Linguistics and Poetics," Roman Jakobson identifies six different functions of language; the "impressive" (or "connotative") function designates all those procedures whereby the aim is not to inform (expressive function) but rather to involve the addressee. Thus, every form of address to the reader or the spectator has to do with the impressive function of language. The advertisement's message exemplifies the use of the impressive function, because it is in the first instance based on an identification with the audience it is addressing.

2. Pierre Rosenstiehl, mathematician and member of the Oulipo, director of studies at the Centre d'analyse et de mathématique sociales (EHESS), works on modelization in the human sciences. His intervention in the seminar was published in an exhibition catalogue entitled *Cartes et figures de la Terre* (Paris: Éditions du Centre Pompidou, 1980), 94–105. A book in French: Paolo Santarcangeli, *Le Livre des labyrinthes: Histoire d'un mythe et d'un symbole*, trans. Monique Lacau (Paris: Gallimard, 1974) → Quite a confused book, primarily an archaeological and ethnological dossier; very little on the symbolic, and banal, we'll come back to this. [*Note by Roland Barthes. References to this book are given by an S followed by the page number in the margin of the lecture notes.*]

3. Jean Racine, *Phaedra*, in *Five Plays*, trans. Kenneth Muir (London: Macgibbon and Kee, 1960), act 2, scene 5 for the first citation (197); act 1, scene 3 for the second (186).

4. Hawara, situated in the Fayyum in Egypt, is famous for the second pyramid that King Amenemhat III of the Twelfth Dynasty built there to contain him for the afterlife. According to Herodotos, the pyramid's funerary temple comprised thousands of chambers organized around a great many courtyards, following an extremely complex plan. It was this vast construction that impressed the Greeks; they named it "Hawara's labyrinth."

5. The exhibition, *Le Surréalisme en 1947: Exposition internationale du surréalisme*, introduced by André Breton and Marcel Duchamp, took place at the Galerie Maeght, Paris, between July 7 and September 30, 1947.

6. Paolo Santarcangeli, *Le Livre des labyrinthes*.

7. Mentioned in Santarcangeli's *Le Livre des labyrinthes*, which refers to W. H. Matthews's *Mazes and Labyrinths* (London, 1922).

8. Marcel Brion, "Hoffmannsthal et l'expérience du labyrinthe," *Cahiers du Sud* 133 (1955).

9. {Émile Littré's *Dictionnaire de la langue française*.}

10. Reference to the *Verleugnung*, the Freudian figure of the disavowal of reality, which Freud develops in *An Outline of Psychoanalysis* (Standard Edition, vol. 23). See also Octave Mannoni "Je sais bien mais quand même...," *Les Temps Modernes* 212 (January 1964); reprinted in *Clefs pour l'imaginaire ou l'autre scène* (Paris: Seuil, 1969).

11. Friedrich Nietzsche, aphorism 169, in *Daybreak: Thoughts on the Prejudices of Morality*, ed. Maudemarie Clark and Brian Letter, trans. R. J. Hollingdale (Cambridge: Cambridge University Press, 1997), 104.

12. At the end of his preface to Paul Morand's *Tendres Stocks* (1920), Proust describes his own style as his "Ariadne's thread"; cited by Léon Pierre-Quint in *Marcel Proust, sa vie, son oeuvre* (Paris: Le Sagittaire, 1925).

13. Proairesis is the ability to rationally determine the outcome of an action. Barthes defines it in the following way: "For Aristotle, praxis, a practical science which produces no work distinct from the agent (in contrast to poiesis) is based on the rational choice between two possible modes of action or proairesis." *Sade, Fourier, Loyola*, trans. Richard Miller (Baltimore, Md.: The Johns Hopkins University Press, 1997), 26fn; OC 3:722. In his reading of Balzac's "Sarrasine," the short story that generated *S/Z* (1970), Barthes identifies five codes of reading, notably the "proairetic code," the "code of actions and behaviors," which "unfolds as [the] process of naming takes place, as a title is sought or confirmed." *S/Z*, trans. Richard Miller (New York: Farrar, Strauss and Giroux, 1974), 19.

14. The program was as follows: December 9, 1978, Marcel Detienne; December 16, 1978, Gilles Deleuze; January 6, 1979, Hubert Damisch; January 13, 1979, Claire Bernard; January 20, 1979, Hélène Campan; January 27, 1979, Pascal Bonitzer; February 3, 1979, Hervé Cassan; February 10, 1979, Françoise Choay; February 17, 1979, Jean-Louis Bouttes; February 24, 1979, Pierre Rosenstiehl; March 3, 1979, Octave Mannoni. The summary in the Col-

lège de France yearbook gives the professional titles of the invited speakers and their research fields. See p. 378.

15. Sigmund Freud, "Revision of the Theory of Dreams," in *New Introductory Lectures on Psychoanalysis* (Standard Edition, vol. 22), 25.

16. Gabriel García Márquez, *One Hundred Years of Solitude*, trans. (French) by Claude Durand and Carmen Durand (Paris: Seuil, 1968); Éric Marty recommended that Barthes read it.

17. {"Lebrun" translates as "The Brown," "Charpentier" as "Carpenter"} "Lefebvre" is a variation of *fèvre*, meaning "smith" or "blacksmith" in old French.

18. Catachresis is a rhetorical figure where a word is used in a metaphor, metonymy, or synecdoche to designate something for which no literal term exists.

19. On the poetic origins of humanity according to Vico, see Barthes's comments on pp. 75–76.

Concluding Session of March 10, 1979

1. Orally, Barthes adds: "Around 1963–64, for personal reasons . . . I planned to undertake a semiology of clothing." This project was conceived in the context of research begun in 1955 under the supervision of Georges Freidmann on the subject of "the symbolism of clothes"; the result was the publication of *The Fashion System* in 1967.

2. Octave Mannoni, the invited speaker for the preceding session (March 3, 1979), opposed literality "which doesn't admit of any possible transformation" to comprehension, defined as the "possibility or illusion that the text could be replaced by another text which says the same thing" (sound recording of the seminar, © Seuil).

Session of December 1, 1979

1. In the section entitled "*Impossibilia*" in *Sade, Fourier, Loyola*, Barthes argues that it is impossible for a book to evoke the real: "everything is left to the power of discourse. This little-considered power is not merely evocative but also negative. Language has this property of denying, ignoring, dissociating reality: when written, shit does not have an odor; Sade can inundate his partners in it, we receive not the slightest whiff, only the abstract sign of something unpleasant." *Sade, Fourier, Loyola*, trans. Richard Miller (Baltimore, Md.: The Johns Hopkins University Press, 1997), 136–137.

2. This is a transcription of the passage that Barthes read out to his audience, from Chateaubriand, *Mémoires d'outre tombe*, ed. Maurice Levaillant and Georges Mouliné (Paris: Gallimard, "Bibliothèque de la Pléaide," 1951), 1:210–211. Note that part of the passage is also cited in Marcel Proust, *In Search of Lost Time*, vol. 6: *Time Regained*, trans. Andreas Mayor and Terence Kilmartin, rev. D. J. Enright (London: Chatto and Windus, 1992), 284 {translation cited here}.

3. A full bibliography of all the works cited can be found at the end of this volume.

4. This is a transcription of a page of around thirty handwritten lines that Barthes inserted among his notes retroactively. It is probably the introduction to a paper delivered at the invitation of Antoine Compagnon at the École Polytechnique on February, 20, 1980. In all likelihood, this short text served as the introduction to the first big section of the lecture entitled "The Desire to Write," and Barthes used part of it again in his presentation at the Polytechnique. Given the care with which Barthes inserted this page into his lecture

notes (new pagination, a linking arrow, etc.), we have retranscribed the text as it appears in the manuscript.

5. François Maspero opened a bookshop called *Joie de lire* {Joy of Reading} on rue Saint-Séverin, in the fifth arrondissement of Paris; by 1978, it had already closed down.

6. Barthes is referring to the passage he read out at the beginning of the lecture, p. 128.

7. This sentence was drafted, crossed out, then eventually read out loud in the lecture.

8. Passage crossed out by Barthes.

9. Pothos, who at times is said to be the son of Zeus and Taygete (one of the Pleiades, wife of Lacedaemon and mother of Himéros) and at others the son of Aphrodite, is the personification of loving desire, more often associated with the figures of Eros and Himéros. In *A Lover's Discourse*, Barthes evokes: "*Pothos*, desire for the absent being, and *Himéros*, the more burning desire for the present being." *A Lover's Discourse: Fragments*, trans. Richard Howard (New York: Hill and Wang, 1978), 15; OC 5:43. *Volupia* is the personification of fully satisfied desire or, according to Georges Dumézil, fully satisfied will. See *La Réligion romaine archaïque* (Paris: Payot, 1974), 341–343.

10. End of the passage crossed out by Barthes.

11. Among the works by Gérard Genette, see in particular *Mimologics*, trans. Thais E. Morgan (Lincoln: University of Nebraska Press, 1994), and *Palimpsests: Literature in the Second Degree*, trans. Channa Newman and Claude Doubinsky (Lincoln: University of Nebraska Press, 1997).

12. Allusion to, among others, the *Roland Barthes sans peine* by Marc-Antoine Burnier and Patrick Rambaud (Paris: Balland, 1978).

13. Reference to Antoine Compagnon's paper entitled "L'Enthousiasme," presented on March 2, 1977, in the context of the seminar "Tenir un Discours" led by Barthes at the Collège de France. For the introduction to this seminar, see Roland Barthes, *Comment vivre ensemble*, ed. Claude Coste (Paris: Seuil, 2002).

14. On the writing of the two *Untimelys* on Schopenhauer and Wagner, Nietzsche also says: "What I did by and large was take to take two famous and still altogether undetermined types . . . in order to say something, in order to have a couple more formulas, signs, means of expression in my hands. . . . It was in this way that Plato used Socrates, as a semiotic for Plato.—Now I look back from a distance at the circumstances of which these essays are a witness, I would not wish to deny that fundamentally they speak only of me." From "The Untimely Essays," in *Ecce Homo*, trans. R. J. Hollingdale (London: Penguin, 1992), 57.

15. Barthes read out this passage (transcribed here) extracted from Marcel Proust, *Against Sainte-Beuve and Other Essays*, trans. John Sturrock (London: Penguin, 1988), 68. {translation modified}

16. Issa (1763–1827); haiku cited by Roger Munier in *Haiku*, with a preface by Yves Bonnefoy (Paris: Fayard, 1978), 79.

17. Probably the texts on art collected in *La Doublure* (Paris: Flammarion, 1982), texts that Barthes, a great friend and admirer of Severo Sarduy, would have been familiar with.

18. {*Fille de joie*, literally, "daughter of joy," is another term for a prostitute}

19. Gustave Flaubert, letter to Louise Colet (November 1847): "Fortunately my admiration for the masters grows and, far from making me despair, that crushing parallel actually rekindles this indomitable fantasy of mine to write." All Barthes's references to Flaubert's correspondence are taken from *Préface à la vie d'écrivain, ou Extraits de la correspondence*, ed. Geneviève Bollème (Paris: Seuil, 1963), 46.

20. Implicit reference to Philippe Lacoue-Labarthe and Jean-Luc Nancy, *The Literary Absolute: The Theory of Literature in German Romanticism*,

trans. Philip Barnard and Cheryl Lester (Albany: State University of New York Press, 1988).

21. Chateaubriand, *Mémoires d'outre-tombe*, 1:1148.

22. See p. 153.

23. Flaubert, letter to his niece (May 20, 1873), in *Préface à la vie d'un écrivain*, 258.

24. Flaubert, letter to Louise Colet (March 6, 1853), in ibid., 104.

25. Cited by Klaus Wagenbach, *Kafka*, trans. Ewald Osers (Cambridge, Mass.: Harvard University Press, 2003), 59.

26. On the notion of *scripturire*, see pp. 8–9.

27. Barthes inserted this paragraph of around twenty lines written on a separate piece of paper into his lecture notes. He does not refer to it in the lecture itself; this paragraph served as the conclusion to his paper delivered at the École Polytechnique on February 20, 1980. See the introductory page, *supra*, p. 130.

28. Barthes is probably referring to Freud's *Introduction to Psychoanalysis*, in particular chapters 10 and 21.

29. Jean-Pierre Richard, *Littérature et sensation*, preface by Georges Poulet (Paris: Seuil, 1954). See, in particular, the discussion of Emma Bovary's wedding meal. Barthes is perhaps also thinking of Jean-Pierre Richard's paper entitled "Plaisir de table, plaisir de texte," delivered at the conference on Roland Barthes at Cerisy-la-Salle in 1977. See *Prétexte: Roland Barthes* (Paris: UGE, 1978; Paris: Christian Bourgois, 2002), 361–382.

30. See Barthes's column entitled "Ne fumez pas" in *Le Nouvel Observateur*; OC 5:637.

31. Flaubert, letter to Louise Colet (August 16, 1847), in *Préface à la vie d'écrivain*, 45.

32. Flaubert, letter to Louise Colet (October 23, 1846), in *The Letters of Gustave Flaubert: 1830–1857*, ed. and trans. Francis Steegmuller (Cambridge, Mass.: The Belknap Press of Harvard University Press, 1979), 86–87.

Session of December 8, 1979

1. This is the moment when Proust, preoccupied with the writing of *Against Sainte-Beuve*, passes from the essay to the novel. From the correspondence, we know that the summer of 1909 was entirely given over to that enormous task, although it has since been claimed that the metamorphosis of the project occurred over a longer period.

2. See "Gérard de Nerval" and "Sainte-Beuve and Balzac," two of the essays in *Against Sainte-Beuve*. Note also that the Narrator of *Time Regained* evokes these works in the Prince de Guermante's library.

3. See, in particular, chapter 5 of *Bouvard and Pécuchet*: "Finally, they resolved to write a play. The difficult thing was the subject." Gustave Flaubert, *Bouvard and Pécuchet*, trans. A. J. Krailsheimer (Middlesex, 1976), 139.

4. On the "motley" in the German Romantic theory of literature, see Friedrich Schlegel's "Critical Fragments": "Many works that are praised for the beauty of their coherence have less unity than a motley heap of ideas simply animated by the ghost of a spirit and aiming at a single purpose" (fragment 103). Friedrich Schlegel, *Friedrich Schlegel's Lucinde and the Fragments*, trans. Peter Firchow (Minneapolis: University of Minnesota Press, 1971), 154. See also Barthes's reference to the term in his rough plan for a novel, *Vita Nova* (OC 5:999). See pp. 397–406, below.

5. Barthes is quoting from the chapter entitled "Les sciences philologiques." Novalis, *L'Encylopédie*, trans. Maurice de Gandillac (Paris: Éditions de Minuit, 1966), 322. {This fragment can be found in Novalis, *Notes for a Romantic*

Encyclopaedia, ed. and trans. by David W. Wood (Albany: State University of New York Press, 2007), 26. The translations of the two further fragments are my own.}

6. Friedrich Nietzsche, *The Birth of Tragedy and Other Writings*, ed. Raymond Geuss and Ronald Speirs, trans. Roland Speirs (Cambridge: Cambridge University Press, 1999), 68–69. {Barthes's emphasis; translation modified}

7. Mikhail Bakhtin (1895–1975), the literary theorist and historian, conceives of language and literary creation not as a code but as the elaboration of an intersubjectivity; the work is polyphonic, and dialogism is the founding principle of all literature.

8. *Rhapsodic*: from the Greek *rhaptein*, "to sew, to stitch together." Here Barthes is repeating the terms of his lecture entitled "Longtemps, je me suis couché de bonne heure," delivered at the *Collège de France* (October 19, 1978); OC 5:459–470.

9. Antoine Compagnon, *La Seconde main ou Le Travail de la citation* (Paris: Seuil, 1979), 284–287. If the jeton, bearing arms and a motto, is the emblem Montaigne chose for himself, the "offspring" {le rejeton}, the book (like the child), is conversely an object that is more produced than invented, an "emblem too perfect to remain as such," which, "a part of his life," will not rest until it escapes its author.

10. On the principle of intransitivity of the verb *to write* in Barthes's oeuvre, see p. 35.

11. This is how the narrator responds to those who question him: "He said: 'Hey, are you working?' I answered: 'I'm writing *Paludes*.'" André Gide, *Paludes* (Paris: NRF-Gallimard, 1925).

12. Émile Benveniste, *Problèmes de linguistique générale I* (Paris: Gallimard, 1966), 168 *sq*. Barthes is paraphrasing parts of chapter 14 entitled "Active and Middle of the Verb" and referring to the examples that Benveniste provides. {The translation of these passages follows (and paraphrases) Mary Elizabeth Meek's translation. See *Problems in General Linguistics*, trans. Mary Elizabeth Meek (Coral Gables, Fla.: University of Miami Press, 1971), 145–150.}

13. Pånini, an Indian grammarian from the fourth century BC, is one of the great theoreticians of Sanskrit, the sacred language of Hinduism. He established the phonological and morphological systems of the Vedic and Sanskrit dialects and, among others, posited the distinction between a "word for oneself" (middle) and a "word for another" (active).

14. This substitution (of "active / middle" by "external / internal") enables Benveniste, with regard to the supposedly intelligible and satisfying symmetry between the active and the passive, to rediscover the traditional indicator of a strong opposition between the two terms. See Benveniste, *Problems in General Linguistics*, 150.

15. Gustave Flaubert, letter to Louise Colet (February 1, 1852), in *Préface à la vie d'écrivain, ou Extraits de la correspondence*, ed. Geneviève Bollème (Paris: Seuil, 1963), 64.

16. Gustave Flaubert, letter to Amédée Pommier (September 8, 1880), in *Préface à la vie d'écrivain*, 214.

17. {In English in the text. Barthes uses the English term *writing* here and elsewhere to designate collective or anonymous writing.}

18. Hegelian idealism considers the Absolute to be a subject, which means that the author is dissolved in the universality of the verb. According to the code of literary copyright, no one can claim ownership of an idea.

19. {In English in the text.}

20. "... idleness is enough for me, provided I am doing nothing, I much prefer waking to a sleeping dream," writes Jean-Jacques Rousseau, referring to his stay on Saint-Pierre island in September 1765. *Confessions*, ed. Patrick

Coleman and trans. Angela Scholar (New York: New York University Press, 2000), 626.

21. Jean Pavans, a writer, translator, and critic of the work of Henry James, sent Barthes the manuscript of *Ruptures d'innocence* (Paris: Éditions de la Différence, 1982).

22. Chateaubriand, *Mémoires d'outre tombe*, ed. Maurice Levaillant and Georges Mouliné (Paris: Gallimard, "Bibliothèque de la Pléaide," 1951), 2:157; Michel de Montaigne, *The Complete Essays*, ed. and trans. M. A. Screech (London: Penguin, 2003), book 1, chap. 3, p. 11.

23. In Michelet's work, and in particular the preface to *History of the Revolution*, the two key figures of grace and justice—the Christianity of the Thousandth year and the Revolution—are often linked. After the Thousandth year, and similarly after the Revolution, came a time of boredom, a "suspension of history": "The certain boredom of tomorrow is already making us yawn today, and the prospect of the days, the years of boredom that lie ahead already weighs heavily upon us, giving us no taste for life" (Jules Michelet, *Histoire de France*, 1871).

24. For Barthes, "*marcottage*" is "that mode of composition by enjambments whereby an insignificant detail provided at the beginning of a novel reappears at the end, having as it were grown, germinated, blossomed." "Ça prend," *Magazine Littéraire* 144 (January 1979); OC 5: 654–656.

25. The name Forcheville circulates throughout *In Search of Lost Time* (the Count of Forcheville, Swann's rival at the Verdurin's home in "Swann in Love"; then, in *The Captive, The Fugitive*, Madame Swann becomes Madame Forcheville; Gilberte Swann becomes Mademoiselle de Forcheville before becoming Madame de Saint-Loup . . .). The appearance of this word on the manuscript of *Albertine disparue*, which Proust was reworking right up until his death, contains the promise of a new narrative development around the name of Forcheville, following the principle of *marcottage* so important to Barthes.

26. "Abraham cannot be mediated, which can also be expressed by saying he cannot speak. As soon as I speak I express the universal, and if I do not do that, then no one can understand me." Søren Kierkegaard, *Fear and Trembling*, trans. Sylvia Walsh (Cambridge: Cambridge University Press, 2006), 52.

27. Cited by Jean-Marie Carré in *La Vie aventureuse de Jean-Arthur Rimbaud* (Paris: Plon, 1926), 166.

28. See "Souvenirs de Louis Pierquin" (1856–1928), in *Lettres de la vie littéraire d'Arthur Rimbaud (1870–1875)*, ed. Jean-Marie Carré (Paris: Gallimard, 1931), 161.

29. See Jean-Marie Carré, *La Vie aventureuse de Jean-Arthur Rimbaud*; and "La pseudo-destruction d'Une saison d'enfer," in *Lettres de la vie littéraire d'Arthur Rimbaud (1870–1875)*, 221–231.

30. See Henri Boulaine de Lacoste, *Rimbaud et le problème des « Illuminations »* (Paris: Mercure de France, 1949).

31. Louis-Gustave Binger, Barthes's maternal grandfather, once Faidherbe's aide-de-camp, tracked the sources of the Niger, Kong, and Mossi rivers between 1887 and 1889. Barthes comments during the lecture: "You know, I'm stunned by the closeness of the dates, and the fact that my grandfather was exploring a part of black Africa at the same time as Rimbaud was exploring Abyssinia never ceases to surprise me."

32. Cited by Jean-Marie Carré, *Lettres de la vie littéraire d'Arthur Rimbaud*, 81.

33. Pascal, *Pensées*, trans. Roger Ariew (Indianapolis, Ind.: Hackett, 2005), 170.

34. Reference to Arthur Rimbaud, *Oeuvres*, ed. Paterne Berrichon, with a preface by Paul Claudel (Paris: Mercure de France, 1912).

35. Taken from Jules Michelet, *Histoire de France*, vol. 3 (Paris: Librairie Internationale, 1871).

36. While at Motiers, Jean-Jacques Rousseau worried about how he would survive: "I saw the little bit of capital that remained to me diminishing daily. Two or three years would be enough to consume the rest, without there being any prospect of my replenishing it unless I again began to write books, a fatal profession, I had already renounced." *Confessions*, 593.

37. This quotation from *La Peau du chagrin* [*The Wild Ass's Skin*] opens Barthes's presentation of Balzac's play, *Le Faiseur*, directed by Jean Villar at the Théâtre national de Chaillot in May 1957, reprinted under the title "Will Burns Us," in *Critical Essays*, trans. Richard Howard (Evanston, Ill.: Northwestern University Press, 1972), 77 {translation modified}; OC 2:348–351.

38. On Barthes embarking on his *Vita Nova*, see the opening pages of *The Preparation of the Novel*, p. 3 sq. See also the plan for a literary work entitled *Vita Nova*, OC 5:994–1001. See pp. 397–406, below.

39. Rousseau, *Confessions*, 626.

40. Ibid.

41. Ibid., 627.

42. The *komboloï* is a rosary made out of large glass beads. Barthes refers to this object in his outline plan for a novel entitled *Vita Nova*. See OC 5:1009 and p. 399, below.

43. Poem from the Zenrin Kushu, translated by Alan W. Watts in *The Way of Zen* (London: Thames and Hudson), 134. Barthes refers to it in part 1 of the course (p. 6) and mentions it a number of times throughout his oeuvre, notably in *A Lover's Discourse: Fragments*, trans. Richard Howard (London: Jonathan Cape, 1979), 233. {translation modified}

44. *Wou-wei* (or *Wu-wei*) is "purposelessness," the "absence of intention." See Watts, *The Way of Zen*, 148. Barthes devotes a chapter of the course on the Neutral to the *Wou-wei*; see *The Neutral*, trans. Rosalind Krauss and Denis Hollier (New York: Columbia University Press), 175–185.

45. Neologism formed on the basis of *sorites* in classical Latin, a term from logic and rhetoric, taken from the Greek *soreties*, "formed through accumulation," itself derived from *soros*, "heap."

46. Neologism from the Greek *bolos*, "lump of earth."

47. {When said aloud, "birch tree," *le bouleau*, is easily confused with *le boulot*, meaning "work."}

48. Martin Heidegger, "Overcoming Metaphysics," in *The End of Philosophy*, trans. Joan Stambaugh (Chicago: University of Chicago Press, 2003), 109.

49. Friedrich Nietzsche, "Why I Am So Wise," in *Ecce Homo*, trans. R. J. Hollingdale (London: Penguin, 1991), 15–16.

Session of December 15, 1979

1. {Eugène de Rastignac, a character in Balzac's *La Comédie humaine* series of novels. At the end of *Le Père Goriot* (1835), after attending Goriot's funeral, Rastignac surveys Paris from the heights of the Père Lachaise cemetery and declares: "*À nous deux!*" ("It's between you and me now!")}

2. Gustave Flaubert, letter to George Sand (July 20, 1873), in *The Correspondence of Gustave Flaubert and George Sand*, ed. Alphonse Jacobs, trans. Francis Steegmuller and Barbara Bray (London: The Harvill Press, 1999), 318.

3. {Barthes is quoting from Marthe Robert's French translation; in Joseph Kresh's translation of Kafka's *Diaries*, the same citation reads: "My novel is the cliff on which I'm hanging, I know nothing of what is going on in the world." Franz Kafka, *Diaries*, ed. Max Brod (New York: Schocken Books, 1979), 204.}

4. Freud created the term *Idealich* in 1914 ("On Narcissism: An Introduction"), which designates the real Ego, object of the first narcissistic satisfactions; however, Freud makes no conceptual distinction between the Ideal Ego and the Ego-Ideal—both have the same function of censorship and idealization. It was after Freud that a number of authors, in particular Jacques Lacan, established two distinct intrapsychic formations. See Jean LaPlanche and J.-B. Pontalis, *The Language of Psychoanalysis*, trans. Donald Nicholson-Smith (London: Karnac and the Institute of Psychoanalysis, 1988), 201–202. See also the texts that Barthes refers to in the margin notes: Freud, *Essays in Psychoanalysis* and especially "The Ego and the Id (the Ego-Ideal)"; Jacques Lacan, *The Seminar of Jacques Lacan*, book 1: *Freud's Papers on Technique 1953–1954*, ed. Jacques-Alain Miller, trans. John Forrester (Cambridge: Cambridge University Press, 1988); Moustapha Safouan, *Études sur l'Oedipe* (Paris: Seuil, 1974).

5. Kafka, *Diaries*, 122.

6. In "Deliberation," a discussion of the diary, Barthes evokes "an insoluble doubt as to the value of what one writes in it." In *The Rustle of Language*, trans. Richard Howard (New York: Hill and Wang, 1986), 359; OC 5:668.

7. Kafka, *Diaries*, 134.

8. See p. 14; see also the paper entitled "Longtemps, je me suis couché de bonne heure"; OC 5:468.

9. Pascal, *Pensées*, fragment 650, trans. Roger Ariew (Indianapolis, Ind.: Hackett, 2005), 196.

10. Ibid., 143.

11. Barthes did not make point (a) in the lecture and so did not read out the extract he mentions. He is probably referring to the narrative of a reading by the writer Bernhard Kellerman, which Kafka attended on November 27, 1910: he was one of the few members of the audience to remain; everyone else left the room.

12. In the first part of the course, Barthes establishes a link between the Joycean epiphany and what he terms the "Incident." See pp. 100–101.

13. Barthes reads out an extract from a letter from Franz Kafka to Max Brod, the content of which was used in *Description of a Struggle*, Kafka's first text (1904–1905). Cited in Klaus Wagenbach, *Kafka*, trans. Ewald Osers (Cambridge, Mass.: Harvard University Press, 2003), 43.

14. Cited by Henri Mondor, who mentions Stéphane Mallarmé's response to Camille Mauclair in a note. See *Vie de Mallarmé* (Paris: Gallimard, 1947), 20.

15. Maurice Blanchot, *The Book to Come*, trans. Charlotte Mandell (Stanford, Calif.: Stanford University Press, 2003), 196 {translation modified}. Barthes is quoting from Marcelin Pleynet's *Lautréamont* (Paris: Seuil, 1967), 5–6.

16. Paragraph crossed out by Barthes.

17. See p. 20.

18. On the role of the stain or mark in pictorial invention, see Leonardo da Vinci's *A Treatise on Painting*, where he describes a new method for "awakening the mind to a series of inventions": "By looking attentively at old and smeared walls, or stones and veined marbles of various colors, you may fancy that you see in them several compositions, landscapes . . . with an infinity of other objects." Leonard da Vinci, *A Treatise on Painting with a Life of Leonardo and an Account of His Works by John William Brown*, trans. John Francis Rigaud (Elibron, 2005), 62.

19. See also Roland Barthes's "The Plates of the Encyclopedia," a preface to *L'Univers de l'Encyclopédie. 130 planches de l'Encyclopédie de Diderot et d'Alembert* (Paris: Libraires associés, 1964), republished in *New Critical Essays* (1972); see also "Le Bas et l'idée" (1967); OC 2:1243–1244.

20. The narrator of André Gide's *Paludes* is writing a book entitled *Paludes*.

21. Sartre's novel closes with the hero's desire for a novel. Antoine Roquentin, who throughout *Nausea* is doing historical research into the Marquis de Rollebon, dreams of "another kind of book": "Naturally, at first it would only be a tedious, tiring job, it wouldn't prevent me from existing or from feeling that I exist? But a time would have to come when the book would be written, would be behind me, and I think that a little of its light would fall over my past." Jean-Paul Sartre, *Nausea*, trans. Robert Baldick (London: Penguin, 2002), 252.

22. In heraldry, the specialist term *abîme*, which designates the center of the shield (1671), furnished Gide with the expression *mise en abyme* (Gide restored the etymological *y*). Gide used the expression for the first time in his Diary while making a number of remarks on the "retroaction of the subject on itself" in September 1893. *Journal, 1887–1925*, ed. Éric Marty (Paris: Gallimard, "Bibliothèque de la Pléiade," 1996), 1:71. The expression refers to a procedure whereby the subject or action is reduplicated.

23. Michel de Montaigne, *The Complete Essays*, trans. and ed. M. A. Screech (London: Penguin, 2003), book 3, chap. 2, p. 909.

24. For a development of the question, see Roland Barthes's "L'ancienne Rhétorique, aide-mémoire," *Communications* 16 (December 1970): 172–229; OC 3:527–601.

25. A rhetorical procedure that consists in appealing to the benevolence of one's audience by apologizing for one's weaknesses or shortcomings in advance.

26. "Indecision" is one of the symptoms of what literary history has termed "Amielism" (along with aboulia, proteism, irresolution, narcissism . . .). Amiel writes in his *Diary*: "I glimpse, I half-open, I set about but I don't enter into" {"*J'entrevois, j'entrebâille, j'entreprends mais je n'entre pas*"}.

27. *Turandot*, a tragicomic theatrical tale, created in Venice in 1762 by Carlo Gozzi (1720–1806). Princess Turandot sets three riddles for each of her suitors to solve and punishes whoever fails with decapitation. The work was set to music by Weber in 1809, Busoni in 1917, and Puccini in 1926. Barthes was also aware of Brecht's *Turandot or the Whitewasher's Congress* (1954), from Schiller's versions of Gozzi's play.

28. On writing as a tendency, see p. 141 sq.

Session of January 5, 1980

1. Marcel Proust, letter to Jacques Rivière (February 7, 1914), in *Selected Letters*, vol. 3: *1910–1917*, ed. Philip Kolb, trans. Terence Kilmartin (London: HarperCollins, 1992), 232–233.

2. Leo Tolstoy, *Master and Man*, trans. Paul Foot (London: Penguin, 1977).

3. See the preceding paragraph, and pp. 15, 104 sq., and 149–50.

4. Nietzsche names Socrates as the representative of a life justified by the idea and the power of theory. Here, the figures of the artist and the priest, which are inscribed within Nietzsche's broader active / reactive typology, echo and support the distinction between science and technology that Barthes sets out in the course.

5. {A reference to *Les Compagnons du devoir*, a guild of artisans who traditionally produce one chef d'oeuvre or masterpiece as part of the apprenticeship to their craft; they then tour the country with the piece to showcase their skills, but it can on no account be sold.}

6. *Volumen*: derived from *volvere*, "to turn around, to roll," designates a "scroll, a roll, a fold." The *volumen* designates papyrus leaves that are pressed together and then rolled around batons made of wood or ivory. By extension, the "volume" designates a collection of written or printed sheets bound together, forming a book.

7. Jacques Scherer, *Le « Livre » de Mallarmé* (Paris: Gallimard, 1957). As Barthes was using the 1977 edition, all further references are to this later edition.

8. In *Les Poèmes d'Edgar Poe*, on "The Raven," Mallarmé writes: "a prodigious idea takes flight from these pages which, written after the fact (and without anecdotal foundation, that's all there is to it), remain no less congenial to Poe than if they were sincere. Namely, that all chance must be banished from the modern work, where it can only be feigned; and that the eternal flap of the wings does not rule out a lucid gaze scrutinizing the space devoured by its flight." *Oeuvres complètes*, ed. Henri Mondor and G. Jean-Aubry (Paris: Gallimard, "Bibliothèque de la Pléiade," 1945), 230. On the dossier compiled by Jacques Scherer, see *Le « Livre » de Mallarmé*, 126.

9. Gustave Flaubert, letter to Louise Colet (January 16, 1852), in *The Letters of Gustave Flaubert, 1857–1880*, ed. and trans. Francis Steegmuller (Cambridge, Mass.: The Belknap Press of Harvard University Press, 1979), 154.

10. Gustave Flaubert, letter to Louise Colet (June 26, 1853), in *Préface à la vie d'écrivain, ou Extraits de la correspondence*, ed. Geneviève Bollème (Paris: Seuil, 1963), 129.

11. {La Hune and PUF (Presses Universitaires de France) are bookshops in the fifth and sixth arrondissements of Paris.}

12. Jean-Jacques Rousseau, *Confessions*, ed. Patrick Coleman, trans. Angela Scholar (Oxford: Oxford University Press, 2000), 5.

13. *Ta Biblia*: "the books" in Greek; root of "the Bible," formed of a number of books.

14. Jean-Michel Gardir, *Les Écrivains italiens, "La Divine Comédie"* (Paris: Larousse, 1978), 47.

15. Friedrich Nietzsche, *Ecce Homo*, trans. R. J. Hollingdale (London: Penguin, 1992), 5.

16. Friedrich Nietzsche, letter to Paul Deussen (November 26, 1888), Turin.

17. Stéphane Mallarmé, "Scribbled at the Theater," in *Divagations*, trans. Barbara Johnson (Cambridge, Mass.: The Belknap Press of the University of Harvard Press, 2007), 142. See also the chapter entitled "Théâtre et religion" in Jacques Scherer's *Le « Livre » de Mallarmé*, 43–45.

18. Barthes refers to this episode in the first half of the Course, p. 105.

19. A novel by Malcolm Lowry (1948). In his introduction to the French edition (1959), Maurice Nadeau evokes "those who left for Mexico, notably in order to follow in the footsteps of the Consul in Quauhnahuac."

20. Franz Kafka, letter to Oskar Pollak (1904), cited in Klaus Wagenbach, *Kafka*, trans. Ewald Osers (Cambridge, Mass.: Harvard University Press, 2003), 42. {translation modified}

21. Stéphane Mallarmé, letter to Paul Verlaine (November 16, 1885), in *Selected Letters of Stéphane Mallarmé*, ed. and trans. Rosemary Lloyd (Chicago: University of Chicago Press, 1988), 143. See also the chapter entitled "Livre et Album," in Jacques Scherer, *Le « Livre » de Mallarmé*, 18–21.

22. See on this topic Mallarmé's letter to Henri Cazalis (May 14, 1867), in *Selected Letters of Stéphane Mallarmé*, 76.

23. Stéphane Mallarmé, manuscript of the "Book," page 181, edited by Jacques Scherer, *Le « Livre » de Mallarmé*.

24. See infra, p. 198.

25. Gustave Flaubert, letter to George Sand (December 2, 1874), in *The Correspondence of Gustave Flaubert and George Sand*, trans. Francis Steegmuller and Barbara Bray (London: The Harvill Press, 1999), 390.

26. Oral: "The novel is a general work with imprecise contours, but it actually resolves the contradiction between knowledge of the world and writing, between learning and writing."

27. "Allusion to a manuscript that Barthes had recently read, in which, he adds orally: "the hero [Audrey] is treated for viral hepatitis, jaundice in other words. And I said to myself: but that's not the same thing! . . . The author made me want to write, because had I been in his shoes, I'd have done some digging to find out whether or not it was the same thing. To know how to write a novel, you need to know a bit about everything in the world."

28. Mallarmé, "Notes, 1869," *Oeuvres complètes*, 851.

29. Scherer, *Le « Livre » de Mallarmé*, 18.

30. Stéphane Mallarmé, "Autobiography," in *Selected Prose Poems, Essays, and Letters*, trans. Bradford Cook (Baltimore, Md.: The Johns Hopkins Press, 1956), 16.

31. Mallarmé, letter to Paul Verlaine (November 16, 1885), in *Selected Letters of Stéphane Mallarmé*, 144.

32. The two citations are taken from Mallarmé's preface to *Divagations*.

33. See infra, p. 189.

34. Charles Baudelaire, "Edgar Poe, sa vie et ses oeuvres," preface to *Histoires extraordinaires*, his translation of *Extraordinary Tales* (Paris: Michel Lévy Frères, 1856). Rhapsodic: see supra, p. 144. The brackets are Barthes's, who uses the two different spellings, "rhapsodic" and "rapsodic."

35. Gilles Deleuze, *Nietzsche and Philosophy*, trans. Janis Tomlinson (New York: Columbia University Press, 1983).

36. See the seminar "Proust and Photography," infra, p. 346.

37. Élisabeth de Clermont-Tonnerre, *Robert de Montesquiou et Marcel Proust* (Paris: Flammarion, 1925), 21.

38. John Cage, public conversation with Daniel Charles in October 1970, reproduced in *For the Birds: In Conversation with Daniel Charles* (Boston: Marion Boyars, 1981), 36.

39. On the instruction Cage received from Schönberg, see ibid., 71–73.

40. January 12, 1911: "what is written down will, in accordance with its own purpose and with the superior power of the established, replace what has been only felt vaguely in such a way that the real feeling will disappear while the worthlessness of what has been noted down will be recognized too late." Franz Kafka, *Diaries*, ed. Max Brod (New York: Schocken Books, 1979), 35.

41. Mallarmé, "Important Miscellaneous News Briefs—Solitude," *Divagations*, 274.

42. Quoted by Barthes in "Deliberation," in *The Rustle of Language*, trans. Richard Howard (New York: Hill and Wang, 1986), 371.

Session of January 12, 1980

1. Stéphane Mallarmé, letter to Henri Cazalis (July 18, 1868), in *Selected Letters of Stéphane Mallarmé*, ed. and trans. Rosemary Lloyd (Chicago: University of Chicago Press, 1988), 87.

2. Leo Tolstoy, note of February 28, 1851, in *Tolstoy's Diaries*, ed. and trans. R. F. Christian (London: The Athlone Press, 1985), 22–23.

3. Cited by Gilles Deleuze in *Nietzsche and Philosophy*, trans. Janis Tomlinson (New York: Columbia University Press, 1983), 21.

4. ". . . in music, there can be much organization or a lot of disorganization—everything is possible. In the same way, the forest includes trees, mushrooms, birds, anything you wish. Although we can still organize a lot and even multiply organizations, in any case, the whole will make a disorganization!" John Cage, *For the Birds: In Conversation with Daniel Charles* (Boston: Marion Boyars, 1981), 53.

5. Barthes is referring here to the polemics around the classification of the *Pensées*: the sequence of the pages that were discovered upon Pascal's death

and how they are organized in different editions are topics that still provoke heated debate.

6. Cited by Michel Le Guerne in his preface to Pascal's *Pensées* (Paris: Gallimard, 1973), 1:10.

7. Paul Valéry, letter to Jeanne Valéry (July 1909), in *Œuvres complètes*, vol. 1 (Paris: Gallimard, "Bibliothèque de la Pléiade," 1957).

8. The karst is an area of irregular limestone shaped by erosion: fissures, sinkholes, and caverns form the karst relief.

9. From the Greek *soma*, "body." Designates, in biology, the ensemble of an organism's nonproductive cells, as opposed to *germen* (reproductive cells).

10. Marcel Proust, letter to Anna de Noailles (mid-December 1908), in *Selected Letters*, vol. 2: *1904–1909*, ed. Philip Kolb, trans. Terence Kilmartin (London: Collins, 1989), 416.

11. {*les "affres du style."* Barthes is referring to Flaubert's famous exclamation, made in a letter to George Sand (November 27, 1866): "I know them well, the Pangs of Style!" *The Letters of Gustave Flaubert, 1857–1880*, ed. and trans. Francis Steegmuller (Cambridge, Mass.: The Belknap Press of Harvard University Press, 1979), 92.}

12. See the long passage on the *Notatio*, p. 90 sq.

13. Franz Kafka, *Diaries*, ed. Max Brod (New York: Schocken Books, 1979), 158.

14. Ibid., 398. {translation modified}

15. Blaise Pascal, *Pensées*, trans. Roger Ariew (Indianapolis, Ind.: Hackett, 2005), 174. {translation modified}

16. Ibid., 157.

17. "A page of the album is moved, deleted or added according to chance—this chance that it is precisely the function of true literature to abolish," writes Jacques Scherer, *Le « Livre » de Mallarmé* (Paris: Gallimard, 1957), 19.

18. Mallarmé, letter to Eugène Lefébure (May 27, 1867), in *Selected Letters of Stéphane Mallarmé*, 77.

19. Allusion to the two "ways," the Guermantes way and the Méséglise way, which form the landscape of the Narrator's childhood; in *Time Regained* he discovers that the two ways—which he thought were irreconcilable—actually meet.

20. Gustave Flaubert, letter to Louise Colet (February 1, 1852), in *Préface à la vie d'écrivain, ou Extraits de la correspondence*, ed. Geneviève Bollème (Paris: Seuil, 1963), 65.

21. Gustave Flaubert, letter to Louise Colet (January 15, 1853), in *The Letters of Gustave Flaubert: 1830–1857*, ed. and trans. Francis Steegmuller (Cambridge, Mass.: The Belknap Press of Harvard University Press, 1979), 179–180.

22. Kafka, *Diaries*, 30.

23. See the citation from Heidegger in the session of December 8, 1979.

24. Cited in Chateaubriand, *Mémoires d'outre tombe*, ed. Maurice Levaillant and Georges Mouliné (Paris: Gallimard, "Bibliothèque de la Pléiade," 1951), 1:450. Blanchot quotes and discusses this note from Joubert's *Notebooks* in *The Book to Come*, trans. Charlotte Mandell (Stanford, Calif.: Stanford University Press, 2003), 62.

25. See pp. 242–43.

26. Chateaubriand, letter to Madame Récamier (January 3, 1829), in *Mémoires d'outre tombe*, 2:285.

27. Kafka, *Diaries*, 31.

28. Ibid., 62.

29. The year 1909 was crucial for Proust in terms of setting out on the path toward writing a novel. Barthes is probably radicalizing the transition from the

essay to the novel, which occurred between 1908 and 1910, while Proust was writing *Against Sainte-Beuve*.

30. Honoré de Balzac, "The Secrets of the Princesse de Cadignan" {my translation}. See also Gaétan Picon, *Balzac* (Paris: Seuil, 1954), 92.

31. Weekly columns that Barthes published in the *Nouvel Observateur* between December 18, 1978, and March 26, 1979. In the final one, Barthes said that he was "disconcerted by" and "unhappy with" his columns.

32. Allusion to the filming of *Les Soeurs Brontës* by André Téchiné (1979), in which Barthes played William Thackeray.

33. Pascal, *Pensées*, 162.

34. Quoted in Klaus Wagenbach, *Kafka*, trans. Ewald Osers (Cambridge, Mass.: Harvard University Press, 2003), 270.

35. Cited by Proust in "Sainte-Beuve and Balzac," in *Against Sainte-Beuve and Other Essays*, trans. John Sturrock (London: Penguin, 1988), 58.

36. Kafka, *Diaries*, 225.

37. Honoré de Balzac, letter to Zulma Carraud (November 21, 1831), in *The Unpublished Correspondence of Honoré de Balzac and Zulma Carraud, 1829–1850*, trans. J. Lewis May (London: John Lane, 1937), 40.

38. Franz Kafka, aphorism 52, cited by Marthe Robert in her preface to the diaries: Franz Kafka, *Journal*, trans. Marthe Robert (Paris: Grasset, 1954), vii.

39. Franz Kafka, cited by Marthe Robert in ibid., ix.

40. Allusion to Roland Barthes, *A Lover's Discourse: Fragments* (1977).

Session of January 19, 1980

1. Because there had been a problem with the microphone during the previous lecture, Barthes wanted to summarize the essential points at the beginning of the next session. This is perhaps why he did not have enough time to read the three pages entitled "Life as Work" and skipped directly to p. 212.

2. Roland Barthes, "The Death of the Author" (1967).

3. Jean Bellemin-Noël, *Vers l'inconscient du texte* (Paris: PUF, 1979), 5.

4. Roland Barthes, *The Pleasure of the Text* (1973). See also the interviews that Barthes gave on this book, notably "L'Adjectif est le 'dire' du desire" (1973); OC 4:465–468.

5. *Camp*—a term coined in the United States by Susan Sontag in 1964—refers to kitsch, to outmoded attitudes promoted as fashionable. The term entered into French common usage as a result of Patrick Mauriès's book *Second manifeste au camp* (Paris: Seuil, 1979).

6. "Notes on Gide and his Journal" (1942); OC 1:33–46. Barthes's first published text was "Culture et tragédie," which appeared in *Cahiers de l'étudiant*, Spring 1942.

7. George D. Painter, *Marcel Proust: A Biography* (London: Chatto and Windus, 1959), 1:xiii.

8. From *biographeme*, a neologism invented by Barthes in a now famous formulation: "were I a writer, and dead, how I would love it if my life, through the pains of some friendly and detached biographer, were to reduce itself to a few details, a few inflections, let us say, to 'biographemes' whose distinction and mobility might go beyond any fate and come to touch, like Epicurean atoms, some future body, destined to the same dispersion." "Preface" to *Sade, Fourier, Loyola*, trans. Richard Miller (Baltimore, Md., The Johns Hopkins University Press, 1997), 9.

9. Marcel Proust, *Against Sainte-Beuve and Other Essays*, trans. John Sturrock (London: Penguin, 1988), 12. Barthes's emphasis.

10. See Chateaubriand, *Mémoires d'outre tombe*, ed. Maurice Levaillant and Georges Mouliné (Paris: Gallimard, "Bibliothèque de la Pléiade," 1951),

1046. Chateaubriand's "Testamentary Preface," dated December 1, 1833, and published in *La Revue des Deux Mondes* (1846) is one of the variations on the Avant-Propos to *Mémoires d'outre-tombe*.

11. Quoted in Painter, *Marcel Proust*, 1:xiii.

12. "I can rescue the Diary on the one condition that I labor it *to death*, to the end of an extreme exhaustion, like a *virtually* impossible Text: a labor at whose end it is indeed possible that a Diary thus kept no longer resembles a diary at all." Barthes, "Deliberation," in *The Rustle of Language*, trans. Richard Howard (New York: Hill and Wang, 1986), 373. {translation modified}.

13. End of the passage crossed out by Barthes.

14. Barthes discusses the sources and the determinations of this *Vita Nova* at length in the first part of the course.

15. Arthur Rimbaud, letter to Georges Izambard (May 13, 1871), in *Complete Works, Selected Letters: A Bilingual Edition*, trans. Wallace Fowlie, rev. Seth Whidden (Chicago: University of Chicago Press, 2005), 371.

16. *Oberman*, a novel by the French writer Étienne Pivert de Senancour (1770–1846), narrates the inner adventures of a young hero who despairs of life, idealizes nature, and shuns all human contact. The novel was misunderstood when it was first published (1804) but was greatly admired by the Romantics.

17. After having evoked the infinite pleasures of solitude and plant collection, Jean-Jacques Rousseau narrates a memorable promenade in the Swiss Alps: "I was alone; I went deep into the winding crevices of the mountain; and passing from wood to wood and boulder to boulder, I arrived at a retreat so hidden that I had never seen a more desolate sight on my life. . . . I . . . began to dream more at ease thinking that I was in a refuge unknown to the whole universe where persecutors would not unearth me." Disturbed by a familiar clanking, Rousseau suddenly comes across a stocking mill in a nearby hollow, and exclaims: "But, after all, who would have expected to find a mill in a ravine? In the whole world, only Switzerland presents this mixture of wild nature and human industry." *The Reveries of the Solitary Walker*, trans. Charles E. Butterworth (Indianapolis, Ind.: Hackett, 1992), 100–101.

18. George Painter, who narrates this event, suggests that the guests of honor were Marcel Plantevignes and two other young people from Cabourg, along with "the unmarried survivors of his single friends," notably Reynaldo Hahn, Emmanuel Bibesco, and Léon Radziwill. See George Painter, *Marcel Proust: A Biography* (London: Chatto and Windus, 1965), 2:147.

19. Jules Michelet (1798–1874) married Athénais Mialaret in 1849. *L'Oiseau* (1856), *La Mer* (1861), *La Montagne* (1868).

20. See p. 156.

21. Idleness, Doing Nothing, the Moroccan Child – these are some of the figures around which the different plans for *Vita Nova*, Barthes's project for a novel, are organized; OC 5:994–1001. See *infra*, pp. 397–406.

22. See the citation from Rousseau on p. 216.

23. Chateaubriand, "Préface testamentaire," in *Mémoires d'outre-tombe*, 1047.

24. Franz Kafka, *Diaries*, ed. Max Brod (New York: Schocken Books, 1979), 105.

25. Gustave Flaubert, letter to Louise Colet (June 7, 1853), in *Préface à la vie d'écrivain, ou Extraits de la correspondance*, ed. Geneviève Bollème (Paris: Seuil, 1963), 125.

26. Jean-Jacques Rousseau, *Confessions*, ed. Patrick Coleman, trans. Angela Scholar (Oxford: Oxford University Press, 2000), 630.

27. See p. 246.

28. {In English in the text.}

29. Gustave Flaubert, letter to Ernest Feydeau (January 1862), in *Préface à la vie d'écrivain*, 222; see *infra*, pp. 269–70.

30. Rousseau, *Confessions*, 629.

31. In *In Search of Lost Time*, Aunt Léonie suffers from such acute digestive problems (dyspepsia) that she "kept two wretched mouthfuls of Vichy water on her stomach for fourteen hours!" Marcel Proust, *In Search of Lost Time*, vol. 1: *Swann's Way*, trans. C. K. Scott Moncrieff and Terence Kilmartin, rev. D. J. Enright (London: Chatto and Windus, 1992), 81. {translation modified}

32. {In English in the original}

33. Sentence crossed out by Barthes. The last words are illegible; we think they read "*à relais*" {by relays}.

34. Gustave Flaubert, letter to Maxime du Camp (April 7, 1846), in *Préface à la vie d'écrivain*, 46.

35. Urt, on the banks of the Adour, a few kilometers from Bayonne, is where Barthes would spend his holidays.

36. The first course at the *Collège de France*, entitled *Comment vivre ensemble* ("How to Live Together") discusses monastic time at length. *Comment vivre ensemble*, ed. Claude Coste (Paris: Seuil, 2002).

37. Christophe Plantin (1520–1589), a famous typographer and printer, occasional poet; his best known work is *Le Bonheur de ce monde*, which Barthes reads aloud. See *infra*, pp. 231–32.

38. Stéphane Mallarmé, *Selected Poems*, trans. C. F. MacIntyre (Berkeley: University of California Press, 1957), 83.

39. These details are taken from Léon Pierre-Quint, *Marcel Proust: His Life and Work*, trans. Hamish Miles and Sheila Miles (New York: A. A. Knopf, 1927), 59.

40. Ibid., 103.

41. Franz Kafka, letter to Max Brod, cited in Klaus Wagenbach, *Kafka*, trans. Ewald Osers (Cambridge, Mass.: Harvard University Press, 2003), 117.

42. In 1934, Barthes suffered a first attack of tuberculosis (hemoptysia and lesions on the left lung), which meant spending a year in free cure in Bedous in the Pyrenees. When he returned to Paris, he enrolled for a literature degree at the Sorbonne. After a relapse, he spent the years between 1942 and 1945 in the Saint-Hilaire-du-Touvet sanatorium; then, between 1945 and 1946, he was in the clinic at Leysin, in French-speaking Switzerland. Barthes published his first articles (on Gide, Camus) in the sanatorium's magazine, *Existences* (see *OC* 1).

43. Prompted by Maurice Nadeau, in August 1947, Barthes published the first of a long series of articles on literature in the journal *Combat*. These texts were collected and published under the title *Le Dégré zéro de l'écriture* {*Writing Degree Zero*} in 1953; *OC* 1:169–225.

44. Georges Rivane, *Influence de l'asthme sur l'œuvre de Marcel Proust* (Paris: La Nouvelle Édition, 1945).

45. Charles-Louis Philippe (1874–1909), French writer, close to the symbolists and then to the naturalists, author of *Père Perdix* (1902) and *Marie Donadieu* (1904); his life and works were marked by illness and poverty. Madame Bocquet was the concierge of the Parisian apartment building where Barthes lived.

46. T. S. Eliot, *The Waste Land* (1922).

47. Stéphane Mallarmé, the first line of the conference on Villiers de L'Isle-Adam (1890). Barthes's emphasis.

48. {In English in the original.}

49. Gustave Flaubert, letter to Guy de Maupassant (August 15, 1878), in *Préface à la vie d'écrivain*, 282.

50. Barthes is alluding to a trip organized by Fabrice Emaer, manager of the "Palace," a famous Parisian nightclub that opened in 1977, to mark the opening of a "Palace" in Cabourg.

51. Joseph Joubert, *Pensées, maximes et essais* (Paris: Perrin et Cie, 1911).

Session of January 26, 1980

1. Friedrich Nietzsche, "Why I Am So Clever," in *Ecce Homo: How One Becomes What One Is*, trans. R. J. Hollingdale (London: Penguin, 1992), 36. {translation modified}.

2. Barthes evoked these texts on p. 142.

3. Nietzsche, "Why I Am So Clever," in *Ecce Homo*, 22.

4. This brief description of Joubert's eating habits, whom Chateaubriand met in the company of Madame de Beaumont, appears in the context of a long page devoted to him. Chateaubriand, *Mémoires d'outre tombe*, ed. Maurice Levaillant and Georges Mouliné (Paris: Gallimard, "Bibliothèque de la Pléaide," 1951), 450.

5. Léon Pierre-Quint, *Marcel Proust: His Life and Work*, trans. Hamish Miles and Sheila Miles (New York: A. A. Knopf, 1927), 109.

6. {Optalidon is used for migraines; Eno for the lungs; Aturgyl for the sinuses; Optanox is a sleeping pill.}

7. See Roland Barthes, *The Neutral*, ed. Thomas Clerc under the direction of Éric Marty, trans. Rosalind E. Krauss and Denis Hollier (New York: Columbia University Press, 2005), 97ff.

8. See p. 263.

9. Martin Flügel, *The Psychology of Clothes* (London: The Hogarth Press, 1950). Barthes often refers to this book; see especially "La mode et les sciences humaines" (1966) and *The Fashion System* (1967).

10. Jean-Jacques Rousseau, *Confessions*, ed. Patrick Coleman, trans. Angela Scholar (Oxford: Oxford University Press, 2000), 587.

11. Chapter 2 of Flaubert's *Bouvard and Pécuchet* is devoted to the Parisians setting up home at Chavignolles, the description of their raptures and their blunders, and the detailed account of their forays into agriculture.

12. Christophe Plantin (1520–1589), whom Barthes referred to in the previous session (see p. 220, *infra*). In the *Anthology of European Poetry*, vol. 1: *From Machault to Malherbe, 13th to 17th Century*, ed. Mervyn Savill, trans. William Stirling (London: Alan Wingate, 1977), 100–101.

13. See Barthes' first lecture at the Collège de France, *Comment vivre ensemble*, ed. Claude Coste (Paris: Seuil, 2002), in particular the section entitled "Proxémie," 155–158 {where Barthes defines "proxemics" as a term coined by E. T. Hall in 1966 that refers to "subjective spaces as they are experienced or lived affectively by subjects."}

14. Lévitan was the best-known furniture retailer in France in the 1970s.

15. Barthes reads out an extract from Proust's *Against Sainte-Beuve*, trans. Sylvia Townsend Warner (London: Chatto and Windus, 1958), 27; translation based on *Contre Sainte-Beuve, suivi de Nouveaux Mélanges*, ed. Bernard de Fallois (Paris: Gallimard, 1954).

16. Gustave Flaubert, letter to Alfred Le Poittevin (May 13 1945), in *The Letters of Gustave Flaubert: 1830–1857*, ed. and trans. Francis Steegmuller (Cambridge, Mass.: The Belknap Press of Harvard University Press, 1979), 31.

17. Marcel Proust, *Against Sainte-Beuve and Other Essays*, trans. John Sturrock (London: Penguin, 1988), 30.

18. Franz Kafka, letter to Max Brod (July 1922), quoted in Klaus Wagenbach, *Kafka*, trans. Ewald Osers (Cambridge, Mass.: Harvard University Press, 2003), 83–84.

19. Franz Kafka, *Diaries*, ed. Max Brod (New York: Schocken Books, 1979), 32.

20. Gustave Flaubert, letter to Louise Colet (April 15, 1852), in *Préface à la vie d'écrivain, ou Extraits de la correspondence*, ed. Geneviève Bollème (Paris: Seuil, 1963), 69.

21. Marcel Proust, letter to Robert de Montesquiou (September 7, 1907), in *Selected Letters*, vol. 2: *1904–1909*, ed. Philip Kolb, trans. Terence Kilmartin (London: HarperCollins, 1992), 330.

22. Let us recall Nietzsche's demand in his foreword to *Ecce Homo*, a demand that could well be the one Barthes makes of his audience: "*Listen to me! For I am thus and thus. Do not, above all, confound me with what I'm not!*" Friedrich Nietzsche, *Ecce Homo*, trans. R. J. Hollingdale (London: Penguin, 1992), 3.

23. Arthur Rimbaud, letter to Ernest Delahaye (June 1872), in *Complete Works, Selected Letters: A Bilingual Edition*, trans. Wallace Fowlie (Chicago: University of Chicago Press, 2005), 391 {translation modified}. The *travaince* (for *travaille*, or work), like the *juinphe* (for *juin*, or June) that Barthes mentions in the margin are from Rimbaud—two of his customary syntactical distortions (Jacques Rivière would say, "he messes about with the most benign words.").

24. Kafka, *Diaries*, 212.

25. Quint, *Marcel Proust*, 70, 65.

26. Kafka, *Diaries*, 61.

27. "They count time not in days but in nights." Tacitus *De Moribus Germanorum* 26.2–3.

28. "Night seems to lead and govern the day."

29. Act 2 of *The Knight of the Rose*, an opera in three acts by Richard Strauss, libretto by Hugo von Hofmannsthal. Octavian is the hero.

30. Honoré de Balzac, "The Exiles" (*Les Proscrits*) {my translation}.

Session of February 2, 1980

1. This passage was drafted but not read aloud.

2. It is precisely this "practical relationship with others" that feeds the "fantasy of idiorrythmy" (*idios*, "proper, particular"; *rhuthmos*, "rhythm"), the principal topic of the first course, *Comment vivre ensemble*, ed. Claude Coste (Paris: Seuil, 2002).

3. Extracts from Marcel Proust's letters to Antoine Bibesco, cited in Marthe Bibesco, *Marcel Proust at the Ball*, trans. Anthony Rhodes (London: Weidenfield and Nicholson, 1956), 8.

4. Chateaubriand, *Mémoires d'outre tombe*, ed. Maurice Levaillant and Georges Mouliné (Paris: Gallimard, "Bibliothèque de la Pléaide," 1951), 450.

5. Léon Pierre-Quint, *Marcel Proust: His Life and Work*, trans. Hamish Miles and Sheila Miles (New York: A. A. Knopf, 1927), 106.

6. Franz Kafka, "Summary of all the arguments for and against my marriage," *Diaries*, ed. Max Brod (New York: Schocken Books, 1979), 225.

7. Ibid., 281.

8. Ibid., 33.

9. Ibid., 229.

10. End of the omitted passage.

11. Marcel Proust, *Against Sainte-Beuve*, trans. Sylvia Townsend Warner (London: Chatto and Windus, 1958), 68–70. {translation modified}.

12. Gustave Flaubert, letter to his niece Caroline (August 6, 1974). Flaubert, who had previously sent her a different version of the first line of his manuscript, writes: "It was in obedience to your command, dear Loulou, that I sent

you the first line of *Bouvard and Pécuchet*. But since you refer to it, or rather exalt it, as a 'holy relic,' and since you mustn't adore relics that are false, please be informed that the one you possess is no longer authentic. Here is the real one: '*With the temperature in the nineties, the Boulevard Bourdon was absolutely deserted.*' So much for that, and you won't know a word more for a long time to come." *The Letters of Gustave Flaubert: 1830–1857*, ed. and trans. Francis Steegmuller (Cambridge, Mass.: The Belknap Press of Harvard University Press, 1979), 21.

13. *Deus absconditus*, Isaiah's "hidden God" (Isaiah 45:15), discussed by Pascal: "That God wanted to be hidden ... God being thus hidden, any religion that does not say God is hidden is not true. And any religion that does not explain it is not instructive." Fragment 224, *Pensées* (Paris: Gallimard, 1973), 71–72.

14. Klaus Wagenbach, *Kafka*, trans. Ewald Osers (Cambridge, Mass.: Harvard University Press, 2003), 82.

15. Gustave Flaubert, letter to Alfred le Poittevin (September 1845), in *The Letters of Gustave Flaubert, 1830–1857*, 36.

16. The essays that comprise *Mythologies* were published in various journals between 1952 and 1956 before being published as a collection by Éditions du Seuil in 1957.

17. Gustave Flaubert, letter to Louise Colet (April 24, 1852), in *The Letters of Gustave Flaubert, 1830–1857*, 158.

18. Gustave Flaubert, letter to Louise Colet (December 13, 1846), in *Préface à la vie d'écrivain, ou Extraits de la correspondence*, ed. Geneviève Bollème (Paris: Seuil, 1963), 43.

19. Honoré de Balzac, letter to Zulma Carraud (March 1833), in *The Unpublished Correspondence of Honoré de Balzac and Madame Zulma Carraud, 1829–1850*, trans. J. Lewis May (London: John Lane, 1937), 159.

20. The two citations are taken from the same letter to Ernest Feydeau (December 19, 1858), in *Letters of Gustave Flaubert, 1857–1880*, 13.

21. These details are taken from Didier Raymond's *Schopenhauer* (Paris: Seuil, 1979), 99.

22. Information taken from Franz Kafka's "Travel Diaries"—Kafka spent the afternoon at Lisztbaus on Tuesday, July 2, 1911: "Liszt worked from five to eight, then church, then slept a second time, visitors from eleven on." *Diaries*, 470.

23. Gaston Bachelard, *The Dialectic of Duration*, trans. McAllester Jones (Manchester: Clinamen Press, 2000), 20, 21.

24. Leo Tolstoy, "Rules for Developing the Rational Will" (March–May 1847), in *Tolstoy's Diaries*, vol. 1: *1847–1894*, ed. and trans. R. F. Christian (London: The Athlone Press, 1985), 14.

25. Using a discrete system of notation that allowed him to specify where he wept and the quantity of tears, Ignatius of Loyola kept a record of every time he cried: *a* [*antes*], tears before mass; *l*, tears during mass; *d* [*después*] tears after mass, etc. See *The Spiritual Journal of St. Ignatius Loyola*, trans. William J. Young (Kessinger Publishing, 2006).

26. Tolstoy, *Tolstoy's Diaries*, 1:12.

27. Tolstoy. See in particular the whole of the year 1847 in *Tolstoy's Diaries*. The margin note refers to Michel Aucouturier's preface to Tolstoy's *Journaux et carnets*, vol. 1: *1847–1889*, trans. Gustave Aucouturier (Paris: Gallimard, 1975).

28. "Here I lie, done in by my fellow men." Paul Valéry requested that his friends inscribe this on his gravestone.

29. Kafka, *Diaries*, 31.{translation modified}

30. Tolstoy, *Tolstoy's Diaries*, 1:185.

31. "He has always put his faith in that Greek rhythm, the succession of *Ascesis* and Festivity, the release of one by the other (and not the banal rhythm of modernity: *work / leisure*)." Roland Barthes, *Roland Barthes*, trans. Richard Howard (Berkeley: University of California Press, 1977), 157.

32. Gustave Flaubert, letter to Maxime du Camp (April 7, 1846), in *Préface à la vie d'écrivain*, 36.

33. For Nietzsche, what is *noble* is on the side of the active, the artist, the sovereign individual—of the affirmative power of life.

34. Proust, *Against Sainte-Beuve*, 70.

35. "It is as though this greed came from my stomach, as though it were a perverse appetite." Kafka, *Diaries*, 114.

36. This great "Active / Reactive" typology structures Nietzschean thought. In *Nietzsche and Philosophy*, Gilles Deleuze writes: "In a body the superior or dominant forces are known as *active* and the inferior or dominated forces are known as *reactive*. Active and reactive are precisely the original qualities which express the relation of force with force." *Nietzsche and Philosophy*, trans. Hugh Tomlinson (London: Continuum, 2006), 37.

37. These citations are taken from "Why I Am So Clever," in *Ecce Homo: How One Becomes What One Is*, trans. R. J. Hollingdale (London: Penguin, 1992), 33–34.

38. Jean-Louis Bouttes, a student and close friend of Barthes.

39. {*Manuel des Études Littéraires* by Pierre-Georges Castex and Paul Surer, a six-volume textbook which ranges from the middle ages to the twentieth century (Paris: Hachette, 1946–1953).}

40. Guy Michaud, *Mallarmé* (Paris: Hatier, 1953). On Mallarmé's crisis of 1866, see the letters he wrote to his close friends and in particular a long letter to Henri Cazalis (May 14, 1867), which retrospectively evokes that "terrifying year: my Thought has thought itself, and reached a pure Concept," or the letter to Villiers de L'Isle-Adam (September 24, 1867): "—and you will be terrified to learn that I have arrived at the Idea of the Universe through sensation alone." *Selected Letters of Stéphane Mallarmé*, ed. and trans. Rosemary Lloyd (Chicago: University of Chicago Press, 1988), 74, 81.

41. The title of Barthes's article for a special edition of the *Magazine Littéraire* on Proust, no. 144 (January 1979); *OC* 5:654–656.

42. Gustave Flaubert, letter to Madame Roger des Genettes (1861[?]), in *The Letters of Gustave Flaubert, 1857–1880*, 20.

43. Barthes had made some contacts among the members of the Proust team that was created by Jacques Bersani, Michel Raimond, and Jean-Yves Tadié in 1971 and in 1974 was attached to the *Centre d'histoire et d'analyse des manuscrits modernes* (now the *Institut des textes et manuscrits modernes*, ITEM / CNRS); central to this research network was the *Bulletin d'informations proustiennes* (Paris: Presses de l'ENS, 1975), founded by Claudine Quémar and Bernard Brun.

44. The most recent research on the work of Marcel Proust confirms this intrication of the two projects and the long, progressive transition between the two. The study of particular letters has revealed that the whole of the summer of 1909 (and not just the month of September) was a period of "intensive writing labor." On this crucial period, see Jean-Yves Tadié, *Marcel Proust* (Paris: Gallimard, 1999), in particular the chapter entitled "La métamorphose de *Contre Sainte-Beuve*, 1909–1911," 2:95–112.

45. Implicit reference to "Ça prend," Barthes's article on Marcel Proust's writing (*OC* 5:654–656).

Session of February 9, 1980

1. Marcel Proust, *Against Sainte-Beuve*, trans. Sylvia Townsend Warner (London: Chatto and Windus, 1958), 66–67.

2. Marcel Proust, letter to René Blum (February 23, 1913), *Selected Letters*, vol. 3: *1910–1917*, ed. Philip Kolb, trans. Terence Kilmartin (London: HarperCollins, 1992), 158.

3. See Roland Barthes's article on Proust, "Ça prend," *Magazine Littéraire* (January 1979); OC 5:654–656). See also "Une Idée de recherche," published in *Paragone* (October 1971); OC 3:917–921.

4. Roland Barthes refers to this principle on pages 104 and 150.

5. Marcel Proust, letter to L. De Robert (July or August 1913), *Selected Letters*, 3:194.

6. *La Valse* (1920), a choreographic poem by Maurice Ravel, begins with what seems to be a distant rumbling; it swells and concludes in "a fantastic and fatal whirling" (Ravel).

7. Gustave Flaubert, letter to Louise Colet (August 26, 1853), in *Préface à la vie d'écrivain, ou Extraits de la correspondence*, ed. Geneviève Bollème (Paris: Seuil, 1963), 144.

8. Paul Valéry, cited by Agathe Rouard-Valéry in her "Introduction biographique" to Valéry's *Oeuvres* (Paris: Gallimard, 1957). Barthes's emphasis. {Also quoted in the context of a discussion of Cy Twombly in Roland Barthes, "The Wisdom of Art," in *The Responsibility of Forms*, trans. Richard Howard (Berkeley: University of California Press, 1985), 182.}

9. Blaise Pascal, *Pensées* (Paris: Gallimard, 1973), 265.

10. Gustave Flaubert, letter to Louise Colet (December 9, 1853), in *Préface à la vie d'écrivain*, 158.

11. Gustave Flaubert, letter to Madame Roger des Genettes, 1861[?], in *The Letters of Gustave Flaubert*, ed. and trans. Francis Steegmuller (Cambridge, Mass.: The Belknap Press of Harvard University Press, 1979), 20. Barthes had already quoted the first part of the citation (see 255), which he gives in full here.

12. Gustave Flaubert, letter to Louise Colet (August 26, 1853), in *Préface à la vie d'écrivain*, 144.

13. Marcel Proust, letter to Gaston Gallimard (around May 22, 1919), in *Selected Letters*, vol. 4: *1918–1922*, ed. Philip Kolb, trans. Joanna Kilmartin (London: HarperCollins, 2000), 75.

14. Barthes repeats here a number of the developments from his text "Variations sur l'écriture" (1973); OC 4:267–316.

15. See Gabriel Monod, *Jules Michelet* (Paris: Hachette, 1905), 165ff.

16. Pascal, *Pensées*, fragment 773, p. 287.

17. This information is taken from Gabriel Monod, *La Vie et pensée de Jules Michelet* (Paris: Champion, 1923), 2:43.

18. Jules Michelet, "The 1869 Preface" to the *History of France*, trans. Edward K. Kaplan and published as an appendix to Edward K. Kaplan, *Michelet's Poetic Vision: A Romantic Philosophy of Nature, Man, and Woman* (Amherst: University of Massachusetts Press, 1977), 166–167.

19. In Buddhism, the Maya Veil represents the world as an illusion.

20. Gustave Flaubert, letter to Louise Colet (April 24, 1852), in *The Letters of Gustave Flaubert, 1830–1857*, 158 {translation modified}. Barthes cites this passage in "Flaubert and the Sentence," *New Critical Essays*, trans. Richard Howard (New York: Hill and Wang, 1980), 69–74; OC 4:78–85. Reference to Flaubert's "marinade" of April 15, 1878, on p. 8.

21. Gustave Flaubert, letter to Monsieur X. (July 22, 1875), in *Préface à la vie d'écrivain*, 193.

22. Tenuate Dospan, 75 mg, a diet pill, is also used in cases of hypersomnia.

23. Gustave Flaubert, letter to Ernest Feydeau (August 8, 1871), in *Préface à la vie d'écrivain*, 249. Barthes's emphasis.

24. These quotations are taken (respectively) from letters to: Louise Colet (June 7, 1853), Ernest Feydeau (January 1862), and Louise Colet (August 9, 1846). Flaubert, *Préface à la vie d'écrivain*, 126, 222, 38.

25. Jean-Jacques Rousseau, *The Reveries of the Solitary Walker*, trans. Charles E. Butterworth (New York: NYU Press, 1971), 8.

26. Charles Baudelaire, "To J. G. F.," *Artificial Paradise*, trans. Ellen Fox (New York: Herder and Herder, 1971), 31.

27. Alfred de Vigny, *Journal d'un poète* (1885), ed. Louis Ratisbonne. We have been unable to locate the edition that Barthes was using.

28. Recorded on October 29, 1947, in the *Cahiers de la Petite Dame*, vol. 4: *1945–1951*, in *Cahiers d'André Gide* no. 7 (Paris: Gallimard), 75.

29. Emmanuel Swedenborg (1688–1772), poet, mathematician, geologist, physician, gave up his scientific research to devote himself entirely to theosophy. His works were well known throughout Europe, and he traveled constantly; a binder, he made his books himself and distributed them widely. His research had a profound impact on Balzac, Nerval, Baudelaire, and Breton.

30. Antiochus in Racine's *Berenice*, act 1, scene 4. The debate between Barthes and Raymond Picard in 1964–1965 around Racine hinged on the question of semantic interpretation. See Barthes, *On Racine* (1963) and *Criticism and Truth* (1966).

31. Barthes develops the notion of *acedy* ("state of depression, melancholy, sadness, boredom") in a session of his first lecture course at the Collège de France, *Comment vivre ensemble*, ed. Claude Coste (Paris: Seuil, 2002), 53–56. Barthes also refers to the notion in the first part of *The Preparation of the Novel*; see p. 5.

32. {*Vaseux*, meaning muddy, sludgy but also muddled, woolly, confused.}

33. Pascal, *Pensées*, fragment 529, p. 193.

34. "My soul is very sorrowful, even to death," says Christ to Peter in the garden of Gethsemane (Matthew 26:38).

35. Arthur Schopenhauer, *The World as Will and Representation*, trans. E. F. J. Payne (Indian Hills, Colo.: The Falcon's Wing Press, 1958), 1:312.

36. Chateaubriand, *Mémoires d'outre tombe*, ed. Maurice Levaillant and Georges Mouliné (Paris: Gallimard, "Bibliothèque de la Pléaide," 1951), 1:187.

37. Gustave Flaubert, letter to Louise Colet (December 2, 1846), in *Préface à la vie d'écrivain*, 44.

38. Chateaubriand, *Mémoires d'outre-tombe*, 1:187.

39. Stéphane Mallarmé, letters to Henri Cazalis (March 23, 1864) and Albert Collignon (April 11, 1864), in *Selected Letters of Stéphane Mallarmé*, ed. and trans. Rosemary Lloyd (Chicago: University of Chicago Press, 1988), 28, 30.

Session of February 16, 1980

1. See *infra*, p. 246.

2. Félix Guattari's letter to Valéry Giscard d'Estaing, the president of the Republic, dated October 5, 1979, was published for the first time in *Libération* on October 10, 1979.

3. {Italian expression: "And yet it moves."}

4. Gisèle, one of Albertine's friends, describes the French composition exam she took for the certificate of studies. The topic, "Sophocles, from the Shades, writes to Racine to console him on the failure of *Athalie*" and how the young girl deals with her response to it is an opportunity for the Narrator to make a number of ironic comments on how literature is taught. See *In Search of Lost Time*, vol. 2: *Within a Budding Grove*, trans. C. K. Scott

Moncrieff and Terence Kilmartin, rev. D. J. Enright (London: Chatto and Windus, 1992), 567.

5. Quotations from Michel Foucault's foreword to the documents associated with the case of Pierre Rivière (sentenced for parricide in 1835). Foucault makes clear that "their principle of existence and coherence is neither that of a composite work nor a legal text" and for this reason advocates the creation of new discursive instruments. See Michel Foucault, "Foreword," *I, Pierre Rivière, Having Slaughtered My Mother, My Sister, My Brother: A Case of Parricide in the Nineteenth Century*, trans. Frank Jellinek (Lincoln: University of Nebraska Press, 1982), ix. This reasoning is also at the heart of *The Order of Discourse*, the text of his inaugural lecture at the Collège de France, delivered December 2, 1970.

6. {In English in the text.}

7. Barthes is referring here to the seminar entitled "Recherches sur la rhétorique," which he led for two years running at the École des hautes études de sciences sociales (EHESS), Paris (1964–1965 and 1965–1966). See the presentation of the seminar published in the prospectus of the EHESS, OC 2:747–749, 2:875.

8. {In English in the text.}

9. This manuscript was presented to Barthes by Thierry Leguay, one of the students he was close to, and published a few years later under the title *La Petite Fabrique de littérature* by Alain Duchesne and Thierry Leguay (Paris: Magnard, 1984).

10. Gustave Flaubert, letter to Monsieur X (April 1858), in *Préface à la vie d'écrivain, ou Extraits de la correspondence*, ed. Geneviève Bollème (Paris: Seuil, 1963), 200–201.

11. Stéphane Mallarmé, "The Evolution of Literature," interview with Jules Huret for *La Revue Blanche*, which concludes with these famous words: "'So you can see,' he said, shaking hands with me, 'that in the final analysis all earthly existence must ultimately be contained in a book.'" In *Selected Prose Poems, Essays, and Letters*, trans. Bradford Cook (Baltimore, Md.: The Johns Hopkins Press, 1956), 24. {The same formulation, which reappears in "The Book as Spiritual Instrument," was recently translated by Barbara Johnson as: "everything in the world exists to end up as a book." In *Divagations* (Cambridge, Mass.: The Belknap Press of Harvard University Press, 2007), 226.}

12. Franz Kafka, letter to Felice Bauer, cited in Klaus Wagenbach, *Kafka*, trans. Ewald Osers (Cambridge, Mass.: Harvard University Press, 2003), 84.

13. Barthes is quoting from Jean-François Lyotard, *La Phénoménologie* (Paris: PUF, 1954), 4.

14. Friedrich Nietzsche, *Ecce Homo: How One Becomes What One Is*, trans. R. J. Hollingdale (London: Penguin, 1992), 62 {translation modified}.

15. Kafka, *Diaries*, 37.

16. Symphony no. 45, known as the "Farewell" symphony, by Joseph Haydn. In 1772, the composer's innovation was to conclude his symphony with an adagio rather than a fast movement. Haydn is said to have written this piece so that Prince Esterhazy would hear the musicians' campaign to be released from a contract that obliged them to be away from their families for months at a time: the instruments stop playing one after another, and each musician snuffs out his candle before leaving the stage.

17. Chateaubriand, "Préface testamentaire," *Mémoires d'outre tombe*, ed. Maurice Levaillant and Georges Mouliné (Paris: Gallimard, "Bibliothèque de la Pléaide," 1951), 1045.

18. Saint Polycarp, bishop of Smyrna, martyred in 167; Flaubert happened across his motto on the base of an old engraving found on the quays. Having decided to make Saint Polycarp his patron saint, Flaubert refers to him frequently in his correspondence. He writes, notably: "Even the slightest contact [with the

world] is painful to me. I'm more irascible, intolerant, unsociable, over-the-top, Saint-Polycarpian than ever. . . . One does not mend one's ways at my age!' Letter to his niece Caroline (December 2, 1873), in *Préface à la vie d'écrivain, ou Extraits de la correspondence*, ed. Geneviève Bollème (Paris: Seuil, 1963), 260.

19. Napoleon Bonaparte was actually born in August 1769.

20. Chateaubriand, "Préface testamentaire," *Mémoires d'outre tombe*, 1046.

21. See in particular György Lukács, *The Theory of the Novel*; and Lucien Goldmann, *Towards a Sociology of the Novel*.

22. See the entry "Roman" in the *Encyclopaedia Universalis* (section on "Roman et société") by Michel Zéraffa.

23. Guergui Plekhanov (1856–1918), a brilliant theoretican of historical materialism, introduced Marxism into Russia in the 1880s.

24. Allusion to the laborious construction of a left-wing Union, in particular the PS and the MRG severing links with the PCF over the actualization of the common Program in September 1977.

25. Gustave Flaubert, letter to Ivan Turgenev (November 13, 1872), in *The Letters of Gustave Flaubert, 1857–1880*, ed. and trans. Francis Steegmuller (Cambridge, Mass.: The Belknap Press of Harvard University Press, 1979), 200–201. {translation modified}

26. Kafka, *Diaries*, 149.

27. Chateaubriand, "Préface testamentaire," in *Mémoires d'outre tombe*, 1046.

28. Philippe Sollers, *Paradis* (Paris: Seuil, 1978). Barthes said: "it's a writing that rediscovers the great Romantic unity of the music, of the scansion, of the profound rhythm of spoken language." Interview for *Wunderblock* (1977); OC 5:384.

29. Quintilian (35–96 AD), the famous Roman orator and master of rhetoric under Vespasian and Domitian; see in particular *Institutio Oratoria* (Education of an Orator), book 1, chap. 1, entitled: "The precautions required by the child when beginning his education. Nannies and Private Tutors."

30. {"Self-made" in English in the original.}

31. For both quotations, see Chateaubriand, *Mémoires d'outre tombe*, 250.

32. {"Le Roi, c'est moi!" ("I am the King!")—although here the silent *e* is still pronounced.}

33. Gustave Flaubert, letter to George Sand (December 4, 1874), in *The Correspondence of Gustave Flaubert and George Sand*, ed. Alphonse Jacobs, trans. Francis Steegmuller and Barbara Bray (London: The Harvill Press, 1999), 293. Barthes entitled one of his columns in *Le Nouvel Observateur* "Tant que la Langue vivra" ("As Long as Language Lives") (1979); OC 5:643.

Session of February 23, 1980

1. Probably because he was running out of time, Barthes skips the next four pages and begins the last session of the Course at "To Finish the Course."

2. Stéphane Mallarmé, "Crisis of Verse," in *Divagations*, trans. Barbara Johnson (Cambridge, Mass.: The Belknap Press of Harvard University Press, 2007), 210.

3. "The author {*l'écrivain*} partakes of the priest's role, the writer {*l'écrivant*} of the clerk's; the former's speech is an intransitive act (hence, in a certain sense, a gesture), the latter's is an activity . . . *the function of the writer {l'écrivant} is to say at once and on every occasion what he thinks*; and this function, he thinks, suffices to justify him." "Authors and Writers," in *Critical Essays*, trans. Richard Howard (Evanston, Ill.: Northwestern University Press, 1972), 147–148. {translation modified}.

4. {In English in the original.}

5. Stéphane Mallarmé, "The Evolution in Literature," in *Selected Prose Poems, Essays, and Letters*, trans. Bradford Cook (Baltimore, Md.: The Johns Hopkins Press, 1956), 19.

6. Stéphane Mallarmé, "Music and Letters," in *Mallarmé in Prose*, ed. Mary Ann Caws, trans. Jill Anderson et al. (New York: New Directions Books, 2001), 32. {translation modified}.

7. *Il Convivio* (1304–1307) proposes to build a modern secular culture grounded in philosophical speculation and with the aim of radically overhauling political structures. Dante justifies the need to write his treatise in the vernacular from the outset and demonstrates its theoretical effectiveness and expressive powers.

8. Robert Boulin (minister for employment in Raymond Barre's government, under the presidency of Valéry Giscard d'Estaing) was found dead in a lake in Rambouillet Forest on October 30, 1979. The official verdict of suicide has always been contested by the victim's family.

9. Friedrich Nietzsche, *The Will to Power*, ed. Walter Kaufmann, trans. Walter Kaufmann and R. J. Hollingdale (New York: Vintage Books, 1968), 380, 381.

10. {In English in the text.}

11. Gustave Flaubert, letter to Louise Colet (April 7, 1854), in *Préface à la vie d'écrivain, ou Extraits de la correspondence*, ed. Geneviève Bollème (Paris: Seuil, 1963), 173.

12. Jena Romanticism, still called the "first phase of Romanticism," a group comprising the Schlegel brothers, Novalis, Tieck, and Schelling, the organ of which was the *Athenaeum* review. Philippe Lacoue-Labarthe and Jean-Luc Nancy write: "In the end, Jena will be remembered as the place where it was claimed that the theory of the novel must itself be a novel." Philippe Lacoue-Labarthe and Jean-Luc Nancy, *The Literary Absolute: The Theory of Literature in German Romanticism*, trans. Philip Barnard and Cheryl Lester (Albany: State University of New York Press, 1988), 12.

13. {"*Information jour au jour et à l'estomac.*" Barthes' formulation here echoes the title of Julien Gracq's famous pamphlet entitled "La Littérature à l'estomac" ("The Literature of Bluff") published in 1950.}

14. Gustave Flaubert, *Sentimental Education*, trans. Robert Baldick (London: Penguin, 2004), 323.

15. End of the long passage skipped by Barthes.

16. Passage crossed out by Barthes to the end of the paragraph.

17. This allusion to the title of his first book, *Writing Degree Zero* (a series of articles published in the journal *Combat* from 1947 on and as a collection by Seuil in 1953) refers implicitly to Barthes' early work, which invoked "a writing free of any servitude to a marked order of language" and designated the work as an "experience of impossibility"; here, thirty years on, Barthes is assigning it another vanishing point: the great classical novel as infinitely new.

18. From 1976, two years after the creation of Fnac {a large chain of shops selling books, music, films, electronics, etc.}, Jérôme Lindon, the director of Les Éditions de Minuit, violently opposed the policy of selling books at discount prices, which posed a serious threat to the network of independent bookshops and, more generally, to the economy of literary creation ("difficult books") that Barthes is referring to here. The dispute went on for a number of years and was only resolved in 1981 with the "law fixing the price of books" introduced by Jack Lang, minister of culture of the new socialist government and unanimously passed by the Assemblée Nationale.

19. See Philippe Hamon's article "Notes sur les notions de norme et de lisibilité," *Littérature* 14 (1974).

20. "A thought has escaped, I wanted to write it down: I write instead that it has escaped me." Blaise Pascal, *Pensées* (Paris: Gallimard, 1973), 146.

21. Tatiana Lipschitz's doctoral thesis, *Style et symptôme: une métanalyse du discours ironique contemporain* (1979).

22. *Deconstructive* thinking was launched by the works of Jacques Derrida. The term, which comes from Heideggerian *Destruktion*, refers to "an operation bearing upon the traditional structure or architecture of the founding concepts of Western metaphysics." This interest in structures is not presented as structuralist: it is in the first instance a matter of "undoing, decomposing, desedimenting" structures, paying special attention to the divergences and *"différances"* at play within the weft of language that explode the very logic of the sign. Clearly, this approach has an affinity with the positions expounded in "From Work to Text" (1971) or *The Pleasure of the Text* (1973). Note that *slippage* (*"glissement"*)—which Barthes appears to be opposing to *deconstruction*—is in fact one of the privileged operators of deconstruction, along with *contamination* or *dissemination*.

23. Barthes is probably referring to a remembered conversation with Elio Vittorini (1908–1966), an Italian writer, essayist, and (with Italo Calvino) editor and co-director of the famous journal entitled *Menabò*, whom Barthes met through Éditions du Seuil and the various journals he was involved in.

24. For the citation and these positions, see Stéphane Mallarmé, "Art for All," in *Selected Prose Poems, Essays, and Letters*, 12.

25. "The best and most delectable wine, and also the most intoxicating . . . by which, without drinking it, the annihilated soul is intoxicated, a soul at once free and intoxicated! Forgetting, forgotten, intoxicated by what it does not drink and will never drink!" Quotation from Ruysbroeck, which concludes *A Lover's Discourse: Fragments*, trans. Richard Howard (New York: Farrar, Straus and Giroux, 1978), 234.

26. Stéphane Mallarmé, "Important Miscellaneous News Briefs—Magic," in *Divagations*, trans. Barbara Johnson (Cambridge, Mass.: The Belknap Press of Harvard University Press, 2007), 264.

27. Barthes is paraphrasing "the story of Zarathustra": Friedrich Nietzsche, *Ecce Homo: How One Becomes What One Is*, trans. R. J. Hollingdale (London: Penguin, 1992), 69.

28. Kafka's saying, cited by Marthe Robert in her introduction to her translation of Kafka's *Diaries*: "Know yourself does not mean: observe yourself. Observe yourself is the serpent's motto. That means: transform yourself into the master of your actions. What the motto means, then, is: 'Fail to know yourself! Destroy yourself!'—and only when one stoops very far down can one hear the good part, which runs: 'in order to make yourself into that which you are.'" Kafka, *Journal*, trans. Marthe Robert (Paris: Grasset, 1954), v. {The saying is partially translated into English in Ritchie Robertson, *Kafka: A Very Short Introduction* (Oxford: Oxford University Press, 2004), 118.}

Proust and Photography: An Examination of a Little-Known Photographic Archive

1. When Barthes met her, Mme Anne-Marie Bernard (Conservateur Général des Bibliothèques), had commissioned an exhibition of Paul Nadar's photographs and was the author of a book that served as the main source of inspiration for this seminar, *Le Monde de Proust* (Paris: Direction des Musées de France, 1978; repr. Éditions du Patrimonie, 1999 and 2003).

2. The Harcourt Studios, a famous photographic agency that imposed a specific iconography of the actor in the fifties: "In France, you are not an actor if you have not been photographed by the Harcourt Studios." "The Harcourt

Actor," *The Eiffel Tower and Other Mythologies,* trans. Richard Howard (New York: Hill and Wang, 1979), 19.

3. *Le Monde de Proust, photographies de Paul Nadar,* catalogue by Anne-Marie Bernard and Agnès Blondel (Musées de France, 1978). The book is a collection of around a hundred photographs accompanied by notes that were drawn, for the most part, from George Painter's two-volume biography of Proust (1959 and 1965); these notes were one of Barthes's sources when composing the biographical notes that were intended to accompany the projection of the photographs.

4. Jeanne Pouquet, see p. 362.

5. George D. Painter, *Marcel Proust: A Biography,* 2 vols. (London: Chatto and Windus, 1959–1965), trans. Georges Cattaui (Paris: Mercure de France, 1966). {In the biographical notes Barthes is frequently either directly quoting or silently paraphrasing passages from Cattaiu's translation of Painter's book. In this translation, I have gone back to Painter's original English text and located the same passages that Barthes quotes in their French translation. For further details on this strategy, see the translator's preface at the front of this volume.}

6. This formulation implicitly refers to the text entitled "One Always Fails in Speaking About What One Loves" (a paper planned for a conference on Stendhal in Milan in the spring of 1980), which Barthes was writing at the same time as the presentation of this seminar. The accident (February 25, 1980) that led to Barthes's death on March 26 meant he was unable to deliver and publish the paper; the text appeared in *Tel Quel* 85 (Fall 1980); *OC* 5:906–914.

7. {Barthes's formulation echoes Lacan's translation of the Freudian expression *Wo Es war, soll Ich werden,* translated in the Standard Edition as "Where Id was, there ego shall be" (*The Standard Edition of the Psychological Works of Sigmund Freud,* 22:80). Lacan proposes two alternative translations: "*Là où c'était . . .*" or "*Là où s'était dois-je advenir*" *(*There where it was, or there where one was . . . I should come to be*). Jacques Lacan,* Écrits *(Paris: Éditions du Seuil, 1966), 417.}

8. Marceline Desbordes-Valmore (1786–1859), a woman of letters, poet, and author of a number of collections including *Pauvres Fleurs* (1839) and *Bouquets et prières* (1843), was admired by Lamartine, Hugo, Baudelaire, and Verlaine and considered to be the female embodiment of French-style Romanticism. Barthes is probably referring here to the story entitled "Le Petit Bègue" ("The Little Stutterer") and, more implicitly, to the theme of hesitant, stammering speech, which runs throughout her work.

9. Reference to Proust's duties as an "unpaid attaché" to the Mazarine library, rue de Grenelle, a post he competed for and obtained in 1895. The post did not suit him, and he was granted leave for two months for reasons of ill health; the leave was extended to 1900, when he was considered to have resigned.

10. Amélie Weil, née Oulman, wife of Georges Weil, Proust's aunt by marriage. See p. 371.

11. Aunt Léonie's house at Combray (novelistic version of Illiers, in Eure-et-Loir, where Proust's family originated) is a version of the house belonging to Mme Élisabeth Amiot, née Proust, Marcel Proust's paternal aunt; the rooms in the cottage (the bedroom and the kitchen are described in *In Search of Lost Time*) are indeed of a modest size.

12. Allusion to Pierre Bordieu's *La Distinction* (Paris: Éditions de Minuit, 1979), recently published.

13. See p. 375.

14. The *gestus.* See note 1, p. 421.

15. See p. 350.

16. {In this passage, Barthes consistently uses the expression "*les clefs*" ("the keys") to refer to the real-life sources of some of the characters in *In Search of Lost Time*.}

17. Barthes is referring here to Marcel Proust's famous dedication to Jacques de Lacretelle in a copy of *Du côté de chez Swann*, dated April 20, 1918—the most important dedication Proust wrote. See Marcel Proust, *Selected Letters*, ed. Philip Kolb, trans. Terence Kilmartin (London: HarperCollins, 1992), 3:412.

18. See Octave Mannoni, "Le Rêve et le transfert," *Clefs pour l'imaginaire ou l'autre scène* (Paris: Seuil, 1969).

19. Baron Doasan (Painter) or Doäzan (Tadié), a regular at Mme Aubernon's salon (who was the model for Mme Verdurin), is one of the models for Charlus, as Proust himself claims in a letter to Montesquiou.

20. Barthes was treated for a pulmonary ailment by Dr. Brissaud, the son of Professor Brissaud. Doctor Brissaud's sons, Jean and Henri, were his classmates at the Lycée Montaigne.

21. Possibly "Callot": rue Jacques-Callot was where Barthes lived as an adolescent.

22. {Marcel Proust, letter to Laure Hayman (May 18, 1922), *Selected Letters*, ed. Philip Kolb, trans. Joanna Kilmartin (London: HarperCollins, 2000), 4:353.}

Haiku

1. Here we present the transcription of the fascicule composed by Barthes and handed out during the session of January 13, 1979. We have reproduced the punctuation as it appears on the original document.

2. {The translations marked * are taken from R. H. Blyth's *Haiku*, 4 vols. (Tokyo: Hokuseido Press, 1949–1952). Those marked with † repeat the translations used in Roland Barthes, *Empire of Signs*, trans. Richard Howard (New York: Hill and Wang, 1982). All other translations are my own, working directly from the French (retaining the name of the French translator for reference). For an account of the strategy adopted here, see the translator's preface.}

Vita Nova

1. Barthes is evidently referring to the death of his mother, which occurred on October 25, 1977.

2. We know nothing specific about this "decision"; nevertheless, it is clear that it is a matter of a mythical conversion—in the manner of Pascal—to a "new life" wherein existence would be entirely taken up by "literature."

3. R. H. are the initials of the character-pretext that led to the writing of *A Lover's Discourse: Fragments*.

4. This Greek term, which is difficult to make out, has been transcribed here as Κομπολόιό {*Komboloï*} rather than Κοβολι, as Barthes writes mistakenly. Meaning "beads" in modern Greek. In this instance *Komboloï* refers to the traditional pastime with which Greek men occupy themselves while the women knit: a secular pastime that involves manipulating a kind of rosary that is passed from one hand to the other.

5. Éric Marty: the word would appear to be "expansion." {Diana Knight, however, suggests "expression," which would fit with the phrase in the fifth plan: "I'm withdrawing from the world to begin a great work that will be an expression of . . . Love."}

6. {A is the first letter of *agir*, or "to act."}

7. The Zenrin poem is a poem in the Zen tradition from *Zenrin Kushu* (fifteenth century). Barthes alludes to it in *Incidents* as a way of characterizing the pose and the attitude of the Moroccan child he mentions here: "A kid sitting on a low wall, alongside a road he isn't watching—sitting, as it were eternally, sitting in order to be sitting, *without procrastinating*. Sitting quietly, doing nothing. Spring comes, and the grass grows of its own accord." See Diana Knight, "Idle Thoughts: Barthes's *Vita Nova*" Nottingham French Studies (Spring 1997): 88–98.

8. This is clearly a reference to Dante. "'Now go, for one same will is in both: you are guide, you lord, and you master.' So I said to him; / and when he had set forth / I set out upon the deep, savage path." *The Divine Comedy of Dante Alighieri*, vol. 1: *Inferno*, ed. and trans. Robert M. Durling (Oxford: Oxford University Press, 1996), 47. {translation modified}

9. {*Mam.* is used here as an abbreviation for *Maman*, a familiar term for Mother}

10. {The Café de Flore, in Paris}

11. {Barthes's term here is *Recherches*, echoing the title of Proust's *A la Recherche du temps perdu* (*In Search of Lost Time*).}

12. This Greek term signifies motleyed, multicolored, changeable. It is notably used apropos of the Romantic novelists to designate the total novel that combines all literary forms. In his 1979–1980 lecture course at the Collège de France, which was cut short by his death but drafted in full, Barthes wrote: "Romantic Novel or Absolute Novel. Novalis (*Encyclopaedia*, Book 2, Section 6, fragments 1441 and 1448): *Art of the Novel*: Shouldn't the novel include all kinds of styles, variously linked to and animated by the common spirit? The art of the novel excludes all continuity. The novel should be an edifice that is built anew in each of its eras. Each little fragment should be something cut out—something circumscribed—a whole worth something in itself." A little further on Barthes adds: "I forgot to give the Greek word: *poikilos*, daubed, spotted, mottled—the root of *pikilia* in modern Greek: various *hors d'oeuvres*—we could also cite the Rhapsodic, the tacked together (Proust: the Work as made by a Dressmaker) → the Rhapsodic distances the Object, magnifies the Tendency, the act of *Writing*." See p. **144**.

13. {Barthes's term here is *reliefs*, signifying remains or remnants but also the raised or visible portions of something. Both meanings are used in the seventh plan. See p. **405**.}

14. Allusion to François Porbus the younger, a Flemish painter, born in Anvers in 1570 and died in Paris in 1622, who appears in Balzac's *The Unknown Masterpiece*, to which Barthes is referring here. Yet Barthes makes a peculiar mistake: the actual author of the chaotic canvas—a "kind of formless fog"—from which a single fragment—a bare foot—emerges is Frenhofer.

15. {Allusion to the fable by La Fontaine: "The Frog Who Wished to Make Herself as Big as the Bull." See *Selected Fables*, trans. Christopher Wood (Oxford: Oxford University Press, 1995), 13–14.}

16. {A term adapted from the Italian *bolgia*, used by Dante to refer to the gulfs or valleys of the eighth circle of the Inferno.}

17. {Barthes's plan reads: "Politique H etc.," with the "H" shorthand for *Homosexuelle*; here the "G" should be read as shorthand for "Gay," as in "Gay Politics etc."}

18. Barthes is alluding here to Jean-Louis Bouttes, one of his closest friends.

19. {Barthes's *Journal of Mourning*, which belongs to that "panorama" of writings that form a background to *The Preparation of the Novel* discussed in the editor's preface (see pp. **xvi–xviii**), has recently been published in French: *Journal de Deuil: 26 octobre 1977–15 septembre 1979*, edited by Nathalie Léger (Paris: Seuil, 2009).}

20. Barthes initially wrote "79" here, but then corrected it by writing "78" over the top.

21. In the 1979–1980 lecture course, Barthes quotes this passage from Heidegger in the section on "Idleness": "Heidegger (*Essays*, XXVII, 'Overcoming Metaphysics'): 'The unnoticeable law of the earth preserves the earth in the sufficiency of the emerging and perishing of all things in the allotted sphere of the possible which everything follows, and yet nothing knows. The birch [the tree, that is!] never oversteps its possibility. The colony of bees dwells in its possibility. It is first the will which arranges itself everywhere in technology that devours the earth in the exhaustion and consumption and change of what is artificial. Technology drives the earth beyond the developed sphere of its possibility into such things which are no longer a possibility and are thus the impossible' → that, I think, is a good description of the Conflict between *Writing* (will, exhaustion, wear, variations, whims, artifices, in short, the *Impossible*) and *Idleness* (Nature, development—"sensitivity"—within the sphere of the Possible)." See pp. 156–57.

BIBLIOGRAPHY

Works in English

Amiel, Henri-Frédéric. *Amiel's Journal: The Journal of Henri-Frédéric Amiel.* Trans. Mrs. Humphrey Ward. London: Macmillan, 1885.

Apollinaire, Guillaume. *Alcools: Poems 1898–1913.* Trans. William Meredith. New York: Doubleday, 1964.

———. *Selected Writings of Guillaume Apollinaire.* Trans. Roger Shattock. New York: New Directions, 1971.

Bachelard, Gaston. *Air and Dreams: An Essay on the Imagination of Movement.* Trans. Edith R. Farrell and C. Frederick Farrell. Dallas: Dallas Institute of Humanities and Culture, 1988.

———. *The Dialectic of Duration.* Trans. Mary McAllester Jones. Manchester: Clinamen, 2000.

Bacon, Francis. *The Advancement of Learning and Novum Organum.* Ed. James Creighton. New York: Colonial, 1900.

Balzac, Honoré de. *The Girl with the Golden Eyes.* Trans. Carol Cosman. New York: Carroll and Grat Publishers, 1998.

———. *The Unpublished Correspondence of Honoré de Balzac and Madame Zulma Carraud.* Trans. J. Lewis May. London: John Lane, 1937.

Barthes, Roland. *Camera Lucida.* Trans. Richard Howard. New York: Hill and Wang, 1981.

———. *Critical Essays.* Trans. Richard Howard. Evanston, Ill.: Northwestern University Press, 1972.

———. *Empire of Signs.* Trans. Richard Howard. New York: Hill and Wang, 1982.

———. *The Eiffel Tower and Other Mythologies.* Trans. Richard Howard. New York: Hill and Wang, 1979.

———. *The Fashion System.* Trans. Matthew Ward and Richard Howard. New York: Hill and Wang, 1983.

———. *The Grain of the Voice.* Trans. Linda Coverdale. Berkeley: University of California Press, 1985.

———. *Image / Music / Text.* Trans. Stephen Heath. New York: Hill and Wang, 1977.

———. "Inaugural Lecture, Collège de France." Trans. Richard Howard. In *A Roland Barthes Reader.* Ed. Susan Sontag. London: Jonathan Cape, 1982.

———. *A Lover's Discourse: Fragments.* Trans. Richard Howard. New York: Farrar, Straus and Giroux, 1978.

———. *New Critical Essays.* Trans. Richard Howard. New York: Hill and Wang, 1980.

———. *The Neutral.* Ed. Thomas Clerc under the direction of Eric Marty. Trans. Rosalind E. Krauss and Denis Hollier. New York: Columbia University Press, 2005.

———. *The Responsibility of Forms.* Trans. Richard Howard. Berkeley: University of California Press, 1985.

———. *Roland Barthes.* Trans. Richard Howard. Berkeley: University of California Press, 1977.

———. *The Rustle of Language*. Trans. Richard Howard. New York: Hill and Wang, 1986.
———. *S/Z*. Trans. Richard Miller. New York: Farrar, Strauss and Giroux, 1974.
———. *Sade/Fourier/Loyola*. Trans. Richard Miller. Baltimore, Md.: The Johns Hopkins University Press, 1997.
———. "To Write: Intransitive Verb?" *The Languages of Criticism and the Sciences of Man*. Ed. Richard Macksey and Eugenio Donato. Baltimore, Md.: The Johns Hopkins University Press, 1970.
———. *Writing Degree Zero*. Trans. Annette Lavers and Colin Smith. New York: Hill and Wang, 1968.
Bataille, Georges. *Visions of Excess: Selected Writings, 1927–1939*. Trans. Allan Stoekl with Carl R. Lovitt and Donald M. Leslie Jr. Minneapolis: University of Minnesota Press, 1985.
Baudelaire, Charles. *Artificial Paradise*. Trans. Ellen Fox. New York: Herder and Herder, 1971.
———. *Les Fleurs du Mal*. Trans. Richard Howard. Boston: Godine, 1982.
Benveniste, Émile. *Problems in General Linguistics*. Trans. Mary Elizabeth Meek. Coral Gables, Fla.: University of Miami Press, 1971.
Bernard, Anne-Marie. *The World of Proust, as Seen by Paul Nadar*. Trans. Susan Wise. Cambridge, Mass.: The MIT Press, 2002.
Bibesco, Marthe. *Marcel Proust at the Ball*. Trans. Anthony Rhodes. London: Weidenfield and Nicholson, 1956.
Blanchot, Maurice. *The Book to Come*. Trans. Charlotte Mandell. Stanford, Calif.: Stanford University Press, 2003.
———. *The Infinite Conversation*. Trans. Susan Hanson. Minneapolis: University of Minnesota Press, 1993.
Blyth, R. H. *Haiku*. 4 vols. Tokyo: The Hokuseido Press, 1949–1952.
———. *A History of Haikus*. 2 vols. Tokyo: The Hokuseido Press, 1963.
Cage, John. *For the Birds: In Conversation with Daniel Charles*. Boston: Marion Boyars, 1981.
Dante. *The Divine Comedy of Dante Alighieri*. Trans. Robert M. Durling. Oxford: Oxford University Press, 1996.
De Quincey, Thomas. *Confessions of an English Opium-Eater*. Vol. 3 of *The Collected Works of Thomas De Quincey*, rev. ed. Ed. David Masson. Edinburgh: Adam and Charles Black, 1890.
De Sade. *Crimes of Love: Heroic and Tragic Tales, Preceded by an Essay on Novels*. Trans. David Coward. Oxford: Oxford University Press, 2005.
Deleuze, Gilles. *Nietzsche and Philosophy*. Trans. Hugh Tomlinson. New York: Columbia University Press, 1983.
Ellmann, Richard. *James Joyce*. Oxford: Oxford University Press, 1959.
Flaubert, Gustave. *Bouvard and Pécuchet*. Trans. A. J. Krailsheimer. New York: Penguin, 1976.
———. *The Correspondence of Gustave Flaubert and George Sand*. Trans. Francis Steegmuller and Barbara Bray. London: The Harvill Press, 1999.
———. *The Letters of Gustave Flaubert: 1832–1857*. Trans. Francis Steegmuller. Cambridge, Mass.: The Belknap Press of Harvard University Press, 1979.
———. *The Letters of Gustave Flaubert: 1857–1880*. Trans. Francis Steegmuller. Cambridge: The Belknap Press of Harvard University Press, 1982.
———. *Sentimental Education*. Trans. Robert Baldick, rev. Geoffrey Wall. London: Penguin, 2004.
———. "A Simple Heart." In *Three Tales*. Trans. Roger Whitehouse. London: Penguin, 2005.
Foucault, Michel. Foreword to *I, Pierre Rivière, Having Slaughtered My Mother, My Sister, My Brother: A Case of Parricide in the Nineteenth

Century. Ed. Michel Foucault. Trans. Frank Jellinek. Lincoln: University of Nebraska Press, 1982.

———. "The Order of Discourse." In *Untying the Text: A Poststructuralist Reader*. Ed. Robert Young. London: Routledge and Kegan Paul, 1981.

Freud, Sigmund. "The Ego and the Id (the Ego-Ideal)." In *Essays in Psychoanalysis*. In *The Standard Edition of the Psychological Works of Sigmund Freud* [*SE*], vol. 19. London: The Hogarth Press and the Institute of Psychoanalysis, 1953–1974.

———. "On Narcissism: An Introduction." In *SE*, vol. 14.

———. "An Outline of Psychoanalysis." In *SE*, vol. 18.

———. "Revision of the Theory of Dreams." In *SE*, vol. 22.

Gérard Genette, *Mimiologics*. Trans. Thais E. Morgan. Lincoln: University of Nebraska Press, 1994.

———. *Palimpsests: Literature in the Second Degree*. Trans. Channa Newman and Claude Doubinsky. Lincoln: University of Nebraska Press, 1997.

Girard, René. *Deceit, Desire, and the Novel: Self and Other in Literary Structure*. Trans. Yvonne Freccero. Baltimore, Md.: The Johns Hopkins University Press, 1976.

Goldmann, Lucian. *Towards a Sociology of a Novel*. Trans. Alan Sheridan. London: Tavistock, 1975.

Heidegger, Martin. *The End of Philosophy*. Trans. Joan Stambaugh. Chicago: University of Chicago Press, 2003.

Jakobson, Roman. "Linguistics and Poetics." In *Style in Language*. Ed. Thomas A. Sebeok. Cambridge, Mass.: The MIT Press, 1960.

Janouch, Gustav. *Conversations with Kafka*. Trans. Goronwy Rees. 2nd ed. New York: New Directions, 1971.

Kafka, Franz. *The Diaries: 1910–1923*. Ed. Max Brod. Trans. Joseph Kresh, Martin Greenberg, et al. New York: Schocken Books, 1976.

Kierkergaard, Søren. *Fear and Trembling*. Ed. C. Stephen Evans and Sylvia Walsh. Trans. Sylvia Walsh. Cambridge: Cambridge University Press, 2006.

Lacan, Jacques. *The Seminar of Jacques Lacan*. Book 1: *Freud's Papers on Technique, 1953–1954*. Ed. Jacques Alain Miller. Trans. John Forrester. Cambridge: Cambridge University Press, 1988.

Lacoue-Labarthe, Philippe, and Jean-Luc Nancy. *The Literary Absolute: The Theory of Literature in German Romanticism*. Trans. Philip Barnard and Cheryl Lester. Albany, N.Y.: SUNY Press, 1988.

La Fontaine, Jean. *La Fontaine: Selected Fables*. Trans. James Michie. London: Penguin, 1982.

Laplanche, J., and J.-B. Pontalis. *The Language of Psychoanalysis*. Trans. Donald Nicholson Smith. London: Karnac Books and the Institute of Psychoanalysis, 1988.

Loti, Pierre. *Aziyadé*. Trans. Marjorie Laurie. London: Kegan Paul International, 1989.

Loyola, Ignatius. *The Spiritual Journal of St. Ignatius Loyola*. Trans. William J. Young. Kessinger, 2006.

Lukács, György. *The Theory of the Novel*. Trans. A. Bostock. London: Merlin Press, 1971.

Mallarmé, Stéphane. *Divagations*. Trans. Barbara Johnson. Cambridge, Mass.: The Belknap Press of Harvard University Press, 2007.

———. *Selected Letters of Stéphane Mallarmé*. Trans. Rosemary Lloyd. Chicago: University of Chicago Press, 1988.

———. *Selected Poetry and Prose*. Ed. Mary Ann Caws. Trans. Paul Auster, Mary Ann Caws, et al. New York: New Directions, 1984.

———. *Selected Prose Poems, Essays, and Letters*. Trans. Bradford Cook. Baltimore, Md.: The Johns Hopkins University Press, 1956.

Maupassant, Guy de. *Pierre and Jean*. Trans. Julie Mead. Oxford: Oxford University Press, 2001.

Michelet, Jules. "The 1869 Preface." In *Michelet's Poetic Vision: A Romantic Philosophy of Nature, Man, and Woman*, by Edward K. Kaplan. Amherst: University of Massachusetts Press, 1977.

———. *Satanism and Witchcraft: A Study in Medieval Superstition*. Trans. A. R. Allinson. New York: Citadel, 1946.

Montaigne, Michel de. *The Complete Essays*. Trans. M. A. Screech. London: Penguin, 2003.

Nietzsche, Friedrich. *The Birth of Tragedy and Other Writings*. Ed. Raymond Geuss and Ronald Speirs. Trans. Roland Speirs. Cambridge: Cambridge University Press, 1999.

———. *Daybreak: Thoughts on the Prejudices of Morality*. Ed. Maudemarie Clark and Brian Letter. Trans. R. J. Hollingdale. Cambridge: Cambridge University Press, 1997.

———. *Ecce Homo*. Trans. R. J. Hollingdale. London: Penguin, 1992.

———. *The Will to Power*. Ed. Walter Kaufmann. Trans. Walter Kaufmann and R. J. Hollingdale. New York: Vintage Books, 1968.

Novalis, Friedrich. *Notes for a Romantic Encyclopaedia*. Trans. David W. Wood. Albany, N.Y.: SUNY Press, 2007.

Painter, George. *Marcel Proust: A Biography*. 2 vols. London: Chatto and Windus, 1959–1965.

Pascal, Blaise. *Pensées*. Trans. Roger Ariew. Indianapolis: Ind.: Hackett, 2005.

Plantin, Christophe. "The Happiness of this World." In *Anthology of European Poetry*, vol. 1: *From Machault to Malherbe, Thirteenth to Seventeenth Century*. Ed. Mervyn Savill. Trans. William Stirling et al. London: Alan Wingate, 1977.

Proust, Marcel. *Against Sainte-Beuve and Other Essays*. Trans. John Sturrock. London: Penguin, 1988.

———. *By Way of Sainte-Beuve* [*Contre Sainte-Beuve*]. Trans. Sylvia Townsend Warner. London: Chatto and Windus, 1958.

———. *In Search of Lost Time*. Vols. 1–5. Trans. C. K. Scott Moncrieff and Terence Kilmartin, rev. D. J. Enright. London: Chatto and Windus, 1992.

———. *In Search of Lost Time*. Vol. 6. Trans. Andreas Mayor and Terence Kilmartin, rev. D. J. Enright. London: Chatto and Windus, 1992.

———. *Marcel Proust: A Selection from His Miscellaneous Writings*. Trans. Gerard Hopkins. London: Allan Wingate, 1963.

———. *Selected Letters*. Vol. 2: *1904–1909*. Ed. Philip Kolb. Trans. Terence Kilmartin. London: Collins, 1989.

———. *Selected Letters*. Vol. 3: *1910–1917*. Ed. Philip Kolb. Trans. Terence Kilmartin. London: HarperCollins, 1992.

———. *Selected Letters*. Vol. 4: *1918–1922*. Ed. Philip Kolb. Trans. Joanna Kilmartin. London: HarperCollins, 2000.

Quint, L. P. *Marcel Proust: His Life and Work*. Trans. Hamish Miles and Sheila Miles. New York: A. A. Knopf, 1927.

Racine, Jean. *Five Plays*. Trans. Kenneth Muir. New York: Hill and Wang, 1960.

Renard, Jules. *Natural Histories*. Trans. Richard Howard. New York: Horizon, 1966.

Rimbaud, Arthur. *Complete Works, Selected Letters: A Bilingual Edition*. Trans. Wallace Fowlie, rev. Seth Whidden. Chicago: University of Chicago Press, 2005.

Robertson, Ritchie. *Kafka: A Very Short Introduction*. Oxford: Oxford University Press, 2004.
Rousseau, Jean-Jacques. *Confessions*. Ed. Patrick Coleman. Trans. Angela Scholar. Oxford: Oxford University Press, 2000.
———. *The Reveries of a Solitary Walker*. Trans. Charles E. Butterworth. New York: NYU Press, 1971.
Sartre, Jean-Paul. *Nausea*. Trans. Robert Baldick. London: Penguin, 2002.
———. *"What Is Literature?" and Other Essays*. Trans. Jeffrey Mehlman. Cambridge, Mass.: Harvard University Press, 1988.
Schlegel, Friedrich. *Friedrich Schlegel's* Lucinde *and the* Fragments. Trans. Peter Firchow. Minneapolis: University of Minnesota Press, 1971.
Silesius, Angelus. *The Cherubinic Wanderer*. Trans. Maria Shrady. New York: Paulist Press, 1986.
Suzuki, Daisetz Teitaro. *Essays in Zen Buddhism*. Vol. 1. New York: Grove Press, 1961.
———. *Essays on Zen Buddhism*. 3 vols. London: Luzac, 1934.
Tolstoy, Leo. *Childhood, Boyhood, Youth*. Trans. C. J. Hogarth. London: Everyman's Library, 1991.
———. *Master and Man*. Trans. Paul Foot. London: Penguin, 1977.
———. *Tolstoy's Diaries*. 2 vols. Trans. R. F. Christian. London: The Athlone Press, 1985.
Valéry, Paul. *Variety*. Trans. Malcolm Cowley. New York: Harcourt, Brace, 1927.
Verlaine, Paul. *Paul Verlaine: Selected Poems*. Trans. Martin Sorrell. Oxford: Oxford University Press, 1999.
Wagenbach, Klaus. *Kafka*. Trans. Edward Osers. Cambridge, Mass.: Harvard University Press, 2003.
Watts, Alan W. *The Way of Zen*. London: Thames and Hudson, 1957.
Zola, Émile. *Germinal*. Trans. Roger Pearson. London: Penguin Books, 2004.

Works in Other Languages

Apollinaire, Sidoine. *Lettres*. Trans. André Loyen. Paris: Les Belles Lettres, 1979.
Barthes, Roland. *Comment vivre ensemble: Simulations romanesques de quelques espaces quotidiens*. Ed. Claude Coste. Paris: Seuil / IMEC, 2004.
———. *Œuvres complètes*. Ed. Éric Marty. 5 vols. Paris: Éditions du Seuil, 1993–1995.
———. *Prétexte: Roland Barthes*. Colloque de Cerisy. Ed. Antoine Compagnon. Paris: Éditions Christian Bourgois, 2003.
Bellemin-Noël, Jean. *Vers l'inconscient du texte*. Paris: PUF, 1979.
Benveniste, Émile. *Problèmes de linguistique générale*. Vol. 2. Paris: Gallimard, 1966.
Bernard, Anne-Marie, and Agnès Blondel. *Le Monde de Proust, photographies de Paul Nadar*. Paris: Musées de France, 1978.
Bonnet, Henri. *Marcel Proust de 1907 à 1914*. Paris: Nizet, 1971.
Bouillane de Lacoste, Henri. *Rimbaud et le problème des "Illuminations."* Paris: Mercure de France, 1949.
Brion, Marcel. "Hofmannsthal et l'expérience du labyrinthe." *Cahiers du Sud* 133 (1955).
Burnier, Marc-Antoine, and Patrick Rambaud. *Roland Barthes sans peine*. Paris: Balland, 1973.

Carré, Jean-Marie. *La Vie aventureuse de Jean-Arthur Rimbaud*. Paris: Plon, 1926.
Cassien. *Institutions cénobitiques*. Paris: Cerf, 1965.
Cattaui, Georges. Introduction. In *Marcel Proust*, by George D. Painter. Paris: Mercure de France, 1966.
Chaix-Ruy, Jules. *La Formation de la pensée philosophique chez Vico*. Paris: PUF, n.d.
Chateaubriand, François-René de. *Mémoires d'outre-tombe*. Vol. 1. Ed. Maurice Levaillant and Georges Moulinié. Paris: Gallimard, 1951.
———. *Vie de Rancé*. Preface by Roland Barthes. Paris: UGE, 1965.
Cioran, E. M. *La Tentation d'exister*. Paris: Gallimard, 1956.
Clermont-Tonnerre, Élisabeth de. *Robert de Montesquiou et Marcel Proust*. Paris: Flammarion, 1925.
Compagnon, Antoine. *La Seconde main ou le Travail de la citation*. Paris: Seuil, 1979.
Coyaud, Maurice. *Fourmis sans ombre. Le Livre du haïku. Anthologie Promenade*. Paris: Phébus, 1978.
Diderot, Denis. *Œuvres complètes*. Vol. 3. Paris: Club français du livre, 1970.
Duchesne, Alain, and Thierry Leguay. *La Petite Fabrique de littérature*. Paris: Magnard, 1984.
Étiemble, René. "Du Japon" (1976), reprinted in *Quelques essais de littérature universelle*. Paris: Gallimard, 1982.
Flahault, François. *La Parole intermédiaire*. Paris: Seuil, 1978.
Flaubert, Gustave. *Préface à la vie d'écrivain, ou Extraits de la correspondance*. Ed. Geneviève Bollème. Paris: Seuil, 1963.
Gardair, Jean-Michel. *Les Écrivains italiens. 'La Divine Comédie.'* Paris: Larousse, 1978.
Gautier, Théophile. *Émaux et camées* (1922). Paris: Librairie Gründ, 1935.
Gide, André. *Paludes*. Paris: Gallimard, 1926.
———. *Journal (1887–1925)*. Vol. 1. Ed. Éric Marty. Paris: Gallimard, 1996.
Grenier, Jean. *L'Esprit du Tao*. Paris: Flammarion, 1957.
Joubert, Joseph. *Pensées, maximes, et essais*. Paris: Perrin et Cie, 1911.
Kristeva, Julia. *La Révolution du langage poétique*. Paris: Seuil, 1974.
La Bruyère. *Les Caractères*. Paris: Gallimard, 1951.
Lacan, Jacques. *Le Séminaire*. Book 11. Paris: Seuil, 1973.
Legendre, Pierre. "Où sont nos Droits poétiques?" *Cahiers du cinéma* 297 (February 1979).
Lyotard, Jean-François. *La Phénoménologie*. Paris: PUF, 1976.
Mallarmé, Stéphane. *Correspondance complète (1862–1871)*. Paris: Gallimard, 1959.
———. *Correspondance*. Ed. Bertrand Marchal. Preface by Yves Bonnefoy. Paris: Gallimard, 1995.
———. *Œuvres complètes*. Ed. Henri Mondor and G. Jean-Aubry. Paris: Gallimard, 1945.
Michaud, Guy. *Mallarmé*. Paris: Hatter, 1982.
Michelet, Jules. Preface to *Histoire de la France*. Paris: Librairie internationale, 1871.
Monod, Gabriel. *La Vie et la pensée de Jules Michelet*. Vol. 2. Paris: Champion, 1923.
———. *Jules Michelet*. Paris: Hachette, 1905.
Morand, Paul. *Tendres Stocks*. Preface by Marcel Proust. Paris: Le Sagittaire, 1920.
Morier, Henri. *Dictionnaire de poétique et de rhétorique*. Paris: PUF, 1961.
Munier, Roger. *Haiku*. Preface by Yves Bonnefoy. Paris: Fayard, 1978.

Novalis, Friedrich. *L'Encyclopédie*. Trans. Maurice de Gandillac. Paris: Éditions de Minuit, 1966.
Picon, Gaétan. *Balzac*. Paris: Seuil, 1954.
Proust, Marcel. *Choix de lettres*. Ed. Philip Kolb. Paris: Plon, 1965.
Rambures, Jean-Louis de. *Comment travaillent les écrivains*. Paris: Flammarion, 1978.
Raymond, Didier. *Schopenhauer*. Paris: Seuil, 1979.
Richard, Jean-Pierre. *Littérature et sensation*. Preface by Georges Poulet. Paris: Seuil, 1954.
Rimbaud, Arthur. *Oeuvres*. Ed. Paterne Berrichon. Preface by Paul Claudel. Paris: Mercure de France, 1912.
———. *Lettres de la vie littéraire d'Arthur Rimbaud (1870–1875)*. Paris: Gallimard, 1931.
Rivane, Georges. *Influence de l'asthme sur l'oeuvre de Marcel Proust*. Paris: La Nouvelle Édition, 1945.
Safouan, Moustapha. *Études sur l'Œdipe*. Paris: Seuil, 1974.
Santarcangeli, Paolo. *Le Livre des labyrinthes. Histoire d'un mythe et d'un symbole*. Trans. Monique Lacau. Paris: Gallimard, 1974.
Sarduy, Severo. *La Doublure*. Paris: Flammarion, 1982.
Schehadé, Georges. *Anthologie du vers unique*. Paris: Ramsay, 1977.
Scherer, Jacques. *Le 'Livre' de Mallarmé*. Paris: Gallimard, 1957.
Sieffert, René. *La Littérature japonaise*. Paris: Armaud Colin, 1961.
Sollers, Philippe. *Paradis*. Paris: Seuil, 1978.
———. *Les Sophistes. Fragments et témoignages*. Paris: PUF, 1969.
Valéry, Paul. Preface to *Sur des livres japonais*, by Kiko Yamata. Paris: Le Divan, 1924.
———. *Oeuvres*. Vol. 1. "Introduction biographique" by Agathe Rouart-Valéry. Paris: Gallimard, 1957.
Vico, Giambattista. *Scienza Nuova (1725)*. Trans. Christina Trivulzio. Paris: Gallimard, 1993.
———. *Oeuvres choisies de Vico*, by Jules Michelet. In *Œuvres complètes*, vol. 1. Ed. Pierre Viallaniex. Paris: Flammarion, 1971.
Villier, Marc, ed. *Dictionnaire de la spiritualité ascétique et mystique*. Vol. 14. Paris: Beauchène, 1937–1995.
Yamata, Kiko. *Sur des livres japonais*. Paris: Le Divan, 1924.

INDEX NOMINUM

Abraham, 151, 433n26
Agostinelli, Alfred, 306, 313, 315, 317
Albaret, Céleste, 334
Albaret, Odolon, 317, 334
Albertine (*In Search of Lost Time*), 62, 315, 337, 448n4
Albufera, Louis d', 306, 318, 346, 360
Alcidamas, 15, 412n14
Alençon, Émilienne d', 337
Amiel, Henri-Frédéric, 36, 92, 172, 416n16, 436n26
Apollinaire, Guillaume, 51, 66, 254, 418n19
Apollinaire, Sidoine, 8, 410n22
Arcimboldo, 56
Ariadne, 114, 115, 117, 118, 121, 428n12
Aristotle, 120, 142, 428n13
Arman de Caillavet, Albert, 306, 329
Arman de Caillavet, Gaston, 362, 365
Arman de Caillavet, Mme Albert (Léontine Lippmann), 307, 309, 319, 329, 339, 362
Arman de Caillavet, Mme Gaston (Jeanne Pouquet), 307, 309, 319, 325, 329, 362, 365, 453n4
Artaud, Antonin, 47, 182, 208, 233
Arthur, King, 105
Aubernon de Nerville, Lydie, 306, 319, 363
Aubert, Edgar, 351
Augustine, Saint, 14, 154
Avedon, Richard, 421n4

Bachelard, Gaston, 16, 49, 130, 247, 412n16, 418n13
Bacon, Francis, 51
Baignères, Laure, 319
Bakhtin, Mikhail, 144, 432n7
Bakunan, 53, 381
Balzac, Honoré de, 94, 103, 132, 185, 289, 434n37, 455n14; clothing of, 230; and painting, 59, 70, 135–36; Proust on, 258–59; and schedules, 246, 247; and secrecy, 243; short stories of, 198; and Swedenborg, 448n29; and Vita Nova, 212; and the work *vs.* the world, 203, 204, 207; and writing at night, 238, 239
Barney, Miss, 337
Barrès, Maurice, 306, 320, 335, 347
Bartet, Julia, 306, 321
Baruzi, Jean, xxi
Basho, 35, 52, 53, 60, 63, 65–69, 72, 78–86, 379, 382–87, 413n7
Bataille, Georges, 143, 415n4
Baudelaire, Charles, 143, 177, 424n5b, 448n29, 453n8; and the Album, 186; and boredom, 274; crises of, 253; and De Quincey, 40, 416n8; and heroism, 281; and individuation, 43; and notation, 93, 95; on not publishing, 270; on synaesthesia, 59
Bauer, Felice, 281
Beatrice (*Divine Comedy*), xxi, 47, 205, 409n10
Beckett, Samuel, 289
Beethoven, Ludwig van, 96
Bellemin-Noël, Jean, 208
Benardaky, Marie, 306, 314, 323, 324, 325, 347
Benardaky, Mme, 306, 322–23, 324
Benardaky, Nicholas, 306, 315, 324
Benjamin, Walter, 45, 417n2
Benveniste, Emile, 74, 130, 145, 146, 422n14, 432n14
Berg, Alban, 96, 425n10
Bergotte (*In Search of Lost Time*), 315, 320, 329, 335, 339
La Berma (*In Search of Lost Time*), 327
Bernard, Anne-Marie, 305, 452n1
Bernard, Claire, 378, 428n14
Bernhardt, Sarah, 306, 326–27
Berrichon, Paterne, 153
Bibesco, Antoine, 317, 444n3
Bibesco, Emmanuel, 317, 441n18
Bibesco, Marthe, 240

Binger, Louis-Gustave, 433n31
Birotteau, César (*Grandeur et décadence de César Birotteau*), 311
Bizet, Georges, 366
Bizet, Jacques, 366
Blanche, Jacques-Émile, 361
Blanchot, Maurice, 6, 46, 47, 69, 82, 282, 300; and breakdown, 269; and Ego-Ideal/Ideal Ego, 167
Bloch (*In Search of Lost Time*), 353
Blum, Léon, 352
Blum, René, 259
Blyth, Robert H., xxix, 28, 32, 63, 414n23; translations by, 29, 39, 41, 45, 48, 49, 54, 57, 58, 65–75, 82, 85, 379–87
Bodhidharma, 69
Bollème, G., 129
Boni de Castellane, Marquis, 306, 314, 331, 342, 364
Boni de Castellane, Marquise (Anna Gould), 306, 331, 342
Bonitzer, Pascal, 71, 428n14
Bonnet, Henri, 236, 256, 262
Bossuet, Jacques-Bénigne, 290
Bouilhet, Louis Hyacinthe, 225, 240
Boulin, Robert, 451n8
Bourdieu, Pierre, 312
Bourget, Paul, 350
Bouttes, Jean-Louis, 378, 428n14, 455n18
Bovary, Emma (*Madame Bovary*), 99, 257, 431n30
Brancovan, Rachel de, 353
Bréauté (*In Search of Lost Time*), 367
Brecht, Bertolt, 88, 107, 313, 423n1, 436n27
Brel, Jacques, 5, 409n9
Breton, André, 428n5, 448n29
Brichot (*In Search of Lost Time*), 319, 359
Briggs, Kate, xxv–xxx
Brion, Marcel, 116
Brissaud, Édouard, 306, 328
Brod, Max, 165, 223, 234, 240, 435n13
Brunot, Ferdinand, 353
Buddha, 157

Buson, 39, 41, 48, 57–59, 65–67, 82, 83, 85, 380–83, 386, 387
Byron, George Gordon, Lord, 274

Cage, John, 32, 48–49, 76, 187, 190, 415n6, 418n12, 423n11, 438n4
Caillaux, Mme, 330
Calmette, Gaston, 306, 330
Campan, Hélène, 378, 428n14
Camp, Maxime du, 225, 240, 257
Caraman-Chimay, Élisabeth (Comtesse Henri Greffulhe), 306, 345
Carré, Jean-Marie, 151
Cassan, Hervé, 378, 428n14
Cassien, 42
Castellane. *See* Boni de Castellane, Marquis
Cazalis, Henri, 446n40
Céard, Henri, 422n3
Céline, Louis-Ferdinand, 233, 278
Cézanne, Paul, 92
Charlotte (*Les Souffrances du jeune Werther*), 325
Charlus, baron de (*In Search of Lost Time*), 37, 210, 257, 259, 315, 345, 359, 364, 416n4, 454n20
Chateaubriand, François-René de, xxvii, 147, 150, 174, 288, 409n7; and the Book, 184, 191; and boredom, 272–73; crises of, 254; and desire, 302; and Ego-Ideal/Ideal Ego, 161–62, 166; and food, 229; friends of, 241; and history, 283, 284; on language, 145, 290, 296; and life writing, 210, 211; *Memoirs from Beyond the Grave*, 128, 129, 131, 161, 184, 198, 207, 210, 211, 215, 284, 302; on methodical life, 199–200, 245; mistress of, 344; and Vita Nova, 215; on wanting-to-write, 138, 139; and the work vs. the world, 203, 207, 211; and writing at night, 238
Chevigné, Comtesse Adhéaume de (Laure de Sade), 306, 314, 315, 332, 345, 367
Choay, Françoise, 378, 428n14
Cholet, Armand-Pierre de, 306, 333
Chomsky, Noam, 98, 425n15
Chrétien de Troyes, 104
Cicero, 97
Cioran, E. M., 94, 289

Claudel, Paul, 41, 75, 153, 278
Clerc, Thomas, xxvi, 408n4a
Clermont-Tonnerre, Élisabeth de, 187, 346
Colet, Louise, 246, 430n19
Colette, 63, 337
Compagnon, Antoine, xxvi, 18, 134, 144, 412n2, 429n4, 432n9
Condillac, Etienne de, 76, 422n20
Conrad, Joseph, 289
Corot, Jean-Baptiste-Camille, 39
Cortazar, Julio, 280
Cottard (*In Search of Lost Time*), 319, 328, 363
Cottard, Mme (*In Search of Lost Time*), 363
Cottin, Céline, 334
Cottin, Nicholas, 306, 334
Coyaud, Maurice, 25, 26, 28, 377; on haiku, 31, 32, 35, 53, 61, 63, 64, 67, 73; translations by, 31, 41, 51, 52, 56, 58, 64–66, 75–80, 83, 85, 86, 88, 379–87
Crécy, Odette de (*In Search of Lost Time*), 259, 323, 350, 356
Croisset, Francis de, 214
Culler, Jonathan, xxviii

Dallemagne, Adolphe, 357
Damisch, Hubert, 378, 428n14
Dante Alighieri, 3, 11, 14, 139, 288, 455n8; on acedy, 271; and the Book, 180, 181, 185, 189; *Divine Comedy* of, 5, 24, 104–5, 118, 180, 181, 187, 191, 205, 283, 392, 408nn2b, 4b; and haiku, 24; on language, 295, 451n7; *Vita Nova* of, xxi, 5, 170, 212
Daudet, Alphonse, 306, 315, 320, 335, 336, 363
Debussy, Claude, 306, 336
Degas, Edgar, 354
Delacroix, Eugène, 424n5b
Delahaye, Ernest, 151, 237
Delarue-Mardrus, Lucie, 306, 337
Deleuze, Gilles, 42, 113, 187, 190, 378, 417n22, 428n14, 446n36
Democritus, 51
De Quincey, Thomas, 40, 57, 416n9
Derrida, Jacques, 113, 452n22
Desbordes-Valmore, Marceline, 310, 453n8
Detienne, Marcel, 23, 114, 121, 123, 378, 428n14
Diderot, Denis, 107, 168–69, 185, 427n38

Dionysius the Areopagite, 14
Doason, Baron Jacques, 315
Dreyfus, Robert, 265
Dufour, Louis, 35, 43
Dumas, Alexandre, 139, 413n3
Dumézil, Georges, 130, 430n9
Duns Scott, John, 100, 426n20

Eisenstein, Sergei, 420n4
Eliot, T. S., 224
Ellmann, Richard, 100, 102
Emaer, Fabrice, 443n50
Emerson, Ralph Waldo, 241
Étiemble, René, 25, 413nn7,8

Faguet, J.-F., 238
Faucon, Bernard, 71, 421n8
Faure, Antoinette, 347
Fauré, Gabriel, 306, 338
Fellini, Federico, 106, 108, 119, 427n36
Feydeau, Ernest, 214
Flahault, François, 37
Flaubert, Gustave, xxvii, 18, 280, 357; on asceticism, 245; bed of, 235–36; and the Book, 184; and boredom, 272; and bourgeoisie, 286–87; *Bouvard and Pécuchet*, 92, 133, 135, 143, 181, 184, 185, 231, 244, 443n11, 444n12, 445n12; and breakdown, 268; crises of, 253; and Ego-Ideal/Ideal Ego, 163, 166; on feminism, 297; and food, 228; friends of, 240; and heroism, 281; on home, 231, 233; and language, 99–100, 291, 296; letters of, 129; *Madame Bovary*, 99, 197, 225, 257, 261, 284; "marinade" of, 410n21; and notation, 91; notebooks of, 90–91, 230; on not publishing, 269; on not writing, 154; on the Novel, 184; philosophy of, 174; and photography, 71; and planning, 259, 261; and pure form, 177–78; and rhetoric, 279; and Romanticism, 303; and Saint Polycarp, 449n18; *Salammbô*, 184; and schedules, 245, 246–47, 248, 249; and secrecy, 242, 243, 244; and sentence, 98, 99–100; *Sentimental Education*, 284, 297, 412n3; *A Simple Heart*, 89; and starting up, 255, 257; on talent, 196–97; *Temptation of Saint Anthony*, 225, 269; on time, 265; and *Vita Nova*, 216, 217, 220; on wanting-to-write, 138, 140, 141–42, 159–60, 172; on writing, 147, 237, 260
Fleming, Ian, 415n10
Flügel, Martin, 230
Forcheville (*In Search of Lost Time*), 150, 433n25
Foucault, Michel, 113, 278, 449n5
Fourier, Joseph, 60
France, Anatole, 278, 306, 319, 320, 329, 335, 339
Francesca de Rimini (*Inferno*), 104, 181
Franck, Henri, 328, 338
Françoise (*In Search of Lost Time*), 106, 334, 420n2
Freud, Sigmund, 15, 51, 117, 141, 160, 435n4; and labyrinth, 119, 124
Friedmann, Georges, 429n1a
Fugyoku, 54, 381

Galliffet, General Marquis Gaston de, 306, 341, 364
Gallimard, Gaston, 263
Gardair, Jean-Michel, 185, 189
Gardet, Louis, 14, 411n11
Gautier, Théophile, 40
Genette, Gérard, 133–34, 430n11
Gérard, J.-M., 310
Gide, André, 106, 270, 274, 278, 435n20; crises of, 253; and Ego-Ideal/Ideal Ego, 163–64; and Life as Work, 209; and *mise en abyme*, 170, 436n22; and notation, 91, 92; and secrecy, 242, 243
Girard, René, 12
Giscard d'Estaing, Valéry, 172, 448n2
Gisèle (*In Search of Lost Time*), 277, 448n4
Goldmann, Lucien, 12, 14, 130, 285
Goncourt brothers, 91, 209, 357
Gonsui, 56, 381
Gorgias, 97, 412n14
Gould, Anna (Marquise Boni de Castellane), 306, 331, 342
Gozzi, Carlo, 436n27
Gracq, Julien, 451n13
Gramont children, 306, 343
Gramont, Élisabeth de, 346
Gramont, Louis René de, 343
Greffulhe, Comte Henri, 306, 344
Greffulhe, Comtesse Henri (Élisabeth de Caraman-Chimay), 306, 345
Grenier, Jean, 417n23
Greuze, Jean-Baptiste, 427n34
Guattari, Félix, 448n2
Guermantes, Duc de (*In Search of Lost Time*), 62, 311, 344, 364
Guermantes, Duchesse de (*In Search of Lost Time*), 62, 315, 332, 345, 364, 366
Guermantes, Princesse de (*In Search of Lost Time*), 321, 366
Guiche, Duc Armand de, 187, 306, 318, 321, 343, 346
Gyp, Comtesse de Martel, 306, 347

Haas, Charles, 306, 315, 340, 341, 345, 348, 354, 364
Hahn, Reynaldo, 306, 335, 336, 349, 356, 441n18
Halévy, Daniel, 43
Halévy, Geneviève (Mme Émile Straus), 307, 332, 348, 363, 366, 367
Harmon, Philippe, 299
Hasuo, 88
Haussman, Baron, 117
Haydn, Joseph, 282, 449n16
Hayman, Laure, 306, 313, 350, 360, 370
Heath, Willie, 306, 351
Hegel, G.W.F., 43, 167, 254
Heidegger, Martin, 156–57, 198, 395, 452n22, 456n21
Herbart, Johann Friedrich, 163, 209
Heredia, José Maria de, 352
Heredia, Marie de, 306, 347, 352
Hermant, Abel, 306, 353
Hocke, Gustav René, 84
Holderlin, Friedrich, 47
Hollier, Denis, xxix
Houville, Gérard d' (Marie de Heredia), 352
Howard, Richard, xxix
Howland, Mme Meredith, 306, 354
Hugo, Victor, 203, 253, 453n8
Huret, Jules, 281, 449n11
Husserl, Edmund, 265, 281
Huysmans, Joris-Karl, 228

Ichiku, 58, 382
Ignatius of Loyola, 248, 445n25
Ilto, 58, 382
Isocrates, 97

Issa, 29, 41, 48, 49, 72, 79, 85, 136, 379–81, 384, 386, 430n16
Izambard, Georges, 212

Jacques-Dalcroze, Émile, 50, 418n15
Jakobson, Roman, 416n2, 427n1
Janouch, Gustav, 21, 95
Jan-Tsen-Tsaï, 202
Jesus Christ, 133, 181
Joubert, Joseph, 46, 191, 198–99, 226, 228, 241, 443n4
Joyce, James, 100–103, 426n20
Jupien (*In Search of Lost Time*), 364

Kafka, Franz, xxvii, 160, 197, 304; and the Book, 180, 181, 251; desk of, 234–35; *Diaries* of, 165, 200, 208, 445n22; and Ego-Ideal/Ideal Ego, 161–62, 163, 165; friends of, 240, 241, 435n13; illness of, 223; Janouch on, 21, 95; *Journal* of, 129; on necessity, 193; and Romanticism, 303; and schedules, 246, 248–49; and secrecy, 242, 243, 244; and separation, 279, 280, 281, 287, 289; on speech *vs.* writing, 188; and Vita Nova, 215; and wanting-to-write, 138, 140, 172; and the work *vs.* the world, 200, 202–3, 204, 205, 208; and writing at night, 237, 238
Kaneko Tota, 56, 381
Kant, Immanuel, 27
Kawabata Bosha, 76
Keats, John, 211
Kellerman, Bernhard, 435n11
Kierkegaard, Søren, 21, 43, 50, 151, 433n26
Knight, Diana, xxvi
Kolb, Philip, 64, 175, 192, 263, 265
Krauss, Rosalind, xxix
Kristeva, Julia, 26
Kusatao, 52, 77, 381

La Bruyère, Jean de, 138, 311
Lacan, Jacques, 26, 70, 160, 421n1, 435n4, 453n7
Lacoste, Bouillane de, 151
Lacoue-Labarthe, Philippe, 430n20, 451n12
Lacretelle, Jacques de, 313, 325, 454n18

Lamartine, Alphonse de, 56, 105, 254, 426n33, 453n8
Laurent, Méry, 306, 356
Lautréamont, Comte de (Isidore Ducasse), 167, 182, 281
Lecoq, Jacques, 50, 418n15
Lefébure, Eugène, 47, 418n8
Legendre, Pierre, 71
Léger, Nathalie, xvii–xxiii, xxvi, xxviii, xxix
Legrand, Marc, 60
Leguay, Thierry, 280, 449n9
Leibniz, Gottfried, 296
Lemaire, Madeleine, 306, 321, 332, 349, 355
Leonardo da Vinci, 435n18
Léonie, Aunt (*In Search of Lost Time*), 218, 312, 442n31
Lessing, Gotthold Ephraim, 107, 427n38
Lévi-Strauss, Claude, 103, 130, 135, 311
Lewinter, Roger, 427n38
Lippmann, Léontine (Mme Albert Arman de Caillavet), 307, 309, 319, 329, 339, 362
Lipshitz, Tatiana, 300, 452n21
Liszt, Franz, 247, 445n22
Littré, Émile, 117, 428n9
Loti, Pierre, 412n4, 419n1
Louauys, Pierre, 352
Lowry, Malcolm, 437n19
Lukács, György, 12, 130, 285
Lyly, John, 84

Machiavelli, Niccolò, 153
Maistre, Joseph de, 297
Malherbe, François de, 56
Mallarmé, Stéphane, 129, 224, 240, 306, 356, 415n12; and the Album, 186; and the Book, 176, 177, 178, 180, 181, 182–83, 185, 189; and boredom, 272, 273, 274; and breakdown, 268; crises of, 254, 446n40; and desire, 302, 303; and Ego-Ideal/Ideal Ego, 163, 167; and filiation, 301–2; and haiku, 26, 27, 46, 47; and heroism, 281; and home, 232; and language, 289, 293, 294; on necessity, 195, 196; and the past, 276; and planning, 261; on Poe, 437n8; and Romanticism, 303; on speech *vs.* writing, 188; and Vita Nova, 220; and wanting-to-write, 172; and the work *vs.* the world, 203, 208

Malraux, André, 184, 278, 283
Mannoni, Octave, 122–23, 124, 315, 378, 428n14, 429n2a
Marino, Giambattista, 84
Maritain, Jacques, 411n11
Martial, 26, 84
Martin, H.-J., 92, 98
Marx, Karl, 286
Maspero, François, 430n5
Massignon, Louis, 411n11
Mathilde, Princesse, 307, 348, 357, 363
Matisse, Henri, 236
Matsuo, 57, 382
Mauclair, Camille, 167
Maupassant, Guy de, 94, 361, 442n49
Mauriac, François, 278
Mauriès, Patrick, 100, 425n19
Mauron, Charles, 129
Maurras, Charles, 347
Medici, Laurent de, 153
Medina of Marrakech, 94
Meisetsu, 31, 75, 379
Mérimée, Prosper, 357
Merleau-Ponty, Maurice, 122
Méséglise (*In Search of Lost Time*), 344, 439n19
Metzger, Heinz-Klaus, 96, 425n10
Mialaret, Athénais, 441n19
Michaud, Guy, 254
Michelet, Jules, xvii, xxi, 41, 80, 150, 441n19; on boredom, 433n23; on Guelph *vs.* Ghibelline, 50, 418n16; *History of France* of, 42, 264, 267; *History of the Revolution* of, 266–67; and individuation, 43; and schedules, 245; vertical style of, 84; and Vita Nova, 212, 214, 219; *Vita Nuova* of, 5, 407n8, 409n11
Milosz, Oscar, 27, 67, 414n21
Mizoguchi Kenji, 50
Mondor, Henri, 167, 281
Monet, Claude, 136
Montaigne, Michel de, 144, 147, 150, 153, 171, 432n9; and Life as Work, 207, 211
Montbazon, Madame de, 409n7
Montesquiou, Robert de, 236, 307, 313, 318, 321, 337, 344, 354, 363; and Charlus, 210, 315, 345; photographs of, 358–59
Montriender, Comtesse de (*In Search of Lost Time*), 357
Moravia, Alberto, 272

Morier, Henri, 25
Mornand, Louisa de, 307, 318, 360
Munier, Roger, 377, 379, 380, 381, 382, 384, 386; translations by, 28, 45, 52, 59, 72, 77, 83, 136
Musset, Alfred de, 134, 254, 264, 268

Nadar, Paul, xviii, xxviii, 305, 308, 452n1
Nadeau, Maurice, 437n19, 442n43
Nancy, Jean-Luc, 430n20, 451n12
Napoleon Bonaparte, 357, 450n19
Nerval, Gérard de, 143, 448n29
Newton, Isaac, 46
Nibor, Yann, 327
Nietzsche, Friedrich, 7, 44, 102, 176, 430n14, 444n22; on active *vs.* reactive, 446nn33,36; and the Album, 187; and the Book, 180, 190; on casuistry of egoism, 227, 228, 236; and desire, 303; *Ecce Homo* of, 129, 135, 157, 180, 227, 228, 236, 267, 281, 304, 430n14; and filiation, 301; and haiku, 50, 55, 102; and labyrinth, 118, 120, 123; and language, 292, 295; on nihilism, 279; on Noble Life, 250; on reading, 251; on Socrates and Plato, 135, 144, 436n4; styles of, 178
Noailles, Anna de, 328, 337, 346, 353
Nodier, Charles, 253
Novalis, Friedrich, 451n12
Nunez, Laurent, xxv

Octavian (*The Knight of the Rose*), 238, 444

Painter, George, xxix–xxx, 75, 210, 214, 314, 441n18, 453nn3,5
Palmer, Evelina, 337
Pånini, 145, 432n13
Paracelsus, 42
Parmigianino (Francesco Mazzola), 84
Pascal, Blaise, 153, 261, 270, 277, 299, 445n13; on acedy, 271–72; and Ego-Ideal/Ideal Ego, 163, 164; on necessity, 193, 194; *Pensées* of, 164, 190, 194, 264, 394, 395, 438n5; and simplicity, 300; on time, 266; and the work *vs.* the world, 202
Pasiphae, 114–15
Paul (*Paul and Virginie*), 105
Pavans, Jean, 149, 433n21
Périer, Florin, 190
Philippe, Charles-Louis, 223, 442n45
Picard, Raymond, 448n30
Picon, Gaétan, 132, 154, 201–4, 212, 238, 246, 247
Pignatelli, Emmanuela (Comtesse Potocka), 307, 361
Plantin, Christophe, 231, 443n12
Plato, 135, 144, 280, 430n14
Plekhanov, Guergui, 450n23
Poe, Edgar Allan, 49, 170, 177, 186, 281, 418n13, 437n8
Polignac, Prince de, 338
Polycarp, Saint, 449n18
Porbus, François, 394, 455n14
Potocka, Comtesse (Emmanuela Pignatelli), 307, 361
Pougy, Liane de, 337
Pouquet, Jeanne (Mme Gaston Arman de Caillavet), 307, 309, 319, 325, 329, 362, 365, 453n4
Pozzi, Dr. Samuel, 307, 319, 363
Prince of Wales (Edward VII), 306, 340, 348, 367
Proust, Adrien, 307, 372
Proust, Jeanne, 4, 307, 373
Proust, Marcel, xxvii, 5, 7, 8, 11, 14, 19, 99; and the Album, 187; on Balzac, 59, 70, 135–36, 258–59; bed of, 236; bedrooms of, 233–34; and the Book, 185, 189; and clothing, 22, 144, 230; crises of, 254; death of, 150, 223; and Ego-Ideal/Ideal Ego, 166; and essay *vs.* novel, 143, 192, 256, 258, 431n1, 439n29, 446n40; and food, 228, 229; friends of, 240, 241, 308–15; and haiku, 35, 37, 39, 40, 43, 51, 53, 60, 64, 68; and handwriting, 265; illness of, 223; and imitation, 134; and labyrinth, 118; on lying, 220; and memory, 16, 39, 49, 50; and Methodical Life, 201, 209–10, 211, 246, 250; mother of, 4, 307, 373; and notation, 53, 91, 93, 103; philosophy of, 175; photograph of, 307, 312, 321, 375; and photography, xviii, xxviii, 70, 308–15; and planning, 259, 260, 262–63, 266; and Proof, 196; and Romanticism, 147, 303; *Against Sainte-Beuve* of, 59, 70, 103, 135–36, 143, 192, 210, 233, 234, 243, 256, 258, 262, 330, 431n1, 439n29, 446n40; and secrecy, 243, 244; and separation, 275, 279, 281, 285, 296; and sleep, 175–76, 229; and starting up, 256–57; tangibilia in, 62; and teaching of literature, 277, 278; and truth, 103–9; and Vita Nova, 214, 221–22, 391–92; and wanting-to-write, 9, 140, 172; and writing at night, 237–38, 239
Proust, Robert, 307, 363, 374

Queneau, Raymond, 200
Quinent, Edgar, 266
Quintilian, 265, 289, 450n29
Quint, L.-P., 221, 222, 229, 236, 237, 241

Rabelais, François, 185
Rachel (*In Search of Lost Time*), 360
Racine, Jean, 12, 23, 114, 291, 419n7, 448n30
Radziwill, Léon, 318, 325, 346, 441n18
Radziwill, Michel, 325
Rambures, Jean-Louis, 22, 413n13
Rancé, Amand-Jean de, 409n7
Rastignac, Eugène de (*Père Goriot*), 159, 434n1
Ravel, Maurice, 85, 260, 423n18, 447n6
Régnier, Henri de, 352
Renan, Ernest, 254, 278, 357
Renard, Jules, 60–61, 85, 420n15
Richard, Jean Pierre, 130, 141–42, 228, 431n30
Rilke, Rainer Maria, 9, 279–80
Rimbaud, Arthur, 129, 136–37, 212, 237, 299, 433n31, 444n23; scuppering by, 151–53, 182
Rinka, 65, 383
Rivane, Georges, 229, 234, 236
Rivière, Jacques, 175, 444n23
Rivière, Pierre, 449n5
Robbe-Grillet, Alain, 412n18
Ronsard, Pierre de, 67
Roquentin, Antoine, 169, 436n21

Rosenstiehl, Pierre, 113, 121, 378, 428n2, 428n14
Rothschild, Baron Alphonse de, 331
Rousseau, Jean-Jacques, xxvii, 43, 149, 432n20, 434n36, 441n17; and boredom, 274; clothing of, 230; *Confessions* of, 129, 154, 155, 179; and Ego-Ideal/Ideal Ego, 164, 166; *Introit* of, 179; on not publishing, 154, 269–70; and Proust, 103, 147; and Vita Nova, 213, 215, 216, 217; and wanting-to-write, 172
Roxane (*Bajazet*), 321
Ruskin, John, 99
Ruysbroek, Jan Van, 302

Sacripant, Miss (*In Search of Lost Time*), 323
Sade, Laure de (Comtesse Adhéaume de Chevigné), 306, 314, 315, 332, 345, 367
Sade, Marquis de, 66, 127, 133, 429n1b; and fantasy, 11, 99; on love, 14, 411n9; and rose motif, 32, 415n4
Safouan, Moustapha, 160
Sagan, Prince Boson de, 307, 314, 364
Saimaro, 72, 384
Sainte-Beuve, Charles Augustin, 4, 254, 258, 357
Saint-Pierre, Bernardin de, 426n33
Saint-Saëns, Camille, 338
Sampu, 45, 380
Sand, George, 148, 159
Santarcangeli, Paolo, 116
Sarduy, Severo, 137, 181, 430n17
Sartre, Jean-Paul, 20, 130, 166, 171, 278, 283, 285, 436n21; on individualism, 42, 417n14
Saussure, Ferdinand de, 7, 70, 421n5
Schehadé, Georges, 27, 28, 41, 51, 67, 414n21
Scherer, Jacques, 129, 177, 180–89, 195, 261, 268, 281, 294, 302
Schlegel, Friedrich, 138
Schönberg, Arnold, 96, 187, 304, 425n10
Schopenhauer, Arthur, 135, 234, 246–47, 272, 448n35
Schubert, Franz, 338
Schumann, Robert, 96, 186, 209
Schwartz, Gabrielle, 307, 365

Seijugo, 83, 386
Seishi, 80, 386
Senancour, Étienne Pivert de, 213, 441n16
Servière, 143, 144
Sévigné, Mme de, 37
Shakespeare, William, 181
Shiki, 29, 30, 75, 77, 379, 384
Shoha, 52, 381
Shusai, 45, 380
Sieffert, René, 31, 64
Silesius, Angelus, 82
Silverman, A. O., 101
Socrates, 135, 176, 251, 280, 430n14
Sollers, Philippe, 7, 26, 201, 279, 450n28
Sonojô, 65, 383
Sontag, Susan, 440n5
Staël, Madame de, 254
Staël, Nicolas de, 92, 424n9
Stendhal, xx, 207, 253, 264
Straus, Émile, 366
Straus, Mme Émile (Geneviève Halévy), 307, 332, 348, 363, 366, 367
Strauss, Richard, 444n29
Suzuki, Daisetz Teitaro, 60, 64, 409n17, 419n13
Swedenborg, Emmanuel, 270, 448n29

Tacitus, 238
Tadié, Jean-Yves, 262
Taigi, 66, 73, 383
Taine, Hippolyte, 254, 357
Talleyrand-Périgord, Hélie de, Prince de Sagan, 342
Téchiné, André, 19, 412n5, 421n9, 440n32
Teishitsu, 80, 386
Thomas Aquinas, Saint, 14, 100, 426n20
Thom, René, 107
Thrasymacus, 97
Thucydides, 97
Tissot, James, 341
Toko, 76
Tolstoy, Leo, 14, 16, 130, 157, 175; and the Book, 189; and Methodical Life, 208, 248, 249; and starting up, 255; and Vita Nova, 392; and wanting-to-write, 172
Turenne, Comte Louis de, 307, 314, 364, 367
Turgenev, Ivan, 287
Twombly, Cy, 97, 425n10

Valéry, Paul, xxi, 93, 195, 278, 424n7b; and the Book, 185, 191; and haiku, 24–25, 26, 29, 59, 61; and planning, 260, 261; on short form, 96; tombstone of, 445n28; and Vita Nova, 220; and writing at night, 237
Van Gogh, Vincent, 203
Verdi, Giuseppe, 301
Verdurin, Mme (*In Search of Lost Time*), 319, 355, 454n20
Verdurin, Monsieur (*In Search of Lost Time*), 329
Verlaine, Paul, 151, 152, 254, 349, 416n17, 453n8; and haiku, 36, 51, 64
Vernant, Jean-Pierre, 23
Vernet, Blandine, 134
Vico, Giambattista, 75, 76, 121, 422n17
Vigny, Alfred de, 51, 270
Villeparisis, Mme de (*In Search of Lost Time*), 355, 416n3
Vinaver, Michael, 68, 420n10
Vinteuil (*In Search of Lost Time*), 259, 336, 338, 357
Virgil, 3, 11
Virginie (*Paul and Virginie*), 105
Vittorini, Elio, 302, 452n23
Vivien, Reneé, 337
Voltaire, 219, 278
Volupia (goddess of fully satisfied Desire), 132, 430n9

Wagner, Richard, 135, 258
Watteau, Antoine, 169
Watts, Alan, 80, 423n6
Webern, Anton von, 96, 97, 425n10
Weil, Adèle, 307, 369
Weil, Amélie, 307, 371
Weil, Georges, 307, 370
Weil, Louis, 342, 350, 370
Weil, Nathé, 307, 368
Werther (*Les Souffrances du jeune Werther*), 317
Wohryzeck, Julie, 242
Woolf, Virginia, 82, 171

Yaha, 34, 379
Yamata Kikou, 28, 61, 81, 96, 379; translations by, 57, 72, 79, 84, 381, 384, 385, 386
Yoshikawa Kazuyoshi, 420n1

Zeami, 50, 418n14
Zola, Émile, 18, 79, 174, 230, 285, 422n3

INDEX RERUM

acedy, 5, 14, 216, 271–72, 390, 395, 409n12, 448n31
advertising, 179, 427n1
advice, 245, 280
affect, 62–63, 68, 107
Against Sainte-Beuve (Proust), 192, 210, 243, 262; on Balzac, 59, 70, 135–36, 258; on bedrooms, 233, 234; and essay *vs.* novel, 143, 256, 258, 431n1, 439n29, 446n40; rejection of, 103, 330
age, 3–5
the Album, 211, 261, 266, 439n17; finishing, 194–95; *vs.* the Book, 182–92, 198
alchemy, 42, 183
animals, 62–63, 73, 82, 119
Anna Karenina (Tolstoy), 13, 285
Artificial Paradise (Baudelaire), 143, 300
asceticism, 150, 158, 245, 249, 250
Atala (Chateaubriand), 283
author, 33, 164, 432n18; collective, 293–94; return of, 207–8; sacralization of, 224–26; *vs.* writer, 450n3
autonymy, 9, 300–301
Aziyadé (Loti), 18, 412n4

bedrooms, 233–34
beds, 235–36
Being and Nothingness (Sartre), 171
bereavement, 4–5, 51, 105, 298, 389, 390, 391, 392, 395
Berenice (Racine), 448n30
Bible, 180; Isaiah, 445n13; John, 4, 408n6; Matthew, 7, 417n12, 448n34
biography, 208–10
The Bird, The Sea, The Mountain (Michelet), 214
Birth of Tragedy (Nietzsche), 144
the Book, 265, 296; as-Guide, 181–82; and fantasy, 177; and filiation, 301–2; as Object, 251; Total, 182–85, 189; typology of, 178–82; Ur-, 180, 181; *vs.* the Album, 182–92, 198
boredom, 159, 271–74, 433n23
Bouvard and Pécuchet (Flaubert), 92, 143, 231, 244, 443n11, 445n12; and the Book, 181, 184, 185; and imitation, 133, 135
Buddhism, 27, 157, 271, 447n19

Camera Lucida (Barthes), xix, 421nn7,12
capitalism, 285, 287
"Ca prend" (article; Barthes), xix
Les Caprices (Musset), 264
Casanova (film; Fellini), 106, 427n36
Castex and Surer. See *Manuel des Études Littéraires*
The Castle (Kafka), 235
cats, 63, 73
La Celestina (Rojas), 181
Cercle de la Rue Royale (Crillon), 341
Cerisy-la-Salle conference (1977), 11, 210, 411n3, 412n18, 431n30
Les Chansons grises (Verlaine), 349
The Charterhouse of Parma (Stendhal), 264
La Chatte (Colette), 63
Christianity, 271–72, 433n23. See also Bible
Chroniques (Barthes), 102
"Le Cimetière marin" (Valéry), 24
Circuit (play; Feydeau and Croisset), 214
circumstance, 52–54, 418n23
cities, 117, 118, 123, 213
classification, 32–33, 35, 116, 127, 141, 148, 211
clothing, 230, 312–13, 429n1a
Le Club des amis du texte (Leguay), 280, 449n9
code: in clothing, 312–13; and fantasy, 10–11; in haiku, 38, 39–40, 41, 68; and *kireji*, 63–64; in language, 293; metalinguistic, 300; in poetry, 31–32

Comédie Humaine (Balzac), 203, 259
Le Comte de Monte-Cristo (Dumas), 108
concetto (conceit), 84–85, 377, 423n14
Confessions (Rousseau), 129, 154, 155, 179
Confessions of an English Opium Eater (De Quincey), 40, 57, 416n9
content, 174, 177–78, 189
Contes (Voltaire), 219
contingency, 50–54
Convivio (Dante), 295
Le Coup de dés (Mallarmé), 182
Crimes of Love (Sade), 14
cruising, 202, 391, 395

dance, 117
death, 4–6, 9, 105–7, 191, 210; and finishing, 150; and labyrinth, 119; of Proust, 150, 223; and return of author, 208; and sexuality, 15, 411n12; and wanting-to-write, 133
"The Death of the Author" (Barthes), 208
deconstruction, 301, 456n22
desire, 159, 171, 184, 246, 280, 302–3; for the absent (*Pothos*), 132, 430n9; cessation of, 153; and doubt, 174; and fantasy, 176, 198; and haiku, 29–36, 377; for the past, 275–77; social, 311–13; *vs.* acedy, 271; to write, 138–42, 150, 172. *See also* wanting-to-write
desks, 234–35
diaphorology, 45, 417n1
Diaries (Kafka), 165, 200, 208, 445n22
Diary (Amiel), 36, 416n16
Diary (Gide), 209
the diary, 187–89, 198, 266, 390, 391, 441n12; and life as work, 207, 208, 210, 211
Divagations (Mallarmé), 186
Divine Comedy (Dante), 5, 118, 180, 187, 191; Beatrice in, xxi, 47, 205, 409n10; as guide book, 181; *Inferno*, 104–5, 181, 283, 392, 408nn2b,4b; *Paradiso*, 24
dogs, 62–63, 95
Don Quixote (Cervantes), 133, 181, 285

Dreyfus Affair, 254, 285, 310, 318, 329, 347, 348
drugs, 91, 229, 242, 256, 268

Ecce Homo (Nietzsche), 129, 135, 157, 180, 267, 304, 430n14; on casuistry of egoism, 227, 228, 236; and heroism, 281
Ego-Ideal/Ideal Ego, 160–67, 435n4
egoism/egotism: casuistry of, 224–28, 240; of haiku, 64–66; and life writing, 211; and the Novel, 411n9; and reading, 251; and Vita Nova, 217–18; and the work *vs.* the world, 204–6
Encyclopaedia (Diderot), 143, 168, 185, 427n38
Encyclopaedia Universalis, 12, 285, 286, 450n22
encyclopedias, 296
epigrams, 84, 96
Epigrams (Martial), 26
epiphanies, xxii, 72, 100–102, 104, 107, 108, 165, 435n12
Epiphanies (Joyce), 100–101, 107
the essay, 260, 390, 391; *vs.* novel, 143, 256, 258, 431n1, 439n29, 440n29, 446nn40,44
Essays (Montaigne), 207, 211
Euphues (Lyly), 84
Exiles (Balzac), 239
Extraits de la Correspondance (Flaubert), 129

Le Faiseur (play; Balzac), 434n37
fantasy, 393; and the diary, 187; of form, 226; of the Novel, 11–12, 15, 17; and obstacles, 263; and patience, 199; sexual *vs.* writing, 10–11; of Vita Nova, 212–14; and the volume, 176–78, 185; and wanting-to-write, 198
fascism, 7, 410n23
feminism, 297
filiation, 136–37, 301–2
film, 34, 50, 61, 118, 192; and Fellini, 106, 119, 427n36; and preparation of the novel, 127, 128, 129; *vs.* photography, 70, 71, 72
food, 141, 228–29
form: fantasized, 226; indecision about, 192, 199; *vs.* content, 174, 177–78, 189
fragments, 18, 191, 198, 228, 245, 255; in Joyce, 101, 102;

in life writing, 210–11; the Novel as, 143–44, 286; in Proust, 103, 187, 192, 210, 256, 262; and Vita Nova, 390, 391, 394, 395
Fragments (Schlegel), 138
French language, 18, 99, 290, 291, 295, 302; and haiku, 37, 59, 77; past in, 77; translations into, 25, 26, 28
French Revolution, 284, 285
friends, 201, 217–18, 240–41, 391

La Genèse d'un poème (Poe, translated by Baudelaire), 177
The Genius of Christianity (Chateaubriand), 161
gesture, 9, 411n6, 414n18, 420n4, 424n5b, 427n39, 450n3; and haiku, 26, 49–50; and notation, 18, 91, 95
gestus, 88, 107, 313, 423n1
The Girl with the Golden Eyes (Balzac), 94
"Gladys Harvey" (short story; Bourget), 350
Goldfinger (film), 34, 415n10
Graziella (Larmartine), 105, 426n33

haiku, xxvi, 19, 23–90, 377–87, 424n2a; code in, 38, 39–40, 41, 68; and contingency, 51–53, 54; co-presence in, 76–77; desire for, 29–36, 377; discretion in, 66–69; individuation in, 52, 65, 67; *kireji* in, 63–64; limits of, 83–86, 88; and memory, 39, 48–49; and moment of truth, 104, 107, 108; and narrative, 88, 89, 424n3a; and notation, 90, 93, 127; and perception, 55–61; and photography, 70–74; and Proust, 35, 37, 39, 40, 43, 51, 53, 60, 64, 68; and quiddity, 100, 102; *satori* in, 39, 75, 76, 77, 78–81, 84; seasons in, 32, 34–36, 38; translation of, xxix, 23, 24–25, 28, 413n8; weather in, 37–39, 40, 43, 45, 47; and Zen, 69, 80, 81, 82
Hamlet (Shakespeare), 181
handwriting, 263–65
the heap, 156, 158, 160, 214, 434n45; and Vita Nova, 219, 220, 390, 391, 395

472 INDEX RERUM

heroism, 281–82, 286
history, 283–85, 288, 296
History of France (Michelet), 42, 264, 267
History of the Middle Ages (Michelet), 266
History of the Revolution (Michelet), 266–67
homosexuality, 10–11, 141, 242, 298, 359, 459n17
hypotyposis, 57–58

idleness, 153–57, 159, 160, 198, 432n20, 441n21, 460n21; and Vita Nova, 214, 220, 390, 391, 392, 393, 395
Iliad, 181
illness, 222–24, 442n42
the imaginary, 3, 98, 188, 244, 252, 314; and breakdown, 269; and desire, 108, 131, 176; and Ego-Ideal/Ideal Ego, 160, 162, 163, 167; and haiku, 67; pharmacopoeia of, 229; and simulation, 171; and wanting-to-write, 172
imitation, 133–37, 181, 281
incident: and haiku, 56, 69, 88, 101, 102, 419n2; and quiddity, 101–2; and truth, 108
individuation: in haiku, 52, 65, 67; and individual, 43–44; and nuance, 45; and photography, 72; and short form, 96; against the system, 42–43; of times of day, 39–42; *vs.* individual, 67
Inferno (Dante). See *Divine Comedy*
In Search of Lost Time (*Á la Recherche du temps perdu*; Proust), xxix, 9, 13–16, 19, 88, 103, 241, 300; as biography, 210; *Within a Budding Grove*, 37; characters in, 313–15; and crises, 254; and death of Proust, 150; and essay *vs.* novel, 143, 256, 258, 431n1, 439n29, 446n40; as fragments, 187; *The Guermantes Way*, 105; and haiku, 39, 53; and heroism, 281; and indecision, 192; as *mise en abyme*, 170; and photographs, 309–15; and planning, 259, 262–63; proof of, 196; publication of, 310; and secrecy, 243, 244; sentences in, 194; starting up, 256–57; themes of, 175–76; *Time*

Regained, 8, 104; and wanting-to-write, 140; weather in, 35, 37
inspiration, 134–35, 136, 192
the instant, xxii, 18, 25, 107, 248, 377, 418n12, 427n38; and haiku, 40, 48–49, 52, 72, 75
Introduction to Psychoanalysis (Freud), 119

Jean Santeuil (Proust), 13, 368
Jews, 311, 312, 348, 349
Journal (Kafka), 129
journalism, 186, 221, 293
Journaux et carnets (Tolstoy), 130

kairos (right opportunity), 50, 90, 260, 310
kireji (Jap.: poetic punctuation), 63–64, 78
Knight of the Rose (opera; Strauss), 238, 444n29
komboloï (beads), 155, 390, 434n42, 458n4

labyrinth, 113–24, 378; Greek myth of, 114–15; as thing, 116–17; as word, 114–16
language, 415n12, 421n5, 422n20, 424n7b, 427n1; and the Book, 179; choice of, 288–92; classical, 289–90, 294–95; desire for, 302; and Flaubert, 99–100; and haiku, 76, 80, 81; intransitive verb in, 144–48; and labyrinth metaphor, 118, 120–21; of modernity, 299; and necessity, 193; and notation, 377; and photography, 72; and the real, 70, 75, 429n1b; and rhetoric, 279; rhythm of, 450n28; separation, 294–95; spoken, 291–96; temporal expression in, 74, 77, 290, 291, 293; of writing, 288–89, 295
Les Soeurs Brontës (play), 421n9
Letters to a Young Poet (Rilke), 9, 280
Lettres de la vie littéraire d'Arthur Rimbaud, 129
Life of Rancé (Chateaubriand), 56, 409n7
life writing, 210–11
linguistics, 168, 423n13
The Literary Absolute (Lacoue-Labarthe and Nancy), 138, 296, 297, 430n20, 455n12

Le Livre de Mallarmé (Scherer), 129
"Longtemps, je me suis couché de bonne heure" (lecture, 1978; Barthes), xix
Lost Illusions (Balzac), 212
Louis XVIII (king of France), 161
love, 5, 6, 12, 271; in Dante, xxi, 104–5, 181; and death, xxi–xxii, 106, 107, 114, 277; of dogs, 62; and Ego-Ideal/Ideal Ego, 160, 163, 165; Eros *vs.* Agapé, 14; and haiku, 30, 33, 67, 82; and labyrinth, 115, 121; and losing face, 20; and the Novel, 15, 17; and other, 134–35; in Proust, 9, 37–38; and weather, 38, 47; and the work *vs.* the world, 202–3, 205, 206, 244
A Lover's Discourse (Barthes), xxii, xxviii, 102, 302

ma (Jap.: interval), 7, 27, 28, 36, 55, 96, 97, 409n17
Madame Bovary (Flaubert), 99, 197, 225, 257, 261, 284
Madame Edwarda (Bataille), 143
Maeght exhibition (1947), 115, 428n5
Mallarmé (Mauron), 129
Manuel des Études Littéraires (Castex and Surer), 213, 253, 259, 446n39
maquette (scale model), 168, 169–70, 180
marcottage (composition method), 150, 187, 196, 259, 426n30, 433nn24,25
marriage, 241–42
Marxism, 3, 42, 130, 285, 286, 450n23
"Master and Man" (short story; Tolstoy), 175
media, 30, 71, 130, 297, 299; language of, 291, 293–96; and nuance, 45, 47; and petite bourgeoisie, 6–7, 287
Memoirs from Beyond the Grave (Chateaubriand), 128–31, 198, 207, 284, 302; and Ego, 161, 184; and life writing, 210, 211; and Vita Nova, 215
Memoirs of an Egotist (Stendhal), 207
memory, 92, 123, 132; and haiku, 39, 48–49, 50; and the Novel, 15–16

metalinguistics, 122, 300
metaphor: of labyrinth, 113–24, 378; and maquette, 169–71; and myth, 121; and necessity, 193; and simulation, 168–69
"The Metaphor of the Labyrinth" (seminar), xviii, xxii
method, 12, 20, 167–71, 187; and haiku, 23, 108
methodical life, 199–250, 251
mid-life ("middle of the journey"), 3–5, 10, 20
mise en abyme (work within a work), 104, 169–70, 274, 426n33, 436n22
Les Misérables (Hugo), 255
modernity, 57, 97, 208, 303; language of, 299, 421n5; and literature, 285, 297; in music, 425n10; rhythm of, 446n31; and Rimbaud, 137, 153
Monsieur Teste (Valéry), 143, 185, 187, 300
morality, 51, 193, 197, 270, 275, 288, 389, 390
"The Mountain Where Old People Were Abandoned," 86–87
music, 96, 194, 249, 304, 338, 425n10; and Cage, 32, 48–49, 76, 187, 190, 415n6, 418n12, 423n11, 438n4; in *Vita Nova*, 389, 390, 395
myth, 103, 114–15, 118, 120, 121, 124
Mythologies (Barthes), 245

Nadja (Breton), 143
narrative, 130, 171–73; and fantasy, 178; and haiku, 85–86, 377, 424n3a; and labyrinth, 118, 122–23; and notation, 94; and readability, 299–300
The Narrow Road to the Deep North (Basho), 53
Natural Histories (Renard), 60, 85, 423n18
Nausea (Sartre), 169, 436n21
necessity, 191–94, 198
The Neutral (lecture course; Barthes), xviii, xxviii, xxix, 7, 15
the neutral, 21, 66, 69, 80, 83, 390, 391, 394
Noh drama, 50, 55, 418n14
notation, 17–19, 23, 108, 127, 192, 377–78, 421n2; and dress, 230; in haiku, 43, 47, 49; levels of, 92–93; and the novel, 88–93; and Proust, 53, 91, 93, 103; and the sentence, 97–100; and speech, 188; structural, 94–95
Notebooks (Tolstoy), 208
"Notes on the Notions of Norm and Readability" (Harmon), 299
Le Nouvel Observateur (periodical), xix, 102, 142, 201, 291, 440n31
nuance, 37, 42–43, 45–47, 49, 53, 60, 99

Oberman (Senancour), 213, 441n16
Odyssey, 181
One Hundred and Twenty Days (Sade), 11
Organum (Bacon), 51
originality, 221–22
the other, 137, 197, 251, 269; and Ego-Ideal/Ideal Ego, 161, 164–65, 166

painting, 27, 39, 137, 147, 195, 390, 395, 427n38; and Balzac, 59, 70, 135–36; as *Mise en abyme*, 169
Paludes (Gide), 274, 435n20
parabase, 129, 167
Paradis (Sollers), 279, 297, 450n28
Paradiso (Dante). See *Divine Comedy*
"Paris Evenings" (diary; Barthes), xix
Parsifal (Wagner), 258
the past, 17, 77, 275–77, 284, 293, 301
pathos, 55–61, 108
Paul and Virginie (Saint-Pierre), 105, 426n33
La Peau ce chagrin (*The Wild Ass's Skin*; Balzac), 154, 434n37
Pelléas (opera; Debussy), 317, 336
Pensées (Pascal), 164, 190, 194, 264, 394, 395, 438n5
perception, 55–60
Père Goriot (Balzac), 259
petite bourgeoisie, 6–7, 286–87, 295
"The Philosophy of Composition" (Poe), 177
photography, 52, 70–74, 76, 394, 421n4; and Proust, 308–15

Picture Gallery (Watteau), 169
Pierre and Jean (Maupassant), 94
Pleasure and Days (Proust), 351
Pleasure of the Text (Barthes), 102, 208
poetry, 49, 58, 75, 177, 186, 414n21, 415n12; code in, 31–32; copying of, 133; French, 24, 25, 26, 30, 31–32, 51, 414n15; Greco-Latin, 32; and nuance, 45–46; planning of, 260, 261–62; and prose, 294; rhythm of, 25. See also haiku
poikilos (daubed, spotted), 144, 211, 394, 459n12
Pothos (desire for the absent thing), 132, 430n9
Pour une histoire de la lecture (Martin), 92
Problems of General Linguistics (Benveniste), 74
Protestantism, 91–92
proxemics, 232, 234, 235, 236, 443n13
psychoanalysis, 14, 130, 176, 414n18; and Ego-Ideal/Ideal Ego, 160, 166; and labyrinth metaphor, 118, 124

quiddity, 100–103, 104

"The Raven" (Poe), 177
readability, 124, 148, 299–300
reading: codes of, 428n13; and Ego-Ideal/Ideal Ego, 166; Imaginary of, 314; and wanting-to-write, 131–32; and writing, 132–33, 137, 139, 142, 250–52
the real, 70–77, 421n1, 429n1b; division of, 75–76, 92
realism, 18, 39, 80
René (Chateaubriand), 283
renga (poetry game), 64
repetition, 4, 5, 6, 94
the rhapsodic, 186, 190, 262, 432n8, 459n12
rhetoric, 279–81
rhythm, 248, 249–50, 444n2, 446n31, 450n28
Road to Sèvres (painting; Corot), 39
Roland Barthes by Roland Barthes (Barthes), 102
Romanticism, 42, 144, 147, 211, 303, 457n8, 459n12; and boredom, 272, 274; Jena, 296, 455n12; and the past, 275–76

sabi (loneliness), 419n13
Salammbô (Flaubert), 184
Sanskrit language, 145, 432n13
satori, 8, 56, 58, 90, 101, 131; and haiku, 39, 75, 76, 77, 78–81, 84; and *kireji*, 64
Satyricon (film; Fellini), 119
science, 12–13, 113, 185, 296, 436n4
scripturire. *See* wanting-to-write
scuppering, 151–53
seasons, 377; code of, 39–40; in haiku, 32, 34–36, 38
secrecy, 242–45
semiotics, 135, 208
the sentence, 97–100, 425n14
Sentimental Education (Flaubert), 284, 297, 412n3
separation, 173, 275–98; of the Author, 294; and language, 294–95; of writer, 287–88
sexuality, 14, 15, 99, 123; in haiku, 66, 68; and wanting-to-write, 141, 143
short form, 96–97, 102, 103. *See also* haiku
A Simple Heart (Flaubert), 89
simulation, 137, 168–71
Snakes and Ladders (game), 117
Les Soeurs Brontës (film), 440n31
solitude, 240–42, 244, 281, 304
Sophists, 15
The Sorceress (Michelet), 41
Souvenirs (Tolstoy), 16
speech, 188, 291–96
Stephen Hero (Joyce), 101, 104, 426n20
stereotypes, 68, 292, 296, 301
structuralism, 130, 208, 285
subjectivity, 3, 44, 147, 166; fragmented, 18; and haiku, 33, 52, 53; and simulation, 171
suchness, 43, 73, 80
Surrealists, 115, 265
the Swan (poem; Mallarmé), 220–21
symbolism, 79, 116, 119, 228–29
Symbolists, 59, 272
synaesthesia, 59–60, 419n11

talent, 196–98
Tales of a Pale and Silvery Moon After the Rain (film), 50
tangibilia, 56, 57–58, 62, 419n3
Tao (path), 20, 21, 69, 157, 219, 390, 391, 425n12
Taoism, 190, 409n17

technology, 157, 278, 317; and impossibility, 460n21; *vs.* science, 12–13, 436n4
Temptation of Saint Anthony (Flaubert), 225, 240, 269
La Tentation d'exister (Cioran), 94
the Text, 73, 143, 148, 169, 244; and return of author, 208, 209
"That's it!", 13, 49, 76–82, 100, 104, 411n6
theater, 129, 180, 183; *Noh*, 50, 55, 418n14
The Three Musketeers (Dumas), 413n3
time: and friends, 240–41; and language, 290, 291; as obstacle, 263; and patience, 199; and Vita Nova, 216; of work, 265–67
Today or the Koreans (Vinaver), 68, 420n10
the Tragic, 296–98
translation, 289; of haiku, 23, 24–25, 28, 413n8
Travel Sketches (Basho), 53
truth, 109, 277, 297; moment of, 104–8
Turandot (play; Brecht), 436n27
Turandot (play; Gozzi), 173, 436n27

Ulysses (Joyce), 100, 104
Under the Volcano (Lowry), 181
Universal Reportage, 293–96, 299
"The Unknown Masterpiece" (short story; Balzac), 198, 459n14
urbanism, 117, 118, 123, 213
Ur-book, 180, 181
urdoxa (study of phenomena), 71, 72, 421n11
"Urt Diary" (Barthes), 60, 159, 220, 416n10, 417n1, 419n12
Utsuroi (Jap.: moment between two states), 7, 55, 82, 106, 409n17

La Valse (poem; Ravel), 447n6
Vita Nova, 154, 212–24; administration of, 217–19; and casuistry of egoism, 227, 228; defense of, 219–24; and home, 230–36; and peace, 215–16; and schedules, 237, 245–49
Vita Nova (Dante), xxi, 5, 170, 212

Vita Nova (outline; Barthes), xix, xxii, xxv–xxvi, 389–95, 441n21
Vita Nuova (Michelet), 5, 407n8, 409n11
the void, 27, 46–48, 55

wanting-to-write (*vouloir-écrire*; *scripturire*), xxviii–xxix, 8–9, 10, 127, 130–73; lack of, 139–40; and night-time, 238; and not writing, 172; and the past, 276; and Proust, 9, 140, 172; and reading, 132–33; and rhetoric, 280; and sexuality, 141, 143; and talent, 197; and *wou-wei*, 158–60
War and Peace (Tolstoy), 13, 14, 15, 16, 105, 249, 255, 283
Will to Power (Nietzsche), 102
the work: archaism of, 279; characteristics of, 298–99; and desire, 303; finished, 224; sacralization of, 224–26
the world (life): social, 201, 217–18, 219; *vs.* the work, 200–206; as the work, 207–11
The World of Proust, as Seen by Paul Nadar (Bernard), 305, 309
wou-wei (*wuwei*; non-action), 156–60, 162, 165, 214, 434n44
writer: de-classed, 287–88, 294; exiled, 282–92, 294; types of, 211; *vs.* author, 450n3
writing: aristocracy of, 301–2; breakdown in, 268–70; choice in, 173, 174–99, 250, 275, 285–92, 303; collective, 293–94; and crises, 253–55; defense of, 219–24; finished, 148–50, 194–95; form *vs.* content of, 174, 177–78, 189; as intransitive verb, 144–48, 410n1; language of, 288–89, 295; and life as work, 207–11; and methodical life, 199–250, 251; and music, 249; in night-time, 237–39; not publishing, 269–70; obstacles to, 263–71; patience in, 173, 199–275; philosophy of, 174–75; planning of, 260–63; praxis of, 250–73; and reading, 251–53; and separation, 173, 275–98; simplicity in, 299–301; speed of, 263–65; starting up, 252–57, 259, 260; to stop,

writing (*continued*)
150–57; as tendency, 141–42, 143, 145, 173; themes of, 175–76; trials of, 173, 271, 275; *vs.* boredom, 272–74; *vs. écrivance*, 293

Writing Degree Zero (Barthes), xvii

wu-shi (nothing special), 80–81, 423n6

Yami (Jap.: that which twinkles), 55

Zarathustra (Nietzsche), 180, 304

Zen Buddhism, 15, 43, 410n17, 419n13, 421n4; and haiku, 69, 80, 81, 82; and music, 418n12; and non-action, 156; and perception, 55–56

Zenrin Kushu, 392, 409n15, 434n43, 459n7

European Perspectives

A Series in Social Thought and Cultural Criticism

Lawrence D. Kritzman, Editor

Gilles Deleuze	*The Logic of Sense*
Julia Kristeva	*Strangers to Ourselves*
Theodor W. Adorno	*Notes to Literature*, vols. 1 and 2
Richard Wolin, editor	*The Heidegger Controversy*
Antonio Gramsci	*Prison Notebooks*, vols. 1, 2, and 3
Jacques LeGoff	*History and Memory*
Alain Finkielkraut	*Remembering in Vain: The Klaus Barbie Trial and Crimes Against Humanity*
Julia Kristeva	*Nations Without Nationalism*
Pierre Bourdieu	*The Field of Cultural Production*
Pierre Vidal-Naquet	*Assassins of Memory: Essays on the Denial of the Holocaust*
Hugo Ball	*Critique of the German Intelligentsia*
Gilles Deleuze	*Logic and Sense*
Gilles Deleuze and Félix Guattari	*What Is Philosophy?*
Karl Heinz Bohrer	*Suddenness: On the Moment of Aesthetic Appearance*
Julia Kristeva	*Time and Sense: Proust and the Experience of Literature*
Alain Finkielkraut	*The Defeat of the Mind*
Julia Kristeva	*New Maladies of the Soul*
Elisabeth Badinter	*XY: On Masculine Identity*
Karl Löwith	*Martin Heidegger and European Nihilism*
Gilles Deleuze	*Negotiations, 1972–1990*
Pierre Vidal-Naquet	*The Jews: History, Memory, and the Present*
Norbert Elias	*The Germans*
Louis Althusser	*Writings on Psychoanalysis: Freud and Lacan*
Elisabeth Roudinesco	*Jacques Lacan: His Life and Work*
Ross Guberman	*Julia Kristeva Interviews*
Kelly Oliver	*The Portable Kristeva*
Pierre Nora	*Realms of Memory: The Construction of the French Past*
	vol. 1: *Conflicts and Divisions*
	vol. 2: *Traditions*
	vol. 3: *Symbols*
Claudine Fabre-Vassas	*The Singular Beast: Jews, Christians, and the Pig*
Paul Ricoeur	*Critique and Conviction: Conversations with François Azouvi and Marc de Launay*
Theodor W. Adorno	*Critical Models: Interventions and Catchwords*
Alain Corbin	*Village Bells: Sound and Meaning in the Nineteenth-Century French Countryside*
Zygmunt Bauman	*Globalization: The Human Consequences*
Emmanuel Levinas	*Entre Nous: Essays on Thinking-of-the-Other*
Jean-Louis Flandrin and Massimo Montanari	*Food: A Culinary History*
Tahar Ben Jelloun	*French Hospitality: Racism and North African Immigrants*
Emmanuel Levinas	*Alterity and Transcendence*
Sylviane Agacinski	*Parity of the Sexes*
Alain Finkielkraut	*In the Name of Humanity: Reflections on the Twentieth Century*
Julia Kristeva	*The Sense and Non-Sense of Revolt: The Powers and Limits of Psychoanalysis*

Régis Debray	*Transmitting Culture*
Catherine Clément and Julia Kristeva	*The Feminine and the Sacred*
Alain Corbin	*The Life of an Unknown: The Rediscovered World of a Clog Maker in Nineteenth-Century France*
Michel Pastoureau	*The Devil's Cloth: A History of Stripes and Striped Fabric*
Julia Kristeva	*Hannah Arendt*
Carlo Ginzburg	*Wooden Eyes: Nine Reflections on Distance*
Elisabeth Roudinesco	*Why Psychoanalysis?*
Alain Cabantous	*Blasphemy: Impious Speech in the West from the Seventeenth to the Nineteenth Century*
Luce Irigaray	*Between East and West: From Singularity to Community*
Julia Kristeva	*Melanie Klein*
Gilles Deleuze	*Dialogues II*
Julia Kristeva	*Intimate Revolt: The Powers and Limits of Psychoanalysis*, vol. 2
Claudia Benthien	*Skin: On the Cultural Border Between Self and the World*
Sylviane Agacinski	*Time Passing: Modernity and Nostalgia*
Emmanuel Todd	*After the Empire: The Breakdown of the American Order*
Hélène Cixous	*Portrait of Jacques Derrida as a Young Jewish Saint*
Gilles Deleuze	*Difference and Repetition*
Gianni Vattimo	*Nihilism and Emancipation: Ethics, Politics, and Law*
Julia Kristeva	*Colette*
Steve Redhead, editor	*The Paul Virilio Reader*
Roland Barthes	*The Neutral: Lecture Course at the Collège de France (1977–1978)*
Gianni Vattimo	*Dialogue with Nietzsche*
Gilles Deleuze	*Nietzsche and Philosophy*
Hélène Cixous	*Dream I Tell You*
Jacques Derrida	*Geneses, Genealogies, Genres, and Genius: The Secrets of the Archive*
Jean Starobinski	*Enchantment: The Seductress in Opera*
Julia Kristeva	*This Incredible Need to Believe*
Marta Segarra, editor	*The Portable Cixous*
François Dosse	*Gilles Deleuze and Félix Guattari: Intersecting Lives*